WRITE
SOURCE

Teacher's Edition

Grade 8

Featuring iwrite
www.greatsource.com/iwrite

Dave Kemper, Patrick Sebranek,
and Verne Meyer

WRITE SOURCE®

GREAT SOURCE EDUCATION GROUP
a division of Houghton Mifflin Company
Wilmington, Massachusetts
www.greatsource.com

Teacher Consultants

Patty Beckstead
St. George, Utah

Amy Goodman
Anchorage, Alaska

Debra McConnell
Williston, Vermont

Steve Mellen
Temple Hills, Maryland

Reviewers

Ilene R. Abrams
Cobb County School District
Marietta, Georgia

Doreen A. Caswell
Mary G. Montgomery
Semmes, Alabama

Marilyn Erbentraut
Randall Consolidated
Bassett, Wisconsin

Mary M. Fischer
Arlington Public Schools
Arlington, Massachusetts

Michelle Gallagher
Pinellas County Schools
Largo, Florida

Cullen Hemstreet
Jefferson Parish Schools
Metairie, Louisiana

Alberta Lantz
School District of Waukesha
Waukesha, Wisconsin

Rita Martin
Jenks Public Schools
Jenks, Oklahoma

Inge Noa
Unified School District 475
Junction City, Kansas

Mary Osborne
Pinellas County Schools
Largo, Florida

Tamara Jo Rhomberg
Rockwood School District
St. Louis, Missouri

Deborah Richmond
Ferry Pass Middle School
Pensacola, Florida

Robert Wright
Sebastian River Middle
  School, Indian River S.D.
Sebastian River, Florida

Great Source Editorial: **Bev Jessen, Michele Order Litant, Patricia Moore**

Write Source Editorial: **Steve Augustyn, Laura Bachman, Mariellen Hanrahan, Dave Kemper, Rob King, Lois Krenzke, Janae Sebranek, Lester Smith**

Production: **April Barrons, Colleen Belmont, Tammy Hintz, Kevin Nelson, Mark Lalumondier**

For further credits, see page 819.

Technology Connections for *Write Source*

This series is supported by two Web sites:

The **Great Source iwrite** site is a writing resource that supports students, teachers, and parents. You'll find tutorials about the forms and traits of writing, as well as the latest articles, features, tips, and contests. Go to **www.greatsource.com/iwrite**.

The **Write Source** site features the materials available from Write Source, as well as handy writing topics, student models, and help with research. You can even read about the history of Write Source. Go to **www.thewritesource.com**.

Printed in China

International Standard Book Number: 978-0-669-00707-7

1 2 3 4 5 6 7 8 9 10 - RRDS - 15 14 13 12 11 10 09 08

Program Overview

Professional Development

THE FORMS, THE PROCESS, AND THE TRAITS

WRITING WORKSHOP AND WRITING ACROSS THE CURRICULUM

GRAMMAR AND TEST PREPARATION

DIFFERENTIATION

LITERATURE AND WRITING

RESEARCH

Teacher Resources

In the Front Matter

In the Wraparound

The Writing Process

The Forms of Writing

DESCRIPTIVE WRITING

NARRATIVE WRITING

EXPOSITORY WRITING

PERSUASIVE WRITING

RESPONSE TO LITERATURE

WRITE SOURCE

Dear Educator,

Welcome to *Write Source,* the only K–12 writing program in existence. With this series, any student can learn to write, and any teacher can teach writing. *Write Source* demystifies writing by fully integrating the six traits of writing with the writing process.

In these pages, you'll find hundreds of

- **models of the major forms of writing:** narrative, expository, persuasive, response to literature, creative, and research.
- **concrete strategies for the writing process:** prewriting, writing, revising, editing, and publishing.
- **assignments and activities** to help your students understand and improve the traits of writing.
- **point-of-use connections** to the grammar instruction and practice provided in the *SkillsBook* and the *Interactive Writing Skills* CD-ROM.

This teacher's edition (TE) makes it easy to implement the program.
1. Scan the next few pages to understand the program and tailor it to your needs.
2. Open the book to any unit overview to plan your teaching schedule.
3. Flip to any wraparound page to present a lesson.
4. Turn to the end of the book to find reproducible teaching aids.

It's that easy.

For over 30 years, we at Write Source have worked hard to place the best writing instructional materials in the hands of teachers and students. This program contains everything you and your students need to succeed at writing . . . well, everything except a pen.

Yours truly,

Dave Kemper
Author

Program Overview

This section of the teacher's edition introduces you to the *Write Source* program. It familiarizes you with the main components—from the pupil's edition and the teacher's edition to the technology available for implementation.

Mini Index

What are the main components in

WRITE SOURCE?

The *Write Source* program at each level includes a pupil's edition and a teacher's edition (implementation guide), plus the Teacher's Resource Pack.

Pupil's Edition

The *Write Source* pupil's edition (PE) reflects the latest and best research on writing and learning and provides everything a student needs, including

- **the six traits of writing** fully integrated in **the writing process**.
- **writing strategies** for planning, drafting, revising, and editing.
- **integrated grammar**, mechanics, and usage activities.
- **writing-across-the-curriculum** models and guidelines.
- **collaborative writing** projects and **peer response** sheets.
- **student models** to read, analyze, and emulate.

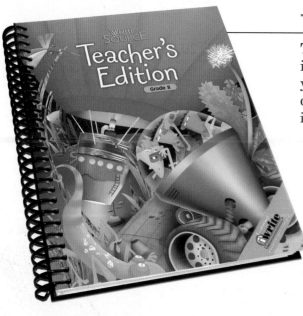

Teacher's Edition

The *Write Source* teacher's edition (TE) makes implementing the new program easy for you—whether you are an experienced teacher, a new teacher, or someone not specifically trained in writing instruction.

- The **Professional Development** section helps you easily set up an effective writing program— or use these materials in an existing program.
- The **Teacher Resources** and **Unit Overviews** provide you everything you need to plan your year, your week, and your day, with pacing for writing units and integrated grammar.
- The tips for **English language learners**, **struggling learners**, and **advanced learners** help you differentiate your instruction.

Teacher's Resource Pack

The Teacher's Resource Pack contains the following resources:

SkillsBook

Designed to help students practice and improve their essential **grammar, mechanics,** and **usage skills,** each *SkillsBook* addresses the skills covered in the pupil edition "Proofreader's Guide" with

- **more than 130 editing and proofreading activities,**
- clear and easy-to-follow activities,
- additional "Next Step" follow-up or enrichment activities.

SkillsBook teacher's edition is also included.

Assessment Book

This convenient teacher's resource provides **copy masters for an editing pretest, a progress test, and a posttest** to help teachers monitor students' progress with writing skills.

Overhead Transparencies

Convenient overhead transparencies feature **graphic organizers and benchmark papers** for whole-class instruction.

Teacher's Resource CD-ROM

The *Teacher's Resource* CD-ROM includes all the blackline masters from the program on a handy CD-ROM.

Write Source *Interactive Writing Skills* CD-ROM

Packed with interactive activities that support six **language and grammar skill** areas—punctuation, mechanics, spelling, usage, understanding sentences, and parts of speech—this student-friendly CD-ROM provides

- **animated lessons that explain key grammar concepts,**
- engaging, interactive activities, and
- printable and electronic reports for students' scores on each activity.

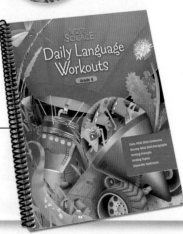

Daily Language Workouts

This flexible teacher's resource builds students' grammar skills through **5- to 10-minute daily (and weekly) editing and proofreading activities. Sentence combining** teaches students to construct more complex, sophisticated sentences.

What technology supports

WRITE SOURCE?

Interactive Writing Skills CD-ROM, **Great Source iwrite, Write Source Eval-U-Write,** and **www.thewritesource.com** each offers you a valuable teaching tool that will help your students become better writers and learners.

Interactive Writing Skills CD-ROM

This highly engaging CD-ROM, which comes in the Teacher's Resource Pack, provides grammar lessons and activities to help students become better writers and editors. The activities address six areas of language study, including punctuation, mechanics, spelling, word usage, sentence construction, and parts of speech. This CD-ROM appeals to a variety of learning styles—including visual, auditory, and textual learners—because of the following features:

- colorful, animated tutorials that explain key grammar concepts;
- interactive activities, ranging from click-in punctuation to highlighting parts of speech in color; and
- guided practice and assessment of concept mastery.

Great Source iwrite

The Great Source iwrite Web site is an ideal complement to the *Write Source* writing program. The Web site is especially helpful when it comes to making the writing process work in the classroom and at home. Great Source iwrite includes the following features:

- lesson plans and minilessons,
- assessment ideas and rubrics,
- grammar help,
- writing prompts, and
- state writing standards.

Write Source Eval-U-Write

Eval-U-Write is a subscription-based online writing practice and evaluating tool powered by the award-winning ETS *Criterion*^{SM} Service. As an evaluating tool, Eval-U-Write provides you with instant holistic and diagnostic feedback of students' essays. Key features of this tool include the following:

- immediate feedback for student writers,
- individualized reporting and tracking for teachers,
- unlimited opportunities for writing assessment and instruction, and
- a wide variety of reporting methods to track student and class performance.

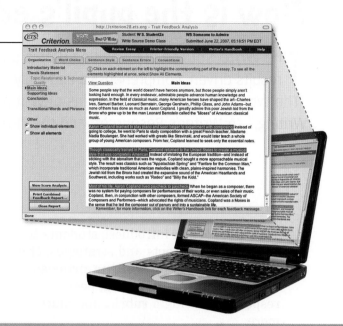

www.thewritesource.com

The Write Source Web site provides even more help for students and teachers. The site features

- writing topics,
- student models,
- MLA and APA guidelines,
- sample multimedia reports, and
- research sites.

Write Source eEditions

The *Write Source* eEditions provide computer access to the full content of student and teacher texts in an easy-to-use, electronic format. Ideal for laptop projector or whiteboard display, these interactive texts provide

- full text search;
- printable graphic organizers, activities, and worksheets;
- interactive glossaries;
- audio support in the student edition;
- links to Web resources; and much more.

How is the pupil's edition organized?

The **Write Source** pupil edition (PE) is student friendly and adaptable, research based and results driven, comprehensive and easy to implement. The text consists of six main sections: "The Writing Process," "The Forms of Writing," "The Tools of Learning," "Basic Grammar and Writing," "A Writer's Resource," and the "Proofreader's Guide."

The Writing Process

The first section introduces students to key writing concepts and strategies: **the integration of the writing process and the traits of writing,** peer responding, using a rubric, and much more.

The Forms of Writing

The second section consists of **in-depth core units** covering descriptive writing, narrative writing, expository writing, persuasive writing, responding to literature, creative writing, and research writing.

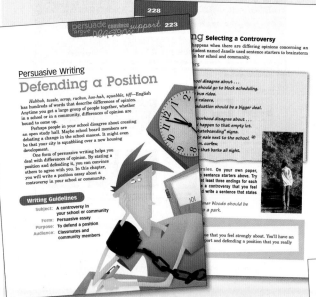

The Tools of Learning

The third section helps students improve **important classroom skills:** listening and speaking, note taking, critical reading, summarizing, and test taking.

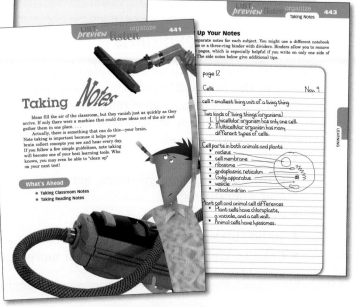

Basic Grammar and Writing

This section (the blue pages) covers **the fundamental building blocks of writing:** words, sentences, and paragraphs. Each lesson increases the students' understanding of basic grammar and writing skills.

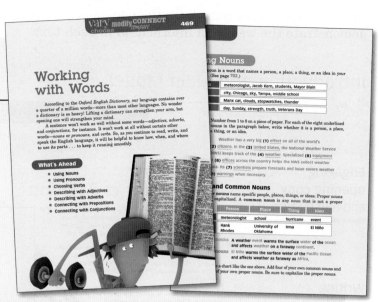

A Writer's Resource

The fifth section (the green pages) functions as **a writing guide** that students can refer to whenever they have questions about the development and presentation of their paragraphs, essays, reports, and stories.

Proofreader's Guide

The final section (the yellow pages) addresses **the conventions of standard English:** punctuation, mechanics, spelling, usage, sentences, and parts of speech.

A Closer Look at the PE Pages

These sample pages come from the persuasive writing core unit. Special features are highlighted to demonstrate the wealth of information in each text.

Introduction and Main Model

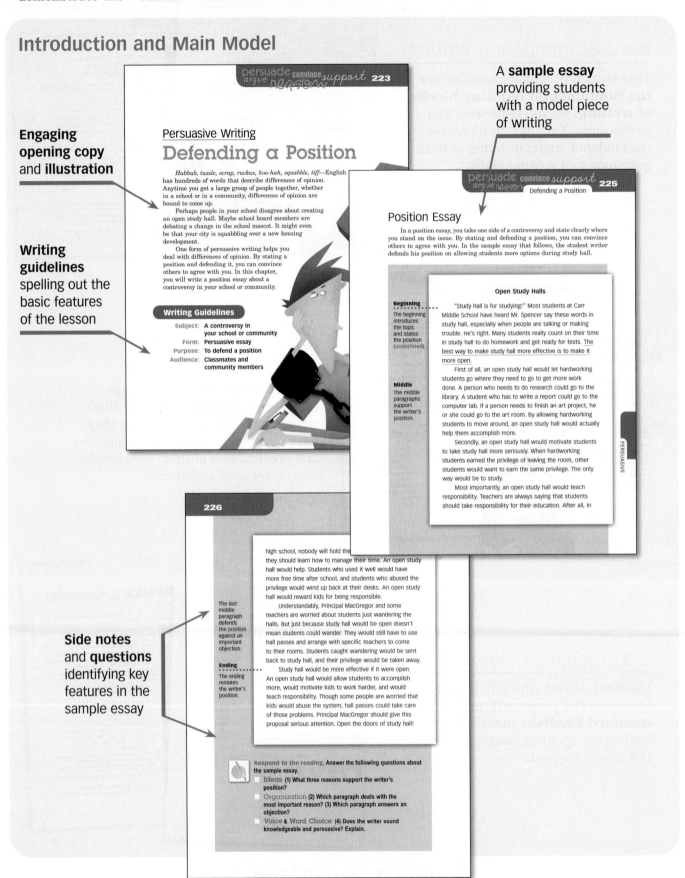

Engaging opening copy and **illustration**

Writing guidelines spelling out the basic features of the lesson

A **sample essay** providing students with a model piece of writing

Side notes and **questions** identifying key features in the sample essay

persuade argue convince reason support 223

Persuasive Writing
Defending a Position

Hubbub, tussle, scrap, ruckus, hoo-hah, squabble, tiff—English has hundreds of words that describe differences of opinion. Anytime you get a large group of people together, whether in a school or in a community, differences of opinion are bound to come up.

Perhaps people in your school disagree about creating an open study hall. Maybe school board members are debating a change in the school mascot. It might even be that your city is squabbling over a new housing development.

One form of persuasive writing helps you deal with differences of opinion. By stating a position and defending it, you can convince others to agree with you. In this chapter, you will write a position essay about a controversy in your school or community.

Writing Guidelines

Subject: A controversy in your school or community
Form: Persuasive essay
Purpose: To defend a position
Audience: Classmates and community members

persuade argue convince reason support 225
Defending a Position

Position Essay

In a position essay, you take one side of a controversy and state clearly where you stand on the issue. By stating and defending a position, you can convince others to agree with you. In the sample essay that follows, the student writer defends his position on allowing students more options during study hall.

Beginning
The beginning introduces the topic and states the position (underlined).

Middle
The middle paragraphs support the writer's position.

Open Study Halls

"Study hall is for studying!" Most students at Carr Middle School have heard Mr. Spencer say these words in study hall, especially when people are talking or making trouble. He's right. Many students really count on their time in study hall to do homework and get ready for tests. The best way to make study hall more effective is to make it more open.

First of all, an open study hall would let hardworking students go where they need to go to get more work done. A person who needs to do research could go to the library. A student who has to write a report could go to the computer lab. If a person needs to finish an art project, he or she could go to the art room. By allowing hardworking students to move around, an open study hall would actually help them accomplish more.

Secondly, an open study hall would motivate students to take study hall more seriously. When hardworking students earned the privilege of leaving the room, other students would want to earn the same privilege. The only way would be to study.

Most importantly, an open study hall would teach responsibility. Teachers are always saying that students should take responsibility for their education. After all, in

PERSUASIVE

226

The last middle paragraph defends the position against an important objection.

Ending
The ending restates the writer's position.

high school, nobody will hold the [...] they should learn how to manage their time. An open study hall would help. Students who used it well would have more free time after school, and students who abused the privilege would wind up back at their desks. An open study hall would reward kids for being responsible.

Understandably, Principal MacGregor and some teachers are worried about students just wandering the halls. But just because study hall would be open doesn't mean students could wander. They would still have to use hall passes and arrange with specific teachers to come to their rooms. Students caught wandering would be sent back to study hall, and their privilege would be taken away.

Study hall would be more effective if it were open. An open study hall would allow students to accomplish more, would motivate kids to work harder, and would teach responsibility. Though some people are worried that kids would abuse the system, hall passes could take care of those problems. Principal MacGregor should give this proposal serious attention. Open the doors of study hall!

Respond to the reading. Answer the following questions about the sample essay.

- **Ideas** (1) What three reasons support the writer's position?
- **Organization** (2) Which paragraph deals with the most important reason? (3) Which paragraph answers an objection?
- **Voice & Word Choice** (4) Does the writer sound knowledgeable and persuasive? Explain.

The Writing Process and the Traits of Writing

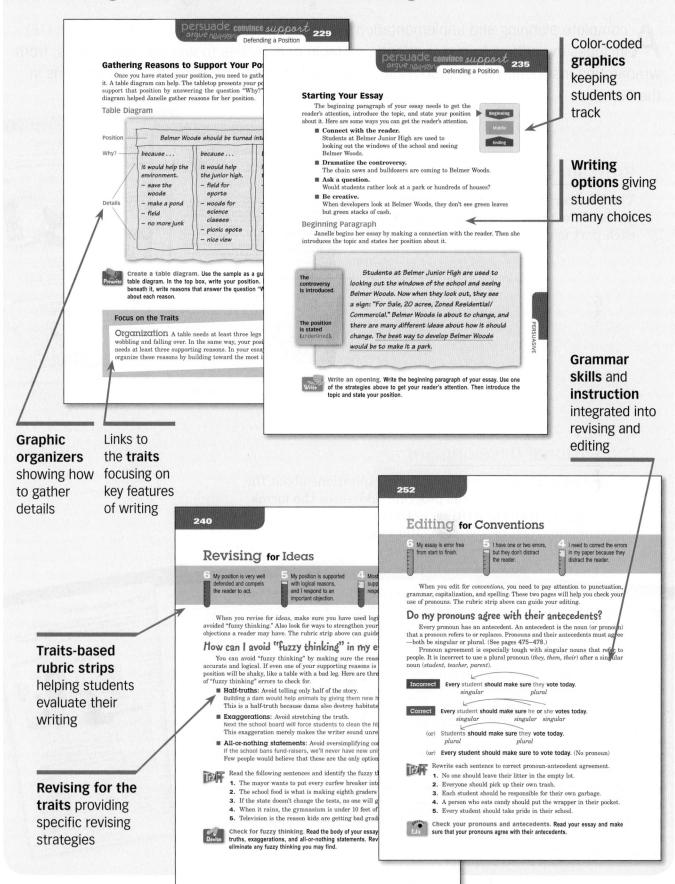

Color-coded graphics keeping students on track

Writing options giving students many choices

Grammar skills and **instruction** integrated into revising and editing

Graphic organizers showing how to gather details

Links to the traits focusing on key features of writing

Traits-based rubric strips helping students evaluate their writing

Revising for the traits providing specific revising strategies

How is the teacher's edition organized?

A complete planning and implementation guide, the **Write Source** teacher's edition (TE) includes everything from a yearlong timetable of activities to weekly lesson plans, from wraparound instructions to reproducible benchmark papers. Here are the main sections in the TE:

Program Overview

The TE overview identifies the main parts of the program and discusses how each part is put together.

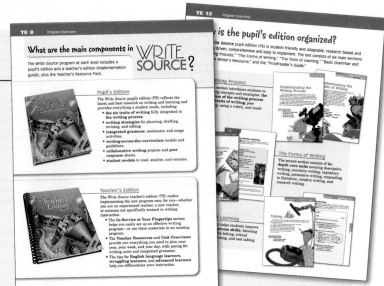

Professional Development

The second part answers all of your key questions about the program. It explains how the program addresses the forms of writing, the traits of writing, grammar, reading skills, differentiation, test preparation, and much more.

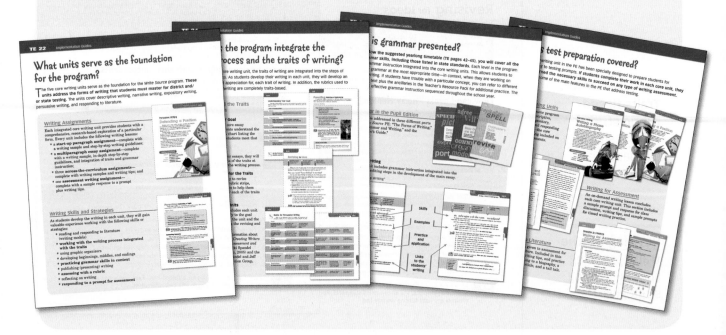

Teacher Resources

The third part of the TE provides charts and tables to help you use the program. Included in this section are a suggested yearlong timetable of activities, a scope-and-sequence chart, a writing framework, and more.

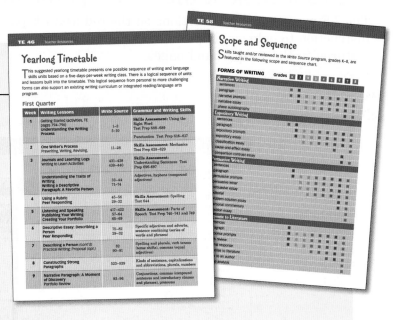

Wraparound Teacher's Edition

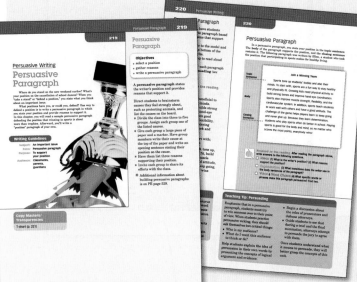

The heart of your TE includes reduced PE pages accompanied by unit overview pages, wraparound guidelines for differentiated instruction, objectives, cross-references, and teaching tips. (See pages i–xviii for a closer look at the wraparound instructions.)

Copy Masters

The fifth part of the TE contains your reproducible copy masters. Included here are rubrics, benchmark papers, graphic organizers, getting-started activities, and a unit-planning sheet.

A Closer Look at the TE Wraparound Pages

The TE wraparound instructions on the reduced PE pages provide a wide range of explicit instruction to help you implement each unit. This two-page spread highlights some of the key features on the wraparound pages.

Unit Overviews

Writing standards blending state and NCTE standards

Traits-based goals for each form of writing

Chapter summaries for quick reference to contents and minilessons to provide warm-ups for the chapters

Lesson plans to provide unit pacing and integration of grammar components

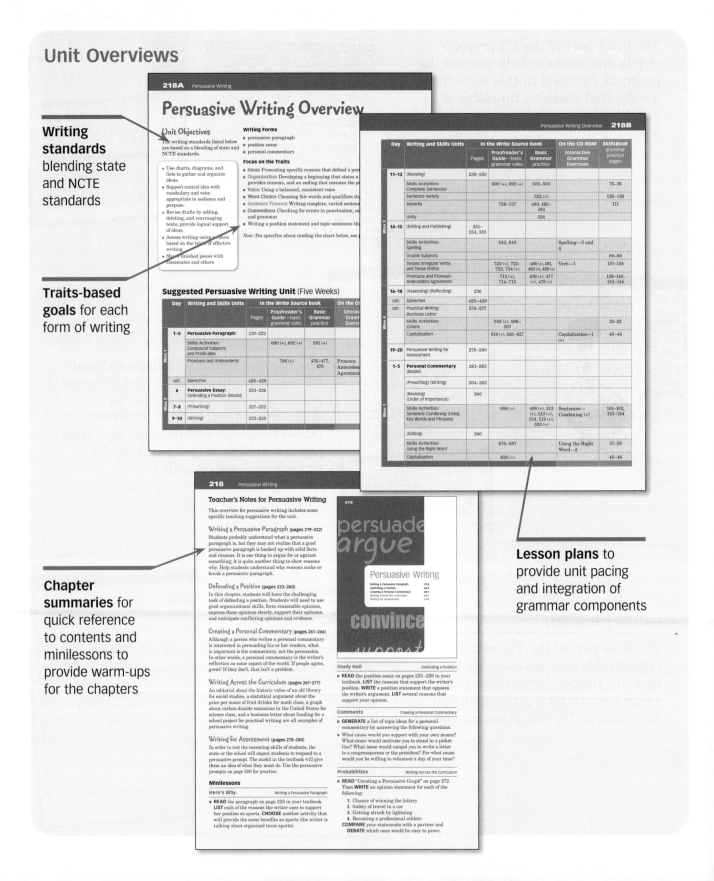

Special Instructions

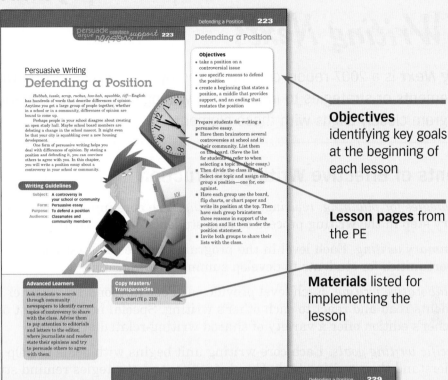

Objectives identifying key goals at the beginning of each lesson

Lesson pages from the PE

Materials listed for implementing the lesson

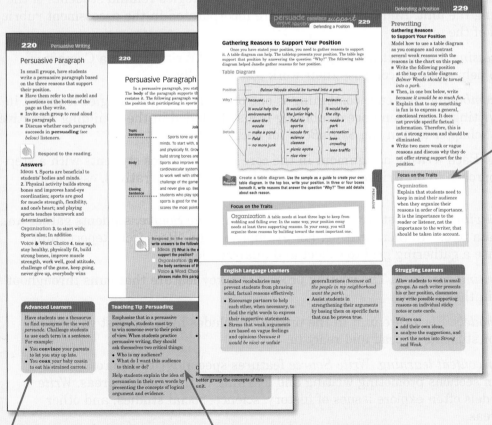

Focus on the traits guiding six-traits instruction

Guidelines for differentiated instruction providing point-of-use teaching strategies

Teaching tips offering useful ideas for helping students with specific aspects of the lessons

How does *Write Source* comply with *Writing Next?*

Writing Next is a 2007 report commissioned by the Carnegie Corporation. It identifies 11 elements or strategies to improve the writing of students in grades 4–12. The *Write Source* program closely aligns with these elements.

Elements of Effective Writing Instruction

1. *Strategies for planning, revising, and editing.* The core units include strategies at every step in the writing process to help students develop their writing.

2. *Summary writing.* Each level in the program provides at least one or two opportunities for students to develop summary paragraphs.

3. *Collaborative writing.* Each level provides a "Peer Responding" chapter to help students read and react to each other's writing. Special notes at point of use in the teacher's edition offer a variety of shared writing-related activities.

4. *Specific writing goals.* Each core writing unit begins with goals to help students understand their writing task. Graphics, tips, and strategies remind students of the goals during the unit. And the same goals are incorporated in the assessment rubric at the end of the unit.

5. *Word processing.* Each text in the program contains a "Writing with a Computer" chapter to help students compose their work electronically.

6. *Sentence combining.* Sentence combining is one of the revising strategies featured in the core writing units. Sentence combining is also included in the "Building Effective Sentences" chapter and in the *SkillsBook* for each level.

7. *Prewriting.* Each writing assignment in the core units provides students with a step-by-step approach to prewriting to help them plan effective narratives, essays, and reports.

8. *Inquiry activities.* For most writing assignments in *Write Source,* students gather and analyze data to use in their writing. For example, in the "Research Report" unit, students use a gathering grid to collect and analyze ideas.

9. *Process writing approach.* The writing process is a key feature that runs throughout each text in the program.

10. *Study of models.* Each core unit in the program includes high-interest writing samples for students to read and react to.

11. *Writing for content learning. Write Source* features special writing-across-the-curriculum sections promoting writing and learning in the content areas. *Write Source* models often explore issues of history, science, social studies, and other content areas.

Graham, S., & Perin, D. (2007). *Writing next: Effective strategies to improve writing of adolescents in middle and high schools—A report to Carnegie Corporation of New York.* Washington, DC: Alliance for Excellent Education. This citation does not constitute an endorsement.

Professional Development

This section provides embedded professional development to help you get the most out of *Write Source*. It explains how the program addresses the forms, the process, and the traits of writing as well as grammar, reading, differentiation, test prep, and much more.

Mini Index

How does *Write Source* teach the forms of writing?

Write Source provides numerous models and assignments for each major form of writing: descriptive, narrative, expository, persuasive, response to literature, creative, and research. Special attention is given to preparing for district and state tests in the forms that are most often tested.

Writing Assignments

Each integrated core writing unit provides students with a comprehensive, research-based exploration of a particular form. Every unit includes the following writing lessons:

- a **start-up paragraph assignment**—complete with a writing sample and step-by-step writing guidelines;

- two **multiparagraph essay assignments**—complete with writing samples; in-depth, step-by-step guidelines; and integration of traits and grammar instruction;

- four **across-the-curriculum assignments**—complete with writing samples and writing tips; and

- one **assessment writing assignment**—complete with a sample response to a prompt plus writing tips.

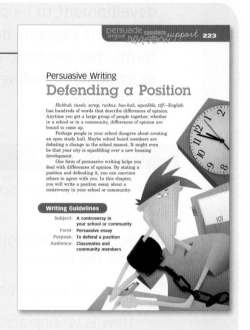

Writing Skills and Strategies

As students develop the writing in each unit, they will gain valuable experience working with the following skills or strategies:

- reading and responding to literature (writing models).

- **working with the writing process integrated with the traits.**

- using graphic organizers.

- developing beginnings, middles, and endings.

- **practicing grammar skills in context.**

- publishing (presenting) writing.

- **assessing with a rubric.**

- reflecting on writing.

- **responding to a prompt for assessment.**

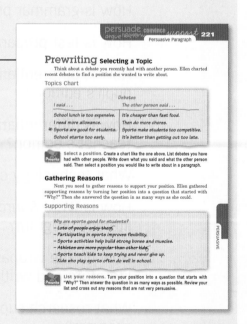

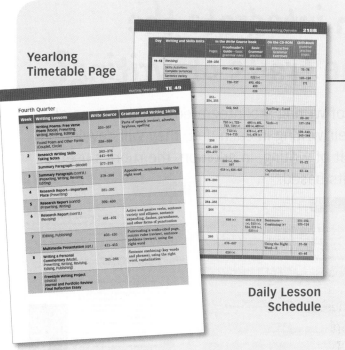

Yearlong Timetable Page

Daily Lesson Schedule

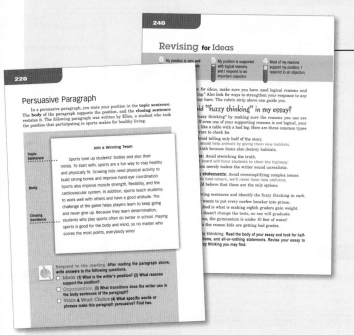

Implementation of the Core Units

The yearlong timetable serves as a suggested quarter-by-quarter guide for implementing the core units. (See pages TE 46–49.) Then the TE overview pages at the beginning of each core unit provide a daily lesson schedule. Each core unit takes two to four weeks to complete if, as suggested, you assign the start-up paragraph, the multiparagraph essay, and the assessment writing assignment.

The timetable suggests optional activities that would affect the length of a unit. If additional grammar options are assigned, that, too, would affect the length of a unit.

Special Instructional Features

The core units work for all students, regardless of their language background and writing experiences. *If students stay on task, they will produce effective pieces of writing.* These special features make the units student friendly:

- **Step-by-Step Approach:** The instructions carefully and predictably guide students through the writing process.
- **Language of Instruction:** Special care is given to the explanations and directions to make sure that students understand what is expected of them.
- **Examples:** At each point during the process, students are provided with examples that they can use as models for their own work.
- **Design:** Graphics and color coding help visual learners stay on task.

How does the program integrate the writing process and the traits of writing?

Throughout each core writing unit, the traits of writing are integrated into the steps of the writing process. As students develop their writing in each unit, they will develop an understanding of, and appreciation for, each trait of writing. In addition, the rubrics used to assess each piece of writing are completely traits based.

The Process and the Traits in the Core Units

Understanding Your Goal

The beginning of each core essay assignment helps students understand the goal of their writing. A chart listing the traits of writing helps students meet that goal.

Focus on the Traits

As students develop their essays, they will find valuable discussions of the traits at different points during the writing process.

Revising and Editing for the Traits

When students are ready to revise and edit, they will find rubric strips, guidelines, and strategies to help them improve their writing for each of the traits of writing.

Rubrics for the Core Units

A traits-based rubric concludes each unit. This rubric ties in directly to the goal chart at the beginning of the unit and to the rubric strips presented on the revising and editing pages.

Special Note: For more information about the traits, we recommend *Creating Writers Through 6-Trait Writing Assessment and Instruction,* 4th ed., by Vicki Spandel (Addision Wesley Longman, 2005) and the *Write Traits®* by Vicki Spandel and Jeff Hicks (Great Source Education Group, 2009).

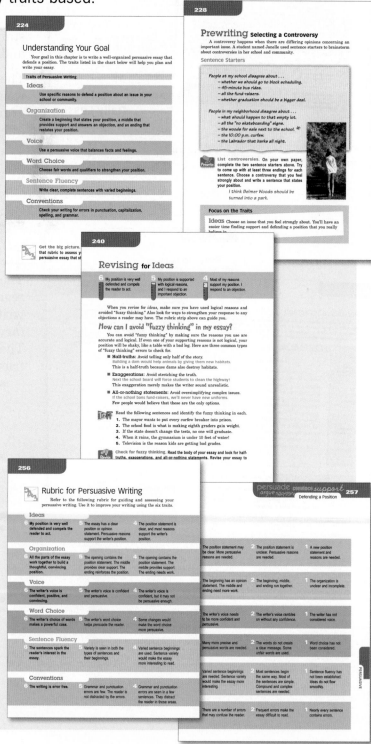

Process and Traits Chart

By design, students address the different traits at the appropriate stages during their core writing. The following chart shows which traits are the focus during the various steps in the writing process.

Prewriting

Ideas
Organization

Writer's Questions:

- What is my topic and focus?
- Who is my audience, and what do they need to know?
- What information supports my focus?
- How should I organize my writing?

Writing

Ideas
Organization
Voice

Writer's Questions:

- Do I have enough information to answer readers' questions?
- Where do I begin?
- Where do I go next?
- How do I know when to stop?
- What transitions should I use?
- How do I want to sound?

Revision

Ideas
Organization
Voice
Word Choice
Sentence Fluency

Writer's Questions:

- What is my main message? Is it clear?
- Does the organizational pattern work?
- Is my opening a grabber?
- Did I end with a thought, surprise, or question that will make my readers think?
- Is this the right tone and voice for this audience, topic, and format?
- Is the language formal or informal enough?
- Do the sentences show enough variety to keep readers interested?

Editing

Conventions
Presentation

Writer's Questions:

- Did I read my work both silently and aloud?
- Is this writing as error free as I can make it?
- Did I use page layout in a way that will attract the reader's eye and make main points easy to find?

How can I implement a writing workshop?

Write Source complements implementation of a writing workshop. The program includes minilessons for instruction, high-quality models to encourage individual writing, support for whole-class sharing, and much more.

Integrated Minilessons

In the core units, each step in the process of the students' writing can serve as a minilesson in a writing workshop. You will find lessons that teach students to do the following:

- preview the trait-based goal of a writing project
- select a topic
- gather details using a graphic organizer
- create a focus (thesis) statement
- organize details using a list or an outline
- create a strong beginning
- develop a coherent middle
- write an effective ending
- receive (and provide) peer responses
- revise for the traits
- edit and proofread for conventions
- publish a finished piece
- use traits-based rubrics

Mon	Tues	Wed	Thurs	Fri
Writing Minilessons (10 minutes as needed)				
Status Checks (2 minutes) Find out what students will work on for the day.				
Individual Work (30 minutes) Writing, Revising, Editing, Conferencing, or Publishing				
Whole-Class Sharing Session (5 minutes)				

Graphic Organizers

Write Source contains many graphic organizers that can serve as the subject of workshop minilessons. The graphic organizers modeled in *Write Source* include the following:

List	Pie graph	Sensory chart	Process diagram	"Why" chart
Web	Plot chart	Venn diagram	Basics of life list	Line diagram
Cluster	Storyboard	Table diagram	5 W's chart	Picture diagram
T-chart	Bar graph	Cycle diagram	Cause-effect chart	Comparison-contrast chart
Outline	KWL chart	Gathering grid	Problem-solution chart	
Time line	Circle graph	Character chart	Topic list	

High-Quality Models

Write Source models strong writing. Each core unit begins with an accessible, high-interest model, complete with annotations pointing out key features in the writing. Once students have read and analyzed each model, they will be ready (and excited) to begin their own writing. Other models and examples throughout each unit introduce and/or demonstrate specific writing techniques that students can experiment with.

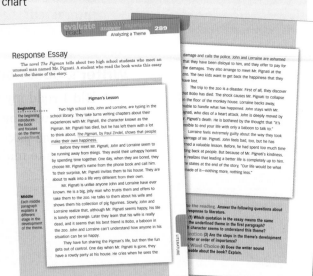

Individual Writing

Write Source makes it easy for writing-workshop students to work on their own. It also provides specific help whenever students have questions about their writing. Here are some of the areas that are addressed:

- catching the reader's interest
- providing background information
- developing strong paragraphs
- elaborating (adding facts, statistics, anecdotes, and so on)
- organizing ideas by time, location, importance, logic
- quoting, paraphrasing, and summarizing
- using transitions
- drawing conclusions
- calling the reader to act

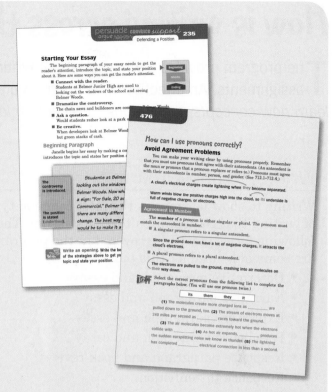

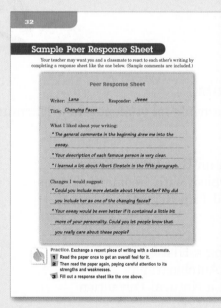

Peer and Teacher Response

Write Source reviews peer responding and provides a peer response sheet. Consistent integration of the traits in the writing process allows students and teachers to speak a common language as they conduct responding sessions. Traits-based checklists and rubrics help pinpoint just what is working—and what could work better—in each piece of writing.

Whole-Class Sharing

Write Source helps students complete their work, preparing it for whole-class presentation. The program provides a wealth of suggestions for publishing student work.

Every writing unit ends with evaluation using traits-based rubrics. Even the evaluation process is modeled with sample essays and assessments. A reflection sheet also helps students think about what they have learned and internalize the lessons to use in the future.

How is writing across the curriculum addressed?

The program provides a wide variety of writing-across-the-curriculum (WAC) activities and assignments. An effective WAC program promotes *writing to show learning, writing to learn new concepts,* and *writing to reflect on learning.*

Writing to Show Learning

Writing to show learning is the most common type of writing that content-area teachers assign. The following forms of writing covered in the program are commonly used for this purpose.

- Descriptive paragraph and essay
- Narrative paragraph and essay
- Expository paragraph and essay
- Persuasive paragraph and essay
- Response paragraph and book review
- Response to nonfiction
- Summary paragraph
- Research report
- Taking classroom tests

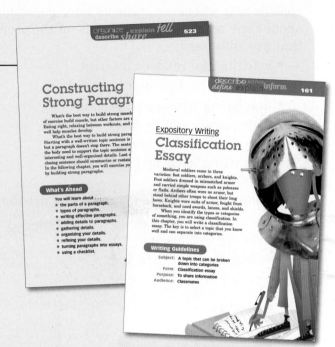

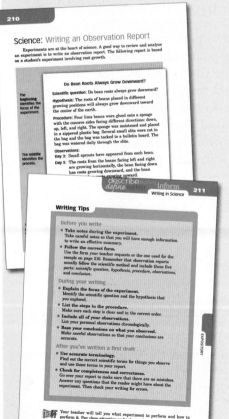

Specific WAC Assignments

Specific content-area assignments let students show learning.

Descriptive Writing

Social Studies: Writing an Eyewitness Report
Math: Describing an Object with Geometric Terms
Science: Writing a Field-Trip Report

Narrative Writing

Social Studies: Recalling a Historical Moment
Math: Writing a Math Autobiography
Science: Writing About a Natural Formation

Expository Writing

Social Studies: Writing a News Report
Math: Explaining a Mathematical Operation
Science: Writing an Observation Report

Persuasive Writing

Social Studies: Writing an Editorial
Math: Developing a Statistical Argument
Science: Creating a Persuasive Graph

Writing to Learn New Concepts

Writing-to-learn activities are unrehearsed and ungraded activities likes those listed below. The purpose of writing to learn is not to produce finished pieces of writing but rather to explore new concepts. *Write Source* discusses and demonstrates the following writing-to-learn activities.

- Clustering
- Freewriting
- Listing
- First Thoughts

Additional Writing-to-Learn Activities

Warm-Ups: Students write for the first 5 to 10 minutes of class. These writings help students focus on the lesson at hand. In warm-ups, students explore what they know about new concepts, sort out their thoughts about what they are learning, and rehearse answers for discussions and exams.

Stop 'n' Write: At any point in a class discussion, students are asked to stop and write. The writing helps them to evaluate their understanding of the topic, to reflect on what has been said, and to question anything that may be unclear.

Summing Up: Students are asked to sum up what was covered in a particular lesson by writing about its importance, a possible result, a next step, or a general impression.

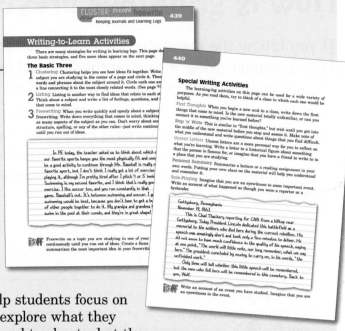

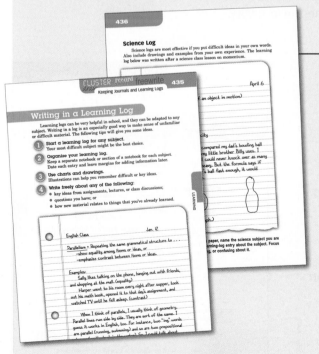

Writing to Reflect on Learning

Exploring personal thoughts and feelings helps students to think beyond first impressions, to search for connections between subjects, and to enlarge their global impressions. *Write Source* discusses and demonstrates the following writing-to-reflect activities.

Keeping a Personal Journal: A personal journal provides a special place for students to explore ideas, feelings, and experiences. They can write about people, events, and anything else in their lives.

Writing in a Learning Log: In a learning log, students write about subjects they are studying. It's a place to explore how new information connects to their own experiences.

How is grammar presented?

If you follow the suggested yearlong timetable (pages TE 46–49), you will cover all the key grammar skills, including those listed in state standards. Each level in the program includes grammar instruction integrated into the core writing units. This allows students to learn about grammar at the most appropriate time—in context, when they are working on their own writing. If students have trouble with a particular concept, you can refer to different parts of the text plus the ancillaries in the Teacher's Resource Pack for additional practice. The end result is effective grammar instruction sequenced throughout the school year.

Grammar in the Teacher's Edition

The yearlong timetable (pages TE 46–49) provides the big picture of grammar integration, and the unit overview at the beginning of each unit shows specifically what grammar to use while teaching writing. Grammar connections at point of use pinpoint the time to present each new concept.

Grammar in the Pupil's Edition

Forms of Writing

Each core unit includes grammar instruction integrated into the revising and editing steps in the development of the main essay.

From "Narrative Writing"

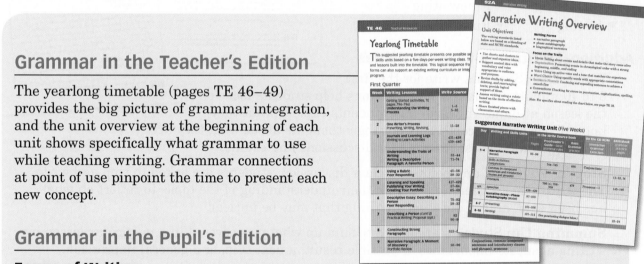

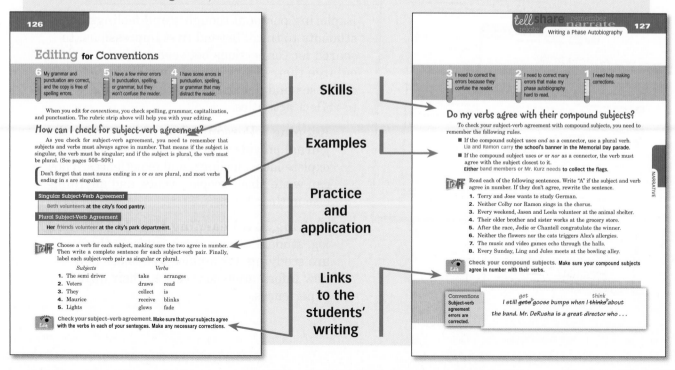

Basic Grammar and Writing

For more grammar in the context of writing, turn to "Working with Words" and "Building Effective Sentences." Use these minilessons to review specific grammar and style issues that students can apply to their writing.

From "Working with Words"

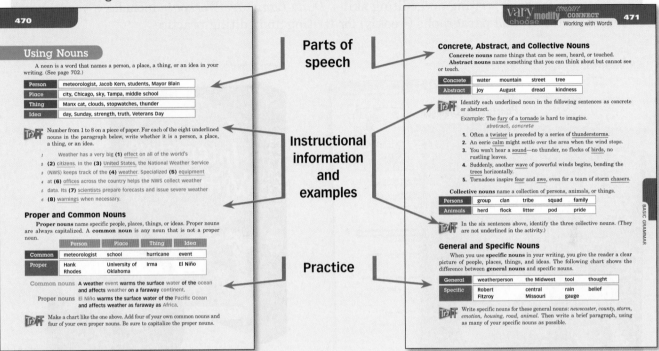

Parts of speech

Instructional information and examples

Practice

Proofreader's Guide

This section serves as a complete grammar and editing guide, providing rules, examples, and activities (including tests in standardized-test format).

From "Marking Punctuation"

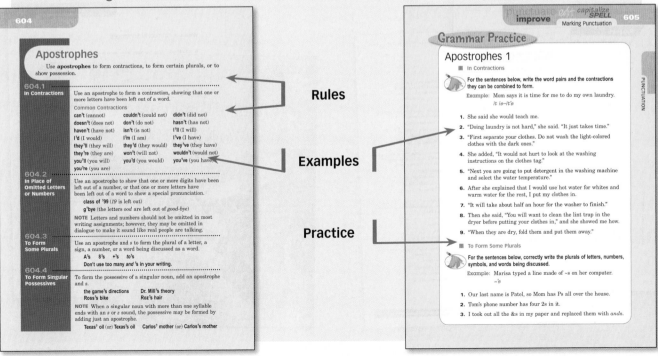

Rules

Examples

Practice

Grammar in the Teacher's Resource Pack

The *SkillsBook* provides more than 130 punctuation, mechanics, spelling, usage, sentence, and parts-of-speech activities. The *Interactive Writing Skills* CD-ROM includes even more practice for mechanics, punctuation, usage, sentences, spelling, and parts of speech. This self-grading resource works well for review or reinforcement. The *Assessment* booklet contains pretests, progress tests, and posttests for basic writing and editing skills. *Daily Language Workouts* includes a year's worth of sentences (daily) and paragraphs (weekly) for writing and editing practice.

SkillsBook

Interactive Writing Skills

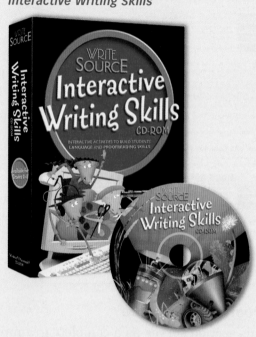

Assessment

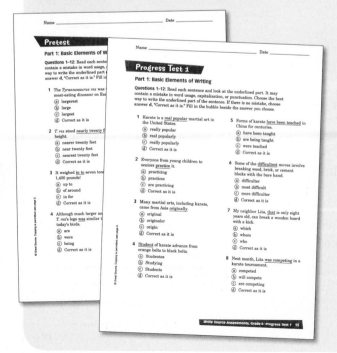

Daily Language Workouts

Planning Grammar Instruction

Should I implement *all* of the suggested basic grammar activities?

In the course of the year, if you assigned every grammar exercise listed in the daily lesson schedules (located in the unit overviews of your TE), your students would complete **all** of the "Basic Grammar and Writing," "Proofreader's Guide," *SkillsBook*, and CD exercises.

Because the most effective grammar instruction happens in context, daily lesson schedules call for these exercises at appropriate times during revising and editing in the core writing units. As the teacher, you must choose the type and number of exercises that will best meet the needs of your students.

How are all the grammar resources related?

Write Source SkillsBook activities parallel and expand on the rules and exercises found in the "Proofreader's Guide." In "Basic Grammar and Writing," the brief exercises function well as minilessons and may be assigned as needed. The interactive CD allows students to return to exercises again and again throughout the year to review and reinforce grammar skills.

How do I use the daily lesson schedule chart?

The sample below from the "Persuasive Writing" unit (week 2) is followed by four points that explain how to read and use the daily lesson schedules.

Day	Writing and Skills Units	In the *Write Source* book			On the CD-ROM	*SkillsBook*
		Pages	Proofreader's Guide—basic grammar rules	Basic Grammar practice	Interactive Grammar Exercises	grammar practice pages
6–7	(Writing)	295–300				
8–10	(Revising)	301–312				
	Skills Activities: Nouns		702–703, 704–705	471–472 (+), 473	Nouns—1	133–134, 135–136, 137–138
	Wordy Sentences			506		83–84
	Combining Sentences with Relative Pronouns		706–707	515		119–120

1. The "Proofreader's Guide" and "Basic Grammar" columns give the PE pages that cover rules, examples, and exercises for each "skills activity" item.
2. The *"SkillsBook"* and "CD-ROM" columns give pages and exercise numbers from those particular resources, not from the PE.
3. When more than one concept is covered on a PE page, the practice to address will be indicated in parentheses.
4. A (+) following a page number means the exercise or practice is called for elsewhere and may have been completed already. You may review the exercise orally if this is the case.

Why would I use *Daily Language Workouts*?

Daily Language Workouts is a teacher resource that provides a high-interest sentence for each day of the year and weekly paragraphs for additional editing and proofreading practice. This regular practice helps students develop the objectivity they need to effectively edit their own writing.

How is test preparation covered?

Each core writing unit in the PE has been specially designed to prepare students for responding to testing prompts. **If students complete their work in each core unit, they will have learned the necessary skills to succeed on any type of writing assessment.** Here are just some of the main features in the PE that address testing.

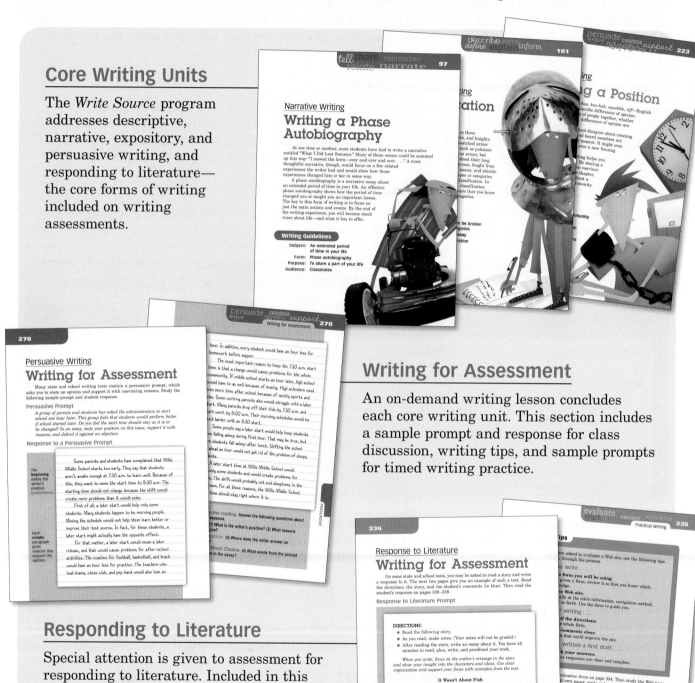

Core Writing Units

The *Write Source* program addresses descriptive, narrative, expository, and persuasive writing, and responding to literature—the core forms of writing included on writing assessments.

Writing for Assessment

An on-demand writing lesson concludes each core writing unit. This section includes a sample prompt and response for class discussion, writing tips, and sample prompts for timed writing practice.

Responding to Literature

Special attention is given to assessment for responding to literature. Included in this unit are samples, writing tips, and practice prompts for responding to a novel, a photo, a Web site, and a nonfiction article.

Taking Classroom Tests

The chapter on test taking includes a section entitled "Taking Essay Tests" that helps students analyze the key words in writing prompts.

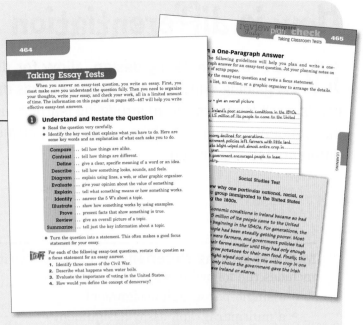

Writing Across the Curriculum

The writing-across-the-curriculum assignments at the end of the core writing units help students prepare for on-demand writing on content-based tests.

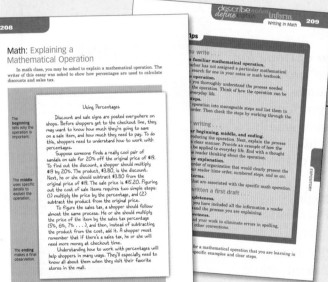

Test Prep for Grammar Skills

The grammar skills tests at the end of each section in the "Proofreader's Guide" follow a standardized test format. Familiarity with this formatting will help students do their best on these important tests.

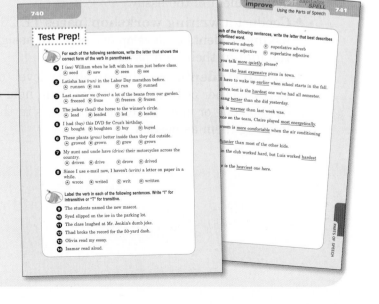

How is differentiation handled in the PE?

*W*rite Source **texts, by design, allow for differentiation in writing instruction.** The key guiding principle for the authors was developing a writing program to meet the needs of all students—from struggling learners and English-language learners to advanced, independent students. A close examination of the writing units shows that they are set up for differentiated instruction.

Core Writing Units

Multiple writing experiences: Each core writing unit includes the following writing experiences:

- a single-paragraph assignment,
- a multiparagraph essay assignment,
- three writing-across-the-curriculum lessons, plus
- a writing-for-assessment prompt assignment.

These different writing experiences give you options for implementation depending on the needs and nature of your students. You can implement the core units, one assignment after another, as delineated in the yearlong timetable (pages TE 46–49), helping individuals or small groups of students as needed. Or you can differentiate instruction in any number of ways. Here are four of the many possibilities:

- Have **struggling learners** focus on the single-paragraph writing assignment while other students complete the multiparagraph essay assignment.
- Have **advanced learners** work individually or in small groups on the multiparagraph essay assignment, while you guide struggling learners step-by-step through the development of the essay.
- Conduct a **writing workshop** (pages TE 26–27), asking students to develop one or more assignments in the unit at their own pace.
- **Group students** according to ability level (or according to some other criterion) and have them help each other develop one or more of the assignments in the unit, guiding them as needed.

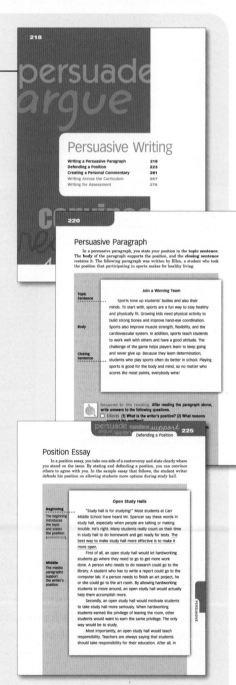

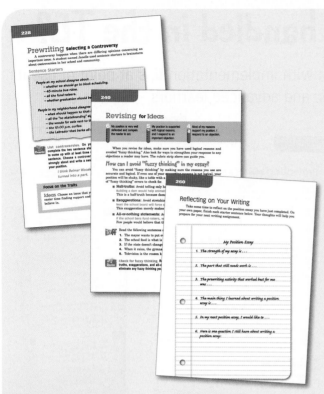

Research-based design and layout:

In his book *Strategies for Struggling Writers* (Guilford Press, 1998), educator and researcher James L. Collins explains that struggling writers need the following aids to help them with their writing:

- color coding and signposts
- graphic organizers
- discreet chunks of copy
- clearly defined, sequential tasks
- skills integrated with the process
- opportunities to reflect on the writing

Write Source core writing units contain all of the above features. As a result, the units are tailor made for struggling learners and English-language learners. These features also facilitate the independent work of the more advanced students.

Basic Grammar and Writing

"Basic Grammar and Writing," a special section (the blue pages), covers the basics in three chapters: "Working with Words," "Building Effective Sentences," and "Writing Paragraphs." You can differentiate instruction with these chapters as needed. For example, advanced students could complete the work in these chapters independently, while you cover the lessons more carefully and selectively with struggling students and English-language learners.

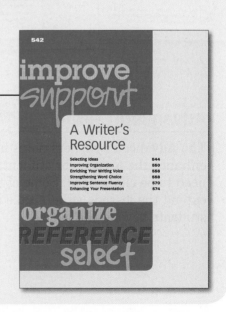

A Writer's Resource

"A Writer's Resource" (the green pages) serves as a writing guide that students can refer to time and again to help them with their writing. Advanced students can find their own answers to writing questions in this section, while you can find minilesson ideas for struggling learners and English-language learners with specific writing needs.

Resource:
Tomlinson, Carol A., and Susan Demirsky Allan. *Leadership for Differentiating Schools & Classrooms.* ASCD, 2000.

How is differentiation handled in the TE?

The teacher's edition addresses differentiation with implementation tips at point of use for struggling learners, English language learners, and advanced learners.

Struggling Learners

The Struggling Learners notes allow you to customize lessons to meet the needs of students who may have difficulty completing the work. These notes provide alternative approaches; others provide extra practice or additional insights.

English Language Learners

The English Language Learners notes help you to guide students with limited language skills through the lessons. These notes provide extra practice, alternative approaches, connections to first languages, glossaries of new terms, demonstration ideas, and more.

Advanced Learners

The Advanced Learners notes help you enhance the lessons for students who need to be challenged. Some of the notes extend the lessons; others take advanced students beyond the page.

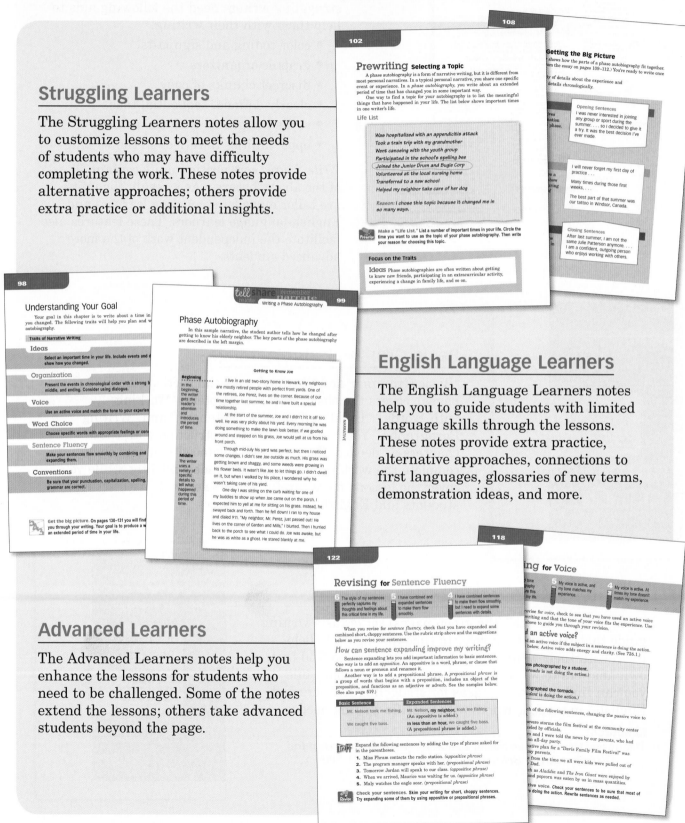

What technology can help with differentiation?

The *Write Source* series includes a number of technologies to help you provide each student the scaffolding—and challenges—he or she needs.

For students who struggle with writing, try Eval-U-Write!

This subscription-based online service helps students plan, write, revise, and edit essays. Eval-U-Write lets students work at their own pace, supporting them throughout the writing process and preparing them for on-demand writing. Eval-U-Write features

- eight interactive prewriting tools,
- real-time, traits-based feedback,
- 90 *Write Source* prompts in tested forms,
- 150+ additional prompts,
- online handbooks drawn from your *Write Source* "Proofreader's Guide," and
- a powerful grade book with many reports for classroom management.

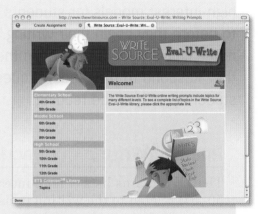

For students who struggle with grammar, try the *Interactive Writing Skills* CD-ROM!

This CD-ROM helps students practice grammar with videos, rules, examples, and interactive activities. Students work at their own pace and log their progress in a session record they can print out or e-mail to you. They practice

- punctuation,
- mechanics,
- spelling,
- usage,
- sentences, and
- parts of speech.

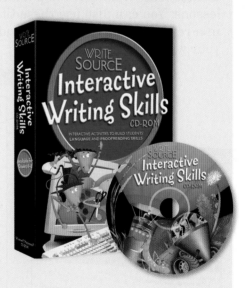

For students, parents, and teachers who need a little more help, visit our Web sites!

Great Source iwrite and thewritesource.com give your students, their families, and you extra support:

- writing tutorials, tips, and minilessons
- grammar help
- writing prompts and sample student essays
- help with research

Go to www.greatsource.com/iwrite and www.thewritesource.com.

GREAT SOURCE
iwrite
www.greatsource.com/iwrite

How is *Write Source* part of a complete literacy program?

*W*rite Source helps your students make the reading-writing connection with many high-interest models for students to respond to before they begin their writing. The side notes point out key features in the model, and the "Respond to the reading" questions help students analyze the reading.

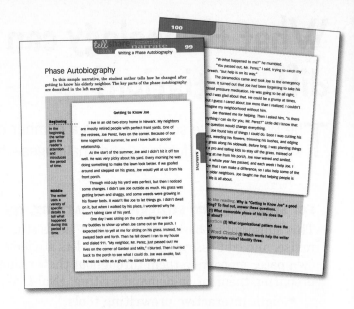

Reading-Writing Connection

The TE contains lists of high-interest titles (pages TE 50–57) related to the writing units. You can select mentor texts from these lists to incorporate into your lessons. You can also use these titles to engage students in a reader's workshop that provides a springboard for your writer's workshop.

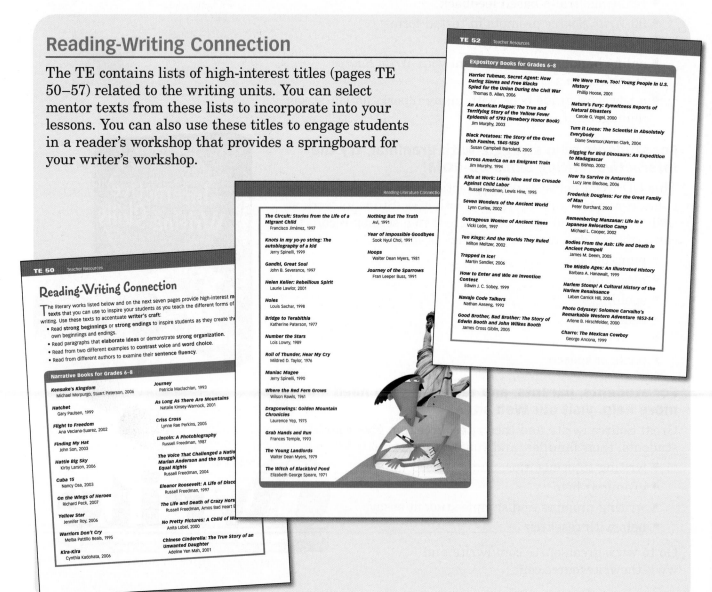

How do the wraparound notes connect literature and writing?

The TE wraparound notes provide tips for connecting writing to literature and for crafting writing the way the pros do.

Literature Connections help you tie your writing instruction to exemplary literature. You'll find

- quotations from famous authors,
- anecdotes about writing,
- tips for helping students learn from literature, and
- suggestions for bridging reading time and writing time.

Literature Connections

Flash fiction: One way to inspire students to write narrative paragraphs is to introduce to them the concept of flash fiction. Flash fiction is any short piece (often under 100 words) that tells a complete story. Professional writers enjoy the challenge of telling a story in such a compact form, and middle-school readers enjoy such quick reads. Of course, your students will be writing about an actual event, not fiction, but the goal is the same: to capture an experience in a small space. Encourage your students to find flash fiction on the Web—and perhaps create some flash fiction of their own.

Craft Connections feature tricks and techniques used by professional writers. You'll find

- practical strategies that professionals use,
- real-life stories to inspire your students,
- quotations from authors about writer's craft,
- discussions of style and voice, and
- ways to apply literary devices in writing.

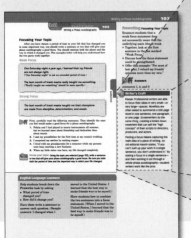

Writer's Craft

Focus: Professional writers are able to focus their ideas in very small—or very large—spaces. Novelists are often asked to summarize a 500-page novel in one sentence, one paragraph, or one page. Screenwriters do the same thing, creating a boiled-down treatment that can sell the "high concept" of their scripts to directors, producers, and actors.

Finding a focus means capturing the main idea of a piece of writing. An old editorial maxim states, "If you can't sum up your work in a single sentence, you don't understand it." By stating a focus in a single sentence—and then working it out through a whole phase autobiography—student writers work like the pros.

What research supports the *Write Source* program?

The *Write Source* program reflects the best thinking and research on writing instruction.

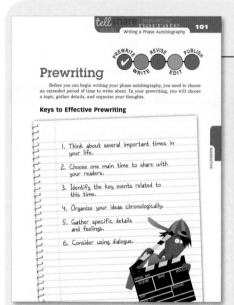

Applying the Process Approach to Writing

Research: The process approach, discussed by educators Donald M. Murray and Donald H. Graves, among others, breaks writing down into a series of steps—prewriting through publishing. Research has shown that students write more effectively, and more thoughtfully, if they approach their work as a process rather than as an end product.

Graves, Donald. H. ***Writing: Teachers & Children at Work.*** Heinemann, 2003.

Murray, Donald. M. ***Learning by Teaching.*** Boynton/Cook Heinemann, 1982.

Write Source: All of the writing units and assignments in the text are arranged according to the steps in the writing process. This arrangement helps students manage their work, especially in the case of longer essay or research report assignments.

Meeting the Needs of Struggling Writers

Research: Many students in today's classrooms struggle with writing and learning. For struggling students, following the writing process is not enough. According to the research done by James L. Collins, struggling students need specific strategies and aids to help them become better writers. Collins found that these students benefit from the following: *skills instruction integrated into the process of writing, color coding and signposts in the presentation of instructional material, the use of graphic organizers, instructions presented in discreet chunks of copy,* and so on.

Collins, James L. ***Strategies for Struggling Writers.*** Guilford Press, 1998.

Write Source: The core writing units contain all of the above features. As a result, the units are perfectly suited for struggling learners and English-language learners.

Sequencing Assignments

Research: Writing instructor and researcher James Moffett developed a sequence of writing assignments—known as the "Universe of Discourse"—that has, over the years, served countless English/language arts classrooms. Moffett sequences the modes of writing according to their connection or immediacy to the writer. Moffett suggests that students first develop descriptive and narrative pieces because the students have an immediate, personal connection to this type of writing. Next, they should develop informational pieces that require some investigation before moving on to more challenging, reflective writing, such as persuasive essays and position papers.

Moffett, James. *Teaching the Universe of Discourse.* Boynton/Cook, 1987.

Write Source: The writing units and assignments in the *Write Source* texts are arranged according to the "Universe of Discourse," starting with descriptive and narrative writing, moving on to expository writing, and so on. These assignments provide students with a comprehensive exploration of the writing spectrum. They are designed to be used in a sequence that supports an existing writing curriculum or integrated reading/language arts program.

Integrating the Traits of Writing

Research: To become better writers, students need to become confident self-assessors. Vicki Spandel, among others, has developed "six-trait writing," an instructional approach that helps students to recognize the characteristics of effective writing and to better understand how to improve their own work. "Six-trait writing" has become recognized as one of the most significant movements in writing pedagogy and assessment.

Spandel, Vicki. *Creating Writers: Through 6-Trait Writing Assessment and Instruction.* Pearson/AB Longman, 2008.

Spandel, Vicki. *Write Traits®.* Great Source, 2002–2004.

Write Source: Traits-of-writing instruction is integrated throughout the core writing units. Special attention to the traits is given during the revising and editing steps, and the assessment rubric for each unit is trait based. *Write Traits* for grades K–12, available from the Great Source, complements the *Write Source* program.

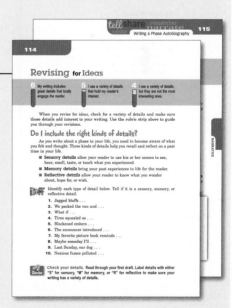

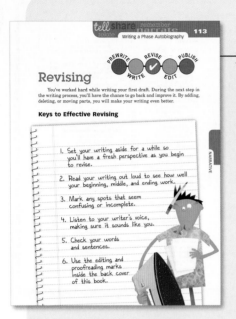

Implementing a Writing Workshop

Research: Countless respected writing instructors and researchers have touted the importance of establishing a community of writers in the classroom. Teachers can establish such a community by implementing a writing workshop. In a writing workshop, students are immersed in all aspects of writing, including sharing their work with their peers.

Atwell, Nancie. *In the Middle: New Understandings About Writing, Reading, and Learning.* Heinemann, 1998.

Write Source: The units in *Write Source* are so clearly presented that most students can work independently on their writing in a workshop. In addition, the core units contain innumerable opportunities for workshop minilessons. (See pages TE 26–27.)

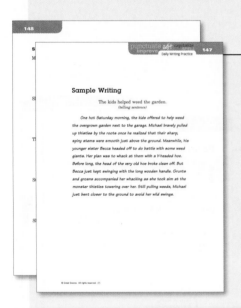

Producing Writing with Detail

Research: Rebekah Caplan learned through her teaching experience that students don't automatically know how to add details to their personal, informational, and persuasive writing. She discovered with her students that adding detail to writing is a skill that must be practiced regularly, much like a musician requires regular warm-up and practice. To address this problem, Caplan came up with the "show-me" sentence strategy in which students begin with a basic idea—"My locker is messy"—and create a brief paragraph that shows rather than tells the idea. As students regularly practice this skill in daily warm-ups, they learn how to write with detail.

Caplan, Rebekah. *Writers in Training: A Guide to Developing a Composition Program.* Dale Seymour Publications, 1984.

Write Source: *Daily Language Workouts* in the Teacher's Resource Packet contains a series of show-me sentences that teachers can implement as a regular classroom warm-up.

Teacher Resources

This section of the TE provides important tools that will help teachers implement the *Write Source* program. Of special interest will be the yearlong timetable. It provides a comprehensive, research-based language arts program that emphasizes writing and grammar skills.

Mini Index

Yearlong Timetable

This suggested yearlong timetable presents one possible sequence of writing and language skills units based on a five-days-per-week writing class. There is a logical sequence of units and lessons built into the timetable. This logical sequence from personal to more challenging forms can also support an existing writing curriculum or integrated reading/language arts program.

First Quarter

Week	Writing Lessons	*Write Source*	Grammar and Writing Skills
1	Getting Started (activities, TE pages 794–796) **Understanding the Writing Process**	1–3 5–10	**Skills Assessment:** Using the Right Word Test Prep 688–689
			Punctuation Test Prep 616–617
2	**One Writer's Process** Prewriting, Writing, Revising,	11–28	**Skills Assessment:** Mechanics Test Prep 628–629
3	**Journals and Learning Logs** Writing to Learn Activities	431–438 439–440	**Skills Assessment:** Understanding Sentences Test Prep 696-697
	Understanding the Traits of Writing Writing a Descriptive Paragraph: A Favorite Person	33–44 71–74	Adjectives, hyphens (compound adjectives)
4	**Using a Rubric Peer Responding**	45–56 29–32	**Skills Assessment:** Spelling Test 644
5	**Listening and Speaking Publishing Your Writing Creating Your Portfolio**	417–422 57–64 65–69	**Skills Assessment:** Parts of Speech Test Prep 740–741 and 749
6	**Descriptive Essay: Describing a Person Peer Responding**	75–82 29–32	Specific adjectives and adverbs, sentence combining (series of words and phrases)
7	**Describing a Person** *(cont'd)* Practical Writing: Proposal *(opt.)*	82 90–91	Spelling and plurals, verb tenses (tense shifts), commas (equal adjectives)
8	**Constructing Strong Paragraphs**	523–539	Kinds of sentences, capitalizations and abbreviations, plurals, numbers
9	**Narrative Paragraph: A Moment of Discovery** Portfolio Review	93–96	Conjunctions, commas (compound sentences and introductory clauses and phrases), pronouns

Second Quarter

Week	Writing Lessons	*Write Source*	Grammar and Writing Skills
1	**Narrative Essay: Phase Autobiography** (Model, Prewriting, Writing)	97–112	Punctuating dialogue
2	**Narrative Essay** *(cont'd)* (Revising, Editing)	113–128	Transitive and intransitive verbs, verbals (participles and infinitives), prepositional phrases, active vs. passive verbs, punctuating dialogue, subject-verb agreement
3	**Peer Responding**	29–32	
	Narrative Essay *(cont'd)* (Publishing)	129	
	Assessing, Reflecting	130–134	
	Expository Paragraph: Classification	157–160	Complete sentences (understood and delayed subjects), using the right word
4	**Writing an Expository Essay: Classification** (Model, Prewriting, Writing)	161–176	
5	**Expository Essay** *(cont'd)* (Revising, Editing)	177–192	Awkward sentences, misplaced modifiers, rambling sentences, combining with subordinating conjunctions, apostrophes (possession), using the right word
6	**Peer Responding**	29–32	
	Expository Essay *(cont'd)* (Publishing)	193	
	Assessing, Reflecting	194–198	
	Response Paragraph: Theme (Model)	283–286	Punctuating titles, capitalizing titles
7	**Response to Literature: Book Review—An Insight** (Model, Prewriting, Writing)	287–300	Quotations
8	**Book Review** *(cont'd)* (Revising, Editing)	301–316	Nouns, wordy sentences, combining sentences (relative pronouns), restrictive and nonrestrictive phrases and clauses, punctuating dialogue, subject-verb agreement
	Peer Responding	29–32	
	Book Review *(cont'd)* (Publishing)	317	
	Assessing, Reflecting	318–322	
9	Portfolio Review	65–69	

Third Quarter

Week	Writing Lessons	*Write Source*	Grammar and Writing Skills
1	**Writing Stories** (Prewriting, Writing)	343–348	
2	**Writing Stories** *(cont'd)* (Revising, Editing, Publishing)	348–349	Punctuating dialogue, interjections, correlative conjunctions, sentence variety (kinds of), combining sentences (compound and complex), sentence problems (review), subject-verb agreement
3	**Writing a Biographical Narrative** (Model, Prewriting, Writing)	135–140	
	(Revising, Editing, Publishing)	141–142	Transitions, end punctuation, using the right word
4	**Persuasive Paragraph**	219–222	Compound subjects and predicates, pronouns and antecedents
5	**Persuasive Essay—Defending a Position** (Model, Prewriting, Writing)	223–238	
6	**Persuasive Essay** *(cont'd)* (Writing, Revising, Editing)	239–254	Complete sentences, sentence variety, unity, adverbs, spelling, tenses (irregular verbs and tense shifts), double subjects, pronouns and pronoun-antecedent agreement
	Peer Responding	29–32	
	(Publishing)	255	
	Assessing, Reflecting	256–260	
	Writing for Assessment	214–216	
7	**Writing a Letter to an Author** (Model, Prewriting, Writing)	323–327	
	(Revising, Editing)	328	Compound and complex sentences, indefinite pronouns, punctuation (review), using the right word
	(Publishing)	328	
8	**Comparison-Contrast Essay** (Model, Prewriting, Writing)	199–204	
	(Writing, Revising, Editing)	204	Comparative and superlative adjectives and adverbs, comma splices and run-ons, double negatives
9	Making Oral Presentations Portfolio Review	423–430	

Fourth Quarter

Week	Writing Lessons	*Write Source*	Grammar and Writing Skills
1	**Writing Poems: Free Verse Poem** (Model, Prewriting, Writing, Revising, Editing)	353–357	Parts of speech (review), adverbs, hyphens, spelling
	Found Poem and Other Forms (Couplet, Circle)	358–359	
2	**Research Writing Skills** **Taking Notes**	363–376 441–448	
	Summary Paragraph—(Model)	377–378	
3	**Summary Paragraph** *(cont'd.)* (Prewriting, Writing, Revising, Editing)	379–380	Appositives, semicolons, using the right word
4	**Research Report—Important Place** (Prewriting)	381–391	
5	**Research Report** *(cont'd)* (Prewriting, Writing)	392–400	
6	**Research Report** *(cont'd.)* (Revising)	401–402	Active and passive verbs, sentence variety and ellipses, sentence expanding, dashes, parentheses, and other forms of punctuation
7	(Editing, Publishing)	403–410	Punctuating a works-cited page, comma rules (review), sentence problems (review), using the right word
	Multimedia Presentation *(opt.)*	411–415	
8	**Writing a Personal Commentary** (Model, Prewriting, Writing, Revising, Editing, Publishing)	261–266	Sentence combining (key words and phrases), using the right word, capitalization
9	**Freestyle Writing Project** (choice) **Journal and Portfolio Review Final Reflection Essay**		

Reading-Writing Connection

The literary works listed below and on the next seven pages provide high-interest **mentor texts** that you can use to inspire your students as you teach the different forms of writing. Use these texts to accentuate **writer's craft**:

- Read **strong beginnings** or **strong endings** to inspire students as they create their own beginnings and endings.
- Read paragraphs that **elaborate ideas** or demonstrate **strong organization**.
- Read from two different examples to **contrast voice** and **word choice**.
- Read from different authors to examine their **sentence fluency**.

Narrative Books for Grades 6–8

Kensuke's Kingdom
Michael Morpurgo, Stuart Paterson, 2006

Hatchet
Gary Paulsen, 1999

Flight to Freedom
Ana Veciana-Suarez, 2002

Finding My Hat
John Son, 2003

Hattie Big Sky
Kirby Larson, 2006

Cuba 15
Nancy Osa, 2003

On the Wings of Heroes
Richard Peck, 2007

Yellow Star
Jennifer Roy, 2006

Warriors Don't Cry
Melba Pattillo Beals, 1995

Kira-Kira
Cynthia Kadohata, 2006

Journey
Patricia Maclachlan, 1993

As Long As There Are Mountains
Natalie Kinsey-Warnock, 2001

Criss Cross
Lynne Rae Perkins, 2005

Lincoln: A Photobiography
Russell Freedman, 1987

The Voice That Challenged a Nation: Marian Anderson and the Struggle for Equal Rights
Russell Freedman, 2004

Eleanor Roosevelt: A Life of Discovery
Russell Freedman, 1997

The Life and Death of Crazy Horse
Russell Freedman, Amos Bad Heart Bull, 1996

No Pretty Pictures: A Child of War
Anita Lobel, 2000

Chinese Cinderella: The True Story of an Unwanted Daughter
Adeline Yen Mah, 2001

Sir Walter Ralegh and the Quest for El Dorado
Marc Aronson, 2000

Spellbinder: The Life of Harry Houdini
Tom Lalicki, 2000

The Greatest: Muhammad Ali
Walter Dean Myers, 2001

The Circuit: Stories from the Life of a Migrant Child
Francisco Jiménez, 1997

Knots in my yo-yo string: The autobiography of a kid
Jerry Spinelli, 1999

Gandhi, Great Soul
John B. Severance, 1997

Helen Keller: Rebellious Spirit
Laurie Lawlor, 2001

Holes
Louis Sachar, 1998

Bridge to Terabithia
Katherine Paterson, 1977

Number the Stars
Lois Lowry, 1989

Roll of Thunder, Hear My Cry
Mildred D. Taylor, 1976

Maniac Magee
Jerry Spinelli, 1990

Where the Red Fern Grows
Wilson Rawls, 1961

Dragonwings: Golden Mountain Chronicles
Laurence Yep, 1975

Grab Hands and Run
Frances Temple, 1993

The Young Landlords
Walter Dean Myers, 1979

The Witch of Blackbird Pond
Elizabeth George Speare, 1971

Nothing but the Truth
Avi, 1991

Year of Impossible Goodbyes
Sook Nyul Choi, 1991

Hoops
Walter Dean Myers, 1981

Journey of the Sparrows
Fran Leeper Buss, 1991

Expository Books for Grades 6–8

Harriet Tubman, Secret Agent: How Daring Slaves and Free Blacks Spied for the Union During the Civil War
Thomas B. Allen, 2006

An American Plague: The True and Terrifying Story of the Yellow Fever Epidemic of 1793 (Newbery Honor Book)
Jim Murphy, 2003

Black Potatoes: The Story of the Great Irish Famine, 1845-1850
Susan Campbell Bartoletti, 2005

Across America on an Emigrant Train
Jim Murphy, 1994

Kids at Work: Lewis Hine and the Crusade Against Child Labor
Russell Freedman, Lewis Hine, 1995

Seven Wonders of the Ancient World
Lynn Curlee, 2002

Outrageous Women of Ancient Times
Vicki León, 1997

Ten Kings: And the Worlds They Ruled
Milton Meltzer, 2002

Trapped in Ice!
Martin Sandler, 2006

How to Enter and Win an Invention Contest
Edwin J. C. Sobey, 1999

Navajo Code Talkers
Nathan Aaseng, 1992

Good Brother, Bad Brother: The Story of Edwin Booth and John Wilkes Booth
James Cross Giblin, 2005

We Were There, Too! Young People in U.S. History
Phillip Hoose, 2001

Nature's Fury: Eyewitness Reports of Natural Disasters
Carole G. Vogel, 2000

Turn It Loose: The Scientist in Absolutely Everybody
Diane Swanson, Warren Clark, 2004

Digging for Bird Dinosaurs: An Expedition to Madagascar
Nic Bishop, 2002

How to Survive in Antarctica
Lucy Jane Bledsoe, 2006

Frederick Douglass: For the Great Family of Man
Peter Burchard, 2003

Remembering Manzanar: Life in a Japanese Relocation Camp
Michael L. Cooper, 2002

Bodies from the Ash: Life and Death in Ancient Pompeii
James M. Deem, 2005

The Middle Ages: An Illustrated History
Barbara A. Hanawalt, 1999

Harlem Stomp! A Cultural History of the Harlem Renaissance
Laban Carrick Hill, 2004

Photo Odyssey: Solomon Carvalho's Remarkable Western Adventure 1853–54
Arlene B. Hirschfelder, 2000

Charro: The Mexican Cowboy
George Ancona, 1999

Rats! The Good, the Bad, and the Ugly
Richard Conniff, 2002

Into the Volcano: A Volcano Researcher at Work
Donna Donovan-O'Meara, 2007

Made You Look: How Advertising Works and Why You Should Know
Shari Graydon, Warren Clark, 2003

Friendly Foes: A Look at Political Parties
Elaine Landau, 2003

The Buffalo and the Indians: A Shared Destiny
Dorothy Hinshaw Patent, William Munoz, 2006

How to Build Your Own Prize-Winning Robot
Edwin J. C. Sobey, 2002

Dragonart: How to Draw Fantastic Dragons and Fantasy Creatures
J. "NeonDragon" Peffer, Jessica Peffer, 2005

How to Drive an Indy Race Car
David Rubel, Gregory Truett Smith, James Westwater, Edward Keating, 1992

How Nature Works
Reader's Digest Editors, 1991

Bravo! Brava! A Night at the Opera: Behind the Scenes with Composers, Cast, and Crew
Anne Siberell, Frederica von Stade, 2001

Lacrosse: The National Game of the Iroquois
Diane Hoyt-Goldsmith, 1998

Dia's Story Cloth: The Hmong People's Journey to Freedom.
Dia Cha, 1998

Extraordinary People with Disabilities
Deborah Kent, Kathryn A. Quinlan, 1997

Black Holes & Supernovae (Secrets of Space)
David E. Newton, 1997

So, You Wanna Be a Rock Star? How to Create Music, Get Gigs, and Maybe Even Make It Big!
Stephen Anderson, 1999

Phineas Gage: A Gruesome but True Story About Brain Science
John Fleischman, 2004

Persuasive Books for Grades 6–8

Free the Children: A Young Man Fights Against Child Labor and Proves That Children Can Change the World
Craig Kielburger, Kevin Major, 1999

The Kid's Guide to Social Action: How to Solve the Social Problems You Choose and Turn Creative Thinking into Positive Action
Barbara A. Lewis, 1998

We Need to Go to School: Voices from the Rugmark Children
Tanya Roberts-Davis, 2003

It's Our World, Too!
Phillip Hoose, 2002

A Kids Guide to Giving
Freddi Zeiler, 2006

Chew on This: Everything You Don't Want to Know About Fast Food
Eric Schlosser, Charles Wilson, 2006

Catch the Spirit: Teen Volunteers Tell How They Made a Difference
Susan K. Perry, 2006

Animal Rights—Yes or No
Marna A. Owen, 1993

School Dress Codes: A Pro/Con Issue
Barbara C. Cruz, 2001

Introducing Issues with Opposing Viewpoints—Gangs
Scott Barbour, 2005

Downloading Copyrighted Stuff from the Internet: Stealing or Fair Use?
Sherri Mabry Gordon, 2005

Separate Sexes, Separate Schools: A Pro/Con Issue
Barbara C. Cruz, 2000

Speak Out! Debate and Public Speaking in the Middle Grades
John Meany, 2005

Advertising: Information or Manipulation?
Nancy Day, 1999

Introducing Issues with Opposing Viewpoints—Advertising
Eleanor Stanford, 2006

Introducing Issues with Opposing Viewpoints—UFOs
Jamuna Carroll, 2006

Causes of Crime: Distinguishing Between Fact and Opinion
Stacey L. Tipp, 1991

Taking Action: How to Get Your City to Build a Public Skatepark
Justin Hocking, 2005

Start Something: You Can Make a Difference
Tiger Woods Foundation and Earl Woods, 2000

Stand Up for Your Rights
Paul Atgwa, 2000

Why It's Great to Be a Girl: 50 Awesome Reasons Why We Rule!
Jacqueline Shannon, 2007

Volunteering to Help in Your Neighborhood
Claudia Isler, 2000

Made You Look: How Advertising Works and Why You Should Know
Shari Graydon, Warren Clark, 2003

Take Action! A Guide to Active Citizenship
Marc Kielburger, 2002

Books About Responding to Literature—Grades 6–8

Dear Author: Students Write About the Books That Changed Their Lives
Weekly Reader's Read Magazine, 1995

The Bookmark Book
Carolyn S. Brodie, Debra Goodrich, Paula K. Montgomery, 1996

What a Novel Idea! Projects and Activities for Young Adult Literature
Katherine Wiesolek Kuta, 1997

Literature Circle Guide: Holes
Tonya Ward Singer, 2002

Literature Circle Guide: Maniac Magee
Perdita Finn, 2001

Literature Circle Guide: Roll of Thunder, Hear My Cry
Rebecca Callan, 2003

10 Ready-to-Go Book Report Projects
Rebekah Elmore, 1999

Wham! Its a Poetry Jam: Discovering Performance Poetry
Sara Holbrook, 2002

Gifted Books, Gifted Readers: Literature Activities to Excite Young Minds
Nancy J. Polette, 2000

Exploring Diversity: Literature Themes and Activities for Grades 4–8
Jean E. Brown, Elaine C. Stephens, 1996

Plays of America from American Folklore for Young Actors: Grade Level 7–12
L. E. McCullough, 199

The Young Actor's Book of Improvisation: Dramatic Situations from Shakespeare to Spielberg
Sandra Caruso, Susan Kosoff, 1998

Teaching Literary Elements: Easy Strategies and Activities to Help Kids Explore and Enrich Their Experiences with Literature (Grades 4–8)
Tara McCarthy, 1999

Big Talk: Poems for Four Voices
Paul Fleischman, 2000

Newbery Authors of the Eastern Seaboard: Integrating Social Studies and Literature, Grades 5-8
Joanne Kelly, Charles Kelly, 1994

50 Fun-Filled Crosswords & Word Searches Based on Favorite Books (Grades 4-8)
Steve Herrmann, 1999

The American Hero in Children's Literature: A Standards-Based Approach
Carol M. Butzow, John W. Butzow, 2005

Reading Response Trifolds for 40 Favorite Novels
Jennifer Cerra-Johansson, 2004

Teaching Writing with Picture Books as Models (Grades 4–8)
Rosanne Jurstedt, 2000

Meet the Authors (Grades 5–8)
Deborah Kovacs, 1999

Song Shoots out of My Mouth: A Celebration of Music
Jaime Adoff, Martin French, 2002

The Place My Words Are Looking For: What Poets Say About and Through Their Work
Paul B. Janeczko, 1990

Children of Promise: African-American Literature and Art for Young People
Charles Sullivan, 2002

Books About Creative Writing—Grades 6–8

Live Writing: Breathing Life into Your Words
Ralph Fletcher, 1999

Poems from Homeroom: A Writer's Place to Start
Kathi Appelt, 2002

Swimming Upstream: Middle School Poems
Kristine O'Connell George, 2002

Seeing the Blue Between: Advice and Inspiration for Young Poets
Paul B. Janeczko, 2006

Neighborhood Odes
Gary Soto, 2005

The Invisible Ladder: An Anthology of Contemporary American Poems for Young Readers
Liz Rosenberg, 1996

I Never Said I Wasn't Difficult: Poems
Sara Holbrook, 1997

Who Do You Think You Are? Stories of Friends and Enemies
Hazel Rochman, 1997

13: Thirteen Stories That Capture the Agony and Ecstasy of Being Thirteen
James Howe, 2003

Shelf Life: Stories by the Book
Gary Paulsen, 2003

Little Worlds: A Collection of Short Stories for the Middle School
Peter Guthrie, 1985

A Kick in the Head: An Everyday Guide to Poetic Forms
Paul B. Janeczko, 2005

Technically, It's Not My Fault: Concrete Poems
John Grandits, 2004

Notebook Know-How: Strategies for the Writer's Notebook
Aimee Buckner, 2005

America Street: A Multicultural Anthology of Stories
Anne Mazer, 1993

Cricket Never Does: A Collection of Haiku and Tanka
Myra Cohn Livingston, Kees De Kiefte, 1997

What's Your Story? A Young Person's Guide to Writing Fiction
Marion Dane Bauer, 1992

Our Stories: A Fiction Workshop for Young Authors
Marion Dane Bauer, 1996

Writing Magic, Creating Stories That Fly
Gail Carson Levine, 2006

Yoga for the Brain: Daily Writing Stretches That Keep Minds Flexible and Strong
Dawn DiPrince, Cheryl Miller Thurston, 2006

Jump Write In! : Creative Writing Exercises for Diverse Classrooms, Grades 6–12
WritersCorps, 2005

350 Fabulous Writing Prompts (Grades 4–8)
Jacqueline Sweeney, Stephanie Peterson, 1999

Reference Books for Grades 6–8

The American Heritage Student Dictionary
Houghton Mifflin, 1994

The American Heritage Student Thesaurus
Paul Hellweg, 2006

The American Heritage® Student Science Dictionary
Editors of the American Heritage Dictionaries, 2002

The Kingfisher Student Atlas
Philip Wilkinson, 2003

The Usborne Internet-Linked Encyclopedia of World History
Jane Bingham, 2001

The Kingfisher History Encyclopedia
Editors of Kingfisher, 2004

The World Almanac for Kids 2007
Editors of World Almanac, 2006

Webster's New Explorer Dictionary of Synonyms & Antonyms
Merriam-Webster, 2003

The Oxford Children's Book of Famous People
Oxford University Press, 1995

The Biographical Dictionary of African Americans
Rachel Kranz, Philip J. Koslow, 1999

Biographical Dictionary of Modern World Leaders: 1992 to the Present
John C. Fredriksen, 2003

Encyclopedia of Native America
Trudy Griffin-Pierce, 1995

New York (Eyewitness Travel Guides)
DK Publishing, 2006 (series)

National Parks Travel Journal (Travel Journal Guides)
AAA, 2003 (series)

Natural Disasters: Atlas in the Round
Clare Oliver, 2001

Hurricanes, Tsunamis, and Other Natural Disasters (Kingfisher Knowledge)
Andrew Langley, 2006

1000 Years of Famous People
Clive Gifford, 2002

The New York Public Library Kid's Guide to Research
Deborah Heiligman, 1998

The New York Public Library Student's Desk Reference
New York Public Library Staff, 1995

The New York Public Library Amazing Hispanic American History: A Book of Answers for Kids
New York Public Library, George Ochoa, 1998

The Facts on File Dictionary of Proverbs
Martin H. Manser, 2007

Kid's Visual Reference of the United States
Blackbirch Press, 2002

Art: An A-Z Guide
Shirley Greenway, 2000

Music: An A-Z Guide
Nicola Barber, 2002

Libraries and Reference Materials (Straight to the Source)
John Hamilton, 2004

Scope and Sequence

Skills taught and/or reviewed in the *Write Source* program, grades K–8, are featured in the following scope and sequence chart.

FORMS OF WRITING	K	1	2	3	4	5	6	7	8
Narrative Writing									
sentences	■	■							
paragraph	■	■	■	■	■	■	■	■	■
narrative prompts		■	■	■	■	■	■	■	■
narrative essay			■	■	■	■	■	■	■
phase autobiography								■	■
Expository Writing									
sentences	■	■							
paragraph		■	■	■	■	■	■	■	■
expository prompts		■	■	■	■	■	■	■	■
expository essay			■	■	■	■	■	■	■
classification essay							■		
cause-and-effect essay								■	
comparison-contrast essay								■	■
Persuasive Writing									
sentences		■							
paragraph		■	■	■	■	■	■	■	■
persuasive prompts			■	■	■	■	■	■	■
persuasive letter			■	■	■	■	■	■	■
persuasive essay				■	■	■	■	■	■
editorial								■	■
problem-solution essay								■	■
personal commentary									■
position essay									■
Response to Literature									
sentences		■							
paragraph		■	■	■	■	■	■	■	■
response prompts		■	■	■	■	■	■	■	■
book review		■	■	■	■	■	■	■	■
journal response						■	■	■	■
response to literature							■	■	■
letter to an author									■
theme analysis									■

	K	1	2	3	4	5	6	7	8
Descriptive Writing									
sentences	■	■							
paragraph		■	■	■	■	■	■	■	■
descriptive essay			■	■	■	■	■	■	■
descriptive prompts				■	■	■			
Creative Writing									
poetry		■	■	■	■	■	■	■	■
story	■	■	■	■	■	■	■	■	■
play			■	■	■	■			
Research Writing									
research report		■	■	■	■	■	■	■	■
multimedia presentation			■	■	■	■	■	■	■
summary paragraph				■	■	■	■	■	■
Research Skills									
interview an expert		■	■	■	■	■	■	■	■
online research/using the Internet		■	■	■	■	■	■	■	■
understanding the parts of a book		■	■	■	■	■	■	■	■
using a dictionary, a thesaurus, or an encyclopedia		■	■	■	■	■	■	■	■
using diagrams, charts, graphs, and maps		■	■	■	■	■	■	■	■
using reference sources		■	■	■	■	■	■	■	■
using the library		■	■	■	■	■	■	■	■
note taking/summarizing		■	■	■	■	■	■	■	■
using a card catalog			■	■	■	■	■	■	■
using periodicals or magazines			■	■	■	■	■	■	■
using time lines			■	■	■	■	■	■	■
asking questions				■	■	■	■	■	■
bibliography (works cited)				■	■	■	■	■	■
The Tools of Learning									
improving viewing skills		■	■	■	■	■			
interviewing skills		■	■	■	■	■	■	■	
giving speeches		■	■	■	■	■	■	■	■
journal writing	■	■	■	■	■	■	■	■	■
learning logs		■	■	■	■	■	■	■	■
listening in class	■	■	■	■	■	■	■	■	■
taking classroom tests		■	■	■	■	■	■	■	■
note taking				■	■	■	■	■	■
completing writing assignments							■	■	■

THE WRITING PROCESS Grades

	K	1	2	3	4	5	6	7	8
Prewriting									
Selecting a Topic									
draw pictures		■	■						
make lists	■	■	■	■	■	■	■	■	■
sentence starters		■	■	■	■	■	■	■	■
chart			■	■	■	■	■	■	■
cluster			■	■	■	■	■	■	■
brainstorm					■	■	■	■	■
character chart					■	■		■	■
freewrite					■	■	■	■	■
Gathering Details									
drawing	■	■							
story map		■	■	■					
cluster	■	■	■	■	■	■	■	■	■
answer questions		■	■	■	■	■	■	■	■
details chart/sheet		■	■	■	■	■	■	■	■
gathering grid		■	■	■	■	■	■	■	■
list details/reasons		■	■	■	■	■	■	■	■
sensory chart	■	■	■	■	■	■	■	■	■
selecting main reasons			■	■	■	■	■	■	■
five W's			■	■	■	■	■	■	■
time line	■			■	■	■	■	■	■
table diagram					■	■	■	■	■
opinion statement							■	■	■
counter an objection								■	■
Organizing Details									
time order		■	■	■	■	■	■	■	■
Venn diagram			■	■	■	■	■	■	■
plot chart			■	■	■	■	■	■	■
time line			■	■	■	■	■	■	■
note cards			■	■	■	■	■	■	■
outline ideas			■	■	■	■	■	■	■
order of importance					■	■	■	■	■
order of location					■	■	■	■	■
Writing									
topic sentence	■	■	■	■	■	■	■	■	■
opinion statement		■	■	■	■	■	■	■	■
facts, examples	■	■	■	■	■	■	■	■	■
supporting details/reasons		■	■	■	■	■	■	■	■
interesting facts/details			■	■	■	■	■	■	■

Grades	K	1	2	3	4	5	6	7	8
make comparisons			■	■	■	■	■	■	■
dialogue			■	■	■	■	■	■	■
transitions			■	■	■	■	■	■	■
call to action			■	■	■	■	■	■	■
closing sentences			■	■	■	■	■	■	■
final comment/interesting thought			■	■	■	■	■	■	■
focus or thesis statement				■	■	■	■	■	■
action words				■	■	■	■	■	■
direct quotations				■	■	■	■	■	■
sensory details				■	■	■	■	■	■
high point of story				■	■	■	■	■	■
explain theme				■	■	■	■	■	■
reflect on a change, a feeling, an experience, a person				■	■	■	■	■	■
restate opinion/thesis					■	■	■	■	■
summarize					■	■	■	■	■
personal details						■	■	■	■
propose a solution							■	■	■
summarize a problem								■	■
share a new insight								■	■
counter an objection						■	■	■	■
emphasize a key idea								■	■
point-by-point discussion									■

Revising

Ideas

	K	1	2	3	4	5	6	7	8
sensory details	■	■	■	■	■	■	■	■	■
topic sentence			■	■	■	■	■	■	■
supporting details			■	■	■	■	■	■	■
dialogue				■	■	■	■	■	■
unnecessary details				■	■	■	■	■	■
focus statement					■	■	■	■	■

Organization

	K	1	2	3	4	5	6	7	8
order of ideas/details	■	■	■	■	■	■	■	■	■
transition words		■	■	■	■	■	■	■	■
order of importance			■		■	■	■	■	■
overall organization			■	■	■	■	■	■	■
order of location			■	■	■	■	■	■	■
logical order			■	■	■	■	■	■	■
clear beginning			■	■	■	■	■	■	■
time order			■	■	■	■	■	■	■

	Grades K	1	2	3	4	5	6	7	8
Voice									
natural		■	■	■	■	■	■	■	■
convincing				■	■	■	■	■	■
interested				■	■	■	■	■	■
dialogue					■	■	■	■	■
fits audience/purpose					■	■	■	■	■
formal/informal					■	■	■	■	■
knowledgeable					■	■	■	■	■
Word Choice									
sensory words/details	■	■	■	■	■	■	■	■	■
specific nouns			■	■	■	■	■	■	■
action verbs				■	■	■	■	■	■
connotation					■	■	■	■	■
modifiers					■	■	■	■	■
onomatopoeia							■	■	■
descriptive words						■	■	■	■
vivid verbs						■	■	■	■
connotation								■	■
Sentence Fluency									
complete sentences		■	■	■	■	■	■	■	■
variety of lengths			■	■	■	■	■	■	■
kinds of sentences			■	■	■	■	■	■	■
combining sentences				■	■	■	■	■	■
compound sentences				■	■	■	■	■	■
complex sentences					■	■	■	■	■
expanded sentences					■	■	■	■	■
variety of beginnings					■	■	■	■	■
types of sentences					■	■	■	■	■
Editing									
capitalization	■	■	■	■	■	■	■	■	■
grammar/punctuation/spelling	■	■	■	■	■	■	■	■	■
proper nouns	■		■	■	■	■	■	■	■
proper adjectives					■	■	■	■	■
Publishing									
publish in a variety of ways	■	■	■	■	■	■	■	■	■
review own work to monitor growth		■	■	■	■	■	■	■	■
self- and peer-assessing writing		■	■	■	■	■	■	■	■
use portfolios to save writing		■	■	■	■	■	■	■	■
use published pieces as models for writing		■	■	■	■	■	■	■	■

WRITING ACROSS THE CURRICULUM

	K	1	2	3	4	5	6	7	8
Narrative Writing									
reading		■							
music		■	■						
social studies			■			■	■	■	■
practical				■			■	■	■
science				■	■		■	■	■
Expository Writing									
social studies		■		■		■	■	■	■
math		■			■	■	■	■	■
reading *		■	■	■	■	■	■	■	■
science			■		■		■	■	■
practical			■	■	■	■	■	■	■
Persuasive Writing									
health		■							
science			■	■	■	■	■	■	■
social studies			■			■	■	■	■
practical				■	■	■	■	■	■
math					■		■	■	■
Descriptive Writing									
math		■	■				■	■	■
science		■	■		■	■	■	■	■
practical			■				■	■	■
social studies					■	■	■	■	■

* The models included in the "Response to Literature" section demonstrate expository writing within the reading curriculum.

GRAMMAR

Understanding Sentences	K	1	2	3	4	5	6	7	8
word order		■	■	■					
declarative		■	■	■	■	■	■	■	■
exclamatory		■	■	■	■	■	■	■	■
interrogative		■	■	■	■	■	■	■	■
complete sentences and fragments		■	■	■	■	■	■	■	■
simple subjects		■	■	■	■	■	■	■	■
simple predicates		■	■	■	■	■	■	■	■
correcting run-on sentences		■	■	■	■	■	■	■	■
compound			■	■	■	■	■	■	■
imperative			■	■	■	■	■	■	■
complete predicates				■	■	■	■	■	■

Understanding Sentences (Continued)

	K	1	2	3	4	5	6	7	8
complete subjects				■	■	■	■	■	■
compound predicates				■	■	■	■	■	■
compound subjects				■	■	■	■	■	■
prepositional phrases				■	■	■	■	■	■
appositive phrases					■	■	■	■	■
clauses, dependent and independent					■	■	■	■	■
complex					■	■	■	■	■
modifiers					■	■	■	■	■
noun phrases					■	■	■	■	■
verb phrases					■	■	■	■	■

Using the Parts of Speech

Nouns

	K	1	2	3	4	5	6	7	8
singular and plural		■	■	■	■	■	■	■	■
common/proper		■	■	■	■	■	■	■	■
possessive			■	■	■	■	■	■	■
singular/plural possessive			■	■	■	■	■	■	■
specific				■	■	■	■	■	■
abstract/concrete					■	■	■	■	■
appositives					■	■	■	■	■
collective/compound					■	■	■	■	■
object					■	■	■	■	■
predicate					■	■	■	■	■
subject					■	■	■	■	■
gender					■	■	■	■	■

Verbs

	K	1	2	3	4	5	6	7	8
contractions with *not*		■	■	■	■	■	■	■	■
action	■	■	■	■	■	■	■	■	■
linking		■	■	■	■	■	■	■	■
past tense		■	■	■	■	■	■	■	■
present tense		■	■	■	■	■	■	■	■
subject-verb agreement		■	■	■	■	■	■	■	■
future tense			■	■	■	■	■	■	■
helping			■	■	■	■	■	■	■
singular/plural				■	■	■	■	■	■
irregular				■	■	■	■	■	■
simple tense				■	■	■	■	■	■
active/passive voice					■	■	■	■	■
direct objects					■	■	■	■	■
indirect objects					■	■	■	■	■
perfect tense					■	■	■	■	■

	Grades	K	1	2	3	4	5	6	7	8
transitive/intransitive						■	■	■	■	■
participles							■	■	■	■
continuous tense								■	■	■
gerunds								■	■	■
infinitives								■	■	■
Pronouns										
personal			■	■	■	■	■	■	■	■
antecedents			■	■	■	■	■	■	■	■
singular and plural			■	■	■	■	■	■	■	■
possessive			■	■	■	■	■	■	■	■
subject and object					■	■	■	■	■	■
demonstrative/interrogative						■	■	■	■	■
gender						■	■	■	■	■
indefinite						■	■	■	■	■
intensive and reflexive						■	■	■	■	■
relative						■	■	■	■	■
Adjectives										
adjectives		■	■	■	■	■	■	■	■	■
comparative/superlative			■	■	■	■	■	■	■	■
articles				■	■	■	■	■	■	■
compound					■	■	■	■	■	■
positive					■	■	■	■	■	■
proper					■	■	■	■	■	■
demonstrative						■	■	■	■	■
equal						■	■	■	■	■
indefinite						■	■	■	■	■
predicate						■	■	■	■	■
Interjections										
Interjections			■	■	■	■	■	■	■	■
Adverbs										
of manner				■	■	■	■	■	■	■
of place		■		■	■	■	■	■	■	■
of time				■	■	■	■	■	■	■
that modify verbs				■	■	■	■	■	■	■
of degree						■	■	■	■	■
that modify adjectives and adverbs						■	■	■	■	■
comparative/superlative						■	■	■	■	■
comparing with adverbs						■	■	■	■	■
irregular forms						■	■	■	■	■
positive						■	■	■	■	■

	K	1	2	3	4	5	6	7	8
Grades									
Conjunctions									
coordinating			■	■	■	■	■	■	■
correlative					■	■	■	■	■
subordinating					■	■	■	■	■
Prepositions									
prepositions	■		■	■	■	■	■	■	■
prepositional phrases				■	■	■	■	■	■
Mechanics									
Capitalization									
pronoun "I"		■	■	■	■	■	■	■	■
days, months, holidays		■	■	■	■	■	■	■	■
first words	■	■	■	■	■	■	■	■	■
names of people	■	■	■	■	■	■	■	■	■
proper nouns		■	■	■	■	■	■	■	■
titles used with names		■	■	■	■	■	■	■	■
titles		■	■	■	■	■	■	■	■
beginning of a quotation		■	■	■	■	■	■	■	■
geographic names			■	■	■	■	■	■	■
abbreviations			■	■	■	■	■	■	■
proper adjectives				■	■	■	■	■	■
words used as names				■	■	■	■	■	■
names of historical events					■	■	■	■	■
names of religions, nationalities					■	■	■	■	■
organizations					■	■	■	■	■
particular sections of the country					■	■	■	■	■
trade names/official names					■	■	■	■	■
letters to indicate form or direction							■	■	■
specific course names							■	■	■
Plurals									
irregular nouns		■	■	■	■	■	■	■	■
most nouns		■	■	■	■	■	■	■	■
nouns ending with *sh*, *ch*, *x*, *s*, and *z*			■	■	■	■	■	■	■
nouns ending in *y*			■	■	■	■	■	■	■
adding an *'s*					■	■	■	■	■
compound nouns					■	■	■	■	■
nouns ending with *f* or *fe*					■	■	■	■	■
nouns ending with *ful*					■	■	■	■	■
nouns ending with *o*					■	■	■	■	■

	Grades	K	1	2	3	4	5	6	7	8
Abbreviations										
days and months				■	■	■	■	■	■	■
state postal abbreviations					■	■	■	■	■	■
titles of people			■	■	■	■	■	■	■	■
addresses				■	■	■	■	■	■	■
acronyms					■	■	■	■	■	■
initialisms					■	■	■	■	■	■
Numbers										
numbers 1 to 9					■	■	■	■	■	■
numbers only					■	■	■	■	■	■
sentence beginnings					■	■	■	■	■	■
very large numbers					■	■	■	■	■	■
numbers in compound modifiers								■	■	■
time and money								■	■	■

Punctuation

	Grades	K	1	2	3	4	5	6	7	8
Periods										
after an initial/an abbreviation			■	■	■	■	■	■	■	■
at the end of a sentence		■	■	■	■	■	■	■	■	■
as a decimal point					■	■	■	■	■	■
after an indirect question								■	■	■
Question Marks										
after questions		■	■	■	■	■	■	■	■	■
after tag questions						■	■	■	■	■
to show doubt						■	■	■	■	■
Exclamation Points										
for words, phrases, and sentences		■	■	■	■	■	■	■	■	■
for interjections			■	■	■	■	■	■	■	■
Commas										
in a series			■	■	■	■	■	■	■	■
in dates			■	■	■	■	■	■	■	■
in friendly letters			■	■	■	■	■	■	■	■
after introductory words			■	■	■	■	■	■	■	■
with interjections		■	■	■	■	■	■	■	■	■
in a compound sentence				■	■	■	■	■	■	■
in addresses				■	■	■	■	■	■	■
to set off dialogue				■	■	■	■	■	■	■
in direct address				■	■	■	■	■	■	■
in numbers					■	■	■	■	■	■
to separate equal adjectives					■		■	■	■	■
to set off appositives						■	■	■	■	■

Commas (Continued)	K	1	2	3	4	5	6	7	8
to set off interrupters					■	■	■	■	■
to set off phrases					■	■	■	■	■
to set off titles of people							■	■	■
Apostrophes									
in contractions	■	■	■	■	■	■	■	■	■
to form plural possessive nouns			■	■	■	■	■	■	■
to form singular possessive nouns			■	■	■	■	■	■	■
to form some plurals					■	■	■	■	■
to replace omitted numbers/letters					■	■	■	■	■
with indefinite pronouns					■	■	■	■	■
to show shared possession					■	■	■	■	■
in possessives w/compound nouns							■	■	■
to express time or amount							■	■	■
Underlining and Italics									
for titles	■	■	■	■	■	■	■	■	■
for special words					■	■	■	■	■
for scientific and foreign words							■	■	■
Quotation Marks									
for direct quotations			■	■	■	■	■	■	■
for titles			■	■	■	■	■	■	■
for special words					■	■	■	■	■
for quotations within a quotation							■	■	■
Colons									
between hour and minutes				■	■	■	■	■	■
in business letter				■	■	■	■	■	■
to introduce a list of items				■	■	■	■	■	■
for emphasis							■	■	■
to introduce sentences							■	■	■
Hyphens									
in word division				■	■	■	■	■	■
in compound words					■	■	■	■	■
in fractions					■	■	■	■	■
to create new words					■	■	■	■	■
to join letters and words					■	■	■	■	■
to avoid confusion or awkward spelling							■	■	■
to make adjectives							■	■	■

	K	1	2	3	4	5	6	7	8
Parentheses									
to add information				■	■	■	■	■	■
Dashes									
for emphasis					■	■	■	■	■
to show a sentence break					■	■	■	■	■
to show interrupted speech					■	■	■	■	■
Ellipses									
to show a pause					■	■	■	■	■
to show omitted words					■	■	■	■	■
Semicolons									
in a compound sentence					■	■	■	■	■
to separate groups (that have commas) in a series					■	■	■	■	■
with conjunctive adverbs							■	■	■

Usage

	K	1	2	3	4	5	6	7	8
Spelling									
high-frequency words	■	■							
consonant endings				■	■	■	■	■	■
i before *e*				■	■	■	■	■	■
silent *e*				■	■	■	■	■	■
words ending in *y*				■	■	■	■	■	■
Using the Right Word	■	■	■	■	■	■	■	■	■

Penmanship

	K	1	2	3	4	5	6	7	8
word space, letter space	■	■							
write legibly	■	■	■	■	■	■	■	■	■
margins/spaces				■	■	■	■	■	■

Meeting the Standards

These six pages clearly show how the *Write Source* program helps you meet national writing standards. In the charts that follow, the standards of the National Council of Teachers of English (NCTE) have been combined with those of numerous states.

National Standards for Descriptive Writing

- Use lists and charts to explore possible topics.
- Draft compositions that have a central idea, a clear thesis, and a thoughtful conclusion.
- Select and use voice and style appropriate to audience and purpose.
- Support ideas with specific, rich vocabulary; sensory and memory details; and anecdotes, descriptions, and specific examples.
- Revise and edit drafts for support of ideas and better word choice, and to ensure standard usage, grammar, and mechanics.

Descriptive Writing in *Write Source*

Descriptive writing, 554
Paragraphs, 71–74, 527, 535
Essay, 75–82,

Assessment support
Assessment sheet, 52, TE 787
Prompts, 546
Test preparation, 464–467

Additional descriptive support
Adjectives, 486–489, 732, 734
Adverbs, 490–493, 736, 738
Details, 531, 532
Eyewitness report, 84–85
Field-trip report, 88–89
Figurative language, 360, 560
Mathematical operation, 86–87
Metaphors, 37, 360, 558
Organizing details, 550–551
Sample topics, 547
Sensory details, 114, 355, 531
Simile, 37, 360, 558
Transitions, 38, 572–573
Word choice, 486–493

National Standards for Narrative Writing

- Use charts and clusters to gather and organize ideas.
- Support central idea with vocabulary and voice appropriate to audience and purpose.
- Revise drafts by adding, deleting, and rearranging texts; provide logical support of ideas.
- Assess writing using a rubric based on the traits of effective writing.
- Share finished pieces with classmates and others.

Narrative Writing in *Write Source*

Narrative writing, 554
Essay, 97–134, 135–142
One Writer's Process, 11–28
Paragraph, 93–96
Review, 155
Story writing, 343–352

Assessment support
Assessment models, TE 763–770
Assessment sheet, TE 787
Assessment, writing for, 152–154
Evaluating,
    a narrative, 25–27
    a phase autobiography, 132–133
Prompts, 152–154, 546
Reflecting on your writing, 28, 134
Rubric, 130–131, 750, 754, 758
Traits of narrative writing, 98

Additional narrative support
Autobiography, 554
Descriptive writing, 554
    essay, 75–91
    paragraph, 71–74
    sensory details, 114,
        355, 531, 557, 559
Dialogue, 348, 556, 557
    in narrative, 116
    punctuating, 556, 588.1,
        598.1, 600.1
E-mail, 150–151
Graphic organizers, 548–549
Historical fiction, 144–145
Math, 146–147
Sample topics, 547
Science 148–149
Transitions, 38, 572–573

National Standards for Expository (Informational) Writing

- Use diagrams, charts, and freewriting to gather and organize ideas.
- Establish a clear focus with topic sentences that explain ideas.
- Support the thesis with a variety of specific, interesting details.
- Revise drafts to create a precise pattern and an interested voice.
- Assess writing using a rubric based on the traits of effective writing.

Expository Writing in *Write Source*

National Standards for Persuasive Writing

- Use charts, diagrams, and lists to gather and organize ideas.
- Support central idea with vocabulary and voice appropriate to audience and purpose.
- Revise drafts by adding, deleting, and rearranging texts; provide logical support of ideas.
- Assess writing using a rubric based on the traits of effective writing.
- Share finished pieces with classmates and others.

Persuasive Writing in *Write Source*

Persuasive writing, 555
Essay, 54, 56, 223–260
Paragraph, 219–222, 529
Review, 281

Assessment support
Assessment models, TE 776–780
Assessment sheet, TE 787
Assessment, writing for, 278–280
Evaluating an essay, 258–259
Prompts, 278–280, 546
Reflecting on your writing, 260
Review, 281
Rubric, 256–257, 752, 756, 760
Traits of persuasive writing, 224

Additional persuasive support
Argument, developing a statistical, 270–271
Business letter, 274–277
Editorial, 268–269
Objections, 230
Personal commentary, 261–266
Proposals, 90–91, 576
Sample topics, 546, 547
Structure, 234, 243
Transitions, 38, 572–573

National Standards for Response-to-Literature Writing

- Develop a response that exhibits an understanding of plot, character, and theme, and that is supported with quotations and details from the piece of literature.
- Use lists, charts, and notes to generate and organize ideas.
- Select a voice and style appropriate to the audience and purpose, and use specific literary vocabulary for clarity.
- Assess writing using a rubric based on the traits of effective writing.
- Share finished pieces with classmates and others.

Responding to Literature in *Write Source*

Response-to-literature writing, 555
Essay, 287–322
Paragraph, 283–286

Assessment support
Assessment models, 781–786
Assessment sheet, TE 787
Assessment, writing for, 336–341
Prompts, 336–341
Reflecting on your writing, 322
Rubric, 318–319, 753, 757, 761
Traits of response-to-literature writing, 288

Additional response-to-literature support
Evaluating a Web site, 334–335
Letter to an author, 323–328
Responding to a historical photo, 330–331
Structure, 296
Summary of a science article, 332–333
Transitions, 38, 572–573

National Standards for Research Writing

- Use research skills to gather ideas and information.
- Write a research report with a thesis statement, several middle paragraphs, and a concluding paragraph.
- Create and present an interactive report.

Research Writing in *Write Source*

Research writing, 555
Report, 363–410
Summary paragraph, 375–378

Assessment support
Evaluating, 410

Additional research support
Computer, writing with, 60–62
Graphic organizer, 389
Internet, 365
Library, 366–374
Multimedia presentations, 411–415
Note cards, 390–391
Outline, 394
Plagiarism, 391
Primary and secondary sources, 364
Reference materials, 370–373
Research skills, 363–374
Sources, citing, 385, 392, 396, 403–404
Thesis (focus) statement, 393, 394
Works-cited page, 403–404

Getting Started Activities

The *Write Source* pupil's edition is full of helpful resources that students can access throughout the year while they are developing their writing skills.

Getting-started activities are provided as copy masters on TE pages 794–796. (See the answer keys on TE page 797.) These activities will

- help students discover the kinds of information available in different sections of the book,
- teach students how to access that information, and
- familiarize students with the layout of the book.

The more familiar students are with the text, the more proficient they will be in using it as a resource.

Scavenger Hunts

Students enjoy using scavenger hunts to become familiar with a book. The scavenger hunts we provide can be done in small groups or as a class. They are designed for oral answers, but you may want to photocopy the pages for students to write on. You may also vary the procedure by first having students take turns finding the items and then, on the next scavenger hunt, challenging students to "race" for the answers.

After your students have completed each scavenger hunt, you can challenge them to create their own versions. For example, small groups can work together to create "Find the Fours" or "Search for Sixes" scavenger hunts and then exchange their "hunts" with other groups.

Special Challenge: Develop questions that teams of students try to answer using the book. Pattern this activity after a popular game show.

Other Activities

- **Problem Resolution** Give students the following assignment: Across the top of a sheet of paper, write down three things you find difficult about school (e.g., taking notes, taking tests, writing essays, spelling, using commas). Then explore your book to find chapters, sections, examples, and so on, that might help you with your problem area. Under each problem, write the titles or headings and the page numbers where you can find help. Keep this sheet to use throughout the year.

- **Help Wanted** A variation on the above activity is to have students write down all the subject areas they study and list under each heading the parts of the book that might help them in that subject.

- **Thought-Trap Poem** Have students write a thought-trap poem: After reviewing the book, close it. The first line of your poem will be the title of the book. Then list thoughts and feelings about the book, line by line. When you have listed everything you want to say, "trap" your thoughts by repeating the title.

- **Poster** Have pairs of students create poster-size advertisements for the book. Each ad should have a headline, list important features (what is in the book) and benefits (whom it can help and how), show an example of illustrations (made by tracing or copying), and urge readers of the ad to get their books now!

- **Pen Pal Letter** Have students imagine that they are each going to send a copy of *Write Source* to a pen pal in another state. Have each student write a letter to send along with it to tell the pen pal about the book.

Written and Compiled by
**Dave Kemper, Patrick Sebranek,
and Verne Meyer**

Illustrated by
Chris Krenzke

WRITE SOURCE®

GREAT SOURCE EDUCATION GROUP
a division of Houghton Mifflin Company
Wilmington, Massachusetts

Welcome to the Wraparound Teacher's Edition!

Writing is a journey to unexplored realms, and *Write Source* can be your guide.

The pupil's edition will guide your students to many destinations. Along the way, they'll meet fellow travelers such as these friendly kids aboard their pencil-lead rover. Your students will also read the work of their fellow explorers in the numerous accessible models.

The teacher's edition will guide you on this journey as well. In the following pages, you'll find not only lesson objectives and instructions but also these special features at point of use:
- Writing Traits Tips
- Teaching Tips
- Integrated Grammar, Literature, Writing Craft, and Technology
- Assessment Options and Test Prep
- Notes for Students of English as a Second Language
- Accommodations and Modifications for Struggling Students
- Enrichments for Advanced Students

Welcome to your writing adventure! Welcome to *Write Source*.

Thanks to the Teachers!

This program would not have been possible without the input of many teachers and administrators from across the nation. As we originally developed this K–12 series, we surveyed hundreds of teaching professionals, and as we revised this series, we have implemented the feedback of even more. Our grateful thanks goes out to each of you. We couldn't have done it without you!

Reviewers

Ilene R. Abrams
Cobb County School District
Marietta, GA

Dawn Calhoun Bray
Houston County School System
Warner Robins, Georgia

Doreen A. Caswell
Mary G. Montgomery
Semmes, Alabama

Tricia Dugger
St. Lucie County Schools District
Ft. Pierce, FL

Vallie J. Ericson
Sheboygan Area School District
Sheboygan, Wisconsin

Paula Denise Findley
Arkansas River Educational
   Cooperative
White Hall, Arkansas

Mary M. Fisher
Arlington Public Schools
Arlington, MA

Michelle Harden-Brown
Savannah-Chatham Southwest Middle
Savannah, Georgia

Kevin F. Harrington
Baldwin Middle School
Baldwin, New York

Beverly Canzater Jacobs
Solon City Schools
Solon, Ohio

Alissa Lowman
Hillside Middle School
Northville, Michigan

Elizabeth F. Manning
A.E. Phillips Laboratory School
Ruston, Louisiana

Rhea Mayerchak
Omin Middle School
Boca Raton, Florida

Steve Mellen
Prince George's County Public Schools
Temple Hills, Maryland

Diana L. Mooney
Lake Denoon Middle School
Muskego, Wisconsin

Ellen Nielsen
Clovis Unified School District
Clovis, California

Geraldine Ortego
Lafayette Parish District Office
Lafayette, Louisiana

Deborah Richmond
Ferry Pass Middle School
Pensacola, FL

Addie Rae Tobey
Shaker Heights Middle School
Shaker Heights, Ohio

Jodi Turchin
Silver Lakes Middle School Board of
   Broward County
North Lauderdale, FL

Bridget Wetton
Alpine Union School District
San Diego, California

Susan Wilson
South Orange/Maplewood School
   District
South Orange, New Jersey

Robert Wright
Sebastian River Middle
Sebastian River, FL

Peggy Zehnder
Bellingham School District
Bellingham, Washington

Technology Connections for *Write Source*

This series is supported by two Web sites:

The **Great Source iwrite** site is a writing resource that supports students, teachers, and parents. You'll find tutorials about the forms and traits of writing, as well as the latest articles, features, tips, and contests. Go to **www.greatsource.com/iwrite**.

The **Write Source** site features all the materials available from Write Source, as well as handy writing topics, student models, and help with research. You can even read about the history of Write Source. Go to **www.thewritesource.com**.

Printed in the United States of America

International Standard Book Number: 978-0-669-00645-2 (hardcover)

1 2 3 4 5 6 7 8 9 10 -RRD- 15 14 13 12 11 10 09

International Standard Book Number: 978-0-669-00904-0 (softcover)

1 2 3 4 5 6 7 8 9 10 -RRD- 15 14 13 12 11 10 09

Using the *Write Source* Book

Your *Write Source* book is loaded with information to help you learn about writing. One section that will be especially helpful is the "Proofreader's Guide" at the back of the book. This section covers all of the rules for language and grammar.

The book also includes four units covering the types of writing that you may have to complete on district or state writing tests. At the end of each unit, there are samples and tips for writing in science, social studies, and math.

Write Source will help you with other learning skills, too—test taking, note taking, and speaking. This makes *Write Source* a valuable writing and learning guide in all of your classes.

Your *Write Source* guide . . .

With practice, you will be able to find information in this book quickly, using the guides explained below.

The **TABLE OF CONTENTS** (starting on the next page) lists the six major sections in the book and the chapters found in each section.

The **INDEX** (starting on page 751) lists the topics covered in the book in alphabetical order. Use the index when you are interested in a specific topic.

The **COLOR CODING** used for "Basic Grammar and Writing" (blue), "A Writer's Resource" (green), and the "Proofreader's Guide" (yellow) make these important sections easy to find.

The **SPECIAL PAGE REFERENCES** in the book tell you where to turn for additional information about a specific topic.

If, at first, you're not sure how to find something in *Write Source,* ask your teacher for help. With a little practice, you will find everything quickly and easily.

The *Write Source* Voice

For over 30 years, our pupil books have spoken directly to students. We see ourselves as writers speaking to other writers.

As a result, the *Write Source* voice is always encouraging, like an older classmate who genuinely wants a younger one to succeed. We believe that every student can learn to write and that every writer can improve. Throughout this book, your students will hear a voice that says, "You can do it!"

In the same way, the material in the wraparound text speaks directly to you. After all, we are simply teachers speaking to other teachers, and so we use the same encouraging voice.

Whether you're a seasoned writing teacher or a fresh new face, we are certain that these materials in your hands can make a big difference for your students. We hope you agree!

Understanding the Writing Process

The first section of the book provides an introduction to (or review of) the writing process.

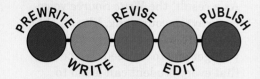

The chapter "One Writer's Process" lets students see how another eighth-grade writer works through the process of prewriting, writing, revising, editing, and publishing.

Integrating the Six Traits

Write Source fully integrates the six +1 traits of writing into the writing process. Prewriting focuses on ideas and organization. Writing adds a focus on voice. Revising focuses on the first three traits and also word choice and sentence fluency. Editing zeroes in on conventions, while publishing features the +1 trait of presentation.

contents

The Writing Process

Wraparound Feature

Focus on the Traits

Organization
Throughout the teacher's edition, trait boxes give you special tips for using the traits to help your students evaluate, discuss, and improve their writing.

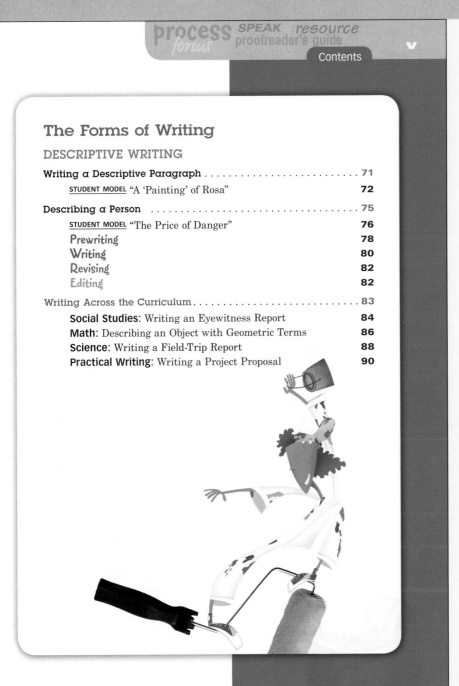

The Forms of Writing

DESCRIPTIVE WRITING

Creating the Forms of Writing

The writing units in *Write Source* focus on creating the fundamental forms of writing:

- Descriptive
- Narrative
- Expository
- Persuasive
- Response to Literature
- Creative
- Research

Each writing assignment includes instruction, examples, and activities that lead students through the writing process. The material works well for whole-class instruction, writing workshop minilessons, and self-paced, individual work time.

Writing Across the Curriculum

Special assignments after each of the major forms help your students write in their content areas: social studies, math, science, and practical writing. Whether you teach these subjects or partner with team teachers, these content-area assignments can help your students succeed throughout their day.

Wraparound Features

Materials

At the beginning of each unit, consult this box to find out what materials you need to have on hand to teach the lesson.

Copy Masters/ Transparencies

These features tell you what classroom presentation aids exist to help you deliver the lesson.

Benchmark Papers

Check this feature to find out what benchmark papers you can use to show your students a range of performance.

Teaching the Core Units

The core writing units focus on the forms that are most often tested—narrative, expository, persuasive, and response to literature.

Each unit begins with an accessible model with response questions.

Afterward, the text leads students step-by-step through the process of creating a similar piece of writing. Activities help students do the following:

- Select a topic.
- Gather details.
- Organize details.
- Create a focus statement.
- Write a strong beginning.
- Build a solid middle.
- Create an effective ending.
- Revise for ideas, organization, voice, word choice, and sentence fluency.
- Edit for conventions.
- Publish work with polished presentation.
- Assess using traits-based rubrics.

Writing Workshop

Each activity in the core writing units can function as a minilesson. Use them . . .

- to direct the whole class before individual writing time,
- to instruct a group of writers who are ready to learn a new skill, or
- to provide scaffolding for an individual writer who gets stuck.

Wraparound Feature

Grammar Connection

Each unit overview suggests grammar activities to cover in the unit. Grammar Connection boxes then help you pinpoint the places to integrate instruction.

Using Rubrics Throughout the Process

You'll find that the traits-based rubrics in *Write Source* help guide your students throughout the process. Each core writing unit begins with a goal rubric that helps your students think about what they are trying to accomplish. Then, as your students revise and edit, rubric strips guide their work, helping them improve their writing in ways large and small.

Preparing for Assessment

Every core unit teaches students process-based strategies, which they internalize as "thinking moves" that will help them in on-demand writing situations. Each unit also ends with a sample on-demand writing prompt and response, as well as additional prompts for practice with high-stakes writing situations.

Efficacy studies in Florida, California, Pennsylvania, Illinois, and Massachusetts have demonstrated significant improvements from pretest to posttest scores for students using the *Write Source* series. See www.greatsource.com for results.

Wraparound Features

Teaching Tip

Throughout the wraparound, you'll find special strategies for making the lesson come alive for your students.

Test Prep!

These features give suggestions for preparing your students for high- and low-stakes writing and grammar tests.

Differentiating Instruction

Each of the core units provides four levels of form-specific assignments:

1. **Paragraph:** Students who are struggling—or who need an introduction to the form—can create a strong paragraph in the appropriate form.
2. **Core Essay:** Middle-level students can create, revise, and edit the first multiparagraph essay in the form.
3. **Challenge Essay:** Advanced students can try their hand at a second, more challenging type of writing in the same basic form.
4. **Cross-Curricular Writing:** All students can apply their new skills by writing in social studies, math, and science and by writing practical forms such as letters and e-mail messages.

Also, because the *Write Source* series follows a consistent format throughout its K–12 line, students who need further differentiation can work at a grade below (or above) their classmates.

PERSUASIVE WRITING

Wraparound Features

English Language Learners

These boxes provide differentiation tips to help English Language Learners.

Struggling Learners

Consult this feature to adjust the lesson for those who are struggling.

Advanced Learners

These boxes feature tips for challenging students who excel.

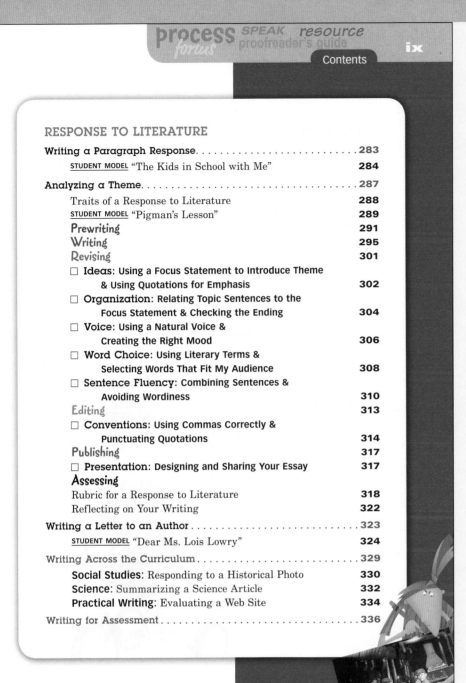

process SPEAK resource
focus proofreader's guide
Contents ix

Literature Connections

Each unit contains numerous student models. By reading them and responding to them, students tune their minds to a given genre before beginning to write in it.

Also, the response-to-literature unit focuses on age-appropriate novels, short stories, biographies, and articles that your students may have read—or may want to read. Here are all the literature-based student models in the response-to-literature unit.

- **Response Paragraph:** "The Kids in School with Me"
- **Response Essay Key Model:** "Pigman's Lesson"
- **Response Essay Working Model:** "Crossing the Line"
- **Response Essay Assessment Model:** "Honest Work"
- **Letter to an Author:** "Dear Ms. Lois Lowry"
- **Response to a Photo (Social Studies):** "No Time to Play"
- **Article Summary (Science):** "Batteries Driving the Future"
- **Evaluation of a Web Site (Practical Writing):** "Making Origami"
- **On-Demand Response to Literature:** "It Wasn't About Fish" prompt and response
- **On-Demand Response to Literature:** "Mountain Encounter"

Wraparound Feature

Literature Connections

These features help you use age-appropriate literary works to teach students special writing techniques. You'll find interesting insights into the works and lives of favorite writers as well as fresh ways to use literature to teach writing.

Tapping Creativity

Write Source promotes creativity in all its writing assignments, but especially in its story and poem chapters. This section allows you and your students to develop forms that are especially inventive.

- Short Story
- Free-Verse Poem
- Found Poem
- Couplet
- Circle Poem

Research shows a direct connection between enjoyment and learning. Think how quickly a student masters a favorite video game or learns all the words to a favorite song. By letting students write for the joy of it, you can awaken in them a lifelong love of writing.

The Craft of Writing

Art teachers teach techniques for creating perspective or formulas for the proportions of a human face, but then art students must internalize these techniques and use them to craft something new and wonderful.

Writing teachers need to do the same. Throughout the core units you will find suggestions for helping students develop their writing style and voice, going beyond concrete skills to discover the craft of writing.

Wraparound Feature

 Writer's Craft

These features help you inspire students to write the way professional writers do. They feature techniques used by the masters as well as interesting anecdotes and quotations.

process SPEAK resource
focus proofreader's guide
xi
Contents

Training Researchers

In this Internet age, strong research skills are more important than ever. Students must be able to evaluate sources and avoid the lure of plagiarism. This section equips students to succeed using traditional and digital source materials.

The step-by-step instructions in the "Research Writing" section help students learn to do the following:

- Use the library.
- Use the Internet.
- Evaluate sources.
- Summarize, paraphrase, and quote.
- Avoid plagiarism.
- Cite sources (according to MLA style).
- Use a gathering grid and create note cards.
- Outline a research report.
- Create a works-cited page.

The section also helps students present their material in a traditional report form—or as a multimedia presentation!

Equipping Students to Learn

This section focuses on the so-called "soft skills" that often get neglected in the modern rush to teach academic subjects. However, the skills of speaking and listening, writing to learn, and conducting oneself in a classroom are crucial to success in all classes.

Organized topically, these six chapters can be taught as minilessons when your students most need them.

- **Use "Listening and Speaking"** when setting up a writing workshop so that students understand the ground rules for group discussion.
- **Present "Giving Speeches"** after students complete a major writing assignment so that they can convert their work into speeches.
- **Assign "Keeping Journals and Learning Logs"** when students are setting up journals at the beginning of a term.
- **Present "Taking Notes"** before students attend a special lecture.
- **Work through "Completing Writing Assignments"** to help students think more deeply.
- **Use "Taking Classroom Tests"** to help students improve performance on assessments.

Wraparound Feature

Technology Connections

In these features, you'll see connections to the *Interactive Writing Skills* CD-ROM, the Great Source iwrite Web site, thewritesource.com, Eval-U-Write, and other technology connections for your students.

The Tools of Learning

SPEAKING TO LEARN

WRITING TO LEARN

process SPEAK resource
forms proofreader's guide **xiii**
Contents

Basic Grammar and Writing

WORKING WITH WORDS

Teaching Grammar and Writing

With clear rules, simple explanations, engaging examples, and fun activities, "Working with Words" provides short minilessons to help students understand and use the different parts of speech.

As you work through the writing units earlier in the book, you will find cross-references to these pages and those in the "Proofreader's Guide." The *Write Source* series fully integrates its grammar components within its writing units—including every activity in the student book, the *SkillsBook,* and the *Interactive Writing Skills* CD-ROM. Integrated grammar instruction allows students to use the rules in context and understand not just the "what" of grammar but also the "why."

You can use all the grammar that is suggested—or target your students' specific needs. The choice is yours.

Avoiding Errors and Creating Style

"Building Effective Sentences" begins on the level of correctness, ensuring that students know how to write complete, error-free sentences. The chapter then covers issues of style, helping students create different types and kinds of sentences, combine or expand choppy sentences, and model the sentences of professional writers. The chapter ends with help for preparing for a sentence-skill test—a component of many state writing tests at this grade level.

xiv

CONSTRUCTING STRONG PARAGRAPHS

Creating Paragraphs

Every core unit begins with a paragraph assignment in the major form: descriptive, narrative, expository, persuasive, and response to literature. This chapter provides further support, guidelines, models, and practice for students who are still working to perfect paragraph-building skills. The chapter also helps students develop a paragraph into a full essay.

Creating Resourceful Writers

This section equips students with specific traits-based strategies that they will use over and over during the writing process. Each new concept is introduced by a question that most eighth-grade writers have asked at one time or another—followed by an answer to the question and a specific strategy for implementing the answer.

A Writer's Resource

Contents **xvii**

process SPEAK resource
forms proofreader's guide **xvii**
Contents

Using the +1 Trait: Presentation

Sometimes the traits are referred to as the six traits +1 because presentation is so crucial to the success of any form of writing. Each of the core units includes a page that focuses on presentation and publishing. This section also provides support for effectively presenting ideas on the page.

Perfecting Conventions

The "Proofreader's Guide" includes the rules of punctuation, mechanics, usage, sentence creation, and parts of speech. The rules are accompanied by engaging example text and activities to test knowledge.

Also, as the "Test Prep" box indicates, the major sections end with test-prep pages to help students study for grammar tests.

Cross-references in this TE connect to other resources—*SkillsBook* activities as well as videos and exercises on the *Interactive Writing Skills* CD-ROM.

Proofreader's Guide

Test Prep!

The "Proofreader's Guide" includes test-prep pages to help you study for tests on punctuation, mechanics, usage, sentences, and the parts of speech.

Why Write?

The following story by Mr. James Pearson, a high school basketball coach, will help answer this question.

> When I was in eighth grade, basketball was my life. But I couldn't try out for the team unless I improved my grades.
>
> I started with language arts and asked Ms. Libby what I could do. She told me to spend more time on my writing, and she gave me this advice: *Write down what you are thinking. Then read your writing. Write some more and then read it again. Do some more writing, and so on. Back and forth.* I followed her advice and found out that I could write.
>
> That advice helped me through middle school, high school, *and* college. It also helped me get the grades to play basketball. If I hadn't listened to Ms. Libby back then, I might not be a coach today.

Writing can do many things if you give it a chance. For one thing, it can help you reach your goals, just like it helped Coach Pearson reach his. Read on to find out more about the value of writing.

What's Ahead

- **Reasons to Write**
- **Creating a Writing "SourceBank"**

Why Write?

Before introducing students to this section, write *Why Write?* on the board.

- Ask students to think about the question for a moment and to jot down a brief answer on a slip of paper.
- Collect the slips of paper and randomly read aloud the responses. You may receive some humorous or offhand responses. You will also receive some thoughtful, insightful responses worthy of discussion.

This activity will get students thinking about their own attitudes and feelings about writing. It can also help you get a sense of the spirit and makeup of the class.

Reasons to Write

Ask students to name things they have gotten better at since they first learned how to do them (for example: reading, playing the piano or any other instrument, playing soccer or any other sport, drawing, painting, or sculpting). Then invite volunteers to describe their first experiences doing these things and how they got better at them. Students may say they got better

- from trying over and over, or
- from being taught or coached.

Help students connect this learning process to writing. Students often think that great writers are born great writers. Be sure they understand that those writers never would have developed their talent if they hadn't started writing, and kept on writing.

As you discuss the reasons to write, ask for a show of hands to find out how many students regularly practice writing for each reason. This will help prepare students for the **Write to learn** activity at the bottom of the page.

Reasons to Write

Writing makes you a better thinker because it helps you explore your experiences. Writing also makes you a better learner because it helps you understand the subjects you are studying. And finally, the writing you do now will make you a better writer next month, next year, and forever.

Writing for All the Right Reasons

Explore Your Personal Thoughts

Writing in a personal journal helps you learn important things about yourself and feel more confident in your ability to write. (See pages 431–434 for more information.)

Better Understand New Ideas

Writing in a classroom journal or a learning log helps you make sense of what you are learning, and it helps you remember things better. (See pages 435–440 for more information.)

Show Learning

Writing essays, developing reports, and answering essay-test questions can show teachers what you have learned. These forms of writing can also help you assess your own understanding of classroom material.

Share Your Ideas

Writing stories and poems to share brings out the best in you as a writer because you are writing for an interested audience, such as your classmates.

 Think of your writing as a special opportunity to learn and to grow, and you will soon understand its value—in school and in life. So what should you do? Just start writing for all the right reasons!

 Write to learn. Write for 5 minutes about the following quotation: "Writing is one of the best learning tools for all students in all subjects." In your writing, explain one or more ways that writing has helped you learn about something in school or in your personal life.

English Language Learners

Use Think-Pair-Share to prepare students for writing about the **Write to learn** quotation. Give them one minute to think about it silently. Then have partners take turns sharing their thoughts aloud. Once students have had time to gather their thoughts, they will be better prepared to write.

learn understand *share*
explore

Why Write? **3**

Creating a Writing "SourceBank"

To think like a writer, you should act like one. You can do this by creating your own "SourceBank" of possible writing ideas. The activities listed below will get you started. (Also see pages **544–547**.)

Look around you for ideas. Be on the lookout for writing inspiration anywhere, anytime. For example, while walking along, you and a friend might see a well-cared-for, healthy plant perched in front of a rundown building. A "flower in the rough" scene like this could give you an idea for a story, a poem, or an essay.

tip Carry a small pocket notebook or a PDA to record ideas. (It's hard to remember everything!) You might also want to write about some of the "found" ideas in your personal journal.

Get involved in your community. Visit museums, historical sites, businesses, and churches. Volunteer your services to a local day care or the park district. Each new experience will give you fresh ideas for writing.

Explore available resources. Surf the Internet and prowl around your library for writing ideas. Make a list of Web sites, articles, and books that you would like to explore. Also become a regular reader of your local newspaper.

Create a personal almanac. Take a close look at your life up to now and list people, places, and things that have mattered the most to you. Here's what you might include:

- Personal skills and interests (singing)
- Memorable firsts (learning to ski)
- Memorable lasts (breaking my ankle)
- School memories (joining the track team)
- Unforgettable people (my great-aunt)
- Unforgettable places (McKinley Hill)
- Favorite books and movies (The Giver)
- Things to change (homework routine)

 Develop an almanac. Copy the headings above into your writing notebook. Leave plenty of space after each. Then list personal ideas under the headings and continue to add ideas throughout the school year. Use some of these ideas as starting points for your writing.

Creating a Writing "SourceBank"

Have students brainstorm additional places or ways they might find writing ideas. Here are some possible suggestions:

- a conversation overheard on a bus or in line at a store
- a sign or advertisement
- a photograph of strangers
- newspaper fillers (small, sometimes humorous articles that often reveal the strangest side of human nature)

Suggest that in addition to carrying a notebook during the day, students can also keep a notebook and pencil by their bed to record thoughts that come to mind at night.

Before assigning the **Try It** activity, discuss different ways students can organize a personal almanac (separate sections in a notebook, etc.). Encourage students to be as creative as they wish when setting up their own almanac.

 **Answers**

No answers are required.

English Language Learners

Rather than have students complete the **Try It** activity individually, approach it as a class brainstorming session. Have students share their ideas about topics that could be listed under each almanac heading. Students can record their own ideas as well as those generated from the brainstorming.

Struggling Learners

In addition to the almanac list, encourage students to include a section on things they've always wondered about. For example:

- How do you become a professional skater?
- Why am I always running late?

These topics may be easier to write about because students will have thought about the ideas already.

Advanced Learners

Have students add a section in their almanac for quotations so that they can record special passages from their reading throughout the year. Advise students to include the title, author's name, and why the quotation has special meaning for them.

The Writing Process Overview

Unit Objectives

The writing standards listed below are based on a blending of state and NCTE standards.

- Learn about the writing process.
- Understand the six traits of effective writing.
- Learn how to use rubrics and the six traits of writing to assess writing.
- Learn about ways to use technology to publish writing.

Writing Process

- **Prewriting** Explore topics, gather details, and plan the organization.
- **Writing** Using the prewriting plan, complete a first draft.
- **Revising** Review the first draft and make changes based on the six traits of effective writing.
- **Editing** Check revised writing for correctness, prepare a final copy, and proofread the final copy for errors.
- **Publishing** Share work with others.

Focus on the Traits

- **Ideas** Establishing a clear focus and collecting specific details
- **Organization** Forming a clear beginning, middle, and ending
- **Voice** Developing a special way of saying things that fits the audience
- **Word** Using specific nouns and verbs that help deliver a clear message
- **Sentence Fluency** Writing sentences that create a smooth flow
- **Conventions** Checking for errors in punctuation, capitalization, spelling, and grammar

Suggested Writing Process Unit (Four Weeks)

| Day | Writing and Skills Units | In the *Write Source* book | | | On the CD-ROM | *SkillsBook* grammar practice pages |
		Pages	Proofreader's Guide—basic grammar rules	Basic Grammar practice	Interactive Grammar Exercises	
1–2	**Getting Started** (activities, TE pages 794–796)	1–3	652–687 and Test Prep, 688–689		Using the Right Word—1,2,3,4	Assessment —Using the Right Word, (61–62)
3	**Understanding the Writing Process**	5–6				
4–5	(cont'd)	7–10	579–615 (+), and Test Prep, 616–617		Marking Punctuation (7)	Skills Assessment —Punctuation, (39–40)
6–7	**One Writer's Process,** (Goals)	11–12				
	(Prewriting, Writing)	13–15				
8–9	(Revising, Editing, Publishing)	16–26	618–627 and Test Prep, 628–629, 630–641		Editing for Mechanics (5)	Skills Assessment —Mechanics, 49–50
10	(Assessing and Reflecting)	27–28				

WEEK 1 / WEEK 2

Day	Writing and Skills Units	In the *Write Source* book			On the CD-ROM	*SkillsBook* grammar practice pages
		Pages	Proofreader's Guide—basic grammar rules	Basic Grammar practice	Interactive Grammar Exercises	
11	**Keeping Journals and Learning Logs**	431–438				
12	Writing-to-Learn Activities	439–440				
13–14	**Understanding the Traits of Writing** (Ideas)	33–36				
	(Organization, Voice)	37–40				
	(Word Choice, Sentence Fluency, Conventions)	41–44	Skills Assessment—Grammar, 690–695 and Test Prep, 696–697, 698–700, 701		Understanding Sentences (5)	Assessment —Grammar (127–128)
15–16	**Using a Rubric**	45–51				
	Assessing	52–56	642–651 (+) Skills Assessment— Proofreading and Spelling 643–644		Spelling (5)	
17–18	**Peer Responding**	29–32				
19	**Publishing Your Writing**	57–64				
20	**Creating a Portfolio**	65–69	702–748 (+) and Skills Assessment— Parts of Speech, 749		Parts of Speech (10)	Assessment —Parts of Speech (185–186)

Note: For specifics about reading the chart above, see page TE 33.

Teacher's Notes for the Writing Process

This overview for the writing process includes some specific teaching suggestions for the unit.

Understanding the Writing Process (pages 5–10)

Many students think that good writing comes naturally. Those who write well simply have a gift, which means that those who don't have the gift won't ever be able to write well. Although it is true that some people do have a knack for expressing themselves in writing, even they have to work at it. Students in every writing skill level can improve if they understand how to take the time to go about the task of writing.

One Writer's Process (pages 11–28)

This may be a student's first exposure to the writing process or a refresher. This chapter models how good writing requires multiple drafts.

Peer Responding (pages 29–32)

Participating in peer responding is one good way to discover whether a student's writing has the desired effect on an audience. It gives students a chance to get feedback from a real audience.

Understanding the Traits of Writing (pages 33–44)

Even the best writers can improve their writing by knowing and implementing specific traits that make writing work. Students who know the six traits can identify strengths and weaknesses in their own and others' writing.

Using a Rubric (pages 45–56)

Have students evaluate the effectiveness of published or student writing using a rubric as a basic guide. At first you may want your students to focus on one specific trait (such as voice) during these sessions. Later on, you can have them evaluate a piece of writing for all of the traits.

Publishing Your Writing (pages 57–64)

This chapter teaches students how to share their writing with an audience. It deals with several publishing opportunities that include the class, school, family, local papers, and so on. It also points out the importance of polishing the work before publishing.

Creating a Portfolio (pages 65–69)

Just as a photo album tells more than a single photo tells, a writing portfolio reveals more about a student writer than any single piece of writing reveals. This chapter emphasizes the importance of self-reflection during the process of becoming a writer.

4

publish EDIT write prewrite revise

Using the Writing Process

Minilessons

Check, Check, Check Understanding the Writing Process

- **READ** the information about revising and editing on page 7 in your textbook. On a separate sheet of paper, **EXPLAIN** why these two steps are important in the writing process.

What a Voice! Understanding the Traits of Writing

- **STUDY** "Understanding Voice" on page 40 of your textbook. **THINK** of your best friend. Then **WRITE** a paragraph, sharing one experience you had with this person. **USE** your best personal voice. **SHARE** your finished paragraph with a classmate.

Raising the Bar Using a Rubric

- **SELECT** a recent essay assignment. **CHOOSE** two traits of writing that you would like to raise on the rubric scale (for example, from 3 to 5). **TELL** how you could make the two traits better in the essay?

Understanding the Writing Process

Most people simply look up at the night sky and say, "Ahh!" Serious stargazers, however, follow a process. They memorize star charts, check weather reports for best viewing times, set up their equipment, and gaze at the right corner of the sky at the right time. The process they follow allows them to see things that most people would miss.

Serious writers also follow a process. There is nothing instant about developing effective writing. It results from prewriting, writing, revising, and editing. This chapter will help you learn more about the writing process and build some valuable writing habits.

What's Ahead

- **Building Good Writing Habits**
- **The Writing Process**
- **The Process in Action**
- **Getting the Big Picture**

Understanding the Writing Process

Objectives
- understand how to build good writing habits
- understand the steps in the writing process
- know the traits of effective writing

Encourage students to think about their writing habits now, so that as they proceed through this section and the rest of the unit, they can understand why their writing is successful or why it is ineffective. Ask students to think about the following questions:

- What kind of writing do you enjoy: stories, poems, reports, letters?
- Do you plan what you're going to write, or do you just sit down and start writing?
- Does revising play a significant role in your process of writing?
- What is the most difficult part about writing for you?
- What is the easiest part about writing for you?

Building Good Writing Habits

Encourage students to look through **specialized journals** *(see below)*, photo albums, souvenir collections, and other mementos from special times in their life. Point out that these materials can be used to trigger ideas for writing.

To get students in the habit of writing every day, set aside five minutes at the beginning or at the end of class for them to do personal writing in their notebook. Assure students that they will not be graded or assessed on this writing; just circulate among them to make sure that they are taking advantage of this time to write.

Give students a chance to reflect on and write about one of the quotations. Then divide students into three (or six, if you prefer) groups. Assign each group one of the quotations, and have them design and create a poster for that quotation to display in the classroom.

6

Building Good Writing Habits

Professional writers aren't born with a special writing gene. They have had to do a lot of practicing to develop their skills. Follow the tips below and you will begin to improve your own writing skills.

Keep a writer's notebook or folder.

Reserve a part of a folder or notebook for your personal writing. Underline any ideas you might want to use in a writing assignment.

> Keep a diary [or writer's notebook]. It's a place to write about things that happen, and also to write about the feelings you're having.   —William Zinsser

Write every day, preferably at a set time.

Get into a regular writing routine, and stick to it. You set aside time to practice other skills. Do the same with your writing.

> The idea is to get the pencil moving quickly.
> —Bernard Malamud

Write with feeling.

How do you truly feel about your subject? Relax and let those emotions hit the page. (You can always tone them down later if you need to.)

> Every time I sit down and write, I know it's going well when it sort of takes over and I get out of the picture.
> —Sandra Bolton

 Write about a quotation. Write nonstop for 5 to 8 minutes about one of the quotations on this page. Consider what it means to you.

Teaching Tip: Specialized Journals

Specialized journals offer students the chance to write about an ongoing event or experience in their lives (for example, taking a trip, learning to do something new, going to a camp). In a specialized journal, students can

- write freely and specifically about one experience that continues over time;

- explore details and feelings while they are still fresh;
- create a valuable source of material for story plots, character sketches, and other writing ideas.
- See PE pages 432–433 for more about keeping a specialized journal.

English Language Learners

Discuss the quotations orally as a class. This will give students an opportunity to hear how others feel about the three ideas and to form their own thoughts about them.

PREWRITE write *revise* **edit** *publish* **7**

Understanding the Writing Process

The Writing Process

Good writing almost always goes through a series of changes before it is ready to share. That is why writing is called a *process*. The steps in this process are described below.

The Steps in the Writing Process

PROCESS

Prewriting

At the start of an assignment, a writer explores possible topics before selecting one to write about. Then the writer collects details about the topic and plans how to use them.

Writing

During this step, the writer completes the first draft using the prewriting plan as a guide. This draft is a writer's *first* chance to get everything down on paper.

Revising

After reviewing the first draft, the writer changes any ideas that are not clear or complete. A smart writer will ask at least one other person to review the draft, as well.

Editing

A writer then checks his or her revised writing for correctness before preparing a neat final copy. The writer proofreads the final copy for errors before sharing or publishing it.

Publishing

This is the final step in the writing process. Publishing is to a writer what an exhibit is to an artist—an opportunity to share his or her work with others.

Analyze your process. How would you classify yourself as a writer? Are you carefree, creative, dramatic, private, public, detailed, and so on? Or are you a combination of some of these? Explain.

The Writing Process

Ask volunteers to read aloud each step in the writing process. After each step, have students share personal writing experiences related to that step. For example, for prewriting, they can describe methods they used to explore topics for past writing assignments.

For the **Analyze your process** activity, you may want to discuss the descriptors (carefree, creative, and so on) before students work on their own.

Most students will probably discover that their writing is a combination of several categories.

English Language Learners

The concept of a process should be encouraging to students. It breaks the complex task of writing into more manageable parts. Make a large, colorful poster with the steps written on it in the order shown here. When the class is focusing on a particular step, paper-clip an arrow or put a sticky note by the word that identifies that step to help students keep track of where they are in the process. Students may need extra time on some steps of the writing process. Offer options, such as meeting in your classroom before or after school or during lunchtime, to get support with any step that is proving difficult.

The Process in Action

Prewriting Selecting a Topic

Remind students that they should always keep in mind the form of writing they have been assigned as they search for a suitable topic. Discuss several forms of writing and encourage students to brainstorm a few topics for each form.

✳ For more about forms of writing, see PE pages 554–555.

Writing
Developing the First Draft

Discuss why the first bulleted item is difficult for some students to follow. Emphasize that it is always commendable for students to write as well as they can. However, they should make every effort to move on when they cannot come up with exactly the right word or when they aren't satisfied with their phrasing of a certain idea. They will have an opportunity to solve these problems during revising.

The Process in Action

The next two pages show you the writing process in action. Use this information as a general guide for each of your writing assignments. The graphic below reminds you that, during an assignment, you can move back and forth between the steps in the writing process.

Prewriting Selecting a Topic

■ Search for possible writing topics that meet the requirements of the assignment.

■ Select a specific topic that really appeals to you.

Gathering and Organizing Details

■ Learn as much as you can about the topic before you start your first draft.

■ Consider the purpose of the assignment and what to emphasize in the writing—either an interesting part of the topic or your personal feelings about it. This will be the focus, or thesis, of your writing.

■ Decide which details you want to include in your writing. Also decide on the best way to organize the details and form a plan.

PREWRITE · WRITE · REVISE · EDIT · PUBLISH

Writing Developing the First Draft

■ When you write your first draft, concentrate on getting your ideas on paper. Don't try to produce a perfect piece of writing.

■ Use the details you collected and your prewriting plan as general guides, but feel free to add new ideas as you go along.

■ Make sure your writing has a beginning, a middle, and an ending.

 Write on every other line and on only one side of the paper when using pen or pencil and paper. Double-space on a computer. This will give you room for revising, the next step in the process.

English Language Learners

When discussing the first bullet under **Developing the First Draft,** be sure students know the leeway they have.

• Tell students that it is okay to substitute a word from their native language if they can't think of the English word they need during this stage.

• Assure them that it is not a problem if they use a sentence structure that they know is not quite right.

• Emphasize that the purpose of a first draft is to get their ideas on paper, much like an artist makes a sketch before actually painting.

• Remind them that during the revising stage, students will have time to fix these things, with your help if needed.

PROCESS

Revising Improving Your Writing

- Review your first draft, but only after setting it aside for a while.
- Use these questions as a general revising guide:
  - **Do I sound truly interested in my topic?**
  - **Do I say enough about my topic?**
  - **Does the beginning draw the reader into the writing?**
  - **Are the ideas clear and in the right order?**
  - **Does the closing remind the reader about the importance of the topic?**
  - **Are the nouns and verbs specific?**
  - **Are the modifiers (adjectives and adverbs) clear and colorful?**
  - **Are the sentences varied? Do they read smoothly?**
- Try to have at least one other person review your work.
- Make as many changes as necessary to improve your first draft.

Editing Checking for Conventions

- Edit for correctness by checking for punctuation, capitalization, spelling, and grammar errors. Also ask someone else to check your writing for errors.
- Then prepare a neat final copy of your writing. (See pages **24–26** for tips and an example.) Proofread this copy for errors before sharing it.

Publishing Sharing Your Writing

- Share your finished work with your classmates, teacher, friends, and family members.
- Consider including the writing in your portfolio.
- Think about submitting your writing to your school newspaper or some other publication. (See pages **57–64** for ideas.)

 Consider the process. The graphic on page 8 reminds you that you sometimes have to go back and repeat a step before you can move forward in your writing. In a brief paragraph, describe a writing assignment in which you had to move back and forth between the steps in the writing process.

Revising
Improving Your Writing

Help students understand the advantages of having a revising stage in the writing process. Ask students if they've ever

- seen a baseball player swing at a ball and miss,
- heard a singer hit a flat note, or
- watched an Olympic ice-skater fall on a jump.

Point out that everyone makes mistakes, but not everyone gets a chance to fix those mistakes before the audience sees them. Writers do have that chance. During revising, writers can improve their writing before they go public with it.

✻ For information on techniques that can be used to improve writing style, see PE pages 558–559.

Stress that writing is not a linear process, and that writers often find themselves moving back and forth between the steps of the writing process. Assignment deadlines often don't allow students this flexibility. Establish criteria early in the year that would allow students to request extensions for writing assignments.

English Language Learners

Explain that it is in the revising stage that writers may rewrite a sentence or a paragraph several times before they are satisfied that it says exactly what they want it to say. Some writers, too, will write more than one complete draft of a piece of writing.

Advanced Learners

Fluent writers may approach the writing process in different ways from other students. They may work through some steps simultaneously; they may skip a step entirely; they may choose to abandon a piece of writing and take a new direction. Stress that evaluations of their work are based on the rubrics and not on the steps in the writing process *per se*.

Getting the Big Picture

After reading the instruction with students, have them share their responses to the matching activity with a partner.

Answers

1. C
2. A
3. E
4. D
5. B

Encourage students who choose to do the **Extra Credit** activity to arrange a time to present their writing-process lesson to younger students.

Getting the Big Picture

Coaches know what it takes to build a successful basketball team: strong rebounders, tough defenders, and good shooters. Experienced writers also know what it takes to produce successful writing: strong *ideas*, clear *organization*, effective *word choice*, and so on.

Of course, these same traits are important in your own writing as well. You should deal with them as they become important at different points in the writing process. Remember that the writing process helps you to slow down and give each trait or part of writing the proper attention.

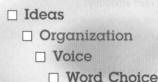

☐ Ideas
  ☐ Organization
    ☐ Voice
      ☐ Word Choice
        ☐ Sentence Fluency
          ☐ Conventions

Use the writing process. Imagine that you are doing a writing assignment. On your own paper, match each activity on the left to its proper place in the writing process on the right.

___ **1.** Check the first draft for voice and personality.   A. Prewriting
___ **2.** Organize your details for writing.   B. Writing
___ **3.** Display the final copy on your Web site.   C. Revising
___ **4.** Double-check the punctuation of dialogue.   D. Editing
___ **5.** Develop an ending that gets the reader thinking.   E. Publishing

Extra Credit: Suppose you had to explain the writing process to a group of younger students who were just beginning to write paragraphs and brief stories. On your own paper, write down what you would say to them.

English Language Learners

Encourage students to do the **Extra Credit** activity. Point out that when talking to younger students, they need to use simpler language. Putting the steps of the writing process into simplified terms will help students to better understand the process.

prewrite **EDIT** *write* *publish*
revise　　**11**

One Writer's Process

Writers need the freedom to choose and to experiment when they write. Without this freedom, writing has little meaning or importance to them. For this reason, you must think of writing as a process. You will do your best work when you select topics that truly interest you and decide how you want to write about them.

This chapter shows the process used by student writer Linda Kerklin as she wrote about her visit to *Freedom Schooner Amistad*. As you will see, this writing had special meaning to Linda because she was writing about people who were fighting for their freedom.

What's Ahead

- Previewing the Goals
- Prewriting
- Writing
- Revising
- Editing
- Publishing
- Assessing the Final Copy
- Reflecting on Your Writing

Copy Masters/ Transparencies

Time line (TE p. 13)

5 W's chart (TE p. 13)

One Writer's Process

Objectives
- trace one writer's steps through the writing process
- evaluate one writer's use of the writing traits: ideas, organization, voice, word choice, sentence fluency, and conventions

After students read the introduction to this section, ask them to
- recall the best piece of writing that they have ever done, and
- explain in their own words why they believe they were so successful with this particular piece of writing.

Students will probably recognize that when they cared about the topic, they communicated that enthusiasm to readers.

Previewing the Goals

After discussing the goals of narrative writing, point out that students can use a **variety of sentence patterns** *(see below)* to achieve sentence fluency.

 **Answers**

Answers will vary. Possible answers:

1. Linda should select a topic that she knows a lot about and cares about. This will make it easier and more enjoyable for her to write.
2. A narrative is a story. The events in a story are usually told in the order in which they happen in time because they're easier to follow that way.
3. She can add personality with specific, vivid details; dialogue that sounds natural; precise language; and a variety of sentence patterns.

12

Previewing the Goals

Before Linda Kerklin began writing, she looked at the goals for her personal narrative assignment, which are shown below. These goals helped her get started. She also previewed the rubric for narrative writing on pages 130–131.

Goals of Narrative Writing

Ideas
Use specific details and dialogue that make the reader want to know what happens next.

Organization
Make sure that the details are organized chronologically, and the beginning, middle, and ending are clear to the reader.

Voice
Make the writing sound like you, and use dialogue to show each speaker's personality.

Word Choice
Use words that express how you feel about the experience.

Sentence Fluency
Use a variety of sentence lengths and beginnings to create an effective style.

Conventions
Be sure that your punctuation, capitalization, spelling, and grammar are correct.

 To understand the important goals for Linda's assignment, answer the following questions:

1. What type of topic should Linda select? Why?
2. Why is a chronological organization important in a narrative?
3. What's one way Linda can add personality to her story?

Teaching Tip: Sentence Variety

Explain that students can make their sentences flow more smoothly by

- varying the sentence beginnings;
- combining short, choppy sentences;
- combining ideas in a series;
- and by using appositives.

Read aloud some published writing examples that demonstrate sentence variety, as students listen for the effect of using different sentence patterns. Encourage students to read aloud their own work when they are checking for variety. Whenever possible, praise students' attempts to vary sentence structure, and provide guidance where needed.

Struggling Learners

Demonstrate sentence-structure variety with this activity. Write these words on the board: *Africa, slavery, sold, kidnapped, people.* Have small groups use the words and any other words they choose to write a sentence. Invite each group to share its sentence and notice how many different sentence patterns evolve.

PROCESS

Prewriting Selecting a Topic

Linda was given the following assignment: Write a personal narrative about an eye-opening or learning experience. To select a topic, she listed experiences and starred the one that interested her the most.

> *Eye-Opening Experiences*
>
> fireworks show at Grant Park   neighborhood mural
> Freedom Schooner Amistad ✱   Statue of Liberty

 List three or four eye-opening experiences in your own life. Put a star next to the one that would make the best topic. Write a brief paragraph (four or five sentences) explaining why you would write about this topic.

Gathering and Organizing Details

Linda wanted to focus on the story of the African captives aboard *La Amistad*. She used the 5 W's and H to gather information about their story.

5 W's and H Chart

> Who?   49 African captives
> What?   the captives took control of the ship
> When?   in 1839
> Where?   aboard La Amistad in the Atlantic Ocean
> Why?   because they had been kidnapped from their homes
> How?   broke free from their captors

Linda also wanted to connect her visit to the *Freedom Schooner* with the story of the African captives. She created a time line. Notes above the line describe her feelings. Notes below the line tell what happened to the captives.

Time Line

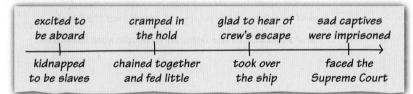

excited to be aboard	cramped in the hold	glad to hear of crew's escape	sad captives were imprisoned
kidnapped to be slaves	chained together and fed little	took over the ship	faced the Supreme Court

---

Prewriting Selecting a Topic

Explain that an eye-opening experience is one in which you learn a truth about life or human nature. Brainstorm a few eye-opening experiences as a class to generate ideas for the **Try It** activity (for example, volunteering at a local hospital, touring a local government office, trying out for a team at a new school).

 Answers

Answers will vary, but paragraphs should show an interest in the topic and an awareness of what was learned from the experience.

If you have the time, as you progress through the rest of this section, suggest that students practice each step of the writing process using the topic they selected here. Explain that this will truly be a practice that won't be graded or assessed.

Prewriting
Gathering and Organizing Details

Discuss the advantages of using graphic organizers such as the 5 W's and H chart and the time line to gather details (TE pages 790 and 792).

✱ For more graphic organizers, see PE pages 548–549 and TE pages 789–793.

English Language Learners

Introduce the term *schooner* and explain that it means a fast sailing ship. If possible, show a picture.

Writing

Developing Your First Draft

Students should read the sample draft three times.

- Read the essay through from beginning to end to understand Linda's ideas.
- Read each side note on the left and the matching passages in the essay to understand how Linda organized and presented her ideas.
- Read one paragraph at a time. After each paragraph, look back at the 5 W's and H chart and the time line on PE page 13 to see how Linda used the details in those graphic organizers in her draft. This will emphasize the importance and usefulness of gathering and organizing details before writing and will prepare students for the **Try It** activity on PE page 15.

Writing Developing Your First Draft

Linda wrote her first draft using her 5 W's and H chart and her time line as a guide. She didn't try to get everything right in this draft. Her only goal was to get all her ideas on paper. (**There are some errors in Linda's first draft.**)

The beginning introduces the experience.	Last summer, the Freedom Schooner Amistad sailed to Chicago. I couldn't wait to get aboard. My excitement at seeing this beautiful ship was soon forgoten when I heard the terrible story.
	I've always loved stories about the high seas. I've always wanted to climb up a ship's pole and shout, Land ho"!
Dialogue helps move the story along.	"The ceiling in here would have been three ft. lower" said the Captain. He lowered his hand from just over his head to the middle of his waist. In this room, the captives sat in chains.
	The wooden ceiling and walls seemed to close on me. The ship moved a little, even docked here. I could only imagine how much it tossed on the high seas. All these people had been kidnaped from there homes
A personal viewpoint is shared.	in Africa and were being sold into slavery. I moved to steady myself, and my ankles and wrists tingled.
	One night, a captive broke free from his chains and freed the other prisoners. He opened the hatch and attacked. In the fight, three people were killed. The

English Language Learners

Be sure students understand the following words and phrases in the sample first draft:

- couldn't wait (was very excited about, anxious to)
- captives (people who are not free)
- tossed on the high seas (thrown back and forth by waves)
- mutiny (rebellion against authority, refusal to obey orders)

Struggling Learners

Although it may be obvious to some students that they would use the first-person point of view to write about a personal learning experience, some students may need to be reminded. Explain first-person point of view (see PE page 352) and the use of personal pronouns and grammar issues with *I* and *me*.

PROCESS

Historical details add interest.

rest of the crew were captured and tied up. The next morning, the captive told the crew to sail toward the rising sun, toward Africa.

The word Africa sounded like "freedom." I felt better. The story wasn't over.

Every night, the crew secretly turned the ship around, heading west. They wasted two months at sea, and without food and water, it killed ten more captives. Then la Amistad was found by an American ship, which brought it to shore.

"That's when they were set free, right?" I asked.

The captain turned toward me and said "that's when they were charged with mutiny and murder."

I couldn't stand up now so I sit down on the floor and listen. The Africans were captive again. The question was are they legal slaves or not? A whole bunch of trials followed after that. The last one was in front of the Supereme Court, which finally said it would be right for the captives to get set free and be able to go back home.

I felt better after that. When we came back up on deck, I felt like shouting Freedom Ho!

The ending ties everything together and gives a final viewpoint.

Try IT   On page 13, you can see how Linda gathered details for her narrative. Does her first draft include all of these details? Does she add any new details? Explain.

Consider having students work in pairs or small groups to discuss the **Try It** activity. Assign the role of recorder to a member of each group, or ask for a volunteer. Tell recorders to take notes during the discussions. After students have completed the activity, have them come together as a class to compare their answers.

Try IT   **Answers**

Linda's first draft uses general details from her 5 W's and H chart but does not use the specific details about

- the 49 African captives;
- 1839, the date of the event;
- the ship in the Atlantic Ocean.

All the details from the time line are included, except for the one about the slaves being fed little. New details include

- the three-foot-lower ceiling;
- the number of people who died (three in a fight and ten because of no food or water);
- the crew secretly turning the ship around;
- and the decision of the Supreme Court to set the slaves free.

Struggling Learners

Remind students that Linda's assignment was to write about an eye-opening experience. Encourage them to discuss whether or not her visit to the *Freedom Schooner* qualifies as an eye-opening experience.

- How was Linda's experience different from what she expected it to be?
- What did Linda learn about life?

Advanced Learners

Challenge students to discover something in history that they consider eye-opening (for example, learning how difficult it was for Michelangelo to paint the Sistine Chapel). After completing their research, students should write a first draft of a personal narrative about their discovery.

Revising

Improving Your Writing

To prepare for the **Try It** activity, try the following:

- Ask for three volunteers and assign each of them one of the three goals shown: Ideas, Organization, Voice.
- Have the volunteers take turns reading aloud Linda's comment (in quotation marks) about that goal.
- Have students tell whether they agree or disagree with the comment and explain why.

Encourage students to make both positive and critical comments. Remind them to be polite and to base their comments on specific details from the draft.

 Answers

Answers will vary.

16

Revising   Improving Your Writing

Once Linda finished her first draft, she looked again at the goals on page 12 and used them as a revising guide. Her thoughts tell you what changes she planned to make.

Ideas

Use specific details and dialogue that make the reader want to know what happens next.

> *"I have covered the basic facts, but some of my ideas aren't clear enough."*

Organization

Make sure that the details are organized chronologically, and the beginning, middle, and ending are clear to the reader.

> *"My second paragraph is out of place. I think it would work better at the beginning."*

Voice

Make the writing sound like you, and use dialogue to show each speaker's personality.

> *"I should add more personal feelings to show that I really care about this experience."*

 Team up with a partner to review Linda's first draft. Write down at least two things that you like about the draft and one or two things that could be improved.

Advanced Learners

As a follow-up to the Advanced Learners activity on TE page 15, have students consider what changes they would make in revising their own first draft.

- Encourage students to make notes about intended changes for *ideas, organization,* and *voice.*

- Afterward, students can meet in groups of three to get positive and critical feedback on their own comments from two peers.
- Remind students to be both polite and specific.

Reviewing Linda's First Revision

After Linda reviewed her first draft, she made the following revisions to the ideas, organization, and voice of her essay.

A key idea is moved.

Last summer, the Freedom Schooner Amistad sailed to Chicago. I couldn't wait to get aboard. My excitement at seeing this beautiful ship was soon forgoten when I heard the terrible story.

I've always loved stories about the high seas. I've always wanted to climb up a ship's pole and shout, Land ho"!

New details make the ideas clearer.

"The ceiling in here would have been three ft.
as we stood in the small cargo bay of the boat
lower" said the Captain. He lowered his hand from just over his head to the middle of his waist. He told us
for three days in the heat of the tropics
that in this room, the captives sat in chains.

The wooden ceiling and walls seemed to close on me. The ship moved a little, even docked here. I could only imagine how much it tossed on the high seas.

A personal feeling is added.

The heat, the room, the fact that
All these people had been kidnaped from there homes
—it all made me feel sick
in Africa and were being sold into slavery. I moved to steady myself, and my ankles and wrists tingled.

One night, a captive broke free from his chains and freed the other prisoners. He opened . . .

Try IT Review Linda's revisions. Identify two of the changes that seem the most effective. Explain your choices.

Reviewing Linda's First Revision

If students need a refresher on using editing and proofreading marks, review the marks shown on this page and on the inside back cover of their book.

As a class, discuss the effect of Linda's revisions before assigning the **Try It** activity.

Try IT Answers

Answers will vary, but responses can suggest the following ideas:

- By moving the idea about climbing up a ship's pole to the top, Linda has created a more exciting beginning that really "hooks" the reader.
- The added details that describe Linda standing in the hold and that tell how long the captives sat in the heat help readers get a better sense of what Linda feels during the tour. This helps readers understand her sympathy toward the captives.
- Adding a personal detail about feeling sick shows how deeply the story of *La Amistad* and its captives affected Linda. It makes readers care, too.

Revising
Using a Peer Response Sheet

Before reading the instruction and discussing the completed "Peer Response Sheet," have students turn to the "Rubric for Narrative Writing" on PE pages 130–131. Give them a minute or two to look over the **rubric** *(see below)* before going on.

As you review each comment in the first section of the "Peer Response Sheet" (What I liked about your writing), have students look back at the essay to see exactly what the responder is referring to and to decide if they agree with the responder (for example, *You got my attention right away* refers to the revision on PE page 17 where Linda changed the beginning of her essay).

Have students work independently or in pairs to complete the **Try It** activity. Suggest that they refer again to the "Rubric for Narrative Writing" on PE pages 130–131 before making a suggestion.

 Answers

Answers will vary but suggestions should be useful, reasonable, and, ideally, based on the goals in the "Rubric for Narrative Writing."

18

Revising   Using a Peer Response Sheet

One of Linda's classmates read her essay. He used a rubric like the one on pages 130–131 and spotted more places that could use improvements. Linda's classmate wrote his comments on a "Peer Response Sheet."

Peer Response Sheet

Writer: *Linda Kerklin*   Responder: *William Becker*

Title: *Freedom Ho!*

What I liked about your writing:

* *You got my attention right away.*

* *You mix the captain's words and your own thoughts.*

* *You sound really interested in the experience.*

Changes I would suggest:

* *In the beginning, could you tell why you like sea stories?*

* *What "terrible story" do you mean?*

* *How many captives were there?*

* *Where is the ship docked?*

 Review the classmate's suggestions for improvements listed above. Which one do you think is the most important? Explain. Also think of one suggestion of your own. Focus on the ideas, organization, and voice in the writing.

Teaching Tip: Rubrics

Rubrics are useful to both teachers and students as evaluation tools. A rubric chart provides a rating scale for each trait being evaluated, ranging from excellent to poor. Each rating also contains a description that can help students (and teachers) arrive at an evaluation.

Students will learn more about using a rubric later in this unit (PE pages 45–56). For now, it may be helpful for them to review the "Rubric for Narrative Writing" on PE pages 130–131 to see what Linda's classmate based his comments and suggestions on, and for making suggestions of their own for the **Try It** activity.

Revising with a Peer Response

Using the comments made by her classmate, Linda revised her story again. She added some important details.

> *with their sailors, cannons, and pirates*
> I've always loved stories about the high seas.
> I've always wanted to climb up a ship's pole and
> shout, Land ho"! Last summer, the Freedom Schooner
> Amistad sailed to Chicago. I couldn't wait to get
> aboard. My excitement at seeing this beautiful ship
>   *of the original Amistad*
> was soon forgotten when I heard the terrible story.
>
> "The ceiling in here would have been three ft.
> lower" said the Captain as we stood in the small
> cargo bay of the boat. He lowered his hand from just
> over his head to the middle of his waist. He told us
>   *forty-nine african*
> that in this room, the captives sat in chains for three
> days in the heat of the tropics.
>
> The wooden ceiling and walls seemed to close on
>   *at navy pier*
> me. The ship moved a little, even docked here. I could
> only imagine how much it tossed on the high seas.
>   *49*
> The heat, the room, the fact that all these people had
> been kidnaped from there homes in Africa and were
> being sold into slavery—it all made me feel sick. I
> moved to steady myself, and my ankles and . . .

What do you love about sea stories?

What terrible story?

What kind of captives? How many were there?

Where is the ship docked?

PROCESS

 Discuss with your classmates the changes the writer makes (shown on pages 17 and 19). Which additions seem the most effective? What other types of changes does she make? How effective are the changes?

Revising with a Peer Response

Invite students to describe their own experiences with peer responding. Have them consider the following questions:
- When is peer responding most helpful?
- What kinds of comments do you find least helpful?

Students who don't feel confident about their writing may feel that they have to make every single change that a peer responder suggests. Point out to students that as the writer, they can decide for themselves when to take a peer responder's advice and when to rely on their own evaluation and judgment.

Do the **Try It** activity as a class.

 Answers

Answers may vary. Students will probably agree that
- the new beginning with the added details is much more interesting;
- and that the specific details about the original *Amistad,* the height of the cargo bay, the number of African captives, and about Navy Pier make the ideas clearer and easier to follow.

English Language Learners

Students may feel especially apprehensive about peer responses if they are not confident about their English skills. Provide frequent modeling and role-playing to help students learn how to give feedback that is both helpful and sensitive. At the initial stages of learning this skill, permit students to select their own peer responders.

Struggling Learners

Focus on the questions on the small pieces of notepaper in the column of Linda's story. Have students discuss how Linda used the suggestions and questions to revise her story.

Revising
Focusing on Words and Sentences

Follow a process similar to the one described on TE page 16 to help students express opinions about word choice and sentence fluency.

- Have volunteers read Linda's comments in quotation marks to the class.
- Have students tell whether they agree or disagree with the comment and explain why.

Have a volunteer demonstrate on the classroom or library computer how they would use the Internet to find specific sailing terms (type "sailing terms" into a search engine). This is a good opportunity to discuss how to **use the Internet** *(see below)* to enhance writing.

When students have finished the **Try It** activity, invite partners to share their responses with the class.

 Answers

Answers will vary.

20

Revising   Focusing on Words and Sentences

Once Linda was done revising for ideas, organization, and voice, she went back to the rubric again, checking her work for *word choice* and *sentence fluency*. Her comments tell how she planned to revise her writing for style.

Word Choice

Use words that express how you feel about the experience.

> "My language is easy to understand, but some of my nouns and verbs could be stronger. I'll also check the Internet for specific sailing terms."

Sentence Fluency

Use a variety of sentence lengths and beginnings to create an effective style.

> "In some places, the sentences don't flow. I'll try using transitions to connect them. Also, I'll combine the short, choppy sentences in the middle paragraphs."

 Team up with a partner to review Linda's revised writing on page 19 for style. Identify two nouns, verbs, or adjectives that could be more specific, vivid, or colorful. Then find one or two sentences that could be improved.

Teaching Tip: Using the Internet

To ensure that students are responsible and careful when using the Internet, take time early in the year to review your school's policy for Internet use. If possible, distribute a handout that provides

- addresses for acceptable search sites with directions for using these sites;

- detailed information about the school's Internet policy;
- a reminder to students to never give their name, address, or telephone number to anyone on the Web;
- and a reminder to know and follow their parents' guidelines.

For more details about using the Internet, see PE page 365.

English Language Learners

Students may have a hard time identifying which words could be replaced by stronger, more vivid synonyms. Pair them with fluent English-speaking students and have the partner underline two or three words that could be replaced. Then have them work together with a dictionary or thesaurus to find replacements.

Checking Linda's Improvements in Style

Linda's next step was to concentrate on the style of her writing. She paid special attention to the clarity and flow of the words and the sentences.

Nautical terms improve the level of language.

Combined sentences and transitions improve fluency.

Stronger words are chosen.

> I've always loved stories about the high seas,
> *swashbuckelers*
> with their ~~sailors~~, cannons, and pirates. I've always
> *mast*
> wanted to climb up a ship's ~~pole~~ and shout, Land
> *So   when*
> ho"! Last summer, the Freedom Schooner Amistad
>
> sailed to Chicago. I couldn't wait to get aboard.
> *though,*
> My excitement at seeing this beautiful ship was
>
> soon forgoten when I heard the terrible story of the
>
> original Amistad.
>
> "The ceiling in here would have been three ft.
>
> lower" said the Captain as we stood in the small
> *schooner*
> cargo bay of the ~~boat~~. He lowered his hand from just
> *and added*
> over his head to the middle of his waist. ~~He told us~~
> *tiny   crouched*
> that in this room, the forty-nine african captives ~~sat~~
> *blistering*
> in chains for three days in the heat of the tropics.
>
> The wooden ceiling and walls seemed to close on
> *rolled*
> me. The ship ~~moved~~ a little, even docked here at navy
> *must have*
> pier. I could only imagine how much it tossed on the
> *cramped quarters*
> high seas. The heat, the ~~room~~, the fact that all
>
> these 49 people had been kidnaped from . . .

 Compare your ideas for changing Linda's writing (page 20) with the changes she has made. How are her changes alike or different from your recommendations?

Checking Linda's Improvements in Style

Have students point out the nautical terms that Linda has added to her draft (*swashbucklers, mast, schooner, rolled, quarters*). Ask them to explain what these words communicate to them as readers. Help them understand that the use of these words
- shows readers that Linda cares about her topic,
- shows that Linda wants to make her essay as precise for readers as possible, and
- makes Linda sound more knowledgeable.

Encourage students who are working on a piece of writing to look for places where they can add specific terms to improve their style.

Consider completing the **Try It** activity as a whole-class exercise. Be sure students have their responses from the **Try It** activity on PE page 20 available so that they can compare and contrast their changes with Linda's changes.

 **Answers**

Answers will vary.

Editing
Checking for Conventions

Give students time to review the "Proofreader's Guide" in the back of their book. Throughout the year they can refer to the instruction, rules, and examples there to clarify any checklist items or to resolve questions about their own writing.

Point out that students are more likely to find all the errors in their own drafts if they make separate passes for each type of error. Use the following activity to illustrate the effectiveness of this process:

- Divide students into four groups to complete the **Try It** activity.
- Have each group use the checklist to look for only one type of error: punctuation, capitalization, spelling, or grammar.
- Have each group share their answers with the class.

 Answers

- Punctuation: "Land Ho!" (add beginning quotation marks and put the exclamation point inside the quotes), <u>Freedom Schooner Amistad, Amistad,</u> lower," (add a comma after *lower*)
- Capitalization: captain, African, Navy Pier
- Spelling: swashbucklers, forgotten, feet, 49
- Grammar: no mistakes

Editing Checking for Conventions

At last it was time for Linda to edit her story for *conventions*. If she had worried about grammar, punctuation, capitalization, and spelling too soon, she may have forgotten to make the other changes that dramatically improved her work. Her comment tells how she planned to edit her writing for one of the conventions.

Conventions

Be sure that your punctuation, capitalization, spelling, and grammar are correct.

> *"I'll carefully check my narrative for punctuation."*

For help with conventions, Linda turned to the "Proofreader's Guide" in the back of her *Write Source* book. She also used the editing checklist shown below.

Editing Checklist

PUNCTUATION

_____ 1. Do I use end punctuation after all my sentences?

_____ 2. Do I use commas correctly?

_____ 3. Do I punctuate dialogue correctly?

CAPITALIZATION

_____ 4. Do I start all my sentences with capital letters?

_____ 5. Do I capitalize all proper nouns?

SPELLING

_____ 6. Have I spelled all my words correctly?

_____ 7. Have I double-checked words my spell-checker might miss?

GRAMMAR

_____ 8. Do I use correct forms of verbs (*had gone*, not *had went*)?

_____ 9. Do my subjects and verbs agree in number? (*Each of them has* a chance to win.)

_____ 10. Do I use the right word (*to, too, two*)?

 Team up with a partner. Using the checklist above, find two or three errors in Linda's revised draft on page 21.

Advanced Learners

Before groups begin the **Try It** activity, invite students to make a poster of the questions on the "Editing Checklist."

- Direct students to copy the headings and questions on the checklist. Tell them to leave space under or beside each question.
- Challenge students to look in their textbooks or reading books to find an example for each question. Have them write the example near the question on the poster.

Display the finished editing checklist poster so that classmates can refer to it during the **Try It** activity and when they do their own writing.

PROCESS

Checking Linda's Editing for Conventions

Linda edited her narrative for spelling, punctuation, capitalization, and grammar. (See inside the back cover of this text for the common editing and proofreading marks.)

Spelling errors are corrected.

I've always loved stories about the high seas, with their (swashbuckelers) *swashbucklers* cannons, and pirates. I've always wanted to climb up a ship's mast and shout, "Land ho!" So last summer, when the <u>Freedom Schooner</u>

Punctuation mistakes are fixed.

<u>Amistad</u> sailed to Chicago, I couldn't wait to get aboard. My excitement at seeing this beautiful ship, though, was soon (forgoten) *forgotten* when I heard the terrible story of the original <u>Amistad</u>.

"The ceiling in here would have been three ~~ft.~~ *feet* lower," said the Ĉaptain as we stood in the small

Treatment of measurements and numbers is corrected.

cargo bay of the schooner. He lowered his hand from just over his head to the middle of his waist and added that in this tiny room, the ~~forty-nine~~ *49* African captives crouched in chains for three days in the blistering heat of the tropics.

The wooden ceiling and walls seemed to close *in* on me. The ship rolled a little, even docked here at

Capitalization errors are corrected.

navy pier. I could only imagine how much it must have tossed on the high seas. The heat, the cramped . . .

Try IT Review Linda's editing for conventions in the paragraphs above. Did you find some of the same errors when you edited her earlier draft on page 21?

Checking Linda's Editing for Conventions

While reviewing the responses for the **Try It** activity on PE page 22, you may have identified kinds of mistakes that students either don't recognize or don't know how to fix. As you review Linda's editing for the **Try It** activity here, you can address those issues. Remind students to

- use quotation marks to enclose the exact words of a speaker;
- always put periods and commas inside quotation marks;
- put an exclamation point or a question mark inside quotation marks when it punctuates the quotation;
- underline (or italicize) the names of ships;
- capitalize titles, such as captain, only when they appear with the person's name, such as Captain Jones;
- spell out measurements, such as inch, foot, or yard;
- use numerals for numbers 10 and over.

Try IT Answers

Answers will vary.

Struggling Learners

✳ Knowing when to capitalize words, such as titles and proper adjectives, can be troublesome for some students. To review capitalization rules, do this K-W-L activity.

● Make a three-column chart with the headings *What We Know, What We Want to Know,* and *What We Learned.*

● List students' responses under the first two headings. They may need help thinking through entries for the second column.

● Refer students to PE pages 618–626 to confirm their knowledge, clarify misconceptions, and identify new learning.

● Complete the chart.

Publishing
Sharing Your Writing

Students are often so relieved to be finished with drafting, writing, revising, and editing, that they do not put effort or thought into their presentation. To emphasize the importance of this step in the writing process, discuss the following questions:

- Why is it important to create a clean final copy of your writing? (Possible response: Revising and editing marks can make ideas difficult to read.)
- What message does a clean copy send to your audience? (Possible response: It says, "I'm proud of what I've written.")
- How would you feel if you turned in a somewhat messy copy of your writing for evaluation? (Possible responses: less confident, embarrassed, not proud)

Some teachers have their own formatting requirements for writing assignments. Make sure students understand any requirements you might have before they turn in their work.

Publishing Sharing Your Writing

Linda used the tips below to help her write the final copy of her story. (See pages **25–26**.)

Focus on Presentation

Tips for Handwritten Copies

- Use blue or black ink and write neatly.
- Write your name according to your teacher's instructions.
- Skip a line and center your title; skip another line and start your writing.
- Indent every paragraph and leave a one-inch margin on all four sides.
- Write your last name and page number on every page after page 1.

Tips for Computer Copies

- Use an easy-to-read font and a 12-point type size.
- Double-space and leave a one-inch margin around each page.

Linda's Final Copy

Linda was proud of her finished story. Presenting it to the class allowed her friends to share the eye-opening experience of being aboard the *Freedom Schooner Amistad*.

Linda Kerklin

Freedom Ho!

I've always loved stories about the high seas, with their swashbucklers, cannons, and pirates. I've always wanted to climb up a ship's mast and shout, "Land ho!" So last summer, when the *Freedom Schooner Amistad* sailed to Chicago, I couldn't wait to get aboard. My excitement at seeing this beautiful ship, though, was soon forgotten when I heard the terrible story of the original *Amistad*.

"The ceiling in here would have been three feet lower," said the captain as we stood in the small cargo bay of the schooner. He lowered his hand from just over his head to the middle of his waist and added that in this tiny room, 49 African captives crouched in chains for three days in the blistering heat of the tropics.

The wooden ceiling and walls seemed to close in on me. The ship rolled a little, even docked here at Navy Pier. I could only imagine how much it must have tossed on the high seas. The heat, the cramped quarters, the fact that all these 49 people had been kidnapped from their homes in Africa and were being sold into slavery—it all made me feel sick. I crouched to steady myself, and my ankles and wrists tingled as if I wore invisible shackles.

Linda's Final Copy

Working as a class, use the goals on PE page 12 and the rubric on PE pages 130–131 to point out elements of Linda's final copy that make it a good example of a narrative essay.

Ideas
- The writer shares a personal, eye-opening experience.

Organization
- The beginning of the story grabs the reader's attention and creates interest.
- The story is told in clear time order and flows smoothly.

Voice
- The writer uses specific details and has a knowledgeable voice.

Struggling Learners

Use the Think-Pair-Share technique to help students explore the relationship between the goals on PE page 12 and the rubric on PE pages 130–131.

- How are these lists organized?
- How can each section of the goals be used while you are developing a piece of writing?
- How can each section of the rubric be used before writing,

during writing and revision, or after writing?

Give students time alone to think and time with a partner to share. Then open a discussion with the class. Help them see that the lists deal with the same basic information and that using the goals can lead to achieving good ratings on the rubric.

Kerklin 2

One moonless night, though, a captive named Sengbe Pieh broke free from his chains and freed the other prisoners. He opened the hatch and crept onto the deck, where the crew slept. Only the man at the helm was awake. Sengbe and the captives attacked. In the fight, one African was killed, as well as two crew members. The rest of the crew were captured and tied up. The next morning, Sengbe told the crew to "sail toward the rising sun, toward Africa."

When the captain said the name "Africa," it was as if he had said the word "freedom." For a moment, I felt better. But the story wasn't over. Every night, the crew secretly turned the ship around, heading west. That way, they wasted two months at sea, and the lack of food and water killed 10 more of the captives. At last, *La Amistad* was found by an American ship, which brought it to shore at Long Island Sound.

"That's when they were set free, right?" I asked.

The captain turned toward me, and his brown eyes looked old and sad, as if he'd seen all these things himself. "That's when they were charged with mutiny and murder."

I couldn't stand up anymore and sat down on those rough boards to listen to the story. The Africans had become captives again. The question was whether they were legal slaves in Cuba or were illegal slaves taken from Africa. Numerous trials led finally to the Supreme Court, where John Quincy Adams argued their case. He helped the captives win their freedom.

When we came up out of that cramped and hot hold into the cool winds off Lake Michigan, I felt like I had been freed. I wanted to climb the mast and shout, "Freedom ho!"

Advanced Learners

Invite students to discuss how and why American culture has romanticized some characters and forms of undesirable behavior, such as pirates and their attacks on other vessels.

- Have students share examples that they're familiar with from books, movies, and even fairy tales.
- Encourage a debate on the practice of romanticizing lawbreakers.

PROCESS

Assessing the Final Copy

Linda's teacher used a rubric like the one that appears on pages 130–131 to assess Linda's final copy. A 6 is the very best score that a writer can receive for each trait. The teacher also included comments under each trait.

5 Ideas

You have selected an excellent experience to share. I want to take the same tour.

5 Organization

Your writing has a clear beginning, middle, and ending.

5 Voice

Your personal feelings come through in your writing.

4 Word Choice

A few more nautical terms would have added a special touch to your narrative.

4 Sentence Fluency

Your sentences are easy to follow. You could have varied some of your sentence beginnings.

6 Conventions

Your essay is free of careless errors.

Review the assessment. Do you agree with the comments and scores made by Linda's teacher? Why or why not? Explain your feelings in a brief paragraph.

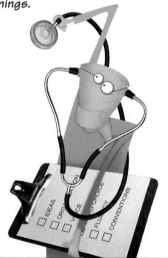

Assessing the Final Copy

If this is the first time students are seeing an assessment based on a rubric, have them

- read the rating for each trait and the teacher's comments, and then
- look at the rubric on PE pages 130–131 to figure out how the teacher arrived at the rating.

Later in the unit, students will review a self-assessment, which is similar in form to the assessment shown here. Students will be well prepared to understand and practice self-assessment if they can understand how the scores and comments were generated for this assessment.

Invite volunteers to share their reviews of the assessment with the class. Students may agree or disagree with the teacher's comments and scores, but they should be able to support their opinions with specific reasons.

Struggling Learners

The writing activity may be too difficult for some students to do on their own, especially if this section is being taught early in the school year. Before they write, have students work in small groups to express their ideas orally. Ask them to look for examples in the essay that support the teacher's comments. Do they agree with the ratings that are given?

Reflecting on Your Writing

Reflecting is a vital part of the writing process. Reflecting can help students

- realize their successes, which will inspire them to write more;
- identify areas that need improvement, which will help them write better in the future.

Reflecting can be difficult and is not something that most students will do without encouragement. Using a reflection sheet like the one shown here can make the task easier to accomplish.

After students read Linda's comments on the reflection sheet, ask them the following questions:

- What do you think is the best part of Linda's narrative?
- What part do you think still needs work?
- What have you learned about writing a personal narrative from Linda's experience?

Reflecting on Your Writing

After the whole process was finished, Linda filled out a reflection sheet. This helped her think about the assignment and plan for future essays.

Linda Kerklin

My Personal Narrative

1. The strength of my narrative is . . .
   that I was able to connect my own experience with a tragic historical event.

2. The part that still needs work is . . .
   the amount of detail I included. I could have made the Africans' experiences easier for the reader to follow.

3. The main thing I learned about writing a personal narrative is . . .
   that it must build in suspense and drama to hold the reader's interest.

4. In one of my next assignments, I would like to . . .
   write a fictionalized story based on the theme of freedom.

5. Here is one question I still have about writing a personal narrative:
   What are some creative ways to write endings for narratives?

respect cooperate SHARE
comment react **29**

Peer Responding

Sharing a piece of writing with your classmates can be a nerve-racking experience. Even professional writers like Mem Fox sometimes get nervous when reading their own work aloud to others: "In those sessions in which each of us reads our writing to the class, we shake with nerves."

The truth is, though, that you—and all writers—need an audience. You need someone to let you know what makes sense and what is unclear. You get the best feedback from your peers in response sessions.

This chapter is all about sharing your writing and making the best possible use of the responses you get from your fellow writers.

What's Ahead

- Peer-Responding Guidelines
- Sample Peer Response Sheet

Peer Respo

Writer: **Lana** Re

Title: **Changing Faces**

What I liked about your writing:
* The general comments in the
  the essay.

* Your description of each famou

* I learned a lot about Albert Eins
  paragraph.

Changes I would suggest:
* Could you include more details ab
did you include her as one of the o
* Your essay would be even

Peer Responding

Objectives
- understand the author's role in peer responding
- understand the responder's role in peer responding
- use a response sheet to practice peer responding

Ask students what they do when they have a good idea. Do they keep it to themselves or share it with their friends? Most people, young or old, can't wait to share their good ideas.

However, when it comes to sharing a piece of writing, most people get really nervous. Remind students that when they write, they are putting their ideas on paper. So, if it will help them feel less nervous, they can think of sharing their writing as just another way of sharing ideas with friends.

Struggling Learners

To help students understand the benefits of peer responses, use the following activity.

- Divide students into groups of three. Distribute to each group photocopies of a movie review and a restaurant review, and have them refer to the peer response on PE page 18.
- Ask students what movie reviews, restaurant reviews, and peer responses have in common. Have the groups discuss their

ideas (they all tell what someone likes and/or doesn't like about something).

- Emphasize that a peer response gives students an opportunity to improve their work, whereas a movie review is given too late for the filmmaker to make improvements. A chef can make changes based on a restaurant review or choose to ignore the comments. This is true for writers, too.

Peer-Responding Guidelines

Emphasize that the key to effective peer responding in a group is practicing good group skills. Students should

- listen carefully,
- think before they speak,
- not interrupt,
- believe that their ideas are important enough to share,
- stay on the topic,
- allow everyone a chance to speak, and
- be honest and respectful.

The Author's Role

Emphasize that peer responders do not expect the writing they are reviewing to be perfect. That is the point of having a peer responder— to help the author identify parts of the writing that could be improved.

30

Peer-Responding Guidelines

At first, you may work with only one person: a teacher or a classmate. This person does not expect your writing to be perfect. He or she knows that you are still working on your paper.

Later, you may have a chance to work with a small group. After a while, you will find that responding to someone's writing is much easier than you thought it would be.

The Author's Role

Select a piece of writing to share and make a copy of it for each group member.

Guidelines	Sample Responses
● **Introduce your piece of writing.** But don't say too much about it.	This paper is about our dependence on the automobile. I decided on this topic after watching a TV show.
● **Read your writing out loud.** Or ask group members to read it silently.	Automobiles are a primary cause of pollution. They are very dangerous. They present many problems. . . .
● **Invite your group members to comment.** Listen carefully.	Okay, everyone, now it's your turn to talk. I'm listening.
● **Take notes** so you will remember what was said.	So, which statistics should I add?
● **Answer all questions** the best you can. Be open and polite.	Yes, the automobile is the number one cause of global warming.
● **Ask for help from your group** with any writing problems you are having.	In my ending, is it clear what I want the reader to do?

English Language Learners

The small group setting can provide a chance for students to observe how others respond before they practice responding in a one-on-one situation.

After they see other students modeling appropriate responses, have them work with a partner to practice responding:

- Provide time for them to read their partner's written piece.
- Encourage them to make notes about points they wish to bring up.

respect cooperate SHARE *react*
comment Peer Responding 31

The Responder's Role

Responders should show an interest in the author's writing and treat it with respect.

PROCESS

Guidelines	Sample Responses
• **Listen carefully.** Take notes so that you can make helpful comments.	Notes: What is the problem with sport utility vehicles?
• **Look for what is good** about the writing. Give some positive comments. Be sincere.	Most of your statistics are convincing.
• **Tell what you think could be improved.** Be polite when you make suggestions.	Could you discuss alternatives to car travel?
• **Ask questions** if you need more information.	Where did you get your statistics about the number of roads in our cities?
• **Make other suggestions.** Help the writer improve his or her work.	Could you include a stronger call to action?

Helpful Comments

In all your comments, be as specific as you can be. This will help the writer make the best changes.

Instead of . . .	Try something like . . .
Your beginning doesn't work.	**Your focus statement sounds a little too wordy.**
Your writing is boring.	**Most of your sentences begin with "It is" or "It may."**
I can't understand one part.	**The part about road rage needs more explanation.**

 Suppose you are the responder to one of the essays on pages 136–137, 200–201, or 262–263. Carefully read the essay. Then write responses to it using the samples at the top of this page as a guide.

The Responder's Role

After reviewing the guidelines and the sample responses, discuss the difference between sincere, **constructive criticism** and negative **put-downs** *(see below)*.

Helpful Comments

After reading the instruction with students, have them practice peer responding in small groups.

- Divide students into groups of four or five students. Distribute the writing that they selected and you photocopied earlier.
- Have groups select a leader to moderate the discussion and make sure everyone follows the guidelines.
- Authors and responders should follow the guidelines listed on PE pages 30–31.
- Circulate, noting which students seem comfortable and which may do better sharing in pairs or with you, for now.

Depending on the results of the group practice, you can choose to do the **Try It** activity as an oral activity with the class or have students work independently.

 **Answers**

Answers will vary.

Teaching Tip: Constructive Criticism vs. Put-Downs

Constructive criticism is thoughtful advice offered in a respectful way. Constructive criticism may point out the flaw in an idea, but it never dismisses the idea outright without an explanation or an alternative suggestion. It never attacks the person who suggested the idea.

Put-downs dismiss an idea without explanation. They criticize the ideas and the people who wrote them.

Constructive criticism: Most students probably won't like the idea of wearing uniforms, but maybe you could suggest that students work together to create a dress code.

Put-down: You're stupid if you think we'll agree to wear uniforms.

Sample Peer Response Sheet

Discuss the purpose of the two main parts of the response sheet.

- The purpose of the first part is to tell what you like about the writing. These comments can compliment the writer's main ideas, specific details, and overall writing skills.
- The purpose of the second part is to suggest changes that will help the writer improve the writing. These comments should be specific, reasonable, and helpful.

Students may recall that they reviewed a peer response sheet earlier on PE page 18. They can look at that response sheet now for another example of the types of comments that are appropriate here.

For the practice activity, students can create their own peer response sheet, using the sample as a model. However, if you require a different written format for peer responding, it makes sense for students to become familiar with that format now.

If you have time, have classmates get together to discuss the comments on their response sheet.

Sample Peer Response Sheet

Your teacher may want you and a classmate to react to each other's writing by completing a response sheet like the one below. (Sample comments are included.)

Peer Response Sheet

Writer: _Lana_   Responder: _Jesse_

Title: _Changing Faces_

What I liked about your writing:

* _The general comments in the beginning drew me into the essay._

* _Your description of each famous person is very clear._

* _I learned a lot about Albert Einstein in the fifth paragraph._

Changes I would suggest:

* _Could you include more details about Helen Keller? Why did you include her as one of the changing faces?_

* _Your essay would be even better if it contained a little bit more of your personality. Could you let people know that you really care about these people?_

Practice. Exchange a recent piece of writing with a classmate.

1 Read the paper once to get an overall feel for it.

2 Then read the paper again, paying careful attention to its strengths and weaknesses.

3 Fill out a response sheet like the one above.

conventions ideas *sentence fluency* **VOICE** *organization* *word choice* 33

Understanding the Traits of Writing

What are your favorite foods? Popcorn? Pancakes? Watermelon? Whatever they are, you wouldn't dump them all into a taco shell and take a bite. That wouldn't make sense.

In the same way, there's more to writing than putting a bunch of words on the page. Effective writing contains well-chosen *ideas,* clear *organization,* and an appropriate *voice.* Experienced writers also pay attention to *word choice, sentence fluency,* and *conventions.* This chapter will teach you how to use these six traits of writing. Before you know it, you'll be using words in ways that clearly express your best thoughts and feelings.

What's Ahead

- **Introducing the Traits**
- **Understanding Ideas . . . Organization . . . Voice . . . Word Choice . . . Sentence Fluency . . . Conventions**

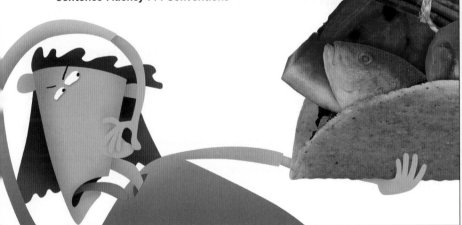

Understanding the Traits of Writing

Objectives

- understand the traits of writing: ideas, organization, voice, word choice, sentence fluency, and conventions
- apply the traits of writing

Earlier in the unit (PE pages 11–28), students traced one writer's progress through the writing process. Suggest that students skim those pages now to recall how the writer applied the six traits of writing to her essay. Make sure students understand the importance of applying all six traits (goals) when they write. Ask them to think about the following:

What would the effect have been

- if Linda had not taken the time to gather and organize details before she started writing?
- if she had left out dialogue?
- if she hadn't included sailing terms?
- if she hadn't included her feelings?
- if all her sentences started exactly the same way?
- if she hadn't corrected spelling and punctuation mistakes?

Introducing the Traits

Three traits relate to the development of the content *and* the form of a piece of writing. They provide a focus during the prewriting and drafting stages of the writing process.

- Ideas
- Organization
- Voice

The other three traits relate more to form. Checking them is more important during the revising and editing processes.

- Word Choice
- Sentence Fluency
- Conventions

✳ The six-point rubric that appears in each of the core units on PE pages 130–131, 194–195, 256–257, and 318–319 is based on these traits. For reproducible rubrics in six-, five-, and four-point scales, see TE pages 750–761.

34

Introducing the Traits

The traits listed below identify the main features found in the best writing. If you write with these traits in mind, you will be pleased with the results.

Ideas
Effective writing has a clear message, purpose, or focus. The writing contains plenty of specific ideas and details.

Organization
Strong writing has a clear beginning, middle, and ending. The overall writing is well organized and easy to follow.

Voice
The best writing reveals the writer's voice—or special way of saying things. The voice also fits the audience.

Word Choice
Good writing contains strong words, including specific nouns and verbs. Strong words help deliver a clear message.

Sentence Fluency
Effective writing flows smoothly from one sentence to the next. Sentences vary in length and begin in a variety of ways.

Conventions
Good writing is carefully edited to make sure it is easy to understand. The writing follows the rules for punctuation, grammar, capitalization, and spelling.

One additional trait to consider is the presentation of your writing. The best writing looks neat and follows guidelines for margins, indenting, spacing, and so on. The way the writing looks on the page attracts the reader and makes him or her *want* to read on.

English Language Learners

In preparation for listing all six traits and explaining what each means, play memory games to help students acquire the information. For example:

- Write the name of each trait on an individual index card. Shuffle the cards and have students put them in order.
- Then display five cards and have students identify which trait is missing.
- Finally, write on individual cards the descriptions that go with the traits and have students match the descriptions with the traits.

Struggling Learners

Invite students to try making up a mnemonic device (a sentence that helps them remember a string of words) as a way to remember the sequence of the traits as well as the first letter of each one. For example: *I Only Vacation With Silly Clowns.* (Ideas, Organization, Voice, Word choice, Sentence fluency, Conventions.)

conventions ideas *sentence fluency*
VOICE *organization word choice* **35**
Traits of Writing

PROCESS

Understanding Ideas

All writing starts, and ends, with ideas. Your job as a writer is to find the best ideas to use in your stories, essays, and reports. As writer Mark Van Doren says, "Bring ideas in and entertain them royally."

How can I select the best topic for writing?

Selecting a topic is different for each form of writing. Use the information below as a guide for selecting the best topics.

Descriptive Writing

Purpose: To present clear pictures of people, places, and objects
Key reminder: Select topics that you know well or that you can observe or research.
Example topics: Describing a neighbor, the bus stop, a special outfit

Narrative Writing

Purpose: To share memorable experiences
Key reminder: Select experiences that you can recall in great detail.
Example topics: Remembering meeting a relative, experiencing stage fright, getting lost

Expository Writing

Purpose: To share information, to explain
Key reminder: Select topics that you can research.
Example topics: Sharing information about tornadoes, pasta, peer pressure

Persuasive Writing

Purpose: To convince the reader to agree with your opinion
Key reminder: Select topics that you have strong feelings about and that you can research to find supporting facts and details.
Example topics: Arguing for or against study halls, final exams, curfews

 Write "Topics for Writing" at the top of a piece of paper. Down the left-hand margin list the following headings (leave five to seven lines after each heading): *Personal Narrative Writing, Descriptive Writing, Expository Writing,* and *Persuasive Writing.* Under each heading, list possible writing topics for each type of writing. Add to the list throughout the school year.

Understanding Ideas

Prepare students for the **Try It** activity.

- Divide students into four groups. Assign each group a writing form: narrative, descriptive, expository, or persuasive.
- Have each group brainstorm at least three new topic ideas for their form of writing. They can look through their writing notebooks and journals for ideas.
- Invite each group to share their topic ideas with the class.

When students do the **Try It** activity, suggest that they list the example topics shown on the page as well as the topics generated by each group. Point out that they may have to reword some of the narrative topics to fit their personal experiences. Students should also write topic ideas of their own, but these ideas will help get them started.

✱ See PE pages 544–545 for additional strategies for selecting a specific writing topic.

 Answers

Answers will vary, but students should list a variety of topics.

Struggling Learners

Students who are having difficulty listing topics may benefit from creating a mind map. Have them write their name in a circle in the center of a piece of paper. Then have them draw five lines radiating out from the circle like the rays of the sun.

On each line, students write one of the 5 W's. Together, brainstorm topics that go with each question word. For example:
- *Who:* family, friends, pets, people they admire
- *What:* hobbies and interests
- *Where:* memorable places
- *Why:* strong feelings
- *When:* time line of important events

Students should then list personal ideas for each of the 5 W's.

Write this sentence on the board:

The peregrine falcon is a bird.

To help students understand how a specific and well-written focus statement can guide how they gather details, ask these questions:

- What main ideas would you expect to read about in an essay with a focus statement like the one on the board? (Possible response: anything to do with why the peregrine falcon is a bird)
- What details would you expect to read about in an essay with a focus statement like the one in the book? (Possible responses: where the peregrine falcon lives, its speed, its skill as a hunter, the fact that it is endangered)

Review the strategies for gathering details. Then point out that this is usually when writers find out if they have picked a suitable topic for the space and time they have to write.

- If they have too many details, the topic may be too broad and may need to be narrowed.
- If they have too few details, the topic is probably too narrow and will need to be expanded.

36

How should I write about a topic?

Writer William Zinsser says, "Clutter is the disease of American writing." You can avoid this disease by creating a focus for your writing. A focus statement tells what specific part of a topic you will cover. With a focus in mind, you won't clutter your writing with unnecessary details.

The peregrine falcon, a lightning-quick bird of prey *(topic)*, is an endangered species *(a certain part)*.

What should I do first to gather details?

The first thing you should do is find out what you already know about a topic. Here are three ways to collect your thoughts about a writing topic:

Freewriting Write freely for at least 5 to 10 minutes, exploring your topic from a number of different angles. The key is to keep your fingers or your pen moving to see what thoughts come to mind.

Listing Jot down things that you already know about your topic, and any questions you have about it. Keep your list going as long as you can.

Clustering Create a cluster with your specific topic as the nucleus word. (See page **95**.)

How can I gather additional details?

Collecting additional details may be a problem unless you have a variety of gathering strategies to use. Here are four of them to choose from.

Ask questions. List questions that come to mind and then find answers to them. You can also ask the 5 W's—*Who? What? When? Where?* and *Why?*—about your topic. Add *How?* for even better coverage.

"Talk" about your topic. Write a dialogue between two people who talk about your topic. (You may or may not want to be one of the speakers.) The two speakers should build on each other's comments as they go along. Keep the conversation going as long as you can.

Focus on a specific audience. Write about your topic to a specific group or audience. You could write to a classroom of preschoolers, a live television audience, the local school board, or the readers of a popular teen magazine. This focus will help you see your topic in new ways.

Read about your topic. Refer to the Internet, nonfiction books, magazines, and newspapers for information. Take notes as you read. (See pages **442–448** for help.)

English Language Learners

Use a K-W-L chart as a way to help students understand how listing and asking questions fit together when gathering details. Demonstrate making a three-column chart.

- The left-hand column is labeled *Know,* and students list anything they already know about their topic there.

- The middle column is labeled *Want to Learn.* There, students list the questions they have about their topic.

- The final column is labeled *Learn.* Students use this column to record the answers they discover to their questions.

conventions ideas *sentence fluency*
VOICE *organization* *word choice* **37**
Traits of Writing

PROCESS

How many different levels of detail should I use?

Usually, each main point in a piece of writing is developed in a separate paragraph. A well-written paragraph should contain at least three different levels of detail.

LEVEL 1: A topic sentence names the main point of a paragraph.
Water is natural and important to life.

LEVEL 2: Secondary sentences make the main point clearer.
It is in rivers, ponds, and lakes, and, of course, inside the human body. Water is the life-giving element that makes up a large percentage of each human being.

LEVEL 3: Additional sentences add specific details to complete the point.
Minerals and salts are essential in the human body, too, but an individual can get enough of these two things from eating healthy food and drinking clear water.

What special features can I use?

To add style to your writing, try including figures of speech and anecdotes.

Figures of speech are creative comparisons that help you explain something or create a special effect. Two common figures of speech are similes and metaphors.

- A **simile** compares two things using *like* or *as*.
  The fire leaped like an attacking panther onto the helpless van in the driveway.

- A **metaphor** compares two things without using *like* or *as*.
  In most high schools across the country, football is king during the fall season.

Anecdotes are brief "slices of life," or ministories, that help you make a point about your topic. They allow you to show your readers something rather than tell them matter-of-factly.
Joe and Ki, two elderly Koreans, shake hands and formally bow to each other. Samantha and Susan, two Americanized Korean teenagers, give each other a kiss on the cheek and then hug.
(These brief anecdotes, or slices of life, come from an expository essay comparing Korean and American culture.)

 Gather details for one of the topics that you listed (page 35). Start by freewriting about the topic; then continue by asking and answering questions about it. Finish by writing a simile, a metaphor, or an anecdote about the topic.

Discuss the three levels of details in a well-written paragraph. For additional practice, have on hand copies of another well-written paragraph, preferably one written by an anonymous, former student. Distribute copies to pairs or small groups of students. Tell them to mark

- the topic sentence with a *1,*
- the secondary sentences that have details that clarify the point with a *2,*
- the additional sentences that have details that complete the point with a *3.*

Emphasize that good writers use figures of speech and anecdotes so that they can **show, not tell** *(see below)* their readers about an idea.

Have students complete the **Try It** activity on their own. Give students the option of using freewriting, listing, or clustering to explore their topic.

Try IT Answers

Answers will vary.

Teaching Tip: Show, Don't Tell

Pair the sentences below with the sample anecdotes to reinforce the difference between showing (the anecdotes) and telling (the sentences below). Ask students to read aloud both versions and point out the differences between them.

- Joe and Ki greet each other.
- Samantha and Susan show each other affection.

Understanding
Organization

Continue the pupil-edition analogy of the carpenter and building a frame by explaining that transitions are like doorways and stairways in a house.

- On each floor of the house, doorways link rooms so that you can walk easily from one room to the next.
- In a paragraph, transitions link sentences to create flow so that you can follow ideas smoothly from one sentence to the next.
- In a house, stairways connect floors (or stories) so that you can climb easily from one level of the house to another level.
- In an essay, transitions connect paragraphs so that you can follow ideas smoothly from one paragraph to the next.

Understanding Organization

Strong writing is well organized from start to finish. Writer Stephen Tchudi (pronounced "Judy") calls organizing a paper the "framing" process: "Just as a carpenter puts up a frame of a house before tacking on the outside walls, a writer needs to build a frame for a paper."

How can transitions help me organize my writing?

Linking words and phrases (transitions) can help you organize the details in each mode of writing. (Also see pages 572–573.)

Descriptive: You can use the following transitions, which show location, to arrange details in your descriptions.

above	across	below	beneath	on top of	to the right	in back of

On top of the track our car groaned to a halt. Then the rain suddenly rushed down. . . . Below us a huge pool of water waited. . . .

Narrative: You can use the following transitions, which show time, to arrange details in your narratives.

after	before	during	first	second	today	next	then

I squeezed my grandmother's hand, holding on with all my strength. First, when we entered the classroom, I let go and walked around. Then I headed back toward my grandmother—only she wasn't there.

Expository: You can use the following transitions to organize comparisons and contrasts.

(when comparing)	like	also	both	in the same way	similarly
(when contrasting)	but	still	yet	on the other hand	unlike

Both fossil fuels and sunlight can produce energy to run cars and heat homes. . . . But solar energy has some distinct advantages. . . .

Persuasive: You can use the following transitions to organize the details in your persuasive essays.

in fact	in addition	equally important	all in all

In fact, more cars and more roads lead to more congestion in busy areas. . . . All in all, the automobile is the leading cause of air pollution. . . .

conventions ideas *sentence fluency*
VOICE *organization* *word choice* **39**
Traits of Writing

PROCESS

How else can I organize my writing?

Many of the essays that you will be asked to write require two different types of thinking about a topic. There's the comparison-contrast essay, the problem-solution essay, and so on. To organize these types of essays you have to consider the two parts of the topic.

Creating a Two-Part Focus Statement

To help you organize a two-part essay, you need to develop an effective focus statement, but only after you have gathered enough facts and details. If you can't think of a focus statement for your two-part essay, complete one of the patterns below. (See pages **548–549** for two-part graphic organizers.)

For problem-solution essays:

. . . could be fixed if . . .
. . . won't change until . . .
   The lack of open gym time for basketball (part 1) could be fixed if **the community center extended its hours** (part 2).

For cause-effect essays:

Because of . . . we now . . .
When . . . happened, I *(we, they)* . . .
   Because of **the stricter grade requirements** (part 1), we now **have fewer students going out for sports** (part 2).

For comparison-contrast essays:

_____ and _____ are both . . . but they differ in . . .
While _____ and _____ have . . . in common, they also . . .
   Sharks and **dolphins** are both **fascinating sea creatures** (part 1), but they differ in **many significant ways** (part 2).

For before-after essays:

Once I *(we, they, it)* . . . , but now . . .
I *(we, they, it)* . . . until . . .
   Once I **had trouble understanding American culture** (part 1), but now **it makes much better sense to me** (part 2).

 Write a focus statement for each two-part essay shown above. Think of topics that you know well or have strong feelings about. Share your statements with your classmates for discussion.

Before having students do the **Try It** activity on their own, work with them to write one focus statement for each type of essay shown (examples follow). For topic ideas, students can look back at the "Topics for Writing" list they began on PE page 35.

Problem-solution: The lack of a safe way to walk to school won't change until the city completes the sidewalk project for all neighborhoods.

Cause-effect: When we have to be at the school bus stop at 6:30 in the morning, we don't get enough sleep and don't have time for breakfast.

Comparison-contrast: While tennis and soccer are both excellent ways to stay physically active, they require totally different sets of physical and emotional skills.

Before-after: I didn't begin to appreciate plays until I saw a movie based on a Shakespeare play.

Try It Answers

Answers will vary, but each focus statement should have two distinct parts and follow a similar pattern to those shown.

Understanding Voice

To help students better understand the effect of a confident voice, have them read the samples with the following questions in mind. Then discuss their responses.

First passage:
- What words and phrases show that the writer lacks interest? (I thought I might, stuff like that)
- What details show that the writer knows very little about the topic? (I will need to learn, figure out, maybe I could, I might be)

Second passage:
- What words and phrases show that the writer is interested in the topic? (I plan to, I will need books about, my project will help)
- What details show that the writer knows the topic well? (construction of castles for protection, base, clay, toilet paper rolls, towers, toothpicks, glue)

After students complete the **Try It** activity, have them exchange notes with a partner who can check to see if it has a confident voice.

 **Answers**

Answers will vary.

40

Understanding Voice

Author Sandra Belton says, "I write for myself because that's who I have to please first." When someone writes for her- or himself, the person's writing voice shines through.

How can I sound confident in my writing?

You will sound confident in your writing if you . . .
- show genuine interest in your topic,
- know a great deal about it, and
- share your honest thoughts and feelings.

Writing Without Confidence

For my history project, I thought I might build a model castle and then write about it.

To build the castle, I will need to learn a lot about castles and figure out how to build one. Maybe I could use some plywood, clay, and stuff like that.

My project should give the class some idea about medieval castles. If you think I might be on the right track, please let me know.

Writing With Confidence

For my history project on medieval life, I plan to build a scale model (2′ x 2′) of an English castle and write an essay on the construction of castles for protection.

To complete this project, I will need books on medieval castles, a 3′ x 3′ plywood board for the base, modeling clay for the walls, toilet paper rolls for the frame of the towers, toothpicks and glue for . . .

My project will help the class understand how a castle was built and how it was used. I would appreciate any suggestions before I get started.

Should I sound enthusiastic in my writing?

Yes, your readers will appreciate it if you sound enthusiastic because it means that you truly care about your topic. However, be careful not to sound too enthusiastic. Too much excitement in your voice will sound phony.

Write a brief note to a coach, a director, an advisor, or a parent displaying a confident voice.

English Language Learners

Provide additional practice to reinforce the concept of voice. Read aloud some examples of writing that sound enthusiastic and some that do not. Letters to the editor of a local newspaper may be a resource for these examples. Help students see which are effective and why.

Advanced Learners

Invite students to work together to write letters in support of an existing community project, such as building a skating park. Or, if students are motivated and committed, they can write letters encouraging the community to begin such a project.
- Tell students to research the project, using the 5 W's and H as a guide (photocopy the reproducible chart on TE page 792), and to write convincing letters to city planning/park officials.
- If students choose an existing project, they should contact the committee in charge of the project and ask to whom they can write letters.
- Encourage students to mail their letters and to become involved in the project.

conventions ideas *sentence fluency*
VOICE *organization* *word choice* **41**
Traits of Writing

PROCESS

Understanding **Word Choice**

Using the best words is an important part of writing. The best words are the ones that sincerely reflect your feelings about your topic. As author Stephen King says, "One of the really bad things you can do is dress up your vocabulary, looking for long words."

How can I improve the verbs that I use?

Here are some strategies that you can use to improve the verbs in your writing:

- After writing a first draft, list the verbs that you have used. If many of your sentences contain linking verbs (*is, are, was, were,* and so on) or overused verbs (*look, see, talk,* and so on), replace some of them.
  A sentence containing an overused verb:
  The play director talked to the unprepared cast members.
  The revised sentence containing a more specific verb:
  The play director lectured the unprepared cast members.

- Use verbs that are active and move the writing forward. Make it clear in your sentences that your subject is actually doing something.
  A sentence that is slow moving because of the verb:
  A surplus of calories is necessary for growth in children.
  The revised sentence that is more direct and active:
  Children require plenty of calories for growth.

How does word choice affect the tone of my writing?

The tone of your writing is the feeling that your writing produces. If the purpose of your writing is to explain or persuade, use words that suggest a serious tone. On the other hand, if the purpose of your writing is to share or to entertain, use words that suggest a more personal tone.

Word choice suggesting a serious, somewhat formal tone:
The automobile has become the main means of transportation, making many aspects of daily life much easier. However, too many people have become overly reliant on the automobile.

Word choice suggesting a personal, more informal tone:
Suddenly I heard these slurping, snorting noises coming from our campsite. I crept to the door. I saw a big brown bear munching on our marshmallows.

 Review one of your latest first drafts and circle any verbs that could be improved. Replace some of these verbs with more effective ones. Also check the tone of your draft. Do all of the words reflect your intended tone?

Understanding Word Choice

Have students work together to create a list of synonyms for overused verbs (*look, see, say, talk, go,* and so on) to keep on display in the classroom. Students can refer to and add to this list all year long.

✳ See PE pages 718–731 for more ways to improve verbs.

Provide examples from literature of writing with a serious, formal tone and writing with a personal, informal tone. Have students identify the tone of each passage and words that suggest the tone.

Before assigning the **Try It** activity, remind students of the Stephen King quotation at the top of the page. Point out that sometimes the simplest word is the best word.

 Answers

Answers will vary.

Have students exchange papers with a partner who can see if they agree with the changes and can check the tone.

English Language Learners

Have thesauruses at various levels available for students to use for the **Try It** activity. Remind students of their practice in using a thesaurus to help with word choice (TE page 20, English Language Learners activity). Ask a student for a verb from his or her draft, and review with students how to find synonyms.

Advanced Learners

Ask students to write about a bicycle accident from two different viewpoints. For example:

- One report could be from a safety officer who witnessed the accident.
- The other one could be an e-mail from the rider to a friend telling about the situation.

Remind students that the reports should clearly refer to the same situation, but that the tone of each should be different and conveyed through word choice.

Understanding
Sentence Fluency

Conduct a revising workshop during which students can test their own sentences for fluency. Have them use the draft they selected for the **Try It** activity on PE page 41, or tell them to choose another work-in-progress or a past piece of writing. Provide time for students to apply each bulleted step shown.

Students will have many chances to practice revising during the year. However, putting revising in the spotlight here can encourage students to view it as a key step in the writing process and not as an afterthought.

Before having students do the **Try It** activity on their own, provide one or two more professional sentences. Work together as a class to write new sentences that follow the pattern of the models.

 Answers

Answers will vary.

42

Understanding Sentence Fluency

All writers build their stories, arguments, or explanations one sentence at a time. Author Gloria Naylor clearly understands the importance of each sentence in her work: "The bottom line for me is the sentence in front of my face. If nine out of ten of them hit the mark, then I am satisfied."

How can I test my writing for fluency?

Sentences are fluent when they all work together to make your writing enjoyable to read. Use the following strategies to test your sentences.

- When you edit your writing, list the opening words in each of your sentences. Decide if you need to vary some of your sentence beginnings.
- Then identify the number of words in each sentence. Consider changing the length of some of your sentences if too many of them have the same number of words.
- Also check your writing for transitions—*first of all, in addition,* and so on. When you revise your writing, add transitions as needed to make the connections between your sentences easier to follow.
- Have someone else read your writing aloud. As this person reads, listen for any sentences that cause the reader to stumble. Then decide if you should revise those sentences to make them easier to read.

How can sentence modeling help me?

You can learn a lot about fluency by studying the sentences and passages of some of your favorite authors. When you come across sentences that you really like, practice writing sentences of your own following that pattern. This process is called **modeling**. (See pages **521–522** for more information.)

A professional sentence from *A Solitary Blue* by Cynthia Voight:

> **Jeff couldn't see the musician clearly, just a figure on a chair on the stage, holding what looked like a misshapen guitar.**

A student model:

> Larisa couldn't identify the person immediately, just a shadow in the dark alley behind the store, carrying what appeared to be a heavy box.

 Search for three well-made sentences in your reading. Then write your own sentences patterned after the originals.

English Language Learners

To provide additional examples of sentence modeling, create a bulletin board.

- Choose appropriate sentences from literature for students to use as models.
- Guide students to write their own sentences following the patterns of the model sentences.
- Display the model sentences and the students' sentences on the bulletin board.

Encourage students to refer to these examples as they write.

conventions ideas *sentence fluency*
VOICE *organization* *word choice* **43**
Traits of Writing

PROCESS

What are different ways I can start my sentences?

You can vary your sentence beginnings in many different ways. Some of the key ways are listed below:

■ **Start with a single-word modifier.**
Before: **Susan Lue confidently stepped into the batter's box.**
After: **Confidently, Susan Lue stepped into the batter's box.**

■ **Start with a participial phrase.**
(See pages **514** and **520**.)
Before: **She tripped and fell right next to us, chasing after the pop fly.**
After: **Chasing after the pop fly, she tripped and fell right next to us.**

■ **Start with an infinitive phrase.**
(See pages **514** and **520**.)
Before: **I decided to interview my grandfather to learn about his days as a baseball player.**
After: **To learn about my grandfather's days as a baseball player, I decided to interview him.**

 Carefully review one of your recent pieces of writing. Look for parts in which the sentences all seem to start in the same way. Vary some of these sentences using the information above as a guide.

What types of sentences add style to writing?

Look for the following types of sentences whenever you read, and practice writing your own versions.

● A **loose sentence** expresses the main idea near the beginning (underlined below) and adds details as needed.

Wil nodded to himself and slipped away, softly as a mouse, toward the back of the house where tourists were never taken.
　　　　　　　　　　—"A Room Full of Leaves" by Joan Aiken

● A **balanced sentence** includes two or more parts that are equal or parallel in structure. (The parallel parts are underlined below.)

He goes out onto his baseball field, spins around second base, and looks back at the academy.
　　　　　　　　　　—*The Headmaster* by John McPhee

When discussing the different ways to start sentences, caution students against creating awkward-sounding sentences just for the sake of variety. Read aloud and discuss this example:

Silently, after the boy's father had gone to bed and the two dogs had curled up, the boy crept down the stairs and out of the house.

Ask students to rewrite the sentence so that it is less awkward. (Possible response: *After the boy's father had gone to bed and the two dogs had curled up, the boy crept silently down the stairs and out of the house.*)

The best way for students to ensure that their sentences sound "right" is to read them aloud.

When students have finished the **Try It** activity, have them read their original and revised sentences to a partner for feedback.

 Answers

Answers will vary.

Tell students to use the sentence-modeling technique they learned on PE page 42 to write a loose sentence and a balanced sentence, based on the two examples. Invite students to share their sentences with the class.

Understanding
Conventions

Throughout this book, students are given a checklist to monitor the revising and editing stages of their work during the writing process. The checklist on this page will help students edit and proofread their revised writing for errors.

Not every piece of writing needs to be taken through every stage of the writing process. You may choose to have students set aside revisions (or even first drafts) of certain assignments, placing them in their portfolios for later work.

Understanding Conventions

Good writing follows the conventions, or basic rules, of the language. These rules cover punctuation, capitalization, grammar, and spelling. When you follow these rules, the reader will find your writing much easier to understand and enjoy.

How can I make sure my writing follows the rules?

A checklist like the one below can guide you as you look over your writing for errors. When you are not sure about a certain rule, refer to the "Proofreader's Guide" (pages 578–749).

Conventions

PUNCTUATION

_____ **1.** Do I use end punctuation after all my sentences?

_____ **2.** Do I use commas correctly in compound sentences?

_____ **3.** Do I use commas correctly in a series?

_____ **4.** Do I use apostrophes correctly to show possession (*that girl's purse* and *those girls' purses*)?

CAPITALIZATION

_____ **5.** Do I start every sentence with a capital letter?

_____ **6.** Do I capitalize the proper names of people and places?

SPELLING

_____ **7.** Have I checked my spelling using a spell-checker?

_____ **8.** Have I also checked the spelling by myself?

GRAMMAR

_____ **9.** Do I use correct forms of verbs (*had gone*, not *had went*)?

_____ **10.** Do my subjects and verbs agree in number (*the boy eats* and *the boys eat*)?

_____ **11.** Do I use the correct word (*to, too,* or *two*)?

 Have at least one other person check your writing for conventions. Professional writers have trained editors to help them with this step in the process. You should ask your classmates, teachers, and family members for help.

English Language Learners

Errors in subject-verb agreement and pronoun-antecedent agreement occur frequently in the early writing of students who are learning English. Encourage them to look up *agreement* in the index at the back of their book so that they will know where to find appropriate information whenever they have questions.

Using a Rubric

How can a writer be measured? A tape measure can tell the writer's hat size, but it can't even begin to measure the person's *ideas,* unique writing *voice,* and *word choice.* A rubric can measure these things.

Rubrics have other uses as well. They can help to prepare a writer at the beginning of a project. They can also guide a writer through the development of a first draft and aid in the revising and editing process. By using the rubric throughout the writing process, a writer can also make sure that his or her final work is ready for assessment. In this chapter, you will learn about all these uses of a rubric—and more!

What's Ahead

- **Understanding Rubrics**
- **Reading a Rubric**
- **Getting Started with a Rubric**
- **Revising and Editing with a Rubric**
- **Assessing with a Rubric**
- **Assessing in Action**
- **Assessing a Persuasive Essay**

Copy Masters/ Transparencies

Assessment Sheet (TE pp. 52, 55, 56)

Using a Rubric

Objectives
- understand the rating scale on a rubric
- learn to read a rubric
- use a rubric for revising, editing, and assessment

Rubric strips appear in the revising and editing sections of the core units in the pupil edition. Emphasize that the rubrics can be used throughout the writing process as well as for assessment.

Have students turn to the "Rubric for Narrative Writing" on PE pages 130–131. Encourage students to discuss how they can use the information on the number scales, particularly number 5, to guide them as they write, revise, and edit. Point out the connection between the rubrics and the traits of writing that appear on PE page 98.

Understanding Rubrics

Have students study the sample rubric strip, which shows the numbers in the rating scale and the single-word ratings that these numbers represent.

Rating Guide

Point out to students that throughout this book, they will use rubric strips to evaluate individual writing traits. Emphasize that for the rubrics to be truly useful to them as writers, students have to understand the meaning of each rating and apply those ratings honestly.

Have volunteers read aloud the meaning of each rating. Ask students if they have any questions about the differences between the ratings.

46

Understanding Rubrics

Rubrics are rating scales. Have you ever rated books or movies on a scale from a high of 10 (perfect) down to a low of 1? With rubrics, you can rate your writing—in this case on a scale from 6 to 1.

| **6** Amazing | **5** Strong | **4** Good | **3** Okay | **2** Poor | **1** Incomplete |

Any piece of writing has a number of different traits or qualities—*ideas, organization, voice, word choice, sentence fluency,* and *conventions.* (For more about the traits, see pages **33–44**). In a single essay, the ideas might be amazing (6), but the word choice might be merely okay (3). See the rating guide below.

Rating Guide

This guide will help you understand the rating scale.

A **6** means that the writing is truly amazing.
It goes way beyond the requirements for a certain trait.

A **5** means that the writing is very strong.
It clearly meets the main requirements for a trait.

A **4** means that the writing is good.
It meets most of the requirements for a trait.

A **3** means that the writing is okay.
It needs work to meet the main requirements for a trait.

A **2** means that the writing is poor.
It needs a lot of work to meet the requirements for a trait.

A **1** means that the writing is incomplete.
It is not yet ready to assess for a trait.

ASSESS
rate *evaluate* improve **47**
measure
Using a Rubric

Reading a Rubric

In this book, the rubrics are color-coded according to the traits. *Ideas* appear in a green strip, *organization* in a pink strip, and so on. Within each strip, the trait is ranked from 6 to 1.

Rubric for Persuasive Writing

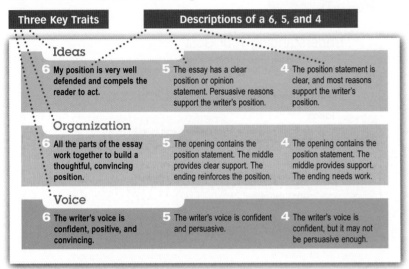

Three Key Traits	Descriptions of a 6, 5, and 4		
Ideas			
6 My position is very well defended and compels the reader to act.	**5** The essay has a clear position or opinion statement. Persuasive reasons support the writer's position.	**4** The position statement is clear, and most reasons support the writer's position.
Organization			
6 All the parts of the essay work together to build a thoughtful, convincing position.	**5** The opening contains the position statement. The middle provides clear support. The ending reinforces the position.	**4** The opening contains the position statement. The middle provides support. The ending needs work.
Voice			
6 The writer's voice is confident, positive, and convincing.	**5** The writer's voice is confident and persuasive.	**4** The writer's voice is confident, but it may not be persuasive enough.

Guiding Your Writing

A rubric helps you . . .

- **plot your course**—knowing what is expected,
- **create a strong first draft**—focusing on *ideas, organization,* and *voice,*
- **revise and edit your work**—considering each trait, and
- **assess your final writing**—rating the traits and the whole assignment.

 Think about the rubric. Read the level 5 descriptions above for *ideas, organization,* and *voice.* What makes an opinion statement clear? What makes reasons persuasive? How are the opening, middle, and ending best organized? What makes a writer's voice confident and persuasive? The following pages will use rubrics to help you answer questions like these.

Reading a Rubric

Have students explain in their own words how to read the rubric, using the sample shown. Be sure they understand that the description for each rating will change depending on the form of writing and the trait being evaluated. For an additional example, have students take a quick look at the rubric for expository writing on PE pages 194–195.

Guiding Your Writing

Direct students' attention to the first bulleted item. Emphasize the importance of reading the entire rubric for a particular form of writing before they write, so that they can understand what to focus on and what to avoid to achieve their goals.

✱ Reproducible six-, five-, and four-point rubrics for persuasive writing are available on TE pages 752, 756, and 760.

Getting Started with a Rubric

Help students understand the difference between the **Understanding Your Goal** list of traits and the main rubric for persuasive writing on PE pages 256–257.

- Before and during writing: The list of traits provides specific directions for planning and developing a writing assignment.
- After writing: The main rubric for each writing form provides descriptions that help writers evaluate how well or how poorly they have addressed each trait and what they need to do to improve their writing.

Suggest that students look back at PE page 47 if they need a reminder of how a rubric for writing is organized.

4

Getting Started with a Rubric

Each of the writing units in this book begins by outlining your writing goals. The page below provides the goals from the persuasive rubric. By previewing the writing rubric, you will understand the main requirements for the unit.

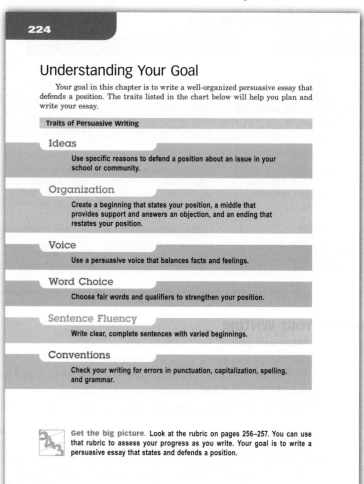

224

Understanding Your Goal

Your goal in this chapter is to write a well-organized persuasive essay that defends a position. The traits listed in the chart below will help you plan and write your essay.

Traits of Persuasive Writing

Ideas
Use specific reasons to defend a position about an issue in your school or community.

Organization
Create a beginning that states your position, a middle that provides support and answers an objection, and an ending that restates your position.

Voice
Use a persuasive voice that balances facts and feelings.

Word Choice
Choose fair words and qualifiers to strengthen your position.

Sentence Fluency
Write clear, complete sentences with varied beginnings.

Conventions
Check your writing for errors in punctuation, capitalization, spelling, and grammar.

Get the big picture. Look at the rubric on pages 256–257. You can use that rubric to assess your progress as you write. Your goal is to write a persuasive essay that states and defends a position.

English Language Learners

Help students understand writing goals by comparing them to another situation. Ask students to imagine that they are going to buy a new bicycle:

- Have them identify qualities they would like the bike to have (good looking, easy to ride, safe, comfortable, and so on).

- Then ask students to tell how one would achieve each quality (for example, to be safe, a bike must be the right size, the brakes need to work well, and the bike should have reflectors and a horn).

Point out that they have listed qualities they want in a bike (safe, comfortable, and so on) just as "Understanding Your Goal" lists qualities of an effective piece of writing (strong ideas, good organization, and so on). Also, they have described how to achieve those qualities in a bike (by buying a bike that is the right size, and so on) just as the traits on this page describe how to achieve an effective piece of writing.

PROCESS

A Closer Look at Understanding Your Goal

The following steps will help you use the "Understanding Your Goal" rubric at the beginning of each writing unit.

1. **Read through the whole chart** to understand your general goals in writing.

2. **Focus on** *ideas, organization,* and *voice* in your prewriting and writing, since these traits are the foundation of excellent writing. (See the chart below.)

3. **Identify goals** for each trait (such as "specific reasons" or "defend a position").

4. **Ask questions** if you aren't sure about any part of the assignment.

A Special Note About the Traits

Different traits are important at different times during your writing. The following chart shows which traits are important at what times.

During **Prewriting** and **Writing**, focus on the *ideas, organization,* and *voice* in your writing.

During **Revising**, focus on *ideas, organization, voice, word choice,* and *sentence fluency.* (For some assignments, your teacher may ask you to concentrate most of your attention on one or two of these traits.)

During **Editing** and proofreading, focus on *conventions.*

When **Assessing** a final copy, consider all six traits. (For some assignments, your teacher may ask you to assess a piece of writing for just a few of the traits.)

 Write a paragraph. Review the goal rubric on page 48. Then write a short paragraph stating your position about an issue in your school or community. Keep the traits in mind as you write.

A Closer Look at Understanding Your Goal

To help students become more familiar with the traits of writing, have them work in small groups to list the similarities and differences in the **Understanding Your Goal** list of traits for the following writing forms:

- narrative writing, PE page 98
- expository writing, PE page 162
- persuasive writing, PE page 224
- response to literature, PE page 288

A copy master for a Venn diagram is available on TE page 791 and can be used to explore similarities and differences.

A Special Note About the Traits

Before students write their paragraph, have them generate a list of possible topics. Have on hand local and school newspapers and a variety of community bulletins and flyers that advertise meetings about local issues and causes. Students can look through these to get ideas.

Make it clear that students are to write a **persuasive paragraph** *(see below).* When they have finished, invite volunteers to read aloud their paragraph and explain how they used the traits to write.

Teaching Tip: Persuasive Paragraph

A persuasive paragraph (see PE pages 219–222) tries to convince readers to agree with the writer's opinion or position. Strong supporting reasons and a confident, knowledgeable voice make the writer's position more convincing.

English Language Learners

Provide a paragraph frame for students who need additional support in writing a persuasive paragraph:

My opinion about _____ is _____. One reason I think that is because _____. An even more important reason is _____. The most important reason is _____. I think you should help by _____.

Revising and Editing with a Rubric

Point out that students should read the rubric strip on PE pages 50–51 from left to right all the way across.

Walk students through the steps for rating a piece of writing. As you read aloud each rating, have students read aloud the corresponding rubric description. Then have students work alone or in pairs to complete the **Try It** activity.

 **Answers**

Answers will vary, but students' ratings should reflect that

- supporting reasons are presented, but they lack specific details to make them sound logical,
- the objection is not clearly stated,
- the response to the objection is not convincing.

50

Revising and Editing with a Rubric

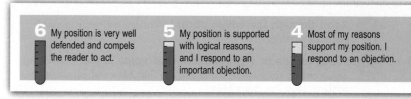

6 My position is very well defended and compels the reader to act.

5 My position is supported with logical reasons, and I respond to an important objection.

4 Most of my reasons support my position. I respond to an objection.

In this book, the sections on revising and editing each start with a rubric strip that focuses on one trait and the activities presented on those pages. It provides ratings from 6 to 1. The rubric strip above focuses on the *ideas* of persuasive writing.

How can rubric strips help me rate my writing?

A rubric strip can help you look objectively at your writing. By knowing how your work measures up, you will be better able to revise or edit. Follow these steps when considering each trait.

1. Begin by checking the number 5 description (a rating of *strong*).
2. Decide if your writing rates a 5.
3. If not, check the 6 or 4 descriptions.
4. Continue until you find the rating that matches your writing.
5. Notice how levels 3, 2, and 1 suggest ways to improve your writing.

 Review the sample persuasive paragraph below. Then rate it for *ideas* using the strip above as a guide and explain your rating. (See pages 46–47 for help.)

> Songs and jingles that get stuck in my head drive me crazy. Songs like this are called earworms because they enter a person's ear and burrow into the brain and won't go away. Pop stars and ad companies come up with the tunes. Special techniques make a song stick. There's no cure for earworms except to turn off all electronic media.

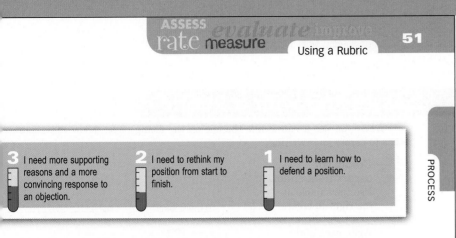

51
Using a Rubric

| 3 I need more supporting reasons and a more convincing response to an objection. | 2 I need to rethink my position from start to finish. | 1 I need to learn how to defend a position. |

PROCESS

How can rubric strips help me revise and edit?

Once you have rated your writing for a given trait, you will see ways to improve your score. The writer of the paragraph on page 50 rated her ideas as a 3. The description of a 3 for ideas told her just what she needed to do to improve her work.

> In the main writing units, each rubric strip is followed by minilessons that will help you revise or edit your writing to improve that trait.

In order to create more logical reasons and provide a convincing response to an objection, the writer made the following changes.

Ideas
Details are made more specific.

An objection is answered in a convincing way.

Songs and jingles that get stuck in my
"The Sweet Escape" once haunted me for weeks.
head drive me crazy. Songs like this are called

earworms because they enter a person's ear and

burrow into the brain and won't go away. Pop
using simple lyrics and catchy rhythms to
stars and ad companies come up with the tunes.
Some people don't mind
Special techniques make a song stick. There's no
but others should just
cure for earworms, except to turn off all electronic

media.

Assessing with a Rubric

A reproducible assessment sheet is available on TE page 787. Students can use this throughout the year whenever they evaluate their writing.

Allow extra time for students to review the sample self-assessment on PE page 55 before they assess their own persuasive paragraph. Answer any questions they have about the self-assessment.

52

Assessing with a Rubric

When you use a rubric like the one on the facing page, follow these four steps to assess your writing.

1 **Create an assessment sheet.** Use the sample at the right to create your own sheet. Write each of the key traits from the rubric, preceded by a short line. Under each trait, leave two or three lines to allow for comments.

2 **Read the final copy.** First, read straight through to get an overall sense of the writing. Then read more carefully, paying attention to the traits.

3 **Assess the writing.** Use the rubric to rate each trait by checking the description for 5 and shifting up or down the scale until you discover the correct rating. Write down the number next to the right trait.

RESPONSE SHEET   Title: _____

_____ IDEAS

_____ ORGANIZATION

_____ VOICE

_____ WORD CHOICE

_____ SENTENCE FLUENCY

_____ CONVENTIONS

Evaluator: _____

4 **Provide comments.** Under each trait, write one thing you liked and one thing that could be improved.

Assess your persuasive paragraph. Make an assessment sheet like the one above. Then evaluate your paragraph (from page 49) using the rubric on pages 256–257. For each trait, write something you did well and something you'd like to improve. (See the sample on page 55.)

Struggling Learners

Some students might find it easier to complete the self-assessment orally first. Have them work with you or with a partner to orally evaluate their paragraph using the rubric. Encourage students to write notes on an assessment sheet as they talk about their writing.

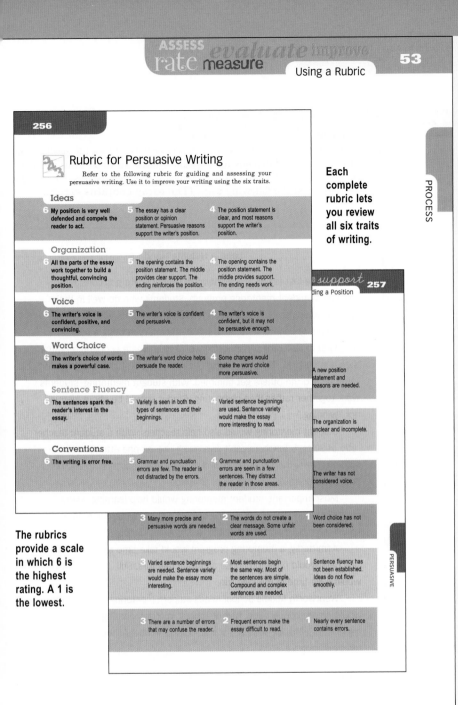

53
Using a Rubric

Each complete rubric lets you review all six traits of writing.

The rubrics provide a scale in which 6 is the highest rating. A 1 is the lowest.

By now, students should be familiar with the organization of the rubric for writing. However, if you think it is necessary, review it one more time. Ask volunteers to explain the purpose of each of the following elements of the rubric:

- headings and colored strips (They identify the trait. There are six headings and colors for the six traits of writing: ideas, organization, voice, word choice, sentence fluency, and conventions.)
- numbers (They rate the writing from a high of 6, which is "amazing," down to 1, which is "incomplete.")
- descriptions (They help the writer evaluate the writing and suggest what to do to improve it.)

✱ The complete six-point rubric for persuasive writing is found on PE pages 256–257. Reproducible six-, five-, and four-point rubrics for persuasive writing are available on TE pages 752, 756, and 760.

Assessing in Action

As students read the essay to themselves, suggest that they jot down notes about the strengths and weaknesses of the essay. The following questions, which are based on the rubric, can help them identify those strengths and weaknesses.

- What is the focus statement that clearly states the writer's position?
- What are some persuasive details and persuasive language the writer includes?
- Does the writer provide enough details?
- How convincing an argument has the writer presented?
- What shows that the writer is interested in the topic?
- What details show that the writer knows the subject well?
- What transition words does the writer use to connect ideas within and between paragraphs?
- What are examples of different sentence patterns and different sentence beginnings?
- Does the writer defend his position against an important objection? What is that objection?

Assessing in Action

In the following persuasive essay, the writer both states his position on an issue in his school and defends his position against an important objection. Read the essay, paying attention to its strengths and weaknesses. Then read the self-assessment on the following page. **(The essay contains errors.)**

Lend a Helping Hand

For the last few years, Wentworth school board has considered creating a student mentoring program. Students who do well in their studies would receive extra credit for helping students who struggle. After years of debate, its time to make student mentoring a reality.

First of all, student mentoring would help create cooperation rather then competition. Right now, after each test, a few students come out "on top" and the others get bummed. With student mentoring, students work together rather than competing. Grades should be about learning, not "winning."

Student mentoring would also help teachers. With a student-teacher ratio of 30 to 1, teachers can't give much one-on-one attention to students. A mentoring program would put extra "teachers" in each class. So more kids could get individual attention.

Most important, student mentoring would help learning. Many struggling students would get the help of a student mentor. Mentors would learn by sharing knowledge. A win-win situation!

Admittedly, a mentoring program would take time to get organized. Teachers would have to choose and train mentors. Still, the program would save time in the long run.

Wentworth Middle School needs student mentoring. The program would create cooperation, help teachers, improve learning, and save time overall. For all these reasons, school board members should vote "yes" for mentoring.

English Language Learners

Prepare students to understand the essay by explaining that a mentor is a person who helps someone else learn and be successful. Point out the similarities between mentors and tutors. Also, be sure students understand that a student-teacher ratio means how many students a teacher has in each class.

Struggling Learners

Provide students with a written version of the questions listed in the left column. Have students answer the questions on a separate sheet of paper as they read the essay.

Then work together with students to identify which trait each question refers to.

PROCESS

Sample Assessment

The student who wrote "Lend a Helping Hand" created an assessment sheet to evaluate his essay. He used the persuasive rubric on pages 256–257. Under each trait, he wrote one strength and one weakness.

RESPONSE SHEET   Title: *Lend a Helping Hand*

_4_ Ideas
  1. My position statement is clear, and I include persuasive details.
  2. A few more details would have made my essay stronger.

_4_ Organization
  1. I followed the plan for my paragraphs.
  2. Some of my transitions sound kind of unnatural.

_4_ Voice
  1. My voice is confident, positive, and persuasive.
  2. In a few places, I'm not formal enough.

_3_ Word Choice
  1. Most of my words are accurate.
  2. The word "bummed" really sticks out.

_3_ Sentence Fluency
  1. I tried to vary sentences.
  2. Two fragments got past me!

_4_ Conventions
  1. I caught many of my errors.
  2. I should have proofed the final copy one more time.

          Evaluator: *Jason Rollingcloud*

Review the assessment. On your own paper, explain why you agree with the response above (or why you don't). Consider each trait carefully.

Sample Assessment

As students write their review of the assessment, tell them to refer to the notes they jotted down while they read the essay. They should probably also look again at the rubric for persuasive writing on PE pages 256–257.

Assessing a Persuasive Essay

Use the following as an alternative to the individual assessing activity.

- Divide students into six groups.
- Assign each group a trait from the "Traits of Persuasive Writing" (PE page 224).
- Tell each group to carefully study the goals (on PE page 224) and the rubric strip (on PE pages 256–257) for their particular trait before they make their comments.

Groups can then come together, and you can work with the class to share their comments and fill out an assessment sheet together (see TE page 787 for a reproducible, blank assessment sheet).

56

Assessing a Persuasive Essay

Read the essay that follows and focus on the strengths and weaknesses in it. Then follow the directions at the bottom of the page. **(The essay contains errors.)**

Our Turn to Shine

Jonesburg Jr. High doesn't have a drama program, so junior high students have to try out for senior high plays. Upper-class actors get all the good parts, and younger students end up in the chorus or as extras. It's time for Jonesburg Jr. High to start its own drama club.

First of all, a junior high drama club would give students a chance at the lead roles. Instead of always standing in the background, they could learn lines, sing solos, and be the stars. As it is, junior high students don't get to feel much pride in senior high plays.

A drama club in the junior high would also help students learn about drama. It doesn't take much acting skill to sit in the background and pretend to make conversation or to stand and hold a spear. Also, junior high students often feel like they are "trespassing" when they participate in senior high plays. Instead of learning about drama, many younger students are learning that they don't want to be involved in drama.

Some people object that a junior high drama club would compete against the senior high program. However, a junior high program would actually support drama at the upper levels. It would train students in acting, singing, and dancing and would help set up drama supporters for the years to come.

Jonesburg Jr. High needs to start its own drama club. It would teach students about drama and help the senior high program. If someone asks about junior high drama, say, "It's long overdue!"

 Use a persuasive rubric. Assess the persuasive essay you have just read using the rubric on pages 256–257 as a guide. Before you get started, create an assessment sheet like the one on page 52. *Remember:* **After each trait, add comments (something good, something to improve).**

English Language Learners

Be sure students understand the specialized vocabulary they will encounter in this essay.

- try out (perform for a judge in order to join a group)
- chorus (in musicals, a group of singers who provide background music; in drama, a group of people speaking together as commentators on the play)
- extras (people who have a small, nonspeaking part in a show, for example, a shopper in a crowded market scene)
- lead roles (main characters or stars of a show)
- standing in the background (being onstage but at the back near the scenery, not at the front where the lead actors are)
- solo (a performance done alone)
- our turn to shine (our chance to perform well and be the stars of the show)

perform *display*
POST print
present **57**

Publishing Your Writing

To build a kite, you begin with simple things: paper, a frame, and plenty of string. Still, when these elements are put together well, the kite will leap into the sky and soar, and everyone for miles around will be able to marvel at it.

Writing is the same way. An essay begins with paper, a framework of ideas, and a string of thought. Put the pieces together well, and you'll create something that will soar. After you finish your work, you'll naturally want everyone to see it. For that, you will need to know your publishing options.

This chapter will help you get your writing ready to publish and give you a variety of publishing ideas. (Also see "Creating a Portfolio" on pages **65–69**.)

What's Ahead

- **Sharing Your Writing**
- **Preparing to Publish**
- **Designing Your Writing**
- **Making Your Own Web Site**
- **Publishing Online**

Publishing Your Writing

Objectives
- explore a variety of publishing options
- understand design features
- plan a Web site
- understand how to publish on the Internet

After students read the introduction to this section, tell them to let their imaginations soar like the kite in the illustration. Have them think up the most fantastic ideas they can for publishing their writing. They could consider ways that will allow them to reach the most people at one time. Provide these two examples to get them started:

- sky books in which their stories, articles, and essays are written across the night sky
- pop-up screens on buses, trains, and planes with a list of all their titles—travelers just click on a title and sit back and read

Sharing Your Writing

Take time to look over the list of publishing ideas here. Decide early in the year which publishing ideas are feasible for your students to try. Offer students the opportunity to try as many of these options as possible during the year.

If your school does not have a newspaper, you can consider starting one. Or you can have your class publish a weekly or monthly literary journal of the class's finest work.

Review students' publishing proposals and encourage them to try the best ones.

✱ For instructions for formatting a proposal and letters to a publisher, see PE pages 576–577.

58

Sharing Your Writing

Some publishing ideas are easy to carry out, like sharing your writing with your classmates. Other publishing ideas take more time and effort, like entering a writing contest. Try a number of these publishing ideas during the school year. All of them will help you grow as a writer.

Performing
- Sharing with Classmates
- Reading to Various Audiences
- Giving a Multimedia Presentation
- Videotaping for Special Audiences
- Performing Onstage

In School
- School Newspapers
- Classroom Collections
- School Literary Magazines
- Writing Portfolios

Self-Publishing
- Family Newsletters
- Greeting Cards
- Bound Writings
- Online Publications

Posting
- Classroom Bulletin Boards
- School or Public Libraries
- School Display Cases
- Business Windows
- Clinic Waiting Rooms
- Literary/Art Fairs

Sending It Out
- Local Newspapers
- Area Historical Society
- Young Writers' Conferences
- Magazines and Contests
- Various Web Sites

Plan your publishing. Select three or four pieces of writing that you feel are your best work. Using the lists above, decide which specific type of publishing (performing onstage, business windows, and so on) would be the best for each of your selected works. Then make specific proposals for publishing each one.

Advanced Learners

If your class chooses to publish a class newspaper or a literary journal, have advanced students investigate some of the organizational details involved.

- jobs: editors, writers, designers, illustrators, photographers
- features: focus on audience
- layout: page design
- printing: who and how, cost
- frequency: discuss deadlines
- distribution: where and how
- adult mentor: teacher and possibly a professional in field

PROCESS

Preparing to Publish

Your writing is ready to publish when it is clear, complete, and correct. Getting your writing to this point requires careful revising and editing. Follow the tips below to help you prepare your writing for publication.

Publishing Tips

- **Ask for advice during the writing process.**
  Be sure that your writing answers any questions your readers may have about your topic.
- **Check the ideas, organization, voice, word choice, and sentence fluency in your writing.**
  Every part of your writing should be clear and complete.
- **Work with your writing.**
  Continue working until you feel good about your writing from beginning to end.
- **Check your writing for conventions.**
  In addition, ask at least one classmate to check your work for correctness. Another person may catch errors that you miss.
- **Prepare a neat finished copy.**
  Use a pen (blue or black ink) and write on one side of the paper if you are writing by hand. If you are writing with a computer, use a font that is easy to read. Double-space your writing.
- **Know your options.**
  Explore different ways to publish your writing. (See page 58.) Start small; then venture into more demanding—and creative—options.
- **Follow all publication guidelines.**
  Just as your teacher wants assignments presented in a certain way, so do the newspapers, magazines, or Web sites. Check for submission guidelines.

> Save all drafts for each writing project. If you are preparing a portfolio (see pages 65–69), you may be required to include early drafts as well as finished pieces.

Preparing to Publish

Publishing Tips

Review the publishing tips with students. Suggest that they flag this page and refer back to it whenever it is time to publish a piece of writing.

Designing Your Writing

Provide examples of past student writing or published magazine or newspaper writing that illustrate each of the guidelines.

✴ See PE pages 574–575 for more about adding graphics to writing.

If possible, also provide examples of what not to do, such as

- using fancy, hard-to-read type fonts,
- using too many sizes of type fonts,
- using too large type fonts,
- using colors that are hard to read,
- making margins too wide (which students sometimes do to avoid writing enough), or
- creating awkward page breaks.

Have several copies of current magazines on hand for students to use as they complete the activity.

60

Designing Your Writing

Whenever you write, always focus on *what you say* before worrying about *how it looks*. Only when you're satisfied with content and style should you concentrate on design. For handwritten papers, write the final copy neatly in blue or black ink on clean paper. When using a computer, follow the guidelines below.

Typography

- Use an easy-to-read font. Generally, a serif font is best for the body, and a sans serif style is used for contrast in headings.

    The letters of serif fonts have "tails"—as in this sentence.
    The letters of sans serif styles are plain—as in this sentence.

- Use a title and headings. Headings break writing into smaller parts, making the writing easier to follow.

Spacing and Margins

- Use one-inch margins on all sides of your paper.
- Indent the first line of every paragraph.
- Use one space after every period and comma.
- Avoid awkward breaks between pages. Don't leave a heading or the first line of a paragraph at the bottom of a page or a column. Never split a hyphenated word between pages or columns.

Graphic Devices

- If appropriate, use bulleted lists in your writing. Often, a series of items works best as a bulleted list (like the ones on this page).
- Consider including graphics. A table, a chart, or an illustration can help make a point clearer. But keep each graphic small enough so that it doesn't dominate the page. A larger graphic can be displayed by itself on a separate page.

 Analyze effective design. Working with a partner, compare the design features of articles from two different magazines. How are the design features of the two articles the same? How are they different? Decide which one is the most effective based on its audience and purpose.

POST Publishing Your Writing **61**

Computer Design in Action

The following two pages show a well-designed student report. The side notes explain the design features.

The title is 18-point type.

The main text is 12-point type and double-spaced throughout.

Headings are 14-point type.

A graphic is inserted for visual interest.

Numbered lists identify main points.

John Swift

Running Toward Health

Joggers, runners, and walkers are everywhere. People who are thinking about taking up running should consider its benefits and what it takes to get started.

Looking at Benefits

Studies have shown that exercise produces definite health benefits. In addition to the proven advantages, people often report other reasons that they like physical activity. Here are three of the most important incentives for staying in shape.

1. **Strength.** Doctors recommend walking, jogging, and running because regular physical activity strengthens muscles and increases stamina.

2. **Weight Control**. Regular exercise helps change the way the body uses calories, which helps control weight.

3. **Long-Term Benefits**. Joggers say they feel better after exercising. Medical studies show that regular exercise early in life helps keep a person fit throughout life.

Computer Design in Action

Have students read the essay from beginning to end (PE pages 61–62) for content. Tell them, for now, not to pay attention to the side notes. When they have finished reading, ask the following questions:

- What is the essay about? (running is good for your health)
- How could you tell what the essay was about even before you read it? (the title, the subheads, the sketch of the runner)
- Was the essay easy to read? Explain why you think so. (Most students will probably say yes because the text is divided into short, visually clear sections, and the headings and bullets make it easy to follow.)

Have students read through the essay again. This time, have them read and pay attention to design. Then have volunteers read aloud each side note and look for that design feature in the essay.

Provide time for students to look through past writing assignments to find a piece for the activity at the bottom of the page. Suggest that they select writing that lends itself to a creative and interesting design. An ideal piece would have one or more of the following elements:

- text that can be separated into small sections with headings and subheadings
- a series of ideas or points that could be bulleted or numbered
- facts and statistics that could go into a chart or diagram

Display students' designs in the classroom.

The writer's name and page number appear on every page starting with page 2.

A bulleted list helps organize the essay.

Margins are at least one inch all around.

Swift 2

Getting Started

Getting started is simple. Compared to many forms of exercise, jogging is easy and inexpensive because a fancy gym or costly equipment is not needed. The following suggestions can help someone start off "on the right foot."

- **Finding the right clothes.** Wear good quality, comfortable running shoes; they are really the only special equipment required. Light, roomy jogging clothes are best. More thin layers can be added in cold weather.
- **Setting aside time.** Block out 30 to 60 minutes for exercise every day. Make jogging a regular part of your schedule.
- **Running regularly.** Gradually increase time and distance. Don't try to run 10 miles the first day.

After a few weeks of regular jogging, the initial aches and pains will disappear. Then more options open up such as jogging for longer periods of time and for longer distances. There are also long-distance races, which can be very rewarding. Joggers who keep running are becoming healthier and stronger all the time.

Design a page. Create an effective design for an essay or a report you've already written. Share your design with a classmate to get some feedback: Does your design make the writing appealing to the reader? Is it clear and easy to follow? Does your design distract the reader in any way?

Struggling Learners

Some students may be unable to find a suitable piece of writing. If possible, have a few appropriate papers on hand for students to use. Or you may want to scan some magazine articles into the computer, delete the art and formatting, and present those.

Making Your Own Web Site

You can make your own Web site if your family has an Internet account. Be sure you get the permission of your parents or guardians. Then ask your provider how to get started. If you are using a school account, ask your teacher for help. Use the questions and answers below as a starting point.

How do I plan my site?

Think about the purpose of your Web site and how many pages you need. Do you want a single page, or would several linked pages work better? Check out other sites for ideas. Then make sketches to plan your pages.

How do I make the pages?

Start each page as a text file by using your computer. Many new word processing programs let you save a file as a Web page. If yours doesn't, you will have to add HTML (Hypertext Markup Language) codes to format the text and make links to graphics and other pages. You can find instructions for HTML on the Net or at the library.

How do I know whether my pages work?

You should always test your pages. Using your browser, open your first page. Then follow any links to make sure they work correctly. Also make sure that all the graphics appear and that the pages look perfect.

How do I get my pages on the Net?

You must upload your finished pages to the Internet. Ask your Internet provider how to do this. After the upload, visit your site to make sure it still works. Also, check it from other computers if possible.

How do I let people know about my site?

Once your site is up, e-mail your friends and tell them to visit it!

Try It Plan your own Web site. You might consider a site about your family or one of your special interests. Answer the following questions to help you get organized: What will be the title of the site? What would be a good picture or illustration for the opening page? Where will the links on the opening page lead your visitors?

PROCESS

Making Your Own Web Site

Some students will be accomplished at Web design and familiar with HTML codes. Encourage these computer experts to share their knowledge with the entire class and to offer advice and guidance to those students who are novices at Web design.

Consider doing the **Try It** activity as a whole-class project. After students complete their plan, invite the school's computer technology person in to explain how students can get the site on the Internet.

 **Answers**

Web site plans will vary.

Publishing Online

Provide students with a list of Web site addresses for online magazines that accept student writing. Remind students that every Web site will have its own guidelines for submission that they should follow carefully.

Look for online writing contests. Print out the information and post it in the classroom, along with the Web site addresses. Help students choose their best work to submit to these contest sites.

Allow time for students to visit the Write Source Web site (**www. thewritesource.com**) on the classroom computer or in the computer lab.

64

Publishing Online

The Internet offers many publishing opportunities, including online magazines and writing contests. The information below will help you submit your writing for publication on the Net. (At home, always get a parent's approval first. In school, follow all guidelines for computer use.)

How should I get started?

Check with your teacher to see if your school has its own Web site where you can post your work. Also ask your teacher about other Web sites. There are a number of online magazines that accept student writing. Visit some of these magazines to learn about the types of writing they usually publish.

How do I search for possible sites?

Use a search engine to find places to publish. Some search engines offer their own student links.

How do I submit my work?

Before you do anything, make sure that you understand the publishing guidelines for each site. Be sure to share this information with your teacher and your parents. Then follow these steps:

- **Send your writing in the correct form.**
  Some sites have online forms. Others will ask you to send your writing by mail or e-mail. Always explain why you are sending your writing.
- **Give the publisher information for contacting you.**
  However, don't give your home address or any other personal information unless your parents approve.
- **Be patient.**
  A site may contact you within a week to confirm that your work has arrived. Be patient, though; it may be several weeks before you hear whether your writing will be used or not.

Does the Write Source have a Web site?

Yes. You can visit our Web site at **www.thewritesource.com**. The "Publish It" link also lists other Web sites that accept student submissions.

Visit the Write Source Web site. Use the "Publish It" link. Find out what forms of writing the Write Source is accepting. (Check for your grade level.) Also visit at least two of the other publishing sites listed by the Write Source.

English Language Learners

Be sure that students who are not yet ready to produce lengthy works are not left out of the publishing stage.

- Help students identify places to publish shorter pieces, such as poems or cartoons.
- Provide opportunities for groups to contribute to other publishing products. For example, students who are not yet ready to produce lengthy written works may be able to illustrate works written by others.

Being involved in the process may motivate students to work hard to reach a level where they can submit their own writing.

collect
reflect grow *choose* 65

Creating a Portfolio

A person who has spent the day fishing may get his or her picture taken while holding up a stringer of fish. Of course, that stringer won't hold the small fish, only the big, beautiful ones—the "keepers."

Writers do the same thing with their writing. Instead of hanging their "keepers" on a string, though, they put them in a portfolio. A portfolio allows a writer to show off his or her best work.

This chapter will help you to assemble a writing portfolio. The following pages include information about the types and parts of portfolios, plus planning ideas.

What's Ahead

- **Types of Portfolios**
- **Parts of a Portfolio**
- **Planning Ideas**
- **Sample Portfolio Reflections**

Creating a Portfolio

Objectives
- understand four types of portfolios: showcase, growth, personal, electronic
- select pieces of writing for a portfolio
- set goals to improve future writing

Even if students have already created a portfolio, they will benefit from the instruction and ideas in this section.

Types of Portfolios

Ask students to read the instruction and information about the different types of portfolios silently. Then discuss the advantages to the writer for each type of portfolio.

- A showcase portfolio encourages writers to do their best work.
- A growth portfolio allows writers to see the progress that comes from practice and experience.
- A personal portfolio gives writers a chance to compile the writing that they want to preserve and share with others.
- An electronic portfolio gives writers a wider audience.

Suggest that students look at any reflection sheets they may have completed for previous writing assignments before they do the activity at the bottom of the page.

Types of Portfolios

There are four basic types of portfolios you should know about: a showcase portfolio, a growth portfolio, a personal portfolio, and an electronic portfolio.

Showcase Portfolio

A showcase portfolio presents the best writing you have done in school. A showcase is the most common type of portfolio and is usually put together for evaluation at the end of a grading period.

Growth Portfolio

A growth portfolio shows your progress as a writer. It contains writing assignments that show how your writing skills are developing:

- writing beginnings and endings,
- writing with voice,
- using specific details, and
- using transitions.

Personal Portfolio

A personal portfolio contains writing you want to keep and share with others. Many professional people—including writers, artists, and musicians—keep personal portfolios. You can arrange this type of portfolio according to different types of writing, different themes, and so on.

Electronic Portfolio

An electronic portfolio is any type of portfolio (showcase, growth, or personal) available on a CD or a Web site. Besides your writing, you can include graphics, video, and sound with this type of portfolio. This makes your writing available to friends and family members no matter where they are!

Showcase your strengths. Review your writing from the most recent grading period and then select the pieces that you consider your best efforts. Write a paragraph that summarizes the strengths of your work. Also mention one skill that you still need to develop.

PROCESS

Parts of a Portfolio

A showcase portfolio is one of the most common types of portfolios used in schools. It may contain the parts listed below, but always check with your teacher to be sure.

- A **table of contents** lists the writing samples you have included in your portfolio.
- A **brief essay** or **letter** introduces your portfolio—telling how you put it together, how you feel about it, and what it means to you.
- A **collection of writing samples** presents your best work. Your teacher may require that you include all of your planning, drafting, and revising for one or more of your writings.
- A **cover sheet for each sample** explains why you selected it.
- **Evaluations, reflections,** or **checklists** identify the basic skills you have mastered, as well as those skills that you still need to work on.

Gathering Tips

- **Keep track of all your work.** Include your prewriting notes, first drafts, and revisions for each writing assignment. Then, when you put together a portfolio, you will have everything that you need.
- **Store all of your writing in a pocket folder or computer file.** This will help you keep track of your writing as you build your portfolio.
- **Set a schedule for working on your portfolio.** You can't put together a good portfolio by waiting until the last minute.
- **Take pride in your work.** Make sure that your portfolio shows you at your best.

Write your cover sheets. For each piece of writing that you include in your portfolio, write a cover sheet. Explain why the writing is a good example of your work. Tell what makes it stand out from other writing you have done. Finally, tell why you included it in your portfolio.

Parts of a Portfolio

If you have already established criteria for student portfolios, review that criteria now and make sure students understand exactly what is expected of them.

Gathering Tips

Throughout each school term, set aside specific times for students to work on their portfolio. This will not only prevent them from waiting until the last minute to work on their portfolio, but it will also allow them time to reflect in depth on the most recent writing experience.

Model how to write a sample cover sheet before asking students to write their cover sheets. (For example: I chose to include this essay in my portfolio because it shows the most improvement from draft to final copy. It was with this essay that I really began to understand how free I was to revise my work.)

Planning Ideas

When it comes time for students to set up their portfolio, they should have ample work space. Consider having students work at long tables in the library or cafeteria where they will have room to spread out and organize their materials.

Suggest that students use different colored sticky notes to label each piece of writing as they review it. For example, they could use a red sticky note for an excellent piece of writing that is sure to go into the portfolio. They could use a blue sticky note for a piece of writing that is a maybe. They could use a yellow sticky note for a piece that is a definite "no."

Make sure students understand that they should set their own goals for future writing, and that they shouldn't just copy three of the goals listed here, unless the goals in the list truly match their own goals. It may help to conduct a brainstorming session in which you ask students to suggest other goals to consider.

Planning Ideas

The following tips will help you choose your best pieces of writing to include in your portfolio.

1 Be patient.

Don't make quick decisions about which pieces of writing to include in your portfolio. Just keep gathering everything—including all of your drafts—until you are ready to review all of your writing assignments.

2 Make good decisions.

When it's time to choose writing for your portfolio, review each piece. Remember the feelings that you had during each assignment. Which piece makes you feel the best? Which one did your readers like the best? Which one taught you the most?

3 Reflect on your choices.

Read the sample reflections on page 69. Then answer these questions about your writing:

- Why did I choose this piece?
- Why did I write this piece? (What was my purpose?)
- How did I write it? (What was my process?)
- What does it show about my writing ability?
- How did my peers react to this writing?
- What would I do differently next time?
- What have I learned since writing it?

4 Set future writing goals.

After putting your portfolio together, set some goals for the future. Here are some goals that other students have set:

I will write about topics that really interest me.
I will spend more time on my beginnings and endings.
I will make sure that my sentences read smoothly.
I will support my main points with convincing details.

Set your goals. After you finish putting together a portfolio, set some goals for your future writing. Review the student goals listed above and then identify three goals that would improve your writing.

Struggling Learners

If time allows, encourage students to revise their favorite pieces of writing once again. Remind them to refer to the appropriate goals and rubric while working. Recommend a peer conference for a final review of their revisions. A new reflection would complete the piece.

PROCESS

Sample Portfolio Reflections

When you take time to reflect on your writing assignments, think about the process that you used to develop each one. Also think about what you might do differently next time. The following samples will help you with your own reflections.

Student Reflections

Of all the writing in my portfolio, I am proudest of my persuasive essay about volunteering at the Humane Society. It was a challenge. To write persuasively, I had to understand my topic, my feelings about it, and my reader's feelings. Every word mattered. I worked hard on that essay, but in the end, it helped convince two of my friends to volunteer.

—Melissa Breen

My expository essay turned out really well because I was interested in my topic. It was easy to break the subject down into its parts because I understood it. I seem to have trouble whenever I have to summarize information from other sources, because it's hard to organize the information in a way that is different from the original. The strongest part of my expository essay is the way I used comparisons with everyday things to help explain difficult ideas.

—Thad Molumba

Professional Reflections

As you continue writing and rewriting, you begin to see possibilities you hadn't seen before.

—Robert Hayden

The only way, I think, to learn to write short stories is to write them, and then try to discover what you have done.

—Flannery O'Connor

Advanced Learners

Challenge students to compose a poem that reflects their feelings about writing.

- Use a group brainstorming session as a catalyst to spur their imagination and stretch their modes of expression.

- Encourage them to use figurative language to capture the moods they experience when writing.
- Have students visualize their ideas, perhaps through analogies, so that the images can influence their poetry.

Sample Portfolio Reflections

Read aloud the instruction to the class.

Student Reflections

Have volunteers read aloud each reflection. Then ask how these reflections might help the student writers with future writing assignments. Students may suggest the following ideas:

- Melissa realized that good persuasive writing can influence readers to do something. The next time she has to write persuasively, she will be sure to choose a topic that she understands well and really cares about.
- Thad identified his strengths (understanding the topic, making comparisons) as well as a weakness (summarizing from sources). The next time he is assigned an expository essay, he can ask his teacher for extra help with summarizing. The more he practices, the better he will become.

Professional Reflections

Have students explain in their own words what these reflections mean to them as writers.

Descriptive Writing Overview

Unit Objectives

The writing standards listed below are based on a blending of state and NCTE standards.

- Use lists and charts to explore possible topics.
- Draft compositions that have a central idea, a clear thesis, and a thoughtful conclusion.
- Select and use voice and style appropriate to audience and purpose.
- Support ideas with specific, rich vocabulary; sensory and memory details; and anecdotes, descriptions, and specific examples.
- Revise and edit drafts for support of ideas and better word choice, and to ensure standard usage, grammar, and mechanics.

Writing Forms

- descriptive paragraph
- descriptive essay about a person

Focus on the Traits

- **Ideas** Creating a detailed picture of a person
- **Organization** Describing physical appearance and personality traits, providing an anecdote, and explaining how a person influenced the writer
- **Voice** Using a natural and engaging voice that expresses feelings and enthusiasm
- **Word Choice** Using specific verbs and adjectives
- **Sentence Fluency** Writing a variety of sentence types to improve sentence flow
- **Conventions** Checking for errors in punctuation, capitalization, spelling, and grammar

Suggested Descriptive Writing Unit (Three Weeks)

Day	Writing and Skills Units	In the *Write Source* book			On the CD-ROM	*SkillsBook*
		Pages	Proofreader's Guide—basic grammar rules	Basic Grammar practice	Interactive Grammar Exercises	grammar practice pages
1–4	**Descriptive Paragraph:**	71–74				
	Skills Activities: Adjectives		732–733	486, 488 (+)	Adjectives and Adverbs	165–166
	Hyphens (compound adjectives)		610–611		Hyphens	35
5	**Describing a Person:** (Model)	75–77				
6	(Prewriting)	78–79				
7–8	(Writing)	80–82				
9–10	(Revising)	82				
	Skills Activities: Specific Adjectives		732 (+), 734–735	488 (+), 489		167–168
	Specific Verbs		718–719	480		163–164
	Sentence Variety (combining with a series of words and phrases)		582–583 (commas in a series)	512		5–6, 103–104
11–13	(Editing)	82				
	Skills Activities: Spelling and Plurals		630–631, 632–633		Plurals	51
	Verb Tenses (and tense shifts)		720–721, 724–725	482–483		153–154, 155–156
	Commas (equal adjectives)		586 (+), 587 (equal adjectives)		Commas (to separate equal adjectives)	13
14–15	**Practical Writing** Proposal	90–91				
	Skills Activities: Pronouns		712–713	474	Pronouns—2	149–150

Note: For specifics about reading the chart above, see page TE 33.

Teacher's Notes for Descriptive Writing

This overview for descriptive writing includes some specific teaching suggestions for this unit.

Writing a Descriptive Paragraph (pages 71–74)

In this chapter students will write a descriptive paragraph about a particular person. The goal is to craft a visual image of the subject. Hair color, face shape, and clothing style are only three examples of the many ways a writer can describe another person. Encourage students to present a positive picture of their subject.

Describing a Person (pages 75–82)

A descriptive essay gives students more room to talk about someone special. A paragraph is limited to a quick image, but an essay allows the writer to go deeper, beyond the obvious facial features or height. Such an essay should let the reader know what kind of person is being described (for example: hopeful, talented, thoughtful, funny, and so on).

Writing Across the Curriculum (pages 83–91)

Descriptive writing is an important part of most classes. To illustrate the application of this writing form, models from the following disciplines are shown: social studies—an eyewitness report of the first phone call; math—the description of an object using geometric terms; science—a field-trip report; and practical writing—a project proposal.

Minilesson

What He/or She Is Like   Descriptive Paragraph

- **CHOOSE** one classmate and carefully **THINK** about how you would describe that person. Then **WRITE** an upbeat descriptive paragraph. **SHARE** what you have written. Can the class figure out whom you described?

SPECIFY *picture*

Descriptive Writing

express describe **portray**

Helpful, Friendly, Courteous . . .   Describing a Person

- On a sheet of paper **LIST** all the qualities of one of your friends. **PICK** out the qualities that best describe your friend. **USE** a thesaurus to replace words that are ordinary and unexciting.

A Horse, of Course   Writing Across the Curriculum

- **IMAGINE** that you have been asked to write a descriptive essay about the quarter horse. **LIST** things you would need to include in your essay. In a small group, **DISCUSS** your lists. Did you forget anything?

Descriptive Writing
Descriptive Paragraph

By skillfully brushing paint onto a canvas, an artist can create a vision of a distant landscape or an image of an amazing person. When you write descriptively, you can do the same thing. By carefully arranging words on a piece of paper, you can create a vision of a faraway place or a wonderful likeness of a person.

In this unit, you will write a paragraph that paints a picture of a person. Your goal is to write a description that makes the person come alive for the reader.

Writing Guidelines

Subject:	**A favorite person**
Form:	**Descriptive paragraph**
Purpose:	**To describe what a person looks like**
Audience:	**Classmates**

Descriptive Paragraph

Objectives

- understand the content and structure of a descriptive paragraph
- choose a topic (a person) to write about
- plan, draft, revise, and edit a descriptive paragraph

A **descriptive paragraph** offers a specific picture of a person, a place, a thing, or an event. The writer creates a vivid picture by using specific nouns and verbs and strong adjectives.

✳ For more information about developing descriptive paragraphs, see PE page 527.

Use the following activity to introduce the idea of painting a description with words. Even if students feel limited by their artistic abilities, this activity will help them visualize details about their friend.

- Have students draw a picture of a friend.
- Ask them to label the picture with words that describe the friend.
- Invite students to share their drawings and describe their friend.

Descriptive Paragraph

Point out that the details in the paragraph describe Rosa's physical appearance rather than her personality.

Respond to the reading.

Answers

Ideas 1. Rosa's height, more than six feet tall

Organization 2. top to bottom; starts at her hair and cap, then her face and teeth, then her jumpsuit, and finally her shoes

Voice & Word Choice 3. Possible answers:
- curly
- red
- paint-speckled
- perfect
- white
- tan
- bulky
- once-white
- paint-chip
- rainbow-colored

72

Descriptive Paragraph

A descriptive paragraph offers a detailed picture of a person, a place, a thing, or an event. It begins with a **topic sentence** that tells what the paragraph is about. The sentences in the **body** include descriptive details about the topic, and the **closing sentence** wraps up the paragraph. In the paragraph below, the writer used specific details to describe a painter.

A "Painting" of Rosa

Topic Sentence

Standing more than six feet tall, Rosa is someone I look up to. Other than her height, the first thing I notice about her is her curly, red hair. It's like sparks of fire peeking out from underneath the paint-speckled cap that she wears backward on her head. When Rosa smiles, her perfect row of white

Body

teeth flashes against her tan face. Whenever I see her heading off to work, she is constantly moving. Zipping back and forth with boxes of rollers, lots of paint buckets, bulky old drop cloths, and new rolls of tape, she loads all her gear into her van. Rosa and her once-white jumpsuit look like the paint-chip aisle at the hardware store—splattered with color from the top of her head to the toes of her now rainbow-colored

Closing Sentence

canvas shoes. If I spot her at the end of the day, I always see a fresh set of freckles from that day's job.

Respond to the reading. On your own paper, answer each of the following questions.

☐ **Ideas (1)** In the first sentence, what detail gets the reader's attention?

☐ **Organization (2)** What order of location did the writer generally follow *(top to bottom, left to right)*? Explain.

☐ **Voice & Word Choice (3)** What adjectives are used to create a clear picture of the person? List three of them.

English Language Learners

To reinforce the idea that writing a description is like painting a picture, have students sketch Rosa after reading the description. Then ask students to reread the description and list the phrases that describe elements they have put in their sketches. Have them list any details they missed and then add those details to the sketch.

express SPECIFY portray
picture describe
Descriptive Paragraph 73

DESCRIPTIVE

Prewriting Selecting a Topic

First, you must choose a person to write about. Listing is a good way to get started. The writer of the paragraph on page 72 made lists of people whose physical appearances were interesting to him.

People I Know	People I See Often
* Dr. Willard, the eye doctor	* The old man who feeds the ducks
* My great-grandpa Salvatore	* The little kid who hangs out near my grandma's
* Ron, the junk guy	
* My oldest sister, the chef	* Rosa the painter

Select a topic. Make lists of interesting people you know or often see during your daily activities. Then circle one to describe in a paragraph.

Gathering Details

Your descriptive paragraph should show instead of tell. Before you write your paragraph, jot down concrete details that show what your person looks like from head to toe.

Collect your details. To get started, answer the following questions about your person.

1. Is there any feature that is immediately noticeable (height, color of hair, smile, freckles, posture, and so on)?
2. How can I describe the person's hair, face, and posture?
3. What type of clothes does this person wear?
4. Do the clothes have anything to do with a particular job?
5. Does the person move in a special way or wear unusual shoes?
6. What one word comes to mind when I see this person?

Prewriting Selecting a Topic

* For information on creating lists as a topic-selecting strategy, see PE page 545.

Prewriting Gathering Details

Help students see how to use vivid details to show rather than tell. Have students complete one-line descriptions from the following telling sentences. Students cannot use the underlined telling word in their showing sentence.

- My mother was angry. (Example: My mother wrinkled her brow, frowned, and yelled.)
- The teacher is tough. (Example: The teacher assigns 75 math problems daily and gives surprise tests.)
- The bus was crowded. (Example: The students had to sit three to a seat with their coats and their backpacks on their laps.)

Writing
Creating Your First Draft

Tell students to choose the most noticeable feature from the list of details they created on PE page 73. Brainstorm how to use the feature in a topic sentence.

Reread the topic sentence in "A 'Painting' of Rosa" on PE page 72. Point out that it starts with a participial phrase, which is one way to compose an effective sentence. Students may refer to PE pages 43, 514, and 520 for other examples of sentences that begin with a participial phrase.

Ask students to use this structure in one possible topic sentence.

Revising
Improving Your Writing

After students have used this checklist to review their writing, have partners exchange their drafts and offer revision suggestions. Peer input can give student writers a fresh view of their work.

Editing
Checking for Conventions

Students exchange their revised writing with a partner and check each other's work for errors in conventions. Meet for informal writing conferences to help students with their work.

Writing Creating Your First Draft

The goal of a first draft is to get all of your ideas and details down on paper. Follow the guidelines below.

- Start with a topic sentence that catches your reader's attention. Include a noticeable feature of the person you're describing.
- Use order of location (head to toe) to organize the details in the body of your paragraph. Include the details that you gathered on page 73.
- End with a sentence that keeps the reader thinking about the person.

 Write your first draft. Get all your ideas and details down on paper, thoroughly describing your topic from head to toe. When you are finished, give your paragraph a title.

Revising Improving Your Writing

Now that you have finished your first draft, you need to review it and make revisions. Add, delete, or move parts to make your paragraph clear and interesting to your reader.

 Revise your paragraph. Use the following questions as a guide.

1. Does my topic sentence introduce the person and mention a noticeable feature?
2. Have I included details that create a clear picture of the person?
3. Have I organized the details from head to toe?
4. Do I sound interested in the description?
5. Do I use specific nouns, verbs, and adjectives?
6. Do I use complete sentences that read smoothly?

Editing Checking for Conventions

Carefully edit your revised paragraph for capitalization, spelling, grammar, and punctuation. Then write a neat final copy.

 Edit and proofread your work. Use the checklist on page 128 to check your writing for errors. Then write a neat final copy of your paragraph.

Grammar Connection

Adjectives
- **Proofreader's Guide** pages 732–733
- **Write Source** pages 486, 488 (+)
- **SkillsBook** pages 165–166
- **CD** Adjectives and Adverbs

Hyphens
- **Proofreader's Guide** pages 610–611
- **SkillsBook** page 35
- **CD** Hyphens

Struggling Learners

Some students may need to review the definitions of a participle and a participial phrase.

- A participle is a verb form ending in -ing or -ed. It is used as an adjective and often begins a participial phrase. (Examples: tired child, crashing waves)

- A participial phrase consists of a participle plus any modifiers. It serves as an adjective in a sentence. (Example: Hearing about the accident, he worried about his friends.)

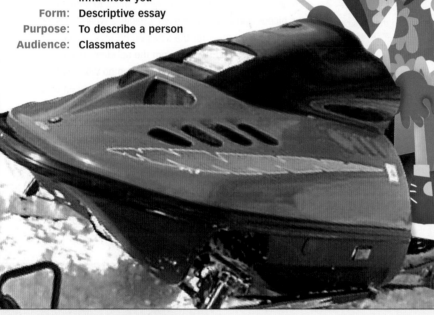

express **SPECIFY** portray
picture describe portray
75

Descriptive Writing
Describing a Person

Every person is unique. Think of people you know and admire. What do they look like? What are their personality traits? What makes them interesting or special? Answering these questions will give you a variety of details to include in a descriptive essay about a person.

In this unit, you will read an essay describing a person who loved to snowmobile. Then you will write an essay that describes a person who has influenced you in a positive way.

Writing Guidelines

Subject: A person who has positively influenced you
Form: Descriptive essay
Purpose: To describe a person
Audience: Classmates

Describing a Person

Objectives
- understand the purpose, content, and form of a descriptive essay
- plan, draft, revise, and edit a descriptive essay

A **descriptive essay** develops a clear and detailed picture of a person, a place, a thing, or an event. In a descriptive essay about a person, the writer
- describes the person,
- creates a strong sense of that person's personality,
- and explains how the person has affected the writer.

Remind students to consider people who have had a positive influence on them or have inspired them.

Copy Masters/ Transparencies

T-chart (TE p. 78)

Descriptive Essay

This sample essay serves as a model for students. The body paragraphs (physical features, personality, and an anecdote) help students understand how to develop an effective description.

Ask students to think about how **words create pictures** (*see below*) in the mind of the reader.

- Ask students to read the first middle paragraph and then draw a picture of Charlie based on the description.
- Display the drawings and have students compare them.
- Then have students do the Teaching Tip activity.

76

Descriptive Essay

In this sample essay, the writer describes his cousin Charlie. As you read the description, look at the notes in the left margin. They explain the important parts of the essay.

Beginning

The beginning introduces the person.

Middle

The first middle paragraph describes the physical appearance (from head to toe).

The next middle paragraph describes the personality.

The Price of Danger

My older cousin Charlie was always up for an adventure, especially if it was dangerous. Charlie took lots of risks. Then, one day, he had a snowmobile accident that changed his life. The doctors said that he might never walk again. Charlie said they were wrong.

Charlie is a big guy who is more than six feet tall and weighs 260 pounds. His size, along with his long, black hair, makes him look strong, like a fullback or a wrestler. Because he works out with weights, his arm muscles are like iron. He likes to wear tight T-shirts to show off his biceps and abs. These days, Charlie is wearing baggy sweatpants to cover up the scars on his legs, which are banged up and twisted from the accident. His feet sometimes drag along the ground when he walks with his forearm crutches. The doctors aren't sure when or if Charlie will ever fully recover.

For me, the best thing about Charlie is that he's not a quitter. If someone tells him he can't do something, he will prove that he can. In the beginning, when Charlie was in rehab, he got tough with himself. At every session, he pushed himself hard to walk again. When the physical therapist told Charlie to take a break, my cousin would say, "No way, man! I want to do this now." Charlie kept

---

**Teaching Tip:
Words Create Pictures**

Students describe with visual details in this activity.

- Draw a simple picture.
- Write a specific description of it on the back of the drawing.
- Each student reads his or her description, hiding the picture.
- Listeners draw the picture.
- Compare the drawings; students suggest how to make the description clearer.

English Language Learners

Explain the following words and phrases from the essay:

- up for an adventure (ready for an exciting activity)
- fullback (a tough, physical runner and blocker on a football team)
- like iron (strong, very hard)
- biceps and abs (muscles)
- banged up and twisted (seriously injured)

- rehab (short for rehabilitation, a time when a person works on getting back to good health, usually by doing special physical exercises)
- got tough with himself, pushed himself (forced himself to work harder)
- pickup football (an informal game of football)

express SPECIFY portray
picture describe
Descriptive Essay

77

DESCRIPTIVE

Middle
The third middle paragraph shares an anecdote.

pushing himself. Before long he was getting around pretty well without any help. However, I know Charlie. He's not going to be satisfied until he can walk without his crutches.

Before the accident, Charlie liked riding his snowmobile and his motorcycle and jogging with his black Lab, Tex. These days he's finding other ways to keep active. When the whole family got together at Thanksgiving, Charlie couldn't play on our pickup football team. That didn't stop him. He did a super job of coaching us from the sidelines.

Ending
The ending tells how the person influenced the writer.

My cousin Charlie has taught me two important lessons. First, I realize I should check out all the safety rules before I try something risky. Second, the best way to get through bad times is to have the right attitude. Charlie's attitude is just as strong as he is. I believe that someday Charlie will walk the way he did before, just like he says he will.

Respond to the reading. Answer the following questions about the essay.

☐ **Ideas** **(1)** What special challenge does the subject of the essay face? **(2)** What physical features does the writer describe to create a picture for the reader? **(3)** What details give the reader an insight into the subject's personality?

☐ **Organization** **(4)** How does the writer organize the middle paragraphs?

☐ **Voice & Word Choice** **(5)** What words or phrases show that Charlie has had a positive influence on the writer? List two.

Respond to the reading.

Answers

Ideas **1.** Charlie is trying to walk again after a snowmobile accident injured his legs.

2. Possible answers:
- more than six feet tall
- 260 pounds
- long, black hair
- muscular arms
- scarred legs

3. Possible answers:
- took lots of risks
- works out
- wears tight T-shirts to show off muscles
- pushed himself hard
- not satisfied until he can walk without crutches
- keeps active
- determined to walk again

Organization **4.** first middle paragraph—physical appearance; second middle paragraph—personality; third middle paragraph—anecdote

Voice & Word Choice **5.** Possible answers:
- not a quitter
- tough with himself
- kept pushing himself
- finding ways to keep active
- didn't stop him
- super job of coaching us
- attitude as strong as he is

Struggling Learners

Have students find the word *anecdote* in a dictionary and a thesaurus and discuss the various meanings and synonyms they find.

- Point out that anecdotes show, rather than tell, what a person is like and are valuable to writers and readers alike.

- An anecdote must be presented within a context so that the story can illustrate something meaningful.
- Have students discuss what the anecdote (the story about Thanksgiving) shows the reader about Charlie, and how the essay sets up the context for the anecdote.

Prewriting Selecting a Topic

Emphasize that students must choose a person who has influenced them in a positive way. They should not choose someone simply because she or he is easy to describe. The essay requires deeper thinking than a descriptive paragraph, so it is important that they select someone meaningful to them.

Brainstorm with students a list of people who might have made a lasting impression on them. Consider

- relatives,
- teachers, and
- friends.

Prewriting Gathering Details

Remind students that they need to describe the subject's **physical details and personality traits** (*see below*) and include an anecdote that illustrates the latter.

✱ For pointers about how to collect details when writing about a person, see PE page 532.

Prewriting Selecting a Topic

Your essay should describe the person's appearance and personality. It should also tell how the person inspired you in a positive way. A chart, like the one below, can help you choose a person to write about and identify the ways in which he or she has influenced you.

Topic Chart

Person	Positive Influence
Dr. Julie, the veterinarian	– caring person – honest person – generous with her time
Mr. Hayes, the chorus director	– patient teacher – explores different types of music – teaches foreign language songs
Adamay, my neighbor	– loves adventure

 Create a topic chart. In the first column, list at least three people who interest you. In the second column, tell how each person has influenced you in a positive way. Choose one of the people as the subject of your essay.

Gathering Details

Next, analyze your subject as you gather details. Think carefully about the person's appearance, personality, special skills, talents, and interests.

 Collect details. Answer the following questions to help you find information to include in your essay.

1. What does the person look like? (Describe him or her from head to toe.)
2. What personality traits does the person have? (Think about feelings and emotions. Is this person quiet? Funny? Outgoing? Kind?)
3. Which of the personality traits is most clear to you? (Think of an experience or event during which this personality trait was evident.)
4. How has this person positively influenced you?

Teaching Tip: Physical Details and Personality Traits

Your students may need help to identify physical details and personality traits. If so, have students work with partners to complete the following activity:

- Create a T-chart (TE page 789). Label one column *Physical Appearance* and the other *Personality Traits*.
- In pairs, choose a famous person who is familiar to the class and write that person's name on the back of the paper.
- Fill in the two columns with words that describe the person physically and that identify personality traits.
- Read aloud the list of physical details and personality traits. The rest of the class tries to identify the famous person.

English Language Learners

Encourage students to list as many details as they can, but point out that they will not use all of those details in their essay. The goal of this activity is to generate as many details as possible.

express SPECIFY portray
picture describe
79
Describing a Person

DESCRIPTIVE

Organizing Your Details

Your essay should describe the person's physical appearance (from head to toe) and personality. You should also include a short story (anecdote) to illustrate your subject's key personality trait. A list can help you organize your details.

Organizing List

Subject	Dr. Julie, the veterinarian
Physical Appearance	short, big smile, white lab coat, blue jeans, red sneakers
Key Personality Trait	kind
Anecdote	caring for Snoops

Organize your details. Create a list like the one above. List details about the person's physical appearance and a key personality trait. Also include an anecdote to illustrate that trait.

Using Verbs and Adjectives

Interesting and specific words help create a strong voice and add personality to your writing. Keep the following tips about word choice in mind as you write:

- Use specific verbs to show action.
  attacked   wandered   examined

- Use adjectives to help readers "see" the scene.
  tiny woman   straight, blond hair   five feet tall

Make a list of specific verbs and adjectives to describe your person's actions and appearance. Use the best ones in your essay.

Prewriting
Organizing Your Details

Tell students that they should choose the details that best show how that person is special or unique.

Tell students to use **action verbs and specific adjectives** (*see below*) to create a vivid picture.

- Encourage students to replace common verbs, such as *laugh*, with specific verbs, such as *giggle, chuckle, snicker,* or *cackle*.
- Ask students to replace an unoriginal adjective, such as *big*, with more specific synonyms, such as *enormous, towering, giant,* and *huge*.

Using Verbs and Adjectives

✳ For examples of how to use action verbs and strong adjectives to write more effectively, see PE pages 480, 488–489.

 Answers

Answers will vary but should include action verbs and specific adjectives.

Teaching Tip: Action Verbs and Specific Adjectives

Give students practice in thinking of exciting and effective adjectives and verbs to use in their writing.

- Form three teams of students.
- Place a general adjective or verb on the board (sample adjectives: *nice, small, good, interesting, hard, happy*; sample verbs: *go, say, make, want*).

- Have the teams move to separate parts of the room. Working together quietly, students list specific adjectives or verbs that could replace the word on the board.
- After a limited period of time (one or two minutes), ask each team to share its list of words.

- Each unique word (one that no other team thought of) scores a point.
- As teams list words, write each new one on the board under the original word.
- Start another round with a new word.

Writing Starting Your Essay

Consider having students write two introductions, one that makes a personal connection and one that shares an interesting detail.

- Writers share both possible beginnings for feedback.
- Then they make their own choice about which one to use.

Writing

Using an Engaging Voice

Remind students to share their feelings about the person in their essay through their choice of words and details.

80

Writing Starting Your Essay

The beginning paragraph should catch your reader's interest and introduce your topic—a person who has positively influenced you. Here are two approaches.

Beginning Paragraph

- **Briefly explain how you know the person.** Is he or she a family member? Friend? Teacher? Include some interesting details to draw the reader into your essay.

> The writer makes a personal connection.
>
> *Dr. Julie is the veterinarian for our family's pets. She gives shots to our dogs and cats every year, and she took care of our parakeet, Squeeker, when he broke his wing last fall. The most important thing she ever did for us was to save our spaniel, Snoops, when he was attacked by a coyote that wandered into our yard.*

- **Begin with an important fact.** Share one important reason why you admire the person; tell something interesting that the person did, or something unusual that happened to him or her.

> The writer shares an interesting detail.
>
> *If it weren't for Dr. Julie, our veterinarian, Snoops would be dead. She saved our spaniel's life after he was attacked by a coyote that had wandered into our yard last fall.*

Using an Engaging Voice

Voice is the special way that a writer expresses ideas and emotions. It shows that the writer really cares about the subject and the audience. When you write, keep the following tips about voice in mind:

- Write as if you were telling a friend about this person.
- Show enthusiasm for your subject.
- Express your true feelings about the person.

 Write your beginning paragraph. Choose one of the approaches above to get started. If you don't like how your first attempt turns out, try another one.

Struggling Learners

If students are unable to make a personal connection and/or share an interesting detail in their beginning paragraphs, they should discuss their opening in a writing conference with you. To help them come up with an intriguing beginning, ask questions such as these:

- What is the most striking physical detail of this person?

- What is his/her most noticeable character trait?
- When was the first time you saw or met the person?
- What was your first conversation about?
- What is the first thing that comes to mind when you think of this person?

If students are still stumped, they should revisit their topic chart (PE page 78) and select a

different person. They will also need to create a new organizing list (PE page 79). Although this will involve some extra work, it will save them from laboring over a difficult subject later on. Reassure students that even professional writers go "back to the drawing board" sometimes.

express SPECIFY portray
picture describe
Describing a Person **81**

DESCRIPTIVE

Developing the Middle Part

The middle part of your essay will include three paragraphs. The first describes the person's appearance, and the second focuses on personality. The third should include an anecdote that demonstrates a key personality trait.

Middle Paragraphs

> **The first paragraph describes Dr. Julie with specific physical details.**
>
> Dr. Julie is a tiny woman, about five feet tall, who always greets everyone with a big smile. Her blond hair is pulled up into a twist. Seeing her in her white lab coat, blue jeans, and red tennis shoes, a person would never guess that she would be strong enough to handle large animals. But the day Snoops was attacked, she hoisted him up onto the examining table just as if she were lifting a cat.
>
> **The second paragraph describes Dr. Julie's personality.**
>
> Dr. Julie is hardworking and caring. Whenever she examines a pet, she talks quietly the whole time to calm the animal. She also carefully explains what she's doing as her strong hands gently feel for a trouble spot. Everyone is thankful that Dr. Julie takes emergency calls both day and night.
>
> **Finally, the writer shares an anecdote about Dr. Julie.**
>
> The day that Dr. Julie examined Snoops, she was honest with her diagnosis. "He has some very bad bites, and he's lost a lot of blood," she said. "However, I'm not going to give up on him." Dr. Julie stated that Snoops needed surgery to save his life. It was hard to leave him at the clinic, but Dr. Julie was very reassuring. That's another great thing about her. She cares about animals, and she also cares about people. When the surgery was over, I could hear the happiness in her voice, and I knew that Snoops was going to be fine.

 Write your middle paragraphs. Use the details you gathered (page 78) and your organizing list (page 79). Describe your person's appearance and personality. Include an anecdote to illustrate a key personality trait.

Writing
Developing the Middle Part

Point out the order of the content of the middle paragraphs:

- physical characteristics
- personality traits
- an anecdote

Ask students why the paragraphs are presented in this order. You might want to compare the arrangement with meeting a new friend. First you notice details about the person's appearance. Then, as you spend time with him or her, you learn about personality traits. Finally, you share activities and experiences with the person.

Read the model essay with students and point out the **dialogue** *(see below)* in the third-paragraph anecdote.

Teaching Tip: Dialogue

Review how to use dialogue effectively. Remind students that hearing a person's own words adds an extra dimension to the description. Ask the following questions:

- What do you learn about Dr. Julie from her words? (She is straightforward, determined, and hopeful.)

- In what way is the quotation effective here? (reader feels that he or she is there; emphasizes how serious the injuries are)

Have students look at the essay on PE page 76. Point out that Charlie's brief spoken words give readers a sense of his personality.

Writing Ending Your Essay

As with the beginning of the essay, encourage students to write more than one possible ending. They can choose the one they like best, or they can get feedback from another student to help them choose.

- Which ending most effectively leaves readers with a final image or something to think about?

Revising and Editing

Suggest that students work with a peer to help with revision.

- Have writers begin by writing a thoughtful answer to this prompt: *What do I want the reader to know about this person?*
- Students should then exchange essays with a peer.
- After students have read their partner's essay, have peer responders answer the following prompt aloud: *What did I learn about this person?*
- Ask writers to compare what they wanted the reader to know with what the reader actually learned. Suggest that they make revisions to correct any discrepancies.

Writing Ending Your Essay

The ending clearly signals that your description is complete. In your last sentence or two, leave the reader with a final idea or image—something that will keep him or her thinking about your topic.

Ending Paragraph

The writer makes a final personal connection.	*From watching Dr. Julie, I've learned that sincerely caring about people and animals is so important. Every time Snoops comes and lays his head in my lap, I think of Dr. Julie and smile.*

 Write your ending paragraph. Wrap things up by explaining how the person has had a positive influence on you.

Revising and Editing

A first draft can always be improved. By adding, deleting, or reorganizing some details, you can make your description better.

 Revise your first draft. Revise your first draft using the questions below as a guide. Then add a title.

- ☐ **Ideas** Have I included enough specific details about the person's appearance and personality? Did I include an anecdote?
- ☐ **Organization** Do I have a clear beginning, middle, and ending? Do I describe my subject from head to toe and share an anecdote according to time order?
- ☐ **Voice** Do I sound interested in the person and in my audience?
- ☐ **Word Choice** Do I use specific verbs and adjectives?
- ☐ **Sentence Fluency** Do my sentences flow smoothly? Do I vary sentence lengths and beginnings?

 Edit your description. Once you have completed your revising, use the checklist on page 128 to edit your essay for errors. Then write a clean final copy to share.

Grammar Connection

Specific Adjectives
- **Proofreader's Guide** pages 732 (+), 734–735
- *Write Source* pages 488 (+), 489
- *SkillsBook* pages 167–168

Specific Verbs
- **Proofreader's Guide** pages 718–719
- *Write Source* page 480
- *SkillsBook* pages 163–164

Sentence Variety
- **Proofreader's Guide** pages 582–583 (commas in a series)
- *Write Source* page 512
- *SkillsBook* pages 5–6, 103–104

Spelling and Plurals
- **Proofreader's Guide** pages 630–631, 632–633
- *SkillsBook* page 51
- **CD** Plurals

Verb Tenses
- **Proofreader's Guide** pages 720–721, 724–725
- *Write Source* pages 482–483
- *SkillsBook* pages 153–154, 155–156

Commas
- **Proofreader's Guide** pages 586 (+), 587 (equal adjectives)
- *SkillsBook* page 13
- **CD** Commas (to separate equal adjectives)

express SPECIFY portray
picture describe **83**

Descriptive Writing
Across the Curriculum

Since its creation in 1876, the telephone has been used to carry descriptions of people, places, and things across the land. A clear phone description lets the listener feel as if he or she is "right there" with the speaker. A clear written description can do the same thing for readers.

You will use descriptive writing in almost all of your classes. In social studies, you may be asked to write an eyewitness report about a famous historical person. In math, your teacher may require you to describe an object using geometric terms. In science class, you may need to describe a place you visited on a field trip. Your description will be successful if your readers can clearly imagine the topic in their minds.

What's Ahead

- **Social Studies:** Writing an Eyewitness Report
- **Math:** Describing an Object
- **Science:** Writing a Field-Trip Report
- **Practical Writing:** Writing a Project Proposal

Across the Curriculum

Objective

- apply what students have learned about descriptive writing to other curriculum areas

The lessons on the following pages provide samples of kinds of descriptive writing students might do in different subject areas. The particular form used in one content area may also be used in a different content area (for example, students could write a field-trip report just as well in social studies as in science).

Assigning these forms of writing will depend on

- the skill level of your students,
- the subject matter they are studying at any particular time, and
- the writing goals of your school, district, or state.

Social Studies: Writing an Eyewitness Report

Help students select an inventor who interests them. Start with the following list:

- Thomas Edison—lightbulb, phonograph, battery
- Gertrude Belle Elion—medical inventions
- Benjamin Franklin—bifocal glasses, lightning rod, Franklin stove
- Galileo—telescope, microscope
- Samuel Morse—telegraph
- James Naismith—basketball
- Jonas Salk—anti-polio vaccine

Encourage students to do research about recent inventions related to computer technology, space exploration, and medicine.

84

Social Studies:
Writing an Eyewitness Report

An eyewitness report is a type of descriptive writing. The writer of the following report describes what it might have been like to witness Alexander Graham Bell inventing the telephone.

The **beginning** shares some important background information.

The **middle** describes the subject and what he is doing.

The **ending** leaves the reader with something to think about.

The World's First Phone Call

It is March 10, 1876. I find myself inside a small, dusty electrical shop in Boston, Massachusetts. Alexander Graham Bell and his assistant, Thomas Watson, are here working on Bell's invention, the electrical speech machine.

Bell is a young man with wavy, black hair and a wild beard. Under his shop apron, he wears a white shirt and brown pants. His right foot taps impatiently as he adjusts the machine's transmitter. A long wire connects it to the receiver, which is with Watson in another room in the shop.

Accidentally, Bell's left elbow knocks over a small container of battery acid. He watches helplessly as the acid oozes onto the wire.

As I rush into the other room, I hear Mr. Bell's voice shouting, "Mr. Watson, come here. I want you!" Watson's eyes widen with surprise as he hears Bell's voice coming through the machine's receiver.

"We've done it!" he shouts to Bell. "We've transmitted human speech through a wire!"

It looks as if this accident has made the invention work! Who knows how the electrical speech machine will be used in the future?

English Language Learners

Point out that the writer presents factual information, but in an intriguing way.

- Discuss what the author does to make the report interesting to read.
- Have students retell the report, including at least one historical fact about Alexander Graham Bell.

Struggling Learners

Have students compare and contrast "The World's First Phone Call" with an encyclopedia entry about Alexander Graham Bell. Discuss the following questions:

- Which one provides the most specific information? Why?
- Which one is the most creatively written? Why?
- Which one do you prefer to read? Why?

Advanced Learners

If time is limited, prior to assigning this report, have students do research outside of class to find some famous inventors who could serve as subjects for the report.

- Ask each student to provide a brief overview of one inventor and his or her inventions.
- Compile a list that the class can use as a source from which to choose topics.

express SPECIFY portray
picture describe portray

85

Writing in Social Studies

Writing Tips

Before you write . . .

- **Choose a famous inventor.** Select an inventor you have studied in class.
- **Do your research.** Learn about the person and his or her invention. Study pictures of the person. From your research, try to imagine the setting in which the person tested the invention and discovered that it worked.
- **Take notes.** Collect important details that will help make your description interesting and clear.

During your writing . . .

- **Write as if you are observing the inventor at the moment the invention first works.** Tell when the event takes place. Briefly describe the inventor and the setting. End with a final thought to keep the reader thinking about the topic.
- **Show, don't tell.** Use descriptive details that show the reader what is happening, as if he or she were seeing it firsthand.
- **Organize your thoughts.** Use order of location (*top to bottom, front to back, left to right, head to toe*) or time order (*first, next, then,* and so on) to organize your details.
- **Use an engaging voice.** Your voice should sound interested, knowledgeable, and excited about being an eyewitness.

After you've written a first draft . . .

- **Check for completeness.** Make sure that you have included enough information to give the reader a clear picture of the inventor and the invention.
- **Check for correctness.** Proofread your essay to make sure there are no mistakes in punctuation, capitalization, spelling, and grammar.

 Choose a famous inventor. Learn about the person and the invention. Write a creative eyewitness account describing the inventor at the moment the invention works.

Writing Tips

Remind students that in order to write an eyewitness account of an actual invention, they must use a combination of

- their imaginations and
- accurate research data.

Discuss the role of eyewitnesses in relationship to courtroom dramas and accident reports. Emphasize that a personal account captures the feeling of an event while incorporating the relevant facts.

 Answers

Answers will vary but should include sensory details that help a reader to see the inventor and the event.

Advanced Learners

To stretch students' researching skills, encourage them to locate and use as many primary sources as possible for this activity.

Math: Describing an Object with Geometric Terms

Use the following suggestions if students have difficulty in thinking of objects to describe in geometric terms:

- Begin by having students describe a simple object, such as a pencil, a shoebox, or a can of soda.
- Have students consult with their math teachers for valuable guidance in using accurate terms for common objects.

Math: Describing an Object with Geometric Terms

Sometimes an object can be described with geometric terms. The writer of this essay describes a quartz crystal as a hexagonal prism.

The **beginning** introduces the object.

The **middle** describes the top, bottom, and side views of the object.

The **ending** makes a final comment.

A Crystal Clear Hexagon

In the world, both natural and man-made objects have geometric shapes. Triangles, rectangles, squares, circles, cubes, cones, and pyramids can be seen in nature and in the world every day. Another common hexagon in nature is the glasslike quartz crystal.

A hexagonal prism crystal is a shape with six sides. The base of a quartz crystal is a hexagon with equal sides and equal angles. A perpendicular rectangle rises from each side from the base. The six rectangles of equal size rising from the base form a six-sided or hexagonal box. The top of the crystal is the same shape as the base.

When looking at the bottom or the top of the crystal, the viewer will see a perfect hexagon. A side view will reveal three long rectangles. From this view, the top and the bottom rectangles are each attached to the middle rectangle at an angle of 60 degrees.

Focusing on geometric shapes to describe an object can help someone else visualize it. Describing something in geometric terms may also make it easier to remember facts and information about the object.

English Language Learners

To help students who are not yet familiar with geometry vocabulary, use these strategies:

- Pair students with proficient English speakers.
- Allow extra time to become familiar with these terms and their usage.
- Ask a math teacher to suggest knowledgeable students as appropriate partners.

Struggling Learners

Ask your library media specialist to locate several *How to Draw . . .* books that students may use for ideas. These books break down objects such as vehicles, buildings, and machines into their basic geometrical shapes before details are added.

express SPECIFY portray
picture describe
picture

87

Writing in Math

DESCRIPTIVE

Writing Tips

Before you write . . .

- **List some geometric terms that could be used to describe a flat or three-dimensional object.**
  Make notes or sketches on the list. Review any terms you are unsure of.
- **Choose an object that can be described with geometric terms.**
  Study the object and look at it from all different angles.
- **Make notes as you observe the object.**
  Jot down specific geometric terms you could use to enable a reader to visualize the object.

During your writing . . .

- **Write a clear beginning, middle, and ending.**
  Introduce the object and then describe it using geometric terms. End with a final comment about your topic or about using geometric terms to describe everyday objects.
- **Organize your description.**
  Describe your object using a spatial method of organization (top to bottom, left to right, and so on).
- **Use correct terms.**
  Include specific and correct geometric terms in your description. The reader should be able to picture the shape you describe.

After you've written a first draft . . .

- **Check for completeness.**
  Have you included enough details to clearly describe your object?
- **Check for correctness.**
  Proofread your writing for punctuation, capitalization, spelling, and grammar errors.

 Write a short essay using geometric terms to describe an object. Share your essay with your classmates.

Writing Tips

Once students have successfully described a simple object in a descriptive paragraph, they can choose a more complex object and write a descriptive essay using geometric terms.

 Answers

Answers will vary.

Struggling Learners

Have some appropriate objects on hand that can be described in geometric terms, such as a flower vase, a cell phone, or a wallet.

- Allow small groups of students to select and study an item.
- Groups work together, or with you, on the prewriting steps.
- Groups work together to write, revise, and edit their description.

Science: Writing a Field-Trip Report

Discourage students from giving a minute-by-minute replay of the field trip (first we did this, next we did this).

- Point out that the middle part of the example essay describes the place, and then the program.
- Note that key details are provided to enable the reader to form a clear mental picture of the planetarium and the program.

88

Science: Writing a Field-Trip Report

In science class, you may be asked to describe your observations on a recent field trip. This student writer describes a field trip to a planetarium.

Blain Planetarium

The **beginning** introduces the topic.

On March 3, our class visited Blain Planetarium. As the bus rounded the curve, I saw the huge white dome. I was anxious to see what was inside.

Stepping into the main room, my eyes followed the curve of the high, dome-shaped ceiling. The guide told us that this would be our movie screen. Scanning the room, I noticed that the planetarium is actually a large circular room. All the seats follow the shape of the room and face the center. We were quickly ushered to a row of red cushioned seats that tilted way back so we could look at the dome. In the center, there is a machine called a star projector.

The **middle** clearly describes the planetarium program.

Then the lights dimmed, quiet music played, and a beautiful sunset in the western sky faded to a black sky filled with stars. A man's voice narrated as we observed the Milky Way, planets, meteorites, and the colorful aurora borealis. Among the stars were constellations like Ursa Major and Orion. Even Halley's comet swept across the sky.

The **ending** makes a final observation.

A sunrise in the eastern sky signaled that the show was finished. I felt as if I had been in a dream. I had been zooming through space so close to the planets that I could almost touch them.

Struggling Learners

To help students understand the importance of sharing the right details, brainstorm a list of the details *not* provided by the writer (how long the trip took, where students ate lunch). Ask these questions:

- Why weren't these details included?
- With what audience would you share this type of information?

express SPECIFY portray
picture describe
89
Writing in Science

Writing Tips

Before you write . . .

- **Choose a topic that interests you.**
  Select a recent field trip related to your class.
- **List main ideas you want to include.**
  You can't tell everything about the field trip, so choose one or two impressive things to write about.
- **Gather specific details.**
  Think about your destination. Use sensory details to describe the sights and sounds of the place.

Sensory Chart

Subject:				
Sights	Sounds	Smells	Tastes	Feelings

During your writing . . .

- **Write a clear beginning, middle, and ending.**
  Introduce the topic in the beginning part. In the middle, describe the place by including specific details. Close by sharing a final thought about the experience.
- **Organize your details.**
  You may organize your details by order of location (*left to right, top to bottom, near to far*) or time order (*first, second, next, last*). Choose the pattern that works best for your description.
- **Use strong words.**
  A strong description contains specific nouns, action verbs, and well-chosen adjectives.

After you've written a first draft . . .

- **Check for completeness.**
  Make sure that you have included all the details that make it possible for the reader to see the place in his or her mind.
- **Check for correctness.**
  Proofread your report for punctuation, capitalization, spelling, and grammar errors.

DESCRIPTIVE

 Select a recent or a past field trip and describe it following the tips above.

Writing Tips

Model an experience that is shared by the students, such as a lunch period in the cafeteria.

- Brainstorm a beginning that introduces the topic.
- Ask students for sentences that describe the cafeteria. Remind them to use sensory details and incorporate action verbs and specific adjectives as they describe the room.
- Then have them describe moving through the lunch line and choosing the meal.
- Finally, encourage students to come up with a last observation about the room and the meal.

 Answers

Answers will vary.

English Language Learners

As a prewriting activity, have students sketch maps showing what they remember about the museum, park, lab, or other science field-trip location they visited.

- Tell students to include on their maps things they want to discuss in their descriptions.

- Have students use a different colored pencil to draw a line representing the path they will take through the map. This path will guide the order in which they discuss things in their report.

Advanced Learners

After students finish writing, encourage them to add a visual component to their report, such as a diorama, map, poster, or collage. Invite class members to compare the written description to the visual aid and comment on how the two work together.

Practical Writing: Writing a Project Proposal

Ask students to describe a project they intend to carry out. They may

- consult with their content area teachers about upcoming projects;
- consider projects that will improve the school or community environment, such as organizing an area cleanup or setting up a recycling program;
- think about a project they could complete for their family or in their home.

90

Practical Writing:
Writing a Project Proposal

Descriptive writing comes in many different forms. For example, you may be asked to describe a project you plan to do. The following proposal, written by a student team, describes a tutoring project.

The **heading** identifies the writers and their proposed project.

Date:	January 12, 2009
To:	Mrs. Munn, Room 210
From:	The Titan Group: Todd Davis, LaToya Wilson, Jacque Trevino, Becky Jackson
Subject:	Volunteer Tutoring

The **beginning** describes the project.

Project Description: An article in our school paper stated that Lincoln Elementary School needed eighth-grade students to tutor third graders in reading. We would like to volunteer our services starting February 3.

The **middle** part gives details about the project.

What We Need: We need written permission from you, our parents, and our principal. We also need written approval from the principal and the third-grade teachers of Lincoln Elementary School.

What We Will Do: On Tuesdays and Thursdays, during our fourth-period study hall, we will walk across the playground to Lincoln School to our assigned classrooms. We will help third-grade students by listening to them read, helping them with their reading assignments, and reading to them.

Outcome: At the end of this project, we will report on the students' progress and show a videotape of our students reading during one of our last sessions. It will show how the tutoring helped.

The **ending** asks for approval of the project.

We hope you will approve our proposal. If you have any suggestions or changes, please let us know.

Advanced Learners

Have students identify the voice used in the proposal and then rewrite it in a very informal tone. Together, compare and contrast the two and discuss why one is appropriate to the task and the other is not.

express SPECIFY portray
picture describe

91

Practical Writing

Writing Tips

Before you write . . .

- **Choose a project that interests you.**
  Working alone or with a team of classmates, choose
  a project you will enjoy doing.
- **Do your research.**
  Decide specifically what you will do and what you will
  need to complete your project.
- **Plan your proposal.**
  Collect details in order to describe the project to your teacher.
  Your goal is to present a clear description of the work you plan
  to do.

During your writing . . .

- **Write a clear beginning, middle, and ending.**
  In the *heading* give the date, your teacher's name and room
  number, the names of your team members, and the subject of
  your project. Next, clearly describe the project. For the other
  parts of your proposal, follow the model on page 90.
- **Order your ideas.**
  Make sure you've included all the information in the
  correct order.
- **Use precise words.**
  Make your description clear and easy to follow. Use specific
  nouns and verbs.

After you've written a first draft . . .

- **Check for completeness.**
  Make sure that you have included all the details that your
  teacher needs to understand the project.
- **Check for correctness.**
  Proofread your proposal for punctuation, capitalization,
  spelling, and grammar errors.

DESCRIPTIVE

 Select a project that you or your team would like to do. Write a project
proposal using the tips above.

Writing Tips

Many of the proposed projects will
require the involvement of several
students, so students should

- form groups based on a common
  project interest,
- work together to create their
  proposal draft,
- cooperatively revise the proposal
  and check for correct use of
  conventions.

Try It Answers

Answers will vary.

Narrative Writing Overview

Unit Objectives

The writing standards listed below are based on a blending of state and NCTE standards.

- Use charts and clusters to gather and organize ideas.
- Support central idea with vocabulary and voice appropriate to audience and purpose.
- Revise drafts by adding, deleting, and rearranging texts; provide logical support of ideas.
- Assess writing using a rubric based on the traits of effective writing.
- Share finished pieces with classmates and others.

Writing Forms

- narrative paragraph
- phase autobiography
- biographical narrative

Focus on the Traits

- **Ideas** Telling about events and details that make the story come alive
- **Organization** Presenting events in chronological order with a strong beginning, middle, and ending
- **Voice** Using an active voice and a tone that matches the experience
- **Word Choice** Using specific words with appropriate connotations
- **Sentence Fluency** Combining and expanding sentences to achieve a smooth flow
- **Conventions** Checking for errors in punctuation, capitalization, spelling, and grammar

Note: For specifics about reading the chart below, see page TE 33.

Suggested Narrative Writing Unit (Five Weeks)

Day	Writing and Skills Units	In the *Write Source* book			On the CD-ROM	*SkillsBook*
		Pages	Proofreader's Guide—basic grammar rules	Basic Grammar practice	Interactive Grammar Exercises	grammar practice pages
1–4	**Narrative Paragraph** (Model)	93–96				
	Skills Activities: Conjunctions		744–745	496	Conjunctions	
	Commas (in compound sentences and introductory clauses and phrases)		590–591	516		11–12, 14
	Pronouns		706 (+), 708–709	479	Pronouns—1	145–146
opt.	*Speeches*	428–429				
5	**Narrative Essay—Phase Autobiography** (Model)	97–100				
6–7	(Prewriting)	101–106				
8–10	(Writing)	107–112				23–24

Day	Writing and Skills Units	In the *Write Source* book			On the CD-ROM	*SkillsBook* grammar practice pages
		Pages	Proofreader's Guide—basic grammar rules	Basic Grammar practice	Interactive Grammar Exercises	
11–14	(Revising)	113–124				
	Skills Activities: Tone (transitive and intransitive verbs)		728–729	484	Verbs—2	159–160
	Verbals (participles, infinitives)		730–731	485, 520	Verbs—3	161–162
	Prepositional Phrases		742–743	519	Prepositions	175–176
	Active vs. Passive Voice		726–727			
	Peer Responding (Model)	29–32				
15–16	(Editing and Publishing)	126–129				
	Skills Activities: Punctuating Dialogue		588–589, 598–599, 600–601		Punctuating Dialogue	
	Subject-Verb Agreement			508–509	Sentences—Subject-Verb Agreement	95–96
17–18	(Assessing) (Reflecting)	130–133, 134				
opt.	*Speeches*	428–429				
opt.	**Practical Writing: E-Mail Message**	150–151				
	Skills Activities: Kinds of Sentences		579 (+), 580 (+)	518 (+)		107–108
	Capitalization		618–619	470	Capitalization	41–42
19–20	Narrative Writing for Assessment	152–154				
1–5	**Biographical Narrative** (Model)	135–137				
	(Prewriting)	138–139				
	(Writing)	140				
	(Revising)	141				
	Skills Activities: Transitions			539		73
	(Editing and Publishing)	142				
	Skills Activities: End Punctuation		579–581	518		3–4
	Using the Right Word		652–661		Using the Right Word—1 and 4	53–54

WEEK 3

WEEK 4

WEEK 1 SECOND FORM

Teacher's Notes for Narrative Writing

This overview for narrative writing includes some specific teaching suggestions for the unit.

Narrative Paragraph (pages 93–96)

A narrative paragraph is a simple short story. It briefly, but succinctly, tells about an experience, a person, or an event. A narrative paragraph may be complete in itself or may be the foundation for a longer account.

Writing a Phase Autobiography (pages 97–134)

In this chapter, students will have an opportunity to explore different phases in their lives. They will select one of those periods and write about it in a phase autobiography. Their work should help them tap into themselves—their best resource about themselves. They may even come to understand more fully who they are.

Writing a Biographical Narrative (pages 135–142)

Once students understand how to write about themselves and learn about themselves, they will be better able to write about and learn about others. This should help them understand that other people also have hopes, fears, dreams, and ideas.

Writing Across the Curriculum (pages 143–151)

Narrative writing applies to other courses. Examples in this chapter include a social studies class imagining being aboard the *Mayflower*, a student's joy in understanding new concepts in math, talk about the form of a cloud in science, and a thank-you to a teacher for a field-trip suggestion in practical writing,

Writing for Assessment (pages 152–154)

Assessment tests as well as college-entrance essays often ask students to tell something about themselves, perhaps an event that changed their lives. In any case, practice with this form of writing will prove useful later when students must write for assessment. Narrative prompts for student practice are included on page 154.

Minilessons

Gym Class   Narrative Paragraph

- **WRITE** a paragraph that shares an experience in a recent gym class. **REWRITE** what you have written using more interesting nouns, dynamic adjectives, and active verbs. **SHARE** your results with a classmate.

tell
relate

Narrative Writing

narrate
remember
share

Once Upon a Time   Phase Autobiography

- **THINK** about a memorable or important time (weeks, or months) in your life. **LIST** facts and feelings surrounding that time.

My Favorite Famous Person   Biographical Narrative

- **STUDY** the "Gathering Details" list on page 138 of your textbook. **LIST** four potential subjects for biographical stories. One subject you should know well; one subject you should know only a little; one subject you should know by name only; and finally, choose one subject who you do not know personally (a famous person).

Landing on Mars   Writing Across the Curriculum

- Some day, people may explore Mars. **RESEARCH** the Red Planet (average temperatures, landing sites, atmosphere, etc.). Then **WRITE** a sentence outline for a narrative that tells the story of landing on Mars and the first couple days of exploration.

Narrative Writing
Narrative Paragraph

Has anyone ever offered you a "penny for your thoughts"? Has anyone ever pulled a quarter out of your ear?

Actually, your thoughts are worth much more than pennies and quarters. By the end of eighth grade, a typical public school system has spent more than $60,000 to educate *each student*. To you, your thoughts are even more valuable. Your mind is a treasure trove of discoveries and "aha!" moments.

One way to count up the treasures in your head is to write about them. A narrative paragraph gives you a chance to record a moment of discovery and share it with others. It's a trick as neat as pulling a quarter out of your ear!

Writing Guidelines

Subject:	**A moment of discovery**
Form:	**Narrative paragraph**
Purpose:	**To entertain**
Audience:	**Classmates**

Narrative Paragraph

Objectives
- select a moment of discovery
- write a narrative paragraph

Narrative paragraphs tell a story about an event, a person, or an experience. Paragraphs usually include a topic sentence, the body, and a closing sentence.

After reading this page as a class, have students do a five-minute freewrite on a moment of discovery, such as
- learning how to ride a bicycle,
- figuring out how to play a new song on an instrument, or
- studying a new subject in school.

Literature Connections

Flash fiction: One way to inspire students to write narrative paragraphs is to introduce to them the concept of flash fiction. Flash fiction is any short piece (often under 100 words) that tells a complete story. Professional writers enjoy the challenge of telling a story in such a compact form, and middle school readers enjoy such quick reads. Of course, your students will be writing about an actual event, not fiction, but the goal is the same: to capture an experience in a small space. Encourage your students to find flash fiction on the Web—and perhaps create some flash fiction of their own.

Narrative Paragraph

Review the parts of a paragraph: topic sentence, body, closing sentence.

✸ Additional information about parts of a paragraph is on PE pages 524–525.

Respond to the reading.

Answers

Ideas 1. The story is about discovering how a magic trick is done.

Organization 2. The details are organized by time.

Voice & Word Choice 3. grinned, snapped, appeared, rolled, vanished, stared, glimpsed, snatched

After students respond to the reading, discuss the order of the paragraph:

■ First, Grandpa did the trick.
■ Next, he did the trick again and Eric stared at his hands.
■ Last, Eric did the trick himself.

Point out how each sentence uses at least one descriptive action word (*snapped, rolled, snatched*). Contrast this style with some sentences that use less descriptive verbs: "Then he *put out* his hand and the coin *was there*. He *took* it away and the coin *was gone*."

94

Narrative Paragraph

A "moment of discovery" is a perfect subject for a narrative paragraph. In the student model below, Eric describes a special moment when he figured out his first magic trick. The **topic sentence** introduces the topic, the **body** explains what happened, and the **closing sentence** wraps things up with a final thought.

Topic Sentence •••••••••••••

Body

Closing Sentence •••••••••••••

A Handy Trick

Grandpa grinned and held out his hand in front of me. He snapped his fingers, and a quarter appeared in his palm. Rapidly, he rolled his fingers, and the quarter vanished. I'd seen this trick a hundred times, but today I was determined to figure it out. The quarter appeared again, and vanished again. I stared carefully at Grandpa's hands. He held his left hand out to his side, palm open. His right hand was in front of him and open underneath, with the back facing me. He turned his right hand over, and I glimpsed the quarter in his clenched fist. I snatched the quarter from his hand and held it just as he had shown me. Then, with a grin of my own, I snapped my fingers, and the quarter appeared. Grandpa still had many tricks up his sleeve, but that was one trick I had learned.

Respond to the reading. Answer the following questions on your own paper.

☐ **Ideas** **(1)** What moment of discovery is the story about?

☐ **Organization** **(2)** Are the details of the paragraph organized by importance, time, or some other pattern of organization?

☐ **Voice & Word Choice** **(3)** What vivid verbs help re-create the moment of discovery?

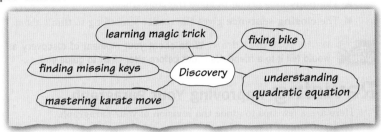

Narrative Paragraph 95

Prewriting **Selecting a Topic**

Whenever you learn something new, you have a moment of discovery. To find a topic for his narrative paragraph, Eric made a cluster of these moments.

Topic Cluster

Create a cluster. On your own paper, write "Discovery" and circle it. Make a cluster of four or five of your own moments of discovery. Choose one of these moments to write a paragraph about.

Gathering Details

One way to gather details about the moment of discovery is to use a before-after chart. Eric created the following chart about his "aha!" moment.

Before-After Chart

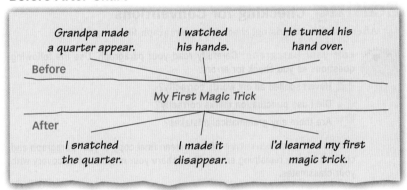

Create a before-after chart. Make a chart like the one above. Write what happened before and after your moment of discovery.

NARRATIVE

Prewriting **Selecting a Topic**

If students have difficulty generating ideas on their own, ask for suggestions from the entire class and record them in a topic cluster.

- Have students do some brainstorming in pairs or small groups, and ask volunteers to report their ideas to the whole class.
- Write the ideas on the board or on chart paper.

Prewriting **Gathering Details**

Explain that an "aha!" moment is one in which a person realizes something important (it can also be called a lightbulb moment). Point out that because an "aha!" moment is a short, isolated thought, it is necessary to explain what happened both before and after the moment in order to understand its importance.

Some students may find it easier to create a before-after chart then a T-chart. Provide photocopies of the reproducible T-chart on TE page 789.

✱ Additional information about writing narrative paragraphs is on PE page 526.

Struggling Learners

If students have trouble coming up with moments of discovery, have them begin by brainstorming lists of people who have taught them things (such as parents, teachers, relatives, neighbors, coaches, or friends). Then have them use a before-after chart to re-create the details for their "aha!" moment.

Writing
Creating Your First Draft

Remind students that in writing about a moment of discovery, they should vividly describe what led up to the discovery and what followed.

Revising
Improving Your Paragraph

Help students understand the importance of "show, don't tell":

- Form a small group of students and give the group a short scene to act out (such as finding a lost pet, learning a new game, meeting someone new, or finding the perfect gift).
- Have the group prepare and perform a short scene.
- During the performance, have the other students record what they see.
- Then have each student write a description showing exactly what happened in the scene.
- Ask students to identify the "showing" words they used in their notes to describe the scene.

Editing
Checking for Conventions

Have students trade their paragraphs with a partner and check each other's work for words that show and build the actions to the moment of discovery.

96

Writing   Creating Your First Draft

A well-written narrative paragraph should have a topic sentence, a body, and a closing sentence.

- The **topic sentence** introduces or starts the narrative.
- The **body** uses action to move the story along.
- The **closing sentence** gives the reader something to think about.

 Write your first draft. Write about your moment of discovery as you would tell it to a friend. Use your before-after chart to guide you.

Revising   Improving Your Paragraph

Here are a few tips to guide the revision of your paragraph.

- **Show, don't tell.** Instead of telling the reader that "Jenna was excited," show it: "Jenna clapped her hands and screamed at the top of her lungs."
- **Build to the high point.** Lead up to the moment of discovery.
- **Rewrite sentences if needed.** Check for sentences that are awkward or unclear. Rewrite them so that they flow nicely.

 Revise your paragraph. Focus on ideas, organization, voice, word choice, and sentence fluency as you revise your narrative paragraph.

Editing   Checking for Conventions

After you finish revising, check your paragraph for conventions.

 Edit your paragraph. Carefully read your paragraph. Use the following questions as you check for errors.

1 Have I spelled all my words correctly?

2 Did I use punctuation marks correctly?

3 Are there any grammatical mistakes?

Proofread your narrative. Make a clean final copy of your paragraph and check it for any remaining errors. Then share your moment of discovery with your classmates.

Grammar Connection

Conjunctions
- **Proofreader's Guide** pages 744–745
- *Write Source* page 496
- **CD** Conjunctions

Commas
- **Proofreader's Guide** pages 590–591
- *Write Source* page 516
- *SkillsBook* pages 11–12, 14

Pronouns
- **Proofreader's Guide** pages 706 (+), 708–709
- *Write Source* page 479
- *SkillsBook* pages 145–146
- **CD** Pronouns-1

tell **share** remember
relate **narrate** 97

Narrative Writing
Writing a Phase Autobiography

At one time or another, most students have had to write a narrative entitled "What I Did Last Summer." Many of those essays could be summed up this way: "I mowed the lawn—over and over and over. . . ." A more thoughtful narrative, though, would focus on a few related experiences the writer had and would show how those experiences changed him or her in some way.

A phase autobiography is a narrative essay about an extended period of time in your life. An effective phase autobiography shows how the period of time changed you or taught you an important lesson. The key to this form of writing is to focus on just the main actions and events. By the end of the writing experience, you will become much wiser about life—and what it has to offer.

Writing Guidelines

Subject:	An extended period of time in your life
Form:	Phase autobiography
Purpose:	To share a part of your life
Audience:	Classmates

English Language Learners

To make sure that students understand what a *phase* is, engage them in creating a word web. Branches of the web can include

- a definition (of *phase* as a period of time);
- synonyms (a while, time, period); and
- examples of ways they have heard the word used (going through a phase; in the early phase of her career).

Copy Masters/ Transparencies

T-chart (TE p. 100)

Time line (TE p. 102)

Sensory chart (TE p. 107)

Writing a Phase Autobiography

Objectives

- choose a period of time to write about
- write a narrative essay telling about an important time in your life

A **phase autobiography** is a narrative essay about an extended period of time in one's life.

- Students are likely to have written narratives about an isolated experience—such as their best day, their most embarrassing moment, or their greatest accomplishment. They might have trouble adopting the longer view that is necessary for any topic as introspective as this.

- Share some extended experiences from your own life or from the life of a person you admire. Be sure to include how the experiences changed the person or taught an important lesson.

Understanding Your Goal

Traits of Narrative Writing

Three traits relate to the development of the content and the form. They provide a focus during prewriting, drafting, and revising.

■ Ideas
■ Organization
■ Voice

The other three traits relate more to form. Checking them is part of the revising and editing process.

■ Word Choice
■ Sentence Fluency
■ Conventions

* The six-point rubric on PE pages 130–131 is based on these traits. Reproducible six-, five-, and four-point rubrics for narrative writing can be found on TE pages 750, 754, and 758.

Test Prep!
When figure skaters prepare a routine for an Olympic competition, they consider jumps, combinations, spins, footwork, choreography, and artistry. These are the "traits" judges use to score an ice-skating routine.

When students use the traits in the process, they are preparing for the assessment at the end of the assignment. They are also preparing for on-demand writing tests.

98

Understanding Your Goal

Your goal in this chapter is to write about a time in your life when you changed. The following traits will help you plan and write your phase autobiography.

Traits of Narrative Writing

Ideas
Select an important time in your life. Include events and details that show how you changed.

Organization
Present the events in chronological order with a strong beginning, middle, and ending. Consider using dialogue.

Voice
Use an active voice and match the tone to your experience.

Word Choice
Choose specific words with appropriate feelings or connotations.

Sentence Fluency
Make your sentences flow smoothly by combining and expanding them.

Conventions
Be sure that your punctuation, capitalization, spelling, and grammar are correct.

 Get the big picture. On pages 130–131 you will find a rubric that will guide you through your writing. Your goal is to produce a well-written essay about an extended period of time in your life.

tell share remember
narrate
relate
Writing a Phase Autobiography   99

Phase Autobiography

In this sample narrative, the student author tells how he changed after getting to know his elderly neighbor. The key parts of the phase autobiography are described in the left margin.

Beginning

In the beginning, the writer gets the reader's attention and introduces the period of time.

Middle

The writer uses a variety of specific details to tell what happened during this period of time.

Getting to Know Joe

I live in an old two-story home in Newark. My neighbors are mostly retired people with perfect front yards. One of the retirees, Joe Perez, lives on the corner. Because of our time together last summer, he and I have built a special relationship.

At the start of the summer, Joe and I didn't hit it off too well. He was very picky about his yard. Every morning he was doing something to make the lawn look better. If we goofed around and stepped on his grass, Joe would yell at us from his front porch.

Through mid-July his yard was perfect, but then I noticed some changes. I didn't see Joe outside as much. His grass was getting brown and shaggy, and some weeds were growing in his flower beds. It wasn't like Joe to let things go. I didn't dwell on it, but when I walked by his place, I wondered why he wasn't taking care of his yard.

One day I was sitting on the curb waiting for one of my buddies to show up when Joe came out on the porch. I expected him to yell at me for sitting on his grass. Instead, he swayed back and forth. Then he fell down! I ran to my house and dialed 911. "My neighbor, Mr. Perez, just passed out! He lives on the corner of Garden and Mills," I blurted. Then I hurried back to the porch to see what I could do. Joe was awake, but he was as white as a ghost. He stared blankly at me.

NARRATIVE

Phase Autobiography

Work through this sample essay with the class, pointing out the elements that make it a good phase autobiography.

Ideas

- The author writes about learning an important lesson.
- The details help show how he changed.

Organization

- There is a strong beginning, middle, and ending.
- The author uses dialogue that shows action.

Voice

- It is written in an active voice.
- The tone matches the experience; it is eager, reflective, honest, and hopeful.

Writer's Craft

Time travel: Writers are time travelers. They can begin at one point in time and move forward or backward. They can skip anything unimportant or uninteresting and can focus on only the most important events.

Understanding this power is key to writing a strong phase autobiography. To tell everything that happens over a long period of time is not only uninteresting—it is also impossible. Instead, writers need to select the moments that really matter, and leap from one moment to another using time transitions.

English Language Learners

Make sure students understand the following words and phrases:

- retired people, retirees (older people who no longer work)
- didn't hit it off (didn't like each other; didn't get along)
- picky (fussy)
- goofed around (behaved in a playful or silly way)
- dwell on it (think a lot about a certain thing)

Focus on the last two paragraphs of the model, in which the author describes a big change in his own behavior and outlook as a result of the experience.

- Point out that the key to the phase autobiography is the conclusion.
- Ask what revelation, change, or consequence arose as a result of this phase in the author's life.

Respond to the reading.

Answers

Ideas 1. last summer

Organization 2. time order

Voice & Word Choice 3. Possible answers: perfect, special, picky, blurted, blankly, little did I know

100

Middle
The writer uses dialogue to explain what was said.

"W-What happened to me?" he mumbled.

"You passed out, Mr. Perez," I said, trying to catch my breath. "But help is on its way."

The paramedics came and took Joe to the emergency room. It turned out that Joe had been forgetting to take his blood pressure medication. He was going to be all right, and I was glad about that. He could be a grump at times, but I guess I cared about Joe more than I realized. I couldn't imagine my neighborhood without him.

Joe thanked me for helping. Then I asked him, "Is there anything I can do for you, Mr. Perez?" Little did I know that one question would change everything.

Joe found lots of things I could do. Soon I was cutting his grass, weeding his flowers, trimming his bushes, and edging the grass along his sidewalk. Before long, I was planting things like a pro and telling kids to stay off the grass. Instead of yelling at me from his porch, Joe now waved and smiled.

Ending
The ending tells how the writer changed.

A whole year has passed, and each week I help Joe. I realize that I can make a difference, so I also help some of the other older neighbors. Joe taught me that helping people is what life is all about.

Respond to the reading. Why is "Getting to Know Joe" a good piece of writing? To find out, answer these questions.

☐ **Ideas** (1) What memorable phase of his life does the writer tell about?

☐ **Organization** (2) What organizational pattern does the writer use?

☐ **Voice & Word Choice** (3) Which words help the writer create an appropriate voice? Identify three.

English Language Learners

Have students create a before-after chart (like the one on PE page 95) for "Getting to Know Joe."

- Provide photocopies of the reproducible T-chart on TE page 789. Direct students to write *Before* at the top of the

left-hand column and *After* at the top of the other.
- Help students complete the chart. Then guide them to see how the young writer's perceptions of his elderly neighbor changed as he took the time to get to know him.

Advanced Learners

Challenge students to predict what the relationship between the writer and Joe will be like in five years. Have them write a brief essay speculating on how the relationship will have developed.

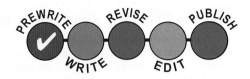

tell share remember narrate relate

Writing a Phase Autobiography

101

Prewriting

Before you can begin writing your phase autobiography, you need to choose an extended period of time to write about. In your prewriting, you will choose a topic, gather details, and organize your thoughts.

Keys to Effective Prewriting

1. Think about several important times in your life.

2. Choose one main time to share with your readers.

3. Identify the key events related to this time.

4. Organize your ideas chronologically.

5. Gather specific details and feelings.

6. Consider using dialogue.

NARRATIVE

Prewriting

Keys to Effective Prewriting

Remind students of the purpose of the prewriting stage in the writing process. (It's when the writer gets ready to write.)

"Keys to Effective Prewriting" explains the process students will be guided through on PE pages 102–106.

After reviewing the items in the list, be sure students can define *chronologically*.

Writer's Workshop

Each of the activities on the following pages teaches a crucial prewriting skill, such as selecting a topic, finding a focus, and gathering details. These activities can function as minilessons for writing workshops. Present the minilessons during whole-class instruction, use them to work with a small group, or assign them to individual students who are struggling with a certain prewriting skill.

You'll find that the writing, revising, editing, and publishing sections of this unit also contain activities that make perfect minilessons for writing workshops.

Prewriting Selecting a Topic

Suggest the following topics:

- starting a new school
- going away to camp
- moving to a new neighborhood
- learning to swim, doing in-line skating, riding a bike, and so on
- making a new friend

Students may think that events like these are uninteresting because so many people have experienced them.

- Point out that it is the unique perspective that each individual brings to the writing process that will make the topic interesting.
- Explain that a common experience (one that readers can relate to because they have had a similar experience) is often an ideal topic for a phase autobiography.

Focus on the Traits

Ideas

After each student makes a "Life List," encourage the class to explore possible topics for a phase autobiography by brainstorming related ideas for each item on their life lists.

✱ Additional information on making a "Basics of Life" list is on PE page 545.

Prewriting Selecting a Topic

A phase autobiography is a form of narrative writing, but it is different from most personal narratives. In a typical personal narrative, you share one specific event or experience. In a *phase autobiography,* you write about an extended period of time that has changed you in some important way.

One way to find a topic for your autobiography is to list the meaningful things that have happened in your life. The list below shows important times in one writer's life.

Life List

> Was hospitalized with an appendicitis attack
> Took a train trip with my grandmother
> Went canoeing with the youth group
> Participated in the school's spelling bee
> Joined the Junior Drum and Bugle Corp
> Volunteered at the local nursing home
> Transferred to a new school
> Helped my neighbor take care of her dog
>
> Reason: I chose this topic because it changed me in so many ways.

 Prewrite **Make a "Life List."** List a number of important times in your life. Circle the time you want to use as the topic of your phase autobiography. Then write your reason for choosing this topic.

Focus on the Traits

Ideas Phase autobiographies are often written about getting to know new friends, participating in an extracurricular activity, experiencing a change in family life, and so on.

English Language Learners

To help students select a topic, have them make a time line of their life, including any important times.

- Provide photocopies of the reproducible time line on TE page 790.

- Guide students in listing the times chronologically. Have them list the related details for each time underneath that time on the time line.
- Then ask them to circle one time and a set of supporting details to use as a topic.

tell share remember
relate narrate **103**
Writing a Phase Autobiography

Focusing Your Topic

After you have chosen a period of time in your life that has changed you in some important way, you should write a sentence or two that will give your phase autobiography a good focus. You should mention both the phase and the way in which it changed you. The examples below will help you understand how the two parts work together.

Weak Focus

> *One Saturday night a year ago, I learned that my friends are not always right.*
> ("One Saturday night" is not an extended period of time.)
>
> *The last month of track meets really taught me something.*
> ("Really taught me something" should be more specific.)

Strong Focus

> *The last month of track meets taught me that champions are made from discipline, determination, and sweat.*

 First, carefully read the following sentences. Then identify the ones you feel would make a good focus for a phase autobiography.

1. Felicia and I had played in tennis tournaments all summer, but we learned more about friendship and dedication than about tennis.
2. I met my grandfather for the first time at my cousin's wedding.
3. I surprised my mother by making supper.
4. I lived with my grandparents for a semester while my parents were busy starting a new business.
5. When my little sister was born, my life changed completely.

 Focus your topic. Using the topic you selected (page 102), write a sentence or two that will give your phase autobiography a good focus. Be sure you state both the period of time and the important way in which your life changed.

NARRATIVE

Prewriting Focusing Your Topic
Reassure students that a weak focus statement does not necessarily mean that the underlying main idea is weak.
- Together, look at the first sentence in the box marked "Weak Focus."
- Discuss how the focus statement could be strengthened.
- Offer this example: "For most of last year, I valued my friends' opinions more than my own."

 Answers

sentences 1, 4, and 5

 **Writer's Craft**

Focus: Professional writers are able to focus their ideas in very small—or very large—spaces. Novelists are often asked to summarize a 500-page novel in one sentence, one paragraph, or one page. Screenwriters do the same thing, creating a boiled-down treatment that can sell the "high concept" of their scripts to directors, producers, and actors.

Finding a focus means capturing the main idea of a piece of writing. An old editorial maxim states, "If you can't sum up your work in a single sentence, you don't understand it." By stating a focus in a single sentence—and then working it out through a whole phase autobiography—student writers work like the pros.

English Language Learners

Help students break down the **Prewriting** task by asking,
- What period of time changed you?
- How did it change you?

Have them write a sentence to answer each question. (Sample answers: I changed when I moved to the United States. I learned that the best way to make friends was to be myself.)

Show students how to combine the two sentences into a focus statement. (When I moved to the United States, I learned that the best way to make friends was to be myself.)

Prewriting **Freewriting**

If your students do not have much experience with **freewriting** *(see below)*, explain that it is a method of writing designed to put ideas down on paper. The purpose is to focus on generating ideas and feelings that are related to the topic.

Test Prep!

One of the main benefits of freewriting is that it helps students gain fluency. Fluency is the ability to pour ideas out onto a page. Fluent writers often score higher on on-demand assessments because they are able to produce more ideas within a limited time frame. Given that they can produce material more rapidly, fluent writers also have more time to plan their work before writing and revise it afterward.

104

Prewriting **Freewriting**

Now that you have chosen a phase to write about, you need to search your memory for information. Freewriting is an excellent way to recall details without worrying about organization or correctness.

The example of freewriting below was done by the writer of the essay on pages 109–112. Notice that after she finished her writing, she located and underlined the key events. These key events eventually became part of the topic sentences in the middle paragraphs.

Freewriting

> The drum and bugle flyer I brought home from school really got Dad talking about his days in the drum corps. His stories convinced me to sign up for summer band camp. I felt excited and nervous on that first day of camp. I heard Mr. D, the director, was very strict. He was! <u>My first day of practice</u> was unbelievable. <u>All of our practices</u> were tough. We marched like soldiers. My friend, Marcia, quit during the first week. I didn't have that choice. (Our family has this rule: Whatever you start, you finish.) I have to admit that I really liked being in the <u>parades</u>. <u>Field competitions</u> were the best. We always placed somewhere in the top three. In August we traveled to <u>Canada for a competition</u>. I thought the name of it—a tattoo—was weird. We came in first and won an international trophy. . . .

 Freewrite. Write nonstop for 5 to 10 minutes about your topic. Write down all your thoughts and don't stop to revise or correct your writing. Then read through your paper and underline the key events that took place.

Teaching Tip: Freewriting

Most students will benefit from watching you model the process of freewriting for them. Use a computer, an overhead projector, or even a piece of paper, as long as students can see that you are writing without stopping.

English Language Learners

Reassure students that their freewriting does not have to look polished. Allow them to use words from their native language if they cannot think of the English words they need. Stress that the most important thing is to keep the ideas flowing and the pen moving.

tell share remember
relate narrate **105**
Writing a Phase Autobiography

Gathering Details

Now that you've listed your key events, it's time to recall specific details and feelings connected with them. As the writer of the essay on pages 109–112 thought about each event, she wrote down specific details and feelings in a chart. Then she used the chart to write her middle paragraphs.

Specific Details Chart

Key Events	Details	Feelings
First day of practice	hot summer day sore feet Mr. D.—very strict	nervous frightened
Daily practices	intense practices kept bumping into people quickly improved	wanted to quit was exhausted determined to get better
Parades and competitions	teamwork performed in all kinds of weather	was overwhelmed could face difficult challenges
The tattoo	packed stadium competed with the best marching bands	felt confident was motivated

Create a chart. Make a details chart like the one above. Record key events in the first column. Jot down details and feelings you remember about each.

Prewrite

Focus on the Traits

Organization Narrative writing is almost always organized chronologically to help the story flow smoothly from beginning to end. For other patterns of organization, see page **551**.

NARRATIVE

Prewriting Gathering Details

If their charts seem to need more structure, suggest that they think of three or four key events and a few details for each key event.

Focus on the Traits

Organization
Review the basic steps involved in organizing a narrative in chronological order. Tell students to think of the progression of steps in a stairway:

- Just as each step in a stairway leads to the next, each part of a narrative should lead naturally to the next part.
- Although all the parts are connected, each one needs enough support so that it can also stand alone.

✱ Additional information on using chronological order is on PE page 534.

English Language Learners

To reinforce the stairway analogy:
- Have students draw a Step Organizer with a series of steps (empty boxes) that climb from lower left to upper right.
- Have them draw a vertical line through the middle of each rectangle (box), to form two parts.

- Working in chronological order, students should write one key event on the top of each rectangle (step).
- Within each box, they may write details on the left side and feelings on the right side.

Struggling Learners

To help students who have difficulty completing the "Specific Details Chart" on this page, modify it by adding a *Graphics* column after *Key Events*. Have students illustrate each key event, which will spawn ideas for their *Details* and *Feelings* columns.

Prewriting
Understanding Tone and Connotation

Explain that the connotation of a word is the feeling that a word suggests.

Write additional examples that contrast words with neutral and strong meanings on the board.

- ask/demand
- said/asserted
- walk/stride

Ask students to add their own word pairs.

 Answers

1. shook
2. spark
3. huddled, football coach
4. conquering army
5. grueling, dominated

Focus on the Traits

Voice
Remind students that the words that they choose affect the voice in a piece of writing.

106

Prewriting
Understanding Tone and Connotation

When you write about an important phase in your life, your voice should show clearly how you feel about the events. Your attitude toward your subject is called *tone*. One way to create tone is to choose words with a strong feeling, or *connotation*.

In the examples below, note how the writer replaces neutral words with words that have a strong connotation.

> *Neutral:* **Mr. D. was a man with short hair.**
> *Strong:* Mr. D. was a drill sergeant with a crew cut.

> *Neutral:* **Mr. D. walked before us and spoke loudly.**
> *Strong:* Mr. D. paced before us and barked loudly.

 Read the following sentences. For each, indicate which of the words in parentheses has the stronger connotation.

1. The tough schedule *(affected, shook)* my confidence.
2. Mr. D. told me my playing added *(spark, something)* to the trumpet section.
3. Before the competition, Mr. D. *(huddled, met)* with us like a *(leader, football coach)*.
4. As we took the field, we marched like a *(conquering army, big group)*.
5. The *(hard, grueling)* practices paid off when we *(won, dominated)* the competition.

 Gather words with feeling. Review your "Specific Details Chart" (page 105). For each feeling shown in the right column, write at least one word or phrase that expresses that feeling strongly. Try to use these words as you write your first draft.

Focus on the Traits

Voice When you write a phase autobiography, you need to use a voice that sounds like you. Since you're writing about an important part of your life, it should be easy for you to use a natural-sounding voice.

English Language Learners

To help students find stronger words that can replace neutral ones, have them practice using a thesaurus (at their reading level) to look up several neutral words, such as *smile, eat,* and *sleep.* Ask them to find a substitute for each word, but one with a stronger connotation.

Struggling Learners

For the **Prewriting** activity, encourage students to use a thesaurus.

- Caution them, however, to consider the connotations of each alternative and how those alternatives would affect the tone of the piece.
- Advise them to make sure that each "word with feeling" will work in context.

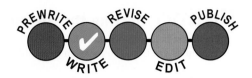

Writing

Now that you have gathered and organized your details, you can begin writing the first draft of your phase autobiography.

Keys to Effective Writing

1. Use the ideas and details you gathered and organized during prewriting.

2. Write on every other line, leaving space to add or change ideas later.

3. Write freely as you develop your beginning, middle, and ending.

4. Add memory and sensory details that bring your experience to life.

5. Use words with feeling to create an appropriate tone.

NARRATIVE

Writing Keys to Effective Writing

Remind students that the writing stage is when they get to write, or draft, their ideas on paper.

"Keys to Effective Writing" explains the process students will be guided through on PE pages 108–112.

Explain that first drafts are not expected to be perfect. Reassure students that they will have several chances to revise their narratives before they have a finished product.

Preview the "Rubric for Narrative Writing" on pages 130–131 to help guide their writing.

 Literature Connections

Mentor texts: Many grade-level appropriate autobiographies can inspire your students:

Finding My Hat by John Son

Chinese Cinderella by Adeline Yen Mah

Knots in My Yo-Yo String by Jerri Spinelli

The Circuit by Francisco Jiménez

Students might also enjoy these excellent biographies:

The Life and Death of Crazy Horse by Russell Freedman

Gandhi, Great Soul by John Severence

Helen Keller: Rebellious Spirit by Laurie Lawlor

Struggling Learners

The fourth item in the "Keys to Effective Writing" checklist instructs students to add memory and sensory details that bring their experience to life.

• Suggest that students use the phone or e-mail to contact family and friends who can assist them in remembering details that will enhance their phase autobiographies.

• Provide photocopies of the reproducible sensory chart on TE page 793 for students to use for note taking during phone conversations and for sorting details from e-mail.

Writing Getting the Big Picture

After students organize their details, check each student's list to make sure that he or she has gathered enough details and arranged them in the proper sequence.

Remind students to use vivid words (including some with strong connotations) while writing their drafts. Assure them, however, that they will have a chance to add more vivid words when they revise.

Technology Connections

The government study *Writing Next* identifies computer use as one of the eleven strategies demonstrated to improve student writing performance. The most obvious way to use a computer for writing is to work on a word processor.

In addition to providing help with drafting narratives, word processors encourage revision because students do not have to recopy their work. Also, using the "Track Changes" feature lets students show their revisions, send drafts to peers for review and response, and keep a record of their various versions.

If your students have access to computers, consider having them use the computers to draft their narratives. You will be helping them not only with traditional literacy but with computer literacy as well.

108

Writing Getting the Big Picture

The chart below shows how the parts of a phase autobiography fit together. (The examples are from the essay on pages 109–112.) You're ready to write once you've . . .

● collected plenty of details about the experience and
● organized the details chronologically.

Beginning

The **beginning** gives background information and focuses on the phase.

> **Opening Sentences**
> I was never interested in joining any group or sport during the summer. . . . so I decided to give it a try. It was the best decision I've ever made.

Middle

The **middle** part uses a variety of details to show how the writer felt during the extended period of time.

> I will never forget my first day of practice . . .
>
> Many times during those first weeks, . . .
>
> The best part of that summer was our tattoo in Windsor, Canada.

Ending

The **ending** explains the importance of this time in the writer's life.

> **Closing Sentences**
> After last summer, I am not the same Julie Patterson anymore. . . . I am a confident, outgoing person who enjoys working with others.

English Language Learners

As students work on organizing details chronologically, have them use a Step Organizer like the one they created while working on PE page 105. Suggest that they use this organizer to map out the details for the middle of their autobiographies.

Starting Your Phase Autobiography

Now that you've selected a topic and gathered details, you are ready to begin writing. In the opening, you need to do three things.

- Grab the attention of your reader.
- Include necessary background information.
- State the topic or phase that you will write about.

Beginning Paragraph

> The writer sets the scene and introduces the phase she plans to write about.

I was never interested in joining any group or sport during the summer. I figured I got plenty of that during the school year. Besides, I liked being free to hang out with my friends and do some odd jobs to earn a little spending money. But then last summer, I saw a flyer for the Warrentown Junior Drum and Bugle Corps. I knew they were a very good group and got to travel a lot, so I decided to give it a try. It was the best decision I've ever made.

Using Transitions

Transitions help you move your reader smoothly through time. You should choose transitions that sound natural in your writing. Below is a chart of transitions that you can use to show time and make your sentences read smoothly. For a chart of other transitions, see pages **572–573**.

Transition Words and Phrases				
about	but	now	this time	usually
as soon as	during	recently	today	when
before	later	so far	until	whenever
besides	next	then	until now	while

Write your beginning. On your own paper, write the beginning of your phase autobiography. Use transitions to connect your ideas.

NARRATIVE

Writing Starting Your Phase Autobiography

When each student has finished writing a beginning paragraph, make sure that she or he has clearly identified the phase that will be the focus of the essay. One effective strategy is to tell how the phase began: I never used to _____, but then I _____.

Another strategy would be to pose a question. For example:
- Do you remember the first time that you _____?
- Have you ever _____?
- Who can forget their _____?

Writing Using Transitions

When students use transitions, encourage them to read aloud that part to make sure that their transitions are smooth and that they have used the correct words and phrases to connect ideas.

✳ Additional information about using transitions is on PE pages 572–573.

Advanced Learners

Ask students to design a chart of transition words that can be used to show time order. It can resemble a time line or timepiece.

✳ Refer students to PE page 572 for a word list.

Display their charts in the classroom.

Writing
Developing the Middle Part

Have students identify the sensory details, words with feeling, and dialogue in the model.

Some of the sensory details include the following:

- nervously tapped
- looked like one of those army drill sergeants
- his voice
- I shivered
- paced back and forth
- his shadow stopped
- went crazy
- standing ovation

Words with feeling include these:

- ordered
- nervously
- exploded
- barked
- almost choking
- shaking my confidence
- dominated

Writing Developing the Middle Part

Now that you have your reader's attention, it's time to add the details that will make the middle of your writing come to life. Stay focused on the most important and interesting information about the extended period of time. Use the tips below to maintain your reader's interest.

- **Use sensory details to add interest.**
- **Choose words with feeling to help create an appropriate tone.** (See page 106.)
- **Use some dialogue.**

Middle Paragraphs

The writer tells about key events related to this period of time.

I will never forget my first day of practice with the drum and bugle corps. The director, Mr. DeRusha, stepped onto the football field and ordered us all to sit along the 50-yard line. I nervously tapped the keys of my trumpet. I'd heard that Mr. D. had a reputation for being tough. He looked like one of those army drill sergeants on TV. He was tall and had a fresh crew cut, and when his voice exploded through the bullhorn, I shivered, even though it was almost 70 degrees outside.

Dialogue is used to show the personality of an important person.

"Listen up, people!" he barked. "Welcome to the Warrentown Junior Drum and Bugle Corps. Being in a drum and bugle corps means you are alert and prepared at all times. Is that understood?"

He paced back and forth in front of us. "By the end of the summer, you will learn to respect this organization, yourselves, and each other." Then his shadow stopped over me. He must have read my name tag.

The writer shows her feelings about the experience.

I couldn't even look up when I heard him call my name and tell me to polish my horn.

"Yes, sir, " I answered, almost choking on the words. Many times during those first weeks, when the demands of practice were shaking my confidence, I thought about quitting. That's when Mr. D. came along and announced, "Miss Patterson, you add a spark to this trumpet section. Good job." Sometimes I wondered if Mr. D. could read minds. He always seemed to know just who needed to hear encouraging words.

Strong sensory details help the reader see and feel the experience.

The best part of that summer was our tattoo in Windsor, Canada. A tattoo is a type of nighttime marching competition. We were competing for an international trophy. Just before our performance, Mr. D. huddled with us like a football coach.

"You are the finest band here tonight," he said. "You know it. I know it. Now go out there and make sure everyone else knows it!"

"Yes, sir!" we shouted.

Marching in a strong, straight line, we were a band with a mission. The explosions of applause we heard during our performance propelled us to hit clearer notes and create sharper steps. We had never sounded so good. At the end, the audience went crazy and rewarded us with a standing ovation. We did it. We dominated the competition and came home with a trophy.

NARRATIVE

Write **Write your middle paragraphs.** Before you begin, review the drafting tips on page 110. Then use your "Specific Details Chart" (page 105) to write the middle part of your essay.

Continue to analyze the model by looking at the dialogue. Point out the following pieces of dialogue:

- "Listen up, people!"
- "Yes, sir," I answered, almost choking on the words.
- "Miss Patterson, you add a spark to this trumpet section. Good job."
- "You are the finest band here tonight," he said. "You know it. I know it. Now go out there and make sure everyone else knows it!"

Discuss what these examples reveal about the speakers and convey to the reader. Ask students to consider why this dialogue was added.

Writer's Craft

Plot line: Fiction writers routinely shape their stories according to a plot line, but this form can also be used to shape nonfiction narratives.

The **beginning** establishes the people and setting.

The **rising action** provides conflict through a series of events.

The **high point** is the moment when the conflict is strongest.

The **ending** tells what happens after the high point.

Writing
Ending Your Phase Autobiography

As students write their ending, remind them of the following:

- A concluding paragraph should do more than repeat what the writer has already said.
- A concluding paragraph should add some new insight that sums up how the time changed the writer.
- The personal change does not have to be a major turning point in the writer's life; the change can simply be that the writer sees things in a different light.

After students finish their first draft, have them review their planning charts (PE page 105) to see whether they omitted any important details. Tell them to highlight the details that they would like to include when they revise their essays.

112

Writing Ending Your Phase Autobiography

The ending explains the importance of the period of time covered in the essay. Your ending should be thoughtful and should come soon after the most important part of your story. Below are several different ideas for endings.

- ### Coming Full Circle
  You can "come full circle" if you include the same key idea in both the beginning and the ending. This approach could have been used in this phase autobiography.

  Key Idea in the Beginning
  I snapped to attention when the band director hurried onto the marching field, barking orders.

  Key Idea in the Ending
  Now, three months later, I still snap to attention whenever Mr. D. barks orders, but I do it because I respect him, not because I'm afraid of him.

- ### Explaining Your Change
  The writer of the essay about the marching band chose to explain how she had changed. (See the model below.)

Ending Paragraph

> *I still get goose bumps when I think about the band. Mr. DeRusha is a great director who taught me about discipline and respect. After last summer, I am not the same Julie Patterson anymore. I now look forward to summer and being with the band. More importantly, I am a confident, outgoing person who enjoys working with others.*

The writer tells how she changed.

Write your ending. Complete your phase autobiography by writing the final paragraph. You may want to use one of the above ways to end your essay.

Form a complete first draft. Put together a complete first draft. Then move on to the revising process.

Struggling Learners

Provide support for students who are struggling to write an ending.

- Invite any student who is having trouble writing an ending to meet with you.
- Ask the student to explain the change that he or she experienced because of this extended period of time.
- Then, together, decide on the best way to shape an effective ending that focuses on this change. (You may suggest that students start the ending paragraph with "I still . . . ," as in the sample ending.)

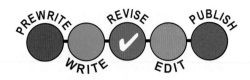

113
Writing a Phase Autobiography

Revising

You've worked hard while writing your first draft. During the next step in the writing process, you'll have the chance to go back and improve it. By adding, deleting, or moving parts, you will make your writing even better.

Keys to Effective Revising

1. Set your writing aside for a while so you'll have a fresh perspective as you begin to revise.

2. Read your writing out loud to see how well your beginning, middle, and ending work.

3. Mark any spots that seem confusing or incomplete.

4. Listen to your writer's voice, making sure it sounds like you.

5. Check your words and sentences.

6. Use the editing and proofreading marks inside the back cover of this book.

NARRATIVE

Revising

Keys to Effective Revising

"Keys to Effective Revising" (*see below*) explains the process students will be guided through on PE pages 114–124.

Point out that in addition to checking for organization, reading aloud your writing is also an effective way to revise for voice.

- Students can read aloud their essay to a classmate. The listener focuses only on the voice, to make sure it is believable.
- Students can check their partner's writing to make sure the dialogue sounds authentic and helps make the story come alive for the reader.
- Students can check for voice by tape-recording their own essays, so they can listen to the language and tone themselves.

Peer Responding

In addition to reading their essays out loud, students should ask a trusted peer to read and respond to their work. Peer response is crucial for helping students understand their strengths and weaknesses—and know which of the following revision lessons can help improve their writing. (See "Peer Responding" on pages 29–32 for more information.)

Teaching Tip: Revising

Many students are reluctant to make changes to their writing. Once they have completed an assignment, they often feel that the writing is set in stone and find it difficult to think about the writing in other ways. Emphasize the importance of revising:

- Tell students that famous writers spend as much time revising their work as they do writing it.

- Stress that making changes to a piece of writing does not mean that someone is a weak writer.
- Explain that revising is actually a sign that the writer cares about producing a strong piece of writing.

Explain that moving sentences and whole paragraphs around becomes routine as you become more comfortable with revising.

Revising for Ideas

The rubric strips that run across the revising pages (PE pages 114–123) are provided to help students focus their revising and are related to the full rubric on PE pages 130–131.

Stress that each detail in the student's phase autobiography should be related to the point they are trying to make. As an example, explain that it would not have been effective for the writer of the model on PE pages 110–111 to add details about Windsor, Canada, because that would not have helped to explain the effect that being in the drum and bugle corps had on her.

 Answers

1. sensory
2. memory
3. reflective
4. sensory
5. sensory
6. memory
7. reflective
8. reflective
9. memory
10. sensory

114

Revising for Ideas

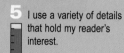

6 My writing includes great details that totally engage the reader.

5 I use a variety of details that hold my reader's interest.

4 I use a variety of details, but they are not the most interesting ones.

When you revise for *ideas*, check for a variety of details and make sure those details add interest to your writing. Use the rubric strip above to guide you through your revisions.

Do I include the right kinds of details?

As you write about a phase in your life, you need to become aware of what you felt and thought. Three kinds of details help you recall and reflect on a past time in your life.

- **Sensory details** allow your reader to use his or her senses to see, hear, smell, taste, or touch what you experienced.
- **Memory details** bring your past experiences to life for the reader.
- **Reflective details** allow your reader to know what you wonder about, hope for, or wish.

 Identify each type of detail below. Tell if it is a sensory, memory, or reflective detail.

1. Jagged bluffs . . .
2. We packed the van and . . .
3. What if . . .
4. Tires squealed as . . .
5. Blackened embers . . .
6. The announcer introduced . . .
7. My favorite picture book reminds . . .
8. Maybe someday I'll . . .
9. Last Sunday, our dog . . .
10. Noxious fumes polluted . . .

 Check your details. Read through your first draft. Label details with either "S" for sensory, "M" for memory, or "R" for reflective to make sure your writing has a variety of details.

Struggling Learners

Encourage students to read aloud or e-mail their first draft to a person who was present during the time period represented in the phase autobiography.

- Have each student request feedback from this person, verifying the accuracy of the details and supplying any new ones that might have been overlooked.
- As an alternative, have students retell to a partner or a teacher the phase they have written about. Then have the listener read the narrative to see if any details were left out.

3 I need to use details that are more varied and interesting.

2 I need to use more details.

1 I need to collect details about my topic.

How do I know if my ideas interest my audience?

One way to find out if your writing interests classmates is to share your first draft with them. The following tips can help you organize a small group to discuss your work. (See also pages **420–421**.)

Group Discussion Tips

1. Provide a copy of your work to two to five classmates.
2. Allow them to read your work before you meet.
3. Ask for title suggestions, which can start the conversation and show whether readers understand the main point of the narrative.
4. Ask group members what they feel or think about different points in the narrative.
5. Ask what could be improved, added, or cut.

Revise

Meet with peers. Gather a small group of classmates and share your work with them. Follow the tips above. (See also pages **29–32**.) Make changes to improve your narrative.

Ideas
A variety of details adds interest.

... *means you are alert and prepared at all times.*

Is that understood?"
                    paced back and forth
   He walked out in front of us. "By the end of the
                  ^
summer, you will learn to respect this organization,

yourselves, and each other." Then his shadow
              He must have read my name tag.
stopped over me.
                  ^

NARRATIVE

Give students 15 minutes to carefully read a classmate's essay and respond to it. Although 15 minutes may sound like a long time, it takes most students at least that long to really absorb what they are reading and come up with helpful tips to improve the writing.

- Have students write down their suggestions as they read, so that they will remember their ideas.
- Remind them to be respectful and constructive when evaluating a peer's writing.

Struggling Learners

To help discussion groups maintain their focus, provide a peer response form. Include the following prompts, and provide space for written responses:

1. Your name:
2. Name of author:
3. Brief summary:
4. Title suggestions:
5. Main point of the narrative:
6. Examples of types of details (sensory, memory, reflective):
7. Something that you liked about the phase auto-biography:
8. Something that could be improved:
9. Something that could be added:
10. Something that could be cut:

Revising for Organization

Some students are hesitant to develop meaningful dialogue because they are unsure of the mechanics involved. These students will benefit from a review of punctuating **dialogue** (*see below*).

116

Revising for Organization

6 The way that my phase autobiography is put together makes it a joy to read.

5 My organization is easy to understand, and I use dialogue.

4 My organization works well, but I need to use dialogue better.

When you revise for *organization*, consider using dialogue to develop your narrative. Also check your beginning, middle, and ending. Use the rubric strip above to guide you.

How can dialogue help me develop my narrative?

Dialogue lets you show what people in your story say. There are two ways to write dialogue.

■ **Direct Dialogue**

Direct dialogue lets you show the exact words of a person. Use direct dialogue when the things a person says reveal an idea very clearly or show something about the person.

> My little brother Jake looked up at me. "When I'm 14, I'll boss you around."
> "When you're 14," I said, "I'll be 22."
> He shook his head sadly. "All right, I'll wait till I'm 23."

■ **Summarized Dialogue**

Summarized dialogue allows you to *tell* what the speaker says. Use summarized dialogue when you want to keep the action moving, rather than show the speaker's actual words.

> I corrected Jake again, telling him I would be 30 when he was 23. He was persistent, upping the age to 31, then 39, and on until I was 111 years old. I told him I probably wouldn't last that long.

 Revise

Check your quotations. Find places where dialogue could help you develop your autobiography. (See page 556 for tips on punctuating dialogue.)

Teaching Tip: Dialogue

To help students with punctuating dialogue, provide these tips:

● Quotation marks always begin and end the dialogue.
● Place periods and commas inside quotation marks.
● Place an exclamation point or a question mark inside the quotation marks when it is part of the quotation. Place it outside the quotation marks when it punctuates the main sentence.
● Place semicolons and colons outside the quotation marks.
● A comma always sets off the speaker's tag (the phrase identifying the speaker) from the quotation, as in the following sentence: Juan says, "Maria belted out her favorite songs while walking to school."
● When a quotation is broken into two parts, commas are often used to set off the speaker's tag in the middle, as in the following sentence: "Why don't you try out for basketball," Willie asked, "since you've played all of your life?"

tell share remember
relate **narrate**
Writing a Phase Autobiography **117**

3 My beginning, middle, or ending needs work. I did not use dialogue.

2 I do not have a beginning, a middle, and an ending.

1 I need to learn how to organize my paper.

Do my beginning, middle, and ending work well?

You will know if your phase autobiography is organized well after you answer the following questions.

1. Does my beginning introduce a phase of my life and grab my reader's attention?
2. Have I presented the middle in chronological order?
3. What time transitions have I used? (See page 109.)
4. In the ending, do I tell the reader how my life changed because of this phase?

 Revise **Check the parts of your phase autobiography.** Read through each part of your essay, while answering the questions above. Make needed changes.

Organization
Direct and summarized dialogue improve the autobiography.

when I heard him call my name and tell
I couldn't even look up. ~~"Miss Patterson. It is~~
me to polish my horn.
~~an important rule here at the Warrentown Junior~~

~~Drum and Bugle Corps for everyone to clean his~~

~~or her trumpet!"~~
"Yes, sir," I answered, almost choking on the words.
~~I mumbled that I understood what he said.~~

Many times during those first weeks, when

the demands of practice were shaking my

confidence, I thought about quitting. . . .

NARRATIVE

Students can have difficulty recognizing weaknesses in their own writing, so having peers evaluate each other's work during the revision process can be helpful.

To initiate peer evaluation, have pairs of students assess each other's first draft using the four questions on PE page 117 as a guide.

 Writer's Craft

Suspension of disbelief: Fiction writers often talk about the reader having a "willing suspension of disbelief." This means that readers willingly look past the words on the page to experience the events the writer describes.

Therefore, the **beginning** of a narrative (whether fictional or factual) should invite readers to suspend their disbelief and spend time experiencing the events.

The **middle** should use sensory details and dialogue to let the reader experience the events. The writer is creating a verbal web that keeps the reader suspended.

The **ending** should gently transition the reader from the narrative back into "real life."

When revising the beginning, middle, and ending, students should try to create narratives that invite readers in, keep their attention, and leave them with something to think about.

English Language Learners

Ask students to use a highlighter to mark any transition words they have included in their writing. If transition words are sparse or missing, help students see where they could be added to make the writing smoother.

✻ Refer students to PE pages 572–573 for a list of transition words.

Revising for Voice

Writing in the active voice is usually preferable to using the passive voice, because an active verb is more forceful than a passive verb. Some students may be unsure of the difference between **active and passive voice** (*see below*).

 Answers

1. Due to severe storms, officials canceled the film festival at the community center.
2. My parents, who had planned an all-day party, told my sisters and me the news.
3. My parents made an alternative plan for a "Davis Family Film Festival."
4. Dad pulled out of storage old videos from the time we all were kids.
5. Everyone enjoyed movies such as *Aladdin* and *The Iron Giant*, and we ate massive quantities of popcorn.

118

Revising for Voice

6 The voice and tone in my autobiography perfectly capture this special time in my life.

5 My voice is active, and my tone matches my experience.

4 My voice is active. At times my tone doesn't match my experience.

When you revise for *voice*, check to see that you have used an active voice in most of your writing and that the tone of your voice fits the experience. Use the rubric strip above to guide you through your revision.

Have I used an active voice?

You have used an active voice if the subject in a sentence is doing the action. See the examples below. Active voice adds energy and clarity. (See **726.1**.)

> **Passive Voice**
>
> **The tornado was photographed by a student.**
> (The subject *tornado* is not doing the action.)
>
> **Active Voice**
>
> **A student photographed the tornado.**
> (The subject *student* is doing the action.)

 Rewrite each of the following sentences, changing the passive voice to active voice.

1. Due to severe storms the film festival at the community center was canceled by officials.
2. My sisters and I were told the news by our parents, who had planned an all-day party.
3. An alternative plan for a "Davis Family Film Festival" was made by my parents.
4. Old videos from the time we all were kids were pulled out of storage by Dad.
5. Movies such as *Aladdin* and *The Iron Giant* were enjoyed by everyone, and popcorn was eaten by us in mass quantities.

 Check for active voice. Check your sentences to be sure that most of your subjects are doing the action. Rewrite sentences as needed.

3 I need to change my passive voice in some sentences. My tone doesn't match my experience.

2 My voice is passive. My tone doesn't match my experience.

1 I need to find out how to write with an active voice.

NARRATIVE

Does my tone match my experience?

Your tone matches your experience if it reveals your attitude about your topic. It's important that your details "show" your reader how you feel.

 Read the following paragraphs. What is the tone of the writer? What details create that tone?

> Having never traveled in the mountains, I tightly close my eyes while the bus chugs up the steep, narrow mountain road. Silently, I pray we don't meet another vehicle coming down the road. The passengers' "ooh's" and "aah's" accompany each bend. After what seems like eternity, the wheels stop and, instinctively, my eyes open.
>
> "We've made it," I say to myself.
>
> Stepping off the bus, the cool air welcomes me. Now I see why everyone is so excited. Towering, snowcapped mountains surround a Cinderella-type castle. I take a deep breath. This view was worth the ride.

Check the tone of your voice. As you read through your writing, think of the attitude you want to reveal. Include details that reflect that attitude.

Voice
A silly phrase is deleted because it doesn't fit the tone.

> The best part of that summer was our tattoo in Windsor, Canada. A tattoo, ~~not the kind that you get on your body,~~ is a type of nighttime marching competition. We were . . .

Again, have pairs of students work in small groups to discuss the tone of their essays. As they read each other's essays, they should focus only on tone. Encourage students to suggest more-vivid words that could express the writer's feelings toward his or her subject.

 Answers

The tone changes from nervous apprehension to relief and awe. The following words reveal the tone:

- tightly close
- I pray
- After what seems like eternity
- cool air welcomes
- Towering . . . mountains surround
- deep breath

Revising for Word Choice

To help students identify places to use more specific words, have them

- use a colored pencil to mark all the general nouns in their essay,
- use a different color to mark all the general verbs,
- use a third color for the general adjectives.

Students may benefit from working on word choice with partners. Tell partners to offer suggestions for replacing general words with more specific ones. Refer them to PE page 41 for a review of word choice.

 **Answers**

Answers will vary.

120

Revising **for** Word Choice

6 The word choice in my autobiography perfectly captures the action for the reader.

5 I use specific nouns. My words create an appropriate tone.

4 My writing contains specific words. I need to change some words to improve the tone.

When you revise for *word choice,* be sure you have used specific nouns, verbs, and adjectives. Also be sure you have chosen words with feeling to create an appropriate tone. Use the rubric strip above to guide your revision.

Have I used specific words?

Specific words present clear details for your reader. The chart below shows how a writer could make a general noun, verb, or adjective more specific.

Nouns		Verbs		Adjectives	
General	*Specific*	*General*	*Specific*	*General*	*Specific*
teacher	instructor coach professor	**tell**	narrate report relate	**good**	well-behaved obedient mannerly
park	square woods commons	**walk**	march stroll plod	**different**	distinct unique unusual

 Do this activity with a partner:

1. Write a sentence that has several nouns, verbs, or adjectives and give it to your partner.
2. Let your partner choose one to three general nouns, verbs, or adjectives in your sentence and make them more specific.
3. See if you can make another round of changes on the same words.
4. Repeat the process, using a sentence your partner wrote.
5. Discuss how these specific words improved the sentences.

 Check for specific words. Look at your nouns, verbs, and adjectives. Have you chosen specific words to make your ideas clear and to match your tone? If not, replace your general words with specific ones.

tell share remember
narrate
relate   **121**
Writing a Phase Autobiography

| **3** I need to choose a few more specific words. I need to develop a tone. | **2** Most of my words are general. I need to develop a tone. | **1** I need to learn more about specific words and developing a tone. |

How can word choice help me develop the tone?

Words that show a specific feeling can help you control the tone of your writing. By changing some neutral words to words with stronger connotations, you can create a more effective tone.

 Read the following sentences. In each, replace the neutral underlined word to create the tone indicated in parentheses.

1. I <u>sat</u> in my seat and waited for the test. *(nervous)*
2. After my name was called, I <u>walked</u> across the room. *(angry)*
3. My friend spent the whole lunch hour <u>talking</u>. *(bored)*
4. Down the alley <u>came</u> a dog. *(fearful)*
5. I walked down a(n) <u>group</u> of hallways. *(confused)*

 Check connotations. **Read through your autobiography, noting words that could be replaced to create a stronger tone. Make changes where appropriate.**

NARRATIVE

Word Choice
Specific words with feeling create a stronger tone.

~~Walking~~ *Marching* in a strong, straight line, we were ~~a big~~ *a band with a mission.*
~~group of people.~~ The ~~sound~~ *explosions* of applause we heard
during our performance ~~made us~~ *propelled to* hit ~~right~~ *clearer* notes and
~~make better~~ *create sharper* steps. We had never sounded so good.

At the end, the audience went crazy and rewarded
us with a standing ovation. We did it.

Before students revise their own writing, review the revisions to the sample essay as a class. Have students speculate on why each change was made.

 Answers

Possible answers:
1. squirmed
2. stormed
3. chattering
4. slunk
5. maze

Writer's Craft

Word choice: English is one of the most expressive languages on the planet because of the vast number of words in it. Traditional estimates of English vocabulary indicate that it contains more than 500,000 words, compared to German (about 185,000) and French (fewer than 100,000).

As a result, in English, a person can *walk, saunter, trot, lope, slink, steal, march, meander, toddle, waddle, shamble, creep, amble, stomp, wander, stroll,* or even *perambulate.* These words have their own colors, sounds, and shapes, and using them strongly affects the tone of a passage. Encourage your students to experiment with word choice, and applaud them when they find (*discover, unearth, capture, nab, scare up*) just the right word.

Revising for Sentence Fluency

Although sentence expanding and sentence combining can improve fluency, students should not aim to eliminate every short sentence.

- Too many long sentences can make for a cumbersome style.
- The ideal writing style mixes simple sentences with complex and compound sentences.

 Answers

Possible answers:

1. Miss Phram, our soccer coach, contacts the radio station.
2. The program manager speaks with her about placing an ad on the station.
3. Tomorrow, Jordan, captain of the basketball team, will speak to our class.
4. When we arrived, Maurice, my cousin, was waiting for us.
5. Maly watches the eagle soar from the mountain peak.

122

Revising for Sentence Fluency

 6 The style of my sentences perfectly captures my thoughts and feelings about this critical time in my life.

5 I have combined and expanded sentences to make them flow smoothly.

 4 I have combined sentences to make them flow smoothly, but I need to expand some sentences with details.

When you revise for *sentence fluency,* check that you have expanded and combined short, choppy sentences. Use the rubric strip above and the suggestions below as you revise your sentences.

How can sentence expanding improve my writing?

Sentence expanding lets you add important information to basic sentences. One way is to add an *appositive.* An appositive is a word, phrase, or clause that follows a noun or pronoun and renames it.

Another way is to add a prepositional phrase. A *prepositional phrase* is a group of words that begins with a preposition, includes an object of the preposition, and functions as an adjective or adverb. See the samples below. (See also page 519.)

Basic Sentence	Expanded Sentences
Mr. Nelson took me fishing.	Mr. Nelson, **my neighbor,** took me fishing. (An appositive is added.)
We caught five bass.	**In less than an hour,** we caught five bass. (A prepositional phrase is added.)

 Expand the following sentences by adding the type of phrase asked for in the parentheses.

1. Miss Phram contacts the radio station. *(appositive phrase)*
2. The program manager speaks with her. *(prepositional phrase)*
3. Tomorrow Jordan will speak to our class. *(appositive phrase)*
4. When we arrived, Maurice was waiting for us. *(appositive phrase)*
5. Maly watches the eagle soar. *(prepositional phrase)*

 Check your sentences. Skim your writing for short, choppy sentences. Try expanding some of them by using appositive or prepositional phrases.

Teaching Tip: Noun Phrases

A noun phrase consists of a noun and any associated modifiers. The noun phrase can act as an adjective. Point out that an appositive is often a noun phrase.

English Language Learners

To help students see whether they have too many short, choppy sentences, ask them to highlight or star simple sentences in one color. Then ask them to highlight or star complex and compound sentences in another color. This color coding should make it obvious whether they need a wider variety of sentence types.

tell share remember
relate **narrate** **123**
Writing a Phase Autobiography

3 I need to combine and expand more of my sentences.

2 I need to combine or expand most of my sentences.

1 Most of my sentences need to be rewritten.

NARRATIVE

How can sentence combining improve my writing?

Sentence combining lets you eliminate short, choppy sentences and improve sentence style. The examples below show sentence combining using an infinitive phrase ("to" followed by a verb) or a participial phrase (a phrase beginning with an *ing* or *ed* word and functioning as an adjective). (See also page **520**.)

Short Sentences	Combined (Infinitive Phrase)
The kids yelled, waved, and jumped. They would attract a crowd.	The kids yelled, waved, and jumped to attract a crowd.

Short Sentences	Combined (Participial Phrase)
The siren blared. It signaled that a tornado was approaching.	Blaring loudly, the siren signaled that a tornado was approaching.

Revise

Combine shorter sentences. Skim your writing, looking for short, choppy sentences. See if you can combine any of them with either an infinitive or a participial phrase.

Sentence Fluency
Prepositional phrases expand short, choppy sentences.

At the end, the audience went crazy and rewarded
with a standing ovation
us. We did it. We dominated the competition and
∧   with a trophy
came home.
∧

Explain that an infinitive phrase consists of an infinitive plus any modifiers it may have. Below are examples of sentences with infinitive phrases:

- I have *to take a science test.*
- Naomi wants *to leave.*
- We try *to help my brother*, but we don't always succeed.

Remind your class that a present participle ends in *-ing*, while a past participle ends in *-ed, -d, -t, -en,* or *-n.* Write the following sentences on the board, and ask students to identify the present participles and the past participles:

- Stopping at his locker, John noticed a mouse race across the hallway floor.
- Tonya collapsed onto the bench, cleverly positioned to save runners time, and took a long drink of water.
- Maria, looking well rested after sleeping for ten hours, was ready for a full day at school.

English Language Learners

Students will need a lot of guided practice with using different types of phrases. Display some examples of appositives, prepositional phrases, infinitive phrases, and participial phrases on a chart. Help students find one example of each type of phrase in the sample paragraphs on PE pages 110–111.

Struggling Learners

After students have revised for sentence fluency, suggest that they exchange papers with a partner. Tell the author to listen for awkward or choppy wording while the partner reads aloud the essay.

Revising Using a Checklist

Make sure that students have completed all of the activities on PE pages 114–123 before they use the checklist.

Point out that presentation is an important final step in the development of a piece of writing. Then review the features of clean copy:

- Use an easy-to-read font (word processing) or neat handwriting.
- Write your name in the upper left-hand corner.
- Skip a line and center your title.
- Skip another line and start your writing.
- Double-space the text.
- Keep a one-inch margin on all four sides.
- Indent the first line of each paragraph.
- Write your last name and the page number in the upper right-hand corner of every page after the first one.

Revising Using a Checklist

 Check your revising. On a piece of paper, write the numbers 1 to 12. If you can answer "yes" to a question, put a check mark after that number. If not, continue to work with that part of your essay.

Ideas

_____ **1.** Do I tell about one phase of my life?
_____ **2.** Do I include a variety of details?
_____ **3.** Do my ideas interest my audience?

Organization

_____ **4.** Do I use dialogue effectively?
_____ **5.** Have I checked my beginning, middle, and ending?
_____ **6.** Do I use transitions effectively?

Voice

_____ **7.** Have I used an active voice?
_____ **8.** Does my tone match my experience?

Word Choice

_____ **9.** Do I use specific words?
_____ **10.** Do I use words with feeling?

Sentence Fluency

_____ **11.** Do I expand short sentences with details?
_____ **12.** Do I combine choppy sentences?

 Make a clean copy. When you've finished revising your essay, make a clean copy before you begin to edit.

Grammar Connection

Active vs. Passive Voice
- **Proofreader's Guide** pages 726–727

Transitive and Intransitive Verbs
- **Proofreader's Guide** pages 728–729
- *Write Source* page 484
- *SkillsBook* pages 159–160
- **CD** Verbs—2

Participles, Infinitives
- **Proofreader's Guide** pages 730–731
- *Write Source* pages 485, 520
- *SkillsBook* pages 161–162
- **CD** Verbs—3

Prepositional Phrases
- **Proofreader's Guide** pages 742–743
- *Write Source* page 519
- *SkillsBook* pages 175–176
- **CD** Prepositions

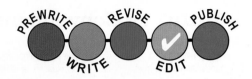

tell share remember **narrate** relate
Writing a Phase Autobiography **125**

Editing

After you have finished revising your writing, it's time to edit your work for conventions: punctuation, capitalization, spelling, and grammar.

Keys to Effective Editing

1. Use a dictionary, a thesaurus, and the "Proofreader's Guide" in the back of this book.

2. Check for any words or phrases that may be confusing to the reader.

3. Check your writing for correctness of punctuation, capitalization, spelling, and grammar.

4. Edit on a printed computer copy and then enter your changes on the computer.

5. Use the editing and proofreading marks inside the back cover of this book.

NARRATIVE

Editing Keys to Effective Editing

"Keys to Effective Editing" explains the process students will be guided through on PE pages 126–128.

Emphasize to students the importance of editing a hard copy of their essay.

- Warn students that a word-processing program will pick up words that do not exist, but it will not correct usage errors. For example, it won't highlight the incorrect use of *there, their,* and *they're.*

- Because computers miss many mistakes, students should not rely on a spell-check program to catch every error.

Editing for Conventions

Subject-verb agreement *(see below)* is not always clear-cut. Students may be unsure whether a certain indefinite pronoun should take a singular or plural verb. The following indefinite pronouns are singular and therefore take a singular verb:

- each
- no one
- everyone
- anyone
- someone
- anybody
- somebody
- everybody

The following pronouns are plural and thus take a plural verb:

- both
- several
- few
- many

 **Answers**

Sentences will vary, but verbs should agree with their subjects:

1. The semi driver arranges
2. Voters read
3. They collect
4. Maurice blinks
5. Lights fade

126

Editing for Conventions

6 My grammar and punctuation are correct, and the copy is free of spelling errors.

5 I have a few minor errors in punctuation, spelling, or grammar, but they won't confuse the reader.

4 I have some errors in punctuation, spelling, or grammar that may distract the reader.

When you edit for *conventions*, you check spelling, grammar, capitalization, and punctuation. The rubric strip above will help you with your editing.

How can I check for subject-verb agreement?

As you check for subject-verb agreement, you need to remember that subjects and verbs must always agree in number. That means if the subject is singular, the verb must be singular; and if the subject is plural, the verb must be plural. (See pages **508–509**.)

> Don't forget that most nouns ending in *s* or *es* are plural, and most verbs ending in *s* are singular.

Singular Subject-Verb Agreement

Beth volunteers at the city's food pantry.

Plural Subject-Verb Agreement

Her friends volunteer at the city's park department.

 Choose a verb for each subject, making sure the two agree in number. Then write a complete sentence for each subject-verb pair. Finally, label each subject-verb pair as singular or plural.

	Subjects	Verbs	
1.	The semi driver	take	arranges
2.	Voters	draws	read
3.	They	collect	is
4.	Maurice	receive	blinks
5.	Lights	glows	fade

 Check your subject–verb agreement. Make sure that your subjects agree with the verbs in each of your sentences. Make any necessary corrections.

Teaching Tip: Subject-Verb Agreement

Because subject-verb agreement can cause so much confusion, remind students to focus on the subject. For example, when a prepositional phrase containing a plural noun follows a singular subject, the subject remains singular, as does the verb. Example: The *movie* about the three musicians *was* fascinating.

The following words may be singular or plural, depending on the meaning of the sentence: *most, all, none, some,* and *any.* Examples:

- *All* of the food *was* stale.
- *All* of the bananas *were* rotten.
- *Most* of the movie *was* scary.
- *Most* of the movies *were* sold out.

English Language Learners

To help students check for subject-verb agreement, underline the subject (with one line) and verbs (with two lines) in the sentences in their phase autobiographies. Then, with your help, ask students to label each subject and verb as singular (S) or plural (P). Together, correct any subject-verb errors that you find.

tell share remember
narrate
relate
Writing a Phase Autobiography   **127**

3 I need to correct the errors because they confuse the reader.

2 I need to correct many errors that make my phase autobiography hard to read.

1 I need help making corrections.

Do my verbs agree with their compound subjects?

To check your subject-verb agreement with compound subjects, you need to remember the following rules.

- If the compound subject uses *and* as a connector, use a plural verb.
  Lia and Ramon carry **the school's banner in the Memorial Day parade.**

- If the compound subject uses *or* or *nor* as a connector, the verb must agree with the subject closest to it.
  Either band members or Mr. Kurz needs **to collect the flags.**

 Read each of the following sentences. Write "A" if the subject and verb agree in number. If they don't agree, rewrite the sentence.

1. Terry and Jose wants to study German.
2. Neither Colby nor Ramon sings in the chorus.
3. Every weekend, Jason and Leela volunteer at the animal shelter.
4. Their older brother and sister works at the grocery store.
5. After the race, Jodie or Chantell congratulate the winner.
6. Neither the flowers nor the cats triggers Alex's allergies.
7. The music and video games echo through the halls.
8. Every Sunday, Ling and Jules meets at the bowling alley.

 Check your compound subjects. Make sure your compound subjects agree in number with their verbs.

Conventions Subject-verb agreement errors are corrected.	*get* I still ~~gets~~ goose bumps when I ~~thinks~~ *think* about the band. Mr. DeRusha is a great director who . . .

NARRATIVE

There are several cases in which subject-verb agreement can be a challenge. Discuss these cases, one at a time.

- The name of an organization or a country takes a singular verb, even when it has a plural form. Example: The Girl Scouts of America *is* sponsoring a food drive.

- Words expressing amount are singular when the amount is viewed as a unit. Example: Ten years *feels* like a long time.

Try IT **Answers**

1. Terry and Jose want to study German.
2. A
3. A
4. Their older brother and sister work at the grocery store.
5. After the race, Jodie or Chantell congratulates the winner.
6. Neither the flowers nor the cats trigger Alex's allergies.
7. A
8. Every Sunday, Ling and Jules meet at the bowling alley.

Editing Using a Checklist

Before students begin using the checklist:

- Suggest that they review their previous writing assignments to search for errors they made in the past. Have them place special emphasis on those areas as they edit.
- Also, encourage them to add any other items that they typically struggle with to the list.

Creating a Title

Recommend that students reread their essays, looking for key words or phrases that are particularly interesting and might be turned into a title. Suggest that they take a creative approach to writing titles. For example, they might use rhyme, alliteration, or words with double meanings. They should make sure, however, that the title matches the tone of their essay. Provide examples of interesting titles of autobiographies.

Editing Using a Checklist

 Check your editing. On a piece of paper, write the numbers 1 to 12. If you can answer "yes" to a question, put a check mark after that number. If not, continue to edit for that convention.

Conventions

PUNCTUATION

_____ 1. Do I use end punctuation after all my sentences?

_____ 2. Do I use commas after introductory word groups and transitions?

_____ 3. Do I use commas between equal adjectives?

_____ 4. Do I punctuate dialogue correctly?

_____ 5. Do I use apostrophes to show possession (a *boy's bike*)?

CAPITALIZATION

_____ 6. Do I start all my sentences with capital letters?

_____ 7. Do I capitalize all proper nouns?

SPELLING

_____ 8. Have I spelled all my words correctly?

_____ 9. Have I double-checked the words my spell-checker may have missed?

GRAMMAR

_____ 10. Do I use correct forms of verbs (*had gone*, not *had went*)?

_____ 11. Do my subjects and verbs agree in number? (She and I *were* going, not She and I *was* going.)

_____ 12. Do I use the right words (*to, too, two*)?

Creating a Title

- Use strong, colorful words: **Marching to Confidence**
- Give the words rhythm: **Step High, Work Hard**
- Be imaginative: **About-Face for Julie**

Grammar Connection

Punctuating Dialogue

- **Proofreader's Guide** pages 588–589, 598–599, 600–601
- **CD** Punctuation—Dialogue

Subject-Verb Agreement

- *Write Source* pages 508–509
- *SkillsBook* pages 95–96
- **CD** Sentences—Subject-Verb Agreement

Struggling Learners

* Before they use the checklist, students may benefit from a punctuation review. Direct them to PE pages 586, 588, 598, and 600.

- Section 586.2 will help students answer question 3 (on commas).
- Sections 588.1, 598.1, and 600.1 will help them answer question 4 (on punctuating dialogue).

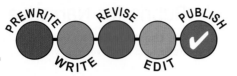

tell share remember
narrate
relate
Writing a Phase Autobiography
129

Publishing

Sharing Your Phase Autobiography

After you have worked so hard to improve your writing, make a neat, final copy to share. You may also decide to present your story in the form of a class magazine, a reading, or a recording. (See the suggestions below.)

Make a final copy. When you write your final copy, follow your teacher's instructions or use the guidelines below to format your story. (If you are using a computer, see pages 60–62.) Create a clean copy of your phase autobiography and carefully proofread it.

Focus on **Presentation**

- Use blue or black ink and write neatly.
- Write your name in the upper left corner of page 1.
- Skip a line and center your title; skip another line and start your writing.
- Double-space your essay.
- Indent every paragraph and leave a one-inch margin on all four sides.
- Write your last name and the page number in the upper right corner of every page after the first one.

NARRATIVE

Create a Class Magazine

Encourage your classmates to submit their writings for a class magazine. Staple them together and keep them in the class.

Share with a Group

Share your writing with a small group of peers. Allow them to ask questions or offer positive comments.

Make a Recording

Record your phase autobiography. Be sure to use an expressive voice. Give the recording and a printed copy of it to someone as a gift.

Publishing

Sharing Your Phase Autobiography

If you create a class magazine, invite students to design a magazine cover featuring an illustration and a relevant title, such as "It's Just a Phase."

- Display the cover designs so that students can vote on which one to use for the magazine cover.
- To ensure that students vote based on design merit, display the designs without artists' names.

Advanced Learners

Tell students that the phase autobiography could be the start of a memoir of their teenage years. Encourage motivated students to write additional essays describing other significant periods in their life. Suggest that they collect several essays in a special folder.

Rubric for Narrative Writing

Have students refer to this rubric throughout the writing process. Tell students to put a sticky note on this page, so that they can refer to the rubric whenever it is needed.

* Reproducible six-, five-, and four-point rubrics for narrative writing can be found on TE pages 750, 754, and 758.

Test Prep!
Throughout *Write Source,* students use formative, traits-based rubrics. These rubrics break the traits apart so that students can learn discrete strategies for improving their writing. Many state writing tests use summative rubrics—sometimes combining all the traits holistically and at other times rating each trait on a smaller scale.

The difference is simple. Formative rubrics are created to help *students.* Summative rubrics are created to help *graders.*

There's no need to worry, though. The formative rubrics in *Write Source* correlate very strongly to the summative rubrics used on most writing tests.

130

Rubric for Narrative Writing

Use this rubric for guiding and assessing your narrative writing. Refer to it whenever you want to improve your writing.

Ideas

6 The narrative captures an unforgettable time. The details make the story come alive.

5 The writer shares an interesting experience. Details help create the interest.

4 The writer tells about an interesting experience. More details are needed.

Organization

6 The way the narrative is put together makes it enjoyable to read.

5 The narrative is well organized, with a clear beginning, middle, and ending. Transitions are used well.

4 The narrative is well organized. Most of the transitions are helpful.

Voice

6 The voice in the narrative perfectly captures the special time or experience.

5 The writer's voice creates interest in the story.

4 The writer's voice could be stronger.

Word Choice

6 The writer's exceptional word choice captures the experience.

5 Specific nouns, verbs, and modifiers create clear pictures.

4 Some of the words need to be more specific to create clear pictures.

Sentence Fluency

6 The style of the sentences captures this time or experience.

5 The sentences are skillfully written and original.

4 The sentences show variety, but some should read more smoothly.

Conventions

6 The narrative is error free.

5 The narrative has a few minor errors in punctuation, spelling, or grammar.

4 The narrative has some errors that may distract the reader.

tell **share** remember
relate   **narrate**   **131**
Writing a Phase Autobiography

NARRATIVE

3 The writer tells about an experience or time. Many more details are needed.

2 The writer needs to focus more specifically on one experience or time.

1 The writer needs to select a topic suitable for a narrative.

3 The order of events needs to be corrected. More transitions need to be used.

2 The beginning, middle, and ending all run together. The order is unclear.

1 The narrative needs to be organized.

3 A voice can sometimes be heard. The writer needs to show more feelings.

2 The voice cannot be heard.

1 The writer has not gotten involved in the story.

3 Many more specific words need to be used.

2 The writer has given little consideration to word choice.

1 The writer has not yet considered word choice.

3 A better variety of sentences is needed. Sentences do not read smoothly.

2 Many short or incomplete sentences make the writing choppy.

1 Few sentences are written well. Help is needed.

3 Several errors confuse the reader.

2 Many errors make the narrative truly confusing and hard to read.

1 Help is needed to make corrections.

Test Prep!
The six traits of writing were first identified in the 1960s by Paul Diederick and a group of 50 professionals who reviewed student papers and brainstormed the qualities that made writing strong. In 1983, a group of educators in Beaverton, Oregon, learned of Diederick's work and replicated it, settling on a similar set of six traits. A separate team in Missoula, Montana, simultaneously ran a study that identified the same basic group of traits.

Thereafter, Northwest Regional Educational Labs (NREL) in Portland and later Great Source in Boston (through Vicki Spandel, who had been a part of the NREL team) did much to teach the world about traits-based instruction.

Put simply, the six traits provide a universal set of criteria for strong writing. They correlate very well to the rubrics used in most state testing. Using the traits throughout the writing process, therefore, prepares students for any writing test they will face.

Evaluating a Phase Autobiography

Ask students if they agree with the sample self-assessment on PE page 133. Then ask them to suggest improvements based on the comments in the self-assessment. If they disagree with any comment, ask them to explain why.

Literature Connections

Metaphors: Jerry Spinelli often uses running as a metaphor for the life of a boy. Here is a quotation from an interview with Mary Capello at City Center in Philadelphia: "I believe [running is] simply an expression of the exuberance of freedom, when a kid is first let out of the house . . . a perfect metaphor for a kid . . . it just comes as naturally as breathing. . . ."

132

Evaluating a Phase Autobiography

As you read the phase autobiography below, focus on the writer's strengths and weaknesses. **(The essay contains some errors.)** Then read the student self-evaluation on page 133.

Under Two Hours!

My heart pounds with excitement, as Dad and I line up for this year's Charity Run. It's my first race. I've been working out. I feel great. I know I'm ready. Bang! We're off. As we run side by side, Dad is panting, "Coop, don't forget . . . how hard you worked . . . to get here."

Yes. Dad and I had started training several months ago. Each day in our early morning walks, we'd go faster and faster. Slowly, the walks turned into jogging. Then they finally turned into running. At first, I had a tough time keeping up with Dad. Sometimes he would slow down for me.

At that time, I have to admit, I was a couch potato. Still, I felt like I should be able to outrun my Dad. So every chance I got, I started working out on my own. After a while, I wasn't panting for breath. I was actually keeping up with Dad. I knew the 10-mile run would be a big challenge. I began to believe that I could do it.

As time went by, I began to think that Dad was actually trying to keep up with me on our morning runs. I would find myself slowing down, so that he wouldn't feel bad just as he had done for me in the beginning.

Suddenly, I hear Dad panting beside me. He tells me to go on. So I take off like a racehorse roaring ahead. My body works in rhythm—legs, arms, muscles, lungs. Just a bit farther . . . pounding toward the waiting crowd . . . I sprint across the finish line. The big race clock shows 1:57:15. I feel so proud, as I turn to cheer on my Dad who is just minutes behind me. He's grinning and panting, "We did it, Coop, under two hours." I think to myself, *Not bad, Coop. Not bad at all.*

English Language Learners

Make sure that students understand the following expressions from the model:

- pounds with excitement (beats fast)
- working out (doing exercises or a physical activity such as jogging)
- couch potato (someone who is not active)

Student Self-Assessment

The assessment below shows how the writer of "Under Two Hours!" rated his essay. He used the rubric and number scales on pages 130–131 to rank each trait. Then he made two comments for each trait. The first one showed something he liked or did well in his essay. The second comment pointed out something that he felt he could have done better.

5 Ideas

1. My topic will interest my classmates.
2. I could tell more about my workouts.

4 Organization

1. Transitions help me tell my story smoothly.
2. My last sentences don't fit well in the narrative.

4 Voice

1. My tone perfectly fits my subject.
2. I could have used more dialogue.

4 Word Choice

1. My title makes readers want to read my narrative.
2. I overused some words, like "panting."

4 Sentence Fluency

1. I use a variety of sentences.
2. I could have combined some short sentences.

4 Conventions

1. I spell all words correctly.
2. Commas give me trouble.

 Use the rubric. Assess your narrative using the rubric shown on pages 130–131.

1 On your own paper, list the six traits. Leave space after each trait to write one strength and one weakness.

2 Then choose a number (from 1 to 6) that shows how well each trait was used.

NARRATIVE

To give students additional practice with evaluating a narrative essay, use a reproducible assessment sheet (TE page 787) and one or both of the **benchmark papers** listed in the Benchmark Papers box below. You can use an overhead transparency while students refer to their own copies made from the copy masters. For your benefit, a completed assessment sheet is provided for each benchmark paper.

Benchmark Papers

Puppy (strong)
- TR 1A–1D
- TE pp. 763–766

A Message for Myself (fair)
- TR 2A–2C
- TE pp. 767–770

Reflecting on Your Writing

Have students keep a folder for reflections of their writing. Tell them to review the contents of the folder every month to assess their writing progress. They may spot repeated problems that need more attention as well as elements that are consistently strong.

Reflecting on Your Writing

You've worked hard to write a phase autobiography that your classmates will enjoy. Now take some time to think about your writing. Finish each of the sentence starters below on your own paper. Thinking about your writing will help you see how you are growing as a writer.

My Phase Autobiography

1. The strength of my phase autobiography is . . .

2. The part that still needs work is . . .

3. The main thing I learned about writing a phase autobiography is . . .

4. In my next phase autobiography, I would like to . . .

5. Here is one question I still have about writing a phase autobiography:

Narrative Writing

Biographical Narrative

What would it be like to live another person's life? Imagine being your brother on his first day at army boot camp or your grandmother as she decided to leave Peru and travel to the United States.

Writing a biographical narrative gives you the chance to take a walk in someone else's shoes. By learning about another person's life experiences and writing about them, you can feel as if you are experiencing the events yourself.

In this chapter, you will read a biographical narrative about a young girl's decision to leave her homeland. Then you will write your own biographical narrative.

Writing Guidelines

Subject:	An experience of someone you know
Form:	Biographical narrative
Purpose:	To tell a story
Audience:	Classmates

Biographical Narrative

Objectives
- choose a topic for a biographical narrative
- create a time line to organize the narrative
- write, revise, and edit a biographical narrative

A **biographical narrative** is a story about an event that happened in someone else's life.

Find out whether students have ever written a narrative essay about someone they know. Discuss whether they have ever interviewed someone to learn more about her or his past. If students have conducted an oral history interview, encourage them to explain how they did it. Ask these questions:

- What kinds of questions did you ask?
- How did you get your subject to tell interesting stories?
- How did you record the interview?
- How did you organize the material after the interview?

Biographical Narrative

Analyze "A Life-Changing Decision" along with your students:

- Discuss the first two paragraphs, paying particular attention to the effect of starting with dialogue. Ask students whether they think this approach is a good one.
- Then focus on the next three paragraphs. What do students think about the organization of this essay?
- Point out that although the writer's grandmother is the central character in the story, the relationship between Maria and the writer is never mentioned. Discuss with students why the writer might have done that.
- Also, instead of using her own voice to tell the story, the writer tells the story as an imaginary observer of her grandmother's experiences. Tell students that this approach is just one way to tell a story. Students may choose to use a more personal voice in writing their own biographical narratives.

Biographical Narrative

A biographical narrative tells a true story from someone else's life. Alayna wrote about her grandmother Maria's decision to come to America as a student from Peru.

A Life-Changing Decision

Beginning
The beginning introduces the main character and the choice she faces.

"So, Maria," asked her father, paging nervously through his newspaper, "have you decided yet?"

"No, Papa," Maria answered as she stared out the living room window.

It was the spring of 1965, and Maria had a life-changing decision to make. Would she stay with her family and friends in Lima, Peru, or accept the scholarship she was being offered at a university in the United States? She knew the choice would change her life forever.

Maria gazed out at the plaza in front of her home and the beautiful cathedral in the distance. Her eyes wandered then to her father's bookstore, where she worked, just walking distance away. Maria sighed. Lima was so comfortable and familiar, but the United States would let her fulfill her dream.

Middle
The middle uses action and dialogue to develop the narrative.

Maria had always wanted to be a nurse, but when she had been a little girl, polio had withered her right leg. The disease had left her with a permanent limp. In Peru, a person like Maria could not easily become a nurse, but in the United States she knew she could follow her dream.

"We need to notify the university by tomorrow," her father said softly, his newspaper crinkling.

English Language Learners

To help students understand how the essay was put together, have them use a Step Organizer (see TE page 105) to outline the middle of the narrative.

tell **share** remember
narrate
relate
Biographical Narrative **137**

NARRATIVE

Middle
The tension builds to a high point.

Maria's heart started pounding, and her mind raced. The future was so uncertain, but part of her loved that fact! Did she have the courage to go to America? Could she bear to stay in Peru?

"Papa, I want to go to America!"

Maria's father jumped up and came to her, hugging her tightly. His eyes looked sad, but he smiled and said, "You will be able to do so much in the United States. They have a modern way of thinking, and if you work hard, they'll give you a chance to live your dreams."

A few months later, Maria's family and friends took her to the airport. They held hands in a circle while they sang "La Flor de la Canela," a Peruvian folk song about love and family. Maria waved one last good-bye before disappearing down the long hallway. With each step, she knew she was growing up.

Ending
The ending shows how the experience changed the person.

As the plane lifted off the ground, Maria felt in her heart that she would never come back to Peru to live. Through tear-filled eyes, she watched the cities, villages, and lush, green mountains of her home get smaller and smaller. She closed her eyes and took a deep breath. Her new life had begun.

 Respond to the reading. Answer the following questions about the biographical narrative.

☐ **Ideas** (1) What details help the reader experience the story?

☐ **Organization** (2) How does the writer organize the details?

☐ **Voice & Word Choice** (3) What words or phrases show how the people in the narrative felt?

Continue to analyze the narrative by looking at one paragraph at a time. Pay special attention to the ideas, the word choice, and the voice. Ask the following questions:

- How does the writer bring readers inside Maria's head?
- What role does dialogue play?
- Which details help you to visualize what you are reading?

 Respond to the reading.

Answers

Ideas **1.** Students' answers will vary.

Organization **2.** in chronological order

Voice & Word Choice **3.** pacing nervously; Maria sighed; Maria's heart started pounding, and her mind raced; His eyes looked sad; She closed her eyes and took a deep breath.

Struggling Learners

Demonstrate how to answer the first **Respond to the reading** question (see above) by pointing out details the writer used (as part of the "show, don't tell" strategy) to help the reader experience the story:

- paging nervously through his newspaper
- stared out the window
- gazed out at the plaza
- Maria sighed
- her heart started pounding, and her mind raced
- her father jumped up and hugged her tightly

Prewriting Selecting a Topic

As an extra challenge, suggest that students choose someone they don't know too well for the biographical narrative, provided they can learn more about the person. Explain that discovering interesting details about their subject will be part of the fun.

Prewriting Gathering Details

Preparing **interview questions** (*see below*) is a skill with which many students may not have had much experience. If students are asking questions based on the 5 W's and H, provide photocopies of the reproducible 5 W's chart (TE page 792) for them to use for note taking.

Prewriting Selecting a Topic

To find a topic for her biographical narrative, Alayna made a line diagram. She began by writing down people she knew well. Under each name, she wrote interesting stories they had told her.

Line Diagram

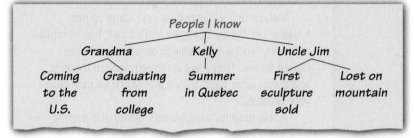

 Choose your topic. Create your own line diagram. Think of people you know and interesting stories they have told you. Choose a story that you would like to learn about and share with others.

Gathering Details

Before you write, gather details about the story. Alayna used the 5 W's and H to interview her grandmother about coming to the United States.

5 W's Chart

1. Who was involved? Maria, Papa, and her family and friends
2. What happened? Maria decided to leave Peru for the U.S.
3. When did the event happen? Spring of 1965
4. Where did the event happen? Lima, Peru
5. Why did it happen? Maria's dream to be a nurse
6. How did she feel about the event? Scared, sad, and excited

 Gather details. Write down questions based on the 5 W's and H. Then ask your subject to tell his or her story. Write down answers to your questions. Afterward, ask any other questions you might have.

Teaching Tip: Interview Questions

Because students may not have had much experience conducting interviews, provide some tips on how to proceed:

- Tell students to conduct a brief phone interview first, to gather some basic facts.
- Next, have them prepare a written list of questions for the face-to-face interview.

Encourage them to ask not only about the facts but also about the person's feelings concerning events in his or her life.

- Tell students that when they conduct the interview, they should feel free to let it take its own course, while using their questions as a road map.

English Language Learners

Have students tape-record their interviews rather than try to keep up with note taking in English. However, they should use recording equipment only if they have the interviewee's permission.

Organizing Details

Most biographical narratives are organized chronologically. Alayna used a time line to organize the details she had gathered about her grandmother's story. Above the line, she wrote events in the story. Below it, she wrote details to include.

Time Line

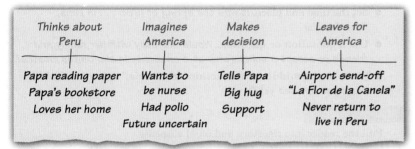

 Create a time line. Use the model above to help you organize your details into a time line. Above the line, list key events. Below it, list details you would like to include in your biographical narrative.

Focus on the Traits

Organization

Narratives follow the classic shape of a plot line. The **beginning** grabs the reader's attention and sets the stage for the narrative. Then **rising action** builds suspense. The **high point** brings the person and the conflict face-to-face, and the **ending** tells how the person is changed.

Story Line

High Point
Decides to go to America

Rising Action
Wants to be nurse and
dreams of America

Beginning
Looks out window
and thinks of home

Ending
Flies from Peru

NARRATIVE

Prewriting *Organizing Details*

After making a time line, students can create a "Specific Details Chart" (see PE page 105) for the biographical narrative. By thinking about the subject's feelings at various points in the story, students will gain insights that will enhance the tone of the piece.

Focus on the Traits

Organization

Another way to shape the organization of a narrative is by creating a storyboard. If students are unfamiliar with storyboards, make a model on the board.

English Language Learners

If students use a storyboard, be sure they understand that they still need to include a beginning (B), rising action (RA) that builds up to a high point (HP), and an ending (E). Have them label each box with one of those codes, to show which narrative element it addresses.

Advanced Learners

Write the words *Senses, Thoughts,* and *Feelings* on the board. For each category, point out some details from the sample time line:

- Senses: hearing the folk song
- Thoughts: plan to be a nurse
- Feelings: loves her home

Challenge students to include details from each category for the events in their time lines.

Writing Creating Your First Draft

Tell students to use the exact words of the person in dialogue, not only at the high point but also wherever it can help bring the person to life.

■ Dialogue reveals personality, conflict, and emotion and can be used throughout students' essays.

■ Explain that biographers often use dialogue when they want to achieve a sense of immediacy and reveal something important about the person they're writing about.

✱ Additional information about using dialogue is on PE page 556.

140

Writing Creating Your First Draft

As you write your first draft, be sure to follow your time line. Use the tips below as a guide.

Beginning

Grab the reader's attention and set the stage for your story.

● **Set the time and place.** *It was the spring of 1965 . . . in Lima, Peru. familiar*

● **Use a quotation or question.** *Would she stay with her family and friends or accept a scholarship at a university in the United States?*

● **Start in the middle of the action.** *"So, Maria," asked her father, "have you decided yet?"*

Rising Action

Pull the reader into the story and build suspense.

● **Include thoughts and feelings.** *Lima was so comfortable and familiar, but the United States would let her fulfill her dream.*

● **Use action.** *Maria's heart started pounding, and her mind raced.*

● **Use sensory details.** *Maria's father jumped up and came to her, hugging her tightly. His eyes looked sad, but he smiled and said, . . .*

High Point

Bring the person face-to-face with the conflict.

● **Describe the high point.** *Did she have the courage to go to America? Could she bear to stay in Peru?*

● **Use dialogue.** *"Papa, I want to go to America!"*

Ending

Describe how the person changed.

● **Describe the final scene.** *Through tear-filled eyes, she watched the cities, villages, and lush, green mountains of her home get smaller and smaller.*

● **Show how the event changed the person.** *She closed her eyes and took a deep breath. Her new life had begun.*

 Write the first draft. Use your time line (page 139) and follow the tips above. Focus on getting all your ideas on paper.

Struggling Learners

Caution students to use end punctuation that corresponds to the tone of the high point in their biographical narratives. Remind them that an exclamation point can indicate excitement, whereas a question mark can heighten the reader's curiosity.

tell share remember
relate narrate **141**
Biographical Narrative

Revising Improving Your Writing

Once you finish your first draft, take a break. When you come back to your story, it will be easier for you to see the parts that need improvement. Check your work for the following traits of writing.

☐ **Ideas** Make sure you have included sensory details as well as thoughts and feelings to bring your story to life.

> *Maria gazed out at the plaza in front of her home and the beautiful cathedral in the distance. Her eyes wandered then to her father's bookstore, where she worked, just walking distance away. Maria sighed.*

☐ **Organization** Add transitions where you need to show a shift in time.

> *A few months later, Maria's family and friends took her to the airport.*
>
> *As the plane lifted off the ground, Maria felt in her heart that she would never come back to Peru to live.*

☐ **Voice** Make sure that the voice fits the person and the event.

> *The future was so uncertain, but part of her loved that fact!*

☐ **Word Choice** Use descriptive and active words.

> *Maria waved one last good-bye before disappearing down the long hallway.*

☐ **Sentence Fluency** Read your story out loud and listen to the flow of your sentences. Combine any short, choppy sentences.

> **Choppy**
>
> *They held hands in a circle. They sang "La Flor de la Canela." It was a Peruvian folk song about love . . .*
>
> **Combined**
>
> *They held hands in a circle while they sang "La Flor de la Canela," a Peruvian folk song about love . . .*

 Revise your narrative. Use the guidelines above as you review your story and make changes.

 NARRATIVE

Revising Improving Your Writing

Before they begin revisions, have students review the section on revising a phase autobiography (PE pages 114–123). Then ask them to use the rubric on PE pages 130–131 to assess their writing.

As students focus on combining sentences, suggest that they check for any run-on or rambling sentences. A run-on sentence results from using a comma (without a conjunction) between two complete sentences. Have students refer to PE pages 504–505 for advice on correcting these types of sentences.

✱ Additional information about combining sentences is on PE pages 512–515.

 Technology Connections

Eval-U-Write, a subscription-based online service, helps students revise by providing feedback for four of the six traits. Using the revision screen, students can target their revisions to the traits that need improvement and can resubmit their work and watch their scores rise.

Grammar Connection

Transitions

- *Write Source* page 539
- *SkillsBook* page 73

Editing

Checking for Conventions

Students have different skill levels in the conventions. Keeping a personal editing checklist can help each student address those areas that are consistently problematic. Be sure students are familiar with the "Proofreader's Guide" (PE pages 578–749) so that they can find explanations and answers to questions that arise during the editing stage.

142

Editing Checking for Conventions

When you're finished revising, it's time to edit your biographical narrative for conventions.

Conventions

Review your punctuation, capitalization, spelling, and grammar. The following checklist can help you.

PUNCTUATION

_____ 1. Do I use commas correctly?

_____ 2. Do I include punctuation at the end of every sentence?

_____ 3. Do I put quotation marks and punctuation in the right place?

_____ 4. Do I use apostrophes to show possession (*Maria's trip*)?

CAPITALIZATION

_____ 5. Do I capitalize all proper nouns?

_____ 6. Do I begin every sentence with a capital letter?

SPELLING

_____ 7. Have I checked my spelling?

GRAMMAR

_____ 8. Do I use correct forms of verbs (*had done*, not *had did*)?

_____ 9. Do my subjects and verbs agree in number? (We *were* going, not We *was* going.)

_____ 10. Do I use the right words (*their, they're, there*)?

 Edit your biographical narrative. After you edit, let someone else look over your work for anything you missed. Then create a final copy and proofread it.

Publishing Sharing Your Writing

A biographical narrative can bring you closer to friends and family. Share your story with the person who lived it.

 Share your biographical narrative. Read your story to the person who experienced it and give him or her a copy to keep.

Grammar Connection

End Punctuation

■ **Proofreader's Guide** pages 579–581

■ *Write Source* page 518

■ *SkillsBook* pages 3–4

Using the Right Word

■ **Proofreader's Guide** pages 652–661

■ *SkillsBook* pages 53–54

■ **CD** Using the Right Word— 1 and 4

English Language Learners

The person who is the subject of a biographical narrative may live in a different country. If so, help each student think of ways that he or she could share the finished essay with that person. Options could include e-mailing the piece to the subject, putting it on a family Web site, or sending a photocopy or tape recording of the essay.

If a translation to the subject's native language is necessary,

● ask the student if he or she feels comfortable translating it,

● try to find a family member or a language teacher who could assist, or

● search for an online translation site that might be helpful.

tell share remember
relate **narrate** **143**

Narrative Writing
Across the Curriculum

Narratives set a course for adventure. In history class, you could write a historical narrative about being the barrel maker aboard the *Mayflower*. In math, you might write about your adventures learning new math concepts. For science class, you might even write a narrative about being a gigantic thunderhead!

This chapter contains samples of narratives like these. It also helps you create e-mails and respond to prompts on writing tests. No matter what the class or assignment, narrative writing can bring any subject to life.

What's Ahead

- **Social Studies:**
  Recalling a Historical Moment
- **Math:** Writing a Math Autobiography
- **Science:** Writing About
  a Natural Formation
- **Practical Writing:**
  Creating an E-Mail Message
- **Writing for Assessment**

Copy Masters/ Transparencies

T-chart (TE p. 148)

Across the Curriculum

Objectives
- apply what students have learned about narrative writing to other curriculum areas
- practice writing for assessment

The lessons on the following pages provide samples of narrative writing students might do in different content areas. The particular form used in one content area may sometimes be used in another content area (for example, students can write a social studies autobiography just as well as a math autobiography).

Assigning these forms of writing will depend on
- the skill level of your students,
- the subject matter they are studying in different content areas, and
- the writing goals of your school, district, or state.

Social Studies:
Recalling a Historical Moment

Analyze the narrative, one paragraph at a time. Point out the details and techniques the author uses, and discuss how they help make the story "come alive":

- In the first paragraph, the sensory details help to establish the setting and reveal the author's feelings.
- In the second paragraph, the dialogue creates a sense of excitement and makes readers feel as if they are right there.
- In the third paragraph, the author describes the actual landing as he sees it and steps on shore.
- In the fourth paragraph, the author uses dialogue again to help create a sense of immediacy.
- In the final paragraph, the author shares his vision of life in the New World and expresses his positive feelings about his new home and the future.

144

Social Studies:
Recalling a Historical Moment

American history is filled with important events. In the narrative below, a student writes about a historical moment as if he had experienced it firsthand.

America the Beautiful

The **beginning** introduces the narrator and sets the scene.

Finally, after months crossing the Atlantic, I see land! As the *Mayflower* brings us closer to shore, I am surprised by how wild the New World looks. There are trees everywhere, a deep, dark forest. The only sounds are the creaking of the ship and the waves crashing against the rocky coast. We are all alone here. My stomach used to feel seasick, but now it feels homesick. What use is a barrel maker in a place like this?

The **middle** builds to a moment of realization.

"Landing party, to the boats!" shouts Mr. Carver, who will govern our colony.

Soon I help row a boatful of settlers ashore. The boat comes aground on a big rock, and I climb out onto it and stand on the New World.

The **ending** reflects on the event.

Mr. Carver follows me. He draws a deep breath and announces, "Our new home!"

Suddenly I can almost see the new settlement. There are rows of houses, people busy with their tasks, and ships from England to trade with us. We have a lot of work ahead of us, but Mr. Carver's confidence makes me believe that we can make this new frontier feel like home.

English Language Learners

If students are unfamiliar with the term *barrel,* show a picture of one. Explain that in colonial times, these containers were used to store items such as flour, beverages, salted and dried fish, and even gunpowder.

Advanced Learners

Have each student write a biographical narrative about a person from the time period they are studying in social studies.

- Have students trade narratives with a partner.
- Then have them write a reflective piece comparing and contrasting the lives of the two people they researched.

tell share remember *narrate* relate
Writing in Social studies **145**

NARRATIVE

Writing Tips

Before you write . . .

● **Select a topic.**
Choose a historic moment to write about, such as Paul Revere's ride, the driving of the golden spike in Utah, or the day Teddy Roosevelt refused to shoot a bear. Page through your history textbook for other ideas. Select a single important moment so that you can write a well-focused narrative.

● **Research your topic.**
Read about the event and gather details about the place and time.

During your writing . . .

● **Write as if you experienced the event.**
Use the "I" voice. Imagine yourself to be part of this event in order to get a feel for the experience. Then record what you would see, hear, and so forth. Include thoughts and feelings.

● **Create other characters.**
Imagine the different kinds of people you might meet. Make them historically accurate. Use dialogue to bring the characters to life.

● **Show how the event affects you.**
Make sure that the moment isn't important only in history, but also to the main character of your narrative—you!

After you've written a first draft . . .

● **Revise your first draft.**
Check your story's organization to be sure it is easy to follow.

● **Check for accuracy.**
Double-check your historical facts—dates, names, and so on.

● **Edit for correctness.**
Check for errors in punctuation, spelling, and grammar.

 Select a moment from American history. Research the event and place yourself in the middle of it. Write a narrative that is both historically accurate and enjoyable to read.

Writing Tips

Suggest that students take one of two approaches to this assignment:

■ Take the role of a reporter or minor character, but use the first-person point of view ("I" voice) to describe what you see and hear and how you feel.

■ Take the role of a famous historical figure who was in the middle of the action.

Tell students to make sure that they give their narrator an authentic voice. Have them try to write dialogue that sounds as if it fits with the time period.

 Answers

Answers will vary.

English Language Learners

Some students may not be familiar with events and characters from American history. If you do not want to provide time for extended research, try the following:

● Ask the class to choose one person or event they would all like to write about.

● Streamline the research process by presenting information to the class and making available books and bookmarked Web sites.

Having everyone focus on the same event or character will make it possible for students to share information and will allow them to concentrate on the writing aspect of the project.

Advanced Learners

Challenge students to write two enjoyable, historically accurate narratives about the same moment from American history—one from the perspective of a girl or boy their age and one from an adult's point of view. Remind them that in each narrative, the writer's voice should reflect how the event would have been experienced by a person of that age.

Math: Writing a Math Autobiography

Ask students to talk about ways in which they use math in their everyday lives. Some students might have earned money for doing chores or odd jobs such as baby-sitting or mowing lawns.

Explain that wherever money is involved, so is math. You might mention the following points:

- You need to multiply to calculate how much to charge for your work.
- You have to understand about percentages in order to calculate a tip.
- You need to use subtraction skills in order to make change.

Technology Connections

The Agnes Scott College in Atlanta, Georgia, has sponsored an ongoing project to highlight the achievements of women in mathematics. The university Web site features numerous math biographies of important female mathematicians. A Web search for "Biographies of Women Mathematicians" will bring up the table of contents page. Check it out, and send your budding mathematicians to the site for reading, research, or inspiration.

146

Math: Writing a Math Autobiography

A math autobiography lets students reflect on their experiences with math. In the following autobiography, a student writes about how she has used math in the past and in the present, and how she expects to use it in the future.

The **beginning** reflects on the student's first experiences with math.

The **middle** gives details about the way the student currently uses math.

The **ending** suggests how she will use math in the future.

Math Matters

I remember the first day I stopped using my fingers to add and subtract. It felt so good to finally "get it." I've come a long way since then, but I still feel just as good every time I learn a new math skill.

I use math a lot in my daily life. When I was younger, I used math to do simple things like make change. Now I can solve more difficult problems. For example, my dad and I put a wood floor in our game room. We took measurements and used equations to find the square footage. That was especially tough because the game room has two small closets. Afterward, Dad and I were able to decide how much wood to buy.

I've come so far in math that now I'm a math tutor. I helped one boy, Chris, understand how to isolate variables. Suddenly, all those equations didn't scare him anymore. He finished his assignment and got an A on it.

I feel great that I can do so many things with math. It's even better now that I can help other kids. I know I'll find many new ways to use my math skills in the future for school, work, and everyday life.

tell share remember
narrate **147**
relate
Writing in Math

Writing Tips

Before you write . . .

- **Remember thoughts and feelings about math.**
  Think of math experiences that made you proud, nervous, excited, or confused. Remember the first time you learned to multiply and the times you've used math in everyday life.

- **Select specific examples to mention.**
  Sift through your memories and choose a few examples of ways that you have used math.

During your writing . . .

- **Focus on examples.**
  Describe specific times that math has been helpful —or difficult—for you.

- **Show the big picture.**
  Demonstrate how you relate to math overall. Let your reader know whether you like math or struggle with it, and why.

After you've written a first draft . . .

- **Revise your first draft.**
  Add any examples that would clarify your experience and remove examples that don't.

- **Check your organization.**
  Make sure the details in your autobiography are organized in a logical way.

- **Edit for correctness.**
  Check for errors in punctuation, capitalization, spelling, and grammar.

NARRATIVE

 Write your own math autobiography. Share specific examples that tell the reader about your overall experience with math.

Writing Tips

After students finish writing their math autobiographies, have them create a math Web site where they can exchange information and tips on using math in their everyday lives. For additional information on making Web sites, see PE page 63.

 Answers

Answers will vary but should show how math plays a role in each student's life.

Science: Writing About a Natural Formation

Discuss the model "I'm All Grown Up!" Help students understand how the writer skillfully uses the first-person point of view to include many interesting details about a cumulonimbus cloud without making the essay sound like a passage from a science textbook. This style of writing is engaging and should be fun for students to tackle.

148

Science:
Writing About a Natural Formation

When you use "personification" in your writing, you give human qualities or characteristics to a nonhuman thing. In science, you can use personification to imagine being a natural formation. In the narrative below, a student personified a thunderhead.

The **beginning** introduces the natural formation.

The **middle** provides details from the point of view of the formation.

The **ending** completes the narrative.

I'm All Grown Up!

People sometimes call me a cumulonimbus. That may not sound like a compliment, but for me it is. In the beginning, I was just a cumulus. That's right, I'm a cloud. I'm made of tiny water droplets that attach to dust, sea salt, and even pollution. As water droplets gather, I grow into a flat-topped thunderhead.

The first half of my name, cumulus, means "heap." That describes how I begin my life, like a heap of puffy cotton balls. I fly low and constantly change shape to look like different animals. It is a fun way to pass the time on warm, sunny days, but I have bigger things in my future.

The second half of my name, nimbus, means "precipitation." As the sun warms the air close to the ground, I grow from a cumulus cloud to a cumulonimbus—a thunderhead. The warm air rises rapidly, pushing the tiny water droplets higher and higher. They bump into each other and form raindrops. I don't even realize what is happening until I am over 40,000 feet tall!

It's exciting to be that tall, but it does make my stomach drop. My negatively charged electrons get attracted to the positively charged protons in the ground. Then the positive and negative charges crash in a shocking bolt of electricity. I immediately hear a rolling round of applause. It's great to be a cumulonimbus.

English Language Learners

To help students understand the technique the writer has used, provide photocopies of the reproducible T-chart on TE page 789.

- In the left column, have students list the science facts in the writing.

- In the right column, have them list examples of personification.
- Point out that most of the essay consists of factual material, but the few instances of personification give the writing its character.

tell share remember
relate **narrate** **149**
Writing in Science

Writing Tips

Before you write . . .

- **Select a topic that interests you.**
  Check your science book for natural formations to write about. Consider formations such as waterspouts, hurricanes, glaciers, fault lines, craters, or canyons.
- **Research the topic.**
  Check your textbook, an encyclopedia, or a Web site to learn about the formation you have chosen.

During your writing . . .

- **Write from the point of view of the formation.**
  Use the "I" voice and imagine yourself as the formation. Tell about where you come from, what you do, and how you change.
- **Include thoughts and feelings.**
  Indicate what your formation does and thinks, likes and dislikes.

After you've written a first draft . . .

- **Revise your narrative.**
  Make sure your essay is organized logically. Check to see that it is informative and easy to follow.
- **Check for accuracy.**
  Double-check the facts in your story.
- **Edit for correctness.**
  Review your work, looking for errors in punctuation, spelling, capitalization, and grammar.

 Select a natural formation that you'd enjoy writing a narrative about. Research your topic and write a story from the point of view of the formation. Share your narrative with your classmates.

NARRATIVE

Writing Tips

Another approach to this kind of assignment is to write a "What Am I?" essay, in which students explain everything about a natural formation without identifying it. If students choose this option, they should read aloud their essays and ask their classmates to identify the formation.

 Answers

Answers will vary.

Practical Writing:
Creating an E-Mail Message

Point out that the writer uses the traditional form for a letter, even though she is writing an **e-mail message** (*see below*). Discuss the importance of not using slang or shorthand language in an e-mail written to a teacher or another adult.

Many people are sloppy when writing e-mails. They do not realize that lazy writing habits, even in an e-mail, are not a good reflection of their abilities. Emphasize that students should

- fill in the subject line with an accurate title,
- select a user name that will be taken seriously, and
- use complete sentences, not instant-message shorthand.

150

Practical Writing:
Creating an E-Mail Message

E-mail has become an important link between teachers and students. In the following narrative e-mail, a student tells a teacher about a tour she went on for extra credit.

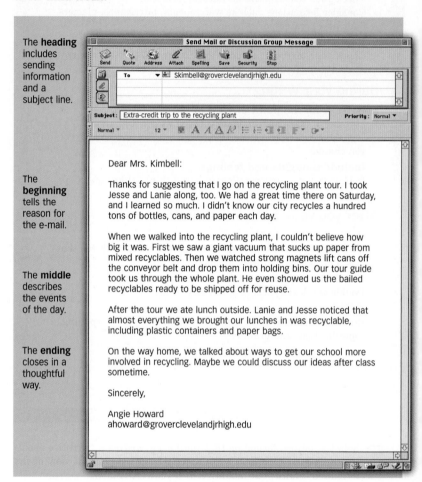

The **heading** includes sending information and a subject line.

The **beginning** tells the reason for the e-mail.

The **middle** describes the events of the day.

The **ending** closes in a thoughtful way.

Dear Mrs. Kimbell:

Thanks for suggesting that I go on the recycling plant tour. I took Jesse and Lanie along, too. We had a great time there on Saturday, and I learned so much. I didn't know our city recycles a hundred tons of bottles, cans, and paper each day.

When we walked into the recycling plant, I couldn't believe how big it was. First we saw a giant vacuum that sucks up paper from mixed recyclables. Then we watched strong magnets lift cans off the conveyor belt and drop them into holding bins. Our tour guide took us through the whole plant. He even showed us the bailed recyclables ready to be shipped off for reuse.

After the tour we ate lunch outside. Lanie and Jesse noticed that almost everything we brought our lunches in was recyclable, including plastic containers and paper bags.

On the way home, we talked about ways to get our school more involved in recycling. Maybe we could discuss our ideas after class sometime.

Sincerely,

Angie Howard
ahoward@groverclevelandjrhigh.edu

Teaching Tip: E-Mail Messages

Because students are becoming increasingly dependent on e-mail correspondence, they need to learn to take a serious approach to writing e-mails.

A whole new, very informal language is emerging as a result of the speed of electronic communication. Unfortunately, many people do not pay careful attention to the content of their e-mail messages.

- If their e-mail application has a spell-check feature, they should get in the habit of using it.
- If you have e-mail set up in your school, have students practice sending messages to you.

tell share remember *narrate*
relate
151
Practical Writing

Writing Tips

Before you write . . .

- **List the details you want to report.**
  Write down your experience, putting events in time order.

During your writing . . .

- **Complete the e-mail heading.**
  Fill in the address line and make sure each character is correct. Then write a subject line that clearly indicates the reason for the e-mail.
- **Greet the reader and give your reason for writing.**
  Start with a polite greeting. Follow by telling why you are sending the e-mail.
- **Be conversational but proper.**
  Make sure your sentences are clear and complete. You may use an informal voice, but your grammar should be correct.
- **Describe what happened and what was said.**
  Describe your experience and include any important conversations you had.
- **End politely.**
  Close with "Sincerely," or another closing you might use in a letter. Type your name below.

After you've written a first draft . . .

- **Reread your e-mail.**
  Don't simply press "Send." Make sure your e-mail is clear and complete.
- **Check for correctness.**
  Check for errors in punctuation, capitalization, spelling, and grammar.

 Think of a school-related event that you enjoyed and select a teacher or mentor who was involved with the event. Write an e-mail message to the person, sharing your experience. (You can send the e-mail or merely treat it as a class assignment.)

NARRATIVE

Writing Tips

Suggest that students print out their e-mail messages, if possible, before sending them. It is much easier to spot mistakes on a printed page than on a computer screen. Encourage students to do all their proofreading of electronic correspondence on hard copy.

 Answers

Answers will vary.

Technology Connections

E-mail is part of a new literacy for modern students, who are increasingly writing in digital formats: e-mail, chat rooms, blogs, instant messages, and text messages. Many of these types of communication include their own lingo, with abbreviations such as LOL (laugh out loud) and emoticons such as :-) . It's important to let students know that these kinds of shorthand may be appropriate in informal communication, but for formal class assignments, they should be avoided.

If students can communicate in both ways—formally in the classroom and informally outside of it—their use of language will be only richer ;-) .

English Language Learners

Remind students to relate the events they experienced in chronological order. Suggest that when they are writing to an audience such as a teacher, it is a good idea to do at least some informal prewriting, such as creating a time line or a Step Organizer. Provide photocopies of the reproducible time line on TE page 790.

Advanced Learners

Have students choose a school-related event that they enjoyed and write a thank-you e-mail to those involved in making it happen. Remind students to describe their experience at the event and to explain why they enjoyed it.

Grammar Connection

Kinds of Sentences
- **Proofreader's Guide** pages 579 (+), 580 (+)
- *Write Source* page 518 (+)
- *SkillsBook* pages 107–108

Capitalization
- **Proofreader's Guide** pages 618–619
- *Write Source* page 470
- *SkillsBook* pages 41–42
- **CD** Capitalization—1

Writing for Assessment

Discuss the narrative with your students. Invite them to analyze the following aspects of the essay:

- voice
- tone
- details—sensory, memory, and reflective
- dialogue

Ask students whether they think the essay could be improved and, if so, what specific changes they would make. Then ask students to score the essay, using the rubric on PE pages 130–131. Discuss the scores, providing the reasons for each score.

Narrative Writing
Writing for Assessment

Many state and school writing tests include a narrative prompt that asks you to recall a personal experience or respond to a "what if" question. Study the following sample prompt and student response.

Narrative Prompt

Life is one long string of learning experiences. From the time that you were a newborn to your eighth-grade year, you have learned many lessons. Think back to an experience that taught you an important lesson. Write a narrative essay describing the experience and what you learned.

Response to a Narrative Prompt

The **beginning** sets up the experience.

Whenever I face a challenging situation, I tell myself, "This will make a good story–if I ever get through it!" Challenges may not be fun, but they often teach important lessons. Just last summer at camp, I faced a rope course that taught me to believe in myself and other people as well.

I stood in front of a 50-foot-tall climbing tower built out of telephone poles. Handholds were bolted to the sides of the poles, and I wore a special harness with belaying ropes. Still, the climb to the top would take all the arm and leg strength I had, as well as faith in two people I hardly knew.

Each **middle** paragraph describes events that took place.

The rope attached to my harness went up over the top of the tower and back down into a locking device held by my cabin mate, Eric. Another boy named Taylor backed him up, but I wasn't sure I could trust either of them. It was too late to turn back, though. I didn't want Eric, Taylor, or other campers to see me lose my nerve.

English Language Learners

To familiarize students with the terminology in this piece, show them a picture of someone on a rope course. Point out the equipment as you explain the following terms:

- rope course (an obstacle course made with ropes and set above the ground)
- climbing tower (a tall tower that is made specifically for people to climb)

- handhold (any object that protrudes from a surface and is held while climbing)
- harness (a device worn around the waist and thighs and used to support the climber)
- belaying ropes (ropes that are used to secure a climber)
- locking device (an object that prevents the belaying rope from slipping out of a person's hands)

- A belaying rope is passed through a pulley that is high above the climbers. One end of the rope is attached to the climber's harness, and the other end is held by a person standing on the ground. If a climber misses a handhold or foothold, the belaying rope will prevent her or him from falling to the ground.

tell share remember
relate **narrate** **153**
Writing for Assessment

Numbly, I stepped to the base of the tower. I grabbed a pair of handholds. The rope on my harness drew tight as Eric pulled on it. Swallowing my fear, I lifted myself up onto the pole. As I rose, Eric and Taylor drew in the slack of my belaying rope. Soon I was 10 feet off the ground, and then 20, and then 30. I paused, smiling as I caught my breath. I should have believed in myself.

Suddenly I slipped, tumbling away from the tower. My belaying line snapped tight, and I hung there, 25 feet up.

"I got you," Eric called out. "Swing back over and grab on."

I did, and realized I should have believed in Eric and Taylor, too. Panting a little, I continued to climb until I reached the platform at the top. When I got there, I cheered, and so did Eric, Taylor, and everyone down below.

That day, I learned that it took two things for me to climb that tower. First, I had to believe in myself. Second, I had to believe in others. That's a lesson I'll be able to use throughout my life.

The ending paragraph reflects on the experience.

NARRATIVE

Respond to the reading. Answer the following questions about the sample response.

- ☐ Ideas (1) What is the focus of this narrative essay?
  (2) What did the writer learn from the experience?
- ☐ Organization (3) How did the writer organize the paragraphs in the essay?
- ☐ Voice & Word Choice (4) What words and phrases express how the writer's mood changed throughout the narrative?

If your students will be taking a state assessment test that requires them to respond to a narrative prompt, provide them with several practice sessions. Devote plenty of time to giving students helpful feedback on their essays.

Respond to the reading.

Answers

Ideas **1.** The focus is a rope course at camp. **2.** The writer learned to believe in himself and others.

Organization **3.** The writer organized the paragraphs in chronological order.

Voice & Word Choice **4.** The following words and phrases show the change in the writer's mood:

- swallowing my fear
- I paused, smiling as I caught my breath.
- I should have believed in myself.
- I did, and realized I should have believed in Eric and Taylor, too.

Writing Tips

Point out that students must approach writing-on-demand assignments differently from open-ended writing assignments and that timed writing creates pressures for everyone.

Narrative Prompts

Allow students the same amount of time to write their response essay as they will be allotted on school, district, or state assessments. Break down each part of the process into clear chunks of time. For example, you might give students

- 15 minutes for reading, note taking, and planning,
- 20 minutes for writing, and
- 10 minutes for editing and proofreading.

Tell students when time is up for each section. Start the assignment at the top of the hour or at the half-hour to make it easier for students to keep track of the time.

Technology Connections

The two narrative prompts on this page appear on Eval-U-Write, along with more than 250 other prompts. You can subscribe to this online service to provide your students with weekly writing assignments, low-stakes assessments (such as unit pretests and posttests), or help preparing for on-demand writing tests.

154

Writing Tips

Use the following tips as a guide when responding to a narrative writing prompt.

Before you write . . .

- **Understand the prompt.**
  Remember that a narrative prompt asks you to tell a story.
- **Plan your time wisely.**
  Take several minutes to plan your writing. Use a graphic organizer like a time line to help with planning your writing.

Time Line

Subject:
First:
Finally:

During your writing . . .

- **Decide on a focus for your narrative.**
  Use key words from the prompt as you write your focus statement.
- **Be selective.**
  Tell only the main events in your experience.
- **End in a meaningful way.**
  Reflect on the importance of the narrative.

After you've written a first draft . . .

- **Check for completeness and correctness.**
  Present events in order. Delete any unneeded details and neatly correct any errors.

Narrative Prompts

- According to an old saying, "The best way to have a friend is to be a friend." Recall a time when you did something to help one of your friends. Write a narrative essay about the experience. Focus on the way that your actions affected your friendship.
- Think about a time when you were new to a group. Perhaps it was your first day at your middle school or junior high. Perhaps it was the first practice for a school play or sports team. Write a narrative about your experience and how you learned to fit in.

 Plan and write a response. Respond to one of the prompts above. Complete your writing within the period of time your teacher gives you. Afterward, list one part that you like and one part that could be better.

English Language Learners

Show students how to turn prompts into questions in their own words, to gain a clearer understanding of what is expected of them. Here are some examples of questions formed from the narrative prompts on this page:

- When did you do something to help one of your friends? What is one way your actions affected your friendship?

- When was a time when you were new to a group? How did you learn to fit in?

Once students have decoded the task by forming their own questions, tell them to outline their response. Remind them to include a beginning, a middle (with events in chronological order), and an ending.

Narrative Writing in Review

Narrative Writing Checklist 155

tell **share** remember **narrate** relate

Purpose: In narrative writing, you *tell a story* about something that has happened.

Topics: Narrate . . . an experience that taught you something,
an experience that covers a period of time,
a story about another person's life,
a time of personal change, or
a memorable event.

Prewriting

Select a topic from your own (or another's) life. List important times in your life to use as a possible topics. (See page 102.)

Organize key events. Do some freewriting to arrange key events in chronological order. (See page 104.)

Remember the details by creating a chart of details and feelings. (See page 105.)

Writing

In the beginning, grab the reader's attention and use transitions to smoothly move the reader through your opening paragraph. (See page 109.)

In the middle, use dialogue, sensory details, and personal feelings. "Show, don't tell," to help the reader understand the experience. (See pages 110–111.)

In the ending, tie the beginning to the ending or explain the importance of the event or experience. (See page 112.)

Revising

Review the ideas, organization, and voice first. Then check **word choice** and **sentence fluency**. Combine and expand sentences to eliminate choppy writing. (See pages 114–124.)

Editing

Check your writing for conventions. Check your writing for subject-verb agreement, and ask a friend to check the writing, too. (See pages 126–128.)

Make a final copy and proofread it for errors before sharing it with other people. (See page 129.)

Assessing

Use the narrative rubric to assess your finished writing. (See pages 130–131.)

NARRATIVE

Narrative Writing in Review

Provide students with strong samples of narrative writing.
- Write your own or do an Internet search for examples, using the key words "narrative prompts."
- Make sure you modify the prompts to match the format of the state assessment that your students will take.

Tell students to refer to the checklist on PE page 155 whenever they have a narrative writing assignment. Have students put a sticky note on this page for handy reference.

Expository Writing Overview

Unit Objectives

The writing standards listed below are based on a blending of state and NCTE standards.

- Use diagrams, charts, and freewriting to gather and organize ideas.
- Establish a clear focus with topic sentences that explain ideas.
- Support the thesis with a variety of specific, interesting details.
- Revise drafts to create a precise pattern and an interested voice.
- Assess writing using a rubric based on the traits of effective writing.

Writing Forms

- expository paragraph
- classification essay
- compare-contrast essay

Focus on the Traits

- **Ideas** Including new and interesting information that explains and defines
- **Organization** Connecting details and following a precise pattern
- **Voice** Using words and details that fit the purpose and connect with the reader
- **Word Choice** Selecting precise nouns, active verbs, and no unnecessary modifiers
- **Sentence Fluency** Constructing sentences that combine ideas, avoid rambling, and flow easily
- **Conventions** Checking for errors in punctuation, capitalization, spelling, and grammar
- Creating a sorting chart to list specific details for each category

Note: For specifics about reading the chart below, see page TE 33.

Suggested Expository Writing Unit (Five Weeks)

Day	Writing and Skills Units	In the *Write Source* book			On the CD-ROM	*SkillsBook*
		Pages	Proofreader's Guide—basic grammar rules	Basic Grammar practice	Interactive Grammar Exercises	grammar practice pages
1–4	**Expository Paragraph:** Classification	157–160				
	Skills Activities: Complete Sentences (Understood and Delayed Subjects)		690–691, 692–693, 694–695	500–501	Sentences— Subjects and Predicates Objects and Indirect Objects	65–66, 74
	Using the Right Word		662–669			55
opt.	*Speeches*	428–429				
5	**Expository Essay: Classification** (Model)	161–164				

WEEK 1

Day	Writing and Skills Units	In the *Write Source* book			On the CD-ROM	*SkillsBook* grammar practice pages
		Pages	Proofreader's Guide—basic grammar rules	Basic Grammar practice	Interactive Grammar Exercises	
6–7	(Prewriting)	165–170				
8–9	(Writing)	171–176				
10–13	(Revising)	177–188				
	Skills Activities: Awkward Sentences			522 (+)		91–92
	Misplaced Modifiers			507		87–88
	Rambling Sentences		690 (+)	505		85
	Combining Sentences with Subordinating Conjunctions		698–699, 744 (+), 746–747	496 (+), 498	Sentence Combining	111–112, 117–118
14–15	(Editing and Publishing)	189–193				
	Skills Activities: Apostrophes (Possession)		604–605, 606–607	472	Apostrophes	27–28, 31–32
	Using the Right Word		670–674		Using the Right Word—3	56
16–18	(Assessing) (Reflecting)	194–197, 198				
opt.	*Speeches*	428–429				
opt.	*Practical Writing: Memo*	212–213				
	Skills Activities: Apostrophes (Possession)		604 (+)			29–30
	Spelling		642 (+), 644		Spelling—1 and 2	
19–20	Expository Writing for Assessment	214–216				
1–5	**Comparison Contrast Essay:** (Model)	199–201				
	(Prewriting)	202–203				
	(Writing)	204				
	(Revising)	204				
	Skills Activities: Comparative and Superlative Adjectives and Adverbs		734 (+), 738–739	491	Adjectives and Adverbs (+)	169–170, 172
	Comma Splices and Run-On Sentences			504		77, 78, 79–80
	(Editing)	204				
	Skills Activities: Double Negatives			510		86

WEEKS 2–3

WEEK 4

WEEK 1 SECOND FORM

Teacher's Notes for Expository Writing

This overview for expository writing includes some specific teaching suggestions for this unit.

Writing an Expository Paragraph (pages 157–160)

When students write an expository paragraph, they organize and present factual information in a way that demonstrates what they have learned or what they understand about a subject.

Writing a Classification Essay (pages 161–198)

Classification is a way to identify the similarities between two or more objects or people. Science depends upon classification to categorize all we see. Before writing a classification essay, a student must find out what makes each group unique. Remind students that classification focuses on general characteristics. Individual items, animals, or people within a group will have their own special features.

Writing a Comparison-Contrast Essay (pages 199–204)

With so many options available, comparing and contrasting are two important skills. Students will have a chance to consider differences between groups and individuals as well as their similarities. Developing this skill will help students make informed decisions about political candidates, car purchases, healthful foods, and so on.

Writing Across the Curriculum (pages 205–213)

Expository (informational) paragraphs or essays are required in most disciplines. Models included in this chapter will show expository essays in social studies, math, science, and practical writing.

Writing for Assessment (pages 214–216)

The model in this chapter will give students an idea of what kind of questions might be posed, and what kind of answers might be expected. Students can't prepare to answer specific questions or even general categories. However, if they learn how to prepare and write an expository essay, they will be ready to deal with state and school writing tests that focus on this writing form.

describe
define

Expository Writing

solve
explain
inform

Minilesson

Class Act   Expository Paragraph

■ For the following subjects, **LIST** the various classifications (categories) you would use to write an expository paragraph: matter, animals, numbers, media, vehicles. **DISCUSS** your results with a classmate.

In a Class by Itself   Classification Essay

■ **PICK** three different types of fruit. **LIST** the general features that make each fruit group special. Then **WRITE** down as many specific features for an individual fruit type as you can. **SHARE** your information with a classmate.

Leaves and Needles   Comparison-Contrast Essay

■ **READ** brief descriptions of a pine tree and an oak tree. **DIVIDE** a sheet of paper into two columns. At the top of one column, **WRITE** "similarities." On top of the other column, **WRITE** "differences." **LIST** the similarities and differences between the two types of trees in their respective columns. **SAVE** your results for a future comparison-contrast essay.

Expository Writing
Expository Paragraph

Astronomers estimate that the universe contains ten thousand billion billion stars. That's a 1 with 22 zeroes after it! Even so, those innumerable stars fall into just seven main types. Seven is a much more manageable number than ten thousand billion billion!

Whenever you separate something into types or parts, you are classifying it. In this chapter, you will write a classification paragraph that will break a topic into categories. When you are finished, you can share with your reader a part of your universe.

Writing Guidelines

Subject:	A topic that can be broken down into categories
Form:	Expository paragraph
Purpose:	To share information
Audience:	Classmates

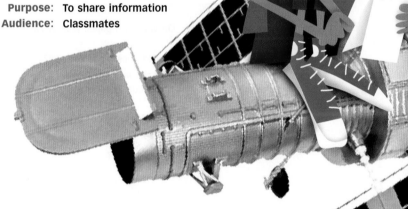

Expository Paragraph

Objectives
- understand the content and structure of an expository paragraph
- choose a topic (one that can be broken into categories) to write about
- plan, draft, revise, and edit an expository paragraph

An **expository paragraph** explains by presenting the steps, the causes, or the kinds of something. A classification paragraph that explains the parts of a topic is an example of an expository paragraph. Like most paragraphs, an expository paragraph contains a topic sentence, body sentences, and a closing sentence.

✱ For more about constructing expository paragraphs, see PE page 528.

Point out that people read for information every day. One way to get information is to read a newspaper. Other sources for information about current events include a magazine article or the Internet.

Expository Paragraph

Before students read the sample paragraph, ask them to suggest ways that they would **classify** (*see below*) the planets (possible responses: by distance from the sun, size, or number of moons).

 Respond to the reading.

Review the questions orally to assess students' understanding of a classification paragraph.

Answers

Ideas **1.** terrestrial planets, gas giants, planetoids

Organization **2.** order of location

Voice & Word Choice **3.** Possible choices:

- terrestrial planets are made of rock and metal; midsize planets Mercury, Venus, Earth, and Mars; rotate slowly
- gas giants, Jupiter, Saturn, Uranus, and Neptune; formed from gases such as hydrogen and helium
- planetoids . . . are too small to be true "planets"; Pluto; don't have moons

158

Expository Paragraph

The classification paragraph is a simple way to present the parts of a topic. It begins with a **topic sentence** that tells what the paragraph will be about. The **body** sentences that follow present the categories along with specific details about each. Finally, the **closing sentence** wraps up the paragraph. The following paragraph classifies the types of "planets" in our solar system.

Topic
Sentence

Body

Closing
Sentence

Three Types of Planets

People often think all planets are alike, but there are actually three types of planets in the solar system. The terrestrial planets are made of rock and metal and are closest to the sun. These include the midsize planets Mercury, Venus, Earth, and Mars. They rotate slowly and don't have many moons. Farther from the sun are the planets called gas giants, Jupiter, Saturn, Uranus, and Neptune. They are called gas giants because they are formed from gases such as hydrogen and helium. Gas giants rotate fast and have many moons. Finally, planetoids are objects made up of rock and ice and are too small to be true "planets." Planetoids sometimes even get pulled into a planet's gravitational field and become moons themselves. Whether they are terrestrials, gas giants, or planetoids, the planets in the solar system are fascinating.

 Respond to the reading. On your own paper, answer each of the following questions.

- [ ] Ideas **(1)** What three categories does the writer give?
- [ ] Organization **(2)** How does the writer organize the specific categories (order of location, order of importance, time order)?
- [ ] Voice & Word Choice **(3)** What words or phrases show that the writer is knowledgeable about the topic?

Teaching Tip: Classify and Categorize

Students may be confused by the words *classifying* and *categorizing*. Point out that these are synonyms that can be used interchangeably. In this unit, however, the verb *classify* is used. It means to put items with similar characteristics into groups. These groups are called categories. The act of grouping things into categories is called classification.

English Language Learners

To provide visual support for the sample paragraph on this page, display a graphic of the planets.

- As you read the paragraph, involve different students in putting different-colored sticky notes with the appropriate descriptors on the planets mentioned.
- For example, one student will put blue sticky notes that say *rock and metal* on the planets

Mercury, Venus, Earth, and Mars.

- Have students continue this process using different-colored sticky notes for the rest of the planets.
- By the end of the activity, students will be able to see the categories by looking at the sticky notes.

Prewriting Selecting a Topic

To select a topic, make a diagram. Select two things you know about and write them at the top. Then list the different categories that can be found in each topic. The writer of the paragraph on page 158 created the following diagram and put a star next to the topic she wanted to write about.

Line Diagram

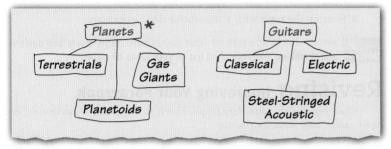

Create a diagram and select a topic. Using the diagram above as a guide, create your own, listing two or three topics that interest you along with their categories. Put a star next to the topic you would like to write about.

Writing a Topic Sentence

Many subjects are too broad for a single paragraph. You can't sum up the universe, for example, in one paragraph. However, you can explain the types of planets in our solar system. Your topic sentence should (1) name the topic, and (2) mention its categories. A simple formula follows.

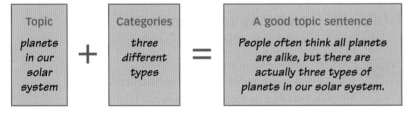

Topic		Categories		A good topic sentence
planets in our solar system	+	three different types	=	People often think all planets are alike, but there are actually three types of planets in our solar system.

Write your topic sentence. Use the basic formula above to write a topic sentence for your paragraph. You may need to try a few different versions to make this sentence say exactly what you want it to say.

EXPOSITORY

Prewriting Selecting a Topic

Model how to make a line diagram by creating one for the topic and sources discussed on TE page 157:

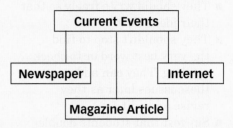

One of the benefits of a classification paragraph (or essay) is that the topic often creates its own organizational plan. Use the sample paragraph on PE page 158 to illustrate this idea.

- One of the characteristics of each category of planets is distance from the sun, so it makes sense to organize the paragraph by order of location.
- As students list categories for a topic, tell them to see if a logical way to organize ideas presents itself.

Prewriting
Writing a Topic Sentence

Point out that if students have more than three or four categories, then their subject is probably too broad. Suggest that they narrow their focus or save the idea for a longer assignment.

✱ See pages PE 552–553 for more on writing good topic sentences.

Struggling Learners

To assist students with topic selection, provide a list of possible topics and help students identify categories for each.

Possible topics and categories include the following:

- army careers: combat, engineering, logistics, health care
- women's gymnastics: vault, uneven bars, balance beam, floor exercise
- ground squirrels: chipmunks, prairie dogs, woodchucks
- alternative fuels: electric, compressed natural gas, hydrogen, ethanol, methanol
- natural fibers: cotton, wool, linen, hemp, jute

Writing
Developing the First Draft

Point out to students the following writing tips:

- They should write freely so that their ideas flow.
- They shouldn't stop to find the very best word or to check spelling. They can address these issues later as they revise and edit.
- Suggest that students double-space their writing so that they will have the space to mark revisions and corrections.

Revising
Improving Your Paragraph

Consider having students revise their paragraphs as part of a revising workshop.

Editing
Checking for Conventions

Have students exchange papers to check for conventions.

160

Writing Developing Your First Draft

A classification paragraph consists of a topic sentence, a body that explains the categories—with supporting details—and a closing sentence.

- Include your topic sentence at the beginning of the paragraph.
- Write body sentences explaining your topic's categories and arrange them in the best possible order: order of importance, chronological (time) order, or order of location. (See page **551**.)
- Sum up the topic with a thoughtful closing sentence.

 Write the first draft of your paragraph. Write freely and don't worry about making mistakes. Just get all your ideas on paper.

Revising Improving Your Paragraph

After you finish your paragraph, check it for *ideas, organization, voice, word choice,* and *sentence fluency.*

 Review your paragraph. Think about the following questions as you revise your writing.

1. Is my topic sentence clear? What details should I add or remove?
2. Are my categories and details organized in the best way?
3. Do I sound knowledgeable about my topic?
4. Are my words clear and precise?
5. Do my sentences flow smoothly? Have I included a thoughtful closing?

Editing Checking for Conventions

After you revise your paragraph, check it for *conventions.*

 Edit your work. Answer the questions below.

1. Did I use correct punctuation and capitalization?
2. Have I checked my spelling and grammar?

Proofread your paragraph. After making a neat copy of your paragraph, check it one more time for errors.

Grammar Connection

Complete Sentences

- **Proofreader's Guide** pages 690–691, 692–693, 694–695
- *Write Source* pages 500–501
- *SkillsBook* pages 65–66, 74
- **CD** Sentences—Subjects and Predicates, Direct Objects and Indirect Objects

Using the Right Word

- **Proofreader's Guide** pages 662–669
- *SkillsBook* page 55

English Language Learners

Point out the second bullet under **Writing**. Explain what each type of organization means. Discuss why the writer used order of location in the sample paragraph on PE page 158. Have students consider topics the class has brainstormed and discuss which type of organization might work best for each topic.

describe *solve*
define explain *inform*   **161**

Expository Writing
Classification Essay

Medieval soldiers came in three varieties: foot soldiers, archers, and knights. Foot soldiers dressed in mismatched armor and carried simple weapons such as poleaxes or flails. Archers often wore no armor, but stood behind other troops to shoot their long bows. Knights wore suits of armor, fought from horseback, and used swords, lances, and shields.

When you identify the types or categories of something, you are using classification. In this chapter, you will write a classification essay. The key is to select a topic that you know well and can separate into categories.

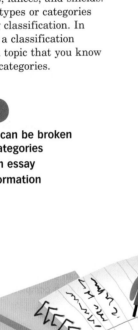

Writing Guidelines

Subject:	A topic that can be broken down into categories
Form:	Classification essay
Purpose:	To share information
Audience:	Classmates

English Language Learners

In order for students to make sense of the first paragraph on this page and to understand the sample essay they will focus on in subsequent pages, be sure they know that *medieval* refers to the time in European history between 500 and 1450 C.E.

- Show students illustrations of soldiers from the period.
- The pictures you show don't necessarily have to depict the exact content of the paragraph, but they should give students a general idea of the time period.

Classification Essay

Objectives
- understand what a classification essay is
- understand the form and content of a classification essay
- plan, draft, revise, edit, and publish a classification essay

A **classification essay** is a piece of writing that
- identifies the main categories of a topic;
- explains the categories, using clear and interesting details; and
- is organized by category.

Have students recall the classification paragraph they wrote earlier. Then tell them to read the introduction on this page silently. When they have finished, ask them what they noticed about the first paragraph. They may note that it
- is a classification paragraph, similar in form but shorter than the paragraph they wrote,
- classifies types of medieval soldiers by their armor and weapons, and
- is organized according to the rank of soldiers, from lowest to highest rank.

Materials

Six-trait checklist (TE p. 193)

Understanding Your Goal

Traits of Expository Writing

Three traits relate to the development of the content and the form. They provide a focus during prewriting, drafting, and revising.

- Ideas
- Organization
- Voice

The other three traits relate more to form. Checking them is part of the revising and editing processes.

- Word Choice
- Sentence Fluency
- Conventions

The more opportunities that students have to apply the writing traits, the sooner these traits will become second nature to them.

- Have students explain how they have applied or plan to apply a writing trait to current writing assignments.
- Refer students to the traits chart as you work through the sample essay on PE pages 163–164 so that they can "see" the traits.

* The six-point rubric on PE pages 194–195 is based on these traits. Reproducible six-, five-, and four-point rubrics for expository writing can be found on TE pages 751, 755, and 759.

162

Understanding Your Goal

When you plan your expository essay, keep the following traits in mind. Understanding these traits will help you reach your goal of writing an excellent expository essay.

Traits of Expository Writing

Ideas

Choose a topic that can be broken down into at least three classes or categories. Then support each with a variety of interesting details.

Organization

Develop a precise pattern of organization for each category and clearly connect your details.

Voice

Use words and details that fit your purpose and connect with the reader.

Word Choice

Select precise words that clearly explain each of the categories.

Sentence Fluency

Write a variety of sentences that connect your ideas smoothly.

Conventions

Use punctuation, capitalization, spelling, and grammar correctly.

 Get the big picture. Review the rubric on pages 194–195 before you get started on your writing. You can use this rubric as a guide to develop your essay and as a tool to assess your completed writing.

Classification Essay

In the expository essay below, the writer identifies and explains three types of armor that have been developed over thousands of years of history. The key parts of the expository essay are listed in the left margin.

Centuries of Protection

Beginning

The beginning introduces the topic and presents the focus statement (underlined).

Middle

The first middle paragraph describes the first category and explains its drawbacks.

The second category is explained.

Officer T. J. Cosford, a guest speaker at Cooper School, showed students a bulletproof vest. This type of body armor once saved his partner's life. While armor has been used throughout the ages, the materials used to make it have changed a great deal over time. From chain mail to steel suits to Kevlar vests, armor has protected people for centuries.

Even though armor had been around for more than 2,500 years, the first important change in armor took place around 1000 C.E. That was when soldiers began wearing chain mail. Chain mail was made of thousands of little metal rings hooked together. The thin rings formed a kind of metal cloth that could be draped around a soldier's body. It was lighter than a metal plate and could cover large areas of a soldier's body. However, chain mail was not perfect. It did very little to stop the impact of a blow from a sword. The chain mail wearer still could be injured or killed.

The next type of armor, the steel suits worn by knights in the 1400s, was a step up from chain mail. A complete suit had the following parts: a breastplate, a back plate, flexible arm and leg covers, gloves, shoes, and a helmet with a hinged door that protected the face. Besides being extremely heavy, the armored suits were expensive to make. Only the rich could afford to wear them. A knight needed people to help him get dressed and mount his horse for battle. Although these steel

EXPOSITORY

Classification Essay

Work through this sample essay with students, pointing out the elements that make it a good classification essay.

Ideas
- The topic is broken down into three categories.
- Each category is supported by interesting details.

Organization
- Each middle paragraph identifies the armor and tells when it was first used. Next it discusses design and materials. Finally, it describes advantages or drawbacks.
- The writer ties the ending to the beginning by commenting on how much the materials have changed over the centuries. The writer also begins and ends the essay by talking about a guest speaker.

Voice & Word Choice
- The writer's use of a story about an uncle shows personal interest.
- Dates and information about how materials affected ease of use show knowledge.

English Language Learners

Support students' understanding of the sample essay by showing related illustrations and pointing out elements, such as chain mail, that might be unfamiliar to them.

- Sources for this information include highly illustrated

books such as *DK Eyewitness Guides: Knight.*
- Another way to find illustrations is to use the Image function of an Internet search engine. Conduct a search using the keyword *armor*.

Respond to the reading.

Answers

Ideas 1. the history of materials used to make protective armor
2. chain mail, steel suits, Kevlar

Organization 3. Each middle paragraph follows this overall pattern:

- First, it identifies the armor and tells when it was first made or worn.
- Next, it discusses the design and materials of the armor.
- Finally, it describes advantages or drawbacks of the armor.

4. In the beginning and in the ending, the writer refers to

- how materials change over time, and
- a guest speaker's experience with armor.

Voice & Word Choice 5. Possible responses:

- Personal interest: the story about a guest speaker whose partner was saved by a bulletproof vest
- Knowledge: specific dates that tell when armor was first worn or invented; specific materials that have been used to protect people

164

Middle
The third middle paragraph describes the third category and explains its advantages.

Ending
The ending considers the overall importance of the topic.

suits offered excellent protection from weapons, they made movement very awkward. If he was knocked from his horse, a soldier in a suit of armor was as good as dead.

Today, the newest armor is made of plastics and man-made fabrics. One of these is Kevlar, invented in the 1970s. Kevlar is a lightweight fiber that is stronger than steel and more flexible than chain mail. With enough layers, Kevlar can stop a speeding bullet. The protective clothing items—helmets, jackets, vests, and boots—worn by today's soldiers contain Kevlar.

People have always needed to protect themselves in battle, and through the years, they found newer and better ways to do it. Types of protection have evolved from chain mail and metal suits to man-made materials. Battle armor will continue to evolve as long as it is needed. Science fiction suggests that someday people may be protected by invisible force fields. In the meantime, people like Mr. Cosford will continue to rely on the latest forms of armor.

Respond to the reading. Answer the following questions about the essay you just read.

☐ **Ideas** (1) What is the writer's topic? (2) What three main categories does the writer cover?

☐ **Organization** (3) Can you find the pattern that is used to organize each middle paragraph? Explain it. (4) How does the writer tie the ending to the beginning?

☐ **Voice & Word Choice** (5) How does the writer show personal interest in and knowledge of the topic? Give an example of each.

English Language Learners

To support students in answering the **Respond to the reading** questions, put the sample essay on an overhead transparency. Use a different-colored transparency pen for each trait to highlight key words in each section. (Ideas: armor, chain mail, steel suits, Kevlar; Organization: first, next, Today; Voice and Word Choice: how materials changed)

Struggling Learners

Point out the circular writing pattern in the sample by showing how the conclusion connects back to the introduction.

- Draw a circle on the board. Divide it into five sections.
- Label the sections of the circle 1–5. Then, as a class, list the parts of the sample and the topics (main ideas) of those parts. (1. Beginning: info about the guest speaker 2.

First middle paragraph: chain mail in 1000 C.E. 3. Second middle paragraph: steel suits in 1400s 4. Third middle paragraph: Kevlar in 1970s 5. Ending: people like the guest speaker continue to rely on armor.)

- Point out that the number 5 comes back to the number 1, and the main idea in the ending comes back to the main idea in the beginning.

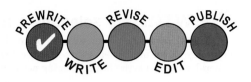

Classification Essay

165

Prewriting

Prewriting is the first step in the writing process. It involves selecting a topic, gathering specific details, and organizing your ideas.

Keys to Effective Prewriting

1. Select a topic that you know well or one you would like to know more about.

2. Write a focus statement that clearly states the topic and mentions its main types or categories.

3. Gather details that will make your essay clear and interesting.

4. Organize your details into three or four main categories.

5. Plan your essay using an organized list or an outline.

EXPOSITORY

Prewriting
Keys to Effective Prewriting

Remind students of the purpose of the prewriting stage in the writing process. (It's when the writer gets ready to write.)

"Keys to Effective Prewriting" explains the process students will be guided through on PE pages 166–170.

- Point out that one of the advantages of an expository writing assignment is that it provides an opportunity to learn something new.
- As students consider ideas for a topic (item 1), suggest that they ask themselves these questions: What have I read about, heard about, or seen recently that captured my interest and made me want to know more? What have I been studying in another class that I'd like to explore from a different angle?
- Emphasize that whatever topic they do finally select should be something that truly interests them.

Writing Workshop

Use the activities in the prewriting, writing, revising, and editing sections as minilessons for your writing workshop. Each activity focuses on a crucial skill and employs concrete strategies to help students succeed.

Prewriting Selecting a Topic

Ask students if there are any other subjects that they would like to add to the list of general subjects. (Possible responses: transportation, communication)

- Provide time for students to brainstorm for topics.
- Circulate among them to make sure that they are following directions and are able to come up with reasonable topic ideas.
- Students who are stuck can look back at the line diagrams they created while exploring topic ideas for their paragraph on PE page 159. One of those topics might be expanded into an essay topic.

* For more ideas for topics, see PE page 547.

Focus on the Traits

Ideas

Be sure students read **Focus on the Traits** before they star their topics.

- After starring topics, students can work in small groups to identify categories for each of the topics.
- If they can't easily identify at least three categories for an item, they should star a different topic.

166

Prewriting Selecting a Topic

The writer of the model essay on protective armor chose a topic that could be broken down into at least three main categories. Choose from the following general subjects for the brainstorming activity below.

clothing	education	health	occupation
exercise	friends	machines	recreation
food	goals	art/music	science

 Brainstorm for topics. To brainstorm for topics, you think freely about all the possibilities. You don't stop to think about any one idea. Just keep listing.

1 Select four general subjects that appeal to you from the list above.

2 On your own paper, draw a gathering chart like the one shown below. Write your four subjects on the top line.

3 List possible writing topics under each general subject.

4 Star the two topics that interest you the most. (You will use these topics in the next exercise.)

Gathering Chart

RECREATION	GOALS	ART/MUSIC	SCIENCE
biking *	climbing a	photography	animal
canoeing	mountain	popular	defenses *
skateboarding		music	storms

Focus on the Traits

Ideas The writer of the sample essay on pages 163–164 wrote about a topic that interested both him and his classmates. The topic worked well because it could be divided into three main categories that could be supported with specific details.

Struggling Learners

Some students may find the gathering chart too challenging.

- If you have already generated a list of several writing topics and related categories as a class (TE page 159), have students choose two of those writing topics and then create clusters (see PE page 264) to organize their details.

- Instruct students to label the center circle with the writing topic and the surrounding circles with the specific categories.

describe *solve* inform
define explain
167
Classification Essay

Sizing Up Your Topic

Once you have selected two possible topics, you should test them to see if they can be broken down into three or four categories. Use the guidelines below to test your topics:

Too Broad . . . Topics that are too broad have too many categories to explore. For example, "animals" has so many categories that you couldn't possibly cover them all in one essay.

Too Narrow . . . If a topic can't be easily broken down into categories, it is too narrow. For example, "octopus ink" would be too narrow.

Just Right . . . "Animal defenses" could include three or four natural methods that animals use to protect themselves. It is just right.

Choose your topic. On your own paper, write the two topics you starred in the exercise on page 166. Beneath each one, list at least three main categories of the topic. When you are finished, ask yourself the following questions about each topic. Then choose the better topic.

1 Does this topic have three or four main categories?

2 Could I find enough details to support each main category?

3 Is this topic *too broad, too narrow,* or *just right*?

Focusing Your Topic

Once you have selected a topic, it's time to write a *focus statement* (also called a *thesis statement*). An effective focus statement identifies the topic you will write about and how it can be broken down. (Sometimes you may wish to actually name the specific categories in your focus statement.)

The following formula was used to write a focus statement for an essay about animal defenses.

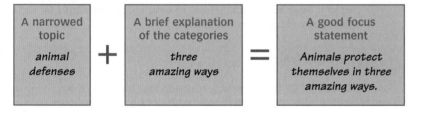

A narrowed topic		A brief explanation of the categories		A good focus statement
animal defenses	**+**	*three amazing ways*	**=**	*Animals protect themselves in three amazing ways.*

Write your focus statement. Using the formula shown above, write a focus statement for your classification essay.

Prewriting Sizing Up Your Topic

If there is time, students might enjoy helping each other evaluate possible topics and determine which are workable.

- Have students appoint three volunteer judges from the class. (Rotate this responsibility during the activity.)
- Give each judge a sign that says *Too Broad, Too Narrow,* or *Just Right.*
- Ask students to take turns presenting their topics, along with the main categories and possible details.
- Have the judges confer to decide if the topic will work. Tell them to hold up the appropriate sign and then be ready to explain their decision.

Prewriting Focusing Your Topic

Strongly encourage students to name the categories in their focus statement. Then the focus statement can truly help focus their writing. Later, if they wish, they can revise their focus statement to include a more general explanation of the categories.

English Language Learners

As students make decisions about topics that will interest them and their readers, provide input about the availability of research materials. Be sure that students will be able to find sufficient material at their reading level to gather information for their topic. If not, steer them toward another choice.

Prewriting
Gathering and Sorting Details

To make sure students are able to generate details, circulate as they create their sorting chart.

- Check the categories they are using and offer advice for gathering details.
- If students cannot generate details or have chosen an unworkable topic, schedule a **writing conference** (*see below*) to discuss options.

✻ For additional instruction about gathering interesting details, see PE page 531.

Focus on the Traits

Organization
Remind students that in a well-constructed paragraph, all the other sentences in the paragraph support the topic sentence.

- Explain that each category and group of details will be arranged in a paragraph.
- Suggest that students number the details in the order in which they might put them in the paragraph.

Prewriting Gathering and Sorting Details

Now that you have selected your topic and written your focus statement, you can begin gathering and sorting details. Sorting helps you see how many details you have for each category. Study the sorting chart below from the student essay about how animals protect themselves.

 If you think of something you would like to add to your list, but you don't know enough about it, write it down as a question and circle it. Do whatever reading or researching is necessary to answer your questions.

Sorting Chart

Changing Colors	Using Chemicals	Releasing Body Parts
- Snowshoe rabbits turn white in winter.	- Skunks spray a stinky liquid.	- Starfish drop arms.
- Cuttlefish turn colors.	- Some frogs taste bad.	*Do they regrow their lost parts?*
Is there a color that cuttlefish can't change to?	- Octopuses shoot dark, cloudy ink.	- Salamanders can regrow a leg or tail.

 Create your sorting chart. On your own paper, draw a sorting chart like the one above. At the top, write the three or four main categories you've chosen to write about. Then, in each column, list specific details for each category and add any questions you may have.

Focus on the Traits

Organization If you are able to divide your topic into three or four main categories, you will also be able to easily divide your essay into clear paragraphs. Remember that each paragraph should address one main category of the topic.

Struggling Learners

Encourage students to leave space beneath each question that is included in their sorting chart. After researching, the students can then write the answer in the reserved space, which will enable them to keep their information organized.

Teaching Tip: Writing Conference

Brief, one-on-one discussions can help some students focus ideas and gain confidence. Many students are more likely to share thoughts and volunteer ideas when they don't feel that their ideas are being scrutinized or judged by their peers.

If you find that a student's topic or categories will not work or the student is having trouble generating details, redirect

his or her efforts, using these questions:
- How interested are you in this topic?
- Can this topic be broken down into other categories that are related?
- What do you know about these categories already?
- How could you find out more about each of these categories?

Writing Topic Sentences

The topic sentence of each middle paragraph should clearly identify one of the categories. Each topic sentence should also include a transition that moves the reader smoothly from one category to the next. The writer of the essay on animal defenses used the topic sentences below to rate the defenses from least to most unusual. (For more information on topic sentences, see pages 552–553.)

Topic Sentences

Topic sentence 1: *One common way animals protect themselves is* by changing color to blend in with their environment.

Topic sentence 2: *A more unusual way animals avoid attack is* by giving off a chemical that smells bad or clouds the surroundings.

Topic sentence 3: *Perhaps the most amazing way animals protect themselves is* by releasing a tail or another body part to get away when captured.

Write your topic sentences. Use the above models to help you write your topic sentences.

1 Keep your focus statement in mind as you write each topic sentence.

2 Be sure each topic sentence addresses one of the main categories mentioned in the focus statement.

3 Include a transition to introduce or say something important about the category. (For more information on transitions, see pages 572–573.)

EXPOSITORY

Focus on the Traits

Voice In a classification essay, you want to sound both interested and knowledgeable. Search for fascinating details and amazing facts to include in your writing.

Prewriting

Writing Topic Sentences

Use the sample topic sentences and the questions below to help students see how transitions can help them connect and organize their ideas.

- What transition words in the sample sentences show the order of animal defenses from least to most unusual? *(One common way, A more unusual way, Perhaps the most amazing way)*.
- What order makes the most sense for your topic sentences?
- What transitions will work to show that order?

Focus on the Traits

Voice
One of the most effective ways for students to show interest in their topic is with a personal anecdote. Ask them to search their memories and their personal journals or discuss their topic with friends and family to trigger ideas for a personal anecdote.

English Language Learners

Make a chart of the types of organization and examples of transition words related to each. Use the headings *Importance, Time Order,* and *Location.*

- Point out that the examples on this page are in order of importance. Write the transition phrases *(One common way, A more unusual way, the most amazing way)* under *Importance.*

- Write the transition words that were used in "Centuries of Protection" (PE pages 163–164) under *Time Order (first, next, Today).*
- Write the transition words *(closest, farther, farthest)* for "Three Types of Planets" (PE page 158) under *Location.*

Keep this chart on display as students write topic sentences for their middle paragraphs.

Struggling Learners

Caution students about two mistakes that are often made when writing topic sentences for middle paragraphs. Write these examples on the board and have students identify the problem with each:

- The cuttlefish changes from orange to yellow. (tells too much, better as a supporting detail)
- My next topic is chemicals. (writer talks to reader)

Prewriting
Organizing Your Ideas

Students may have more than two details for each category.

- Suggest, however, that they limit the details to a maximum of four.
- Assist students as needed with listing the detail sentences for each topic sentence.

Writer's Craft

Two approaches: Some writers are builders. They outline their writing as if creating a blueprint for a building and then construct their writing carefully, step-by-step. Here is a quotation from Frank Yerby, who was one such writer. "Writing a novel is like building a wall, brick by brick; only amateurs believe in inspiration."

Other writers are gardeners. They plant seeds and nurture them and weed them and see what comes up. Here is a quotation from Robert Frost, who followed this approach. "A poet never takes notes. You never take notes in a love affair."

Though the two sides disagree on how to approach writing, both have to cover the same ground. The builder needs to make a structure come to life, and the gardener needs to make a living thing follow a structure. Either approach succeeds if the writer follows it through to completion. Either approach fails if the writer stops short.

Prewriting Organizing Your Ideas

The focus statement identifies the overall topic and main categories of the classification essay. Each category becomes a topic sentence in the actual essay.

Directions   **Organized List**

| Write your focus statement (thesis). | *Animals protect themselves in three amazing ways.* |

Write the first category.	1. *Changing color to blend in with surroundings*
List your first example.	– *Rabbit turns brown in summer, white in winter*
List your second example.	– *Cuttlefish changes to color of surroundings*

Write the second category.	2. *Using chemicals*
List your first example.	– *Skunk repels attackers with foul-smelling liquid*
List your second example.	– *Octopus squirts dark, inky fluid*

Write the third category.	3. *Releasing body parts*
List your first example.	– *Salamander and starfish drop a limb*
List your second example.	– *Gecko drops its tail to get away*

Make sure you have approximately the same number and kinds of details for each main category in your essay. When you revise, you will check for a balance of information from one paragraph to the next.

 Make an organized list. To create your list, follow the "Directions" in the sample above. You will use this list as you write your essay.

Advanced Learners

Pair advanced learners with students who have difficulty organizing their information into a logical order. Have the writer put each topic sentence on a separate strip of paper. Then the partners can arrange the strips in different orders and discuss why a certain type of organization might work best.

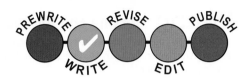

describe solve inform
define explain
Classification Essay **171**

PREWRITE REVISE PUBLISH
WRITE EDIT

Writing

Once you've finished your prewriting, it's time to write your first draft. You're ready to write a first draft when you know enough about your topic and have written a clear focus statement.

Keys to Effective Writing

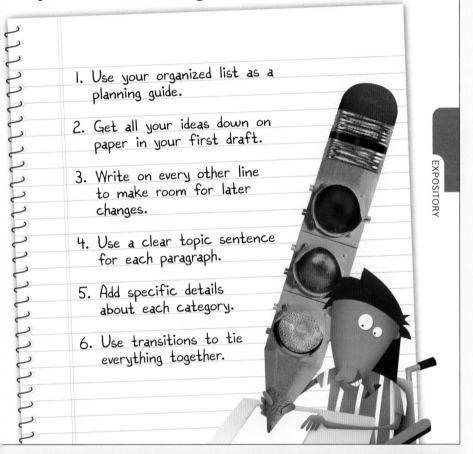

1. Use your organized list as a planning guide.

2. Get all your ideas down on paper in your first draft.

3. Write on every other line to make room for later changes.

4. Use a clear topic sentence for each paragraph.

5. Add specific details about each category.

6. Use transitions to tie everything together.

EXPOSITORY

Writing Getting the Big Picture

Direct students' attention to the descriptions in the graphic of a good **beginning** *(see below),* middle, and ending. Then work together as a class to complete the **Try It** activity.

 Answers

■ **Middle paragraph 1** Topic sentence: That was when soldiers began wearing chain mail. Details: 1000 C.E., made of thousands of metal rings, rings formed a kind of metal cloth, lighter than metal plate, did little to stop impact of a sword blow, wearer could be injured or killed

■ **Middle paragraph 2** Topic sentence: The next type of armor, the steel suits . . . . Details: suit parts, extremely heavy, expensive to make, knight needed help getting dressed and mounting his horse, excellent protection from weapons, made movement awkward, soldier knocked from horse as good as dead

■ **Middle paragraph 3** Topic sentence: One of these [fabrics] is Kevlar . . . . Details: lightweight fiber, stronger than steel, more flexible than chain mail, can stop a speeding bullet, worn by today's soldiers

---

Writing Getting the Big Picture

Now that you have organized your categories into a logical order, you can begin writing your first draft. The graphic below shows how a classification essay is put together.

The opening paragraph contains a clear focus statement. The middle contains several supporting paragraphs, each one covering one main category of the topic. The closing paragraph sums up the essay. (The examples used below are from the sample essay shown on pages 173–176.)

Beginning The **beginning** captures the reader's interest, introduces your topic, and gives your focus statement.	**Focus Statement** Animals protect themselves in three amazing ways.
Middle The **middle** presents each category of your topic. Each middle paragraph includes one category and strong supporting details.	**Three Topic Sentences** One common way animals protect themselves is by changing color to blend in with their environment. A more unusual way animals avoid attack is by giving off a chemical that smells bad or clouds the surroundings. Perhaps the most amazing way animals protect themselves is by releasing a tail or another body part to get away when captured.
Ending The **ending** reminds the reader of the essay's focus and suggests the importance of the topic.	**Closing Sentence** However, without their amazing defenses, some animals would not survive.

TryIt Look at the three middle paragraphs of the model essay on pages 163–164. On your own paper, list the details that support the topic sentence in each paragraph.

Teaching Tip: Beginnings with Purpose

Help students understand the effect of a beginning that not only captures the reader's attention but also helps the writer connect with readers. Ask students to look at the beginning of the sample essay on PE pages 163–164 and to answer these questions:

● How does the writer capture the reader's attention right away? (tells how a guest speaker's partner was saved by a bulletproof vest)

● Why do you think the writer uses the story of the guest speaker? (It is exciting. It helps to create a bond between the writer, the topic, and the reader. It says, "This is a topic that could and should matter to everyone.")

Students will learn more about writing effective beginnings on PE page 173 and more about connecting with their audience on PE page 183.

Starting Your Essay

Begin by writing your opening paragraph as freely as you can. This paragraph should make the reader want to read your entire paper. It should also introduce the focus statement.

Several ways to begin a classification essay are shown below. Each of these examples is written in a different voice, but any would offer an interesting beginning. You might use one or more of these to start your essay.

> Beginning
>
> Middle
>
> Ending

- **Share interesting or surprising details about the subject.** *They sting! They stink! They taste bad! What could "they" possibly be? They are animals that protect themselves in amazing ways.*
- **Ask a question.** *What if you could suddenly change colors and blend into the background?*
- **Give interesting background information.** *For years, people have found many ways to protect themselves. Today, they wear camouflage uniforms and shoot pepper spray.*

Beginning Paragraph

In the beginning paragraph below, the writer combines interesting details with a question to introduce the focus statement.

The writer provides interesting background information and asks a question. **The writer includes a focus statement (underlined).**

> *For years, people have found many ways to protect themselves. Today, they wear camouflage uniforms and shoot pepper spray. Where did people get the ideas for these forms of protection? They may have come from the unusual ways animals defend themselves. Animals protect themselves in three amazing ways.*

EXPOSITORY

Write an opening. Write two beginning paragraphs, using one or more of the techniques given above. Ask yourself which opening will better capture the reader's attention and which one has a stronger voice.

Writing Starting Your Essay

To help students better understand how these three different techniques can affect the voice (or tone) of an essay, ask students to read the example beginnings and the sample beginning paragraph and decide

- which opening sentence they would have chosen, and
- how their choice might have affected the voice (or tone) of the rest of the essay.

English Language Learners

Provide additional models of engaging openings.

- Read opening sentences from a variety of sources, such as nonfiction books and magazine articles at an appropriate reading level.
- Help students identify which approach each opening sentence represents.

Struggling Learners

Present the following three openings for an essay on types of nuts, and ask students to identify the type of beginning used:

- Believe it or not, if stranded on a tropical island, a person could actually survive on coconuts! (share surprising details)
- Vegetarians often substitute nuts as an excellent source of protein. (give background information)
- Have you ever heard a person described as a "hard nut to crack?" (ask a question)

Writing
Developing the Middle Part

To give students a better understanding of the different ways to add specific details to their writing, have them find examples of each of these ways in the paragraphs here and in the sample essay on PE pages 163–164. Analyzing these essays will help students be more aware of how to use these tips when they write their own middle paragraphs. Here are examples students might find:

- Include facts and examples: snowshoe rabbit turns from brown in summer to white in winter.
- Explain a term: gecko, a tropical lizard.
- Make a comparison: chain mail—lighter than a metal plate; Kevlar—stronger than steel, more flexible than chain mail.
- Write about a personal experience: a guest speaker's partner was saved by a bulletproof vest.

Technology Connections

To find more student models of expository writing, go to the Write Source Web site at www.thewritesource.com.

Writing Developing the Middle Part

After writing your beginning paragraph, you are ready to develop the middle of your essay. Each middle paragraph should focus on one main category of your topic and include the specific details from your organized list (page 170). A well-organized paragraph uses a variety of details.

1. The **topic sentence** introduces the topic of the paragraph. (See the underlined sentence in the paragraph below.)

2. The **specific details** in each paragraph support the topic sentence. Here are several different ways to add details to your writing:
   - **Include facts and examples.**
   - **Explain a term.**
   - **Make a comparison.**
   - **Write about a personal experience.**

3. The **closing sentence** ends the paragraph and provides a final thought.

Middle Paragraphs

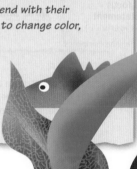

Topic Sentence

Specific Details

Closing Sentence

One common way animals protect themselves is by changing color to blend in with their environment. A good example of this is the snowshoe rabbit. This rabbit turns from brown in summer to white in winter. Its change in color makes it hard for predators to see the rabbit in dry summer grass and winter snow. Cuttlefish also change color to blend with their surroundings. Without the ability to change color, some species of animals would probably be extinct by now. Humans have borrowed this idea to make camouflage clothing.

Topic Sentence	*A more unusual way animals avoid attack is by giving off a chemical that smells bad or clouds the surroundings.* The skunk defends itself by releasing a foul-smelling chemical from glands found beneath its
Specific Details	tail. Because the chemical can severely sting eyes, and the smell is enough to send predators hurrying away, any animal that tangles with a skunk surely won't do it twice! An octopus squirts a dark, inky fluid in front of its attackers. The ink clouds the water and lets the octopus escape. **Did these protective methods give**
Closing Sentence	**someone the idea for pepper spray?**
Topic Sentence	*Perhaps the most amazing way animals protect themselves is by releasing a tail or another body part to get away when captured.* When a limb is trapped, these animals simply release it and go. A salamander's
Specific Details	tail will fall off to allow escape, and a starfish's detached arm will grow into a new starfish! The gecko, a tropical lizard, can drop its tail, which then keeps moving to distract the attacker. After the animal escapes, the lost body part will grow back. **Wouldn't it**
Closing Sentence	**be amazing if humans possessed the ability to regrow parts?**

EXPOSITORY

Write your middle paragraphs. Use your organized list (page 170) to help you write your middle paragraphs. Also consider the drafting tips listed below.

Drafting Tips

Here are some tips for writing your middle paragraphs.
- **Keep your purpose and audience in mind.**
- **Follow your plan or outline.**
- **Add new details if they fit the topic sentence.**

Review the drafting tips for writing middle paragraphs before asking students to draft their own middle paragraphs.

If necessary, remind students about their
- purpose (to write a classification essay about a topic that can be broken down into several categories) and
- audience (their classmates).

Point out that they are likely to write a strong essay that will receive a good assessment if they
- write with their audience in mind *(see below)* and
- follow all the other drafting tips.

Teaching Tip: Audience

Students may benefit from a refresher about why it is important to keep their audience in mind as they write. Discuss the different audiences students may write for during the course of the year, including
- teachers,
- classmates and friends,
- younger students,
- parents or adults, and
- the general public.

Explain that the basic difference among the various audiences is the extent of their knowledge of a topic. Writers who keep their audience in mind as they write choose details that are geared to what their audience knows about their topic. Ask students what kinds of details a writer might include in an essay about skateboarding for each of these different audiences:

- people who skateboard (advanced/new techniques),
- adults who have never skateboarded (history, terminology, how to get started), and
- younger children who are learning to skateboard (brief history, equipment, beginning techniques, safety tips).

Writing Ending Your Essay

Emphasize that each of the two possible endings shown is a good ending paragraph.

- Invite volunteers to tell which ending they prefer and to explain why.
- If students choose to follow the pattern of the first ending paragraph, emphasize that they should ask meaningful questions that will inspire readers to think about the topic, even after they finish reading the essay.
- Tell students to try to avoid asking questions that focus readers' attention on themselves and not on the topic, such as "What would you do if (your leg fell off)?"
- If time allows, have students gather in groups to brainstorm questions they might ask in an ending paragraph.

176

Writing Ending Your Essay

In your ending paragraph, you need to restate your focus and make a final statement. Below are two different ending paragraphs for the essay on animal defenses.

Ending Paragraphs

> **The writer asks the reader to think about the topic and then offers a final thought.**
>
> *Imagine that an individual's skin turned color when he or she went from a red carpet to green grass. What if someone simply dropped a leg if he or she got hurt in an accident, only to have a new leg grow back? Some ways animals use to protect themselves may seem like science fiction. However, without their amazing defenses, some animals would not survive.*

Your final paragraph could also

- summarize all your main points, and
- emphasize the special importance of the overall topic.

> **The writer suggests the importance of the essay and its information.**
>
> *Nature has provided animals with many different ways to protect themselves. They blend in with their surroundings, give off bad-tasting or bad-smelling chemicals, or even drop a captured limb. Over the years, humans have observed and copied many of these defenses. Human beings may be more intelligent, but they can still learn a lot from animals.*

Write your ending paragraph. Write a final paragraph for your essay using the suggestions above.

Write your complete first draft. Bring all the parts of your first draft together to form a complete essay.

Revising

A first draft never turns out quite right. One part may need more details. Another part may not be clear enough. Another part may be too dull. To fix or improve these parts, you need to carefully revise your first draft.

Keys to Effective Revising

1. Read through your entire draft to get a feeling for how well your essay works.

2. Make sure your focus statement states your topic clearly.

3. Check your paragraphs to make sure the details relate to the topic sentence and are in logical order.

4. Be sure you've used a knowledgeable, interested voice.

5. Check your writing for precise words and a variety of sentences.

6. Use the editing and proofreading marks inside the back cover of this book.

EXPOSITORY

Revising

Keys to Effective Revising

"Keys to Effective Revising" explains the process students will be guided through on PE pages 178–188.

Invite volunteers to share personal revising tips. Be sure to share your own tips for revising. Examples could include the following:

- using a graphic organizer to check that each paragraph has all its parts (topic sentence, supporting details that relate to the topic, closing sentence)
- waiting at least 24 hours after you finish a piece of writing to begin revising
- tape-recording a piece of writing and then playing it back to listen for precise words and sentence variety
- asking two people to read a piece of writing and suggest revisions

Peer Responding

Have students trade papers and read and respond to each other's writing. Peer responding helps writers know what to revise. It also helps create a writing community. For more on constructive peer responses, see pages 29–32.

Revising for Ideas

The rubric strips that run across all of the revising pages (PE pages 178–187) are provided to help students focus their revising and are related to the full rubric on PE pages 194–195.

Review the rubric strip at the top of PE pages 178–179. Students will use this rubric to look in their draft for

- different kinds of details, including definitions, explanations, and comparisons; and
- fascinating and surprising facts.

 Answers

1. definition
2. comparison
3. comparison
4. explanation
5. definition
6. explanation

178

Revising for Ideas

 6 My essay presents a variety of fascinating and surprising details for each category.

 5 My essay presents different kinds of interesting details.

 4 My essay has different kinds of details, but they are all basic details.

As you revise for *ideas*, check to see if you used different kinds of details. In a classification essay, you should also be offering information that is new and interesting to your reader. Use the above rubric strip to help you check your ideas.

How can I use different kinds of details?

You can use details to define, explain, or compare ideas in your essay.

- **Definitions** usually answer the question "What is it?"
  Octopus ink makes it hard for predators—the animals attacking the octopus—to see where the octopus is going.

- **Explanations** answer the question "What does it do?" or "Why or how does it do it?"
  An octopus squirts ink to cloud the water and let the octopus escape.

- **Comparisons** answer the question "What is it like?"
  The ink the octopus squirts is like the dust that hides a car on a dirt road.

 Below are six sentences from a classification essay on types of clocks. For each, tell whether the detail used is an explanation, a definition, or a comparison. Use the above questions to help you.

1. Ancient people often used the sun to tell time with an obelisk, a tall, tapered structure with a pyramid-like top.
2. Like obelisks, sundials also use the sun to tell time.
3. Modern watches are more accurate than nature's clocks.
4. Quartz crystals keep accurate time by using an electric field.
5. Quartz watches use an LCD, or liquid crystal display, to show time.
6. Atomic clocks are accurate to one-millionth of a second per year.

 Review your writing. Look for ideas that may need more explanation and for terms that need defining. Also consider making a comparison if it would make your ideas clearer.

English Language Learners

With your help, have students label the details— definition (D), explanation (E), and comparison (C)—in their essays. If students haven't used a variety of details, help them identify different kinds they might use.

describe solve inform
define explain **179**
Classification Essay

3 I need to use a variety of details to add interest.

2 I need to gather more details.

1 I need to understand the different kinds of details.

How can I go beyond basic details?

You know you have gone beyond basic details if a reader says, "Wow, I didn't know that!" For example, most people are familiar with the way a hedgehog rolls up into a ball to protect itself. But many people would not know that when it curls up, the animal also crawls into a protective bag created by its own skin! That's a detail that goes beyond "basic."

■ **Basic detail**

A frog can use its eyeballs for more than just seeing.

■ **Surprising detail**

A frog's eyeballs can drop down against the roof of its mouth to help push food down its throat.

 Read the following paragraph. Then write down two details that are surprising or especially interesting. Explain why you chose them.

1   Whales breathe through blowholes, exhaling air at over 300
2   mph. These watery explosions don't happen that often because
3   whales can hold their breath for as long as 90 minutes. Then they
4   must actually remember to breathe. When whales sleep, they float
5   near the surface with half of their brain awake. It's that half that
6   reminds the whales to breathe.

 Check your writing. Read through your essay to check for surprising details. If necessary, add some details that go beyond basic information.

Ideas
A surprising detail is added.

which then keeps moving to distract the attacker
The gecko, a tropical lizard, can drop its tail. After
the animal escapes, the lost body part . . .

EXPOSITORY

Discuss the difference between the **basic and surprising detail** in the instruction and in the examples. Invite students to provide surprising details about other animals they have studied.

Students will enjoy finding fascinating facts to add to their writing. Be sure to provide time for them to do the research.

After students do the **Try It** activity, invite them to share their responses with the class.

Try It Answers

Choices will vary depending on students' prior knowledge of the subject. Possible choices:

■ exhaling air at over 300 mph
■ whales can hold their breath for as long as 90 minutes
■ they must remember to breathe
■ they float with half of their brain awake

English Language Learners

Rather than having students labor over trying to search out amazing facts in books and encyclopedias, show them an easier way. Tell them to enter the word for their topic, such as *frogs,* and the key words *amazing facts* in a search engine to find Web sites that list amazing facts about specific subjects. (Screen the Web sites for reliability.)

Discuss the rubric strip. Students will use this rubric to review their writing for

- details that are clearly connected by transitions or by the repetition of key words, and
- a precise pattern that is repeated for each category.

Have students work independently to complete the **Try It** activity.

 **Answers**

Possible choices: walrus, tusks, spots, shore(s), teeth

Tell students to focus on one paragraph at a time as they check for connecting details.

- Remind them to also check for links between paragraphs.
- Their organizational plan should have included a specific order for presenting categories.
- Using transition words that suggest this order at the beginning of each middle paragraph is a good way to link ideas. If students need a reminder of how to do this, have them look back at the topic sentences in the sample essay on PE pages 174–175.

180

Revising **for** Organization

6 My details are connected and follow a precise pattern, making my essay clear and engaging.

5 My details are clearly connected with key words and transitions. I follow a precise pattern.

4 My details are connected, but the pattern isn't clear.

When you revise for *organization*, you need to check your details carefully. In a classification essay, the details should be clearly connected. They should also be arranged in the same pattern in each middle paragraph. The above rubric strip will help you check your essay for organization. (For additional information on organization, see pages **550–551**.)

Are my details clearly connected?

Your details are clearly connected when they build from one idea to the next. Here is a strategy to help you tie your ideas together.

- **Repeating a key word.**

The hermit crab's shell does not cover its soft abdomen. **To protect its** abdomen, **the crab backs into an abandoned shell and adopts it as its own.** (The key word *abdomen* connects the details.)

 Read the following paragraph and then list four key words that help to connect the sentences.

1 Seals, sea lions, and walruses are members of the same family,
2 but each has its unique characteristics. The walrus, for example,
3 has unique tusks that make it easy to pick out in a crowd. The tusks
4 are actually huge canine teeth that the walrus uses to establish
5 dominance and secure the best basking spots. To get to these
6 prime spots, the walrus uses its tusks to help pull itself onto rocky
7 or icy shores. Once on shore, the walrus is able to keep other sea-
8 going mammals away by simply displaying its super-sized teeth.

Revise **Check your details.** Read through your essay to check for clearly connected details. If you need to, add key words or transitions to create a link between your ideas.

English Language Learners

Have students use different-colored highlighters to mark instances of repetition of key words. If they find few or no instances of these connections, help them determine places where this type of repetition would be helpful.

describe *solve*
define explain *inform* **181**
Classification Essay

3 I connect some details, but I do not use a pattern.

2 Most of my details are not connected. I do not use a pattern.

1 I need to completely reorganize my paragraphs.

Do I follow a precise pattern in my essay?

You have followed a precise pattern if each main category is covered in the same way, with about the same number and types of details. You can establish this pattern in your organized list or outline. (See page 170.)

 Read the following paragraph. Then number your paper from 1 to 4 and arrange the four sentences below so they follow the same pattern used in the paragraph.

> The folk guitar neck is designed for playing popular music. The neck is tightly glued or bolted to the body to hold up to the tension of the steel strings. The strings are close together on the slender neck, making it easier to use a pick. Because the neck joins the body at the 14th fret, the musician can reach very high notes.

1. Because nylon strings cause less pressure, the wide neck can be carved together with the body.

2. The neck joins the body at the 12th fret to keep the tones low.

3. If you enjoy playing "art" music, the classical guitar is for you.

4. The wide neck keeps the strings spaced for easy finger picking.

 Check for paragraph pattern. Review each middle paragraph of your essay to see if you have followed the same pattern for each category.

Organization
A sentence is moved for a more precise pattern.

> A good example of this is the snowshoe rabbit. Its change in color makes it hard for predators to see the rabbit in dry summer grass and winter snow. This rabbit turns from brown in summer to white in winter.

EXPOSITORY

Complete the **Try It** activity orally.

 Answers

1. If you enjoy playing "art" music, the classical guitar is for you.
2. Because nylon strings cause less pressure, the wide neck can be carved together with the body.
3. The wide neck keeps the strings spaced for easy finger picking.
4. The neck joins the body at the 12th fret to keep the tones low.

If students discover that they did not follow a precise pattern in their draft, it is likely that they did not establish a pattern when they created their organizational list. Assure them that they probably have all the details they need; they just need to rearrange them.

As they reorder details, students will learn whether they have the right kinds of details to re-create the pattern of the first paragraph or if they have to find more details.

Struggling Learners

To help students determine the sample paragraph's pattern, help them identify the purpose of each sentence:

- the type of music identified with this type of guitar (popular)
- how the neck and body are attached (glue, bolts); type of strings (steel)
- positioning of the strings (close together)
- at what fret the neck joins the body (14th)

Encourage students to follow this model to establish a precise pattern in their own writing and to determine if any details are missing.

Revising for Voice

Remind students that *voice* is the way a piece of writing sounds to its audience. The best way for students to recognize voice is to read aloud a piece of writing or to ask someone else to read it aloud. The language used to present ideas will determine how the writing sounds.

Ask students to explain their responses to the **Try It** activity.

 **Answers**

1. presents facts in a clear and interesting way
2. too casual and informal (really cute, kind of like water pitchers, gross nectar, slimy, plop)
3. too personal, slangy (I was bowled over, It's true, Cool)
4. presents facts in a clear and interesting way

Point out to students that they can tell if their essay is too casual or personal if they have

- used the pronoun *I* repeatedly;
- included colloquial expressions, such as *cool, neat, awesome,* and *believe me*; or
- included overused or doubled modifiers, such as *really* or *very, very.*

182

Revising for Voice

6 My voice makes my reader feel I am speaking directly to him or her.	**5** My voice is appropriate for my purpose and connects with my audience.	**4** My voice is acceptable for my purpose, but it does not always connect with my audience.

When revising for *voice* in a classification essay, you must be certain that your voice fits your purpose and reaches the audience. The above rubric strip can guide you in your revising.

How can I tell if my voice fits my purpose?

You can tell if your voice fits your purpose in a classification essay if your writing presents interesting information without sounding too informal.

Try It Below are four passages from classification essays. Decide which of the passages present the facts in a clear and interesting way without sounding too personal or informal.

1 The saguaro cactus survives in the desert by storing water in its stem. The stem tissue can swell up to three times its size as it absorbs the rain.

2 Pitcher plants are really cute. Their leaves are kind of like water pitchers filled with a gross nectar that attracts insects. The bugs then slip on the slimy sides, plop into the liquid, and become plant food.

3 I was bowled over when I learned that the giant redwood tree actually needs a forest fire to reproduce! It's true—the heat of the fire forces the pine cones to open and drop their seeds. Cool!

4 Prairie grasses have adapted to the many fires common to their habitat. The growing structure of the plant is actually located under the ground. This way, when the top of the plant is burned away, new growth can spring up within a few days.

 Check your voice. Answer the following questions. If your voice is not quite right for the purpose of your essay, change some words or sentences.

1 Do I state the facts in a clear and interesting way?

2 Do I avoid words that sound too informal or personal?

describe solve
define explain inform **183**
Classification Essay

3 I need to use a more formal voice when connecting with my audience.

2 I need to use a voice throughout my essay and connect to my audience.

1 I need to learn about voice.

Does my voice connect with my audience?

Your voice will connect with your audience if your essay is informational and engaging. You can make this connection with your audience in several ways.

■ **Use specific examples.** Specific examples can make your thoughts clearer and more interesting to the reader.

Giant redwood trees can have bark two feet thick. The bark helps the trees survive droughts, insect attacks, and even forest fires.

■ **Share an anecdote.** A brief anecdote or story can make your information easier to understand.

People who are sprayed by a skunk try everything from bathing in tomato juice to covering themselves in baking soda.

■ **Relate your topic to the reader.** Allow your audience to see how the topic affects their lives.

If prairie grasses hadn't adapted to survive fires, the prairies would have eventually dried up and blown away. The loss of prairies would have changed the ecology of the entire country.

 Revise **Check reader reaction.** Ask a classmate to read your essay and suggest ways you could create a stronger connection. Use the strategies above as you revise.

EXPOSITORY

Voice
A sentence has been added to connect the topic with the reader's life.

After the animal escapes, the lost body part will
Wouldn't it be amazing if humans possessed
grow back.ʌ *the ability to regrow parts?*
   Imagine that an individual's skin turned color
when he or she went from a red carpet to green
grass. . . .

Ask students to suggest reasons writers would want to connect with their audience. Help them realize that writers want readers to

■ stay interested so that they'll keep reading;

■ say to themselves as they read, "I always wanted to know more about . . . " or "I didn't know that . . . "; and

■ understand, enjoy, and remember what they read.

Suggest that students use a three-point rubric to **check reader reaction** *(see below)*.

Teaching Tip: Checking Reader Reaction

Divide the class into small groups (three students per group) and have students make a copy of their essays for each group member. Then have students take turns reading aloud their essays as group members focus on the trait of voice.

Provide a three-point rubric to help responders offer quick and

easy-to-comprehend feedback. For example:

● Interest Level:
  3 some amazing facts
  2 interesting
  1 few facts
● Level of Knowledge:
  3 clear definitions and/or explanations
  2 some precise words and terms

  1 only general words and information
● Audience Fit:
  3 clear and interesting
  2 too personal or informal
  1 very informal and uninteresting

You may also want to include an open-ended prompt, such as "Suggestions for Improvement."

Revising for Word Choice

After discussing the sample thesaurus entry, demonstrate how to look up a word in a thesaurus and read the entry.

 **Answers**

Answers may vary. Accept all reasonable responses. Possible answers:

1. dash, hurry
2. be in charge of, organize
3. gushes, floods

When given a thesaurus, many student writers will replace words at random without considering if the new words make sense. Before asking students to use a thesaurus to revise, tell them not to replace words that work well already. They should choose words that fit the meaning and tone of their writing.

184

Revising for Word Choice

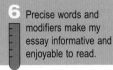 **6** Precise words and modifiers make my essay informative and enjoyable to read.

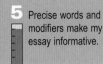 **5** Precise words and modifiers make my essay informative.

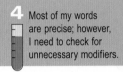 **4** Most of my words are precise; however, I need to check for unnecessary modifiers.

Use precise words and phrases to give your writing clarity. Also avoid the trap of overusing modifiers. The above rubric can help you check for *word choice*.

How can I find precise words?

One way to find just the right word for your essay is to use a thesaurus. A thesaurus is a book that lists synonyms and antonyms. If your thesaurus is arranged alphabetically, look up your word as you would in a dictionary. If you are using a traditional thesaurus, look up your word in the index.

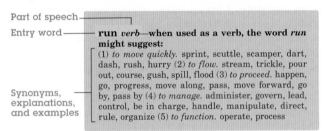

Part of speech
Entry word

run *verb*—when used as a verb, the word *run* might suggest:
(1) *to move quickly.* sprint, scuttle, scamper, dart, dash, rush, hurry (2) *to flow.* stream, trickle, pour out, course, gush, spill, flood (3) *to proceed.* happen, go, progress, move along, pass, move forward, go by, pass by (4) *to manage.* administer, govern, lead, control, be in charge, handle, manipulate, direct, rule, organize (5) *to function.* operate, process

Synonyms, explanations, and examples

Not every synonym for a word has the same meaning. Note how the above thesaurus entry is numbered to show the different meanings of the word. When you use a synonym, be sure it fits your meaning.

 Using the thesaurus entry above, find two synonyms to replace the word "run" in each of the following sentences. Make certain your choice fits the meaning of each sentence.

1. Once the skunk has stopped the attack, it can <u>run</u> to safety.
2. Li was selected to <u>run</u> the school garage sale.
3. Whenever it rains, the water <u>runs</u> over the dam.

 Check your essay for precise word choice. Go through your essay and circle two or three plain words. Use a thesaurus to replace them with more interesting words. Be sure each new word has the precise meaning you need.

English Language Learners

Make available a selection of thesauruses in a variety of formats and at various levels. Help students choose one that is appropriate for them.

Advanced Learners

To sharpen students' word-choice skills, ask them to provide two or three sentences (from a newspaper article, novel, textbook, etc.), each of which contains a vague or general word. Ask for volunteers to write some of these sentences on the board. After consulting a thesaurus, students should offer alternatives for the vague words. Discuss the suitability of each suggestion.

describe solve inform
define explain
Classification Essay **185**

3 Some of my words are not precise or necessary.

2 My words are not precise, and I need to delete unnecessary modifiers.

1 I need help finding precise words and identifying unnecessary modifiers.

Have I used any unnecessary modifiers?

You can check your writing for wordiness by being sure to avoid the problems shown below.

■ **Unnecessary Modifiers** (Delete "kind of," "sort of," and "really.")

> It's sort of important to really keep these fish well fed.

Better: It's important to keep these fish well fed.

■ **Strings of Adjectives** (Select the best one or two.)

> The tiny, cute red sea horse was fun to watch.

Better: The tiny red sea horse was fun to watch.

■ **Unnecessary Adjectives** (Don't restate the obvious.)

> The penguins waddled across the cold, frozen ice.

Better: The penguins waddled across the ice.

 Rewrite each sentence to eliminate wordiness.

1. The hippopotamus can kind of walk on the bottom of the river.
2. The giraffe's horns are really hard, bony, hairy knobs.
3. A giraffe has the same number of neck bones as a small, little child has.

Revise **Check for wordiness.** Circle unnecessary modifiers in your essay and rewrite any sentences that seem wordy.

Word Choice
Precise words are used, and unnecessary modifiers are cut.

> camouflage uniforms
> Today, they wear ~~kind of different-colored outfits~~ and
> pepper spray.
> shoot ~~sort of different stuff from cans.~~ Where did
> people get the ideas for these forms of protection?

EXPOSITORY

Ask students if they recognize their own **poor writing habits** *(see below)* in any of the samples and what they do to avoid these problems.

■ Students may find it difficult to recognize vague or unnecessary adjectives in their writing, believing instead that more words add emphasis to their ideas.

■ As students revise, suggest that they look for places where they have used two or more adjectives together. If any of these words mean the same or nearly the same thing, then one of the adjectives is unnecessary and should be deleted.

✳ For more help with selecting the best adjectives, see PE page 489.

 Answers

Answers may vary. Possible wording:

1. The hippopotamus can walk on the river bottom.
2. The giraffe's horns are bony, hairy knobs.
3. A giraffe has the same number of neck bones as a child.

Teaching Tip: Breaking Poor Writing Habits

Most young writers will admit to using modifiers such as *kind of, sort of, really,* and *like.*

● Point out that they probably use these expressions in their writing because they use them when they speak.

● Explain that even though writers should try for a natural-sounding voice, not all speech patterns are appropriate in writing.

● Expressions such as *kind of, sort of, really,* and *like* do not add any information. In fact, they suggest a lazy or less confident form of expression.

● Encourage students to try to avoid using these expressions when they write and when they speak.

Revising for Sentence Fluency

Caution students against beginning all of their sentences with dependent clauses or making all of their sentences complex. Remind students that a variety of sentence beginnings and a good mix of sentence patterns will make their writing flow smoothly, which will make it easy to follow. It will also be more interesting to read.

 **Answers**

Answers may vary. Possible responses:

1. Because their bodies are covered with sharp spines, porcupine fish are usually left alone by predators.
2. When puffer fish gulp water to expand their size, larger fish can't get puffer fish into their mouths.
3. Although the red panda, like the giant panda, has an extra thumb, it is more closely related to the raccoon.

186

Revising **for** Sentence Fluency

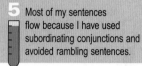

6 My sentences are skillfully written and easy to follow.

5 Most of my sentences flow because I have used subordinating conjunctions and avoided rambling sentences.

4 Most of my sentences are well written, but I could combine some.

When you revise for *sentence fluency*, you should consider combining short sentences by using dependent clauses. At the same time, you should watch out for long, rambling sentences that have too many conjunctions. Your goal is to write smooth sentences of varying types and lengths.

How can I combine sentences using subordinating conjunctions?

You can combine two closely related sentences into one complex sentence by using a subordinating conjunction. (See pages **517** and **744** for a list of conjunctions.)

> Cats get frightened by loud noises. They arch their backs and hiss.

By adding the subordinating conjunction "when," you create a subordinate clause and turn the two short sentences into one complex sentence.

> When cats get frightened by loud noises, they arch their backs and hiss.
>
> (or) Cats arch their backs and hiss when they get frightened by loud noises.

 When the dependent clause begins a sentence, it is followed by a comma. Usually, when the dependent clause comes at the end of a sentence, no comma is used.

 Combine the following sentence pairs by using the subordinating conjunction given in parentheses.

1. Porcupine fish are usually left alone by predators. Their bodies are covered with sharp spines. *(because)*
2. Puffer fish gulp water to expand their size. Larger fish can't get puffer fish into their mouths. *(when)*
3. The red panda has an extra thumb like the giant panda. It is more closely related to the raccoon. *(although)*

 Combine short sentences. Underline any closely related sentences in your essay. Try to combine some of them using subordinating conjunctions.

Grammar Connection

Combining Sentences with Subordinating Conjunctions

- **Proofreader's Guide** pages 698–699, 744 (+), 746–747
- **Write Source** pages 496 (+), 498
- **SkillsBook** pages 111–112, 117–118
- **CD** Sentence Combining

English Language Learners

To help students determine whether they have too many short sentences, have them write on the left side of a sheet of paper *Sentence 1:, Sentence 2:,* and so on.

- Tell students to count the number of words in each of their sentences and record the number beside that heading.

- Then have students examine their list to notice any instances of unusually short sentences in a row.
- Have students revisit these sentences to see if sentence combining would be helpful.

3 Most of my sentences do not flow. I need to combine some closely related sentences and fix a few rambling sentences.

2 Many of my sentences are choppy or rambling. I need to fix them.

1 I need to learn about subordinating conjunctions and rambling sentences.

How can I fix rambling sentences?

You can start fixing a rambling sentence by removing some of the *and*'s and replacing them with periods. Capitalize words as needed. (See page **505**.) After you break up a rambling sentence, you may also improve the flow of the writing by using a subordinating conjunction or another sentence-combining method.

 On your own paper, correct the rambling sentence below by cutting some of the *and*'s and adding periods. Then try to combine a couple related sentences.

> Small animals need the most protection and they might use chemicals to keep themselves safe and these chemicals often cause pain to attacking animals and this pain teaches attackers to leave the small animals alone.

 Check for rambling sentences. Review your essay for sentences that go on and on. Make whatever corrections are needed.

Sentence Fluency

A rambling sentence is made into two sentences. The second sentence begins with a subordinating conjunction.

> The skunk defends itself by releasing a foul-smelling chemical from glands found beneath its tail and̸
> *Because*
> ∧the chemical can severely sting eyes, and the smell is enough to send predators hurrying away, s̶o̶ any animal that tangles with a skunk surely won't do it twice! An octopus squirts a dark, inky fluid in . . .

EXPOSITORY

Before asking students to do the **Try It** activity or to check their own drafts for rambling sentences, direct their attention to the sample at the bottom of the page.

- Tell students to read the side note that explains the correction and then to read the passage.
- Then ask students to suggest another way to revise it. (Possible suggestion: This chemical can severely sting eyes. Its smell is enough to send predators hurrying away, so any animal . . .)
- This will reinforce the idea that there can be more than one way to correct rambling sentences.

Suggest that students use a **peer response sheet** *(see below)* to suggest improvements.

✱ See PE page 505 for more about rambling sentences.

 Answers

Answers may vary.

Because small animals need the most protection, the chemicals they use to keep themselves safe often cause pain to attacking animals. This pain teaches attackers to leave them alone.

Teaching Tip: Peer Response Sheet

Peer responding offers students an opportunity to share their writing with a classmate and to get objective, honest, useful responses that can help them revise effectively.

- Using a peer response sheet allows the peer responder a chance to offer positive comments as well as suggestions for making improvements.

- If students choose to use a peer response sheet here, tell them to focus on sentence fluency, but they can also make helpful comments related to the other traits.

For more about peer responding and using a peer response sheet, see PE pages 29–32.

Grammar Connection

Rambling Sentences
- **Proofreader's Guide** page 690 (+)
- *Write Source* page 505
- *SkillsBook* page 85

Revising Using a Checklist

To make sure students give each of the questions in the revising checklist serious consideration, have them exchange papers with a partner.

- After the partner has a chance to read the essay, the writer can ask her or his partner the questions.
- Partners are likely to give straightforward and honest responses, even if it means the writer has to check the writing again and make additional revisions.

If students are writing the essay as an in-class assignment, provide time for them to make a clean draft. You may again want to remind them to double-space to make it easy for them to edit their work.

188

Revising Using a Checklist

 Check your revising. On a piece of paper, write the numbers 1 to 15. If you can answer "yes" to a question, put a check mark after that number. If not, continue to revise that part of your essay.

Ideas

_____ **1.** Do I cover at least three specific categories of my topic?

_____ **2.** Do I have a clear focus statement?

_____ **3.** Do I include different kinds of interesting details?

Organization

_____ **4.** Does my beginning grab the reader's attention?

_____ **5.** Do the details in each paragraph support the topic sentence?

_____ **6.** Are my ideas and details clearly connected?

_____ **7.** Do I follow a precise pattern?

_____ **8.** Does the ending paragraph restate my focus and make a final statement?

Voice

_____ **9.** Does my voice fit my purpose?

_____ **10.** Have I used different ways to connect with my audience?

Word Choice

_____ **11.** Do I know how to use a thesaurus?

_____ **12.** Do I use precise words?

_____ **13.** Have I deleted unnecessary modifiers?

Sentence Fluency

_____ **14.** Have I combined closely related sentences?

_____ **15.** Is my writing free of rambling sentences?

Grammar Connection

Awkward Sentences

- *Write Source* page 522 (+)
- *SkillsBook* pages 91–92

Misplaced Modifiers

- *Write Source* page 507
- *SkillsBook* pages 87–88

English Language Learners

Use a K-W-L chart as a way to help students understand how listing and asking questions fit together in gathering details. Demonstrate making a three-column chart.

- The left-hand column is labeled *Know,* and students list anything they already know about their topic there.

- The middle column is labeled *Want to Learn.* There, students list the questions they have about their topic.
- The final column is labeled *Learn.* Students use this column to record the answers they discover to their questions.

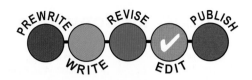

Editing

After you've finished revising your essay, it's time to edit your work for conventions: punctuation, capitalization, spelling, and grammar.

Keys to Effective Editing

1. Use a dictionary, a thesaurus, and the "Proofreader's Guide" in the back of this book.

2. Check your writing for correctness of punctuation, capitalization, spelling, and grammar.

3. If you're using a computer, edit on a printed computer copy. Then enter your changes on the computer.

4. Use the editing and proofreading marks located inside the back cover of this book.

EXPOSITORY

Editing **Keys to Effective Editing**

"Keys to Effective Editing" explains the process students will be guided through on PE pages 190–192.

Direct students' attention to item 2. Remind them to pay particular attention to sentences they combined during the revising process to make sure that they have

- capitalized the first letter of each new sentence they created,
- put a comma after dependent clauses that begin a sentence and before conjunctions in compound sentences,
- added end punctuation when removing *and*'s from rambling sentences to make new sentences, and
- made subjects and verbs in new sentences agree.

Advanced Learners

Encourage one or more students to design a large poster or a bulletin board display that lists the editing and proofreading marks located inside the back cover of the pupil edition. Choose an unobstructed location in the classroom to display the poster or display.

Editing for Conventions

Have students complete the **Try It** activity on their own or with a partner. Review the responses and have students identify the rule that they used to form the possessive.

 Answers

1. grasses'
2. men's
3. crow's, dove's, and robin's
4. ibis's or ibis'
5. Luz's

190

Editing for Conventions

6 My grammar and punctuation are correct, and I have no spelling errors.

5 I have a few minor errors in punctuation, spelling, or grammar.

4 I need to correct errors in punctuation, spelling, or grammar.

When you edit for *conventions*, you are checking your essay for spelling, grammar, capitalization, and punctuation. Use the rubric strip above to guide you through this step in the editing process.

How can I use apostrophes to show possession?

You can show possession of singular words by adding an apostrophe and *s*. For plural words ending in *s*, just add an apostrophe. Be careful, though, because there are some exceptions to these rules. (See 604.4 and 606.1–606.4.)

- When a singular noun of two or more syllables ends with an *s* or *z* sound, add either an apostrophe or an apostrophe and *s*.
  cactus' needles *(or)* **cactus's needles**

- Plural words not ending in *s* need an apostrophe and an *s*.
  children's books   **women's decisions**

- To show shared possession of more than one noun, add an apostrophe and *s* to the last noun in the series.
  Sadako, Nina, and Kim's project (The three share one project.)

- When possession is by individuals in a series of nouns, add an apostrophe and *s* to each noun.
  Sadako's, Nina's, and Kim's projects (Each has her own project.)

 Write the correct possessive form of each underlined noun in the following sentences.

1. The <u>grasses</u> long blades offered excellent camouflage.
2. The <u>men</u> tan clothing hid them so they could watch the birds.
3. They heard the <u>crow</u>, <u>dove</u>, and <u>robin</u> calls.
4. The <u>ibis</u> red feathers were sighted at last.
5. <u>Luz</u> binoculars were passed around.

 Check your work. Look through your essay for any possessives you may have used and make sure you have punctuated them correctly.

Grammar Connection

Apostrophes (possession)

- **Proofreader's Guide** pages 604–605, 606–607
- *Write Source* page 472
- *SkillsBook* pages 27–28, 31–32
- **CD** Apostrophes

English Language Learners

Provide additional practice in the correct use of apostrophes. Copy onto an overhead transparency the following sentence from the sample essay on PE page 175:

A salamanders tail will fall off to allow escape, and a starfishs detached arm will grow into a new starfish!

Have students identify the corrections needed. Then write a version of the sentence using plurals and have them repeat the procedure.

Continue to provide practice by adapting other sentences from the selection and having students punctuate them. (Example: The rabbits color turns from brown in summer to white in winter.)

describe solve inform
define explain **191**
Classification Essay

3 Some of my errors may confuse the reader. I need to fix them.

2 I need to correct many errors that make my essay confusing and hard to read.

1 I need help making corrections, especially with my commas.

How should I use commas with subordinating conjunctions?

When the dependent clause is at the beginning of the sentence, place a comma after it. Generally, do not use a comma when the dependent clause comes after the main clause. (See page **503** and **746.1**.)

Because the viceroy butterfly looks like the bad-tasting monarch, **many predators leave it alone.**

The stonefish is often ignored by predators because it looks just like a rock on the ocean floor.

 Write the following complex sentences on your paper, placing commas where necessary.

1. Because some birds can puff up their feathers to appear larger than they are predators leave them alone.
2. The turtle's shell is a fortress when the animal is under attack.
3. Unless it moves a fawn can hide in the brush from a predator.
4. Hedgehogs can avoid being eaten when they roll into a tight ball.
5. Though the lowland gorilla seems aggressive it is passive.

 Edit your essay. Check to be sure that you correctly punctuated any dependent clauses.

Conventions
Errors with apostrophes and commas are corrected.

When a limb is trapped these animals simply release it and go. A salamander's tail will fall off to allow escape, and a starfish's detached arm will . . .

EXPOSITORY

Explain that commas function for readers the same way yellow traffic lights function for drivers.
- The comma tells the reader to slow down and pause slightly before going on.
- The comma gives readers an opportunity to process ideas that come before the comma and prepare for new ideas that come after the comma.

Understanding this, writers should use commas wisely (and correctly) so that their writing is clear and flows smoothly.
- Too few commas can make ideas unclear.
- Too many commas can create a choppy flow.

 Answers

1. Because some birds can puff up their feathers to appear larger than they are, predators leave them alone.
2. Correct
3. Unless it moves, a fawn can hide in the brush from a predator.
4. Correct
5. Though the lowland gorilla seems aggressive, it is passive.

Struggling Learners

Some students may need additional instruction on punctuating sentences with dependent clauses.

✳ Review PE pages 503 and 746.1.

Demonstrate how comma placement can prevent ambiguity.

- Write on the board **Try It** sentences 1 and 3, leaving out commas.
- Read each sentence without a pause.
- Guide students to identify the dependent clauses and to place commas after them.
- Read each sentence again, pausing and pointing out the commas.

Editing Using a Checklist

Give students a few moments to look over the "Proofreader's Guide" in the back of the pupil edition. Throughout the year, they can refer to the instruction, rules, and examples to clarify any checklist items or to resolve questions about their own writing.

Consider having students use the checklist only after they have completed two editing passes through their essay.

Creating a Title

Students may benefit from working in a group to create a title for their essay.

- Have students try out different titles using the three approaches listed here (name the topic, catch the reader's imagination, establish the tone), and then the group can give feedback on their ideas.
- Group members can also suggest titles after doing a quick read of the essay.

192

Editing Using a Checklist

 Check your editing. On a piece of paper, write the numbers 1 to 10. If you can answer "yes" to a question, put a check mark after that number. Continue editing until you can answer all the questions with a "yes."

Conventions

PUNCTUATION

_____ 1. Do I correctly punctuate dependent clauses?

_____ 2. Do I use apostrophes to show possession?

CAPITALIZATION

_____ 3. Do I capitalize proper nouns and adjectives?

_____ 4. Do I begin each sentence with a capital letter?

SPELLING

_____ 5. Have I spelled all my words correctly?

_____ 6. Have I used the spell-checker on my computer?

_____ 7. Have I double-checked the words my spell-checker may have missed?

GRAMMAR

_____ 8. Do I use correct forms of verbs (*had come,* not *had came*)?

_____ 9. Do my subjects and verbs agree in number?

_____ 10. Have I used the right words (*there, their, they're*)?

Creating a Title

For a classification essay, the title should do one of the following:

- Name the topic: **Ways Animals Defend Themselves**
- Catch the reader's imagination: **Animal Armor**
- Establish the tone: **Staying Alive: Animal Adaptations**

Grammar Connection

Using the Right Word

- **Proofreader's Guide** pages 670–674
- *SkillsBook* page 56
- **CD** Using the Right Word—3

describe *solve* *inform*
define explain **193**
Classification Essay

Publishing

PREWRITE • WRITE • REVISE • EDIT • PUBLISH ✓

Sharing Your Essay

After you have worked so hard writing your essay, you'll want to proofread it and make a neat copy to share. You may also decide to display your essay in the library or present it as a book or a poster. (See the suggestions below.)

Publish

Make a final copy. Follow your teacher's instructions or use the guidelines below to format your essay. (If you are using a computer, see pages 60–62.) Create a clean final copy of your essay and carefully proofread it.

Focus on Presentation

- Use blue or black ink and write neatly.
- Write your name in the upper left corner of page 1.
- Skip a line and center your title; skip another line and start your writing.
- Indent every paragraph and leave a one-inch margin on all four sides.
- Write your last name and the page number in the upper right corner of every page after the first one.

Produce a Book
Turn your essay into a picture book by adding pictures with captions. Make a cover out of cardboard and include your title and name. Punch holes along the left side and fasten the pages together with yarn or secure with brads.

Display Your Essay in School
Ask your teacher if there is a special section or showcase for student papers.

Create a Poster
Attach your essay pages to a large piece of tagboard and add illustrations and informative side notes for each section. Include Web-site addresses for further information on each main idea.

EXPOSITORY

Publishing Sharing Your Essay

Encourage students to suggest ideas for publishing. Because the classification essay is organized according to categories, students may suggest unique visuals to accompany their final copy, including

- a leveled or sectioned diorama (number of levels or sections matches number of categories),
- a sectioned poster or mural,
- a slide show (see PE pages 411–414 for help with preparing multimedia presentations).

Attach a filled-out photocopy of the reproducible six-trait checklist (TE page 762).

- When reviewing a student's final essay, consider reserving lengthy comments and corrections for a one-on-one conference.
- At that time, you can discuss corrections using the "Rubric for Expository Writing" (PE pages 194–195).
- This will help students retain pride in their work while learning to improve as writers.

Advanced Learners

Consult a technology specialist or school librarian to see if your school has purchased a site license for a desktop publishing software program. If so, encourage students with advanced computer skills to turn their essay into an illustrated book to be viewed online or e-mailed to other students.

Rubric for Expository Writing

Remind students that a rubric is a chart that helps them evaluate their writing.

- The rubrics in this book are based on a six-point scale, in which a score of 6 indicates an amazing piece of writing and a score of 1 means the writing is incomplete and not ready to be assessed.
- The rubric is organized according to the basic traits of writing—ideas, organization, voice, word choice, sentence fluency, and conventions.
- Point out that rubrics are also helpful during the writing process. They can guide students whenever they write because they tell them what elements to include in their writing.

✱ Reproducible six-, five-, and four-point rubrics for expository writing can be found on TE pages 751, 755, and 759.

194

Rubric for Expository Writing

Use this rubric for guiding and assessing your expository writing. Refer to it as you improve your writing using the six traits.

Ideas

6 The topic, focus, and details make the essay truly memorable.

5 The essay is informative with a clear focus and specific details.

4 The essay is informative with a clear focus. More specific details are needed.

Organization

6 The organization and transitions make the essay clear and easy to read.

5 The beginning interests the reader. The middle supports the focus. The ending works well. Transitions are used.

4 The essay is divided into a beginning, a middle, and an ending. Some transitions are used.

Voice

6 The writer's voice sounds confident, knowledgeable, and enthusiastic.

5 The writer's voice sounds knowledgeable and confident. It fits the audience.

4 The writer's voice sounds knowledgeable most of the time and fits the audience.

Word Choice

6 The word choice makes the essay very clear, informative, and enjoyable to read.

5 Specific nouns and action verbs make the essay clear and informative.

4 Some nouns and verbs could be more specific.

Sentence Fluency

6 The sentences are skillfully written, and readers will enjoy them.

5 The sentences read smoothly.

4 Most of the sentences read smoothly, but some are short and choppy.

Conventions

6 The essay is error free.

5 The essay has a few minor errors in punctuation, spelling, or grammar.

4 The essay has some errors in punctuation, spelling, or grammar.

3 The focus of the essay needs to be clearer, and more specific details are needed.

2 The topic needs to be narrowed or expanded. Many more specific details are needed.

1 A new topic needs to be selected.

3 The beginning or ending is weak. The middle needs a paragraph for each main point. More transitions are needed.

2 The beginning, middle, and ending all run together. Paragraphs and transitions are needed.

1 The essay should be reorganized.

3 The writer sometimes sounds unsure, and the voice needs to fit the audience better.

2 The writer sounds unsure. The voice needs to fit the audience.

1 The writer needs to learn about voice.

3 Too many general words are used. Specific nouns and verbs are needed.

2 General or missing words make this essay difficult to understand.

1 The writer needs help finding specific words.

3 Many short, choppy sentences need to be rewritten to make the essay read smoothly.

2 Many sentences are choppy or incomplete and need to be rewritten.

1 Most sentences need to be rewritten.

3 Several errors confuse the reader.

2 Many errors make the essay difficult to read.

1 Help is needed to make corrections.

EXPOSITORY

Technology Connections

For video tutorials on each of the six traits of writing—as well as a tutorial on writing expository essays—go to the Great Source iwrite Web site: www.greatsource.com/iwrite.

Evaluating an Expository Essay

Ask students to suggest improvements based on the comments in the self-assessment.

Possible suggestions:

Ideas strengthen ending—Give tips for making selections, delete *read a book,* reorder types of shows in ending to match order in beginning.

Organization follow a precise pattern—Start the third middle paragraph with "Finally, if you . . . ," and then talk about show length, viewer age, and laugh track.

Voice remember purpose—Provide more-specific details about reality shows.

Word Choice more-effective modifiers—Replace *plenty of* with *an abundance of* or *a multitude of;* replace *scary* with *frightening.*

Sentence Fluency fix rambling sentences—If you like serious dramas, you can find plenty of those on TV as well. These are usually an hour long. Some are on late at night when kids shouldn't be up to see them. Some are on at earlier times.

Conventions correct punctuation—In the fourth paragraph, delete dashes, replace with commas.

196

Evaluating an Expository Essay

As you read through Simcha's classification essay below, focus on its strengths and weaknesses. (**The essay contains several errors.**)

Choose Your Entertainment

Once there were only three or four TV channels available. Now, with cable and satellite TV, people might have to choose from hundreds of channels and thousands of programs. It's easy to choose a show if they know what type they are looking for. Three popular types of TV shows include sitcoms, dramas, and reality shows.

If viewers want to laugh and forget their troubles, they could watch a sitcom. Sitcoms—short for situation comedies—are half-hour shows that have one group of people with a different problem each week. These problems are always solved in 30 minutes—minus commercials. They can be either adult or family shows. They have a live audience or a recorded laugh track to let the viewers know when something is funny.

If viewers like serious dramas, they can find plenty of those on TV as well these are usually an hour long. Some are on late at night, when kids shouldn't be up to see them, but some dramas are on at earlier times. Dramas also usually focus on one group, but the story can go on for the whole season. These shows do not have a laugh track.

Finally, there are the so-called "reality" shows. These shows take people and place them in funny or dangerous situations—and then videotape how they react. These shows can be funny—or embarrassing—depending on the people. Sometimes they are scary. They are usually an hour long, but "specials" can be longer and the same people are usually on the show for a while.

People can choose the kind of TV show they want to watch. Depending on their mood, they might want to laugh, have a good scare, or enjoy a classic drama. Thinking about it, though, there are times they'll be better off just reading a good book!

describe solve inform
define explain
Classification Essay **197**

Student Self-Assessment

The assessment below includes comments by Simcha, who evaluated his own essay (on page 196). Notice that he includes a positive comment first. Then he points out an area of his writing that could be improved. (The writer used the rubric and number scale on pages 194–195.)

3 Ideas

1. *I know my audience will be interested in my topic.*
2. *My ending is weak, and I don't have enough details.*

5 Organization

1. *I include a clear topic sentence for each paragraph.*
2. *I should rearrange my last middle paragraph to fit the pattern.*

3 Voice

1. *The reader can tell I like TV.*
2. *What I say about reality shows is too negative.*

3 Word Choice

1. *I explain terms like "sitcom."*
2. *I could use more-effective modifiers.*

4 Sentence Fluency

1. *I vary my sentence beginnings.*
2. *I have a run-on sentence and sometimes ramble.*

4 Conventions

1. *I don't have many spelling errors.*
2. *I use too many dashes where I should use commas.*

Use the rubric. Assess your essay using the rubric on pages 194–195.

1 On your own paper, list the six traits. Leave room after each trait to write one strength and one weakness.

2 Then choose a number (from 1 to 6) that shows how well you used each trait.

EXPOSITORY

Have students share their essays and self-assessments with partners or in small groups for peer evaluation.

- Peers can tell whether they think the assessment is accurate, too lenient, or too critical.
- They should also be prepared to offer concrete examples to support their evaluations.
- Remind students to be considerate when making suggestions.

To give students additional practice with evaluating an expository essay, use a reproducible assessment sheet (TE page 787) and one or both of the **benchmark papers** listed in the Benchmark Papers box below. You can use an overhead transparency while students refer to their own copies made from the copy masters. For your benefit, a completed assessment sheet is provided for each benchmark paper.

Advanced Learners

To extend this activity, pair students and have them exchange their self-assessments. Instruct them to

- offer their opinions of their partner's self-assessment, and
- offer suggestions for any comment about improvements with which they agree.

Benchmark Papers

911! (strong)
- TR 3A–3C
- TE pp. 771–773

Storm Cells (fair)
- TR 4A–4B
- TE pp. 774–775

Reflecting on Your Writing

Tell students to date and save their reflections so that they can easily track their progress throughout the school year.

- Encourage students to review any reflections they may have written earlier in the year.
- This will remind them of their past writing achievements and also help them to recall the areas of their writing that needed work.
- They can then evaluate their classification essay to determine if they have shown improvement in those areas that need work.
- Consider having students complete items 5 and 6 after they have received feedback from you on the assignment. This will encourage them to be more forthright in their reflections.

198

Reflecting on Your Writing

Now that you've completed your classification essay, take a moment to reflect on it. Complete each starter sentence below on your own paper. These thoughts will help you prepare for your next writing assignment.

My Classification Essay

1. The strength of my essay is . . .

2. The part that still needs work is . . .

3. The main thing I learned about writing a classification essay is . . .

4. The prewriting activity that worked best for this essay was . . .

5. In my next essay, I would like to . . .

6. Here is one question I still have about writing a classification essay:

Expository Writing
Comparison-Contrast Essay

"Day One: I was about to begin my dive in the Amazon when I noticed a strange school of fish below my canoe. They look like harmless pacus, but they may be their close cousins, piranhas. I wish I could decide which they were. . . ."

Whenever you are trying to decide between two things, you are comparing and contrasting them. You look at how they are similar, and how they are different. Then you make a decision based on that information.

On the following pages, you'll read an expository essay comparing and contrasting two American cities. The guidelines that follow will help you write your own comparison-contrast essay.

Writing Guidelines

Subject:	Two similar topics that interest you
Form:	Comparison-contrast essay
Purpose:	To explain
Audience:	Classmates

Copy Masters/ Transparencies

T-chart (TE p. 789)

Venn diagram (TE p. 791)

Comparison-Contrast Essay

Objectives
- know what a comparison-contrast essay is
- use what was learned about expository writing to create a comparison-contrast essay
- plan, draft, revise, edit, and share a comparison-contrast essay

A **comparison-contrast** essay explains the similarities and differences between two topics.

- Ask students why it would be important for the diver in the introduction to know whether the fish are pacus or piranhas. (Piranhas are deadly fish that could attack and kill the diver.)
- Point out that understanding the similarities and differences between two things can affect students' lives in a variety of ways.
- Knowing how to compare and contrast can help them decide where to go to college, where to work, where to live, and so on.

Comparison-Contrast Essay

Help students make the connection between a classification essay and a comparison-contrast essay. Point out the following characteristics:

- A classification essay breaks down a topic into categories and then discusses the features of each category.
- A comparison-contrast essay compares and contrasts the features of two similar topics.

Prepare students to select a topic for their own essays.

- Invite them to brainstorm a list of cities, animals, sports, historic figures, landmarks, monuments, plants, and flowers that they know well enough to compare.
- List these ideas on the board so that students can refer to them when selecting their topics.

Review the expository essay rubric on PE pages 194–195. Tell students to keep these traits and scores in mind as they read and respond to the sample essay.

Comparison-Contrast Essay

Making comparisons can result in new insights about a topic: two American cities, two types of sports, two admirable people. For the following essay, the writer compares two cities.

Beginning

The topics are introduced, and the focus statement (underlined) sets up the comparison.

Middle

The first middle paragraph addresses the differences point by point.

Cities Between the Waters

Brad Janty lives in Madison, Wisconsin, and loves it. When his cousin Jim from Seattle visits, Brad shows him the sights. They shop for music on State Street, visit the farmer's market on the capitol square, and end the day listening to jazz on the Union Terrace overlooking Lake Mendota. When Brad visits Jim in Seattle, Jim shows him the sights there. They go to the shops in Pike Place Market, explore Underground Seattle, and eat lunch in the Space Needle. Madison and Seattle may seem different, but they have much in common.

Of course, there are plenty of differences between the cities. At 540,000 people, Seattle is more than twice the size of Madison, which has 205,000 people. Seattle is the largest city in its state, and though Madison is not Wisconsin's largest city, it is the state capital. The Madison area's main products are milk and cheese. Seattle, on the other hand, is known for its cutting-edge technology. Seattle is surrounded by majestic natural wonders, such as mountains, rain forests, and the ocean. Madison's surroundings are a little more humble. It has hills instead of mountains, oak groves instead of rain forests, and lakes instead of the ocean. Madison is in the Midwest and has hot summers and cold winters, while Seattle is on the West Coast and has a temperate climate.

describe solve inform
define explain **201**
Comparison-Contrast Essay

The second middle paragraph addresses the similarities point by point.

Despite their differences, Madison and Seattle have many similarities. Both cities sit on narrow strips of land between two bodies of water. In Madison, we have Lake Mendota and Lake Monona. Seattle lies between Lake Washington and Puget Sound. Both cities are in the northern part of the country. Madison's latitude is 43 degrees, and Seattle's is 47. Each has a huge state university, the University of Wisconsin and the University of Washington, and both are UW's. Madison and Seattle even lie on the same Interstate, I-90, although they're 2,000 miles apart. Either is worth a trip, though, because both are exciting and fun places to visit.

Ending

The ending adds a final reflection about the comparison.

In some ways, none of these features define the two cities. Madison and Seattle have the same soul. Both places are full of tie-dyed clothes, well-worn jeans, and leather sandals. Both have an exciting music scene. It's the atmosphere in each city that most makes them similar. Whether Jim is visiting Brad or Brad is visiting Jim, they always feel at home.

EXPOSITORY

Respond to the reading. On your own paper, write answers to the following questions about the sample essay.

☐ **Ideas** (1) What two things does the writer compare?
(2) What two similarities and two differences interest you?

☐ **Organization** (3) How do the two middle paragraphs support the focus statement?

☐ **Voice & Word Choice** (4) What words and phrases reveal how the writer feels about the two cities? (5) How does the writer show knowledge about the two cities?

Respond to the reading.

Ask students to explain their responses.

Answers

Ideas **1.** Madison, Wisconsin, and Seattle, Washington—two cities
2. Possible choices:
Similarities: on narrow strips of land between two bodies of water, located in North, huge state universities with the initials UW, on Interstate I-90
Differences: Seattle—largest city in state; cutting-edge technology; mountains, rain forests, and ocean; West Coast; temperate climate

Madison—state capital; milk and cheese; hills, oak groves, and lakes; Midwest; hot summers and cold winters

Organization **3.** The focus statement says the two cities seem different but have a lot in common. First middle paragraph explains the differences. Second middle paragraph explains what they have in common.

Voice & Word Choice **4.** Loves it, shows him the sights, always feel at home
5. names specific places to shop, listen to music, and eat; gives specific details about geography, including population and latitude

Struggling Learners

Draw students' attention to the two middle paragraphs in the sample essay.

- Point out that the first paragraph contrasts *(plenty of differences),* while the second uses a transition phrase *(despite their differences)* to redirect the writing.
- The second middle paragraph then compares the two subjects.

- Emphasize that an alternating A/B/A/B organizational pattern is used throughout the middle paragraphs: One sentence reflects subject A, followed by a sentence that reflects subject B.

Explain that this is a good model for organizing the middle paragraphs when students write their own comparison-contrast essays.

202

Prewriting Selecting a Topic

If you plan to assign a general subject, consider asking teachers from other curriculum areas for comparison-contrast ideas related to topics students are studying in their classes.

- Students can then draw on the knowledge that they have previously acquired to write their essays.
- Additionally, as they gather details for their essays, they will probably increase their knowledge and understanding of the topic, which can be beneficial to them during class discussions and test-taking situations in that content area.

Prewriting Gathering Details

Have students use the reproducible T-chart (TE page 789) for gathering details.

- Even if students know their topics well, they will probably have to do some research to find specific details.
- Since specific details will make students' essays more interesting, provide time for research as they complete their gathering charts.

Prewriting Selecting a Topic

Your teacher may assign a general subject for your essay. For the subject "American Cities," the writer used freewriting to find two cities to write about.

Freewriting

Well, let's see. American cities. There's the big three, of course: New York, Chicago, and L.A. But I've never visited any of these cities. The only city I know something about is Madison from visiting my good friend there. Mad Town's cool. I've also heard from my friend that Seattle is cool. I think I'll compare these two cities, if I can find enough about both of them. . . .

 Select your topic. Do a freewriting to find two topics you know enough about to compare and contrast.

Gathering Details

After you have finished your freewriting and found two topics, list details you can use in your essay. Make a gathering chart with two columns like the one below. In each column, write details for one of the topics. If you think of additional details, add them as you go.

Gathering Chart

Madison, WI	Seattle, WA
Lakes Mendota and Monona, Farm products, Latitude 43°, UW, 205,000 people, State capital, Snowy–31", Babcock Hill ice cream, Historical museums, Hills, Near Wisconsin Dells . . .	Largest city in state, 540,000 people, Rainy-34", I-90, Mountains, Space Needle, Puget Sound, West Coast, Known for technology, Latitude 47°, UW, Pike Place Market . . .

 Create a gathering chart. Fill in a gathering chart like the one above. If you can't think of many details, you may want to find another topic.

describe solve inform
define explain
Comparison-Contrast Essay
203

Organizing Details

The writer used the following Venn diagram to organize ideas for his essay. In the center, he wrote the similarities between the cities. In the outer circles, he listed the contrasting ideas from his gathering chart, matching a point about one city to a corresponding point about the other city. If a fact for one city did not have a matching idea for the other, he did not use it in the essay.

Venn Diagram

Madison, WI	Both Cities	Seattle, WA
Midwest	I-90	West Coast
Hills, trees	UW	Mountains, rain forest
Population 205,000	Lots to see	Population 540,000
Milk and cheese	Latitude (43°/47°)	Computers, technology
State capital	Precipitation	Largest city in state
Snowy	(31"/34")	Rainy

 Create a Venn diagram. Make a Venn diagram like the one above to organize the similarities and differences of your topics.

Forming a Focus Statement

A good focus statement gives the topics to be compared and introduces a general comparison.

Sample Focus Statements

> *Madison and Seattle may seem different, but they have much in common.*

> *Many people confuse viruses and bacteria, but if you examine them closely, you'll find they are totally different organisms.*

> *Although the sequoia and giant redwood seem similar, they are in fact very different.*

 Write a focus statement. Using the samples given above, write a focus statement for your comparison-contrast essay.

EXPOSITORY

Prewriting Organizing Details

If it would benefit the majority of students, model the process of filling in a Venn diagram.

- Ask students to suggest two things that they know well to compare and contrast (see PE page 546 for suggestions).
- Use the transparency for a Venn diagram (TR 12) and display it using an overhead projector.
- Have students help you label and fill in the Venn diagram. Make sure to show matching details for each topic.

✱ For more about how a Venn diagram can be used to organize details for a comparison-contrast essay, see PE page 537.

Distribute copies of the Venn diagram (TE page 791) to students, so they can use this type of chart to organize their own details.

Prewriting
Forming a Focus Statement

Use the sample sentences to help students understand that their focus statement should

- introduce the topic, and
- establish a plan to follow in the middle paragraphs for comparing and contrasting the subjects.

English Language Learners

To help students fill in their Venn diagrams, have them refer to their gathering charts (PE page 202).

- Explain that any highlighted information should be written in the middle of the diagram (similarities).
- Information that they connected by a line (differences) should be included in the outside circles.

Struggling Learners

Modify the Venn diagram activity for students with fine motor or spatial organization difficulties. Suggest that they use a marker on a transparency sheet that is placed over their photocopy of the diagram. This allows them to wipe off mistakes when attempting to fit and align details, thereby eliminating frustration that can sabotage successful completion.

Writing Creating Your First Draft

Ask students to look back at the sample essay on PE pages 200–201 and the sample Venn diagram on PE page 203.

- Point out that the writer was able to use the Venn diagram to plan the point-by-point discussion in the middle paragraphs of the essay because there were matching ideas for both cities listed in the Venn diagram.
- Encourage students to look over their Venn diagram to make sure they have matching ideas for both topics. If not, they should cross out or add ideas.

✱ For information about using an essay plan, see PE page 540.

Revising Improving Your Writing

Before students revise, have them review their essay using the rubric on PE pages 194–195.

Editing

Checking for Conventions

Encourage students to use the "Proofreader's Guide" (PE pages 578–749) to help them edit their essays.

Writing Creating Your First Draft

When you write your comparison, pay close attention to each of the main parts: beginning, middle, and ending.

- **Beginning** Grab your reader's attention by starting strong. Then provide details that lead up to your thesis, or focus statement.
- **Middle** Organize your middle paragraphs by discussing each topic point by point, as the writer did on pages 200–201.
- **Ending** Bring the writing to an effective close. One way is to sum up the comparison. Another way is to reflect or comment on it.

 Write your first draft. Refer to your Venn diagram and focus statement to help you write the first draft of your comparison-contrast essay.

Revising Improving Your Writing

After you finish your first draft, review your work for the following traits.

- ☐ **Ideas** Does the focus statement name my two topics and state my focus? Will the details grab the reader's attention?
- ☐ **Organization** Does the essay have a clear beginning, middle, and ending? Does each paragraph focus on one part of the comparison-contrast theme?
- ☐ **Voice** Is my voice appropriate for the topic?
- ☐ **Word Choice** Do I use strong nouns, verbs, and modifiers?
- ☐ **Sentence Fluency** Do my sentences vary in length?

 Revise your writing. Ask yourself the questions listed above after each trait. Decide how you will revise for *ideas, organization, voice,* and so on. Make whatever changes are needed.

Editing Checking for Conventions

When you finish revising, edit your essay for conventions.

- ☐ **Conventions** Have I checked my punctuation, capitalization, and spelling? Have I checked for grammar errors?

 Edit your work. Ask yourself the above questions. Make your corrections, write a neat final copy, and proofread it carefully.

English Language Learners

Direct students' attention to the second bullet ("Middle") under **Writing**. Clarify what point-by-point organization is by having students revisit the sample essay on PE pages 200–201.

- Help students identify examples of sentences or pairs of sentences that tell about one aspect of both cities before going on to discuss another aspect of both cities.

Grammar Connection

Comparative and Superlative Adjectives and Adverbs

- **Proofreader's Guide** pages 734 (+), 738–739
- *Write Source* page 491
- *SkillsBook* pages 169–170, 172
- **CD** Adjectives and Adverbs

Comma Splices and Run-On Sentences

- *Write Source* page 504
- *SkillsBook* pages 77, 78, 79–80

Double Negatives

- *Write Source* page 510
- *SkillsBook* page 86

describe solve,
define explain inform **205**

Expository Writing
Across the Curriculum

Explanations are handy in all sorts of places. For example, imagine that you and six hungry friends need to share one pizza. Can you explain a way to cut the pizza so everyone gets a fair share? Perhaps you could divide 360° by 7 to discover that each piece should be 51.42°. The rest is a matter of working with the protractor and the pizza cutter. On the other hand, you could simply let each person cut a piece of the pizza, and afterward, in reverse order, choose the piece he or she will eat!

This section includes many amazing explanations. You will read a news report about the death of Julius Caesar, an explanation of a mathematical operation, a summary of a science experiment, and a memo giving an update. You'll even learn how to respond to an expository writing prompt. So turn to these pages anytime you've got some explaining to do.

What's Ahead

- **Social Studies:** Writing a News Report
- **Math:** Explaining a Mathematical Operation
- **Science:** Writing an Observation Report
- **Practical Writing:** Writing a Memo
- **Writing for Assessment**

Materials

5 W's chart (TE pp. 206, 207, 211)

Across the Curriculum

Objectives
- apply what students have learned about expository writing to other curriculum areas
- practice writing for assessment

The lessons on the following pages provide samples of expository writing students might do in different content areas. The form used in one content area may also be used in another area (for example, students can write a news report for science just as well as for social studies).

Assigning these forms of writing will depend on
- the skill level of your students,
- the subject matter they are studying in different content areas, and
- the writing goals of your school, district, or state.

Test Prep!
In addition to addressing high-stakes writing assessments, this section focuses on types of writing that students may do in low-stakes situations in their content-area classes.

Social Studies:
Writing a News Report

Invite volunteers to share what they know about Caesar's life and death before reading the sample news report.

- Caesar was a great Roman general and statesman who ruled Rome as a dictator from 49 to 44 B.C.E.
- Although he was a respected leader, many people feared his power.
- He was stabbed to death on March 15, 44 B.C.E., by a group of aristocrats, including two men (Brutus and Cassius) whom Caesar had pardoned after a major military battle.

Divide students into groups.

- Have them read and discuss the sample news report.
- Tell them to look for answers to the 5 W and H questions as they read (*Who? What? When? Where? Why?* and *How?*). Provide photocopies of the reproducible 5 W's chart (TE page 792) for note taking.

Social Studies: Writing a News Report

One way to understand a historical event is to write a news story about it. The following news story was written for a history class. Notice how the student reports the story as if it were a current event.

The **beginning** includes a strong headline that grabs the reader's attention. The most important details come first.

The **middle** includes facts reported in an interesting way.

The **ending** avoids editorializing (giving an opinion).

Caesar Slain on Senate Floor

MARCH 15, ROME: Julius Caesar is dead. Caesar had just arrived in the senate when a mob of senators with knives leapt up and attacked him. Caesar's own friend, Brutus, was allegedly among the attackers. He reportedly stabbed Caesar, too.

Caesar's autopsy recorded 23 stab wounds, though witnesses estimate the number of attackers to have been much higher. One senator, who did not want his name given, stated, "The conspiracy included at least 60 senators, but Brutus and Cassius were the ringleaders."

Brutus and Cassius did little to hide their guilt. Following the attack, they and other conspirators paraded through the streets. Crowds picked up the shouts, "Tyranny ends" and "The Republic returns!"

This latest shock comes just five years into Caesar's reign. Though always popular with the people, Caesar had many enemies in the senate.

"I warned him," a soothsayer outside the senate building claimed. Asked how he knew about the plot ahead of time, the soothsayer denied any involvement in the conspiracy.

Hope for the empire now rests with a new group: Gaius Octavius, Marcus Anthony, and Marcus Lepidus. Though hiding in undisclosed locations, the three have made pledges to raise armies and battle Brutus and Cassius across the whole empire.

Struggling Learners

Before assigning the **Try It** activity, provide practice by working with students to write a news report based on "The Three Little Pigs."

- Use the transparency of the 5 W's chart (TR 13) and add *How?* to it. Have students gather details to complete the chart.
- Then help students identify their audience (other local pigs, other wolves) and discuss objectivity in news reporting.
- On chart paper, record the date, place, and first line. (Example: APRIL 10, LONDON: Local wolf known as "Big Bad" is dead.)

Have volunteers complete the article by adding sentences that incorporate the details from the 5 W's and H chart.

describe solve inform
define explain

207

Writing in Social Studies

Writing Tips

> ### Before you write . . .
>
> - **Select a topic.**
>   Your teacher may assign a topic, or you may choose an event you are familiar with or are studying about.
> - **Gather details.**
>   Use the 5 W's and H to help you gather key information.
> - **Consider the participants.**
>   Consider the event and the people involved.
> - **Think of your audience.**
>   What information would be most important to them?
>
> ### During your writing . . .
>
> - **Organize your report.**
>   Use the inverted pyramid style of organization. Place the most important information in the very first sentence. Then answer as many of the 5 W and H questions as you can. Add less important information later.
>
>
>   Most Important
>   Least
>
> - **Focus on voice.**
>   As you write, use active verbs, strong sentences, and brief paragraphs. Avoid editorializing (giving your opinion).
>
> ### After you've written a first draft . . .
>
> - **Write a strong headline.**
>   Make sure your headline grabs the reader's attention and has a subject and a verb.
> - **Check for completeness and correctness.**
>   Read to make sure you have included the information your reader needs to understand the story. Check your use of conventions.

EXPOSITORY

 Choose an interesting historical event from the time period you are studying. Write it up as a news story. Get your facts right, but make it interesting, too.

Writing Tips

To help students understand the form, tone, and style of a news report, provide them with examples of current news articles. Have them notice the following:

- headline (subject and verb)
- lead sentence (the sentence that begins the article and draws readers into the story)
- organization of details (inverted pyramid: the most important or exciting details appear near the beginning; less important details appear at the end)
- use of precise nouns, active verbs, and quotations

Suggest that students skim their social studies textbook to get ideas for topics. Point out that it is important for them to choose an event they understand and can explain in detail so that readers will understand it and recognize its importance in history.

Make copies of the reproducible 5 W's chart (TE page 792) for students to use when they are gathering and organizing details.

Try IT **Answers**

Stories will vary, but they should provide a clear explanation of the event and contain accurate facts.

English Language Learners

This assignment combines two challenging processes:

- conducting research into a historical event and
- using an inverted pyramid style to create a news report.

Do this task as a class activity. Move methodically through each stage with students to produce a class news report.

Advanced Learners

Extend the activity by having students research and write an obituary about a historical person they admire. Details about the person should include

- childhood,
- education,
- notable achievements, and
- death.

Encourage students to write a thoughtful memorial, not just a list of facts.

Math: Explaining a Mathematical Operation

This assignment helps students explore the connection between math and everyday life, something students often have a difficult time recognizing.

Divide students into pairs, and have them work together to read and analyze "Using Percentages." As they read, tell them to list examples of the following:

- a connection between the operation and everyday life in the introduction and in the ending
- steps that explain the math operation
- specific, real-life details

Writer's Craft

Writing as thinking: In math, students are often asked to show their work. Usually, this involves numbers on a page, but another way to show your work—and your thinking—is to write an explanation such as "Using Percentages." By writing out an explanation, students deepen (or even correct) their thinking about a mathematical process.

208

Math: Explaining a Mathematical Operation

In math class, you may be asked to explain a mathematical operation. The writer of this essay was asked to show how percentages are used to calculate discounts and sales tax.

Using Percentages

The **beginning** tells why the operation is important.

Discount and sale signs are posted everywhere on shops. Before shoppers get to the checkout line, they may want to know how much they're going to save on a sale item, and how much they need to pay. To do this, shoppers need to understand how to work with percentages.

The **middle** uses specific details to explain the operation.

Suppose someone finds a really cool pair of sandals on sale for 20% off the original price of $19. To find out the discount, a shopper should multiply $19 by 20%. The product, $3.80, is the discount. Next, he or she should subtract $3.80 from the original price of $19. The sale price is $15.20. Figuring out the cost of sale items requires two simple steps: (1) multiply the price by the percentage, and (2) subtract the product from the original price.

To figure the sales tax, a shopper should follow almost the same process. He or she should multiply the price of the item by the sales tax percentage (5%, 6%, 7% . . .), and then, instead of subtracting the product from the cost, add it. A shopper must remember that if there's a sales tax, he or she will need more money at checkout time.

The **ending** makes a final observation.

Understanding how to work with percentages will help shoppers in many ways. They'll especially need to know all about them when they visit their favorite stores in the mall.

describe solve inform
define explain
209
Writing in Math

Writing Tips

Before you write . . .

- **Choose a familiar mathematical operation.**
  If your teacher has not assigned a particular mathematical operation, search for one in your notes or math textbook.
- **Study the operation.**
  Make sure you thoroughly understand the process needed to perform the operation. Think of how the operation can be applied to everyday life.
- **Plan the steps.**
  Break your operation into manageable steps and list them in the correct order. Then check the steps by working through the process.

During your writing . . .

- **Write a clear beginning, middle, and ending.**
  Begin by introducing the operation. Next, explain the process (or steps) in a clear manner. Provide an example of how the operation can be applied to everyday life. End with a thought that leaves the reader thinking about the operation.
- **Organize your explanation.**
  Decide on the order of organization that would clearly present the operation to your reader (time order, numbered steps, and so on).
- **Use specific terms.**
  Include words that are associated with the specific math operation.

After you've written a first draft . . .

- **Check for completeness.**
  Make sure that you have included all the information a reader needs to understand the process you are explaining.
- **Check for correctness.**
  Edit and proofread your work to eliminate errors in spelling, punctuation, and other conventions.

EXPOSITORY

 Write directions for a mathematical operation that you are learning in math class. Use specific examples and clear steps.

Writing Tips

Encourage students to look through their math notes, math books, and past math tests to identify mathematical operations that they have mastered and can explain completely and clearly in manageable steps.

- Math teachers often use different scenarios in word problems that require students to apply math operations to real-life situations. If possible, collect examples of these kinds of problems for students to review.
- Provide time for students to choose an operation and discuss how it can be applied to everyday life.
- Point out that if they can tell someone how an operation connects to everyday life, using specific examples and clear steps, then they can also explain it in writing.

 Answers

Answers will vary but should make a clear connection between the mathematical operation and everyday life, include specific examples, and break the operation into easy-to-follow steps.

English Language Learners

Modify this assignment by having students choose a simple mathematical operation to explain to a younger audience.

- This change will allow students to focus on the clarity of their writing rather than get bogged down in grappling with a more sophisticated mathematical concept.

- Students may want to share their finished product with younger children, after sharing their explanation with several peers, who can check it for accuracy and clarity.

Science: Writing an Observation Report

Discuss the format of the sample observation report with students.

- Help students make the connection between writing a good science observation report and good expository writing. (Both require the skills of observation and description.)
- Ask students to point out specific details in the report that help them understand the different stages of the experiment.
- Have them explain why it's important to write clear, well-organized explanations for their reports. (Possible responses: so their teacher can see that they did the experiment correctly and that they understand the results; so other readers can understand the experiment process and the results)
- Invite volunteers to share observation or lab reports they have written for science class.

210

Science: Writing an Observation Report

Experiments are at the heart of science. A good way to review and analyze an experiment is to write an observation report. The following report is based on a student's experiment involving root growth.

The **beginning** identifies the focus of the experiment.

The **middle** identifies the process.

The **ending** explains what the writer has learned.

Do Bean Roots Always Grow Downward?

Scientific question: Do bean roots always grow downward?

Hypothesis: The roots of beans placed in different growing positions will always grow downward toward the center of the earth.

Procedure: Four lima beans were glued onto a sponge with the concave sides facing different directions: down, up, left, and right. The sponge was moistened and placed in a zippered plastic bag. Several small slits were cut in the bag and the bag was tacked to a bulletin board. The bag was watered daily through the slits.

Observations:

Day 3: Small sprouts have appeared from each bean.

Day 5: The roots from the beans facing left and right are growing horizontally, the bean facing down has roots growing downward, and the bean facing up has roots growing upward.

Day 7: The roots from the left- and right-facing beans have bent downward. The bean facing down grew its roots straight down. The roots from the bean facing up have curved to the right and now go over the bean.

Day 9: The roots from all of the beans are growing downward.

Conclusion: Lima bean roots may initially sprout upward or horizontally but will always bend to finally grow downward.

English Language Learners

Assist students in understanding the sample report.

- Read it aloud, slowly.
- During the reading, ask students to quickly sketch each stage explained in the report.
- Use the resulting drawings as clues to any confusion about the content or organization of the piece, so you can clear up any misunderstandings.

describe solve inform
define explain
Writing in Science **211**

Writing Tips

Before you write . . .

● **Take notes during the experiment.**
Take careful notes so that you will have enough information to write an effective summary.

● **Follow the correct form.**
Use the form your teacher requests or the one used for the sample on page 210. Remember that observation reports usually follow the scientific method and include these five parts: *scientific question, hypothesis, procedure, observations,* and *conclusion.*

During your writing . . .

● **Explain the focus of the experiment.**
Identify the scientific question and the hypothesis that you explored.

● **List the steps in the procedure.**
Make sure each step is clear and in the correct order.

● **Include all of your observations.**
List your personal observations chronologically.

● **Base your conclusions on what you observed.**
Make careful observations so that your conclusions are accurate.

After you've written a first draft . . .

● **Use accurate terminology.**
Find out the correct scientific terms for things you observe and use those terms in your report.

● **Check for completeness and correctness.**
Go over your report to make sure that there are no mistakes. Answer any questions that the reader might have about the experiment. Then check your writing for errors.

 Your teacher will tell you what experiment to perform and how to perform it. Pay close attention and take good notes.

EXPOSITORY

Writing Tips

Take time to review the writing tips before assigning the **Try It** activity.

■ Consult with students' science teachers. Try to coordinate this assignment with an actual lab experiment that students are conducting in science class.

■ If that's not possible, ask teachers to suggest several ideas for a science experiment that students can conduct in your classroom.

■ If students are required to use a standard form for science lab reports, ask for copies of the form, so that students can use it for this assignment.

 Answers

Answers will vary.

Literature Connections

Mentor texts: Students who enjoy writing in science may want to check out these examples of expository writing in the sciences.

Nature's Fury: Eyewitness Reports of Natural Disasters by Carole G. Vogel

Digging for Bird Dinosaurs: An Expedition to Madagascar by Nic Bishop

Into the Volcano: A Volcano Researcher at Work by Donna Donovan-O'Meara

Black Holes & Supernovas (Secrets of Space) by David E. Newton

Struggling Learners

✳ Encourage students to use graphic organizers, such as the following, to record procedures and observations (see PE pages 229, 264, and 548–549; and TE pages 789–793):

● charts
● graphs
● lists
● diagrams

Emphasize that these visual aids will help students gather and organize details for their reports.

Practical Writing:
Writing a Memo

Discuss the variety of reasons people have for writing a memo. Some ideas are

- to prepare people for an event or a meeting;
- to provide notes following an event or a meeting;
- to provide feedback on a book, play, or other presentation; and
- to offer suggestions for making improvements to a proposed plan.

If possible, create a memo board to display actual memos as models for students to refer to when they do the **Try It** activity. This will also help reinforce the connection between classroom writing and real-world writing.

Before displaying the memos, check to see that they are appropriate for classroom display and that they follow a clear format.

- To begin, display appropriate memos you have written and received in school.
- Students can also ask their parents for memos they have written and received at work. Emphasize that all memos should be about general topics, such as listed above, and should not include private or confidential information.

Practical Writing: Writing a Memo

In school and in the workplace, memos allow people to communicate quickly and effectively. Memos also provide a handy written record. The following memo reports the progress on the "sets" for a school musical.

Standard memo format is used.

Date: Friday, March 6, 2009

To: Mrs. Lee, Technical Director

From: Corrine Stier, Student Director

The subject of the memo is clearly stated.

Subject: Progress on the *Brigadoon* Sets

Here is the first weekly update on the progress of the *Brigadoon* sets.

Important details are listed.

- Dave Dye has sketched a 15-foot-long set. One side will show the living room of the Campbell cottage, with a thatched roof on top and a window at the back. The other side will be cathedral ruins for the wedding scene. The whole piece will be on wheels, so we can spin it around for scene changes.

- Julie Reynolds primed the four old flats from *My Fair Lady* and drew trees on them. We'll use them on a dark stage along with two freestanding trees to make the forest for the chase scene.

- I want to repaint an old drop curtain to look like the backdrop in the movie. I've attached my drawings for your approval.

A polite but businesslike voice is used.

Thanks for your confidence in me, Mrs. Lee. I won't let you down!

define explain describe solve inform
Practical Writing **213**

Writing Tips

Before you write . . .

● **Use the correct format.**
At the left margin, write or type these four headings: *Date*, *To*, *From*, and *Subject*. Each word should be followed by a colon and the appropriate information. Double-space between each line; triple-space before beginning the body of the memo.

● **Get right to the point.**
Make sure the subject line states the topic of the memo. Then, in the body, begin with the most important information.

During your writing . . .

● **Keep it short.**
Include only the essential information.

● **Organize your thoughts.**
Provide information in a clear, well-organized way. If you need a response, state your request clearly and politely.

● **Use an appropriate voice.**
Be polite and businesslike.

After you've written a first draft . . .

● **Check for completeness.**
Revise your work, asking yourself these two questions:
  • *What does the reader already know?*
  • *What does the reader need to know?*

Then fill in any missing information and delete the unnecessary details.

● **Check for correctness.**
Remember: A memo represents you. In order to make a good impression, check your writing for errors. Once everything is clear and correct, your memo is ready to share.

 Write a memo updating your teacher about your progress on a current school project or assignment.

EXPOSITORY

Grammar Connection

Apostrophes
■ **Proofreader's Guide** page 604 (+)
■ *SkillsBook* pages 29–30

Spelling
■ **Proofreader's Guide** pages 642 (+), 644
■ **CD** Spelling—1 and 2

Writing Tips

Review the steps for formatting a memo.
■ If students will be using a computer to type their memos, consider creating a memo template for them to use.
■ You can also ask a student who is adept at creating computer forms to create the template.
■ Be sure to provide students with directions for accessing and using the template.

It is possible that students will not have an ongoing project or assignment to write about. In that case, suggest that students write a memo about a recently completed project or assignment.

 Answers

Memos will vary but should follow the correct format and the "Writing Tips."

 Technology Connections

Point out to students that an e-mail is basically an electronic memo. The benefits of e-mail are obvious: speed, wide distribution, and electronic copies. The drawbacks are also obvious: e-mail is not confidential, and with a click of the mouse, it can end up in all the wrong hands. Lead a class discussion about the benefits and drawbacks of electronic and paper memos.

Writing for Assessment

If your students must take school, district, or state assessments this year, focus on the writing form they will be tested on.

If time allows, have students work together to create a booklet of test-taking strategies and tips for writing. Ideas may include the following:

■ Think about the traits, content, and structure of the required writing form.

■ Use charts, outlines, and Venn diagrams to plan and organize ideas.

■ Pace your writing according to the amount of time allowed.

■ Allow enough time at the end for rereading and editing.

■ Review the main traits of expository writing. Ask students to look for these traits as they read the sample essay:

☐ a clearly stated focus statement
☐ specific, interesting details
☐ middle paragraphs that support the focus
☐ a clear plan with transitions
☐ a knowledgeable, interested voice
☐ use of specific nouns and action verbs, and effective adjectives

Expository Writing
Writing for Assessment

Many state and school writing tests ask you to respond to an expository prompt. An expository prompt will ask you to explain something or share information. Study the sample prompt and the student response below.

Expository Prompt

There are many inventions that have made life easier. Think of one invention that has had a significant impact on modern life. Then write an expository essay explaining several ways this invention has changed the way people live.

Response to an Expository Prompt

The **beginning** paragraph states the focus or thesis (underlined).

Each **middle** paragraph covers one main point.

Technology is everywhere: supercomputers, MP3 players, hybrid cars, GPS tracking systems, and even greeting cards that play "Celebration." But sometimes the best tech is the old tech. Just now, a library full of students sits at writing carrels, crouching over tests, and every one of them holds a pencil. The lowly pencil has shaped the world.

The pencil put writing in everybody's hands. In the old days, writing was limited to professors with hand-carved goose quills and pots of India ink. Now, carpenters have pencils sticking out of their jeans. Kindergartners and congresspeople use pencils, too. The pencil has made writing democratic.

The pencil also introduced the world to a new concept: the eraser. Before that, writing was permanent. From the time of calligraphy on

describe solve inform
define explain

215

Writing for Assessment

The writer's engaging voice will be a welcome relief to essay graders.

a letter sealed with a wax blob all the way back to Egyptians chiseling hieroglyphics in rocks—writing had been permanent. Then, along came the eraser, and for the first time writers got to change their minds with no trouble at all. Watch out for a writer with a pencil, because that person is probably a free spirit.

Varied examples make the writing lively.

Maybe the biggest way the pencil has changed the world is that it was a computer before there were computers. Pencils can do word processing. They can perform the most complex mathematical calculations. They can create art and doctor photos—often by adding mustaches and beards. And instead of costing $500.00, the typical pencil costs $.05. That's one ten-thousandth of the price—a fact that this very pencil calculated.

The **ending** adds an amusing final thought.

While most people get excited by all the new technology around them, a few people should take the time to admire the old technology, too. Write with it, erase with it, chew on it, but don't forget the pencil.

EXPOSITORY

Respond to the reading. Answer the following questions about the sample essay.

☐ Ideas (1) What is the writer's topic? (2) What three main parts of the topic does the writer cover?

☐ Organization (3) Does the writer organize the essay by time, by order of importance, or by location?

☐ Voice & Word Choice (4) What words tell that the writer cares about the subject?

Respond to the reading.

Ask students to offer their opinions of the essay before they answer the questions.

Answers

Ideas **1.** the lowly pencil
2. The pencil made writing accessible to everyone, it made erasing possible, and it was a computer before there were any computers.

Organization **3.** order of importance

Voice & Word Choice **4.** Possible choices: students sit at writing carrels, crouching over tests, hand-carved goose quills and pots of India ink, from the time of calligraphy on a letter sealed with a wax blob all the way back to Egyptians chiseling hieroglyphics in rocks, free spirit, often by adding mustaches and beards, one ten-thousandth of the price, chew on it

English Language Learners

Have students organize their responses to **Ideas** (under **Respond to the reading**) by making a line diagram like the one they made on PE page 159.

• Tell students to write the topic in a box at the top of their diagram.

• Ask them to draw three boxes below it and to write one of the three main parts of the topic in each box.

• Have them number the boxes to show the order in which the writer addressed the main parts of the topic.

Writing Tips

Point out that students must approach writing-on-demand assignments differently from open-ended writing assignments.

Expository Prompts

Allow students the same amount of time to write their response essay as they will be allotted on school, district, or state assessments. Break down each part of the process into clear chunks of time. For example, you might give students

- 10 minutes for reading, note taking, and planning,
- 25 minutes for writing and revising,
- 10 minutes for editing and proofreading.

Tell students when time is up for each section. Start the assignment at the top of the hour or at the half hour to make it easier for students to keep track of the time.

Technology Connections

The two prompts on this page are also available on the Eval-U-Write online essay grader. Eval-U-Write includes 90 prompts drawn from the *Write Source* series, as well as over 150 other prompts. For more information about this subscription service, go to www.greatsource.com.

216

Writing Tips

Before you write . . .

- **Understand the prompt.**
  Remember that an expository prompt asks you to explain.
- **Plan your time wisely.**
  Take several minutes to plan your writing. Use a graphic organizer like a cluster to help with planning your writing.

Cluster

During your writing . . .

- **Decide on a focus for your essay.**
  Keep your main idea or purpose in mind as you write.
- **Be selective.**
  Use examples and explanations that directly support your focus.
- **End in a meaningful way.**
  Remind the reader about the importance of the topic.

After you've written a first draft . . .

- **Check for completeness and correctness.**
  Present your details in a logical order and correct errors in capitalization, punctuation, spelling, and grammar.

Expository Prompts

- Each of us owns something we treasure. Your object may not seem special to anyone else, but it has meaning to you. Write an essay explaining why this object is so important in your life.
- Write an essay explaining why a certain person is deserving of your admiration. You may or may not personally know this individual.

 Plan and write a response. Respond to one of the prompts above. Complete your writing within the period of time your teacher gives you. Afterward, list one part of your essay that you like and one part that could have been better.

English Language Learners

Before students undertake the assignment, tell them to create a cluster with their topic in the center.

- Instruct students to make three branches and write either three reasons the object they plan to write about is important or three things they admire about the person they identified.

- Then tell students to jot down under each branch the supporting details they will cover.

- As the final step before writing, instruct students to decide what kind of organization would be best and number the branches to show the order in which they will be addressed.

describe solve inform
define explain

Expository Writing Checklist **217**

Expository Writing in Review

Purpose: In expository writing, you *explain something* to readers.

Topics: Explain . . . the kinds of something,
how things are similar or different,
how to do or make something,
the causes of something, or
the definition of something.

Prewriting

Select a topic that you know something about or one you want to learn more about. (See pages 166–167.)

Gather and sort details and organize them chronologically, point by point, or in order of importance. (See pages 168 and 170.)

Write a focus statement, telling exactly what topic you plan to write about. (See page 167.)

Writing

In the beginning, introduce your topic, say something interesting about it, and state your focus. (See page 173.)

In the middle, use clear topic sentences and specific details to support the focus. (See pages 169 and 174–175.)

In the ending, summarize your writing and make a final comment about the topic. (See page 176.)

Revising

Review the ideas, organization, and voice first. Then review for **word choice** and **sentence fluency.** Make sure that you use terms that are precise and connect with the reader. (See pages 178–188.)

Editing

Check your writing for conventions. Also have a trusted classmate edit your writing. (See pages 190–192.)

Make a final copy and proofread it for errors before sharing it. (See page 193.)

Assessing

Use the expository rubric to assess your finished writing. (See pages 194–195.)

EXPOSITORY

Expository Writing in Review

Refer students to this page whenever they write an expository paragraph or essay.

■ Allow them to refer to this review while they are doing a sample assessment.

■ As they become more familiar with the writing form during the year, they will need to refer to the list less frequently.

Persuasive Writing Overview

Unit Objectives

The writing standards listed below are based on a blending of state and NCTE standards.

- Use charts, diagrams, and lists to gather and organize ideas.
- Support central idea with vocabulary and voice appropriate to audience and purpose.
- Revise drafts by adding, deleting, and rearranging texts; provide logical support of ideas.
- Assess writing using a rubric based on the traits of effective writing.
- Share finished pieces with classmates and others.

Writing Forms

- persuasive paragraph
- position essay
- personal commentary

Focus on the Traits

- **Ideas** Presenting specific reasons that defend a position
- **Organization** Developing a beginning that states a position, a middle that provides reasons, and an ending that restates the position
- **Voice** Using a balanced, consistent voice
- **Word Choice** Choosing fair words and qualifiers that strengthen position
- **Sentence Fluency** Writing complete, varied sentences
- **Conventions** Checking for errors in punctuation, capitalization, spelling, and grammar
- Writing a position statement and topic sentences that support it

Note: For specifics about reading the chart below, see page TE 33.

Suggested Persuasive Writing Unit (Five Weeks)

Day	Writing and Skills Units	In the *Write Source* book			On the CD-ROM	*SkillsBook*
		Pages	Proofreader's Guide—basic grammar rules	Basic Grammar practice	Interactive Grammar Exercises	grammar practice pages
1–5	**Persuasive Paragraph:**	219–222				
	Skills Activities: Compound Subjects and Predicates		690 (+), 692 (+)	501 (+)		67–68, 105–106
	Pronouns and Antecedents		706 (+)	476–477, 478	Pronoun-Antecedent Agreement	141–142
opt.	*Speeches*	428–429				
6	**Persuasive Essay:** Defending a Position (Model)	223–226				
7–8	(Prewriting)	227–232				
9–10	(Writing)	233–238				

| Day | Writing and Skills Units | In the *Write Source* book | | | On the CD-ROM | *SkillsBook* grammar practice pages |
		Pages	Proofreader's Guide—basic grammar rules	Basic Grammar practice	Interactive Grammar Exercises	
11–13	(Revising)	239–250				
	Skills Activities: Complete Sentences		690 (+), 692 (+)	502–503		75–76
	Sentence Variety			522 (+)		125–126
	Adverbs		736–737	490, 492–493		171
	Unity			538		
14–15	(Editing and Publishing)	251–254, 255				
	Skills Activities: Spelling		642, 643		Spelling—3 and 4	
	Double Subjects					89–90
	Tenses (Irregular Verbs and Tense Shifts)		720 (+), 722–723, 724 (+)	480 (+), 481, 482 (+), 483 (+)	Verb—1	157–158
	Pronouns and Pronoun-Antecedent Agreement		712 (+), 714–715	476 (+), 477 (+), 478 (+)		139–140, 143–144
16–18	(Assessing) (Reflecting)	256				
opt.	*Speeches*	428–429				
opt.	*Practical Writing: Business Letter*	274–277				
	Skills Activities: Colons		596–597			21–22
	Capitalization		618 (+), 626–627		Capitalization—1 (+)	43–44
19–20	Persuasive Writing for Assessment	278–280				
1–5	**Personal Commentary** (Model)	261–263				
	(Prewriting) (Writing)	264–265				
	(Revising) (Order of Importance)	266		536		
	Skills Activities: Sentence Combining (Using Key Words and Phrases)		698 (+)	498 (+), 512 (+), 513 (+), 514, 519 (+), 520 (+)	Sentences— Combining (+)	101–102, 123–124
	(Editing)	266				
	Skills Activities: Using the Right Word		676–687		Using the Right Word—2	57–58
	Capitalization		626 (+)			45–46

WEEK 3 · WEEK 4 · WEEK 1 SECOND FORM

Teacher's Notes for Persuasive Writing

This overview for persuasive writing includes some specific teaching suggestions for the unit.

Writing a Persuasive Paragraph (pages 219–222)

Students probably understand what a persuasive paragraph is, but they may not realize that a good persuasive paragraph is backed up with solid facts and reasons. It is one thing to argue for or against something; it is quite another thing to show reasons why. Help students understand why reasons make or break a persuasive paragraph.

Defending a Position (pages 223–260)

In this chapter, students will have the challenging task of defending a position. Students will need to use good organizational skills, form reasonable opinions, express those opinions clearly, support their opinions, and anticipate conflicting opinions and evidence.

Creating a Personal Commentary (pages 261–266)

Although a person who writes a personal commentary is interested in persuading his or her readers, what is important is the commentary, not the persuasion. In other words, a personal commentary is the writer's reflection on some aspect of the world. If people agree, great! If they don't, that isn't a problem.

Writing Across the Curriculum (pages 267–277)

An editorial about the historic value of an old library for social studies, a statistical argument about the price per ounce of fruit drinks for math class, a graph about carbon-dioxide emissions in the United States for science class, and a business letter about funding for a school project for practical writing are all examples of persuasive writing.

Writing for Assessment (pages 278–280)

In order to test the reasoning skills of students, the state or the school will expect students to respond to a persuasive prompt. The model in the textbook will give them an idea of what they must do. Use the persuasive prompts on page 280 for practice.

Minilessons

Here's Why.   Writing a Persuasive Paragraph

■ **READ** the paragraph on page 220 in your textbook. **LIST** each of the reasons the writer uses to support her position on sports. **CHOOSE** another activity that will provide the same benefits as sports (the writer is talking about organized team sports).

Study Hall   Defending a Position

■ **READ** the position essay on pages 225–226 in your textbook. **LIST** the reasons that support the writer's position. **WRITE** a position statement that opposes the writer's argument. **LIST** several reasons that support your opinion.

Comments   Creating a Personal Commentary

■ **GENERATE** a list of topic ideas for a personal commentary by answering the following questions.

■ What cause would you support with your own money? What cause would motivate you to stand in a picket line? What issue would compel you to write a letter to a congressperson or the president? For what cause would you be willing to volunteer a day of your time?

Probabilities   Writing Across the Curriculum

■ **READ** "Creating a Persuasive Graph" on page 272. Then **WRITE** an opinion statement for each of the following:

1. Chance of winning the lottery
2. Safety of travel in a car
3. Getting struck by lightning
4. Becoming a professional athlete

COMPARE your statements with a partner and **DEBATE** which ones would be easy to prove.

Persuasive Writing
Persuasive Paragraph

Where do you stand on the new weekend curfew? What's your position on the cancellation of school dances? When you "take a stand" or "defend a position," you state what you think about an important issue.

What positions have you, or could you, defend? One way to defend a position is to write a persuasive paragraph in which you state your position and provide reasons to support it. In this chapter, you will read a sample persuasive paragraph defending the position that winning in sports is about more than trophies. Afterward, you'll write a "position" paragraph of your own.

Writing Guidelines

Subject:	An important issue
Form:	Persuasive paragraph
Purpose:	To support your position
Audience:	Classmates, parents, guardians

Copy Masters/ Transparencies

T-chart (p. 221)

Persuasive Paragraph

Objectives
- select a position
- gather reasons
- write a persuasive paragraph

A **persuasive paragraph** states the writer's position and provides reasons that support it.

Direct students to brainstorm causes they feel strongly about, such as protecting animals, and list the causes on the board.

■ Divide the class into three to five groups. Assign each group one of the listed causes.

■ Give each group a large piece of paper and a marker. Have group members write their cause at the top of the paper and write an opening sentence stating their position on the cause.

■ Have them list three reasons supporting their position.

■ Invite each group to share its efforts with the class.

✱ Additional information about building persuasive paragraphs is on PE page 529.

Persuasive Paragraph

In small groups, have students write a persuasive paragraph based on the three reasons that support their position.

- Have them refer to the model and questions on the bottom of the page as they write.
- Invite each group to read aloud its paragraph.
- Discuss whether each paragraph succeeds in **persuading** *(see below)* listeners.

Respond to the reading.

Answers

Ideas **1.** Sports are beneficial to students' bodies and minds.
2. Physical activity builds strong bones and improves hand-eye coordination; sports are good for muscle strength, flexibility, and one's heart; and playing sports teaches teamwork and determination.

Organization **3.** to start with; Sports also; In addition

Voice & Word Choice **4.** tone up, stay healthy, physically fit, build strong bones, improve muscle strength, work well, good attitude, challenge of the game, keep going, never give up, everybody wins

---

220

Persuasive Paragraph

In a persuasive paragraph, you state your position in the **topic sentence**. The **body** of the paragraph supports the position, and the **closing sentence** restates it. The following paragraph was written by Ellen, a student who took the position that participating in sports makes for healthy living.

Topic Sentence

Body

Closing Sentence

Join a Winning Team

Sports tone up students' bodies and also their minds. To start with, sports are a fun way to stay healthy and physically fit. Growing kids need physical activity to build strong bones and improve hand-eye coordination. Sports also improve muscle strength, flexibility, and the cardiovascular system. In addition, sports teach students to work well with others and have a good attitude. The challenge of the game helps players learn to keep going and never give up. Because they learn determination, students who play sports often do better in school. Playing sports is good for the body and mind, so no matter who scores the most points, everybody wins!

Respond to the reading. After reading the paragraph above, write answers to the following questions.

- ☐ Ideas **(1)** What is the writer's position? **(2)** What reasons support the position?
- ☐ Organization **(3)** What transitions does the writer use in the body sentences of the paragraph?
- ☐ Voice & Word Choice **(4)** What specific words or phrases make this paragraph persuasive? Find two.

Advanced Learners

Have students use a thesaurus to find synonyms for the word *persuade*. Challenge students to use each term in a sentence. For example:

- You **convince** your parents to let you stay up late.
- You **coax** your baby cousin to eat his strained carrots.

Teaching Tip: Persuading

Emphasize that in a persuasive paragraph, students must try to win someone over to their point of view. When students practice persuasive writing, they should ask themselves two critical things:

- Who is my audience?
- What do I want this audience to think or do?

Help students explain the idea of persuasion in their own words by presenting the concepts of logical argument and evidence.

- Begin a discussion about the roles of prosecutors and defense attorneys.
- Guide students to see that during a trial and the final summation, attorneys attempt to persuade the jury to agree with them.

Once students understand what it means to persuade, they will better grasp the concepts of this unit.

persuade convince *support* 221
argue reason
Persuasive Paragraph

Prewriting Selecting a Topic

Think about a debate you recently had with another person. Ellen charted recent debates to find a position she wanted to write about.

Topics Chart

Debates	
I said . . .	*The other person said . . .*
School lunch is too expensive.	It's cheaper than fast food.
I need more allowance.	Then do more chores.
✳ Sports are good for students.	Sports make students too competitive.
School starts too early.	It's better than getting out too late.

 Select a position. Create a chart like the one above. List debates you have had with other people. Write down what you said and what the other person said. Then select a position you would like to write about in a paragraph.

Gathering Reasons

Next you need to gather reasons to support your position. Ellen gathered supporting reasons by turning her position into a question that started with "Why?" Then she answered the question in as many ways as she could.

Supporting Reasons

Why are sports good for students?
- Lots of people enjoy them.
- Participating in sports improves flexibility.
- Sports activities help build strong bones and muscles.
- Athletes are more popular than other kids.
- Sports teach kids to keep trying and never give up.
- Kids who play sports often do well in school.

 List your reasons. Turn your position into a question that starts with "Why?" Then answer the question in as many ways as possible. Review your list and cross out any reasons that are not very persuasive.

PERSUASIVE

Prewriting Selecting a Topic

Ask students to brainstorm topics that might cause debates with friends, such as having a school dress code or building a town skatepark.

- List the topics on the board, and encourage students to present both sides of the argument. Leave the list on the board for students to refer to.
- Provide photocopies of the reproducible T-chart on TE page 789 for students to use to create their topics chart.

Prewriting Gathering Reasons

To model how to gather reasons, choose one of the topics from your class list.

- Ask students to come up with an appropriate *Why?* question for the chosen topic.
- Brainstorm a list of reasons that answer the *Why?* question, and write them on the board.
- Examine the reasons, one at a time, and discuss which ones are weak and should be eliminated. Explain that weak reasons are often based on emotion, not fact.

Struggling Learners

Use a cluster diagram to show how strong reasons relate to and support a particular position.

- In the center circle, write the position *Saturday is the best day of the week because . . .* This position is an opinion that must be supported with factual reasons.
- Ask students to think of and write down reasons for the position.

- Ask volunteers to write reasons in outer circles on the board. Examples might include *Soccer games are on Saturday; There's more time to hang out with friends;* and so on.
- Encourage students to use cluster diagrams to state their positions and list their reasons.

English Language Learners

Discuss and clarify these terms:

- A *debate* involves examining two sides of a question or issue (such as school lunch vs. fast food, or allowance vs. chores). People debate when they have different points of view.
- A *position* is an opinion or a belief about a situation. Stating a position is sometimes called "taking a stand."

Writing Creating the First Draft

Remind students that their paragraph should state their position and provide solid reasons to support it. Emphasize that reasons that are merely personal feelings, such as *because I like it,* are not going to persuade the reader of the value of the writer's position.

Revising Improving Your Writing

After students use the questions for revising, have them exchange papers with a partner. Partners can then review each other's paragraphs, using the questions in their book as a guide.

Editing

Checking for Conventions

If students need a refresher course in editing, spend a few minutes reviewing some of the major points in the "Proofreader's Guide" at the back of the pupil edition.

* Additional information about the "Proofreader's Guide" is on PE pages 579–749.

222

Writing Creating Your First Draft

As you write the first draft of your paragraph, follow these tips.

■ Write a **topic sentence** that clearly states your position. Try different versions until you feel satisfied with the sentence.

■ Create **body sentences** that provide your supporting reasons. Use transitions to help connect the ideas in your sentences.

■ Write a **closing sentence** that restates your position in a fresh, different way.

 Write your first draft. Use the tips above and your prewriting to guide you. The purpose of your first draft is to get your ideas on paper.

Revising Improving Your Writing

Once your first draft is finished, it's time to revise it. Check your *ideas, organization, voice, word choice,* and *sentence fluency.*

 Revise your paragraph. Let the questions below guide the revision of your paragraph.

1 Does the topic sentence clearly state my position?

2 Do the reasons support my position?

3 Do my reasons appear in an effective order? Do I use transitions to tie my ideas together?

4 Does my word choice make my paragraph sound persuasive?

5 Do my sentences flow smoothly?

Editing Checking for Conventions

After you revise your paragraph, check it for *conventions.*

 Edit your paragraph. Ask yourself the following questions.

1 Have I used the correct spelling, punctuation, and capitalization?

2 Have I checked for errors in grammar?

Proofread your paragraph. Make a final copy of your paragraph and check it one more time before sharing it with your audience.

English Language Learners

Encourage partners to work together to discuss ideas for a topic sentence and methods for supporting it in the body and restating it in a closing sentence. Have partners work through the revising and editing steps. Direct them to check each other's work for sentence order and flow; effective persuasive language; and mistakes involving grammar, spelling, and mechanics.

Grammar Connection

Compound Subjects and Predicates

■ **Proofreader's Guide** pages 690 (+), 692 (+)

■ *Write Source* page 501

■ *SkillsBook* pages 67–68, 105–106

Pronouns and Antecedents

■ **Proofreader's Guide** page 706 (+)

■ *Write Source* pages 476–477, 478

■ *SkillsBook* pages 141–142

■ **CD** Pronoun-Antecedent Agreement

Persuasive Writing
Defending a Position

Hubbub, tussle, scrap, ruckus, hoo-hah, squabble, tiff—English has hundreds of words that describe differences of opinion. Anytime you get a large group of people together, whether in a school or in a community, differences of opinion are bound to come up.

Perhaps people in your school disagree about creating an open study hall. Maybe school board members are debating a change in the school mascot. It might even be that your city is squabbling over a new housing development.

One form of persuasive writing helps you deal with differences of opinion. By stating a position and defending it, you can convince others to agree with you. In this chapter, you will write a position essay about a controversy in your school or community.

Writing Guidelines

Subject:	A controversy in your school or community
Form:	Persuasive essay
Purpose:	To defend a position
Audience:	Classmates and community members

Advanced Learners

Ask students to search through community newspapers to identify current topics of controversy to share with the class. Advise them to pay attention to editorials and letters to the editor, where journalists and readers state their opinions and try to persuade others to agree with them.

Copy Masters/ Transparencies

5 W's chart (TE p. 233)

Defending a Position

Objectives

- take a position on a controversial issue
- use specific reasons to defend the position
- create a beginning that states a position, a middle that provides support, and an ending that restates the position

Prepare students for writing a persuasive essay.

- Have them brainstorm several controversies at school and in their community. List them on the board. (Save the list for students to refer to when selecting a topic for their essay.)
- Then divide the class in half. Select one topic and assign each group a position—one for, one against.
- Have each group use the board, flip charts, or chart paper and write its position at the top. Then have each group brainstorm three reasons in support of the position and list them under the position statement.
- Invite both groups to share their lists with the class.

Understanding Your Goal

Traits of Persuasive Writing

Three traits relate to the development of the content and the form. They provide a focus during prewriting, drafting, and revising.

- Ideas
- Organization
- Voice

The other three traits relate more to form. Checking them is part of the revising and editing processes.

- Word Choice
- Sentence Fluency
- Conventions

✱ The six-point rubric on PE pages 256–257 is based on these traits. Reproducible six-, five-, and four-point rubrics for persuasive writing can be found on TE pages 752, 756, and 760.

224

Understanding Your Goal

Your goal in this chapter is to write a well-organized persuasive essay that defends a position. The traits listed in the chart below will help you plan and write your essay.

Traits of Persuasive Writing

Ideas

Use specific reasons to defend a position about an issue in your school or community.

Organization

Create a beginning that states your position, a middle that provides support and answers an objection, and an ending that restates your position.

Voice

Use a persuasive voice that balances facts and feelings.

Word Choice

Choose fair words and qualifiers to strengthen your position.

Sentence Fluency

Write clear, complete sentences with varied beginnings.

Conventions

Check your writing for errors in punctuation, capitalization, spelling, and grammar.

 Get the big picture. Look at the rubric on pages 256–257. You can use that rubric to assess your progress as you write. Your goal is to write a persuasive essay that states and defends a position.

Position Essay

In a position essay, you take one side of a controversy and state clearly where you stand on the issue. By stating and defending a position, you can convince others to agree with you. In the sample essay that follows, the student writer defends his position on allowing students more options during study hall.

Beginning

The beginning introduces the topic and states the position (underlined).

Middle

The middle paragraphs support the writer's position.

Open Study Halls

"Study hall is for studying!" Most students at Carr Middle School have heard Mr. Spencer say these words in study hall, especially when people are talking or making trouble. He's right. Many students really count on their time in study hall to do homework and get ready for tests. The best way to make study hall more effective is to make it more open.

First of all, an open study hall would let hardworking students go where they need to go to get more work done. A person who needs to do research could go to the library. A student who has to write a report could go to the computer lab. If a person needs to finish an art project, he or she could go to the art room. By allowing hardworking students to move around, an open study hall would actually help them accomplish more.

Secondly, an open study hall would motivate students to take study hall more seriously. When hardworking students earned the privilege of leaving the room, other students would want to earn the same privilege. The only way would be to study.

Most importantly, an open study hall would teach responsibility. Teachers are always saying that students should take responsibility for their education. After all, in

PERSUASIVE

persuade convince support 225
argue reason
Defending a Position

Position Essay

Work through this sample essay with the class, pointing out the elements that make it a good persuasive essay.

Ideas

- Clear, specific reasons and examples show the benefit of an open study hall.

Organization

- The opening paragraph supports an open study hall.
- The middle paragraphs use transitions (*first of all, secondly,* and *most importantly*) to show reasons in order of importance.
- The final middle paragraph offers a solution (hall passes) to the principal's possible objection.
- The ending paragraph restates reasons for an open study hall.

Voice

- Facts and specific suggestions support feelings.

Word Choice

- Fair words (*effective, hardworking, accomplish, responsibility, privilege, reward*) sound knowledgeable and persuasive.
- Reasonable qualifiers (*most, many, actually, more, some*) strengthen the position.

English Language Learners

This unit contains many models of student writing. As students read, discuss, and respond to these models, make sure that they understand the meanings of American idioms. In this persuasive essay, clarify the meanings of the following words:

- count on (depend on)
- nobody will hold their hands (No one will set all the rules for them or provide step-by-step guidance. They will have to set rules for themselves.)
- wind up (find themselves)

As you analyze the last two paragraphs, point out the following:

- In the second-to-last paragraph, the writer presents an opposing view and refutes it.
- In the final paragraph, the writer reiterates the reasons stated earlier and asks the principal to consider the proposal.

 Respond to the reading.

Answers

Ideas 1. Students would get more work done; students would take study hall more seriously; students would learn responsibility.

Organization 2. The fourth paragraph gives the most important reason (open study hall would teach responsibility). **3.** The fifth paragraph answers an objection.

Voice & Word Choice 4. The writer does sound knowledgeable and persuasive. He balances solid reasons for the position stated at the beginning with his feelings. The writer uses fair words *(he's right, count on, best way, hardworking students, motivate, the only way, take responsibility, privilege, more effective)* and qualifiers *(most, some).*

226

The last middle paragraph defends the position against an important objection.

Ending
The ending restates the writer's position.

high school, nobody will hold their hands. Now is when they should learn how to manage their time. An open study hall would help. Students who used it well would have more free time after school, and students who abused the privilege would wind up back at their desks. An open study hall would reward kids for being responsible.

Understandably, Principal MacGregor and some teachers are worried about students just wandering the halls. But just because study hall would be open doesn't mean students could wander. They would still have to use hall passes and arrange with specific teachers to come to their rooms. Students caught wandering would be sent back to study hall, and their privilege would be taken away.

Study hall would be more effective if it were open. An open study hall would allow students to accomplish more, would motivate kids to work harder, and would teach responsibility. Though some people are worried that kids would abuse the system, hall passes could take care of those problems. Principal MacGregor should give this proposal serious attention. Open the doors of study hall!

 Respond to the reading. Answer the following questions about the sample essay.

- ☐ **Ideas** (1) What three reasons support the writer's position?
- ☐ **Organization** (2) Which paragraph deals with the most important reason? (3) Which paragraph answers an objection?
- ☐ **Voice & Word Choice** (4) Does the writer sound knowledgeable and persuasive? Explain.

Struggling Learners

Help students understand the importance of voice and word choice in influencing potential readers.

- Carefully review the essay.
- Decide who will be the primary target audience for the essay (the adults who make school policy decisions).

- List key terms and phrases that would appeal to the essay's audience, beginning with the following: *count on, hardworking students, research, accomplish more, motivate, study, responsibility, manage our time, effective.*

Prewriting

PREWRITE REVISE PUBLISH WRITE EDIT

In prewriting, you will select a controversial issue, gather reasons and details, and organize your ideas. Solid prewriting makes persuasive writing much easier.

Keys to Effective Prewriting

1. Select a controversial issue in your school or community and decide what your position is.

2. Gather reasons and details that support your position.

3. Select an important objection that you can address.

4. Write a clear position statement to guide you.

5. Create a list or an outline as a planning guide.

PERSUASIVE

Prewriting

Keys to Effective Prewriting

Remind students of the purpose of the prewriting stage in the writing process. (It's when the writer gets ready to write.)

"Keys to Effective Prewriting" explains the process students will be guided through on PE pages 228–232.

- Before students begin, have the class brainstorm a list of possible ideas.
- Tell students to feel free to choose a topic from the class list or to come up with their own ideas.
- Review students' ideas before they begin, to be sure that they have chosen a topic that lends itself to a persuasive essay.
- Check students' lists of reasons to make sure that they have selected valid ones that can be supported.

Writing Workshop

The prewriting, writing, revising, and editing sections of this unit each contain activities that teach important strategies, such as selecting a topic or gathering reasons. You can use these activities as minilessons in your writing workshop. Present the minilessons to the whole class or to a small group, or use them to provide support for individual students during independent writing time.

Prewriting
Selecting a Controversy

Remind students they can work from the list the class brainstormed (see TE page 227) to pick a controversy.

Focus on the Traits

Ideas

After students list their controversies, have them work in pairs to test out their positions.

- Ask students to determine if there are enough valid reasons to support their partner's position.
- Encourage students to ask one another questions aimed at finding out more about each other's position.

This exercise should help students clarify their thinking and decide whether their topic is one they feel strongly about.

228

Prewriting Selecting a Controversy

A controversy happens when there are differing opinions concerning an important issue. A student named Janelle used sentence starters to brainstorm about controversies in her school and community.

Sentence Starters

People at my school disagree about . . .
- *whether we should go to block scheduling.*
- *45-minute bus rides.*
- *all the fund-raisers.*
- *whether graduation should be a bigger deal.*

People in my neighborhood disagree about . . .
- *what should happen to that empty lot.*
- *all the "no skateboarding" signs.*
- *the woods for sale next to the school.* ✱
- *the 10:00 p.m. curfew.*
- *the Labrador that barks all night.*

 List controversies. On your own paper, complete the two sentence starters above. Try to come up with at least three endings for each sentence. Choose a controversy that you feel strongly about and write a sentence that states your position.

I think Belmer Woods should be turned into a park.

Focus on the Traits

Ideas Choose an issue that you feel strongly about. You'll have an easier time finding support and defending a position that you really believe in.

Gathering Reasons to Support Your Position

Once you have stated your position, you need to gather reasons to support it. A table diagram can help. The tabletop presents your position. The table legs support that position by answering the question "Why?" The following table diagram helped Janelle gather reasons for her position.

Table Diagram

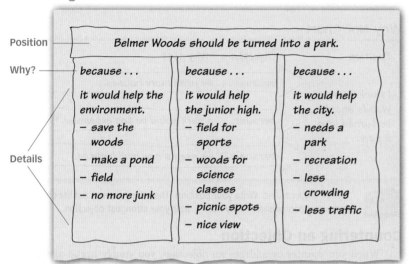

Position

Why?

Details

Belmer Woods should be turned into a park.

because . . .
it would help the environment.
− save the woods
− make a pond
− field
− no more junk

because . . .
it would help the junior high.
− field for sports
− woods for science classes
− picnic spots
− nice view

because . . .
it would help the city.
− needs a park
− recreation
− less crowding
− less traffic

Create a table diagram. Use the sample as a guide to create your own table diagram. In the top box, write your position. In three or four boxes beneath it, write reasons that answer the question "Why?" Then add details about each reason.

Focus on the Traits

Organization A table needs at least three legs to keep from wobbling and falling over. In the same way, your position essay needs at least three supporting reasons. In your essay, you will organize these reasons by building toward the most important one.

PERSUASIVE

Prewriting
Gathering Reasons to Support Your Position

Model how to use a table diagram as you compare and contrast several weak reasons with the reasons in the chart on this page.

- Write the following position at the top of a table diagram: *Belmer Woods should be turned into a park.*
- Then, in one box below, write *because it would be so much fun.*
- Explain that to say something is fun is to express a general, emotional reaction. It does not provide specific factual information. Therefore, this is not a strong reason and should be eliminated.
- Write two more weak or vague reasons and discuss why they do not offer strong support for the position.

Focus on the Traits

Organization
Explain that students need to keep in mind their audience when they organize their reasons in order of importance. It is the importance to the reader or listener, not the importance to the writer, that should be taken into account.

English Language Learners

Limited vocabularies may prevent students from phrasing solid, factual reasons effectively.

- Encourage partners to help each other, when necessary, to find the right words to express their supportive statements.
- Stress that weak arguments are based on vague feelings and opinions (*because it would be nice*) or unfair

generalizations (*because all the people in my neighborhood want the park*).
- Assist students in strengthening their arguments by basing them on specific facts that can be proven true.

Struggling Learners

Allow students to work in small groups. As each writer presents his or her position, classmates may write possible supporting reasons on individual sticky notes or note cards.

Writers can
- add their own ideas,
- analyze the suggestions, and
- sort the notes into *Strong* and *Weak*.

Prewriting
Gathering Objections

Instruct students to choose the objection that will have the strongest impact on the greatest number of people. Suggest that they ask themselves the following questions:

- Who would raise or agree with this objection?
- Does this objection affect many people?
- What impact would this objection have?

Prewriting
Countering an Objection

Have students work in pairs to read each other's arguments and to counter any objections they might raise.

Writer's Craft

Anticipating opposition: Countering an objection requires a strong understanding of audience. Your students display this understanding on a daily basis:

- "If I ask Mom about the party, she'll say no because . . ."
- "Now, I know what you're going to say, but . . ."

Role-play similar encounters to demonstrate that your students already know how to counter objections out loud. Now they just need to do so in writing.

230

Prewriting Gathering Objections

Answering the question "Why?" helped you gather support for your position. Next, answering the question "Why not?" will help you gather possible objections. If you understand objections the reader might have, you can defend against them and make your position stronger. One way to think of objections is to imagine arrows the reader might shoot at your position. Janelle wrote her objections inside arrows.

Why Not Chart

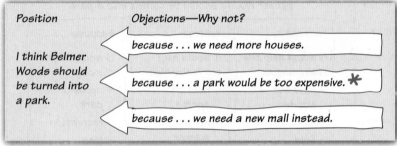

Position

Objections—Why not?

I think Belmer Woods should be turned into a park.

because . . . we need more houses.

because . . . a park would be too expensive.

because . . . we need a new mall instead.

 Gather objections. Write your position. Then draw arrows that list objections to your position (answer "Why not?"). Star your strongest objection.

Countering an Objection

When you counter or address an objection, you simply argue against it. Janelle countered the following objection with the reasons listed below it.

Counterargument Chart

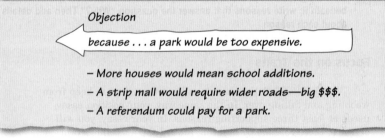

Objection

because . . . a park would be too expensive.

– More houses would mean school additions.

– A strip mall would require wider roads—big \$\$\$.

– A referendum could pay for a park.

 Counter an important objection. Write down the strongest objection to your argument and list the reasons you disagree.

Writing a Position Statement

Your position statement should clearly tell what you think about the controversy. Janelle wrote down her position. Then she tried two other ways to state it. She put a star next to the statement that worked best.

Position Statements

> Belmer Woods should be turned into a park.
>
> The best way to develop Belmer Woods would be to make it a park. ✱
>
> Instead of more houses or stores, the land should become a park.

 Write your position statement. Write three different versions. Then choose the statement you feel works best.

Writing Topic Sentences

Next, you need to write topic sentences for your middle paragraphs. Janelle used a chart. She wrote her reasons in the left column and corresponding topic sentences in the right column.

Outline Chart

Reasons	Topic Sentences
It would help the environment.	First of all, a park would be the right choice for the environment.
It would help the junior high.	Turning Belmer Woods into a park would also help the junior high.
It would help the city.	The most important reason to create a new park is that the whole city would benefit.
Objection: A park would be too expensive.	Some people say the city doesn't have enough money to create a park.

 Write topic sentences. Make an outline chart like the one above. In the left column, list the reasons from your table diagram (page 229) and the objection you chose (page 230). In the right column, create topic sentences.

Prewriting
Writing a Position Statement

Emphasize that readers should be able to identify the topic and understand the writer's view from reading the position statement.

One way for students to learn how to write position statements is to use the technique called modeling.

- Encourage students to write down good focus statements (position statements) that they find in their nonfiction reading.
- Then they should write their own sentences, following the patterns used in the examples they have found.

✱ Additional information about modeling sentences is on PE page 521.

Prewriting
Writing Topic Sentences

Suggest that students use transition words at the beginning of the topic sentences in their middle paragraphs.

PERSUASIVE

Struggling Learners

Have students cut out advertisements—the ultimate persuasive texts—from magazines and newspapers. Then have them highlight the primary message in each ad, which may or may not be a complete topic sentence. Together, practice modeling full sentences from these professional samples.

Prewriting
Organizing Your Essay

As students compose an organized list, remind them that they should try to come up with two or three facts and details for each topic sentence.

Technology Connections

Eval-U-Write contains eight different graphic organizers to help students plan their writing. This subscription-based online tool allows students to create an outline and then port their prewriting right into the work space in which they will develop their essays.

To find out more about Eval-U-Write, go to www.greatsource.com.

232

Prewriting Organizing Your Essay

The following directions can help you create an organized list for your essay. The organized list brings together all the ideas of your prewriting and prepares you to write your first draft.

Directions   **Organized List**

| Write your position statement. | The best way to develop Belmer Woods would be to make it a park. |

| Write your first topic sentence. |
| List facts and details. |

1. First of all, a park would be the right choice for the environment.
   - save part of forest
   - make pond and field
   - stop pollution and graffiti

| Write your second topic sentence. |
| List facts and details. |

2. Turning Belmer Woods into a park would also help the junior high.
   - field for sports teams
   - forest for science classes
   - picnic areas for clubs

| Write your third topic sentence. |
| List facts and details. |

3. The most important reason to create a new park is that the whole city would benefit.
   - no parks on west side
   - west side already crowded
   - houses/strip mall not needed

| Write your fourth topic sentence. |
| List facts and details. |

4. Some people say the city doesn't have enough money to create a park.
   - new houses = school additions
   - new strip mall = road work
   - cheaper to make park

Create an organized list. Use the "Directions" above to organize your position statement, topic sentences, and details. This list will guide you as you write your first draft.

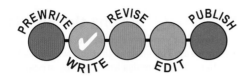

persuade convince support 233
argue reason
Defending a Position

Writing

PREWRITE · WRITE · REVISE · EDIT · PUBLISH

After you create a plan for your essay, you are ready to get all of your ideas on paper.

Keys to Effective Writing

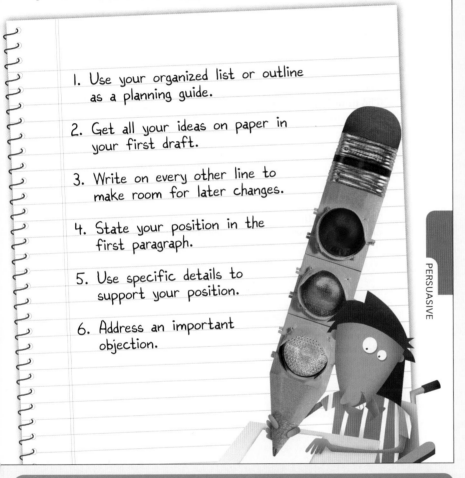

1. Use your organized list or outline as a planning guide.

2. Get all your ideas on paper in your first draft.

3. Write on every other line to make room for later changes.

4. State your position in the first paragraph.

5. Use specific details to support your position.

6. Address an important objection.

PERSUASIVE

Writing Keys to Effective Writing

Remind students that the writing stage is when they get to connect their ideas on paper.

"Keys to Effective Writing" explains the process students will be guided through on PE pages 234–238.

■ Tell students to use a bookmark or put a sticky note on this page so they can refer to it as they write their first draft.

■ As students prepare to write, review the goals of a **first draft** *(see below)*. Emphasize that they don't need to strive for perfection at this point in the writing process. They should concentrate on getting their ideas on paper.

Writing Workshop

Don't just teach your students how to write: write along with them. This is one of the key concepts of the writing workshop approach. You are a writer, just like your students. Let students see you compose a beginning or part of a paragraph. Let them see the mistakes you make and the successes you have.

If you lead by example—one writer among many—you can create a truly supportive and dynamic writing community in your classroom.

Teaching Tip: First Draft

Students may benefit from a review of how to write a first draft.

● As students gather information, remind them to answer the 5 W's and H (Who? What? When? Where? Why? and How?). Provide photocopies of the reproducible 5 W's chart on TE page 792.

● Tell students to review the goals for a persuasive essay on PE page 224.

● Emphasize that the goal of a first draft is to get the ideas on paper. Students will have a chance to make changes and corrections during the revising process.

Writing Getting the Big Picture

Direct students' attention to the descriptions in the graphic of a good **beginning, middle,** and **ending.** The descriptions of the middle paragraphs reveal the development of the main point of the writer's argument.

Writing Getting the Big Picture

Now that you have finished prewriting, you are ready to create a first draft of your essay. The graphic that follows shows how the parts of your essay will fit together. (The examples are from the student essay on pages 235–238.)

Beginning

The **beginning** introduces the controversial issue and states the writer's position.

Position Statement
The best way to develop Belmer Woods would be to make it a park.

Middle

The **middle** paragraphs support the writer's position.

Topic Sentences
First of all, a park would be the right choice for the environment.

Turning Belmer Woods into a park would also help the junior high.

The most important reason to create a new park is that the whole city would benefit.

The **last middle** paragraph answers an important objection.

Some people say the city doesn't have enough money to create a park.

Ending

The **ending** revisits the position.

Closing Sentence
Many people have ideas about developing Belmer Woods, but only a park would be best for the community.

English Language Learners

Explain that the expression *the big picture* in the title on this page means the whole essay or project.
- Tell them to think of a large classroom wall map.
- If they stand close to it, they can see small details.
- However, if they step back, they can see "the big picture"—the entire area covered by the map.
- When discussing the **Ending** portion of the chart, be sure students understand that *revisits* means "restates."

Struggling Learners

Have students copy the sample position statement and closing sentence. Tell students to
- highlight words that appear in both (*develop/developing, Belmer Woods, park, best*),
- follow the same steps with their own beginnings and endings, and
- note that the beginning and ending should not be identical but must have similar points.

persuade convince support **235**
argue reason
Defending a Position

Starting Your Essay

The beginning paragraph of your essay needs to get the reader's attention, introduce the topic, and state your position about it. Here are some ways you can get the reader's attention.

- **Connect with the reader.**
  Students at Belmer Junior High are used to looking out the windows of the school and seeing Belmer Woods.
- **Dramatize the controversy.**
  The chain saws and bulldozers are coming to Belmer Woods.
- **Ask a question.**
  Would students rather look at a park or hundreds of houses?
- **Be creative.**
  When developers look at Belmer Woods, they don't see green leaves but green stacks of cash.

| Beginning |
| Middle |
| Ending |

Beginning Paragraph

Janelle begins her essay by making a connection with the reader. Then she introduces the topic and states her position about it.

> **The controversy is introduced.**
>
> Students at Belmer Junior High are used to looking out the windows of the school and seeing Belmer Woods. Now when they look out, they see a sign: "For Sale, 20 acres, Zoned Residential/Commercial." Belmer Woods is about to change, and there are many different ideas about how it should change. <u>The best way to develop Belmer Woods would be to make it a park.</u>
>
> **The position is stated** (underlined).

 Write an opening. Write the beginning paragraph of your essay. Use one of the strategies above to get your reader's attention. Then introduce the topic and state your position.

PERSUASIVE

Writing Starting Your Essay

To help students develop an effective beginning, consider this activity:

- Select a topic that concerns your school community to model each of the four strategies for capturing the reader's attention.
- Discuss the four approaches and ask students to analyze the differences between them.
- Instruct students to write two opening paragraphs for their essays, using two different strategies.
- Have each student work with a partner to give each other feedback on which approach is most effective.

English Language Learners

Discuss the meaning of the first bullet. Make sure students understand that in order to "connect with the reader," the writer must try to predict how the reader may think and feel. The writer can then organize reasons that target that point of view.

Advanced Learners

Have students search through the classified section of a newspaper and cut out samples that represent the four attention-getting approaches mentioned. For example:

- Connect with the reader: *Here is the starter home you've been looking for.*
- Dramatize the controversy: *Don't waste your gas driving to garage sales—come to a collector's paradise!*
- Ask a question: *Do you need a flexible work schedule?*
- Be creative: *Our inn is full—these six adorable puppies must go!*

If students have difficulty finding ads that fit one or more of the approaches, invite them to write their own persuasive ads.

Writing
Developing the Middle Part
Remind students to draw on the information they have compiled in their organized lists (PE page 232) as they draft their middle paragraphs.

Using Transitions
Examine how the writer uses order of importance in the model.

- Discuss how the writer builds up to the most important reason, which would probably have the most positive impact on the writer's audience.
- Ask students to identify the transitions that are used. Note that the writer has used one from each box on the page.

✱ Additional information about order of importance is on PE page 536.

Writing Developing the Middle Part

Now it's time to write the middle paragraphs of your essay. You start each paragraph with a topic sentence and add details that support it. Your last middle paragraph should address an objection.

Beginning

Middle

Ending

Using Transitions

Transitions will help you show the order of importance in your paragraphs. The following sets of transitions would work well with your first three middle paragraphs.

First of all, Also, Most importantly,	To begin, Also, Finally,	To start with, In addition, Most significantly,

Middle Paragraphs

The topic sentence introduces the topic (underlined).

The body supports the topic sentence.

First of all, a park would be the right choice for the environment. Part of the forest could be saved, and earthmovers could dig out a pond. The grassy part on the north could remain as a field for soccer or baseball. Making the land into a park would also help protect the environment. Nobody would be able to dump junk or car tires there anymore or carve graffiti into the trees. A park would both preserve and protect the environment.

Turning Belmer Woods into a park would also help the junior high. Gym classes and sports teams could use the field on the north side. Science classes could study the plants, trees, and insects

English Language Learners

Help students understand and use transitions by relating these words to a sequence of numbers.

- Refer to the model on PE page 225, pointing out that this writer began the first middle paragraph with the phrase *first of all*. Relate that phrase to the number 1.
- The student used the word *secondly* to begin the next

paragraph. Relate that word to the number 2.

- Associate a number with each of the transitions shown in the three boxes on PE page 236. The words and phrases in each box can become a sequence of 1-2-3.
- Encourage students to keep these word-number associations in mind as they use transitions in their drafts.

The middle paragraphs build to the most important reason.

in the wooded spots. In addition, any clubs in the school would be able to hold events in the picnic areas. Belmer Junior High would be a better place if students had a park next door.

The most important reason to create a new park is that the whole city would benefit. Currently, there are no parks on the west side of town, but there are plenty of houses. A park would give all those people somewhere to go for recreation. A new subdivision or a new strip mall would just make the west side overcrowded.

The last middle paragraph counters an objection.

Some people say the city doesn't have enough money to create a park. However, a subdivision or a strip mall would cost even more. If a hundred new families moved in, the city would have to add on to the schools. If a strip mall were built, the city would have to widen the roads. Those projects would cost a lot more than creating a park.

 Write your middle paragraphs. Create middle paragraphs that support your position for your persuasive essay.

Drafting Tips

- **Follow the plan** in your organized list.
- **Use transitions** to show order of importance.
- **Include clear reasons** and avoid sounding emotional.
- **Respond to an objection.**

PERSUASIVE

Have pairs of students review one another's middle paragraphs. Check each other's writing for the following:

- clear organization
- use of transitions
- strong, fact-based reasons
- a response to an objection

Provide in-class time for revising paragraphs.

 Writer's Craft

Your day in court: Think of a persuasive essay as "your day in court."

In a courtroom, you get to make an opening argument (the introductory paragraph), state your plea (your opinion statement), back up your position with reasons (testimony), cross-examine witnesses for the opposition (countering an objection), and give a closing statement (the concluding paragraph).

A well-written persuasive essay can win your case—and a badly written one can lose it.

Writing Ending Your Essay

Model how to write an effective ending. Using a topic that you have discussed previously, show how to restate the main points without repeating them verbatim.

After students finish writing their endings, have them trade with a partner to see if they have followed the guidelines at the top of the page. Encourage students to make suggestions for improvements.

 Literature Connections

Mentor texts: For professional models of persuasive writing, check out the following books:

It's Our World, Too by Phillip Hoose

Animal Rights—Yes or No by Marna A. Owen

Causes of Crime: Distinguishing Between Fact and Opinion by Stacey L. Tipp

Start Something: You Can Make a Difference by the Tiger Woods Foundation and Earl Woods

Take Action! A Guide to Active Citizenship by Marc Kielburger

Writing Ending Your Essay

The hard work is done. You have stated your position, supported it with reasons, and responded to an objection. Now you are ready to write your ending paragraph. If you aren't sure what to write in your ending paragraph, follow these guidelines.

Sentence 1: Revisit your position.

Sentence 2: Sum up the main support for your position.

Sentence 3: Sum up the objection and your response to it.

Sentence 4: Leave the reader with a strong final thought.

Ending Paragraph

The position is restated.

The paragraph sums up support for the position.

The best way to improve Belmer Woods is to make it into Belmer Park. The park would help the environment, the junior high, and the city. In addition, the park would cost the city less than a new subdivision or strip mall. Many people have ideas about developing Belmer Woods, but only a park would be best for the community.

 Write your ending. Write the final paragraph of your essay. Restate your position and sum up the reasons for it. Leave the reader with something to think about.

Form a complete first draft. Write a complete copy of your essay. Skip every other line if you write by hand, or double-space if you use a computer. This will give you room for revising.

persuade convince support 239
argue reason
Defending a Position

Revising

When you revise, you add or remove details, shift parts of the essay, and work on creating a more persuasive voice. You also check your word choice and refine your sentences.

Keys to Effective Revising

1. Read your essay aloud to get a feeling for how well it works.

2. Make sure you clearly state your position.

3. Check your paragraphs to make sure they follow your writing plan.

4. Polish your voice so that it sounds convincing.

5. Check your words and sentences.

6. Use the editing and proofreading marks inside the back cover of this book.

PERSUASIVE

Revising

Keys to Effective Revising

The "Keys to Effective Revising" explains the process students will be guided through on PE pages 240–250.

Remind students to check the following:
- Make sure each paragraph has a topic sentence that is supported with effective details.
- Check for one strong objection that is countered with logic and reason.
- Check the last paragraph, which should restate the points made in the essay in a new way and wrap up with a strong concluding thought.

English Language Learners

Students may have difficulty understanding direction 4—
Polish your voice so that it sounds convincing.

- Point out that *to polish* something means "to make it bright and shiny." Use a bicycle or a car as an example.

- When writers revise their drafts, they polish the way they have expressed their position and supported it. They fine-tune their arguments so that they are stronger, clearer, and more convincing.

Reassure students that they will have help during this process.

Revising for Ideas

The rubric strips that run across all of the revising pages (PE pages 240–249) will help students focus their revising. They relate to the full rubric on PE pages 256–257.

Have students read their essays to a partner.

- Have listeners focus on "fuzzy thinking."
- Listeners should point out any unclear reasoning they hear.
- Readers should highlight any "fuzzy" sentences.
- Partners should cooperate to strengthen weak sentences.

 Answers

1. exaggeration
2. half-truth
3. all-or-nothing statement
4. exaggeration
5. half-truth

Discuss why each **Try It** sentence contains "fuzzy thinking." Tell students to rewrite the sentences to make them more logical. Have the class work together to agree on the best solution for each sentence.

Revising for Ideas

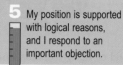

6 My position is very well defended and compels the reader to act.

5 My position is supported with logical reasons, and I respond to an important objection.

4 Most of my reasons support my position. I respond to an objection.

When you revise for *ideas*, make sure you have used logical reasons and avoided "fuzzy thinking." Also look for ways to strengthen your response to any objections a reader may have. The rubric strip above can guide you.

How can I avoid "fuzzy thinking" in my essay?

You can avoid "fuzzy thinking" by making sure the reasons you use are accurate and logical. If even one of your supporting reasons is not logical, your position will be shaky, like a table with a bad leg. Here are three common types of "fuzzy thinking" errors to check for.

- **Half-truths:** Avoid telling only half of the story.
  Building a dam would help animals by giving them new habitats.
  This is a half-truth because dams also destroy habitats.

- **Exaggerations:** Avoid stretching the truth.
  Next the school board will force students to clean the highway!
  This exaggeration merely makes the writer sound unrealistic.

- **All-or-nothing statements:** Avoid oversimplifying complex issues.
  If the school bans fund-raisers, we'll never have new uniforms.
  Few people would believe that these are the only options.

 Read the following sentences and identify the fuzzy thinking in each.

1. The mayor wants to put every curfew breaker into prison.
2. The school food is what is making eighth graders gain weight.
3. If the state doesn't change the tests, no one will graduate.
4. When it rains, the gymnasium is under 10 feet of water!
5. Television is the reason kids are getting bad grades.

 Check for fuzzy thinking. Read the body of your essay and look for half-truths, exaggerations, and all-or-nothing statements. Revise your essay to eliminate any fuzzy thinking you may find.

Advanced Learners

Students can explore the concept of fuzzy thinking by brainstorming half-truths, exaggerations, and all-or-nothing statements for the following topics:

- To save money, the school library will close at noon.
- Before-school hall monitors will be eighth graders.
- Students have a 30-minute lunch period; teachers have an hour.

English Language Learners

Help students understand the term *fuzzy thinking*.

- Brainstorm experiences students may have had that involved tuning or adjusting an unclear image to bring it into focus (camera viewfinder, binoculars, slide or overhead projector).

- Discuss how the fuzzy image becomes clear. Relate these situations to bringing fuzzy thinking into focus by using accurate and logical information.
- Review why each of the examples in the **Try It** activity is "fuzzy" and how it might be revised to be clear.

persuade convince support   241
argue reason
Defending a Position

3	I need more supporting reasons and a more convincing response to an objection.	2	I need to rethink my position from start to finish.	1	I need to learn how to defend a position.

How can I check my response to an objection?

When you are defending a position, you should answer a key objection your reader may have. The best way to check your answer or response to an objection is to ask yourself the following questions:

1. Is the objection *important*?
2. What is the *main point* of the objection?
3. Do I deal with the *main point*?

 Read the following objection paragraph. Use the three questions above to decide what changes could improve the paragraph.

> 1   Some teachers object to cell phones because they are
> 2 too disruptive in class. That's a serious concern, but why can't
> 3 teachers just start every class saying, "Please turn off all cell
> 4 phones"? For that matter, students with cell phones can talk
> 5 quietly enough that everyone else can still hear the lecture. Finally,
> 6 students could just use cell phones for sending text messages
> 7 back and forth. They are silent.

 Review your objection paragraph. Ask yourself the three questions above and revise as needed to make the paragraph more effective.

Ideas
Weak reasons are replaced with more logical ones.

> say the city doesn't have enough money to create
> Some people ~~are against creating~~ a park.
>   would cost even more.
> However, a subdivision or a strip mall ~~isn't any~~
>
> ~~good, either.~~ If a hundred new families moved in, the
>   to add on to the schools
> city would have ~~all kinds of problems~~. If a strip mall
>   to widen the roads
> were built, the city would have ~~even more trouble~~. . . .

PERSUASIVE

Try It Answers

1. The objection is important.
2. The main point of the objection is that cell phones are disruptive in class.
3. The writer deals with the main point by suggesting that cell phones be turned off during class, although this shouldn't have to be announced every day. The writer's other arguments do not address the main point. The writer focuses on ways that cell phones could still be used, but these ways would continue to disrupt the class or, at the very least, the attention of students using the phones.

As you review the revised objection paragraph at the bottom of the page, point out how each change makes a general point more specific and, in so doing, strengthens the argument. Emphasize the importance of using specific examples to refute objections.

Advanced Learners

Brainstorm ways to overcome the objections raised in the following scenarios:

- Aunt Victoria said I could work at her store for two hours after school each day, but Mom is afraid I won't get my homework done.
- I want to play on the summer league baseball team, but the play-offs are the same week as our family reunion.
- I want to go to Marc's birthday party, but I'm supposed to watch my little brother.

Revising for Organization

Remind students to refer to the rubric strip as they make organizational revisions.

 Answers

1. For one thing, parents want to make the junior high graduation a bigger event.
2. Junior high graduation also marks a big change for students.
3. The most important reason to treat junior high graduation more seriously is that it tells students their work is important.
4. It is true that the school board is concerned about the cost of a more elaborate graduation.

Technology Connections

Organization is one of the four traits assessed by Eval-U-Write, a subscription-based online writing tool. Eval-U-Write checks student writing for introductory material, a position statement, main points or reasons, supporting points, and a concluding paragraph. For more on Eval-U-Write, go to www.greatsource.com.

242

Revising for Organization

6 All the parts of my essay work together to build a thoughtful, convincing position.

5 My overall organization is clear, and my reasons are arranged effectively.

4 Most parts of my essay are organized well except for one part.

When you revise your writing for *organization*, check the overall structure of your essay. Also be sure you have placed your reasons in the most convincing order. The rubric strip above can guide your revision.

How can I check the arrangement of my reasons?

The best way to check the arrangement of your reasons is to follow the three guidelines below.

- Save your most important reason until last.
- Use words such as "first of all," "in addition," and "most importantly" to help the reader understand the organization of your reasons.
- Use the final middle paragraph to answer an objection.

 Read the following topic sentences from an essay about junior high graduation. Put them in the most effective order. Transition words and phrases will help you.

1. Junior high graduation also marks a big change for students.
2. The most important reason to treat junior high graduation more seriously is that it tells students their work is important.
3. It is true that the school board is concerned about the cost of a more elaborate graduation.
4. For one thing, parents want to make the junior high graduation a bigger event.

 Check the order of your reasons. Do you build to the most important reason? Do you respond to an objection? Do you tie your paragraphs together with transitions? Revise until you can answer each of these question with a "yes."

persuade convince *support* **243**
argue *reason*
Defending a Position

To help students find out whether their organization follows the pattern of the chart on this page, ask them to

- make a larger version of the chart on a clean sheet of paper,
- fill in each section with a sentence from their essay, and
- identify any blank sections that indicate something may be missing.

3 I need to reorganize the middle part of my essay.

2 I need to include a beginning, a middle, and an ending in my essay.

1 I need to learn how to organize a persuasive essay.

How can I check the overall organization of my essay?

You can use the questions and the chart below to help you check the overall structure of your essay.

Beginning Paragraph
Do I get the reader's attention?
Do I state my position clearly?

Middle Paragraphs
Do I support my position with sound reasons?

Do I answer an important objection with a counterargument?

Ending Paragraph
Do I restate my position?
Do I end with a strong final thought?

Position Statement
Reason 1
Reason 2
Reason 3
Counterargument
Position Summary

 Revise

Check your overall organization. Review your essay and ask yourself the questions listed above. If you can answer "yes" to every question, your overall organization is strong. If not, revise your essay until you can answer "yes" to each question.

PERSUASIVE

Organization
A change helps to show the order of importance.

The most important reason is that   would benefit
To create a new park ~~would help~~ the whole city.
Currently, there are no parks on the west side . . .

Struggling Learners

It is important to make sure that students understand the difference between an objection and a counterargument.

- Discuss the meaning of the prefix *counter–*. Have students use a dictionary to look it up.
- Point out that when they revised their objection

paragraph (PE page 241), they should have included reasons that counter, or oppose, any objections that might be raised.

- Assist students who still need help with writing effective counterargument.

Revising **for** Voice

Have students revise their essays to make the voice more balanced. As students are working, walk around the room and hold a brief **writing conference** *(see below)* with each student, to make sure that she or he understands the concept.

Writer's Craft

Tone: The word *tone* refers to the author's feeling about the topic. To write persuasively, the tone has to have a bit of fire in it: no one is convinced by an apathetic argument. However, too much fire makes a writer sound unreasonable, perhaps even irrational.

244

Revising **for** Voice

6 My mature and reliable voice creates total confidence in my position.

5 My voice is persuasive and consistent. I balance facts and feelings.

4 My voice is consistent, but I need to balance facts and feelings.

To revise for *voice*, make sure your writing voice is persuasive, consistent, and balanced. The rubric strip above can guide you.

Do I balance facts and feelings?

You use a balanced voice if you focus on facts first and back them up with feelings. If your essay focuses on feelings first, it will sound emotional and unconvincing.

> **Too Emotional**
>
> The Qwik-E-Stop is a bad place. The manager seems distrustful of kids. The whole time you feel just awful. You feel as if you need to get out of there as soon as possible.

On the other hand, if your essay focuses solely on facts, it will sound too dull. Feelings give meaning to facts.

> **Too Dry**
>
> The Qwik-E-Stop is on Main Street. It allows only two students in at a time. The manager enforces this rule. If two kids are inside, other kids wait outside.

A persuasive voice balances facts and feelings.

> **A Balanced Voice**
>
> The Quik-E-Stop on Main Street allows only two students in at a time, and the manager closely watches any students who enter the store. This policy and the attitude of the manager make kids feel unwelcome.

 Check your voice for balance. Read through your essay. Do you include both facts and feelings? If your voice sounds too emotional, add facts. If it sounds too dull, add feelings. Revise until you reach a balance.

Teaching Tip: Writing Conferences

Hold one-on-one conferences to clarify how to write in a balanced voice.

- Check each student's progress.
- Discuss the difference between a balanced voice and one that is too emotional or too dry or detached.
- Suggest improvements to create a consistent and balanced voice.

persuade convince support **245**
argue reason
Defending a Position

3 My voice has a few problems with consistency and balance.

2 My voice is inconsistent, and I sound too emotional and unconvincing.

1 I need to learn how to create a consistent and balanced voice.

Do I use a consistent point of view?

You can check for a consistent point of view by looking at the pronouns in your essay. A persuasive essay should use mostly third-person pronouns: *he, she, it, they*. Your teacher may also allow you to use some first-person pronouns: *I, me, we, us*. However, you should avoid second-person pronouns: *you, your*.

 Read the following paragraph. Find five places where the voice shifts from third person to second person. Then suggest what changes would make the voice consistent.

1   Whenever students go into Quick-E-Stop, the manager
2 watches your hands and your pockets. He asks the students if you
3 plan to buy something. Even if the students pull out their money,
4 the manager still scowls as if he doesn't want you there. He
5 doesn't thank them or tell them to have a nice day, but just stares
6 at you until you leave.

 Check consistency of voice. Read your essay, paying special attention to pronouns. Revise any spot where the voice shifts.

Voice
An inconsistent point of view is corrected.

> Students at Belmer Junior High are used to looking out the windows of the school and seeing Belmer Woods. Now when ~~you~~ they look out, ~~you~~ they see a sign: "For Sale, 20 acres, Zoned Residential/Commercial." Belmer Woods is about to . . .

PERSUASIVE

After students revise their essays for consistent point of view, have them trade papers with a partner.

- Tell partners to read only for consistency in point of view.
- Have students use a colored pencil or a highlighter to underline or highlight inconsistencies.

 **Answers**

Whenever students go into Quick-E-Stop, the manager watches **their** hands and **their** pockets. He asks the students if **they** plan to buy something. Even if the students pull out their money, the manager still scowls as if he doesn't want **them** there. He doesn't thank them or tell them to have a nice day, but just stares at **them** until **they** leave.

Revising for Word Choice

Have pairs of students

- exchange and read each other's essays for negative or unfair words,
- use a colored pencil to circle words that they think are unfair, and
- write suggestions for more-neutral words.

 **Answers**

Possible answers:

1. The Quick-E-Stop shouldn't hire people who don't trust customers.
2. The referendum failed because the voters don't want to spend the money.
3. Our principal checks our lockers once a month.
4. The old gymnasium is in poor condition.
5. The study hall monitors won't let anyone talk.
6. Senior women volunteer over 10,000 hours annually at Fairmont Hospital.
7. Careless drivers cause car accidents.

246

Revising for Word Choice

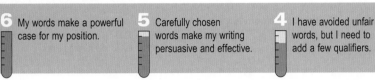

6 My words make a powerful case for my position. **5** Carefully chosen words make my writing persuasive and effective. **4** I have avoided unfair words, but I need to add a few qualifiers.

When you check your essay for *word choice*, make sure you have chosen your words carefully and avoided unfair words. In addition, see if qualifiers (page 247) can make your writing more persuasive. The rubric strip above can guide you.

Did I use unfair words in my essay?

You used unfair words in your essay if some of them are overly negative. Unfair words make your writing seem biased and less persuasive. Notice below how unfair words can be replaced by neutral words.

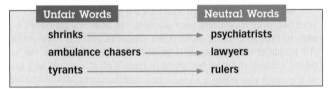

Unfair Words	Neutral Words
shrinks ⟶	psychiatrists
ambulance chasers ⟶	lawyers
tyrants ⟶	rulers

 Read the following sentences and find the unfair words in each. Suggest a replacement word or phrase for each unfair word.

1. The Quick-E-Stop shouldn't hire paranoid people.
2. The referendum failed because the voters are cheap.
3. Big Brother checks our lockers once a month.
4. The old gymnasium is a real pit.
5. The prison guards in study hall won't let anyone talk.
6. Old ladies volunteer over 10,000 hours annually at Fairmont Hospital.
7. Idiots cause car accidents.

 Check your essay for unfair words. Read your essay and watch for overly negative words. Delete or replace them.

English Language Learners

Students with limited vocabularies may not be able to distinguish between unfair and neutral words. In addition, they may not be familiar with the American colloquialisms *shrinks* and *ambulance chasers*.

- Provide easier examples, such as *cheap/inexpensive* and *skinny/slender*.
- Use each example in a sentence that shows its connotative values.
- Then partner students with English-proficient students to work on the **Try It** activity.

3 I need to change some unfair words and add qualifiers.

2 I need to change my unfair language to make a believable position.

1 I need to learn what words are unfair and how to add qualifiers.

How can qualifiers make my writing more persuasive?

Qualifiers can make your writing more persuasive because they limit or "qualify" a statement. Few statements are *always* true for *everyone*. By adding a qualifier to a sentence, you can make your point or claim more believable.

Qualifiers

some	others	many	often	frequently
few	most	several	occasionally	usually

 Read the following sentences. Rewrite each sentence and add a qualifier to make the claim more believable.

1. Students don't take responsibility for their own education.
2. Drivers are careless on the road behind the school.
3. Teachers don't attend the school productions.
4. Students don't care about the student council elections.
5. Parents ignore the parking rules.

Revise **Check your use of qualifiers.** Review your essay, looking for sentences that need qualifiers to make your claims easier to believe.

Word Choice
A qualifier makes a claim more believable, and an unfair word is replaced.

In addition, the park would cost the city less than a new subdivision or strip mall. ^Many People have ideas about ~~exploiting~~ ^developing Belmer Woods, but only a park would be best for the community.

PERSUASIVE

The meanings of some of the **qualifiers** *(see below)* are very similar. Help students understand the distinctions by offering a review of common qualifiers such as *few, some, several, many, most, frequently, usually, often, occasionally,* and *others*.

 Answers

Possible answers:
1. *Some* students don't take responsibility for their own education.
2. Drivers are *often* careless on the road behind the school.
3. Teachers *usually* don't attend the school productions.
4. *Many* students don't care about the student council elections.
5. Parents *occasionally* ignore the parking rules.

Teaching Tip: Qualifiers

As you provide the following definitions, point out the different shades of meaning. After you discuss those that are close in meaning (*several, many, most*), ask students to use the words in sentences.

- few (a small number of things that can be counted)
- some (an unknown or unspecified number)
- several (more than two or three, but fewer than many)
- many (a large number of)
- most (the largest number of)
- frequently (with little time between occasions)
- usually (regularly or normally)
- often (many times)
- occasionally (now and then)
- others (additional ones)

English Language Learners

Remind students that qualifiers make arguments more believable. Provide examples of sentences that are "looking for a qualifier." Have students rephrase the sentences, using qualifiers to make them fair. Start with the following:

- Boys are great baseball players.
- Parents never listen.
- There is nothing good on television these days.

Revising for Sentence Fluency

Have students review the sentences in their essays, making sure they

- have a subject,
- have a verb, and
- create a complete thought.

If students find a group of words that is not a sentence, have them turn the idea into a sentence or connect the idea to an existing sentence.

 Answers

1.	S	6.	S
2.	F	7.	F
3.	S	8.	S
4.	F	9.	F
5.	F	10.	F

Writer's Craft

Intentional fragments: Professional writers sometimes use fragments for effect. They intentionally create an incomplete thought but punctuate it as if it were a sentence. Honestly. The previous word is an example of an intentional fragment. Most fragments in printed material are intentional because editors can't resist fixing unintentional fragments. In fact, if this "writer's craft" feature remains in the book—fragment and all—you know there is a copyeditor somewhere who is still wishing she had taken it out.

248

Revising for Sentence Fluency

6 My sentences spark my reader's interest in my position.

5 My sentences are skillfully written with varied beginnings.

4 My sentences are complete, and most of the beginnings are varied.

To revise for *sentence fluency*, check to see that your sentences are complete and have varied beginnings. The rubric strip above will guide you.

How do I know if my sentences are complete?

Your sentences are complete if each one includes at least one subject and one predicate and expresses a complete thought. If a group of words is missing a subject, a predicate, or is not a complete thought, it is a fragment. (See pages 500–502.)

 Number your paper from 1 to 10. Read the following groups of words. If a group is a complete sentence, write an "S" after its number. If a group is a fragment, write an "F" after it. Rewrite any fragments to make them complete sentences.

1. The city should tear out the old railroad tracks and convert them into a bike path.
2. An exceptional idea.
3. Bike riders and joggers could reach the downtown with ease.
4. Would be a great way to stay in shape.
5. If the city wants to give citizens a new way to get around.
6. The trains currently go under all the major thoroughfares, so the route wouldn't stop traffic.
7. Giving people an alternative way to get to work or school.
8. Because gas prices continue to rise, bike riding and jogging are becoming more popular.
9. Although some people say that the old rail lines are too dirty for foot traffic.
10. Wish the city council would consider the proposal.

Review your sentences. Check the sentences in your essay and make sure that each contains at least one subject and one predicate. Revise any incomplete sentences.

Grammar Connection

Complete Sentences
- **Proofreader's Guide** pages 690 (+), 692 (+)
- *Write Source* pages 502–503
- *SkillsBook* pages 75–76

English Language Learners

Review how to make a fragment into a sentence. Give these examples of sentence fragments that are missing a subject or a verb:

- A great plan.
- Running out of gas.
- Went to the ball game.

Ask students to tell what each sample item is missing and to turn it into a complete sentence.

persuade convince support **249**
argue reason
Defending a Position

3 Most of my sentences are complete, but I need to vary the beginnings.

2 I have many incomplete sentences.

1 I need to learn what makes a sentence complete and how to vary the beginnings.

How can I vary my sentence beginnings?

If most of the sentences in a paragraph begin with a subject followed by a verb, you need to vary the beginnings. You can do so by adding a word, a phrase, or a clause. Note the difference between the following paragraphs.

Similar Beginnings

The school auditorium should be torn down and rebuilt. The roof leaks. The chairs are uncomfortable. People don't enjoy coming to our concerts. They might come if the auditorium were fixed.

Varied Beginnings

The school auditorium should be torn down and rebuilt. When it rains, the roof leaks. To make matters worse, the chairs are uncomfortable. People don't enjoy coming to our concerts. However, they might come if the auditorium were fixed.

 Check your sentence beginnings. Read your essay, looking for places where your sentences all begin with a subject followed by a verb. In such places, revise by adding words, phrases, or clauses to some sentences.

Sentence Fluency
A sentence beginning is improved, and incomplete sentences are corrected.

> Part of the forest could be saved, and
> ∧Earthmovers could dig out a pond. The grassy part
> on the north could remain, ᴀs a field for soccer or
> baseball. Making the land into a park would also
> help. To protect the environment. Nobody would be
> able to dump junk or car tires there anymore . . .

PERSUASIVE

Discuss with students how to vary sentence beginnings. Model how to expand with phrases or clauses.

Then, on the board, compose with students a four- or five-sentence paragraph in which all of the sentences begin in the same way.

■ Use a description of the classroom as a topic.

■ Begin with sentences such as "The classroom is large. The walls are a beige color."

■ Have each student revise the paragraph so that the sentence beginnings vary.

■ Ask students to share their new sentences.

■ Write some of their new sentences on the board to compose a new class paragraph.

✳ Additional information about expanding with phrases is on PE pages 519–520.

Struggling Learners

To help students vary the sentence beginnings in their essays, follow these steps:

● First, have students underline the first few words in their sentences.

● Next, instruct them to check for any series or groups of sentences that start in basically the same way.

● Then tell students to circle those sentences.

● Finally, help each student vary some of these sentences.

Revising Using a Checklist

As students use the revising checklist, remind them to

- carefully reread their essay several times, each time focusing on a different trait; and
- take their time with the checklist, making sure to check each item on the list in their essay.

250

Revising Using a Checklist

Check your revising. On a piece of paper, write the numbers 1 to 12. If you can answer "yes" to a question, put a check mark after that number. If not, continue to work with that part of your essay.

Ideas

_____ **1.** Do I state my position clearly?

_____ **2.** Have I included reasons that support my position?

_____ **3.** Do I effectively respond to an objection?

Organization

_____ **4.** Does the overall structure of my essay work well?

_____ **5.** Are my reasons in the most persuasive order?

_____ **6.** Have I used transitions to help establish the order of importance?

Voice

_____ **7.** Are my facts and feelings balanced?

_____ **8.** Is my point of view consistent?

Word Choice

_____ **9.** Have I avoided unfair words?

_____ **10.** Have I used qualifiers to make my essay more persuasive?

Sentence Fluency

_____ **11.** Are all my sentences clear and complete?

_____ **12.** Do I vary my sentence beginnings?

Make a clean copy. When you've finished revising, make a clean copy before you edit. This makes checking for conventions easier.

Grammar Connection

Sentence Variety

- *Write Source* page 522 (+)
- *SkillsBook* pages 125–126

Adverbs

- **Proofreader's Guide** pages 736–737
- *Write Source* pages 490, 492–493
- *SkillsBook* page 171

Unity

- *Write Source* page 538

English Language Learners

Students may find it easier to hear which sentences can be strengthened if they read aloud their essay.

- Students work with a partner or in a small group.
- Each student reads aloud his or her essay.
- Students suggest revisions to their partners or group members.

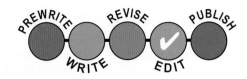

persuade *convince* *support* **251**
argue reason
Defending a Position

Editing

PREWRITE · WRITE · REVISE · EDIT ✓ · PUBLISH

After you finish revising your essay, you are ready to edit for *conventions*: punctuation, capitalization, spelling, and grammar.

Keys to Effective Editing

1. Use a dictionary, a thesaurus, and the "Proofreader's Guide" in the back of this book.

2. Check for any words or phrases that may be confusing to the reader.

3. Check your writing for correctness of punctuation, capitalization, spelling, and grammar.

4. If you are using a computer, edit on a printed computer copy. Then enter your changes on the computer.

5. Use the editing and proofreading marks inside the back cover of this book.

PERSUASIVE

Editing Keys to Effective Editing

"Keys to Effective Editing" explains the process students will be guided through on PE pages 252–254.

- Write the keys to effective editing on the board or on a poster displayed in a prominent place in the classroom.
- Remind students to refer to the list as they begin to edit their essays for conventions.

Technology Connections

For more practice with the rules of writing, see the *Interactive Writing Skills* CD-ROM. It includes fun videos that teach the conventions of writing, rules and examples drawn from the "Proofreader's Guide" of this book, and interactive exercises that help students apply the rules to their writing.

Editing for Conventions

Students should pay attention to two additional points when using pronouns:

- ambiguous pronoun references

  Ambiguous: My dad chose Thomas to drive because *he* knew *he* would drive safely.

  Correct: My dad chose Thomas to drive because Dad knew Thomas would drive safely.

- general pronoun references (where a pronoun refers to a general idea)

  General: The girls ate in the hallway, *which* Mr. Neely was angry about.

  Correct: Mr. Neely was angry that the girls ate in the hallway.

 Answers

Possible answers:

1. No one should leave litter in the empty lot.
2. People should pick up their own trash.
3. Each student should be responsible for her or his own garbage.
4. People who eat candy should put the wrappers in their pockets.
5. Students should take pride in their school.

252

Editing for Conventions

6 My essay is error free from start to finish.

5 I have one or two errors, but they don't distract the reader.

4 I need to correct the errors in my paper because they distract the reader.

When you edit for *conventions*, you need to pay attention to punctuation, grammar, capitalization, and spelling. These two pages will help you check your use of pronouns. The rubric strip above can guide your editing.

Do my pronouns agree with their antecedents?

Every pronoun has an antecedent. An antecedent is the noun (or pronoun) that a pronoun refers to or replaces. Pronouns and their antecedents must agree —both be singular or plural. (See pages 475–478.)

Pronoun agreement is especially tough with singular nouns that refer to people. It is incorrect to use a plural pronoun (*they, them, their*) after a singular noun (*student, teacher, parent*).

Incorrect   Every student should make sure they vote today.
                 singular   *plural*

Correct   Every student should make sure he or she votes today.
               singular   *singular   singular*

(or)   Students should make sure they vote today.
        plural   *plural*

(or)   Every student should make sure to vote today. (No pronoun)

 Rewrite each sentence to correct pronoun-antecedent agreement.

1. No one should leave their litter in the empty lot.
2. Everyone should pick up their own trash.
3. Each student should be responsible for their own garbage.
4. A person who eats candy should put the wrapper in their pocket.
5. Every student should take pride in their school.

Edit **Check your pronouns and antecedents.** Read your essay and make sure that your pronouns agree with their antecedents.

Grammar Connection

Pronouns and Pronoun-Antecedent Agreement

- **Proofreader's Guide** pages 712 (+), 714–715
- *Write Source* pages 476 (+), 477 (+), 478 (+)
- *SkillsBook* pages 139–140, 143–144

English Language Learners

Conduct one-on-one editing conferences to help students check for pronoun-antecedent agreement. As a student reads his or her essay aloud, listen for problems with pronoun-antecedent agreement. When (or if) you notice a problem, help the students understand and correct the error.

persuade convince support
argue reason
Defending a Position
253

3 I need to correct the errors in my paper because they confuse the reader.

2 I need to correct the many errors because they make my essay difficult to read.

1 I need help making corrections.

(See page 510.)

How can I avoid creating a double subject?

You can avoid creating a double subject by making sure that you do not place a pronoun immediately after the subject of a sentence. (See page 510.)

Incorrect

Principal Jenson he **should support the mentoring program.**

Correct

Principal Jenson **should support the mentoring program.**
(or) He **should support the mentoring program.**

 Rewrite each sentence to correct the double subject.

1. Students and teachers they need this mentoring program.
2. Ms. Dorn she will be the sponsor.
3. Students with special skills they will be the mentors.
4. Principal Jenson he should provide a work space.
5. Parents and students they should support this plan.

 Check for double subjects. Read your essay and look for pronouns that immediately follow the subject. Correct any double subjects.

Conventions
A pronoun-antecedent agreement error is removed, and a double subject is corrected.

> Nobody would be able to dump junk or car tires
> there anymore, and they wouldn't be allowed to
>   or
> carve graffiti into the trees. A park it would both
> preserve and protect the environment.

PERSUASIVE

Grammar Connection

Double Subjects
■ *SkillsBook* pages 89–90

1. Students and teachers need this mentoring program.
2. Ms. Dorn will be the sponsor.
3. Students with special skills will be the mentors.
4. Principal Jenson should provide a work space.
5. Parents and students should support this plan.

Editing Using a Checklist

Give students a few moments to look over the "Proofreader's Guide" at the back of the pupil edition. Throughout the year, they can refer to the instruction, rules, and examples to clarify any checklist items or to resolve questions about their own writing.

For additional input, have students exchange their work with a partner.

■ Have each student complete a conventions checklist for their partner's writing.
■ They should be able to point out specific errors for any item that they do not check off.

Creating a Title

Tell students to write down three possible titles for their essay, including one example of each type.

■ Then have small groups review each other's list of titles and give each other feedback on the choices.
■ Encourage students to be creative with their titles. Rhymes, alliteration, and puns are all catchy ways to title an essay. Provide examples of some of your favorite catchy titles.

254

Editing Using a Checklist

 Check your editing. On a piece of paper, write the numbers 1 to 12. If you can answer "yes" to a question, put a check mark after that number. If not, continue to edit for that convention.

Conventions

PUNCTUATION

_____ **1.** Do I use end punctuation after all my sentences?

_____ **2.** Do I use commas before coordinating conjunctions in compound sentences?

_____ **3.** Do I use a comma after a dependent clause at the beginning of a complex sentence?

_____ **4.** Do I leave out commas when a clause or phrase gives necessary information?

_____ **5.** Do I use quotation marks around direct quotations?

CAPITALIZATION

_____ **6.** Do I start all my sentences with capital letters?

_____ **7.** Do I capitalize all proper nouns and proper adjectives?

SPELLING

_____ **8.** Have I spelled all words correctly?

_____ **9.** Have I checked the words my spell-checker may have missed?

GRAMMAR

_____ **10.** Do my subjects and verbs agree in number? (She and I _are_ going, not She and I _is_ going.)

_____ **11.** Do my pronouns agree with their antecedents?

_____ **12.** Have I avoided double subjects?

Creating a Title

■ Sum up the controversy: **Where Will the Woods Go?**
■ Write a slogan: **Equal Rights for Young Shoppers!**
■ Be creative: **Exploring the Halls of Education**

Grammar Connection

Spelling
■ **Proofreader's Guide** pages 642–643
■ **CD** Spelling—3 and 4

Tenses
■ **Proofreader's Guide** pages 720 (+), 722–723, 724 (+)
■ *Write Source* pages 480 (+), 481, 482 (+), 483
■ *SkillsBook* pages 157–158
■ **CD** Verbs—1

English Language Learners

Direct students to look at the sample position statement on PE page 235. Point out that a title could be created from the end of the sentence: *Make It a Park!*

● Encourage students to look for words or phrases in their essay that might work as a title. Provide help as needed.

Advanced Learners

Invite students to find persuasive slogans in business and product advertisements. Students should

● record ad slogans on individual index cards,
● post the cards on an ongoing bulletin board display, and
● create original slogans, such as Best Prices on the Planet, Back-to-School Essentials, or Where the Pros Go.

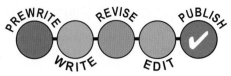

Publishing
Sharing Your Essay

After writing, revising, and editing your position essay, you'll want to make a neat final copy to share. You may also want to present your essay in a debate, publish it in a newspaper, or turn it into a speech.

 Make a final copy. Follow your teacher's instructions or use the guidelines below to format your essay. (If you are using a computer, see page 60.) Create a clean final copy of your essay and carefully proofread it.

Focus on Presentation

- Use blue or black ink and write neatly.
- Write your name in the upper left corner of page 1.
- Skip a line and center your title; skip another line and start your writing.
- Indent every paragraph and leave a one-inch margin on all four sides.
- Write your last name and the page number in the upper right corner of every page after the first one.

Stage a Debate
Gather a group of classmates who have opposite opinions about the same issue. Stage a debate. Present your position, allow others to present theirs, and defend each position.

Create a Speech
Make your essay into a persuasive speech. (See pages 423–430.) Create visual aids that will help you get your point across. Then present your position to an audience that you want to persuade.

Publish in a Newspaper
Format your essay as a letter to the editor of your school or community newspaper. Check submission guidelines. Then send your work in.

PERSUASIVE

Publishing Sharing Your Essay

Since students have written a position paper about a real issue, you can encourage them to share their work with appropriate officials or in a suitable forum.

- Review students' essays before guiding them through the submission process. Make sure the issues are current.
- Coordinate the submissions. If more than one student has written about a topic, submitting their letters together will create more impact.
- If students have written an essay about a school controversy, encourage them to submit their piece to the principal, student council, or school newspaper.
- If students have written about an issue of concern to the community, suggest that they send it to the appropriate local officials or a local newspaper.

Rubric for Persuasive Writing

Tell students to read each description carefully and try to be honest in their self-assessment.

■ Assure them that it's okay to give themselves a 6 for **Ideas** but a 4 for **Organization.**

■ Explain that the purpose of the rubric is to help them break down the assessment process by evaluating each of the six traits individually.

✱ Reproducible six-, five-, and four-point rubrics for persuasive writing can be found on pages 752, 756, and 760.

256

Rubric for Persuasive Writing

Refer to the following rubric for guiding and assessing your persuasive writing. Use it to improve your writing using the six traits.

Ideas

6 My position is very well defended and compels the reader to act.

5 The essay has a clear position or opinion statement. Persuasive reasons support the writer's position.

4 The position statement is clear, and most reasons support the writer's position.

Organization

6 All the parts of the essay work together to build a thoughtful, convincing position.

5 The opening contains the position statement. The middle provides clear support. The ending reinforces the position.

4 The opening contains the position statement. The middle provides support. The ending needs work.

Voice

6 The writer's voice is confident, positive, and convincing.

5 The writer's voice is confident and persuasive.

4 The writer's voice is confident, but it may not be persuasive enough.

Word Choice

6 The writer's choice of words makes a powerful case.

5 The writer's word choice helps persuade the reader.

4 Some changes would make the word choice more persuasive.

Sentence Fluency

6 The sentences spark the reader's interest in the essay.

5 Variety is seen in both the types of sentences and their beginnings.

4 Varied sentence beginnings are used. Sentence variety would make the essay more interesting to read.

Conventions

6 The writing is error free.

5 Grammar and punctuation errors are few. The reader is not distracted by the errors.

4 Grammar and punctuation errors are seen in a few sentences. They distract the reader in those areas.

Struggling Learners

Students who have low self-confidence may not evaluate their own essays fairly, tending to assign low scores. Provide guidance as students use the rubric. Encourage them to look for what they have done well, as well as for what needs improvement.

persuade convince *support*
argue reason
257
Defending a Position

3 The position statement may be clear. More persuasive reasons are needed.	**2** The position statement is unclear. Persuasive reasons are needed.	**1** A new position statement and reasons are needed.
3 The beginning has an opinion statement. The middle and ending need more work.	**2** The beginning, middle, and ending run together.	**1** The organization is unclear and incomplete.
3 The writer's voice needs to be more confident and persuasive.	**2** The writer's voice rambles on without any confidence.	**1** The writer has not considered voice.
3 Many more precise and persuasive words are needed.	**2** The words do not create a clear message. Some unfair words are used.	**1** Word choice has not been considered.
3 Varied sentence beginnings are needed. Sentence variety would make the essay more interesting.	**2** Most sentences begin the same way. Most of the sentences are simple. Compound and complex sentences are needed.	**1** Sentence fluency has not been established. Ideas do not flow smoothly.
3 There are a number of errors that may confuse the reader.	**2** Frequent errors make the essay difficult to read.	**1** Nearly every sentence contains errors.

PERSUASIVE

Test Prep!
The six traits of writing were first identified in the 1960s by Paul Diederick and a group of 50 professionals who reviewed student papers and brainstormed the qualities that made writing strong. In 1983, a group of educators in Beaverton, Oregon, learned of Diederick's work and replicated it, settling on a similar set of six traits. A separate team in Missoula, Montana, simultaneously ran a study that identified the same basic group of traits.

Thereafter, Northwest Regional Educational Labs (NREL) in Portland and later Great Source in Boston (through Vicki Spandel, who had been a part of the NREL team) did much to teach the world about traits-based instruction.

Put simply, the six traits provide a universal set of criteria for strong writing. They correlate very well to the rubrics used in most state testing. Using the traits throughout the writing process, therefore, prepares students for any writing test they will face.

Evaluating a Persuasive Essay

Ask students if they agree with the sample self-assessment on PE page 259. If they agree with the criticisms, ask them to suggest improvements based on the comments in the self-assessment. If they disagree with any comment, ask them to explain why.

Possible suggestions:

Ideas include more positive ideas—The third paragraph might focus on how students will benefit more from devoting time to their education and family commitments.

Organization add transitions— Begin the third paragraph with the words *In addition. . .*

Voice be less emotional and more consistent—In the third paragraph, remove the phrase *staring at you;* condense the list of things students must do each day.

Word Choice use more qualifiers— Add to the third paragraph as follows: ***Most** kids; you **usually** have two hours . . .; that **often** leaves.*

Sentence Fluency vary sentence— patterns—Change sentences that begin with *Now;* do not list a series of activities within a sentence.

Conventions pronoun-antecedent agreement—Clarify pronouns in the fourth paragraph's last sentence

Evaluating a Persuasive Essay

Read the position essay that follows and focus on its strengths and its weaknesses. Then read the student self-assessment on the next page. **(The student essay below contains some errors.)**

Service with a Smile

Delacor high schoolers don't graduate unless they have 40 hours of service learning. Now, some people are saying that middle schoolers should do service learning, too. That program works fine for high schoolers, but it wouldn't work in the middle school.

First of all, middle-school kids can't drive. It would be hard to get to the nursing home or the Humane Society. Most moms and dads already "taxi" their kids all over the place. Many of the places kids would need to get to are too far away to walk to, and too dangerous to ride a bike to. Transportation would be tough.

Middle school students are already busy. It takes time to get ready for school, time to get to school, and almost seven hours at school. Once they're home, they could have two hours of homework staring at them. Then its time for dinner, then piano practice and chores for another hour. Now, if a student gets eight hours sleep, that leaves just a couple hours to do other things. Kids certainly need a couple hours a day for themselves.

Most importantly, community service works best when it is voluntary. Already many middle school students volunteer to march in the Hope Walk for cancer research or to go door to door collecting food for the homeless. They learned the value of community service not because they were required to do it, but because they were inspired to do it.

Parents say kids aren't learning to be responsible. Actually, when those same parents were young, they didn't have to do service learning even in high school. Somehow they learned to be responsible.

Service learning works great in the high school, but it wouldn't work for middle school. Middle school students should volunteer rather than be required to serve.

Advanced Learners

Before students look at PE page 259, ask them to read the essay and evaluate it.

- Have them assign a score from 1 to 6 for each of the six traits—ideas, organization, voice, word choice, sentence fluency, and conventions.
- Share and discuss all results.
- Try to reach agreement on one score for each trait.

persuade convince *support*
argue *reason*
Defending a Position **259**

Student Self-Assessment

The assessment that follows includes the student's comments about his essay on page 258. In the first comment, the student mentions something good about the essay. In the second comment, the student points out an area for possible improvement. (The writer used the rubric and number scale on pages 256–257 to complete this assessment.)

4 Ideas
1. *I have a clear position, and I support it pretty well.*
2. *Some of my ideas sound too negative.*

4 Organization
1. *I've organized my paper just the way I was supposed to.*
2. *Transitions might have helped.*

3 Voice
1. *My voice is strong.*
2. *I sound a little too emotional sometimes, and my point of view shifts.*

3 Word Choice
1. *I use pretty good words throughout.*
2. *If I used more qualifiers, my writing could sound more persuasive.*

4 Sentence Fluency
1. *All of my sentences are complete.*
2. *A little more variety could have made them better.*

4 Conventions
1. *I checked grammar, punctuation, and spelling pretty closely.*
2. *I still have problems with pronoun-antecedent agreement.*

 Use the rubric. Assess your essay using the rubric on pages 256–257.

 On your own paper, list the six traits. Leave room after each trait to write at least one strength and one weakness.

 Then choose a number (from 1 to 6) that shows how well you think you used each trait.

PERSUASIVE

To give students additional practice with evaluating a persuasive essay, use a reproducible assessment sheet (TE page 787) and one or both of the **benchmark papers** listed in the Benchmark Papers box below. You can use an overhead transparency while students refer to their own copies made from the copy masters. For your benefit, a completed assessment sheet is provided for each benchmark paper.

Test Prep!
When students perform self-assessments, they trade places with you—or with whoever scores their writing. By working through this activity, students get a perspective on how readers use rubrics. As a result, next time they write in an on-demand setting, students should be able to anticipate the scorer's response—and increase their score.

Benchmark Papers

Yes, Skateboarding (strong)
- TR 5A–5C
- TE pp. 776–778

Help the School Band (fair)
- TR 6A–6B
- TE pp. 779–780

Reflecting on Your Writing

Students should place their completed reflections in a folder devoted to personal reflections. Ask students to

- date each reflection,
- put all of them in chronological order, and
- reread their reflections from time to time to gain a sense of their writing progress.

Reflecting on Your Writing

Take some time to reflect on the position essay you have just completed. On your own paper, finish each starter sentence below. Your thoughts will help you prepare for your next writing assignment.

My Position Essay

1. The strength of my essay is . . .

2. The part that still needs work is . . .

3. The prewriting activity that worked best for me was . . .

4. The main thing I learned about writing a position essay is . . .

5. In my next position essay, I would like to . . .

6. Here is one question I still have about writing a position essay:

persuade *convince* argue *reasonsupport* **261**

Persuasive Writing
Creating a Personal Commentary

Everyone is unique. Each person has a one-of-a-kind personality and a special way of looking at life. Even identical twins have their own viewpoints to share with the world.

In a personal commentary, a writer can express his or her personal views. News programs often provide commentaries about politics, the economy, or current events; but a commentary can deal with just about any aspect of life.

On the next few pages, you'll read a student's personal commentary about what she has learned from playing violin. Then you will learn to write a commentary of your own.

Writing Guidelines

Subject: **A reflective look at life**
Form: **Personal commentary**
Purpose: **To state your personal view**
Audience: **Classmates**

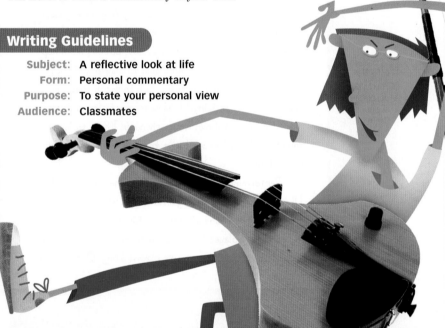

Creating a Personal Commentary

Objectives
- select a topic
- express a personal viewpoint
- write a personal commentary

In a **personal commentary** *(see below)*, a writer expresses his or her personal view about an aspect of life.

- Distribute examples of appropriate personal commentaries from newspapers or news magazines.
- Have students read the commentaries to become familiar with the form.
- Have students discuss with a partner what main feature is shared in each other's commentaries (writer's personal view about an issue, experience, or event).

Teaching Tip: Personal Commentary

Help students develop a clear idea of what a personal commentary is. A personal commentary is not only an expression of one's views but also an analysis of an issue.

- Analyzing involves looking closely at an issue by breaking it into separate parts and examining each part and all the parts together.

- Point out that students may have seen examples of commentaries on television or in a magazine or newspaper. A news analyst or a columnist gives her or his perspective on events in the news.

In writing a personal commentary, students will analyze and give their personal view of a topic.

Personal Commentary

Help students analyze the ideas, organization, voice, and word choice in "Music Teaches Harmony." Tell students to follow these directions:

- Identify the main idea or focus.
- List the topic sentences for each middle paragraph.
- Explain the feeling or viewpoint expressed in the last paragraph.

When students are finished, have them share and discuss their answers.

 Writer's Craft

Intentional ambiguity: The writer of this essay uses the word *harmony* in two different ways simultaneously. She uses harmony to refer to musical notes that complement each other or that work well with a melody. She also uses harmony to mean the peaceful cooperation of people in a group. The ambiguity of the term actually helps her make her point.

For scientists and mathematicians, ambiguous language is never a good thing. For writers, though, careful and conscious use of ambiguity can create new connections in the minds of readers.

262

Personal Commentary

A personal commentary expresses your unique view of some aspect of life. In the commentary that follows, Aimee tells how music has taught her some important lessons about life, lessons that the whole world should learn.

Beginning
The topic is introduced, and the personal view is given (underlined).

Middle
The middle paragraphs support the writer's viewpoint.

Music Teaches Harmony

Some people think music is just a hobby that doesn't have any value in real life. After all, how often does a person need to know how to read notes? To me, though, music teaches some of the most important lessons of life. Music teaches me how to work hard while staying in harmony with others.

My experience with music began with hard work. When I was eight years old, I took my first violin lesson. It was frustrating because I didn't even get to use a real violin! Sometimes I wanted to give up, but my mom kept telling me, "Someday you'll be able to play any kind of music you want on your violin. But to reach that day, you have to keep practicing." I did keep practicing, and hard work has rewarded me. Now, whenever I have to learn something hard, I know I have to stick with it until the job is done.

Performing music brings me together with people. I'll never forget the day I joined the middle school orchestra. The sound of everyone tuning up was music to my ears! As I played the notes in front of me, I looked around at all the other people playing along. Our bows and

English Language Learners

Explain the following musical terms and American idioms that appear in this sample personal commentary:

- read notes (understand and use the symbols on a sheet of music)

- stick with it (keep trying; keep working)
- tuning up (adjusting a musical instrument so that it will make the correct tones)
- music to my ears (delightful) Point out that this expression is a pun as it is used here.

persuade convince reason support **263**
argue
Personal Commentary

fingers moved together to create a sound I could never have made by myself. Even though I knew only a couple other kids in the group, suddenly, I belonged.

Playing with others teaches me about harmony. Every instrument has its own voice, but all the instruments together make a bigger, more wonderful sound. When I play alone, my violin sounds sweet and sad. But when a viola plays along, there's a new dimension to the music. A cello adds its deep harmony, and clarinets and flutes seem to dance. Then come drums and trumpets, and the music comes alive.

Ending
The writer's viewpoint is summed up in a thoughtful way.

I've met a lot of people who aren't exactly like me, but music reminds me that differences are important. Without differences, there's no harmony. On the other hand, harmony doesn't just happen. It takes practice, hard work, and dedication. I wish everybody in the world could learn the lessons music has taught me.

PERSUASIVE

Respond to the reading. On your own paper, answer each of the following questions about the personal commentary.

☐ Ideas (1) What is the main point of Aimee's commentary?

☐ Organization (2) What reasons support Aimee's viewpoint?

☐ Voice & Word Choice (3) What words or phrases show her passion about the topic?

Respond to the reading.

Answers

Ideas **1.** Music teaches Aimee how to work hard and stay in harmony with others.

Organization **2.** Learning to play the violin taught Aimee that hard work is rewarded with success. Playing music with others makes her feel part of the group. Harmony is created by instruments that have different voices, but together they make a more wonderful sound than they can on their own.

Voice & Word Choice **3.** most important lessons of life; I did keep practicing, and hard work has rewarded me; I'll never forget the day I joined the middle school orchestra. The sound of everyone tuning up was music to my ears! It takes practice, hard work, and dedication.

Struggling Learners

Have students look up the word *harmony* in the dictionary, and then explore the way the word is used in this personal commentary to refer to music and relationships. Discuss how activities such as playing music and participating in sports are often used as analogies (comparisons) for life.

Prewriting Selecting a Topic

If students need help choosing a topic, brainstorm a list of ideas. You might include the following:

- playing a team sport
- working at a first job
- going away to camp
- competing on an individual basis
- keeping a diary
- having a talent or hobby
- spending time with family members

Prewriting

Connecting Your Topic to Life

As students make their clusters, tell them to make the lessons as specific as possible. They will find it easier to write their personal commentaries if they think about the specific lessons they have learned.

✱ Additional information about making clusters is on PE page 544.

Prewriting Selecting a Topic

Everyone has a different idea of what is important in life. Whatever is most important to you can teach you a great deal about life in general.

Aimee used freewriting to think about what was most important in her own life. She wrote until she found a topic for her personal commentary.

Freewriting

> What's most important in my life? Definitely music. I want to be a great violinist. It's not just that, though. When I joined the school orchestra, I realized music was a group thing. A whole bunch of people get together to make something beautiful. You have to cooperate. You have to work hard but stay in harmony. It's kind of like life. . . .

 Choose your topic. Freewrite about the things that are most important to you. Continue to write until you discover a topic you would like to write about in a personal commentary.

Connecting Your Topic to Life

Now that you've chosen a topic, it is time to connect your topic to life. Aimee used a cluster to think about the lessons that music teaches her.

Cluster

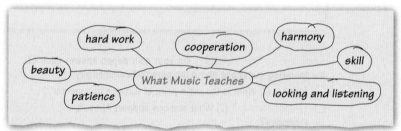

 Create a cluster. Write "What _____ Teaches" in the center of a piece of paper and circle it. Around this circle, add more circles and write the lessons that your topic teaches in each. Choose three or four lessons you want to focus on.

Advanced Learners

Invite students to extend their thinking about "connecting topics to life" by brainstorming lessons that could be learned from the following objects:

- a quilt
- a book
- a rose bush
- a hand-knit sweater

Encourage students to think creatively as they explore connections between these objects and aspects of their lives.

Suggest that students come up with other items from which lessons might be drawn. If they have trouble, offer your own ideas.

persuade convince argue reason support 265
Personal Commentary

Gathering Details

Each lesson you chose from your cluster (page 264) will become a paragraph in your commentary. Now you need to gather details about each lesson. Aimee made a chart, listing the lessons at the top and the details underneath.

Gathering Chart

hard work	cooperation	harmony
– tough to start	– joined orchestra	– different sounds
– kept practicing	– listened to others	– different rhythms
– practice rewarded	– suddenly belonged	– new dimension

Gather details. Create a chart like the one above. List details about three or four lessons your topic teaches about life.

Developing Your Viewpoint

Before you write your essay, you need to state your basic viewpoint and write topic sentences. Use the tips that follow.

- **Personal viewpoint**
  Write a sentence that expresses what the activity has taught you. Try three versions and choose the best one. This sentence will appear in your first paragraph and will guide your writing.
  Music teaches me how to work hard while staying in harmony with others.

- **Topic sentences**
  Write a topic sentence that sums up each lesson your topic teaches. Each of these sentences will begin a middle paragraph.
  My experience with music began with hard work.
  Performing music brings me together with people.
  Playing with others teaches me about harmony.

Develop your viewpoint. Use your chart and the tips above to write your personal viewpoint and topic sentences.

PERSUASIVE

Prewriting Gathering Details

When students finish gathering details, have them share their charts with a partner. Partners should read each other's charts carefully and give feedback on the details.

Prewriting
Developing Your Viewpoint

Remind students that their topic sentences should sum up each lesson related to their topic.

Writer's Craft

Personal commentaries: Personal commentaries abound on Internet blogs. Go online and find a few positive examples and share them with your students to help inspire them as they develop their personal commentaries.

Writing
Developing Your First Draft

As students write their first drafts, have them refer to the paragraph checklist on the top of the page.

✱ Additional information about using a paragraph checklist is on PE page 541.

Revising
Improving Your Writing

As students revise, remind them of some of the points they learned while writing their position essays.

- Make sure you have used effective transition words.
- Check your voice to see that it is strong but not too emotional.
- Reread for precise and persuasive words.
- Make sure that your sentences are complete and varied.

Editing
Checking for Conventions

If students are unsure of any grammatical points, remind them to use the "Proofreader's Guide," which begins on PE page 579.

266

Writing Developing Your First Draft

Use the following tips as you write your first draft.

- **Opening paragraph:** Get your reader's attention, introduce your topic, and provide your basic viewpoint.
- **Middle paragraphs:** Begin each middle paragraph with a topic sentence. After it, include details that support the sentence. Use transitions to link ideas.
- **Closing paragraph:** Thoughtfully summarize your topic and the lesson it teaches about life.

 Create your first draft. Follow the tips above and focus on getting your ideas on paper.

Revising Improving Your Writing

The following questions will help you revise your commentary.

- ☐ **Ideas** Have I stated my topic clearly? Do I connect it to life?
- ☐ **Organization** Does each middle paragraph begin with a topic sentence? Does each include supporting details?
- ☐ **Voice** Does my voice sound clear and interested?
- ☐ **Word Choice** Have I chosen the most effective words?
- ☐ **Sentence Fluency** Do my sentences flow smoothly?

 Revise your writing. Ask yourself the questions above and revise your commentary to improve these traits of writing.

Editing Checking for Conventions

The following questions will help you edit your commentary.

- ☐ **Conventions** Have I checked for capitalization, punctuation, and spelling errors? Have I checked for errors in grammar?

 Edit your work. Check the conventions in your commentary, create a clean final copy, and proofread it.

English Language Learners

Help students apply skills they have practiced in earlier writing activities.

- Guide them to complete these three steps in the writing process (drafting, revising, and editing).
- After each step, students should meet with a partner to check each other's progress.

Grammar Connection

Sentence Combining
- **Proofreader's Guide** page 698 (+)
- *Write Source* pages 498 (+), 512 (+), 513, 514, 519 (+), 520 (+)
- *SkillsBook* pages 101–102, 123–124
- **CD** Sentences—Combining (+)

Using the Right Word
- **Proofreader's Guide** pages 676–687
- *SkillsBook* pages 57–58
- **CD** Using the Right Word—2

Capitalization
- **Proofreader's Guide** page 626 (+)
- *SkillsBook* pages 45–46

persuade convince
argue reason support **267**

Persuasive Writing
Across the Curriculum

Persuasive writing can help you present a convincing case in any class. In social studies, you may be asked to write a newspaper editorial about a community issue in which you call readers to action. Your math teacher may ask you to gather statistics and use them in an argument. In science, you may have to use a graph to make a point about pollution. A persuasive letter can also bring about changes in your school or community—such as lights for a popular soccer field.

The following pages will teach you about all these forms of persuasion and will also prepare you for responding to a persuasive prompt on a timed writing test.

What's Ahead

- **Social Studies:** Writing an Editorial
- **Math:** Developing a Statistical Argument
- **Science:** Creating a Persuasive Graph
- **Practical Writing:**
  Drafting a Business Letter
- **Writing for
  Assessment**

Across the Curriculum

Objectives
- apply what students have learned about persuasive writing to other curriculum areas
- practice writing for assessment

The lessons on the following pages provide samples of persuasive writing students might do in different content areas. The particular form used in one content area may also be used in another content area (for example, students can create a persuasive graph in social studies just as well as in science).

Assigning these forms of writing will depend on
- the skill level of your students,
- the subject matter they are studying in different content areas, and
- the writing goals of your school, district, or state.

Struggling Learners

Help students think about situations in which people need to present a persuasive and convincing argument. Ask the following questions:

- In what classes have teachers asked you to develop a persuasive argument?
- What are the titles of books, movies, or TV programs in

which the characters must be persuasive? (Students may suggest dramatic shows featuring lawyers, doctors, and judges. They may also think of teen dramas or popular sitcoms in which teenagers try to persuade their parents or others to do something.)

Advanced Learners

Invite students who enjoy writing and/or performing plays to collaborate on some short "real-life" skits about presenting a convincing case to parents, siblings, neighbors, relatives, or friends. Other class members may contribute ideas from their own experiences (as part of prewriting) and serve as the audience (as part of publishing).

Social Studies:
Writing an Editorial

Ask a volunteer to read aloud the sample editorial while the rest of the class listens for positively and negatively charged words. Have the listeners create a T-graph and list the two types of words. Their lists should look like the following.

Positive Words	Negative Words
grown	dying
fix	losing
heart	tear down
history	can't happen
center	destroyed
100 years	vote "no"
saved	
historic	
symbol	
official	
renovation	

Discuss how these positively and negatively charged words persuade the reader and affect the writer's voice.

268

Social Studies: Writing an Editorial

An editorial or a letter to the editor expresses a writer's opinion about a current issue or problem. The following editorial was written in a social studies class and focuses on a downtown library.

The **beginning** introduces the topic and gives an opinion.

Protect the Future of Our History

Springfield has grown in the past 10 years, but the center of the city is dying. People would rather build on the outskirts than fix up the downtown. As a result, the city is losing its heart and its history. Now the mayor proposes that the city tear down Springfield Public Library in the old courthouse and build a new library at the city limits. This can't happen.

The **middle** provides supporting reasons for the opinion.

The library building was built in 1893 as the first county courthouse. It became the library in 1982, when the new courthouse was built. The building has been the center of town for more than 100 years and should be saved, not destroyed.

This historic building is a symbol of the city. It's on the postcards and afghans sold at the Historical Society Museum. The library building even appears on the city's official stationery—the same paper used to propose tearing it down.

The **ending** gives a call to action.

Citizens of Springfield should save the public library and save the downtown! If Springfield is willing to spend $6 million on a new library, why not spend the same money fixing up the old one? Even if the renovation costs more, the city shouldn't care only about money. The city's history is important as well. On November 15th, citizens of Springfield should vote "no" for the new library.

Struggling Learners

Share with students additional editorials (or letters to the editor) to help them better understand the working parts of this form of writing. In each example, point out how the writer develops the beginning, the middle, and the ending parts.

persuade convince support **269**
argue reason
Writing in Social Studies

Writing Tips

Before you write . . .

● **Select an issue that you care about.**
Think about problems or issues in your school or community.
Choose a topic that you feel strongly about.

● **Do your research.**
Gather facts and details
that will help you explain
the topic to readers. Use
the information to come
up with a realistic solution.

During your writing . . .

● **State your opinion.**
Explain the problem and why you are concerned about it.

● **Support your opinion.**
Back up your argument with the facts from your research.
Address opposing points of view. Then offer a solution.

● **Restate your opinion and call for action.**
Ask readers to get involved.

After you've written a first draft . . .

● **Review your argument.**
Make sure that your opinion is clear and well supported.

● **Check your facts.**
Read your editorial carefully to make sure your facts are
correct.

● **Check for conventions.**
Correct any errors in punctuation, capitalization, spelling,
and grammar.

 Create your own editorial on a current issue by using the tips above.
Then submit your editorial to your school paper or a local newspaper.

PERSUASIVE

Writing Tips

Brainstorm possible topics by
discussing problems or issues
facing the school or community.
Ask students to look for ideas in the
school and community newspapers.

Students should also think
about good resources for finding
information to support their ideas.
They might check with

■ the library,
■ the local historical society, and
■ officials in the community
or school.

Try IT Answers

Editorials will vary.

Math: Developing a Statistical Argument

It is critical for students to be able to explain their mathematical thinking in clear sentences. Many standardized tests require students to explain in words the reasoning they use in mathematical processes.

Math: Developing a Statistical Argument

A statistical argument uses numbers to prove the value of something. For the following assignment, a student used statistics to decide which pack of blended fruit drinks provides a better value.

The beginning sets up the problem.

Get the Best Value

Which pack of blended fruit drinks gives a better value for the money?

* a 12-pack of 12-ounce cans that costs $3.95
* a 6-pack of 16.9-ounce bottles that costs $2.50

First, one must find out how many ounces are in each pack. To do this, a person should multiply the ounces per can or bottle by the number of cans or bottles in a pack.

The middle provides statistics and equations.

Ounces per can/bottle	x	Number of cans/bottles	=	Total ounces
12	x	12 cans	=	144
16.9	x	6 bottles	=	101.4

Then a person should find the price per ounce by taking the total price for each pack and dividing it by the total number of ounces.

Total price	÷	Total ounces	=	Price per ounce
$3.95	÷	144	=	.027
$2.50	÷	101.4	=	.025

The ending gives the solution.

So, on an ounce-by-ounce basis, the 6-pack of larger bottles is cheaper. The 12-pack costs a little more per ounce, but if the juice is for school lunches, the smaller cans may avoid waste and allow individual servings. So value depends partly on use.

Advanced Learners

Instruct students to look through newspaper advertising supplements for deals that can be analyzed for value. Remind them to look for deals that can be compared. For example:

- a package of six pairs of socks for $5.50 and a package of eight pairs of socks for $6.75

- ten guitar lessons for $95 and twelve guitar lessons for $125

Make this list available to class members for the **Try It** activity on the next page.

persuade convince reason support **271**
argue
Writing in Math

Writing Tips

Before you write . . .

- **Begin by asking a "value" question.**
  Ask a question about the value of something. For example, which package of dog food gives the best value, or which amusement park provides the best value for the entertainment dollar.

- **Plan your steps.**
  Make a list of steps and equations that you need to follow to answer the value question. Check your equations and answers for accuracy.

During your writing . . .

- **Introduce the question.**
  Begin your paper by indicating what question your argument will address.

- **Provide statistics.**
  Let readers know the facts and figures you will be using to argue your point.

- **Show the process step-by-step.**
  Write the equations you use to make your statistical argument. Lead readers through each step.

- **Interpret the statistics.**
  End by telling readers what the statistics mean.

After you've written a first draft . . .

- **Check for completeness.**
  Make sure you haven't left out important variables and steps.

- **Check for correctness.**
  Fix any errors in math, punctuation, capitalization, spelling, or grammar.

 Write your own statistical argument. Choose a question of value that you can argue using statistics. Then lead your readers through the equations needed to argue your point.

PERSUASIVE

Writing Tips

Make a class list of possible topics or let students come up with their own ideas. The list below includes ideas for students to consider:

- two different travel packages to the same destination
- two different cell-phone plans

If students completed the Advanced Learners activity (PE page 270), include their list of ideas here.

 Answers

Arguments will vary.

When students finish writing their statistical arguments, have volunteers share their work with the class. Invite the class to respond to each argument with positive comments and suggestions for improvements.

Science: Creating a Persuasive Graph

Point out that a bar graph is one effective way to display information. Consult with a math teacher about which types of graphs should be familiar to students. Review with students several other kinds of graphs that are useful, including

- pie charts,
- line graphs,
- double bar graphs, and
- pictographs.

✳ For more examples of graphs, see PE page 575.

Literature Connections

Honest reporting: Mark Twain once famously said, "There are three kinds of lies. Lies, damned lies, and statistics" (quoting British Prime Minister Benjamin Disreali). Point out to students that many people make persuasive graphs for the purpose of deceiving readers. It's important when creating a persuasive graph to honestly represent the figures and not distort your evidence. An untrustworthy graph can actually damage the cause of the person who created it.

272

Science: Creating a Persuasive Graph

A graph can quickly persuade readers about a problem. The following graph shows the increase in automobile pollution since 1998.

The **beginning** introduces the graph.

The **middle** presents the figures visually.

The **ending** provides the student's call to action.

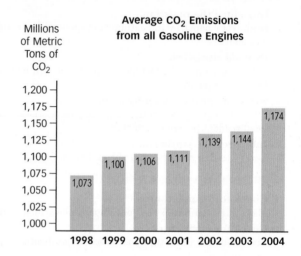

Absolutely Exhausted

Although the United States produces more carbon dioxide (the greenhouse gas CO_2) than any other country, China will soon produce more according to the Environmental Protection Agency. In the United States, total gasoline CO_2 emissions have risen by 9% since 1998.

Average CO_2 Emissions from all Gasoline Engines

Millions of Metric Tons of CO_2

Year	Value
1998	1,073
1999	1,100
2000	1,106
2001	1,111
2002	1,139
2003	1,144
2004	1,174

This bar graph shows the increase in carbon dioxide gases per year from all gasoline engines since 1998. Carpooling, using less air conditioning, and walking are some simple ways to reduce emissions.

persuade convince support 273
argue reason
Writing in Science

Writing Tips

Before you write . . .

● **Select a topic.**
Think about a science issue that involves numbers: water quality, food production, or weather patterns, for example. Select a topic you care about and state your position about it.

● **Research your topic.**
Find out the facts and figures behind the issue. Decide which facts would make the most persuasive graph.

● **Choose a type of graph.**
Select a type that works best to present your argument. (See page 575 for different types of graphs.) Make sure you have all the facts you need.

During your writing . . .

● **Introduce your topic and your argument.**
Write one or two brief paragraphs that put the facts in perspective.

● **Draw your graph.**
Lay out your graph so that the information is clear.

● **Provide your viewpoint.**
Sum up the figures in a persuasive way.

After you've written a first draft . . .

● **Check for completeness.**
Make sure that you included all the necessary details and facts to support your argument. Ask another student to look at your graph to see if it is easy to understand.

● **Check for conventions.**
Correct any errors in punctuation, capitalization, spelling, and grammar.

 Pick a science issue that you care about and that includes statistics (numbers). Gather information about it and create a persuasive graph that demonstrates your position.

PERSUASIVE

Writing Tips

As an alternative to having individual students make their own graphs, have pairs of students complete this activity.

■ After each pair chooses a science issue, encourage the partners to do research on the Internet or in the school library. Give students plenty of time to gather facts. Tell them to try to find the most current information.

■ Have each pair make copies of their completed graph for the class.

■ Invite partners to explain their graph to the class.

 Answers

Graphs will vary.

Advanced Learners

Have students find a graph to share with the rest of the class. Students should explain the topic of the graph and its purpose: to inform, to persuade, to analyze, etc. They should also discuss its strengths, its weaknesses (if any), its visual impact, and so on.

English Language Learners

Talk about graphs as a different way to read (and share) information. Provide several examples to read and discuss together.

Practical Writing:
Drafting a Business Letter

As you review the sample business letter, make the following points:

- The writer explains his position in the first paragraph and bases his request on a safety issue.
- In the second paragraph, the writer states an expected objection and counters it.
- The writer summarizes by naming the people who would be affected by the decision.

274

Practical Writing:
Drafting a Business Letter

Sometimes the best way to make a change in your school or community is to write a persuasive letter. In the following letter to his principal, Alex Hastings asks for lights on a soccer field.

The letter follows the correct format. (See pages 276–277.)

1080 Burns Road
Orange Park, FL 32000
May 5, 2008

Principal Joseph Rodriguez
Greenberg Middle School
116 Shelton Street
Orange Park, FL 32000

Dear Mr. Rodriguez:

The **beginning** introduces the student and his request.

As a soccer team member at Greenberg Middle School, I have a suggestion. We need lights for nighttime games. When school starts in the fall, it gets darker earlier and earlier. It's hard for our teams to finish games safely.

The **body** provides details to persuade the reader.

I realize that lighting is expensive. However, a lighted field could be used by the whole community, so the community could help pay for it. The soccer team could even run a citywide fund-raiser.

The **closing** includes a polite call to action.

Adding lights to our soccer field would make a huge difference for my teammates and me. Please make the request at the next school board meeting.

Sincerely,

Alex Hastings

Alex Hastings

Struggling Learners

Discuss the importance of using a formal voice when writing a business letter. Point out that the persuasive letter should be

- long enough to get the main points across, but
- short enough that the recipient can read it fairly quickly.

persuade convince reason support **275**
argue
Practical Writing

Writing Tips

Use the following tips as a guide when you are asked to write a persuasive letter. (Also see pages 276–277.)

Before you write . . .

- **Choose a topic that you care about.**
  Make a list of problems in your school or community and think of possible solutions. Choose a problem that is important to you.
- **Gather information.**
  Learn as much as you can about the problem. Find facts to support your solution.
- **Consider your reader.**
  Determine what the person you are writing to needs to know.

During your writing . . .

- **Keep it short.**
  Make your point quickly and stay focused on the main idea. Your letter should not be longer than one page.
- **State the problem and your solution.**
  Explain why the situation exists and how it can be fixed.
- **Be polite.**
  Use a courteous voice to persuade the reader.

After you've written a first draft . . .

- **Check for completeness.**
  Make sure you did not leave out any important facts or reasons.
- **Check for correctness.**
  Read your letter several times. Double-check the address and spelling of all names. Correct any errors in punctuation, capitalization, spelling, and grammar.

 Think of a problem in your school or community. Find out who can help solve it. Write a persuasive letter to that person or organization and make a strong but polite argument. (You may send the letter or simply treat it as a school assignment.)

PERSUASIVE

Writing Tips

Brainstorm a list of possible topics.

- Invite students to choose a topic from the class list or to come up with an idea of their own.
- Tell students that what they request in their persuasive letters must be reasonable.

 Answers

Answers will vary but should include a request, details to persuade the reader, and a polite call to action.

Have each student exchange his or her business letter with a partner. Tell partners to check each other's letter using the **Writing Tips** as a guide (especially the tips under **During your writing . . .** and **After you've written a first draft** . . .).

Grammar Connection

Colons

- **Proofreader's Guide** pages 596–597
- *SkillsBook* pages 21–22

Capitalization

- **Proofreader's Guide** pages 618 (+), 626–627
- *SkillsBook* pages 43–44
- **CD** Capitalization—1 (+)

Parts of a Business Letter

Discuss situations in which students will need to send business letters:

- to make a change
- to apply for something
- to request information

Tell students it is important to format a business letter correctly, so that it makes a positive impression on the person who receives it. Then the recipient will be persuaded to respond.

Check students' final drafts to make sure they understand and are following the correct format.

276

Parts of a Business Letter

1 The heading includes your address and the date. Write the heading at least one inch from the top of the page at the left-hand margin.

2 The inside address includes the name and address of the person or organization you are writing to.

- If the person has a title, be sure to include it. (If the title is short, write it on the same line as the name. If the title is long, write it on the next line.)
- If you are writing to an organization or a business—but not to a specific person—begin the inside address with the name of the organization or business.

3 The salutation is the greeting. Always put a colon after the salutation.

- If you know the person's name, use it in your greeting.
    Dear Mr. Christopher:
- If you don't know the name of the person who will read your letter, use a salutation like one of these:
    Dear Store Owner:
    Dear Sir or Madam:
    Dear Madison Soccer Club:

4 The body is the main part of the letter. Do not indent the paragraphs in your letter; instead, skip a line after each one.

5 The closing comes after the body. Use **Yours truly** or **Sincerely** to close a business letter. Capitalize only the first word of the closing and put a comma after the closing.

6 The signature ends the letter. If you are using a computer, leave four spaces after the closing; then type your name. Write your signature in the space between the closing and the typed name.

See page 577 for more about writing letters as well as a set of guidelines for addressing envelopes properly.

persuade convince reason support argue **277**
Practical Writing

Business-Letter Format

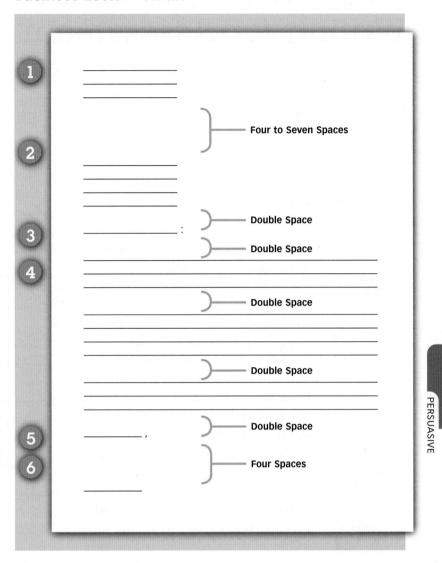

1

2   Four to Seven Spaces

3   Double Space
            Double Space

4   Double Space

            Double Space

5   Double Space

6   Four Spaces

278

Writing for Assessment

As you review the model, discuss the following points:

- The writer starts by stating a position.
- The writer begins each of the middle paragraphs with transition words.
- The writer ends by restating the position.

Engage students in a discussion about the strengths and weaknesses of this essay. Ask them to identify places where they might make changes to improve the writing. Ask them to name parts that they think work especially well.

Persuasive Writing
Writing for Assessment

Many state and school writing tests contain a persuasive prompt, which asks you to state an opinion and support it with convincing reasons. Study the following sample prompt and student response.

Persuasive Prompt

A group of parents and students has asked the administration to start school one hour later. This group feels that students would perform better if school started later. Do you feel the start time should stay as it is or be changed? In an essay, state your position on this issue, support it with reasons, and defend it against an objection.

Response to a Persuasive Prompt

The **beginning** states the writer's position (underlined).

Each **middle** paragraph gives reasons that support the opinion.

Some parents and students have complained that Willis Middle School starts too early. They say that students aren't awake enough at 7:30 a.m. to learn well. Because of this, they want to move the start time to 8:30 a.m. The starting time should not change because the shift would create more problems than it would solve.

First of all, a later start would help only some students. Many students happen to be morning people. Moving the schedule would not help them learn better or improve their test scores. In fact, for these students, a later start might actually have the opposite effect.

For that matter, a later start would mean a later release, and that would cause problems for after-school activities. The coaches for football, basketball, and track would have an hour less for practice. The teachers who lead drama, chess club, and pep band would also lose an

English Language Learners

Discuss the prompt, pointing out that there are three key parts identified in the final direction line:

- state your position
- support it with reasons
- defend it against an objection

Work with students to rephrase the prompt in their own words.

- Write the paraphrase on the board. Encourage students to follow a similar routine when they are taking a test.
- Emphasize that taking the time to analyze and rephrase the prompt will help them to answer the question thoroughly and accurately.

hour. In addition, every student would have an hour less for homework before supper.

The most important reason to keep the 7:30 a.m. start time is that a change would cause problems for the whole community. If middle school starts an hour later, high school would have to as well because of busing. High schoolers need even more time after school because of varsity sports and jobs. Some working parents also would struggle with a later start. Many parents drop off their kids by 7:30 a.m. and start work by 8:00 a.m. Their morning schedules would be much harder with an 8:30 start.

Some people say a later start would help keep students from falling asleep during first hour. That may be true, but more students fall asleep after lunch. Shifting the school day ahead an hour would not get rid of the problem of sleepy students.

A later start time at Willis Middle School would help only some students and would create problems for others. The shift would probably not end sleepiness in the classroom. For all these reasons, the Willis Middle School start time should stay right where it is.

The **final middle** paragraph answers an objection.

The **ending** restates the position and its supporting reasons.

PERSUASIVE

Respond to the reading. Answer the following questions about the sample response.

☐ Ideas (1) What is the writer's position? (2) What reasons does he give?

☐ Organization (3) Where does the writer answer an objection?

☐ Voice & Word Choice (4) What words from the prompt also appear in the essay?

Ask students the following questions:
- How does the writer make his position clear?
- What main point supports the position?
- What makes the writer's voice persuasive?
- Where does the writer use good qualifiers?

 Respond to the reading.

Answers

Ideas 1. The writer's position is that the school start time should remain the same.

2. He says that a later start time would mean a later release, and that would result in less time for after-school activities. He also says that a later start time would negatively impact the entire community (because of issues related to working parents and busing) and would not end the problem of students falling asleep in class.

Organization 3. The writer answers the objection in the fifth paragraph.

Voice 4. *start time should stay*

Writing Tips

Point out that students must approach writing-on-demand differently from open-ended writing assignments.

Persuasive Prompts

Provide students the same amount of time to write their response essay as they will be allotted on school, district, or state assessments. Break down each part of the process into clear chunks of time. For example, you might give students

- 15 minutes for note taking and planning,
- 20 minutes for writing, and
- 10 minutes for editing and proofreading.

Tell students when time is up for each section. Start the assignment at the top of the hour or at the half hour to make it easier for students to keep track of the time.

Technology Connections

The two prompts on this page are also available on Eval-U-Write, a subscription-based online writing tool. Eval-U-Write includes 90 prompts drawn from the *Write Source* series, as well as over 150 other prompts. The service provides real-time essay evaluation for four of the six traits: organization, word choice, sentence fluency, and conventions. To find out more about Eval-U-Write, go to www.greatsource.com.

280

Writing Tips

Before you write . . .

- **Understand the prompt.**
  Remember that a persuasive prompt asks you to state and support an opinion.
- **Plan your response.**
  Spend a few minutes planning before you start to write. Use a graphic organizer (table diagram) as a guide.

Table Diagram

Opinion		
Reason	Reason	Reason

During your writing . . .

- **Share an opinion statement.**
  Think of an opinion that you can clearly support.
- **Build your argument.**
  Think of reasons that support your opinion.
- **End effectively.**
  Explain what you would like to see done.

After you've written a first draft . . .

- **Check for clear ideas.**
  Rewrite any ideas that sound confusing.
- **Check for conventions.**
  Correct errors in punctuation, capitalization, spelling, and grammar.

Persuasive Prompts

- If you could change one rule at your school, what would it be? Write a letter to your school board asking for a school rule to be changed. Make sure to give reasons why the change should happen and answer a possible objection to your idea.

- Your parent or guardian is planning a big vacation. Where would you most like to go? Write an essay proposing a trip you would like to take and indicate why it would be the best choice for your family.

 Plan and write a response. Respond to one of the prompts above. Complete your writing within the period of time your teacher gives you. Afterward, list one part that you like and one part that could have been better.

English Language Learners

Timed assessment tests may be extremely challenging for these students.

- Discuss the directions and prompts.
- Stress the key words that lead to the goal of each essay.
- Call on volunteers to rephrase the prompt in their own words.

- Write the rephrased prompt on the board.

Encourage students to relax, and remind them to use the strategies they have been practicing to help them write strong, persuasive essays.

persuade convince support
argue reason 281

Persuasive Writing Checklist

Persuasive Writing in Review

Purpose: In persuasive writing, you work to *convince people* to think the way you do about something.

Topics: Persuade readers . . . to agree with your opinion or position,
to take an action,
to support a cause, or
to solve a problem.

Prewriting
Select a topic that you care about, one that you can present confidently and that is appropriate for your audience. (See page 228.)

Gather ideas about your topic. (See pages 229–230.)

Write a position statement that identifies your opinion. (See page 231.)

Organize your ideas in a list or an outline with your position statement at the top, followed by topic sentences with supporting facts or details beneath each. (See page 232.)

Writing
In the beginning, grab the reader's attention and clearly state your position. (See page 235.)

In the middle part, devote a paragraph to each reason; include supporting facts and examples. Address an objection to your position. (See pages 236–237 and 241.)

In the ending, restate your position and sum up your reasons for it. (See page 238.)

Revising
Review the ideas, organization, and voice first. Next check for **word choice** and **sentence fluency.** Avoid unfair words. Use a confident voice and a variety of sentence structures. (See pages 240–250.)

Editing
Check your writing for conventions. Ask a friend to edit the writing, too. (See pages 252–254.)

Make a final copy and proofread it for errors before sharing it with your audience. (See page 255.)

Assessing
Use the persuasive rubric as a guide to assess your finished writing. (See pages 256–257.)

PERSUASIVE

Persuasive Writing in Review

Review the list of writing tips with the class. Tell students to refer to these points as they respond to one of the persuasive writing prompts on the bottom of PE page 280.

Response to Literature Overview

Unit Objectives

The writing standards listed below are based on a blending of state and NCTE standards.

- Develop a response that exhibits an understanding of plot, character, and theme, and that is supported with quotations and details from the piece of literature.
- Use lists, charts, and notes to generate and organize ideas.
- Select a voice and style appropriate to the audience and purpose, and use specific literary vocabulary for clarity.
- Assess writing using a rubric based on the traits of effective writing.
- Share finished pieces with classmates and others.

Writing Forms

- paragraph response
- essay that analyzes a theme
- letter to an author

Focus on the Traits

- **Ideas** Developing a clear focus statement that explains the interpretation of the theme, and providing details that support that statement
- **Organization** Establishing a beginning that identifies the title, author, and theme and an ending that sums up the theme's importance
- **Voice** Using a natural voice that creates the appropriate mood
- **Word Choice** Using literary terms for clarity and words appropriate to the audience
- **Sentence Fluency** Improving sentence flow by joining short, choppy sentences and cutting unnecessary words
- **Conventions** Checking for errors in punctuation, capitalization, spelling, and grammar

Note: For specifics about reading the chart below, see page TE 33.

Suggested Response to Literature Unit (Four Weeks)

| Day | Writing and Skills Units | In the *Write Source* book | | | On the CD-ROM | *SkillsBook* |
		Pages	Proofreader's Guide—basic grammar rules	Basic Grammar practice	Interactive Grammar Exercises	grammar practice pages
1–3	**Response Paragraph:** Theme (Model)	283–286				
	Skills Activities: Punctuating Titles		600 (+), 602–603, 624–625		Punctuation— Titles, Capitalization—2	25–26
opt.	Speeches	428–429				
4–5	**Book Review: An insight**	287–290				
	(Prewriting)	291–294				

(WEEK 1)

Week	Day	Writing and Skills Units	In the *Write Source* book: Pages	In the *Write Source* book: Proofreader's Guide—basic grammar rules	In the *Write Source* book: Basic Grammar practice	On the CD-ROM: Interactive Grammar Exercises	*SkillsBook* grammar practice pages
Week 2	**6–7**	(Writing)	295–300				
	8–10	(Revising)	301–312				
		Skills Activities: Nouns		702–703, 704–705	471–472 (+), 473	Nouns—1	133–134, 135–136, 137–138
		Wordy Sentences			506		83–84
		Combining Sentences with Relative Pronouns		706–707	515		119–120
Week 3	**11–12**	(Editing)	313–316				
		Skills Activities: Subject-Verb Agreement		690 (+), 692 (+)	475, 508, 509	Subject-Verb Agreement	97–98
		Restrictive and Nonrestrictive Phrases and Clauses		584–585		Commas with Nonrestrictive Clauses	7–8, 18
		Punctuating Quotations		588 (+), 598 (+), 600 (+)		Punctuating Dialogue (+)	9–10
	13	(Assessing) (Publishing) (Reflecting)	318–321, 317, 322				
	opt.	*Speeches*	428–429				
	14	Practical Writing: Evaluating a Web Site	334–335				
	15	Response Writing for Assessment	336–341				
Week 4	**1**	**Letter to an Author:** (Model)	323–325				
	2–3	(Prewriting) (Writing)	326–327				
	4–5	(Revising)	328				
		Skills Activities: Compound and Complex Sentences		698 (+), 700	516 (+), 517(+)		113–114, 115–116
		Indefinite Pronouns		710–711, 712 (+), 714 (+)	474 (+), 475 (+)	Pronouns—3	147–148, 151–152
		(Editing, Publishing)	328				
		Skills Activities: Punctuation (review)		578–615 (+)	500–510 (+)		39–40
		Using the Right Word		652–655			

Teacher's Notes for Response to Literature

This overview for response to literature includes some specific teaching suggestions for this unit.

Writing a Paragraph Response (pages 283–286)

Writing about literature is an active experience that demands critical and evaluative skills. This section shows how to write a paragraph response as the first step to a much longer evaluative essay.

Analyzing a Theme (pages 287–322)

Some books can be read just for fun. There are books, however, that beg the reader to think. Students will discover that such books are challenging, yet very interesting and worth thinking about. This chapter will help them become accustomed to figuring out the theme, the point of a book. Sample models included will show students how to do that.

Writing a Letter to an Author (pages 323–328)

Most authors do appreciate hearing from their readers, especially readers who purchased a book. They are willing to answer questions as well. However, even if the students don't actually send their letters to an author, this exercise will help them dig a bit deeper in the theme than they might have otherwise.

Writing Across the Curriculum (pages 329–335)

Here students will look at responses to different kinds of material. For example, one student in a social studies class wrote about an early 20th century photograph, another put together a summary of a science article, and a third evaluated a Web site. The response skills they have learned will make these kinds of responses possible.

Writing for Assessment (pages 336–341)

Because students are often asked to respond to a literature prompt on assessment tests, an example has been included with a student's reaction. A prompt has also been added to give your students practice.

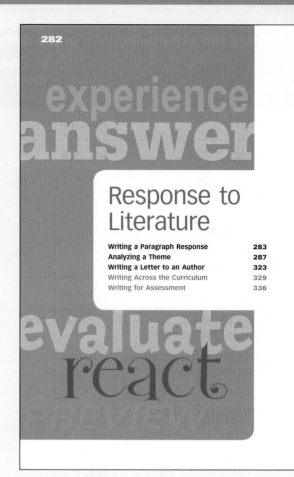

Minilesson

Sail Away   Writing a Paragraph Response

■ **READ** the poem "Old Ironsides." **STUDY** the first stanza and then **WRITE** a topic sentence. **DISCUSS** the poem with a classmate. Then **WRITE** a paragraph response. Change your topic sentence if your discussion points you in a different direction.

A Difficult Lesson   Analyzing a Theme

■ **READ** the response essay on pages 289–290 in your textbook. **IDENTIFY** which character seems most like you. **EXPLAIN** why you chose that character. After reading the essay, are you interested in reading this book? **DISCUSS** your thoughts with a classmate.

Dear Author   Writing a Letter to an Author

■ **CHOOSE** a book you have enjoyed reading. **LOOK UP** the author's name to find out what other books he or she has written. **WRITE** a list of questions you would like to put in a letter to the author. In addition, **LIST** anything else you want to know about the author and his or her work.

Paragraph Response

Response to Literature
Paragraph Response

Just as the ABC's are the building blocks of words, paragraphs are the building blocks of essays. Once you can write solid paragraphs about literature, you'll be better prepared to write whole essays about the poems, stories, and novels that you read.

On the next page, you will read a sample paragraph that responds to Langston Hughes's poem, "The Kids in School with Me." It deals with learning the fundamentals of life—not just the ABC's. Then you will write a paragraph response about a short story or poem you have read recently.

Writing Guidelines

Subject:	A short story or poem
Form:	Paragraph
Purpose:	To respond to the theme
Audience:	Classmates

Objectives

- understand the content and structure of a paragraph response
- choose a topic (a short story or poem) to write about
- plan, draft, revise, and edit a paragraph response

A **paragraph response** examines the meaning, or theme, of a piece of literature. The topic sentence identifies the piece, its author, and its theme. The body sentences explain the theme, and the closing sentence tells why the theme is important.

Writer's Craft

Summary writing: Professional writers learn to put big ideas in small spaces. Often novelists are asked to sum up their 400-page works in a single paragraph. Screenwriters often have to boil their 110-page scripts down to a single "high-concept" sentence. The key to writing a successful response to literature paragraph is to grasp the central idea.

Paragraph Response

If possible, obtain a copy of the poem "The Kids in School with Me" by Langston Hughes and read it aloud to the class.

Explain that a paragraph response may take other forms, such as a story summary or an analysis of a character. In this case, students

- interpret the theme, or message, of a short story or poem, and
- support their focus with details from the story or poem.

Respond to the reading.

Possible answers:

Ideas 1. Students of all backgrounds should learn together and appreciate their differences.

Organization 2. It tells about the poet's dream school.
3. It says that if people see past differences, the dream will come true.

Voice & Word Choice 4. Yes. There are many details from the poem; the motto is quoted; and Mark explains the poet's message.

284

Paragraph Response

When you write a paragraph about a short story or poem you've read, you may be asked to focus on a theme. The **topic sentence** identifies the story, the author, and the theme. The **body sentences** explain the theme, and the **closing sentence** tells something important about it. In the following response, Mark writes about the theme of diversity in "The Kids in School with Me," a poem by Langston Hughes.

Topic Sentence · · · · · · · · · · ·

Body

Closing Sentence · · · · · · · · · ·

"The Kids in School with Me"

In the poem "The Kids in School with Me," Langston Hughes dreams about a school where diversity would be appreciated. The poet describes kids in a classroom. The students have dark skin, freckles, black hair, or other features. Some kids are from different countries around the world, including Russia, China, Poland, Spain, and Greece. Although every student is unique in some way, they are all in the classroom together. Together they study reading and math. All of them work toward graduation, and their motto is "One for All and All for One!" This poem says that if people could only look past color and race, all students would just be kids in school.

Respond to the reading. On your own paper, answer each of the following questions.

☐ **Ideas (1)** What theme in the poem does the writer think is most important?

☐ **Organization (2)** How does the topic sentence introduce the theme? **(3)** How does the closing sentence sum up the theme?

☐ **Voice & Word Choice (4)** Does the writer sound knowledgeable about the poem? Explain.

evaluate react PREVIEW answer experience **285**
Paragraph Response

Prewriting Selecting a Topic

Your first step in writing a response to literature is choosing a short story or poem to write about. Mark began by listing some of his favorites.

Topic List

> "Raymond's Run" by Toni Cade Bambara
>
> "The Kids in School with Me" by Langston Hughes ✱
>
> "Mr. Misenheimer's Garden" by Charles Kuralt

 Choose a short story or poem. Make a list of your favorite short stories or poems. Place a star (✱) next to the one that interests you most.

Finding a Theme

A theme is the lesson about life in a piece of literature. The details in a story or poem are clues to the themes. Mark began his search for a theme by listing details from the poem. Then he reviewed the details and listed some possible themes.

Theme Chart

Details	Themes
– America – students from around the world – different hair, eyes, smiles, skin colors – studying together – "One for All and All for One!" – public school – Polish, Greek, Russian, Chinese	getting along learning together appreciating ✱ diversity

 List details and themes. Create a list of details from the short story or poem you have chosen. Beside it, list themes that relate to those details. Finally, choose one theme to write about.

LITERATURE

Prewriting Selecting a Topic

Do the following as a class.

■ Brainstorm classic short stories and poems that students have read over the years. Students can add to the list on their own, but this will give them a start.

Offer some anthologies and collections for students to scan. Students may also consult with the school librarian for suggestions.

✱ For information about how to punctuate the titles of poems, short stories, and books, see PE pages 600 and 602.

Prewriting Finding a Theme

Explore how to **find the theme** *(see below)* of a piece of writing. Examine the sample theme chart with the class. Point out that Mark has found more than one theme in the poem. Explain that often in a piece of literature there may be more than one theme.

Writing Creating Your First Draft

Encourage students to
- compose several topic sentences, and
- choose the one that best states the theme, or focus.

Remind them that they will have an opportunity to revise and edit their work at a later stage in the writing process.

Revising
Improving Your Paragraph

Suggest that students
- revise their own work, and
- exchange their writing with a partner who will review it.

Peer input can help students see parts of their response that could be improved.

Editing
Checking for Conventions

✱ For examples of words that students may use incorrectly, see Using the Right Word on PE page 652.

286

Writing Creating Your First Draft

A paragraph has three main parts: a topic sentence, the body, and a closing sentence. The following tips will help you create each part.

- **Topic sentence:** Write a sentence that names the short story or poem, its author, and the theme you will focus on.
- **Body:** Write sentences that explain the theme using examples from the piece of literature.
- **Closing sentence:** End with a sentence that sums up the theme.

 Write the first draft of your paragraph. Use the tips above as you write your response paragraph.

Revising Improving Your Paragraph

After you've written your first draft, you need to revise your paragraph to improve on your *ideas, organization, voice, word choice,* and *sentence fluency.*

 Review your paragraph. Use the following questions as a guide to your revision.

1 Have I written about one important theme?

2 Do my sentences appear in the best order?

3 Does my interest in the story or poem show in my voice?

4 Have I used some of the same words the author used?

5 Do my sentences flow smoothly?

Editing Checking for Conventions

Next, check your paragraph for *conventions.*

 Edit your work. Use the following questions to guide your editing.

1 Have I checked my punctuation, capitalization, and spelling?

2 Have I used the right words (*to, two, too*)?

Proofread your paragraph. After you make a neat copy of your final paragraph, check it one more time for errors.

Grammar Connection

Punctuating Titles

- **Proofreader's Guide** pages 600 (+), 602–603, 624–625
- *SkillsBook* pages 25–26
- **CD** Punctuating—Titles, Capitalization-2

English Language Learners

Some students may have difficulty completing this assignment independently. Walk them through the sample paragraph on PE page 284 and help them find

- the topic sentence,
- the examples in the body that explain the theme, and
- the closing sentence.

Assist students with organizing their own paragraphs this way.

Struggling Learners

As part of the response to questions 1, 3, and 4 in the revising process, ask students to cite specific examples from their writing. This will ensure that they have reviewed their paragraphs effectively.

Response to Literature
Analyzing a Theme

A great work of art is more than just paint on canvas. A masterpiece gives viewers a reason to stop and stare and get lost in the painting. It has depth and meaning.

When people talk about the depth and meaning of a piece of literature, they are referring to the literature's theme. Theme is the lesson that a book or story teaches the reader about life. In this chapter, you will write an essay that examines how the theme develops through the characters and events in a piece of literature.

Writing Guidelines

Subject:	**A novel or a story**
Form:	**Essay**
Purpose:	**To analyze a theme**
Audience:	**Classmates**

Pigman's Lesson

Two high school kids, John and Lorraine, are typing in school library. They take turns writing chapters about their experiences with Mr. Pignati, the character known as the Pigman. Mr. Pignati has died, but he has left them with a lot to think about. *The Pigman*, by Paul Zindel,

...life is up to the person living it.
...meet Mr. Pignati, John and Lorraine see ...ay from things. They avoid their unhapp ...pending time together. One day, when they a ...ey choose Mr. Pignati's name from the phone b ...im. To their surprise, Mr. Pignati invites them to ...y are about to walk into a life very different f

...r. Pignati is unlike anyone John and Lorraine have ...nown. He is a big, jolly man who trusts them and offer ...o take them to the zoo. He talks to them about his wif ...d shows them his collection of pig figurines. Slowly, J ...and Lorraine realize that, although Mr. Pignati seems ha ...his life is lonely and strange. Later they learn that his w ...is really dead, and it seems that his best friend is Bobo ...baboon in the zoo. John and Lo... ...understand ...anyone in his situation can be...

...They have fun sharing th... ...en ...gets out of control. One day w... ...le, ...ave a rowdy party at his hou... ...se

Analyzing a Theme

Objectives
- understand how to write an essay that analyzes a theme
- understand the content and form of an essay that analyzes a theme
- plan, draft, revise, edit, and publish an analysis of a theme

An **analysis of a theme** is an essay that examines how the theme, or lesson, in a piece of literature develops through the characters and unfolding events. A theme can often be expressed as a statement about life.

Understanding Your Goals

Traits of a Response to Literature

Three traits relate to the development of the content and the form. They provided a focus during prewriting, drafting, and revising.

- Ideas
- Organization
- Voice

The other three traits relate more to form. Checking them is part of the revising and editing processes.

- Word Choice
- Sentence Fluency
- Conventions

✳ The six-point rubric on PE pages 318-319 is based on these traits. Reproducible six-, five-, and four-point rubrics for responses to literature can be found on TE pages 753, 757, and 761.

288

Understanding Your Goals

Your essay on a theme should explain the lesson or main idea of a story. A theme can usually be expressed as a statement about life. The chart below lists the key traits in a response to literature, with specific suggestions for this assignment.

Traits of a Response to Literature

Ideas
Write a focus statement that explains your interpretation of the theme and then select details to support that statement.

Organization
Write an opening that includes the theme, the book's title, and the author. Close with the theme's importance.

Voice
Make your writing sound natural and create a mood appropriate for the novel or story.

Word Choice
Use literary terms and words that your audience can understand and relate to.

Sentence Fluency
Write sentences that flow smoothly.

Conventions
Correct all punctuation, capitalization, spelling, and grammar errors.

 Get the big picture. Review the rubric on pages 318–319 before you begin writing. The rubrics on pages 302–311 and on 314–315 will guide you throughout the revising and editing steps.

Response Essay

evaluate react answer experience **289**
Analyzing a Theme

The novel *The Pigman* tells about two high school students who meet an unusual man named Mr. Pignati. A student who read the book wrote this essay about the theme of the story.

Beginning
. . . .
The beginning introduces the book and focuses on the theme (underlined).

Middle
Each middle paragraph explains a different stage in the development of the theme.

Pigman's Lesson

Two high school kids, John and Lorraine, are typing in the school library. They take turns writing chapters about their experiences with Mr. Pignati, the character known as the Pigman. Mr. Pignati has died, but he has left them with a lot to think about. *The Pigman,* by Paul Zindel, shows that people make their own happiness.

Before they meet Mr. Pignati, John and Lorraine seem to be running away from things. They avoid their unhappy homes by spending time together. One day, when they are bored, they choose Mr. Pignati's name from the phone book and call him. To their surprise, Mr. Pignati invites them to his house. They are about to walk into a life very different from their own.

Mr. Pignati is unlike anyone John and Lorraine have ever known. He is a big, jolly man who trusts them and offers to take them to the zoo. He talks to them about his wife and shows them his collection of pig figurines. Slowly, John and Lorraine realize that, although Mr. Pignati seems happy, his life is lonely and strange. Later they learn that his wife is really dead, and it seems that his best friend is Bobo, a baboon in the zoo. John and Lorraine can't understand how anyone in his situation can be so happy.

They have fun sharing the Pigman's life, but then the fun gets out of control. One day when Mr. Pignati is gone, they have a rowdy party at his house. He cries when he sees the

LITERATURE

Response Essay

Work through this sample essay with students, pointing out the elements that make it a good response to literature.

Ideas
- The focus statement identifies the theme.
- The beginning introduces the title and author of the piece.
- The writer tells about several events from the book and analyzes the feelings and behavior of the main characters.

Organization
- The opening includes the theme, the book's title, and the author.
- The ending revisits the theme.

Voice
- The writer uses a natural voice.
- The serious voice is appropriate for the theme.

Word Choice
- The words used show that the writer has read and analyzed the story.
- The vocabulary used is appropriate to the audience.

English Language Learners

Before students read the sample essay, make sure they understand the following **idioms:**
- running away from (avoiding)
- gets out of control (turns into a bad situation)
- unable to handle (unable to take care of or participate in)
- getting back at (seeking revenge against)

Respond to the reading.

Answers

Ideas **1.** Final sentence: "Our life would be what we made of it—nothing more, nothing less."
2. John

Organization **3.** time order

Voice & Word Choice **4.** The writer discusses the similarities between John and Lorraine (run away from issues, unhappy homes, enjoy Mr. Pignati, throw a wild party and are ashamed) and the differences (Lorraine runs away, John stays; Lorraine feels guilty but is unchanged, John views his life differently.) The writer also uses direct quotations from the book to develop the response.

 Literature Connections

Mentor texts: The Literature Circle Guide series helps students find their way through classic works of literature. For example, students might like to check out the following titles:

Literature Circle Guide: Holes by Tonya Ward Singer

Literature Circle Guide: Maniac Magee by Perdita Finn

Literature Circle Guide: Roll of Thunder, Hear My Cry by Rebecca Callan

Middle
The last middle paragraph covers the final stage in the development of the theme.

Ending
The ending paragraph revisits the theme.

damage and calls the police. John and Lorraine are ashamed that they have been disloyal to him, and they offer to pay for the damages. They also arrange to meet Mr. Pignati at the zoo. The two kids want to get back the happiness that they have lost.

The trip to the zoo is a disaster. First of all, they discover that Bobo has died. The shock causes Mr. Pignati to collapse on the floor of the monkey house. Lorraine backs away, unable to handle what has happened. John stays with Mr. Pignati, who dies of a heart attack. John is deeply moved by Mr. Pignati's death. He is bothered by the thought that "it's possible to end your life with only a baboon to talk to."

Lorraine feels extremely guilty about the way they took advantage of Mr. Pignati. John feels bad, too, but he has learned a valuable lesson. Before, he had spent too much time getting back at people. But because of Mr. Pignati's kindness, John realizes that leading a better life is completely up to him. As he states at the end of the story, "Our life would be what we made of it—nothing more, nothing less."

 Respond to the reading. Answer the following questions about the sample response to literature.

☐ Ideas **(1)** Which quotation in the essay means the same thing as the underlined theme in the first paragraph? **(2)** Which character seems to understand this theme?

☐ Organization **(3)** Are the steps in the theme's development in time order or order of importance?

☐ Voice & Word Choice **(4)** Does the writer sound knowledgeable about the book? Explain.

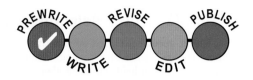

Prewriting

The first step in the writing process is prewriting. Begin by thinking about books and stories you have read recently and their themes.

Keys to Effective Prewriting

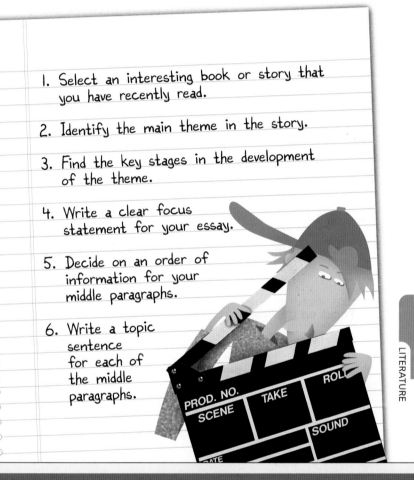

1. Select an interesting book or story that you have recently read.

2. Identify the main theme in the story.

3. Find the key stages in the development of the theme.

4. Write a clear focus statement for your essay.

5. Decide on an order of information for your middle paragraphs.

6. Write a topic sentence for each of the middle paragraphs.

LITERATURE

Prewriting

Keys to Effective Prewriting

Remind students of the purpose of the prewriting stage in the writing process. (It's when the writer gets ready to write.)

Keys to Effective Prewriting explains the process students will be guided through on PE pages 292–294.

- Advise students to use the step-by-step list in the text as a guide whenever they begin prewriting an essay response to literature.
- To help students understand their writing goals, review the rubric for a response to literature on PE pages 318–319. Focus on the ideas, organization, and voice rubric strips at this stage of the writing process.

Writing Workshop

The activities throughout the prewriting, writing, revising, and editing sections of this unit were designed to work as minilessons in a writing workshop. Each activity introduces an important skill, models it, and invites students to try it. You can use these minilessons for whole-group or small-group instruction, or to support students during independent work time.

Advanced Learners

Encourage students to get in the practice of keeping a reading journal. Tell them that as they read, they should make notes on the following ideas:

- what they do and don't like about a story
- interesting things they learn about the characters
- things that puzzle them
- pertinent events and quotations

This kind of journal often serves as a great place to start when looking for topics and details to write about. It also provides a useful record of what students have read and how they felt about it.

✽ For more information on reader-response journals, see PE page 434.

Prewriting **Selecting a Topic**

Provide additional practice in discovering themes. Use Aesop's well-known fable "The Tortoise and the Hare" as a simple example. Read the fable to the class, or tell it in your own words. Discuss possible themes or morals of the story:

- Slow and steady wins the race.
- The race isn't always to the swift.
- Too much confidence and conceit can slow you down and lead to failure.

Ask students which kind of **theme clues** *(see below)* provide the best hints about the theme of "The Tortoise and the Hare." Discuss which interpretation of the story's theme would be the best lesson to apply to students' lives.

Answers

Answers will vary, but students should list the titles and important themes of at least two stories.

Focus on the Traits

Ideas Discuss characters in other familiar stories and tales that authors use to teach life lessons.

Prewriting **Selecting a Topic**

Think about books and stories that you have read recently. What main characters are the most interesting? What do these characters learn during the story? A chart can help you think about main characters and what they learn.

Character Chart

Main Character	What the Character Learns
Crispin (from <u>Crispin</u> by Avi)	Crispin learns that the most important things in life are friendships and courage—things nobody can take away.
Adam Zebrin (from "Zebra" by Chaim Potok)	Adam learns that art can help heal his body and his mind.
Phoebe (from <u>Walk Two Moons</u> by Sharon Creech)	Phoebe learns that every person she meets, no matter how odd, has value.

 Prewrite **Create a character chart.** Use the chart above as a model and follow these directions.

1 In the first column, list the main character from books and stories you have read recently.

2 In the second column, write down what the character learns in the story.

3 Then choose one character to write about. Write one sentence telling why you chose this character.

I chose Adam because art is my favorite class.

Focus on the Traits

Ideas When people talk about the theme of a book or short story, they are talking about the message the story tells about life. One way to discover the theme in a book or story is to ask yourself what the main character learns.

Teaching Tip: Theme Clues

Emphasize that most often a story's theme is *not* openly stated in a work of literature. Students must be detectives and look for clues to find the theme.

Students will need practice in finding clues that will point them toward the author's message. Using popular books and stories that students have

read, model how to find the theme by thinking about the following types of clues:

- analyzing the title,
- identifying statements a character or the narrator makes about life, or
- stating the lesson (or lessons) that a character learns.

English Language Learners

Have students work with partners or in groups to

- think of stories they can analyze,
- identify their themes, and
- discuss how the characters' words and actions give clues about the theme.

Have students save the notes from this discussion and use them for the charting activity on PE page 293.

evaluate PREVIEW experience
react answer **293**
Analyzing a Theme

Gathering Details

Now that you have selected a story and a theme, you should think about how the theme develops. By reviewing the key thoughts, feelings, and actions of the main character, you can chart important stages in the development of the theme. The sample chart below is for the essay on pages 297–300.

Theme Chart

Title: *"Raymond's Run"*

Theme: *Winning isn't the most important thing in life.*

First Stage: The theme in the early part of the story

Squeaky thinks that winning the May Day race again will make her important, but she doesn't think that taking care of her brother Raymond is anything special.

Middle Stages: Important developments that follow the first stage

As the race day approaches, Squeaky concentrates so hard on training that she thinks the only way she can be successful is to win.

On the day of the race, Squeaky loses her concentration because she suddenly realizes that Raymond is kneeling down and getting ready to run, too.

Final Stage: The last stage of the theme's development

Squeaky is confused as she crosses the finish line because she realizes that something has become more important to her than winning.

Prewrite

Chart your theme. Write the theme at the top of a chart like the one above. Then identify three or more stages in the story that help develop or show the theme. Under each stage, list some of the main character's thoughts, feelings, and actions at that time.

LITERATURE

Prewriting Gathering Details

As students develop their theme chart, suggest that they

- record phrases or sentences from the piece of literature that support each stage of the theme, and
- use the completed theme chart to plan their essays and incorporate quotations effectively.

English Language Learners

Make sure students understand that a *stage*, as it is used in this context, is a step in a sequence.

- Practice finding the stages that develop the theme in several simple stories.
- Encourage students to number each stage in their theme chart so that they form an easy-to-follow list to use during drafting.

Struggling Learners

Before students begin the **Prewrite** activity, have them create a chart with four columns that are labeled *Thoughts, Feelings, Actions,* and *Dialogue.* Have students record what the main character thought, felt, did, and said at key times in the story. This may help them identify what the stages in the theme chart should be.

Prewriting
Writing a Focus Statement
Meet in informal writing conferences to help students compose their focus statements.

Prewriting
Organizing the Middle Paragraphs of Your Essay
Emphasize that students should use the elements in the story to show how the author develops the theme. Discuss how to decide whether to use chronological order or order of importance as the organizational pattern for the middle paragraphs.

Students can improve the clarity of their writing by using transition words (*before, first, next, later, finally, most importantly, secondly,* and so on) in topic sentences and middle paragraphs.

Prewriting Writing a Focus Statement

Now that you have identified the main character and the stages in the development of the theme, you are ready to write your focus statement.

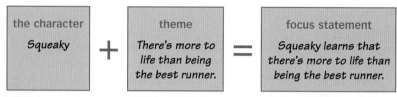

the character		theme		focus statement
Squeaky	+	There's more to life than being the best runner.	=	Squeaky learns that there's more to life than being the best runner.

 Form a focus. Write a focus statement for your analysis of a theme using the formula above.

Organizing the Middle Paragraphs of Your Essay

After you write a focus statement, plan the middle paragraphs of your essay. Each middle paragraph should cover a different stage in the development of the theme.

Below, the writer of the sample essay on pages 297–300 planned the order of the middle paragraphs. She wrote a topic sentence for each stage.

Topic Sentences

> **Topic Sentence 1**
> *Along with being a great runner, Squeaky does another thing well, too, although she doesn't take credit for it.*
>
> **Topic Sentence 2**
> *Competition is important to Squeaky, so she concentrates more and more on winning as the race day approaches.*
>
> **Topic Sentence 3**
> *The day of the race is a special day for Squeaky.*
>
> **Topic Sentence 4**
> *Squeaky can't believe what she's seeing, but she knows that something very important is about to happen.*

 Plan your middle paragraphs. Review your "Theme Chart." Add any stages you feel may be necessary. Then write a topic sentence for each of your middle paragraphs and decide the best order for the paragraphs.

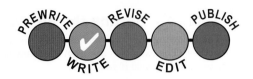

Writing

PREWRITE · WRITE · REVISE · EDIT · PUBLISH

After you've done your prewriting, you can begin writing your essay. Use your focus statement, theme chart, and topic sentences as a guide.

Keys to Effective Writing

1. Write on every other line so that you can make changes later.

2. Use your focus statement and topic sentences to organize your paragraphs.

3. Support your topic sentences with specific details from the story.

4. Refer to your theme chart for details, adding more if needed.

5. Get all of your thoughts on paper.

6. Tie your thoughts together with transitions.

LITERATURE

Writing Keys to Effective Writing

Remind students that the writing stage is when they get to write, or draft, their ideas on paper.

Keys to Effective Writing explains the process students will be guided through on PE pages 296–300.

Review the goals that students should keep in mind as they plan and begin to write their essays.

- Turn back to PE page 288 and reread the goals together.
- Remind students to focus on the goals for these traits—ideas, organization, and voice—as they write a first draft.
- Tell students to refer to the list of Keys to Effective Writing whenever they are about to begin a draft.

Writing Workshop

Let your students see you write. They will be inspired to know that their teacher is a writer, just as they are, and you will foster a writing community in your classroom.

For example, when you present the idea of creating a beginning or an ending for your essay, go ahead and write a few lines. The outcome doesn't have to be perfect. First drafts never are. But if you model the drafting step for your students, they will be emboldened to dive right in and try it themselves.

Writing Getting the Big Picture

If students need more practice in understanding the parts of a response to literature, discuss as a class Aesop's fable "The Tortoise and the Hare" (see TE page 292) in terms of the three main parts of an analysis.

Writer's Craft

Structure: The reason that every essay has a beginning, a middle, and an ending is that it is experienced over time. Any work of art or any event that unfolds over time has a beginning, middle, and ending—a song, a church service, a speech, a TV show, a play. . . . Things that can be experienced all at once, such as a painting, a photograph, or a sculpture, do not have boundaries in time (a beginning, middle, and ending), but only boundaries in space.

Writing Getting the Big Picture

The following chart shows how the three parts of a response to literature fit together. (The examples are from the essay on pages 297–300.) You're ready to write your response if you have . . .

- discovered the theme,
- written a clear focus statement that includes the theme and other information, and
- planned your paragraphs.

Beginning

The **beginning** paragraph introduces the character and states the theme.

Focus Statement
Eventually, Squeaky learns that there's more to life than being the best runner.

Middle

The four **middle** paragraphs show four stages in the development of the theme.

Four Topic Sentences
Along with being a great runner, Squeaky does another thing well, too, although she doesn't take credit for it.

Competition is important to Squeaky, so she concentrates more and more on winning as the race day approaches.

The day of the race is a special day for Squeaky.

Squeaky can't believe what she's seeing, but she knows that something very important is about to happen.

Ending

The **ending** paragraph revisits the theme and summarizes it.

Closing Sentence
The theme of the story is clear: Winning isn't the most important thing in life.

evaluate ~~PREVIEW~~ experience
react answer **297**
Analyzing a Theme

Starting Your Essay

The opening of your essay should include . . .

- background about the events and characters that help develop the theme,
- the title and author of the work, and
- your focus statement about the theme of the story.

> Beginning
>
> Middle
>
> Ending

Beginning Paragraph

The beginning paragraph below starts with background information about the main character and ends with the focus statement about the theme.

The first part gives background.

The last sentence is the focus statement (underlined).

> *The main character in Toni Cade Bambara's story "Raymond's Run" is Squeaky, an aspiring runner. Squeaky is the reigning champion for her age group in the 50-yard dash at the Harlem May Day celebration. She practices running and thinks about it almost constantly as she prepares to defend her title. Eventually, Squeaky learns that there's more to life than being the best runner.*

 Write your beginning. Write the beginning paragraph of your essay. Include background information, the title and author, and your focus statement.

Drafting Tips

- **Talk about the story with a classmate** before you start writing.
- **Write freely,** letting your ideas flow without worrying about neatness.
- **Be sure that you have included enough details** to help your reader understand the point you're making.

LITERATURE

Writing Starting Your Essay

Point out that in the sample beginning paragraph, the focus statement is the last sentence. Explain that often a writer gives background information about the story and the character that leads up to the focus statement. Have students review the sample response essay on PE 289 for the development of the beginning paragraph.

Writing

Developing the Middle Part

Note that the topic sentence of the first middle paragraph creates a smooth transition from the beginning paragraph.

- Point out that the topic sentence for the second and third middle paragraphs also connect back to the beginning paragraph.
- These topic sentences discuss aspects of the focus statement.
- Each middle paragraph should detail a stage in the development of the theme.

298

Writing Developing the Middle Part

Each middle paragraph tells about one of the stages in the development of the theme. These paragraphs focus on the thoughts, feelings, and actions of important characters during each stage. Every middle paragraph should contain a topic sentence.

Middle Paragraphs

These paragraphs show the theme's development.

> The first sentence forms a transition from the previous paragraph to this one.

> Each topic sentence covers a stage of the theme (underlined).

Along with being a great runner, Squeaky does another thing well, too, although she doesn't take credit for it. Taking care of her older brother Raymond is a major responsibility in her life. Squeaky says, "He needs looking after 'cause he's not quite right." She does her duty without really thinking about it.

<u>Competition is important to Squeaky, so she concentrates more and more on winning as the race day approaches.</u> Her main worry is a new girl named Gretchen, who everybody says is very fast. Squeaky psychs up by picturing herself running, almost flying, to the finish line far ahead of Gretchen and the other competitors. She thinks that winning this race is the only way that she can be successful.

<u>The day of the race is a special day for Squeaky.</u> She has to take care of Raymond, so she sits him down on the playground swings and goes to the starting line. However, just before the

evaluate PREVIEW experience
react answer
299
Analyzing a Theme

race, she looks to the side, and there's Raymond on the other side of the fence, kneeling down like he's in the race, too.

Squeaky can't believe what she's seeing, but she knows that something very important is about to happen. When the gun starts the race, she sprints off, still watching Raymond. He keeps up with the leaders, and people start cheering for him. Raymond is running faster than anyone thought he could, and that makes his sister proud of him. When Squeaky crosses the finish line, she is confused and doesn't think that she has won.

> The last stage in the theme's development is described in the last paragraph.

Write your middle paragraphs. Write the middle paragraphs of your essay, using your topic sentences and theme chart as a guide. Fill in details as they are needed.

Using Key Words for Transitions

To create a smooth flow of ideas in your middle paragraphs, tie them together with transitions. Repeating key words is a good way to connect a paragraph to the one before it. The key words below (colored) create a transition between the second and third middle paragraphs shown on page 298.

. . . She thinks that winning this race is the only way that she can be successful.

The day of the race is a special day for Squeaky. . . .

LITERATURE

Writing
Using Key Words for Transitions
Repeating key words is a useful strategy for making smooth transitions between paragraphs.

In the model, repeating the key word (*race*) helps create coherence and smooth transitions between sentences and paragraphs.

✳ For practice in using transitions to develop coherence in writing, see PE page 539.

Struggling Learners

Students may feel that because there are four middle paragraphs in the sample, they also need to write four paragraphs.

- Emphasize that the number of paragraphs depends on the number of topic sentences they've written.
- Invite students to review their paragraphs with you to decide if they have enough to develop their theme.

Advanced Learners

Writing an effective literary analysis is based on a clear understanding of the characters and the plot line. Have pairs of students review each other's middle paragraphs to make sure that every sentence demonstrates a careful "reading" of the story and advances or supports the focus statement.

Writing Ending Your Essay

Discuss with students ways to embed, or smoothly place, a quotation in their writing. Analyze how the writer of "Pigman's Lesson" successfully incorporates quotations at the end of two paragraphs in the sample on PE page 290. Brainstorm a list of common stems (sentence starters) to help students do this in their own essays. Begin the list with:

- The author states that . . .
- According to the author, . . .
- As the main character says, . . .
- At the end of the story, it is clear that . . .

Remind students to use correct **quotation punctuation** *(see below)*.

300

Writing Ending Your Essay

Your essay starts with a statement about the theme. It then goes on to show how the theme develops in stages through the characters and events. Here are some suggestions to help you make your final comments about the theme.

- Show how a character has changed.
- Quote significant lines from the story.
- Predict how the theme might affect a character in the future.
- State the theme as a basic rule of life.

 Quoting lines directly from the book or story can lend support to your ideas and make them stronger in the eyes of the reader.

Ending Paragraph

The ending paragraph below tells about Squeaky's realization of what is really important in life.

> **The last sentence restates the theme (underlined).**
>
> *Finally, when things calm down, the announcer says that Squeaky came in first, and Gretchen was second. Squeaky suddenly realizes that Raymond's happiness is what is really important to her. In the past, she and Gretchen had focused on competing against each other. Now she smiles at Gretchen and thinks that maybe Gretchen would like to help her coach Raymond. Squeaky has a new reason to feel pride in her accomplishments. The theme of the story is clear: Winning isn't the most important thing in life.*

 Write your ending. Write the last paragraph of your essay. Be sure to end by revisiting the theme. (Use one of the four suggestions at the top of this page.)

Form a complete first draft. Make a complete copy of your essay. Double-space or write on every other line so that you have room for revising.

Teaching Tip: Quotation Punctuation

Help students review how to punctuate direct quotations.

- When quoting material from a piece of literature, place quotation marks before and after the exact words from the source.
- When quoting a complete sentence, begin it with a capital letter and include ending punctuation inside the quotation marks.

- Use a comma to set off a speaker tag.

Refer students to the sample response essay on PE page 290. Note that the quotation in the middle paragraph is *not* a complete sentence, so it does not begin with a capital letter.

✻ Review PE page 598 and have students practice punctuating quotations from their literature.

Advanced Learners

Challenge each student to write two versions of the ending paragraph by using two of the four suggestions listed at the top of the page. Then have students work with peers to review the two endings and decide which is more effective.

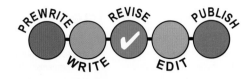

Revising

Now that you've finished your first draft, you're ready to begin revising. Focus on ideas, organization, and other traits to make changes that will improve your writing.

Keys to Effective Revising

1. To get a feel for how well your essay works, read it aloud.

2. Check your focus statement to see if it includes the topic of the essay.

3. Be sure that each detail supports its topic sentence.

4. Check your voice to see if it sounds natural.

5. Review your word choice and sentence fluency.

6. Use the editing and proofreading marks inside the back cover of this book.

LITERATURE

Revising

Keys to Effective Revising

Keys to Effective Revising explains the process students will be guided through on PE pages 302–312. Emphasize the importance of the first item on the list. Reading a first draft aloud helps students immediately identify trouble spots.

Remind students to refer to the list as they get ready to revise their work. After they have made their changes, have them exchange work with a partner to receive additional suggestions.

Peer Responding

Ask your students to get a peer response prior to revising their work. The peer response will help them understand just what changes they need to make as they work through revision.

Writing Workshop

Instead of assigning all of the revision strategies on the following pages, treat them as minilessons on improving ideas, organization, voice, word choice, and sentence fluency. If a student or a group of students is having trouble with one of the traits, select the appropriate strategy and work through it with them. The purpose of the following pages is not to make revision interminable, but rather to demystify the process so anyone can do it.

Revising for Ideas

The rubric strips that run across all of the revising pages (PE pages 302–311) are provided to help students focus their revising and are related to the full rubric on PE pages 318–319.

 Answers

1. Relate the main theme to the story.
2. Give specific information about what the character learns and explain the relationship to the story.
3. Tell the specific theme and how it is expressed in the story.
4. Give the title of the book and tell who the boy is and how he learns the lesson in the story.
5. Relate this theme to the specific title and character.

302

Revising **for Ideas**

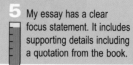

6 My ideas show a complete and careful analysis of the theme.

5 My essay has a clear focus statement. It includes supporting details including a quotation from the book.

4 My essay has a focus statement, but I need to add more supporting details.

Ideas are the key elements of an essay. Use the rubric strip above and the information below as a guide to revising the ideas in your essay about a theme.

Does my focus statement introduce the story's theme?

You know your focus statement is effective when it states a specific theme and relates it to the story through the author, the title, or the characters.

> **Poorly Developed Focus**
>
> **People don't understand each other.**
> (The theme is too general, and it is not related to a story.)

> **Well-Developed Focus**
>
> **In *To Kill a Mockingbird*, the three children learn that it sometimes takes a crisis before people can see the good in others.**
> (The theme is specific, and it is clearly related to the story.)

 The following focus statements are poorly developed. What kind of information should be added to make each one better?

1. *The Call of the Wild* is about wildness.
2. The story's main character, Vicki, realizes something about hope.
3. "The Gift of the Magi" has an interesting ending.
4. In Mark Twain's book, a boy learns that freedom carries responsibilities.
5. The story is about a boy who recovers from his injuries when he stops feeling sorry for himself.

 Check your opening. Review your opening paragraph. Pay close attention to the theme in your focus statement and how it relates to the story.

Struggling Learners

As a visual reminder to use the rubric strips to revise their essay, have students make a "Rubric Rating" column in the left margin of their first draft. Students should

- list each trait,
- leave space below each heading, and
- draw a line where they can fill in each rating.

The margin will look like this:

Ideas

———

Organization

———

This will prompt students to use the rubric strips as they consider each trait.

evaluate answer experience **303**
react
Analyzing a Theme

 3 I need to make my focus statement clearer. I also need to add more supporting details.

2 I need a focus statement and supporting details.

1 I need to learn how to analyze a theme.

Did I use quotations to emphasize certain ideas?

Quoting directly from a book or story can be an effective way to emphasize important ideas in your essay. The quotation could . . .

■ highlight an important statement by the author,

■ reflect something about the character being quoted, or

■ express the theme.

 Read the sentences below, which come from the closing paragraph of a student essay. Why did the writer include the direct quotation? Refer to the list above to help you decide.

1   Atticus Finch's earliest lesson to Scout is simple: "You never
2 really understand a person until you consider things from his
3 point of view . . . until you climb into his skin and walk around in
4 it." Throughout the novel, Scout is learning to understand people.

 Review your first draft for ideas. Be sure that your theme is clearly stated in your opening. Also check to see whether you have used quotations effectively.

Ideas
A direct quotation is inserted.

Taking care of her older brother Raymond is a
Squeaky says, "He needs looking after 'cause
major responsibility in her life. She does her   he's not
                                                  quite right."
duty without really thinking about it.

LITERATURE

Encourage students to use quotations, but stress that any quotation they use should clearly elaborate on one of their own thoughts or feelings.

 **Answer**

The quotation expresses the theme.

Writer's Craft

Balanced quotations: When a response to literature contains no quotations, the reader "feels he or she is looking in a mirror dimly." To use too many quotations, however, is to overwhelm the reader with bits and pieces of the original. Students need to find a balance. The best quotations should be carefully selected and integrated into the student's own thought.

Also, caution students against ending paragraphs with quotations. Each time a quotation is used, it should be explained—not simply left to dangle.

Struggling Learners

If students have not included a direct quotation in their analysis, have them complete this activity.

● Instruct students to list two or three quotations that seem important from their source novel or story.

● Ask them to explain to you why each quotation is important.

● Then help them incorporate one or more of the quotations into their analysis.

Revising for Organization

By checking that the words in their **topic sentences** relate back to the focus statement, students ensure that their writing flows in a unified and coherent way.

 Answers

Topic sentences:
- great runner, does another thing well
- important to Squeaky, concentrates . . . on winning
- race is special
- knows that something very important is about to happen

304

Revising for Organization

6 All the parts work together to create an insightful analysis.

5 The beginning, middle, and ending of my essay work well together.

4 All my topic sentences in the middle relate to the focus, but I need to improve the ending.

Organization is the way that you arrange your ideas within the essay. Use the rubric strip above and the following information to review and revise the organization of your essay.

Do my topic sentences relate to the focus?

The topic sentences in your middle paragraphs will relate to the focus if they sound like they flow from the focus statement in the first paragraph.

 Read the focus statement and the topic sentences below. On your own paper, write the words in each topic sentence that relate to the focus.

Focus Statement
> *Eventually, Squeaky learns that there's more to life than being the best runner.*

Topic Sentences
> *Along with being a great runner, Squeaky does another thing well, too, although she doesn't take credit for it.*

> *Competition is important to Squeaky, so she concentrates more and more on winning as the race day approaches.*

> *The day of the race is a special day for Squeaky.*

> *Squeaky can't believe what she's seeing, but she knows that something very important is about to happen.*

 Check your topic sentences. Write your focus statement at the top of a sheet of paper. Then write the topic sentences from your middle paragraphs under the focus. Rewrite any topic sentences that do not relate to the focus.

evaluate answer experience **305**
react
Analyzing a Theme

3 I need to change all the topic sentences and rewrite the ending.

2 I need to redo the middle part because the topic sentences do not relate to the focus.

1 I need to learn how to organize a response to literature.

What's the best way to end my essay?

Your ending should revisit the theme and leave the reader with something to think about. A good way to emphasize the theme is to use one of the following suggestions.

- Show how a character has changed.
- Quote an important line from the story.
- Predict how the theme might affect a character in the future.
- State the theme as a basic rule of life: *Winning isn't the most important thing in life.*

 For each of the following endings, identify the suggestion (listed above) that the writer used.

1. John now realizes that how he lives his life is completely up to him.

2. The author sees José, the "born worker," as a boy with a fine future.

 Review your essay for organization. Be sure that the theme is explained clearly in the beginning and restated effectively in the ending.

Organization
A restatement of the theme is added.

> Now she smiles at Gretchen and thinks that
> maybe Gretchen would like to help her coach
> Raymond. Squeaky has a new reason to feel
> pride in her accomplishments. The theme of the story is clear: Winning isn't the most important thing in life.

LITERATURE

Provide additional practice with endings by directing students to reread the ending of "Pigman's Lesson" on PE page 290.

- Note that the final paragraph in the sample essay shows how John has changed.
- Point out that the final sentence of the ending paragraph quotes an important line from the story.
- Explain that the writer has used two of the suggestions listed here to write an effective ending.

 Answers

1. Show how a character has changed.
2. Predict how the theme might affect a character in the future.

Revising for Voice

Here is another way to check a sentence for a natural-sounding voice.

- Rewrite the sentence once so that it is overly formal.
- Rewrite it another time so that it is very, very informal.

By exaggerating the voice in both directions, students may get a better feel for reworking the original sentence so that it sounds more natural.

306

Revising for Voice

6 My voice sounds distinctive and insightful from start to finish.

5 My voice sounds natural. It creates the right mood for the story.

4 My voice sounds natural, but it needs to reflect more clearly the mood of the story.

Voice is the "sound" of your writing. The rubric strip above and the information below will help you revise your essay so that it sounds natural and creates an appropriate mood.

How do I know whether my writing has a natural voice?

Your writing has a natural voice if it sounds like you and is neither too formal nor too informal. Writers sometimes create language that is too formal because they think that it sounds impressive. Others use language that is too casual or informal. Neither one will sound natural.

> **Too Formal**
>
> The consequence of the experience was that the adolescent female came to a new realization of what was right and what was wrong.

> **Too Informal**
>
> That girl sure did learn her lesson all right.

The voice in the revised sentence below sounds more natural.

> **Natural**
>
> Because of the experience, the girl learned a lesson about how to tell right from wrong.

 The best way to hear how your essay sounds is to read it aloud. If you think it sounds unnatural, so will the reader.

 Check for natural voice. Reread your essay, marking any sections that sound too formal or too informal. Rewrite those parts so that they sound more natural.

English Language Learners

Some students may not be able to discriminate between a formal voice and an informal voice.

- Explain that the vocabulary in the too-formal example is difficult, and the sentence is unnecessarily long.
- Point out that the idioms and colloquialisms in the too-informal example are not appropriate for this type of written work.

- As students begin to revise for voice, have them read aloud their essay to a partner who might provide constructive tips on how to revise for a more natural voice.
- As students continue the revising process, explain that word choice and fluency influence voice. Assist students with revising for these traits.

evaluate ~~PREVIEW~~ experience **307**
react answer
Analyzing a Theme

3 My voice needs to sound natural and match the mood of the story more clearly.

2 I need to create a natural voice.

1 I need to learn more about voice.

Does my voice create the right mood?

Mood is the feeling or reaction that your writing creates in the reader.

  Read the following sentences. For each one, describe the mood (sad, suspenseful, happy, silly, fearful) that is produced by the writing.

1. At the beginning of the story, Charlise felt that something very unusual was about to happen.

2. Charlise turned from the kitchen counter, fell over the cat, dropped the pie on the floor, and sat on it as though it were a comfortable cushion.

3. Mr. Pignati felt so alone that he collapsed on the floor.

  Be sure that your voice creates the right mood. Think about the mood that you wish to create in your essay. Review your writing and make necessary changes in your voice.

Voice
A sentence is deleted to keep the mood consistent. Overly formal language is rewritten.

The day of the race is a special day for Squeaky. ~~She doesn't really have a life.~~ She has to ~~give substantial assistance to~~ *take care of* Raymond, so she sits him down on the playground swings and goes to the starting line. However, just before the race, she looks to the side, and there's Raymond . . .

LITERATURE

Before students work on the activity, share with them a series of "telling" sentences from short stories and novels. Ask students to describe the mood that each sentence suggests.

 **Answers**

1. suspenseful
2. silly
3. sad

Advanced Learners

Invite students to write short stories that clearly demonstrate mood (sad, suspenseful, happy, silly, fearful, and so on).

- Remind students that their story should have a theme, and that the theme will help determine the mood of the story.
- When pieces are finished, have students publish them in a magazine for the class to enjoy.

Revising **for** Word Choice

Review the definitions of the terms in the box. Have students check PE pages 351–352 or refer them to a dictionary.

Remind students to include literary terms in their writing.

- Have them highlight any terms they may have used in their first drafts.
- When students revise their drafts, encourage them to include a few of the literary terms listed in the exercise on this page.

 Answers

1. character
2. theme
3. mood
4. protagonist
5. narrator
6. dialogue
7. tone

308

Revising **for** Word Choice

6 My word choice reflects my analytical thinking about literature.

5 My word choice, including literary terms, is appropriate for my reader.

4 My word choice is appropriate, but I need to add more literary terms.

When you revise your writing for *word choice*, be sure that your words effectively describe the story and that they are on the right level for your audience.

How can I improve my word choice?

When you write about literature, literary terms like *dialogue* and *mood* can help make your essay clear and effective. (See pages 351–352 for terms that you can use to write about novels and stories.)

Try IT Use each word in the following chart to complete the sentences below.

character	dialogue	mood	narrator
theme	tone	protagonist	

1. A _____ is a person or an animal in a story.

2. A story's _____ is its lesson about life.

3. _____ is the feeling that a piece of writing creates in the reader.

4. The _____ is the main character of a story.

5. The person or character who actually tells the story is the _____ .

6. _____ is the words spoken between the characters.

7. A writer's attitude toward his or her subject is the _____ .

 Revise for literary terms. Check your essay for places where you might use literary terms to add clarity to your writing.

evaluate react PREVIEW answer experience **309**
Analyzing a Theme

3 I need to make the word choice more appropriate for the reader.

2 I need to pay more attention to word choice.

1 I need help with word choice.

Are my words appropriate for the reader?

Your words will be appropriate if they are not too slangy or too showy.

Lorraine thought that John was acting dumb.

(This use of *dumb* is slang.)

Lorraine thought that John was acting nonsensically.

(*Nonsensically* is too showy.)

Lorraine thought that John was acting foolishly.

(*Foolishly* is an appropriate word.)

 Read the paragraph below and decide whether the underlined words are too slangy or too showy. Choose more appropriate words.

1　　They have fun sharing the Pigman's life, but then everything
2　gets nuts. One day when he is gone, they have a happening party.
3　He cries when he sees the damage and calls the law enforcement
4　authorities. John and Lorraine are disconsolate when they realize
5　how much they have hurt Mr. Pignati.

 Revise for word choice. Look back at the way you have used words in your essay. Replace words that are not appropriate.

Word Choice
More appropriate language is used.

　　　　　Competition
　~~Domination in athletics~~ is important to
　　　　　concentrates more and more on
Squeaky, so she ~~freaks about~~ winning as the race

day approaches. Her main worry is a new girl named

Gretchen, who everybody says is very fast.

LITERATURE

Advise students to be careful that the voice in their essay stays consistent. If they occasionally use slang words or words that are too showy, for example, the result may be an uneven or unnatural voice that distracts the reader.

 Answers

The replacement words may vary. Possible answers:

- gets nuts—too slangy; use *gets confusing*
- happening—too slangy; use *wild* or *rowdy*
- law enforcement authorities—too showy; use *police*
- disconsolate—too showy; *use sorry* or *ashamed*

Teaching Tip: Slang

Discuss how some words (slang) that are common in speech may be inappropriate in writing.

- Note that slang may be popular for a while but then disappear.
- Point out that new words often reflect cultural changes.
- Brainstorm slang terms used today.

Revising for Sentence Fluency

Write the following sentence pairs on the board and have students combine them using a relative pronoun.

- Micah and Sara want to see a movie.
  Sara is Micah's cousin.
- Sara wants to see the latest horror movie.
  The horror movie opens today.
- Micah doesn't like horror movies.
  Horror movies scare him.

✳ For more information about using relative pronouns to combine sentences, see PE page 706.

 Answers

Possible answers:
1. José, who comes from a hardworking family, is a boy with a fine future.
2. José and Arnie get a job cleaning a swimming pool that is owned by a friend of Arnie's father.

310

Revising for Sentence Fluency

6 The sentences in my analysis make my ideas really stand out!

5 My sentences are skillfully written and keep the reader's interest.

4 Most of my sentences flow smoothly, but I need to cut unneeded words.

To revise for *sentence fluency*, check the clarity, flow, and smoothness of your sentences. The rubric strip above and the information below will help you.

How can I make my sentences flow more smoothly?

You can make your sentences flow more smoothly by using a relative pronoun (*who, that, which*) to join short sentences. The following example shows (1) two short sentences and (2) a combined sentence with a relative pronoun.

> **Two Short Sentences**
>
> **José works harder than his cousin Arnie. Arnie avoids physical labor whenever possible.**

> **Combined Sentence with a Relative Pronoun**
>
> **José works harder than his cousin Arnie, who avoids physical labor whenever possible.**

 Rewrite the following sentences, using relative pronouns to combine each pair of short sentences into a longer one.

1. José is a boy with a fine future. José comes from a hardworking family.
2. José and Arnie get a job cleaning a swimming pool. The pool is owned by a friend of Arnie's father.

 Use commas to set off a clause beginning with a relative pronoun if the clause is *not necessary* to the basic meaning of the sentence. (See **706.3** and **684.6**).

> **Soccer, which is a favorite sport in many other countries, is becoming popular in the United States.**

Commas should not set off a clause that is necessary to understand the meaning of the sentence.

> **Soccer that is played indoors is a very high-scoring game.**

Grammar Connection

Combining Sentences with Relative Pronouns

- **Proofreader's Guide** pages 706–707
- *Write Source* page 515
- *SkillsBook* pages 119–120

Struggling Learners

Help students understand the difference between a **restrictive clause** (one that is necessary to the meaning of the sentence) and a **nonrestrictive clause** (one that is not essential for meaning).

- Have a volunteer read aloud the first example in the tip section.
- Then have the volunteer read the same sentence aloud, leaving out the clause (in blue). Help students see that although the clause adds information, it is not essential to the meaning.
- Repeat this process with the second example. Explain that if you omit this clause, the meaning of the sentence changes, because the clause tells what kind of soccer is high-scoring.

✳ For more information about restrictive and nonrestrictive clauses, see PE page 584.

evaluate *PREVIEW* experience
react answer 311
Analyzing a Theme

3 I need to combine short, choppy sentences and cut unneeded words.

2 I need to pay much more attention to the flow of my sentences.

1 I need to learn more about sentences.

Are some of my sentences wordy?

Your sentences may be wordy if you have used more words than you need or repeated yourself unnecessarily. (See page 506.)

> **When Mia opened her mouth to speak, everyone in the area around her listened.**
>
> When Mia spoke, everyone in the area listened.
> (Unneeded words have been removed.)
>
> **Beyonce practices soccer on the soccer field with the other girls on her team at 3:30 p.m. in the afternoon.**
>
> Beyonce practices soccer with her team at 3:30 p.m.
> (Repetitious wording has been removed.)

 Rewrite the paragraph below so that it is less wordy.

> **Arnie goes out and gets them a job cleaning Mr. Clemens's pool at his house. While José is in the pool scrubbing the walls of the pool, Mr. Clemens accidentally falls into the pool without meaning to.**

Revise **Revise for sentence fluency.** Check your essay for short sentences that can be combined. Also check for wordiness.

Sentence Fluency
Repetitious wording and unnecessary wording are deleted.

> *Finally, when things calm down ~~later,~~ the announcer says that Squeaky came in first, and Gretchen was second. Squeaky ~~hears the announcement and~~ suddenly realizes that Raymond's happiness is what is really important to her.*

LITERATURE

Grammar Connection

Wordy Sentences
- *Write Source* page 506
- *SkillsBook* pages 83–84

To help students identify repeated or unnecessary words in their essays, suggest that they highlight words and phrases that say the same thing.

- Make sure they understand that the words eliminated in the sample sentences say the same thing as other words in the sentences.
- If needed, have pairs of students review each other's writing for repetitious and unnecessary words.

 Answers

Answers will vary. Possible rewritten paragraph:

> Arnie gets them a job cleaning Mr. Clemens's pool. While José is scrubbing the walls of the pool, Mr. Clemens accidentally falls in.

Revising Using a Checklist

Advise students to use the checklist as a serious tool to help them edit their writing.

- Ask them to respond to the questions by noting specific examples in their drafts rather than simply checking off the boxes.
- For more feedback, each student should have a partner edit their writing using the checklist as a guide.

312

Revising Using a Checklist

 Check your revising. On a piece of paper, write the numbers 1 to 12. If you can answer "yes" to a question, put a check mark after that number. If not, continue to work with that part of your essay.

Ideas

_____ 1. Have I written a focus statement that introduces my topic?

_____ 2. Have I given the reader enough information?

_____ 3. Did I use significant quotations?

Organization

_____ 4. Have I included a beginning, a middle, and an ending?

_____ 5. Do my topic sentences relate to my focus?

_____ 6. Did I leave my reader with a clear idea of the theme's importance?

Voice

_____ 7. Does my voice sound natural?

_____ 8. Have I created the right mood?

Word Choice

_____ 9. Have I used literary terms, if appropriate?

_____ 10. Have I avoided words that are too slangy or too showy?

Sentence Fluency

_____ 11. Have I combined short sentences?

_____ 12. Have I eliminated unnecessary words?

 Make a clean copy. When you've finished revising your essay, make a clean copy before you begin to edit.

Grammar Connection

Pronouns (person, number)

- **Proofreader's Guide** pages 702–703, 704–705
- *Write Source* pages 471, 472 (+), 473
- *SkillsBook* pages 133–134, 135–136, 137–138
- **CD** Nouns—1

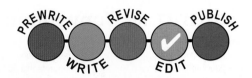

Editing

After you've finished revising your essay, it's time to edit for the following conventions: punctuation, capitalization, spelling, and grammar.

Keys to Effective Editing

1. Use a dictionary, a thesaurus, and the "Proofreader's Guide" in the back of this book.

2. Check quotations for correct punctuation.

3. Check your writing for correctness of punctuation, capitalization, spelling, and grammar.

4. If you use a computer, edit on a printed copy and enter your changes on the computer.

5. Use the editing and proofreading marks inside the back cover of this book.

LITERATURE

Editing **Keys to Effective Editing**

Keys to Effective Editing explains the process students will be guided through on PE pages 314–316. Advise students to review this list as they prepare to edit their work.

Technology Connections

The *Interactive Writing Skills* CD-ROM can offer your students a fun way to practice the conventions of English. Students will find informative videos about each rule, examples drawn from the *Write Source* series, and enjoyable exercises that will let them apply their knowledge.

Editing **for Conventions**

This page illustrates that commas set off a word or phrase if the information is *not needed* to understand the basic meaning of the sentence.

Remind students that commas also should set off a clause beginning with a relative pronoun if the clause is *not necessary* to the basic meaning of the sentence.

✱ For a quick review, students can turn back to PE page 310 or refer to pages 584 and 684.6.

 Answers

1. commas
2. no commas
3. commas

314

Editing **for Conventions**

6 My grammar and punctuation are correct, and the copy is free of all errors.

5 My essay has one or two errors that do not interfere with the reader's understanding.

4 I need to correct the few errors in punctuation, spelling, or grammar.

Conventions are the rules you follow for punctuation, capitalization, grammar, and spelling. To edit for conventions, use the rubric strip above and the information below.

Have I used commas correctly to set off words and phrases?

A word or phrase should be set off with commas if the information *is not* needed to understand the basic meaning of the sentence. No commas are used if the information *is* needed to understand the sentence. (See 584.1.)

> **Jem,** taking a shortcut home, **was badly injured.**
>
> Hiding in his house, **Boo Radley watched what went on in the neighborhood.**
>
> **Jem didn't see the man** who attacked him.
> (*Who attacked him* is needed to understand which man the sentence is referring to.)

 Read the following sentences. Decide whether the italicized words should be set off with commas.

1. Scout *who is only six when the book begins* is quick to judge.
2. She lives in a place *where people are known by what their families are like.*
3. The Cunninghams *as Scout explains to her teacher* do not like to owe people.

 Edit for commas. Check your essay to make sure that you have used commas correctly to set off words and phrases.

evaluate PREVIEW experience
react answer **315**
Analyzing a Theme

3 I need to correct the errors because they confuse the reader.

2 I need to pay more attention to conventions so the reader can follow my writing.

1 I need to learn about conventions.

How do I punctuate direct quotations?

Use quotation marks to enclose direct quotations. An indirect or reworded quotation needs no quotation marks. Read the following paragraph and note the way the blue quotations are punctuated.

Colonel Sanders said, "Mr. Leghorn won't be with us tonight." The Colonel also told us that Leghorn had been detained in the kitchen. Everyone in the audience was upset by the news, and one of the dancers asked, "Can it be true?" Others wondered who could possibly call the square dance as well as the trusty Mr. L. Finally, a voice from the back of the room suggested that Mr. Terpsichore would make a good substitute. At that, Mr. Terpsichore stepped forward, looked at the band, and said, "Hit it, boys!"

 Copy the following paragraph, inserting any punctuation needed for quotations. (See 598.1 and 600.1.)

1   José's father sometimes exclaims, Life is hard! But José is not
2   discouraged. He feels that his muscles need to work hard, and
3   he tells his cousin Arnie that he will not rest until he finds a job.
4   Arnie then asks, Do you want to work together?

 Edit for conventions. Check your essay for punctuation, especially punctuation used in direct and indirect quotations.

Conventions
Commas are added and quotation marks are removed.

Finally when things calm down the announcer says that, "Squeaky came in first, and Gretchen was second." Squeaky suddenly realizes that . . .

LITERATURE

The distinction between direct quotations and paraphrasing (an indirect or reworded quotation) is an important one.

■ Emphasize that direct quotations are not necessarily dialogue.

■ Any phrases or sentences taken *directly* from a work of literature and used in a student's essay must be set off by quotation marks.

Model this on the board. Write a few sentences about a novel students have read, and include a direct quotation from the book that is not dialogue.

 Answers

José's father sometimes exclaims, "Life is hard!" But José is not discouraged. He feels that his muscles need to work hard, and he tells his cousin Arnie that he will not rest until he finds a job. Arnie then asks, "Do you want to work together?"

Struggling Learners

For practice in distinguishing between and punctuating direct and indirect quotations, play this game:

● One student says something (a direct quotation) and writes it on the board with correct punctuation.

● A second student paraphrases the statement as an indirect quotation (*She said that . . .*) and then writes the paraphrase on the board with correct punctuation.

● Repeat with different pairs of students.

Grammar Connection

Punctuating Quotations
■ **Proofreader's Guide** pages 588 (+), 598 (+), 600 (+)
■ *SkillsBook* pages 9–10
■ **CD** Punctuating Dialogue (+)

Editing Using a Checklist

Give students a few moments to look over the Proofreader's Guide in the back of the pupil's edition. Throughout the year, they can refer to the instruction, rules, and examples to clarify any checklist items or to resolve questions about their own writing.

Ask students to focus on one question at a time when they use the checklist. First they should check *every* sentence for end punctuation; then they should check *every* sentence for long introductory phrases or clauses, and so on.

Creating a Title

An effective title adds meaning and interest to an essay. Explain that although using the book or story title may be an easy way to get a title, it is not a very creative option. Have students
- create several possible titles,
- share them with other students, and
- get feedback on the most inviting version.

316

Editing Using a Checklist

 Edit Check your editing. On a piece of paper, write the numbers 1 to 12. If you can answer "yes" to a question, put a check mark after that number. If not, continue to edit for that convention.

Conventions

PUNCTUATION

_____ 1. Does each sentence have end punctuation?

_____ 2. Do I use commas after introductory word groups?

_____ 3. Do I use commas to set off parenthetical expressions?

_____ 4. Have I correctly punctuated my quotations?

_____ 5. Do I use apostrophes to show possession (*my parents' house*)?

CAPITALIZATION

_____ 6. Do I start all my sentences with capital letters?

_____ 7. Have I capitalized all proper nouns?

SPELLING

_____ 8. Have I spelled all my words correctly?

_____ 9. Have I double-checked the words my spell-checker may have missed?

GRAMMAR

_____ 10. Do I use correct forms of verbs (*lying in bed,* not *laying in bed*)?

_____ 11. Do my subjects and verbs agree in number? (*Mathematics is,* not *Mathematics are,* my favorite subject.)

_____ 12. Have I used the right words (*its, it's*)?

Creating a Title
- Use the title of the book or story: **"Raymond's Run"**
- Refer to the character: **Squeaky's Victory**
- Be creative: **Crossing the Line**

Grammar Connection

Subject-Verb Agreement
- **Proofreader's Guide** pages 690 (+), 692 (+)
- *Write Source* pages 475, 508, 509
- *SkillsBook* pages 97–98
- **CD** Subject-Verb Agreement

Restrictive and Nonrestrictive Phrases and Clauses
- **Proofreader's Guide** pages 584–585
- *SkillsBook* pages 7–8, 18
- **CD** Commas with Nonrestrictive Phrases

Advanced Learners

Point out that the third title example above, "Crossing the Line," employs a play on words. Challenge students to
- search for words in their essay that have double meanings, and
- think of similar types of expressions that could be used as a title for their essay.

(For example: "Bank On It" could be used for an essay about the virtue of financial responsibility; "Age-Old Wisdom" could be used for an essay about learning to appreciate the wisdom of grandparents.)

evaluate PREVIEW experience
react answer
Analyzing a Theme 317

Publishing
Sharing Your Essay

Now that you've finished writing, revising, and editing your essay, it's time to make it look good. You may also want to present your essay in some other form: illustrations, sharing with your classmates, or a submission to a literary magazine. (See the suggestions in the boxes below.)

Make a final copy. Follow your teacher's instructions or use the guidelines below to format your paper. (If you are using a computer, see pages 60–62.) Write a final copy of your essay and proofread it for errors.

Focus on Presentation

- Use blue or black ink and write neatly.
- Write your name in the upper left corner of page 1.
- Skip a line and center your title; skip another line and start your writing.
- Indent every paragraph and leave a one-inch margin on all four sides.
- Write your last name and the page number in the upper right corner of every page after the first one.

Make Illustrations
Draw one or more illustrations of key scenes in the development of the theme. Write a caption at the bottom of each illustration and post them in your classroom.

Submit Your Essay to a Literary Magazine
If your school has a literary magazine, submit your essay for publication. Write a cover letter explaining why classmates might be interested in your essay.

Share It with Your Classmates
Give a short introduction to the book or short story you wrote about and then read your essay to the class.

LITERATURE

Advanced Learners

There are many Web sites and Web quests created by students to publish responses to literature. Supervise students as they access appropriate sites by

- using an Internet search engine,
- referring to a student Web-site publication, or
- seeking help from a school librarian.

Be sure that you screen every site that students locate. Encourage students to publish their essays by adding a link to an existing Web site or by creating their own.

Allow students to be creative in deciding how to share their essays. Here are some possible suggestions:

- Organize a display of their illustrated work in a prominent location in the school.
- Present their responses to the class as a panel of literary experts discussing the works of literature.
- Put together an issue of a classroom magazine that focuses on works of literature.

Rubric for a Response to Literature

Remind students that a rubric is a chart that helps them evaluate writing.

- The rubrics in this book are based on a six-point scale, in which a score of 6 indicates an amazing piece of writing and a score of 1 means the writing is incomplete and not ready to be assessed.

- There is a strip in the rubric for each of the basic traits of writing—ideas, organization, voice, word choice, sentence fluency, and conventions.

A rubric can guide students as they write because it tells what elements to include in the writing and how to present them.

✻ Reproducible six-, five-, and four-point rubrics for responses to literature can be found on pages 753, 757, and 761.

Rubric for a Response to Literature

Use this rubric for guiding and assessing your writing. Refer to it whenever you want to improve your writing using the six traits.

Ideas

6 The ideas show a complete understanding of the reading.

5 The essay has a clear focus statement and all the necessary details.

4 The essay has a clear focus statement. Unnecessary details need to be cut.

Organization

6 All the parts work together to create an insightful essay.

5 The organization pattern fits the topic and purpose. All parts of the essay are well developed.

4 The organization pattern fits the topic and purpose. A part of the essay needs better development.

Voice

6 The voice expresses interest and complete understanding. It engages the reader.

5 The voice expresses interest in and understanding of the topic.

4 The voice expresses interest but needs to show more understanding.

Word Choice

6 The word choice reflects careful thinking about the reading.

5 The word choice, including the use of literary terms, creates a clear message.

4 The word choice is clear, but more literary terms would improve the essay.

Sentence Fluency

6 The sentences in the essay make the ideas really stand out.

5 The sentences are skillfully written and keep the reader's interest.

4 No sentence problems exist. More sentence variety is needed.

Conventions

6 Grammar and punctuation are correct, and the copy is free of all errors.

5 The essay has one or two errors that do not interfere with the reader's understanding.

4 The essay has a few careless errors in punctuation and grammar.

3 The focus statement is too broad. Unnecessary details need to be cut.	**2** The focus statement is unclear. More details are needed.	**1** The essay needs a focus statement and details.
3 The organization fits the essay's purpose. Some parts need more development.	**2** The organization doesn't fit the purpose.	**1** A plan needs to be followed.
3 The voice needs to be more interesting and express more understanding.	**2** The voice does not show interest in or an understanding of the topic.	**1** The writer needs to understand how to create voice.
3 The word choice is too general and more literary terms are needed.	**2** Little, if any, attention was given to word choice.	**1** The writer needs help with word choice.
3 A few sentence problems need to be corrected.	**2** The essay has many sentence problems.	**1** The writer needs to learn how to construct sentences.
3 The errors in the essay confuse the reader.	**2** The number of errors make the essay hard to read.	**1** Help is needed to make corrections.

LITERATURE

Technology Connections

Eval-U-Write can score student essays for four of the six traits:
- organization,
- word choice,
- sentence fluency, and
- conventions.

In this way, Eval-U-Write does the heavy lifting for you, so that you can focus on the ideas and voice of student writing.

To find out more about this subscription-based online tool, go to www.greatsource.com.

Evaluating an Analysis

Ask students if they agree with the sample self-assessment on PE page 321. If they agree with the criticisms, ask them to suggest improvements based on the comments in the self-assessment. If they disagree with any comment, ask them to explain why.

Possible suggestions:

Ideas **a direct quotation from Arnie**—Include a quotation that reveals Arnie's personality.

Organization **add an additional middle paragraph**—Illustrate the differences between José and Arnie.

Voice **more emotion in focus statement**—The differences between these two characters show that those who do honest work . . .

Word Choice **stronger verbs and modifiers**—José *is eager* to work . . . so the idea that Arnie will *take care of* that part *appeals to José*.

Sentence Fluency **vary sentence patterns**—In the third paragraph, change *Arnie is not only lazy* . . . to *Not only is Arnie lazy, but* . . .

320

Evaluating an Analysis

Read through the following analysis of a theme, focusing on the essay's strengths and weaknesses. Then read the student's self-evaluation on the next page. **(There may be errors in the essay below.)**

Honest Work

In the story "Born Worker," writer Gary Soto's main character, José, is a boy who comes from a hardworking family. José himself enjoys hard work, and even though his father complains, "Life is hard," the boy loves to use his muscles doing physical labor. His cousin, Arnie, thinks that he can make money without working. Soto's theme is that those who do honest work are more responsible than those who avoid it.

José wants to work whenever he is not in school. Arnie has a plan for both of them to make money. The plan is that Arnie will find jobs, José will do the work, and they will split the money. José hates asking people for jobs, so the idea that Arnie will do that part sounds good. They agree to give the plan a try, even though José will have to do all of the work.

Arnie gets them a job cleaning Mr. Clemens's swimming pool. While José is in the pool scrubbing the walls, Mr. Clemens accidentally falls in and hits his head on the bottom. José rushes to save the bleeding man, but Arnie screams that they should take off and leave him in the pool. Arnie disappears. José calls 911 and waits with Mr. Clemens, putting ice on his injured head. When the rescue team comes, Arnie suddenly reappears as though he had been there the whole time. He acts like he is in charge of Mr. Clemens's rescue. Arnie is not only lazy, he's also dishonest and irresponsible.

With Arnie telling his lies in the background, José thinks about his father, who "would have seen that José was more than just a good worker. He would have seen a good man." Gary Soto sees José, the "born worker," as a boy with a fine future. Arnie, however, will have a future full of trouble if he doesn't change.

Student Assessment

The assessment below is the student's evaluation of her essay, including her comments. The first comment is something positive, and the second comment is something she could improve. (The writer used the rubric and number scale on pages 318–319 to complete this assessment.)

5 Ideas

1. My focus states the theme.
2. A direct quotation from Arnie would help readers understand him.

4 Organization

1. My opening and closing express the theme in different ways.
2. One more middle paragraph would help show the differences between José and Arnie.

5 Voice

1. My voice creates a serious mood that fits the topic.
2. My voice sounds too unemotional in the focus statement.

4 Word Choice

1. My words are on the right level for my audience.
2. I need to choose stronger words, especially verbs and modifiers.

5 Sentence Fluency

1. My sentences are well developed, not short and choppy.
2. Too many of my sentences start with names.

6 Conventions

1. I think my paper is free of careless errors.
2. I'm not sure how to use commas around quotations.

Use the rubric. Assess your essay using the rubric on pages 318–319.

1 On your own paper, list the six traits. Leave room after each trait to write one strength and one weakness.

2 Then choose a number (from 1 to 6) that shows how well you used each trait.

LITERATURE

To give students additional practice with evaluating a response essay, use a reproducible assessment sheet (TE page 787) and one of the **benchmark papers** listed in the Benchmark Papers box below. You can use an overhead transparency while students refer to their own copies made from the copy masters. For your benefit, a completed assessment sheet is provided for each benchmark paper.

Struggling Learners

Before reviewing the assessment, work as a class to score the sample essay.

- Divide the class into six groups. Assign a writing trait to each group.
- Using the rubric on PE pages 318–319, each group lists a strength and a weakness for their assigned trait.
- Compare group comments with those of the student evaluator (writer).

Advanced Learners

Have students work in pairs to revise "Honest Work" using the comments in the sample student assessment. Then ask them to

- present their revised essays to the class, and
- ask classmates to assess the revised versions.

Benchmark Papers

Number the Stars (strong)
- TR 7A–7C
- TE pages 781–783

Across Five Aprils (fair)
- TR 8A–8C
- TE pages 784–786

Reflecting on Your Writing

Emphasize that students need to think about their work after they complete a final copy. Analyzing their writing strengths and weaknesses will help students improve their future work.

- Have students save their written reflections.
- Each time they prepare to write a new analysis, they should review their written reflections to know what they should work on.
- Students will notice that they are becoming more skilled writers over time.

322

Reflecting on Your Writing

Reflect on your finished analysis of a theme by completing each starter sentence below. These comments will help you check your progress as a writer.

My Analysis

1. The strength of my essay is . . .

2. The part that most needs change is . . .

3. The main thing I learned about writing an analysis of a theme is . . .

4. In my next response to literature, I would like to . . .

5. Here is one question I still have about writing an analysis of a theme:

6. Right now I would describe my writing ability as . . . (excellent, good, fair, poor)

evaluate *PREVIEW*
react **answer** experience **323**

Writing a Letter to an Author

Response to Literature
Writing a Letter to an Author

Have you ever gotten to the last page of a novel and wished it wouldn't end? What happens next? Do the characters have any more adventures? Why didn't the author write more? The best way to get answers to these questions is to write to the author.

Writing a letter to an author is a creative way to respond to literature. You can share what you liked most about the work and ask any questions you might have. Also, when you write a letter to an author, you switch roles. You're the writer for a change!

The following pages provide a sample letter to an author. Afterward, you will find guidelines to help you create your own letter.

Writing Guidelines

Subject:	**A book or short story**
Form:	**Letter**
Purpose:	**To show understanding and ask questions**
Audience:	**Author**

Objectives
- understand the reasons for writing a letter to an author
- use what was learned about writing in response to literature to write a letter to an author
- plan, draft, revise, edit, and share a letter to an author

A **letter to an author** is a creative way to gain a better understanding of a piece of literature. In a letter, students can share what they liked about the author's work and possibly get answers to any remaining questions.

Letter to an Author

Ask students to think about stories they have recently read. Brainstorm some questions they may have about a story when they come to the end of a book.

- What will the character(s) do next?
- Will changes in the characters last?
- Why did the characters behave as they did?

Ask students how they can find out information about authors (biographical information on book jacket, Internet, reference books about authors in the library).

Find out if students have ever written letters to a favorite author and whether they received any replies.

 Literature Connections

Mentor texts: To inspire your students in their letters to authors, read to them from *Dear Author: Students Write About the Books That Changed Their Lives,* from Weekly Reader's *Read* Magazine.

Letter to an Author

Writing a letter to an author is one way to gain a better understanding of a special book or short story that you have read. In this sample, Lupita shares her thoughts and feelings about Lois Lowry's book *The Giver*.

4214 Rose Lane
Highfield, IL 60600
October 11, 2010

Dear Ms. Lois Lowry,

Beginning

The beginning introduces the reader and gives her reason for writing to the author.

I am an eighth grader in Creekside Middle School. As part of a literature class assignment, we are supposed to write to the author of a book we've read this semester. Since I really enjoyed reading *The Giver,* I decided to write you.

Before I started the book, our teacher read to us from your 1994 Newbery Medal acceptance speech. We learned that you got the ideas for the book from several things. You remembered growing up in an American part of Tokyo, Japan, and secretly riding your bike to explore the city. You also got inspiration for *The Giver* from your dad. When he got old, your dad had lost most of his memory, but he seemed content. How did you turn those ideas into an entire book?

The first thing I noticed about *The Giver* was its cover. Our teacher told us that you took the picture of the old man on the cover. Who is that man? It looks like he is thinking about something very sad. On the corner of the cover, there are some bare trees. I wondered if the man was from that place. The cover made me curious about the story.

Middle

The middle provides the reader's response to the book.

I like how you told the story. At first, everything is perfect and there are no problems in the world. Everyone is taken care of and happy. When Jonas becomes the

Receiver, everything changes for him. He realizes that something is missing from the world. Jonas searches to discover what's going on. It was really hard for me to put the book down, since I wanted to keep reading.

At first I was disappointed by the ending, but then I realized that you were leaving it up to the reader. Each person can have his or her own ending. Are you planning to write a sequel to *The Giver* someday?

Our teacher told us about an interview you gave. You said, "Reading is what makes you a great writer." I think reading your work has made me a better writer. You also said that writing letters is a wonderful way to practice writing. I've started writing my grandmother a letter every week. I tell her stories about school, family, and friends. Thank you for the writing ideas and all the wonderful books you've written.

I look forward to reading more of your books.

Sincerely,

Lupita Marquez

Ending
The ending reflects on the importance of the book to the reader.

 Respond to the reading. Answer the following questions about the sample letter.

☐ **Ideas** (1) What book or short story does the writer talk about? (2) Where does the writer get her information?

☐ **Organization** (3) Where does the writer introduce herself and give her reason for writing?

☐ **Voice & Word Choice** (4) How does the writer personally connect with the author?

LITERATURE

 Respond to the reading.

Answers

Ideas 1. *The Giver* by Lois Lowry
2. from an acceptance speech made by the author, from the book and its cover, and from an interview the author gave

Organization 3. opening paragraph

Voice & Word Choice 4. She tells her impressions of the cover and the story, she asks the author questions, and she tells how the book has affected her.

Prewriting
Selecting a Literary Work

Work with students to generate a list of their favorite authors and books. Suggestions may include:

- Beverly Cleary: *Dear Mr. Henshaw*
- Louis Sachar: *Holes*
- Gary Paulsen: *Hatchet*
- Jack London: *The Call of the Wild*

Consider allowing students to include on their lists movies and the directors or producers.

Prewriting Gathering Details

These sentence starters will help students focus the story line. They can easily be applied to a movie as well as a printed story.

326

Prewriting Selecting a Literary Work

To get started, select a book or story you would like to write about. Lupita began by listing novels and stories she had recently read.

Topics List

Books and Stories	Author
Rocket Boys	Homer Hickman
"Rules of the Game"	Amy Tan
The Giver	Lois Lowry *

 Select a literary work. List books and short stories that you have read, along with the authors' names. Put a star (*) next to the author that you would like to write to. Have your teacher approve your choice.

Gathering Details

Sentence starters provide one way to gather information for a letter to an author. Lupita used sentence starters to think about *The Giver*.

Sentence Starters

> The most interesting thing about the background of this story is . . .
> *that it was based on growing up in Japan.*
> The first thing I noticed about the story was . . .
> *the picture of the old man on the cover.*
> The thing I liked most about the story was . . .
> *the way it was told.*
> I think that the ending . . .
> *is open-ended; you have to decide yourself.*
> This story is important to me because . . .
> *it made me want to read more and write more.*

 Gather details. On your own paper, complete each of the sentence starters above for your book or story. Also jot down questions to ask the author.

English Language Learners

If students struggle with any of the sentence starters, have them

- create a cluster diagram (for example, diagram background information or things they liked about the book), and
- use the information they generate in their clusters to complete the sentence starters.

Struggling Learners

For questions to ask the author, students should consider . . .

- one or more of the main characters actions,
- something one of the characters had said,
- a specific action or event in the story,
- the ending,
- why the author chose this story idea, or
- what other ideas interest him or her.

evaluate
react
PREVIEW experience
answer
Letter to an Author
327

Writing Creating Your First Draft

Now that you've selected a book and gathered details, you are ready to write the first draft of your letter. Follow the guidelines below.

- **Follow the correct format.** See the friendly letter formatting guidelines at the bottom of this page.
- **Use a polite but personable voice.** Write in a conversational voice, but avoid slang or incorrect English. Make sure your sentences are clear and complete.
- **Let your sentence starters guide your writing.** Use the sentences you completed on page 326 to help you develop each paragraph in your letter.
- **Ask questions.** Encourage the author to respond to your letter by asking questions.

 Write the first draft. Follow the format and guidelines on this page as you write the first draft of your letter.

Focus on the Traits

Organization A friendly letter has five basic parts. Use the following guidelines to format your letter.

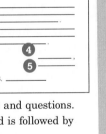

1. **Heading:** The heading appears in the upper right-hand corner and includes your address and the date.
2. **Salutation:** This polite greeting begins two lines below the heading. It starts with *Dear* and ends with a comma.
3. **Body:** The body identifies the writer and the reason for writing and includes details and questions.
4. **Closing:** The closing politely says good-bye and is followed by a comma. Common closings follow:
   Sincerely,   Your friend,   Regards,
5. **Signature:** The signature is your signed name.

✻ **P.S.:** A postscript gives an optional afterthought.

LITERATURE

Writing Creating Your First Draft

Point out that popular authors receive many letters from readers.

- Discuss how students can catch the attention of an author by writing in an enthusiastic voice and asking thought-provoking questions.
- Encourage them to show a sincere interest in and knowledge of the author's work, which will increase the possibility of getting a reply to their letter.

Focus on the Traits

Organization
Find each of the five basic parts of the **friendly letter** *(see below)* in the sample on PE pages 324–325. Have students pay attention to these specifics:

- The date is in the heading.
- The term *salutation* means the same as *greeting*; the salutation ends with a comma.
- Each paragraph begins with an indented line.
- *Sincerely* is often misspelled in the closing; it ends with *-ely*.

Teaching Tip: Friendly Letters

Students may have little experience in writing friendly letters if they are frequent users of e-mail and instant messaging. To give them practice in writing in this form, have students write a letter to a partner in the class.

Direct students to write a letter telling their partner about the book they've selected and the author they've chosen to write to.

Have students

- include the five basic parts of a friendly letter,
- use an appropriate voice and word choice to briefly describe the book and the questions they plan to ask the author, and
- "send" letters by delivering them to their partner's desk.

Revising Improving Your Writing

Encourage students to use this checklist as they revise their letters. Have them exchange their revised drafts with another student to get additional input about changes that might improve the letter.

Editing

Checking for Conventions

Correct conventions are critical because the letter may, in fact, be sent to an author or a professional writer.

- Insist that students take time to edit thoroughly.
- Set up writing conferences with as many students as possible to provide input at this final stage.

✳ For a review of some spelling rules, see PE page 642.

Publishing

Sharing Your Writing

Students may be unfamiliar with addressing an envelope. Provide the appropriate guidelines.

✳ To find out how to address an envelope, see PE page 577.

328

Revising Improving Your Writing

After you finish your first draft, revise it for the following traits.

- ☐ **Ideas** Does my letter focus on one short story or book?
- ☐ **Organization** Do I follow the proper format? (See page **327**.)
- ☐ **Voice** Do I sound as though I have read the book or short story and understand it?
- ☐ **Word Choice** Are my words clear and accurate?
- ☐ **Sentence Fluency** Are my sentences complete? Do they have different lengths and beginnings? Do they flow well?

 Revise your letter. Ask yourself the questions above. Revise your letter to improve these traits of writing.

Editing Checking for Conventions

When you edit your letter to an author, focus on the *conventions* of your writing.

- ☐ **Conventions** Have I checked punctuation and capitalization? Have I checked spelling and grammar?

 Edit your work. Ask yourself the questions above as you edit your letter. Make a clean final copy and proofread it.

Publishing Sharing Your Writing

Once you've finished your letter, share it. Here are some suggestions.

- Send the letter to the author if your author is still living. Check online to find the contact information for the author's publisher. Address your envelope to the author in care of (c/o) the publisher. Then attach appropriate postage and send it.
- Read the letter to your class. If any other students have read the same book or story, discuss your questions with them.
- Post the letter on a school or local library bulletin board. Ask permission first.

 Share your ideas. Choose one of the publishing ideas above or come up with your own.

Grammar Connection

Compound and Complex Sentences

- **Proofreader's Guide** pages 698 (+), 700 (+)
- *Write Source* pages 516 (+), 517 (+)
- *SkillsBook* pages 113–114, 115–116

Indefinite Pronouns

- **Proofreader's Guide** pages 710–711, 712 (+), 714 (+)
- *Write Source* pages 474 (+), 475 (+)

- *SkillsBook* pages 147–148, 151–152
- **CD** Pronouns—3

Punctuation

- **Proofreader's Guide** pages 578–615 (+)
- *Write Source* pages 500–510 (+)
- *SkillsBook* pages 39–40

Using the Right Word

- **Proofreader's Guide** pages 652–655

Response to Literature
Across the Curriculum

An old saying goes, "A picture is worth a thousand words." That's because a picture can show something that happened a thousand miles away or a hundred years ago. By responding to pictures, articles, and Web sites, you can learn about the world around you. In social studies, you can study photos from another time or place. In science, you can read articles that push the frontiers of technology. And by exploring the Web, you can see things on the other side of the world—or the universe!

After working with the different forms of response writing on the following pages, you will get a chance to practice responding to a timed test prompt.

What's Ahead

- **Social Studies:** Responding to a Historical Photo
- **Science:** Summarizing a Science Article
- **Practical Writing:** Evaluating a Web Site
- **Writing for Assessment**

Copy Masters/ Transparencies

Sensory chart (TE p. 331)

Across the Curriculum

Objectives
- apply what students have learned regarding writing about literature
- practice writing for assessment

The lessons on the following pages provide samples of response writing students might do in different content areas. The particular form used in one content area may also be used in another area (for example, students can summarize an article in social studies just as well as in science).

Assigning these forms of writing will depend on
- the skill level of your students,
- the subject matter they are studying in different content areas, and
- the writing goals of your school, district, or state.

Social Studies:
Responding to a Historical Photo

Analyze the sample paragraph response.

- Have students read the topic sentence and the closing sentence.
- Point out that the topic sentence (the first sentence) introduces the subject of the photograph.
- Note that the last sentence explains what the photo can teach the viewer.

Ask students to find the phrases used to clearly describe the **photograph details** *(see below)* that relate to the topic sentence. Have students list the words and phrases that help readers visualize the picture. (Possible answers include: dark room, crowded, smoky, covered with dirt, shirt with a big hole, ripped, tired.)

Literature Connections

Mentor text: To further explore the relationship between stories and visual arts such as photography and drawing, see *Sketching Stories, Stretching Minds: Responding Visually to Literature* by Phyllis Whitlin.

330

Social Studies:
Responding to a Historical Photo

Social studies explores the way people have lived in different places and at different times. A picture tells a story without any words. You can use your observational skills and information from social studies class to write a response to a historical photograph.

In her social studies textbook, Sydney saw a picture of kids working at midnight in a glass factory in the early 1900s. It showed her what life must have been like for kids who had to work to help their families make enough money.

No Time to Play

The **beginning** introduces the photo.

In the past, kids worked long hours in factories with terrible working conditions. This picture from 1908 shows child laborers at midnight in a glass factory. The dark room is crowded with pipes, tables, glass bottles, and a brick oven.

The **middle** describes the photo.

Everything is smoky and covered with dirt. One of the boys wears a shirt with a big hole on the shoulder. His pants are ripped, too. A few of the boys look up toward the camera, very tired and a little surprised. Maybe they are wondering why someone would take a picture of them. Pictures like this made people want to outlaw child labor. Today, kids spend

The **ending** reflects on the photo's value.

their time at school or at home with family and friends. Even though a picture may be sad to look at, it can teach valuable lessons about the country's past.

Teaching Tip: Photograph Details

Writing a response to a photograph requires careful visual study and use of strong, specific adjectives and nouns. Help students practice observing details and describing them in clear language.

- Show the class a historical photograph, preferably one like the sample that contains several details.
- Let students study it for 5 or 10 seconds.

- Put the photograph out of sight, and then have students do a 1-minute freewrite to describe the details in the photograph as clearly as they can.
- Compare student descriptions and then show them the photograph again.
- Discuss how students could improve their descriptions.
- Repeat this exercise with different photographs.

evaluate *PREVIEW* experience
react **answer**

331

Writing in Social Studies

Writing Tips

Before you write . . .

- **Choose a picture.**
  Search through your history book or the Internet to find a historical picture to write about.

- **Imagine being a person in this picture.**
  Think about what it must have been like to live in another time and place.

- **Think about why this picture is important.**
  Ask yourself what this picture shows about the society of the time. Ask yourself how pictures such as this one may have brought about the changes evident in today's society.

During your writing . . .

- **Focus on the main features of the picture.**
  Start with the first thing you notice. Describe it and then shift to other details in a logical fashion.

- **Share interesting details.**
  Let the images in the photograph suggest sounds, smells, textures, and other details.

After you've written a first draft . . .

- **Revise your response.**
  Make sure you have connected the picture's historical setting to the present day. Check to see that your details appear in the best possible order.

- **Double-check important facts.**
  Make sure the names and dates in your paragraph are correct.

- **Check for correctness.**
  Check the conventions in your response. Then make a final copy of your work and proofread it for errors.

 Search your textbook, the library, or the Internet for a historical photograph that interests you. Look for information that can help you understand the historical significance of the picture. Write a paragraph that responds to the photo. Use the information above as a guide.

LITERATURE

Writing Tips

Discuss with social studies teachers and the school librarian the selection of photographs available to students in their textbooks or other school materials.

- Look over the choices to be sure they are appropriate for the assignment.
- Invite each student to share with the class the photograph he or she chose and the accompanying paragraph response.

You may wish to provide photocopies of the reproducible sensory chart on TE page 793 to help students include a variety of details.

 **Answers**

Paragraphs will vary, but students should refer to details in the picture and explain why the picture is important.

Advanced Learners

Ask a social studies teacher what era students are currently studying. Have each student

- find a photograph from that time period (or a realistic illustration, if they are studying an era before photography was invented),

- write a response to the photograph, and
- organize the photographs and response paragraphs as a classroom collection to be posted in the social studies classroom or school library.

Science: Summarizing a Science Article

Make sure that students understand how to write an effective topic sentence for a summary. The sentence should

- give the name of the article and the author's name, if known;
- state the main idea or overview; and
- contain a strong main verb.

Examine the topic sentence in the sample paragraph "Battery Included." Have students find the key features (the author's name is not given here).

Tell students to avoid writing a weak topic sentence that begins like this: This article was about . . .

Science: Summarizing a Science Article

Every day, magazines, newspapers, and Web sites report the fascinating discoveries of science. Summarizing an article can help you understand it. The following article, "Batteries Driving the Future," explains the technology of hybrid cars. The paragraph "Battery Included" summarizes the article.

Batteries Driving the Future

As the world's population swells, the demand for cars increases. More cars mean more pollution, but scientists and the automotive industry have found a way to reduce this problem: the hybrid car.

Hybrid cars use an electric motor and a gasoline engine. The electric motor is powered by a long-lasting battery, which is charged by a generator built into the car. This combination of devices provides an extremely efficient use of gasoline. Here's how hybrid cars work:

- When a hybrid car is starting and going slowly, the electric motor powers the car.
- At higher speeds, the gasoline engine takes over. The engine sends power to a generator, which charges the battery.
- If the car is going uphill or speeding up, the electric motor and gasoline engine work together.
- During slowing down and braking, the generator charges the battery.

Hybrid cars are becoming increasingly popular as consumers seek vehicles that lessen environmental impact. Their sleek designs make them visually appealing and aerodynamic. The fuel efficiency of hybrid cars reduces reliance on gasoline. As hybrids grow in popularity, there's no doubt that batteries will drive the future of the automotive industry.

Topic Sentence

Body

Closing Sentence

Battery Included

The article "Batteries Driving the Future" explains how hybrid cars use an electric motor and a gasoline engine. The electric motor, which works at low speeds, gets its power from a battery. The battery doesn't need to be plugged in, since it is charged by a generator in the car. Hybrid cars have a smooth shape for both style and aerodynamics, and they use less fuel, making them better for the environment. The world and its people are beginning to benefit from hybrid cars.

evaluate react answer experience **333**
Writing in Science

Writing Tips

Before you write . . .

- **Gather science magazines.**
  Check your school library for magazines such as *National Geographic* or *Current Science*. Also check the Internet for scientific articles from sources such as www.nasa.gov. Your teacher may know of other sources.
- **Read the article and take notes.**
  Read your selection once to get the overall idea of the article. Then reread the material and take notes about important information.
- **Organize your paragraph.**
  Identify the main idea of the article. Gather only the details needed to support the main idea.

During your writing . . .

- **Focus on the main idea.**
  Use your topic sentence to identify the main idea in the article. In the body, include key details to support it. End with a clear closing sentence.
- **Be brief.**
  Make sure your summary is only about a third of the length of the original article.

After you've written a first draft . . .

- **Check your facts.**
  Make sure that you have accurately recorded key facts from the article.
- **Check for conventions.**
  Correct any errors in spelling, punctuation, capitalization, and grammar.

 Find an interesting science article in a magazine or on the Internet. Read the article and write a summary of it using the tips above as a guide. Make sure to double-check the facts in your response.

LITERATURE

Writing Tips

To help students identify important information for summaries, they should . . .

- pay special attention to headings, words in italics or boldface, and the first word of each paragraph;
- learn the meaning of any new words; and
- ask themselves: *What main idea in the reading connects all of the details?*

Before students begin to write their summary, make sure they understand the difference between **summarizing and paraphrasing** *(see below)*.

 Answers

Summaries will vary but should present a main idea supported by accurate facts.

Teaching Tip: Summarizing vs. Paraphrasing

Remind students that when they summarize an article, they must use their own words and be careful not to plagiarize. In addition, remind them of the difference between summarizing and paraphrasing.

- Explain that summarizing is writing the main idea of an article briefly, in their own words. It is a way of noting the overall idea of an article and providing material that supports that idea. It is shorter than the article.
- Paraphrasing is using their own words to repeat all of the information in a passage.

Advanced Learners

To help students find an interesting science article in a magazine, suggest that they use the *Readers' Guide to Periodical Literature*. This reference work is available in print and electronic formats. Students can look up any subject area, and article titles and sources will be listed. Guide them in selecting articles that are at an appropriate reading level.

Practical Writing:
Evaluating a Web Site

Ask students to discuss the three purposes of Web sites (inform, persuade, entertain). Ask the following questions:

- What kind of site do you use when you do research for a history report? (one that informs)
- Why is it important to know if the purpose of a Web site is to persuade? (The site may not present objective information.)
- What kind of site would you visit when you want to read about your favorite movie star? (one that entertains)

Go over the evaluation form with students. Make sure that students understand terms such as *navigation* (ease in finding one's way around a site) and *layout* (how text and graphics are arranged on the screen).

Practical Writing:
Evaluating a Web Site

Web sites combine words and graphics to inform, persuade, or entertain. One student filled out the following form to evaluate a Web site about origami.

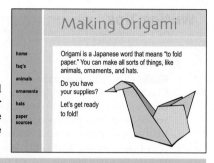

Making Origami

Origami is a Japanese word that means "to fold paper." You can make all sorts of things, like animals, ornaments, and hats.

Do you have your supplies? Let's get ready to fold!

home
faq's
animals
ornaments
hats
paper sources

Web Site Evaluation

Complete this form by filling in the subject of the Web site, circling its purpose, and rating its parts. Then add your overall comments at the bottom.

Web-site subject and address: *Origami, www.origami.hby.net*

Purpose:	inform	persuade	(entertain)

Information

incomplete	1	2	(3)	4	5	thorough

Navigation

confusing	1	2	(3)	4	5	simple

Layout

distracting	1	2	3	(4)	5	helpful

Text (words)

muddled	1	2	3	4	(5)	legible

Graphics (pictures)

dull	1	2	3	(4)	5	engaging

Colors

boring	1	2	3	(4)	5	appealing

The strong points: *The green and gold colors grabbed my attention. The different letter style for the title makes it stand out.*

Possible improvements: *Information about what supplies are needed and what to click next should be included.*

Practical Writing **335**

Writing Tips

If you are asked to evaluate a Web site, use the following tips to guide you through the process.

Before you write . . .

● **Study the form you will be using.**
If you are given a form, review it so that you know which details to judge.

● **Review the Web site.**
Look carefully at the site's information, navigation method, layout, and so forth. Use the form to guide you.

During your writing . . .

● **Follow all of the directions.**
Complete the whole form.

● **Make your comments clear.**
Give criticism that could improve the site.

After you've written a first draft . . .

● **Double-check your answers.**
Make sure your responses are clear and complete.

 Review the evaluation form on page 334. Then study the Web page below. On your own paper, write at least two "strong points" and two "possible improvements" for the Web page.

 Lawrence Middle School

home calendar clubs courses schedule library sports staff contact

The field trip to Chicago is coming up. We'll visit the Museum of Natural History. They have full-size dinosaur skeletons on display. Be sure to get your permission slip in soon.

LITERATURE

Writing Tips

Note that some Web sites are more reliable than others. Encourage students to use sites with addresses that end in *.gov, .edu,* or *.org* whenever possible.

■ Have students evaluate this text's related Web site at **www. thewritesource.com**.

■ Supervise students when they evaluate other Web sites.

■ Ask a school librarian to recommend appropriate sites for students to evaluate.

Try IT Answers

Possible answers:

Strong points:
■ very legible type
■ attractive design
■ many links on the site

Possible improvements:
■ Provide a link to a permission slip that can be printed out.
■ Tell where and when to turn in the permission slip.
■ Include detailed information about the field trip.
■ Provide links to the museum and/or sites that offer data about Chicago for tourists.

Writing for Assessment

If your students must take school, district, or state assessments this year, focus on the writing form on which they will be tested.

Find out whether writing notes directly on a state test is possible. Discuss other options with students. They may be required to include a graphic organizer or instructed to write notes on a separate piece of notebook paper instead.

336

Response to Literature
Writing for Assessment

On some state and school tests, you may be asked to read a story and write a response to it. The next two pages give you an example of such a test. Read the directions, the story, and the student's comments (in blue). Then read the student's response on pages 338–339.

Response to Literature Prompt

DIRECTIONS:
- Read the following story.
- As you read, make notes. (Your notes will not be graded.)
- After reading the story, write an essay about it. You have 45 minutes to read, plan, write, and proofread your work.

When you write, focus on the author's message in the story and show your insight into the characters and ideas. Use clear organization and support your focus with examples from the text.

It Wasn't About Fish

Jake sat on his front porch and watched the road. "Any time now." Under his left elbow was a bag stuffed with a week's worth of clothes and a pair of hip waders. Under his right elbow was a five-gallon bucket loaded with a tackle box and three rods, broken down to fit in Dad's hatchback.

✱ "Where is he?" Jake muttered, checking his watch.

"Maybe he decided to cancel."

Jake glanced irritably over his shoulder to see his little sister grinning at him through the living room window. Her blond hair stuck out in ponytails on the sides of her face. Jake shook his head. "Yeah, right. Not two years in a row." ← Canceled before

Sarah vanished from the window and opened the front door, dragging her own pack.

"You're not going, Sarah. Mom said you couldn't."

"It's not up to Mom," she replied, sitting down beside the fishing gear. "Dad gets to decide."

English Language Learners

Provide help as necessary with the fishing terms, slang, and other difficult words and phrases in the sample story:

- hip waders (long boots worn when fishing in a stream)
- tackle box (a case for holding fishing lures, hooks, and other supplies)
- hatchback (a car that has a back window that opens like a door)
- muscle in on (intrude upon)
- spring-break trip (a trip taken during spring school vacation)
- gut a fish (remove the organs from a dead, freshly caught fish)
- a still lake (a quiet, smooth lake with no waves)
- cracking the door (opening the door just a little bit)
- felt rotten (felt bad or ashamed)
- eyes were brimming (eyes were full of tears about to fall)
- fire up (start the engine)

evaluate
react   answer   experience   **337**
Writing for Assessment

Just what I need, Jake thought, *a 10-year-old sister trying to muscle in on my spring-break trip.* "You're not going. You'll get to go when you're 11. I have one more year, just me and Dad." Since the separation, Jake and Sarah had had to fight over chances like these. "Besides, you don't even like fishing."

"Maybe I do," she said. "I just need somebody to show me how."

Jake leaned back, smiling cruelly. "All right, Sis—first I'll teach you how to put worms on a hook. Then I'll teach you how to gut a fish and skin it and cut off its head."   ↖ Not nice

"Gross!" Sarah said, retreating into the house.

Laughing, Jake sighed and settled in. The fact was, he wasn't crazy about any of that stuff, either. Fishing was more about sitting in a boat with Dad and just talking, just being together on a still lake. It wasn't about fish.

"Where is he?"   He knows.

The phone rang. Jake felt his breath leave in a great gush. He knew what this call was about, even before Mom answered it. His teeth creaked against each other as he waited for the inevitable.

"Honey," Mom said, cracking the door open behind him. "Sorry. That was your dad. He's stuck at work again. He's going to have to cancel the trip. I'm sorry, Jakey."

"Don't call me Jakey," he snapped, crouching forward as if he'd just been punched in the gut. He caught his head in his hands. *Instead of fishing, I'll be stuck at home all week with Little Miss—*

The door creaked open again, and soft footsteps came on the porch behind Jake. Sarah sank down beside the fishing gear. She picked at her pack of clothes. "I wanted him to change his mind."

Jake's face flushed with anger. "You wanted him to cancel?"

Sarah stared at him, her eyes wide between her ponytails. "No, Jake. I wanted him to take me along, too."

The red in Jake's face dissolved. *Sarah wants this trip as much as I do.* Jake suddenly felt rotten. "You really want to learn to fish?"

Sarah's eyes were brimming as she nodded.

"Well, I can teach you. I know everything Dad knows."

"Honest?"   ↖— Thinks about someone else

"Sure." Jake stood up, lifting Sarah's pack and his own in one hand. His other hand hoisted the fishing gear. "Mom, fire up the minivan. I'm going to teach you two how to fish!"

LITERATURE

Discuss the notes that have been made on the sample test. Discuss why these particular words, phrases, and sentences are marked. (Possible answers: They provide details about background and the current situation, help the reader focus on what is going on between and within the characters, and highlight the changes in the main character.)

Ask students these questions:

- Do you agree with the selection of parts that have been marked?
- Would you highlight any other parts of the story?
- Would you ignore any of the ones that are underlined or circled?

Ask students to find two places in the sample essay where the writer uses quotations. Reinforce the idea that using quotations from the text can also help with writing effective conclusions.

- Ask students to find a quotation from the story on PE pages 336–337 that they could add to the last paragraph of the sample response. They might need to revise the last paragraph to make the quotation work.

- Show them how to "slide in" the quotation. (Possible last sentence: He turns his disappointment into a positive experience when he tells his mom and Sarah, "I'm going to teach you two how to fish!")

- Ask students to decide whether adding a quotation improves the overall feel of the essay and the conclusion in particular.

- Point out that sometimes a quotation is effective, but at other times it is not useful. Students must use their judgment as writers to make that decision. Emphasize that when they are uncertain, they should ask a writing partner for another opinion.

338

Student Response

The following essay shows a student response to the story "It Wasn't About Fish." Note how the student uses details from the story to support the focus.

Beginning

The first paragraph names the story and gives a focus statement (underlined).

"It Wasn't About Fish" is a coming-of-age story in which a big disappointment tests the main character. Jake's father, who is separated from Jake's mother, had promised to take the boy on a fishing trip. Jake is eager to be with his dad and away from his 10-year-old sister. Then Jake's dad calls to cancel the trip for the second year in a row. The way that Jake handles this disappointment shows that he is growing up.

Middle

The middle paragraphs include examples and details from the story to explain characters and themes.

At first, Jake is only thinking about himself. He has packed all his things and is waiting impatiently for his dad to drive up. When Jake's sister, Sarah, says she wants to go on the trip, too, he tells her she can't. He isn't paying any attention to her feelings. Sarah doesn't give up, so Jake even scares her off by telling her, "I'll teach you how to gut a fish and skin it and cut off its head." Jake wants the fishing trip all to himself.

When Jake's dad calls to cancel the trip, Jake starts thinking in a different way. First of all, he is crushed. He feels abandoned. Afterward, when Sarah comes out, Jake gets angry. He thinks she wanted their dad to cancel. Really, she wanted to go along. Once Jake sees that Sarah feels as left out as he does, he starts to act more mature. Instead of just thinking about himself, Jake actually thinks about spending more time with his mom and his little sister.

I think the title tells a lot about the theme of this story. Jake realized that the trip "wasn't about fish," but about spending time with his dad. When the trip is canceled, Jake realizes he can go fishing anyway with the rest of his family. Instead of counting on his dad to teach him, Jake becomes the teacher.

At the beginning, Jake thinks only about himself and is pretty unhappy. By the end, he is thinking about others, and he is happy. Jake has learned that the trip is about being with family.

Ending
The ending sums up the character's change and the theme.

Respond to the reading. Answer the following questions about the student response.

☐ Ideas (1) What is the focus of the student's response? (2) What feelings does this student describe?

☐ Organization (3) How did the notes on pages 336–337 help the student organize the response?

☐ Voice & Word Choice (4) What words or phrases from the story does the writer quote? (5) Were these examples effective?

LITERATURE

Respond to the reading.

Answers

Ideas **1.** that Jake grows up through dealing with his disappointment by thinking of others **2.** disappointment, selfishness, impatience, anger, empathy, happiness

Organization **3.** helped gather details and retell the important points in the story to support the interpretation of the theme

Voice & Word Choice **4.** his words about fishing to discourage Sarah

5. Yes, because they show how little Jake thinks of Sarah's feelings at that point and highlight the change in his attitude toward her at the end.

Practice Writing Prompt

Point out that students must approach writing-on-demand differently from open-ended writing assignments.

Give students the same amount of time to write their response essays as they will be allotted on school, district, or state assessments. Break down each part of the process into clear chunks of time. For example, you might give students

- 15 minutes for note taking and planning,
- 20 minutes for writing, and
- 10 minutes for editing and proofreading.

Tell students when time is up for each section. Start the assignment at the top of the hour or at the half-hour to make it easier for students to keep track of the time.

Practice Writing Prompt

Response to a literature prompt. Carefully read the directions below. Use 10 minutes at the beginning to read the story, make notes, and plan your writing. Also leave time at the end to proofread your work.

DIRECTIONS:

- Read the following story.
- As you read, make notes *on your own paper.*
- After reading the story, write an essay about it. You have 45 minutes to read, plan, write, and proofread your work.

When you write, focus on the author's message in the story and show your insight into the characters and ideas. Use clear organization and support your focus with examples from the text.

Mountain Encounter

Keira leaned against a large boulder and gasped for breath. She stared at the clear blue sky overhead. A small bird flew along, disappearing into the trees. Keira sighed and wished that she could fly like that bird. Instead, she was stuck here, slogging along on the trail. She looked ahead at the dirt path that switched back and forth up the steep mountainside. Her parents and little brother, Ethan, were already at the next bend.

"C'mon, Keira!" shouted Ethan. He smirked back at her as he skipped along the path.

Taking a deep breath, Keira pushed herself away from the coolness of the boulder. Her feet ached with each step. Her back was hot and sweaty under a backpack that held snacks, a bottle of water, sunscreen, and her camera. "Why did I have to come along?" Keira grumbled as she stumbled over a tree root. She just couldn't keep up with her family on these hikes. They set one pace, and Keira set another.

The voices of her family echoed from the trail ahead, and her mother's laughter floated down through the trees. Keira glared at her own feet. Puffs of dust rolled up around the boots with each arduous step. If only she could catch up . . .

Thirty agonizing minutes later, Keira slouched on a rock. "I'm taking another break!"

A faint response came from the trail ahead: "We're at the next lookout point. We'll wait for you here."

At the next lookout point . . . What beautiful things were they seeing while Keira was stuck in the dust of the trail? She slid her backpack off and grabbed her water bottle. The water was warm and tasted like plastic. Yuck. She spit it onto the ground and watched the water slowly seep into the dirt.

Maybe next year, I won't come on the family vacation. Keira reached for her backpack. Then her mouth dropped open in shock.

Just a few feet ahead on the trail stood a doe and two fawns. The deer stared at Keira with their soft brown eyes. The doe waited as her fawns skipped across the trail. They were so close, Keira wanted to reach out and touch their velvety reddish-brown coats. Instead, she held her breath and watched in quiet wonder. The fawns were so tiny and delicate. She couldn't believe how fragile they looked, and yet they playfully hopped and bounced about. All too soon, the fawns wandered off with the doe patiently following behind. As suddenly as they had appeared, the deer faded away into the woods.

Keira stared in amazement at the empty trail.

"C'mon, Keira!" Ethan called from ahead. "You're missing the view."

Nope, she thought, *I have my own view.* But out loud she replied, "I'm coming!" Keira smiled and started back up the trail, walking at her own pace.

LITERATURE

Remind students that they will take notes on a piece of notebook paper. Advise them to number the paragraphs and to refer to them that way in their notes in order to save time.

- Recommend that they look for a strong quotation to support the theme of the literature as they take notes.
- Suggest that they include the quotation in their conclusion.

Creative Writing Overview

Unit Objectives

The writing standards listed below are based on a blending of state and NCTE standards.

- Use lists and charts to generate and organize ideas.
- Demonstrate an understanding of story patterns and elements of fiction.
- Choose a conflict, and present a character through internal and external dialogue and actions.
- Use literary devices, such as dialogue, figurative language, and poetic sounds, effectively.
- Gather sensory details and use poetry techniques to write a free-verse poem and other forms of poetry; and revise, edit, and share poems.

Writing Forms

- short story
- poems

Focus on the Traits

- **Ideas** Presenting a character and a conflict clearly through dialogue, thoughts, and action
- **Organization** Building to a high point (moment of change) and then ending quickly
- **Voice** Sounding natural, showing the writer's personality and originality
- **Word Choice** Using action words to show rather than tell
- **Sentence Fluency** Experimenting with special poetic techniques to create an appealing rhythm
- **Conventions** Checking for errors in punctuation, capitalization, spelling, and grammar

Note: For specifics about reading the chart below, see page TE 33.

Suggested Creative Writing Unit (Three Weeks)

| Day | Writing and Skills Units | In the *Write Source* book | | | On the CD-ROM | *SkillsBook* grammar practice pages |
		Pages	Proofreader's Guide—basic grammar rules	Basic Grammar practice	Interactive Grammar Exercises	
1	**Writing Stories** (Model)	343–345				
2–3	**Short Story** (Prewriting)	346–347				
4–5	(Writing)	348				

WEEK 1

Day	Writing and Skills Units	In the *Write Source* book			On the CD-ROM	*SkillsBook*
		Pages	Proofreader's Guide—basic grammar rules	Basic Grammar practice	Interactive Grammar Exercises	grammar practice pages
6–7	(Revising)	349				
	Skills Activities: Punctuating Dialogue		588 (+), 598 (+), 600 (+)		Punctuating— Dialogue (+)	
	Interjections		746 (+)		Commas to Set Off . . . Interjections . . .	181–182
	Correlative Conjunctions		744 (+)	496 (+), 497		177–178
	Sentences Variety (Kinds of Sentences)		579 (+), 580 (+)	518 (+)		109–110
	Sentence Combining (Compound and Complex)		698 (+), 700 (+)	516 (+), 517		69–70, 71–72, 179–180
8–9	(Editing, Publishing)	349				
	Skills Activities: Sentence Problems (Review)			502 (+), 503 (+), 504 (+)		81–82
	Subject-Verb Agreement			508 (+), 509 (+)	Subject-Verb Agreement (+)	99–100
10 opt.	Other Story Patterns	350				
1–2	**Writing Poems:** Free Verse Poem (Model)	353–354				
	(Prewriting)	355–356				
	(Writing) Prepositional Phrases	356	742 (+)	494, 519 (+)	Prepositions	174
3–4	(Revising)	357				
	Skills Activities: Parts of Speech Review		702–748 (+), 749	470–498 (+)		183–184
	Adverbs		736 (+), 738 (+)	490 (+), 492(+), 493 (+)		173
	Hyphens		608–609, 610 (+), 732 (+)		Hyphens (+)	33–34
5	(Editing)	357				
	Skills Activities: Spelling		642 (+)		Spelling Review—1	
opt.	*Writing a Found a Poem*	358				
opt.	*Other Forms— (Couplet, Circle)*	359		519 (+)		

WEEK 2

WEEK 3

Teacher's Notes for Creative Writing

This overview for creative writing includes some specific teaching suggestions for the unit.

Writing Stories (pages 343–352)

Young writers are encouraged to use their imaginations to invent stories through creative writing. This chapter contains a clear explanation of how stories develop, together with a model story, writing guidelines, story patterns, tips on how to improve a story, and the elements of fiction.

Writing Poems (pages 353–361)

Poetry comes in many shapes, sizes, and forms. This chapter offers students a thoughtful explanation of just what poetry is, showing them how to read and appreciate it, too. Writing guidelines, sample poems, and poetry techniques and forms complete this chapter.

Minilessons

We . . . They	Writing Stories

- **READ** the explanations about point of view on page 352 of your textbook. **WRITE** a brief story about a trip to a zoo, a lake, a store, or a park. **TELL** the story from a first-person point of view. Then **WRITE** the story in one of the third-person points of view.

Sounds That Sound the Same	Writing Poems

- **READ** the definition of alliteration on page 360 of your textbook. **WRITE** alliterative words to go with each of the following words: bank, lake, snake, and turtle. **COMPARE** your results with a classmate.

342

imagine
entertain

Creative Writing

show
create
discover

Creative Writing
Writing Stories

"I'm not a kid anymore!" At some time, you may have said these words to the adults in your life. But when you cross over from adolescence to adulthood, it's a gradual process. You may not even feel it happening. Even so, at some point you suddenly realize that you have grown up.

Stories about growing up are called "coming of age" stories. The main character has a significant experience, whether big or small, that makes him or her more mature. In this chapter, you will read a "coming of age" story and then develop a story of your own to share.

Writing Guidelines

Subject:	**Growing up**
Form:	**Short story**
Purpose:	**To entertain**
Audience:	**Classmates**

Copy Masters/ Transparencies

T-chart (TE pp. 346, 347)

Sensory chart (TE p. 355)

343

Writing Stories

Objectives
- understand the content and structure of a short story
- choose a topic (a coming-of-age experience) to write about
- plan, draft, revise, and edit a short story

A **short story** generally presents a main character and a conflict.
- The opening paragraphs introduce the character, setting, and conflict.
- Then the rising action, composed of a series of events or actions, builds toward a high point or a moment of change.
- At the high point, the character comes face-to-face with the conflict.
- The story ends soon after this climax with the main character having changed in some way.

Short Story

Ask students to think about the following questions as they read or listen to "Shifting Gears":

- How would you describe Ted at the beginning of the story? (Possible answers: excited, selfish, hopeful, insensitive)
- How would you feel in his place? (Answers will vary.)
- What is the high point of the story? (when Ted understands his father's feelings and feels ashamed of himself)
- How does Ted change? How would you describe him at the end of the story? (Ted recognizes his family's situation and appreciates his dad's efforts. He becomes unselfish, sensitive, and grateful.)

Short Story

The following story is about how a young man learns to be more sensitive to others in his family.

Shifting Gears

Beginning

The beginning introduces the characters, the setting, and the conflict.

Ted pressed his nose against the store window that stood between him and a metallic-blue 21-speed racer. "Look at that bike, Sam! I WANT that bike!"

"Get away from there before Mr. Huan makes you clean the drool from his store window!" His friend Samantha laughed and pulled Ted away.

"Well, my birthday's tomorrow, and I've been dropping a lot of hints at home, like ads and pictures of the bike. I've just got to have it so I can go anywhere I want!"

"Your dad's out of work," Sam said quietly, "and I bet that bike's awfully expensive."

Ted didn't answer. *Yeah*, he thought, *but you only turn 13 once. Mom and Dad always promised me something special when I became a teenager.* He jumped on a hydrant and balanced a moment before jumping down again. "He'll find a job soon."

Rising Action

The rising action builds the suspense.

When he got home, his parents were in the kitchen talking. Ted waved to them on his way to the living room. Flopping down on the couch, he dug between the cushions for the remote. As he flipped through TV stations, he caught snatches of his parents' conversation. There were words like "overqualified" and "mortgage" and something about unemployment checks. Ted turned the volume higher.

The next morning, Ted's father woke him. "Hey, Champ, Mom had to go to work early, so I'll be making your birthday breakfast. Do you want anything special? Maybe something with wheels?"

Ted was suddenly wide awake. He threw back the covers and bounded into the kitchen. There, clumsily wrapped in newspaper and tied with a crooked bow, was a bicycle-shaped package.

entertain create imagine discover
show **345**
Writing Stories

CREATIVE

"Dad!" Ted tore through the newspaper, and then suddenly stopped and stared. There stood not the shiny racing bike but a secondhand 10-speed. The chrome had been shined up, and the frame was freshly painted, but it was not new—and it was not what he had hoped for. There was an awkward silence as he stared at the gift shining hopefully amidst the crumpled newspaper.

He looked away, swallowing down a lump. *Dad knows I wanted a new bike,* he thought, *not an old used one.*

"I know it's not exactly what you wanted, but . . . " his dad's words trailed off. Ted looked up at him and saw his own disappointment mirrored in his father's eyes. He thought of the hours his father must have spent sanding and painting, shining and oiling, to give his son something special. Suddenly, he was ashamed of himself.

"Are you kidding, Dad?" Ted hugged his father. "Hey, now I can get a paper route and help out around here." It had been a long time since they had hugged, and Ted was surprised to find he was nearly as tall as his father. "Thank you, Dad!"

The phone rang, and Ted ran to answer it.

"Hi, Sam! Come on over and see my new bike! We can go for a ride down to the river." Ted looked over at his father, who smiled back as he picked up the crumpled paper.

High Point

The high point is when the main character has a moment of realization and moves toward adulthood.

Ending

The ending shows how the character has matured.

Respond to the reading. Review the story and answer the following questions.

- [ ] **Ideas** (1) What does Ted want? (2) What could keep him from getting it?
- [ ] **Organization** (3) What events make up the rising action? Name three.
- [ ] **Voice & Word Choice** (4) What words or phrases suggest the bike was disappointing? List at least two. (5) What statements suggest Ted has changed? List at least two.

Respond to the reading.

Answers

Ideas **1.** an expensive, new 21-speed racing bike
2. His dad is out of work and might not be able to afford it.

Organization **3.** Possible answers: Ted's parents talk about his dad's unemployment and money issues; his dad wakes him on his birthday; his gift is wrapped in newspaper; he unwraps the bike; it is a fixed-up, used 10-speed

Voice & Word Choice **4.** Possible answers: not the shiny racing bike, second-hand, not new, not what he had hoped for, old, used, not exactly what you wanted, saw his own disappointment, swallowing a lump
5. Possible answers: thought of the hours his father must have spent, he was ashamed of himself, hugged his father, I can get a paper route and help out, thank you, see my new bike

Prewriting *Finding a Character*

Remind students of the purpose of the prewriting stage in the writing process. (It's when the writer gets ready to write.)

Offer students an alternative to creating their own main character. Prepare slips of paper on which you describe a character and his or her qualities (appropriate to a "coming of age" story). Students may randomly choose a slip and consider using that character in their story.

Model additional characters using these as samples:

- an 8-year-old girl from another country: sad, curious, quiet, eager, worried, artistic
- a teenage boy starting in a new school: bright, moody, lonely, anxious, determined, resentful
- an injured athlete: bitter, frustrated, ambitious, strong, talented, confident, caring

Prewriting *Selecting a Conflict*

Provide photocopies of the reproducible T-chart on TE page 789. If students have trouble generating conflict ideas, refer them to the list of different kinds of conflicts on PE page 351.

Prewriting **Finding a Character**

When writing a story, you should first select a main character. Next make a quick list of qualities that person might have at the beginning of your story.

The writer of "Shifting Gears" chose a teenage boy as the main character for his story and made the following quick list. He underlined the qualities he decided to use for the character.

Quick List

> Character: *a boy turning 13, Ted*
>
> Qualities: <u>*active*</u>, <u>*heroic*</u>, <u>*selfish*</u>, <u>*unrealistic*</u>, <u>*enthusiastic*</u>,
>   *helpful, nasty, cheerful*

Make a quick list. Start with any type of person and list qualities that person might have. Underline the ones you might want to use.

Selecting a Conflict

Every story needs a conflict. A conflict is created when a character wants something and has to overcome an obstacle to get it. The writer of the story on pages 344–345 used a "What If?" chart to develop the conflict for his story.

"What If?" Chart

Character's Want	What If? (Conflict)
Character wants a new bicycle.	Parents feel it's not safe.
	* The father is unemployed (no money).
	The character has a physical handicap.

Create a "What If?" chart. Imagine what your character wants. Then list three or four conflicts that might keep the character from getting it. Select the conflict that you think would make the best story. (For more information on developing your story, see the plot-line graphic on page 351.)

English Language Learners

Be sure students understand the meaning of *conflict* in this context (a problem that needs to be solved). Clarify that story conflict does not necessarily mean that the characters are angry at each other. Point out the following:

- Ted and his father didn't argue.
- They had different needs and desires, and both of them had to work out a solution.

Advanced Learners

Ask students to brainstorm titles of stories they have read in which a conflict is created by something a character wants, and then have them explain the conflict. (For example, in *Sarah, Plain and Tall* by Patricia MacLachlan, Anna wants to convince Sarah to stay on the Plains as their new mother rather than return to her beloved ocean state.)

entertain create imagine discover
show **347**
Writing Stories

CREATIVE

Changing a Main Character

In a "coming of age" story, you need to focus on how your main character becomes more mature. One way to chart the change in your main character is to think about what he or she is like before and after the high point of the story.

The writer of "Shifting Gears" created a character chart to show the change in his main character. On the chart, he listed things that Ted said, thought, and did both before and after unwrapping his birthday present. The differences show that Ted is becoming more mature.

Character Chart

	What he says	What he thinks	What he does
Before	needs an expensive bike to go anywhere	doesn't want to be disappointed	avoids his parents and ignores what they are saying
After	will use the bike to get a job	realizes his father is also disappointed	hugs and thanks his father

Create a character chart. Make a chart like the one above, listing things your character could say, think, and do before and after the change.

Showing Rather Than Telling

When you focus on what a character does, you "show" instead of "tell." You can show your character's personality by describing *what* the person does and *how* he or she does it.

Instead of telling: **Kai felt happy.**

Show: **Kai jumped for joy.**
Kai smiled a huge grin.

Gather your details. Write down things you could have your character do to show the reader how the character feels. Write as many details as you can, even though you won't use them all. Select the details you think are clearest and most powerful.

Prewriting
Changing a Main Character

A character chart is a way to help the writer plan how to show changes in the character. Explain that students may

- list more details in the chart than they actually use in the story or
- revise the chart as they go along.

Prewriting
Showing Rather Than Telling

To review the concept of show, don't tell, invite students to participate in this group activity:

- Groups list details that show what a less vivid word would tell. (For the word *smart*, details could be *solves crossword puzzles in pen, rarely has to study for math tests,* and so on.)
- Groups share their lists, but not the less vivid word.
- Other groups guess which telling word the details reveal.

✳ For strategies about show, don't tell, see PE page 557.

English Language Learners

Help students focus on how a character may change during a story. Work with students to complete a reproducible T-chart on TE page 789. Discuss and contrast childish traits with mature traits. Ask these questions:

- How does a young child usually behave? (often impatient, self-centered; needs help in many basic activities)

What kinds of behaviors show that someone is more grown up? (Examples: can wait for things, sometimes thinks of others' needs, can take charge of many aspects of life)

Recording their ideas will help students figure out how to show changes on a character chart through specific words, thoughts, and actions.

Prewriting Using Dialogue

Point out similarities and differences between internal and external dialogue.

- In internal dialogue, the interrupter ("he thought") serves the same purpose as a speaker tag does in external dialogue.
- Words that would be within quotation marks in external dialogue could be underlined or italicized in internal dialogue if the writer really wanted to set these words off.

Compare the effects of the **dialogue** *(see below)* in "Shifting Gears" on PE pages 344–345. What does each kind add to the story? (External dialogue makes readers feel that they are there and gives insight into characters. Internal dialogue lets the reader share the character's thoughts.)

✱ To learn more about how to use dialogue, see PE page 556.

Writing

Developing Your First Draft

Remind students that the writing stage is when they get to develop their ideas on paper. Encourage students to refer to these tips whenever they begin to write.

348

Prewriting Using Dialogue

There are two types of dialogue. **External dialogue** is when people speak out loud. **Internal dialogue** is when the writer lets the reader know what the character is thinking.

Yeah, he thought, but you only turn 13 once.

 Write internal dialogue. Imagine what your character might be thinking at some point. Be sure the internal dialogue shows the reader something important about your character.

Writing Developing Your First Draft

Once you have developed a character and a conflict, you are ready to write your first draft. The following tips will help you.

1 Introduce your character and what he or she wants.
For example, the writer showed what Ted wanted through his actions.
Ted pressed his nose against the store window that stood between him and a metallic-blue 21-speed racer.

2 Introduce your conflict.
The writer used dialogue to present the obstacle.
"Your dad's out of work," Sam said quietly, "and I bet that bike's awfully expensive."

3 Use action verbs.
He jumped on a hydrant and balanced a moment before jumping down again.

4 Build to the high point.
Show the character's struggle leading up to the point of decision.
Suddenly, he was ashamed of himself.

 Write your first draft. Introduce your character and conflict. Be sure the conflict is clear, and use action to build to the point when your character changes.

Struggling Learners

Help students get started with their writing by making a storyboard.

- Fold a blank sheet of paper in fourths.
- Label each quarter of the paper *Beginning, Rising Action, High Point,* and *Ending.*
- In each section, sketch ideas for key events in each part of the plot before writing a draft.

Teaching Tip: Internal and External Dialogue

Students may need practice in writing internal and external dialogue. Write this dialogue on the board, but do *not* include the punctuation.

"Luke, please see me after class," requested Mrs. Reilly. "I'd like to speak with you about your essay."

"Okay," replied Luke.

- Direct students to punctuate the sentences.

- Then ask what Luke might think about this request. (He might worry that he had done poorly.)
- Invite students to add internal dialogue to show Luke's thoughts, and ask them to punctuate it correctly. (For example, *Well,* Luke thought, *I hope I didn't fail the assignment.*)

CREATIVE

Revising Improving Your Writing

Once you have finished your first draft, set it aside for a while. Later, look at your story with a fresh perspective and review it for the following traits.

☐ **Ideas** Do I clearly present the conflict? Do I show my character through dialogue, thoughts, and action?

☐ **Organization** Do I build up to the moment of change? Do I end quickly after the high point?

☐ **Voice** Does my voice (including dialogue) sound natural and keep the reader's interest?

☐ **Word Choice** Do my words fit the characters? The situation?

☐ **Sentence Fluency** Do my sentences smoothly move the reader along?

 Revise your story. Use the questions above as a guide when you revise your first draft.

Editing Checking for Conventions

After you finish revising your story, you should edit it for *conventions*.

☐ **Conventions** Have I begun each sentence with a capital letter? Have I ended each sentence with end punctuation and punctuated dialogue correctly? Have I checked my spelling?

 Edit your story. Use the questions above to guide your editing. Then use the tips below to write a title. Create a clean final copy, proofread it, and see page 129 for publishing ideas.

Creating a Title

Your title is your first opportunity to hook the reader, so make it memorable. Here are some tips for writing a strong title.

■ Use a metaphor: **Riding Through Life**
■ Borrow a line from the story: **Something Special**
■ Be creative: **Shifting Gears**

Revising Improving Your Writing

At the revising stage, students should be sure that they have clearly
■ presented the conflict;
■ shown the character through dialogue, thoughts, and actions; and
■ developed the plot, building to the high point.

Editing
Checking for Conventions

These questions target a few specific conventions.

✱ To focus on end punctuation, have students see PE pages 579–580.

Creating a Title

Discuss the metaphor in the first title, "Riding Through Life," comparing life to a bike ride. The story is about a bike and Ted's journey toward maturity in life.

Grammar Connection

Punctuating Dialogue
■ *Proofreader's Guide* pages 588 (+), 598 (+), 600 (+)
■ **CD** Punctuating Dialogue (+)

Interjections
■ *Proofreader's Guide* page 746 (+)
■ *SkillsBook* pages 181–182
■ **CD** Commas to Set Off-Interjections

Correlative Conjunctions
■ *Proofreader's Guide* page 744 (+)
■ *Write Source* pages 496 (+), 497
■ *SkillsBook* pages 177–178

Sentence Variety
■ *Proofreader's Guide* pages 579 (+), 580 (+)
■ *Write Source* page 518 (+)
■ *SkillsBook* pages 109–110

Sentence Combining
■ *Proofreader's Guide* pages 698 (+), 700 (+)
■ *Write Source* pages 516 (+), 517
■ *SkillsBook* pages 69–70, 71–72, 179–180

Sentence Problems
■ *Write Source* pages 502 (+), 503 (+), 504 (+)
■ *SkillsBook* pages 81–82

Subject-Verb Agreement
■ *Write Source* pages 508 (+), 509 (+)
■ *SkillsBook* pages 99–100
■ **CD** Subject-Verb Agreement

Story Patterns

To help students remember **story patterns** *(see below),* have them make a story-pattern booklet:

1. Hold a piece of paper horizontally and fold it into thirds like a business letter. Then fold the thirds in half to make six rows.
2. Unfold the paper and then fold it in half vertically. Unfold it again to find two columns, each with six boxes.
3. To make flaps, cut along the horizontal creases in the left column, stopping at the vertical fold.
4. Label the front of each flap: *Coming of Age, Rescue, Union, Underdog, Decision, Rivalry.*
5. On the inside of each flap, write a brief description of the pattern. In the facing box on the right-hand side, write a one-sentence summary of a story idea for each pattern.

 **Answers**

Answers will vary but should reflect one of the story patterns and include a conflict.

350

Story Patterns

A "coming of age" story is one of many patterns of stories you could write. Below are a few examples of common plot patterns used by writers.

The Rescue	In a *rescue* story, the main character is either in need of rescue or must rescue someone else. Adventure stories often follow this pattern. **Jori must somehow get her little brother out of a ravine.**
The Union	In the *union* story, two characters must overcome one or more obstacles to be together. Many stories about friendship, family, and love use the union pattern. **Amee and Sondra are sisters adopted by different families. They must work out a way to be together.**
The Underdog	In the *underdog* plot, someone overcomes adversity to achieve a goal. Main characters who are underdogs often appeal to readers. **Zhora overcomes her blindness to become a concert pianist.**
The Decision	In a *decision* story, the main character is faced with a decision that will test him or her. Tension builds in the story as the decision approaches. **Anapat must choose between going on a class trip or staying with his hospitalized grandfather.**
Rivalry	In a *rivalry* story, the main character must face a challenger. In this pattern, the main character is the *protagonist,* and the challenger is the *antagonist.* **Bo's team must face the team that defeated them for the state championship last year.**

 Choose one of the story patterns above. Think of a story that would fit that pattern. Write a single sentence that sums up the story. Be sure to include the conflict.

Teaching Tip: Story Patterns

Review the story patterns on PE page 350, form six groups, and assign a story pattern to each group.

- Have each group list the titles of at least two stories *(short stories, novels, movies, television shows)* that follow the pattern.

- Also have them state a one-sentence description of one or two story ideas that follow the pattern.
- Then instruct each group to introduce the pattern and share their findings: two existing stories and one or two new story ideas that follow the pattern.

CREATIVE

Elements of Fiction

The following list includes many terms used to describe the elements or parts of literature. This information will help you discuss and write about the novels, poetry, essays, and other literary works you read.

Action: Everything that happens in a story

Antagonist: The person or force that works against the hero of the story (See *protagonist.*)

Character: A person or an animal in a story

Characterization: The way in which a writer develops a character, making him or her seem believable
Here are three methods:

● Sharing the character's thoughts, actions, and dialogue
● Describing his or her appearance
● Revealing what others in the story think or say about this character

Conflict: A problem or clash between two forces in a story
There are five basic conflicts:

● **Person Against Person** A problem between characters
● **Person Against Himself or Herself** A problem within a character's own mind
● **Person Against Society** A problem between a character and society, the law, or some tradition
● **Person Against Nature** A problem with some element of nature, such as a blizzard or a hurricane
● **Person Against Destiny** A problem or struggle that appears to be beyond a character's control

Dialogue: The words spoken between two or more characters

Foil: The character who acts as a villain or challenges the main character

Mood: The feeling or emotion a piece of literature or writing creates in a reader

Moral: The lesson a story teaches

Narrator: The person or character who actually tells the story, giving background information and filling in details between portions of dialogue

Plot: The action that makes up the story, following a plan called the plot line

Plot Line: The planned action or series of events in a story (The basic parts of the plot line are the beginning, the rising action, the high point, and the ending.)

PLOT LINE — High Point — Rising Action — Beginning — Ending

● The **beginning** introduces the characters and the setting.
● The **rising action** adds a conflict—a problem for the characters.
● The **high point** is the moment when the conflict is strongest.
● The **ending** tells how the main characters have changed.

Elements of Fiction

Review the **elements of fiction** *(see below)* and their definitions with the entire class.

Focus on any terms that appear to be unfamiliar or confusing to students.

■ For example, point out the differences in the definitions of the terms *protagonist* and *antagonist.*
■ Ask students to name the protagonists and antagonists of some popular books or movies.
■ Have students think of a scenario that would demonstrate each of the five basic conflicts on PE page 351.

Use PE pages 350–352 as resources throughout this unit.

Teaching Tip: Elements of Fiction

Remind students that the four basic elements of fiction are character, plot, setting, and theme. Students should know these terms and use them in writing about literature. Also point out that many of the terms in this two-page glossary are related. For example, *action, conflict,* and *plot line* deal with plot; *characterization, antagonist,* and *protagonist* deal with character; and so on.

Ask three students to assist you in a simple demonstration of the third-person point of view. You serve as the narrator, and the three students serve as characters who act out according to your instructions, but do not say anything. (Rehearse the three scenarios below before presenting them to the rest of the class.)

Sample scene: Three students have just taken a test.

- Omniscient: *(Narrator tells how the students feel, and each character reflects these feelings.)* "After the unit test, Jacob is relieved, Yoko is upset, and Juan is ecstatic."
- Limited omniscient: *(Only one student shows the emotion the narrator describes.)* "Juan was sure he had failed the test, and he felt like crying as he left the room with Jacob and Yoko."
- Camera (objective) view: *(The narrator describes what can be seen, but not the feelings of the characters.)* "Jacob, Yoko, and Juan walked slowly out of the classroom. Silently, they headed in separate directions."

 Answers

Answers will vary but should identify and describe the conflict in one sentence and describe the protagonist in another.

352

Point of View: The angle from which a story is told (The angle depends upon the narrator, or person telling the story.)

- **First-Person Point of View**
  This means that one of the characters is telling the story: "We're just friends— that's all—but that means everything to us."
- **Third-Person Point of View**
  In third person, someone from outside the story is telling it: "They're just friends—that's all—but that means everything to them." There are three third-person points of view: *omniscient, limited omniscient,* and *camera view.* (See the illustrations on the right.)

Protagonist: The main character or hero in a story (See *antagonist.*)

Setting: The place and the time period in which a story takes place

Theme: The message about life or human nature that is "hidden" in the story that the writer tells

Tone: The writer's attitude toward his or her subject (Tone can be described by words like *angry* and *humorous.*)

Total Effect: The overall influence or impact that a story has on a reader

Third-Person Points of View

Omniscient point of view allows the narrator to tell the thoughts and feelings of all the characters.

Limited omniscient point of view allows the narrator to tell the thoughts and feelings of only one character at a time.

Camera view (objective view) allows the story's narrator to record the action from his or her own point of view without telling any of the characters' thoughts or feelings.

 Select a story that you have read that fits one of the five basic conflicts on page 351. In one sentence, describe its conflict. Add a sentence that describes the protagonist.

Struggling Learners

Assist students in identifying point of view in stories they have read. Point out that stories written in the first-person point of view are easily identified by the use of *I, me, us,* and *we* outside of dialogue. These personal pronouns indicate that the narrator is telling a story about himself or herself.

entertain create imagine **discover** 353
show

Creative Writing
Writing Poems

The camera clicks and captures an image of one moment in time. Another way to capture a special moment is to write a poem. A well-written poem, like a thought-provoking photograph, goes beyond the surface of things and touches the heart. Poets select special words to share their deepest thoughts, feelings, and sensations.

In this chapter, you will have the best of both worlds. You'll be writing a poem based on a photograph. Your challenge, like that of the master photographer, will be to take the "picture," the photo, and then delve deeper and capture the heart of the moment.

Writing Guidelines

Subject:	A picture that gives you a special feeling
Form:	Free-verse poem
Purpose:	To entertain
Audience:	Family and classmates

English Language Learners

Allow students a few minutes to browse through books of poetry. Encourage them to think about poetry or song lyrics in their native language or in English. Point out that poems do not have to rhyme.

- Suggest that they list some words that come to mind when someone says the word *poetry*.

- After allowing them a few minutes to make the list, have them freewrite about poetry.
- Share a few favorite poems with them. Discuss some of the special features in these poems.

Writing Poems

Objectives

- understand the content and structure of a free-verse poem and other forms of poetry
- choose a topic (a photograph or some words and phrases) to inspire a poem
- use poetry techniques, including figures of speech and special sounds, in a poem
- plan, draft, revise, edit, and share a free-verse poem and a found poem, as well as a couplet or a circle poem

To determine what experiences students have already had with poetry, direct students to complete a 5-minute freewrite about writing, reading, or listening to poetry. Then discuss how poets use language in special ways to capture moments and create images and feelings.

Free-Verse Poem

Some students may be unfamiliar with free-verse poetry.

- Explain that the images and feelings created in free verse can be vivid and powerful.
- Point out that writing in free verse requires a command of vocabulary. It employs word play that challenges the reader to observe the ordinary in an exceptional way.

Read aloud "The Biplane" so students can hear how it sounds. Then ask:

- How does the photograph help the reader?
- What words stand out to you?
- Do any of the lines rhyme?
- Are all the lines the same length?

Respond to the reading.

Answers

Ideas 1. Possible answers: dance; spiraling upward; swooping downward; chase its shadow; waggling its wings

Organization 2. empty sky, taking off, maneuvering in the air, its shadow moving below it as the plane flies on

Word Choice 3. Possible answers: dance, spiraling, freedom, swooping, chase, waggling, playful

---

354

Free-Verse Poem

Traditional poetry follows a specific pattern of rhythm and rhyming lines. **Free-verse poems**, on the other hand, create their own patterns and seldom use rhyming lines.

Poets who write free-verse poems carefully consider every word. The following free-verse poem expresses the poet's feelings about the photo of a soaring biplane in flight.

The Biplane

Alone
in a wide sky,
heaped clouds crowding back
against heaped hills
to make room for its dance.

Spiraling upward
for no reason, but
freedom!

Swooping downward
to chase its shadow,
waggling its wings
with a playful growl.

Its shadow passes coolly
over me,
alone and free
on this wide earth.

—Carter Williams

Respond to the reading. On your own paper, reflect on the ideas, organization, and word choice of the free-verse poem above.

- ☐ **Ideas** (1) Which details capture the flight of a biplane? List at least two.
- ☐ **Organization** (2) The poem is divided into four stanzas. Which special part of flight does each stanza deal with?
- ☐ **Word Choice** (3) What words work to convey a feeling of joy in this poem? List at least three.

English Language Learners

Help students with challenging metaphoric words and images, including the following: "heaped clouds," "heaped hills," "danced," "spiraling," "swooping," "waggling," and "growl."

Advanced Learners

Invite students to search through poetry anthologies for other examples of free-verse poems that are accompanied by photographs or drawings to share with the class. Discuss how the poetry and the visual images fit together.

Prewriting Selecting a Topic

To write your poem, first find a picture that gives you a special feeling. You might search family photo albums, magazines, or the Web. (Many search sites have a special option for searching pictures.) Your teacher may also offer you a choice of pictures, or you can choose one of the photos below.

CREATIVE

Gathering Details

Poets use sensory details to create an image in the reader's mind. As you view your photo, notice visual details. Then imagine that you are in the scene and jot down what you might hear, smell, taste, and feel. Carter created the following sensory chart, based on his biplane photo.

Sensory Chart

See	Hear	Smell	Taste	Feel
wide, brown ground	engine buzzing,	dry grass	dust	sun breeze!
wide, pale blue sky	sputtering,			flying
heaped shadowy mountains	growling			grit
heaped white clouds	hiss of wind			heat
sunlight on trees				

Prewrite

Create a sensory chart. Create a chart like the one above to gather sensory details about your photo. Include specific details that are in the photo as well as additional sensations that simply come to mind.

Prewriting Selecting a Topic

Give students time to find an image that inspires them. They may need to search through sources at home or in a library.

Prewriting Gathering Details

Provide photocopies of the reproducible sensory chart on TE page 793. Depending on the photographs they select, students may need help finding sensory details for smell, taste, or feel.

- Tell students that pictures will vary in the way that they stimulate the senses.
- Encourage them to be creative in imagining several details for those senses that are most appropriate for their image.

* For examples of using adjectives with the right feeling, see PE page 488.

English Language Learners

If students simply list nouns on the sensory chart (such as ground, sky, mountains), ask them to

- take a closer look at their photo,
- add adjectives to the nouns they have listed, and
- use a thesaurus at their reading level to find interesting and precise descriptive words.

Advanced Learners

Encourage students to notice how the writer of "The Biplane" uses emotion as well as sensory images to involve the reader in the poem. Point out words that evoke feelings, such as *alone, dance, freedom,* and *playful.* Discuss other emotions that could be explored in a poem about flying. (A pilot might feel afraid, proud, or brave.)

Prewriting
Using Poetry Techniques

To practice onomatopoeia, brainstorm a list of words that sound like the noises they name.

■ Begin with *growl* and *hissing* from the text.

■ Invite students to think of more examples (*splash, gush, buzz, crash, boom, clang, squeak*).

Explore how line breaks affect poems by doing the following:

■ Have students write out "The Biplane" without line breaks in each stanza.

■ Have them compare the two versions for meaning and emotional impact.

Point out that line breaks and punctuation are often used differently in poetry. Students should consider the breaks and punctuation as "meaning markers" and think about the purpose of each mark or break. (For example, in the poem on PE page 354, have students notice that the word *Alone* has more impact because it is by itself on the first line.)

Writing
Developing Your First Draft

Encourage students to use their imagination and write about their picture or photograph without attention to form or conventions at this stage of the process.

356

Prewriting Using Poetry Techniques

Poets play with the sounds of words. **Onomatopoeia** (ŏn′ə-măt′ə-pē′ə) is one example. It means using words that sound like the noises they name.

with a playful growl   **wind hissing over wings**

Poets also play with the way words are placed on the page. **Line breaks**, for instance, help control the way a poem reads. In the following selection, line breaks emphasize the plane's climb and the word "freedom."

Spiraling upward for no reason, but freedom!

 Use special techniques. On your sensory chart, underline any words that use onomatopoeia. List any other special techniques you want to use from pages 360–361.

Writing Developing Your First Draft

Now it's time to have some fun writing the first draft. Follow the tips below.

■ **Study** the photo you have chosen to refresh your memory. Review your sensory chart for details.

■ **Imagine** yourself in the picture. What types of things do you see and hear? Also think of experiences you have had that can help you connect with the photo.

■ **Write** whatever comes to mind. There will be plenty of time for revision later.

 Write your first draft. Use the tips above to guide your writing. Experiment with onomatopoeia, line breaks, and other special techniques.

Grammar Connection

Prepositional Phrases

■ **Proofreader's Guide** page 742 (+)

■ *Write Source* page 494–495, 519 (+)

■ *SkillsBook* page 174

■ **CD** Prepositions (+)

Struggling Learners

Model the process of writing a free-verse poem. Show students your illustration and sensory words. Then begin crafting the poem, explaining the imagery and structure (stanzas, line breaks) as you go along.

Advanced Learners

Have students choose a favorite poem and write a letter (real or imagined) to the poet, quoting their favorite lines in the letter. Have them refer to a writing handbook for guidelines about quoting lines of poetry and incorporating them into expository text.

entertain create discover **357**
show imagine
Writing Poems

CREATIVE

Revising Improving Your Poem

"Success," you may have heard, "is 10 percent inspiration and 90 percent perspiration." Even though the first draft of your poem may be truly inspired, the work of revision can improve it. Keep these traits in mind when revising your poem.

☐ **Ideas** Do I use sensory details? Does my poem convey special thoughts and feelings that stem from the photo?

☐ **Organization** Do my line breaks and indents help express my thoughts and feelings?

☐ **Voice** Does my poem show personality and originality?

☐ **Word Choice** Are my words precise and interesting?

☐ **Sentence Fluency** Do my phrases and sentences have an appealing rhythm? Do I use any special poetic techniques?

 Revise your poem. Using the questions above as a guide, keep revising until your poem is the best that it can be.

Editing Fine-Tuning Your Poem

Because poems are shorter than most other types of writing, every word and detail is important. Focus on the conventions of writing as you edit your poem.

☐ **Conventions** Is my poem free of errors that could distract the reader?

 Edit your poem. Poems sometimes break the rules, but never by accident. So check your final copy one last time for errors.

Publishing Sharing Your Poem

When your poem is finished, share it with other people. Here are some good ways to do that. (See pages **57–64** for other publishing ideas.)

● **Post it.** Put it on a bulletin board, a Web site, or your refrigerator.
● **Submit it.** Send your poem to a contest or magazine.
● **Perform it.** Read your poem aloud to friends and family.

 Publish your work. Poems are made to be shared, so give people a chance to read yours or hear it. Ask your teacher about other publishing ideas.

Revising Improving Your Poem

Advise students to set aside their work for a while so that they can look at it from a fresh perspective. Encourage them to experiment with features that are not usually the main focus in other forms of writing, such as

■ metaphoric language,
■ rhythm, and
■ structure.

Editing Fine-Tuning Your Poem

Before students edit their poems, discuss how poets often use conventions differently than other writers. For example, point out that some poems do not use capital letters or end punctuation.

Examine the conventions in "The Biplane" on PE page 354. Explain that students have some creative leeway in how they apply conventions in their poems.

Publishing Sharing Your Poem

Encourage students to read their work to parents and siblings and then to read it to the class. Invite students to listen for the rhythms, poetic techniques, and sounds that their classmates use. Display students' poetry.

Advanced Learners

Discuss the saying "taking poetic license" and the kinds of circumstances under which it is used. Ask students to find examples of poetic license in poems they have read.

Grammar Connection

Parts of Speech Review
■ **Proofreader's Guide** pages 702–748 (+), 749
■ *Write Source* pages 470–498 (+)
■ *SkillsBook* pages 183–184

Adverbs
■ **Proofreader's Guide** pages 736 (+), 738 (+)
■ *Write Source* pages 490 (+), 492 (+), 493 (+)
■ *SkillsBook* page 173

Hyphens
■ **Proofreader's Guide** pages 608–609, 610 (+), 732 (+)
■ *SkillsBook* pages 33–34
■ **CD** Hyphens (+)

Spelling
■ **Proofreader's Guide** pages 642 (+)
■ **CD** Spelling Review—1

Writing a Found Poem

Provide pairs of students with magazines or sections of a newspaper. Instruct them to cut out at least 10 words and phrases within a certain time limit.

- Display one pair's set of "found" words.
- Have the class suggest ways to arrange the words and phrases to form a poem. Point out that hyphens can be used to join words.
- Then ask partners to make a poem using their own word sets. When they like their poem, they should glue the words in place.

✳ For information on how to use hyphens, see PE page 608.

Writing Tips

A found poem has a strong visual component. Explain that the form of the poem, including the size and style of different fonts, can add interest to the poem.

Writing a Found Poem

A found poem borrows words from day-to-day sources like street signs, package labels, recipe books, and so on. The poet then arranges those words in an interesting way. For example, the following poem uses words found at a post office and arranges them to suggest amusing meanings.

COD

BUSINESS   REPLY
MAIL   FIRST-CLASS
          MAIL
PERMIT NO.   MAIL
POST OFFICE WILL
NOT MAIL
          WITH-
OUT STAMP
                    HELP
STAMP OUT
     POSTAGE SCALE

Writing Tips

- **Select a topic.** Watch for interesting words and phrases all around you—at school, at the mall, on signs, or in junk mail. What possibilities do those words and phrases suggest?
- **Gather details.** Keep a journal of things you see that could become a found poem. Collect advertisements and photographs with interesting possibilities.
- **Create a form.** Arrange your found words in unusual ways. Experiment with line breaks and indents to make your found poem one of a kind.

Create your found poem. Following the tips above, write your own found poem. Have fun making it as thought provoking as possible.

Struggling Learners

Help students get started by
- giving them a set of words that you have clipped from magazines or
- allowing them to experiment with arranging words from magnetic poetry kits.

Advanced Learners

Encourage students to combine art and poetry using this technique.
- Arrange found words into the shape of an object named in the poem. For example, words and phrases from instructions on how to set up a tent could be arranged within the outline of a tent sketched onto the paper.

CREATIVE

Writing Other Forms of Poetry

Poetry can take many, many forms. Here are two types that could be inspired by a photograph.

Couplet

A couplet is two rhyming lines, usually of the same length and rhythm. Most couplets are in iambic pentameter format—five pairs of syllables with each pair following an unstressed-stressed pattern—like the following lines from William Shakespeare's sonnet XVIII:

> Sŏ lóng ăs mén căn bréathe, ŏr éyes căn sée,
>
> Sŏ lóng lĭves thís, ănd thís gĭves lífe tŏ thée.

The couplet is an important building block for many rhyming forms. Taken alone, a couplet can make a concise poem itself, as in the following example.

> **Amber Light**
> Time pauses now, it seems, as this day ends
> and I pause, chatting timelessly with friends.

 Note that it's okay to vary from this pattern for effect. Even Shakespeare varied his rhythms sometimes!

Circle Poem

A circle poem suggests a relationship between a series of individual words or phrases. It makes these connections in a chain, eventually coming full circle to end with something close to the opening idea.

> *streetlight*
> *porch light*   *wet road*
> *clock face*   *night river*
> *floating moon*

 Write a poem. Choose one of the forms on this page and write your own poem. Remember to follow the writing process on pages 355–357.

Writing Other Forms of Poetry

Couplet
To help students hear the rhythm in a couplet, have them read aloud the lines and tap out the rhythm gently on their desks.

Circle Poem
Examine the relationship between each pair of words or phrases in the poem. Help students see that each line leads to or is connected in some way to the line that follows.

English Language Learners

To help students understand the concept of circle poems, play a word-association game.

- Place six to eight students in a circle.
- Give one student a word (such as *elephant*) to say.
- Have the next student say the first word that comes to mind.
- Continue until each student has contributed a word.

- Record the words on a piece of paper, and then transfer them to the board.
- If the last word doesn't seem to relate to the first, invite the group to think of another word that might link them together and bring the circle poem to a conclusion.

Struggling Learners

Demonstrate a phone-number poem using 745-2031 (the number of syllables per line corresponds to each digit, with zero represented by punctuation alone).

> *It's already time for lunch!*
> *What will you have?*
> *A tall glass of milk?*
> *Yes, please*
> *!*
> *Some pizza?*
> *Yum!*

Using Special Poetry Techniques

Figures of Speech

Direct students to create their own examples of each figure of speech, following these steps:

- Fold a piece of paper into quarters, and label each section with one figure of speech.
- In each section, copy the example from the text, and add an example of your own.

Place your examples in your writing folder so you can use them in the future.

Sounds of Poetry

Emphasize that the sound techniques on PE pages 360–361 are used mostly in poetry.

Use these pages as a resource throughout this unit.

360

Using Special Poetry Techniques

Poets use a variety of special techniques in their work. This page and the next define some of the most important ones.

Figures of Speech

- A **simile** (*sĭm´ə-lē*) compares two unlike things with the word *like* or *as*.

  The scrap of paper fought
  like a fish on a hook.

- A **metaphor** (*mĕt´ə-fôr*) compares two unlike things without using *like* or *as*.

  Her eyes were searchlights.

- **Personification** (*pər-sŏn´ə-fĭ-kā´shən*) is a technique that gives human traits to something that is nonhuman.

  The leaves gossiped among themselves.

- **Hyperbole** (*hī-pûr´bə-lē*) is an exaggerated statement, often humorous.

  When Guadalupe showers, the Pacific goes dry.

Sounds of Poetry

- **Alliteration** (*ə-lĭt´ə-rā´shən*) is the repetition of consonant sounds at the beginning of words.

  The kids rode a cute little carousel.

- **Assonance** (*as´ə-nəns*) is the repetition of vowel sounds anywhere in words.

  A green apple gleams at me.

Advanced Learners

Invite students to write similes or metaphors that appeal to each of the five senses. For example:

- Her eyes shone like sunbeams.
- When the pots and pans clattered, it was a drum solo.
- The honey was gleaming like liquid gold.
- Gram is the queen bee.

CREATIVE

■ **Consonance** (*kŏn´sə-nəns*) is the repetition of consonant sounds anywhere in words.

> They plucked the anchor from the aching deep.

■ **Line breaks** help to control the rhythm of a poem as it is read. Readers naturally tend to pause at the end of a line. That gives added emphasis to the last word in a line.

> In liquid heat the swimming sun
> hangs on the horizon.

■ **Onomatopoeia** (*ŏn´ə-măt´ə-pē´ə*) is the use of words that sound like what they name.

> The crackling bag crumpled in his fist.

■ **Repetition** (*rĕp´ĭ-tĭsh´ən*) uses the same word or phrase more than once, for emphasis or for rhythm.

> She forced her tired feet, her tired soul, to slog along.

■ **Rhyme** means using words whose endings sound alike. *End rhyme* happens at the end of lines.

> Flowers grow in sidewalk cracks,
> And children grow near railroad tracks.

> *Internal rhyme* happens within lines.

> The smoke could choke a chimney.

■ **Rhythm** (*rĭth´əm*) is the pattern of accented and unaccented syllables in a poem. The rhythm of free-verse poetry tends to flow naturally, like speaking. Traditional poetry follows a more regular pattern, as in the following example.

> Ĭn Lóndŏntówn, whĕre úrchĭns híde,
> Thĕre líves ă mán ŏf wóefŭl mínd. (a regular rhythm)

Write your own example for two or more of the techniques explained on these two pages. Then expand at least one of your examples into a complete poem.

English Language Learners

Give the following instructions to provide additional practice with individual techniques:

• Write a simile to describe today's weather.

• Write an alliterative sentence related to your school.

• Write a sentence that includes onomatopoeia about a sound you are hearing right now.

Advanced Learners

Encourage students to create rhyming dictionaries as an ongoing project. Remind them that rhyming words do not always end in the same spelling patterns. Provide examples such as *caught/ bought* and *few/blue*.

Have students find examples of the "Sounds of Poetry" in poems included in their literature anthologies. Discuss the examples as a class. Then ask students to find additional examples of three or four of the techniques on their own.

Try IT Answers

Answers will vary. Give examples for two or more poetry techniques and provide a complete poem.

Research Writing Overview

Unit Objectives

The writing standards listed below are based on a blending of state and NCTE standards.

- Use research skills to gather ideas and information.
- Write a research report with a thesis statement, several middle paragraphs, and a concluding paragraph.
- Create and present an interactive report.

Writing Forms

- summary paragraph
- research report
- multimedia presentation

Focus on the Traits

- **Ideas** Developing an interesting topic that is researched through reliable sources
- **Organization** Creating an outline that includes a thesis statement, topic sentences that support the thesis statement, and details that support each topic sentence
- **Voice** Using a knowledgeable, interested, and informative voice
- **Word Choice** Using one's own words to summarize and paraphrase information, using quotations for exact words, and explaining unfamiliar technical terms in context
- **Sentence Fluency** Developing sentences that flow smoothly from one to another
- **Conventions** Checking for errors in punctuation, capitalization, spelling, and grammar

Note: For specifics about reading the chart below, see page TE 33.

Suggested Research Writing Unit (Four Weeks)

	Day	Writing and Skills Units	In the *Write Source* book			On the CD-ROM	*SkillsBook* grammar practice pages
			Pages	Proofreader's Guide—basic grammar rules	Basic Grammar practice	Interactive Grammar Exercises	
WEEK 1	1–3	**Research Writing Skills**	363–374				
	4	**Taking Notes**	441–448				
	5	**Summary Paragraph** (Model)	376				
WEEK 2		(Prewriting)	377				
	6	(Writing)	378				
		(Revising)	378				
		Skills Activities: (Appositives)		586 (+), 587 (appositives)	472 (appositives), 513 (+)	Commas to Set Off Appositives . . .	17

Day	Writing and Skills Units	In the *Write Source* book			On the CD-ROM	*SkillsBook* grammar practice pages
		Pages	Proofreader's Guide—basic grammar rules	Basic Grammar practice	Interactive Grammar Exercises	
7	(Editing)	378				
	Skills Activities: Semicolons		594–595			19–20
	Using the Right Word		652–686 (+)			59–60
8	**Research Report:** (Model)	381–385				
9–10	(Prewriting)	386–389				
11–12	(Prewriting)	390–391				
13	(Prewriting)	392–394				
14–15	(Writing)	395–402				
16	(Revising)	405–406				
	Skills Activities: Active and Passive Verbs		726 (+)			
	Sentence Variety and Ellipses		614–615			127–128, 129–130
	Sentence Expanding			511, 521–522		121–122
	Dashes and Parentheses and Other Forms of Punctuation		612–613			36, 37–38
17–18	(Editing)	407–408				
	Skills Activities: Comma Rules Review		582–591 (+)			15–16
	Sentence Problems Review			506 (+), 507 (+), 508 (+), 509 (+), 510 (+)		93–94
	Using the Right Word		652–686 (+)			61–62
19	(Publishing)	409				
20 opt.	**Multimedia Presentations**	411–415				
	Skills Activities: Spelling Review		642 (+)		Spelling Review—1 (+)	

WEEK 2 CONTINUED / WEEK 3 / WEEK 4

Teacher's Notes for Research Writing

This overview for research writing includes some specific teaching suggestions for the unit.

Building Research Skills (pages 363–374)

This chapter tells about the kinds of sources of information available to researchers and where to find that information. Equally important for students is knowing how to evaluate the sources before spending a lot of time in research and then inadvertently including false information in their papers.

Writing a Summary Paragraph (pages 375–378)

Writing good summaries contributes to academic success because such an ability shows that the student understands what he or she has read or heard. This chapter contains guidelines as well as a model of a summary paragraph.

Writing a Research Report (pages 379–410)

Everyone has questions about things that especially interest them. Writing a research report about the subject of interest is one way to find the answers. This chapter includes a model report about a particular region of the country and a works-cited page. Students will then be asked to pick a part of the country and write about it using proper documentation.

Developing Multimedia Presentations (pages 411–415)

Successful multimedia presentations can bring a topic to life for the audience. Students will learn important guidelines for the use of media in their presentations. The proper balance of media forms makes a good presentation better. Too much media can be overwhelming and confusing. A sample interactive storyboard is included.

Minilessons

As I Recall . . .   Building Research Skills

■ **CHOOSE** a biography of Lincoln or Washington. **CHECK** the sources listed in the back of the book. On a sheet of paper make two columns, one for primary sources and one for secondary sources. **WRITE** the title of each source listed in the appropriate column.

To Sum Up   Writing a Summary Paragraph

■ **READ** pages 376-378 in your textbook on writing a summary paragraph. In a small group, try to **WRITE** the main idea about the Krakow salt cellars (page 376) in one sentence.

Outer Space   Writing a Research Report

■ **ASSUME** that you have been asked to write a research report for a group of visitors from another planet. These visitors want to go to one place that is representative of the United States. **LIST** what you think they need to know about our country, then **CHOOSE** the spot. **EXPLAIN** why you think your choice is a good one.

Ready. Action.   Developing Multimedia Presentations

■ **LIST** the types of media that you are able to use. **LIST** the ones you don't have access to, but you would like to use. **DESCRIBE** how you would use each item (for example, a DVD player) in a presentation.

Research Writing
Building Skills

People often describe history in terms of "Ages"—Stone, Bronze, Iron, Dark, Middle, and so on. Some people call today the "information age." Print and electronic media supply a sea of information. That is why research skills—knowing how to find what you need, and how to judge what you find—are more important than ever.

In this chapter, you will learn how to use the Internet and the library to find the information you need. You'll also learn how to evaluate the sources of that information. These may be some of the most important skills you learn during your school years.

What's Ahead

- Primary vs. Secondary Sources
- Using the Internet
- Using the Library
- Using Reference Materials
- Evaluating Sources

Building Skills

Objectives

- distinguish between primary and secondary sources
- understand how to use the Internet to do research
- understand how to access and use library reference materials
- know the elements of a dictionary page
- learn how to evaluate sources

Use these questions to assess students' research skills.

- How do you start when you research a topic? What sources can you use?
- Is it easier to find information in library reference materials or on the Internet? Explain.
- How do you know if a resource is reliable or not?

Primary vs. Secondary Sources

Use the following questions to continue the discussion about primary and secondary sources:

- Why might a primary source be more reliable than a secondary source? (A primary source has firsthand knowledge.)
- What kinds of situations could make either source unreliable? (Possible responses: Primary source—A person you talk to could be biased. Secondary source—An author could mix up facts or be led astray by an unreliable source.)

Types of Primary Sources

Point out that e-mail has made it much easier for researchers to conduct interviews, surveys, and questionnaires.

- A greater number of people can be reached at one time by sending the same e-mail.
- Responders can reply instantaneously. They are also more likely to give more complete answers than they might give during a telephone call.

 **Answers**

1. secondary source
2. primary source

364

Primary vs. Secondary Sources

Primary sources of information are original sources. They provide you with firsthand information.

Secondary sources contain information that has been gathered by someone else. Most nonfiction books, newspapers, magazines, and Web sites are secondary sources.

Primary Sources	Secondary Sources
1 Visiting a grocery store	**1** Visiting a Web site about salt in foods
2 Interviewing a nutritionist	**2** Reading an article about salt in foods
3 Talking to a person on a salt-free diet	**3** Watching a TV program about salt in the diet

Types of Primary Sources

- **Diaries, Journals, and Letters** You can find these sorts of primary sources in libraries and museums.
- **Presentations** Historical sites, museums, guest speakers, and live demonstrations can give you firsthand information.
- **Interviews** You can interview an expert in person, by phone, by e-mail, or through the mail.
- **Surveys and Questionnaires** To gain information from many people at once, have them answer a list of questions. Then study the results.
- **Observation and Participation** Observing a person, place, or thing is a common method of gathering firsthand information. So is participating in an event yourself.

 Decide whether each of the following is a primary or a secondary source of information.

1. Listening to a scholar's presentation about an artist's life
2. Viewing an artist's work in a museum

Using the Internet

The Internet is a great place to start your research. All you need is a computer with an Internet connection to surf the World Wide Web and to send and receive e-mail. On the Web, you can find online encyclopedias, government publications, and university sites, as well as pages posted by businesses and private individuals. The tools available for searching all these sources of information are improving all the time.

If you have never used the Internet before, your teacher or librarian can show you how. Keep the following points in mind as you do your Internet research.

Points to Remember

- **Use the Web carefully.** Look for sites that have *.edu, .org,* or *.gov* in the address. These are educational, nonprofit, or government Web sites and will offer the most reliable information. If you are not sure about the reliability of a site, check with your teacher or librarian. (Also see page **374**.)

- **Use a search site.** A search site such as www.google.com or www.yahoo.com is like a computer catalog for the Internet. You can enter keywords to find Web pages about your subject.

- **Look for links.** Often, a Web page includes links to other pages dealing with your topic. Take advantage of these links.

- **Be patient.** The Web is huge and searches can get complicated. New pages are added all the time, and old pages may change addresses or even disappear completely.

- **Know your school's Internet policy.** To avoid trouble, be sure to follow your school's Internet policy. Also follow whatever guidelines your parents may have set up for you.

 Visit **www.thewritesource.com** and go to the "Research Links" page. Spend a few minutes exploring one of the "Homework Help" sites listed there. Write a paragraph explaining what helpful or interesting things you found on that site.

RESEARCH

Using the Internet

Take time to review your school's policy for using the Internet.
- If possible, distribute a copy of the policy to each student.
- Remind students to close all pop-up windows (ones that pop up when a user is browsing a Web site) immediately.
- Explain that some pop-ups are advertisements that help pay for the maintenance of the Web sites, but others are capable of installing hidden programs on computers, which can affect computer functions.

After students complete the **Try It** activity, have them share their paragraphs in a group.

 Answers

Answers will vary.

For additional practice, ask students to suggest a few topics related to what they are studying in science and social studies. Then have partners use a search engine to find a list of Web sites for each topic. Tell students to look for URLs (Web-site addresses) that end in *.edu, .org,* or *.gov,* as these sources are generally more reliable.

English Language Learners

Beforehand, on a classroom computer or on one in the media center, bookmark an example of each kind of site mentioned on this page. Use those bookmarked locations as concrete examples when you help students with this page.

Struggling Learners

Students who have difficulty in other areas may excel at using the Internet to find information. Take advantage of this opportunity to make these students "leaders" or "advisers" for Internet research.

Using the Library

If possible, arrange a library tour with a school or local librarian and have students complete the **Try It** activity during that tour.

 Answers

Student notes will vary.

Many libraries have reference librarians who are experts at finding information, especially using the library computer system.

- Encourage students to introduce themselves to the reference librarian at their public library.
- If possible, arrange a class tour during which the reference librarian demonstrates computer search techniques.
- Some students may enjoy creating a map showing the different sections of their school or public library.
- Suggest that they tape the map to the inside cover of their writing notebook for quick reference.

366

Using the Library

While the Internet is a good place to start your research, the library may be a better place to continue your research. Library materials are often more in-depth and reliable than what you may find on the Net. In libraries, you can find books, magazines, newspapers, and videos (and maybe even a computer with Internet access). Most libraries contain the following sections.

1 Books are usually divided into three sections.

- The **fiction** section includes stories and novels. These books are arranged in alphabetical order by the authors' last names.
- The **nonfiction** section contains books that are based on fact. They are usually arranged according to the Dewey decimal system. (See page **369**.)
- The **reference** section has encyclopedias, atlases, dictionaries, directories, and almanacs.

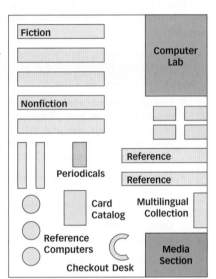

2 The periodicals section includes magazines and newspapers.

3 The computer lab has computers, often connected to the Internet. You usually sign up to use a computer.

4 The media section includes music CD's, cassettes, videotapes, DVD's, and CD-ROM's. Computer software (encyclopedias, games, and so on) may be found in this section as well.

 During your next visit to the library, explore a section of the library you rarely use. Take notes about the type of materials available in that section. Put your notes in your writing folder so you can use them as a reference later.

Struggling Learners

Have partners help each other find out which sections of the library have information on a given topic. Ask them to

- divide a piece of paper into four equal sections;
- label the sections *Nonfiction, Periodicals, Computer Catalog,* and *Reference;* and
- list several titles of articles or books they find in each section.

English Language Learners

If students make a map of their school media center, tell them to leave a two-inch margin all the way around their map.

- Ask them to draw a line from each section on the map to the margin.
- In the margin, have them write two or three examples

of the specific materials that can be found there. For example, in the margin beside the reference section, they might write *World Book Encyclopedia;* and next to the periodicals section, they could write *National Geographic.*

Searching a Computer Catalog

Every computer catalog is a little different. Therefore, the first time you use a particular computer catalog, it's a good idea to check the instructions for using it or to ask a librarian for help. With a computer catalog, you can find information on the same book in three ways:

1 If you know the book's title, enter the title.

2 If you know the book's author, enter the author's name. (When the library has more than one book by the same author, there will be more than one entry.)

3 Finally, if you know only the subject you want to learn about, enter either the subject or a keyword. (A *keyword* is a word or phrase that is related to the subject.)

If your subject is . . .	your keywords might be . . .
paper folding,	origami, paper art, paper folding, paper work.

Computer Catalog Screen

Author:	Montroll, John
Title:	African Animals in Origami
Published:	Dover Publications, 2004
Subjects:	Animals in art, decoration and ornament, origami, paper work
STATUS:	**CALL NUMBER:**
Available	736.9822Mon
LOCATION:	
Adult nonfiction	

RESEARCH

 Create a computer catalog screen like the one above for a book you have read or one you are reading.

Searching a Computer Catalog

The best way for students to become familiar with a computer catalog system is with practice.

- Prepare a list of book titles, authors' names, and subjects.
- Encourage students to look up each item, using a computer in the school library or one in the public library.
- Invite volunteers to describe differences, if any, between the two systems.

Many public libraries belong to larger networks with several branches. The computer catalog often shows search results for the whole network.

- If a book is not available at the local branch, the librarian can usually request it from another branch.
- Have students ask their librarian if this option is available at their library and if so, to explain how it works.

Take students to the school library for the **Try It** activity, or have them go to a library on their own.

 Answers

Answers will vary.

Searching a Card Catalog

Most libraries have either a computer catalog or a card catalog, but not both.

- If your school library has a card catalog, ask the media specialist to review with students how to use it.
- Make sure that they recognize title, author, and subject cards and know how to use the information on each type of card to find a book on the shelf.

368

Searching a Card Catalog

If your library has a card catalog, it will most likely be located in a cabinet full of drawers. The drawers contain title, author, and subject cards, which are arranged in alphabetical order.

1 To find a book's title card, ignore a beginning *A, An,* or *The* and look under the next word of the title.

2 To find a book's author card, look under the author's last name. Then find the author card with the title of the book you want.

3 To find a book's subject card, look up an appropriate subject.

All three cards will contain important information about your book—most importantly, its call number. This number will help you find the book on the library's shelves.

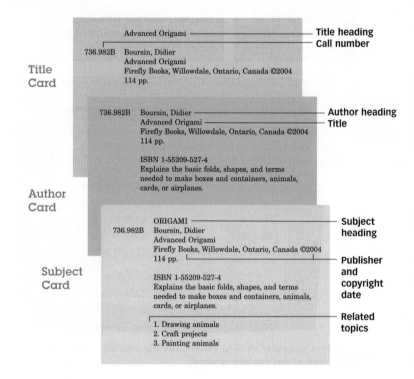

369
Building Skills

Finding Books

Each catalog entry for a book includes a call number that tells where to find the book on the library shelves. Most libraries organize nonfiction books by the Dewey decimal system, which has 10 subject categories.

000–099	**General Works**	500–599	**Sciences**
100–199	**Philosophy**	600–699	**Technology**
200–299	**Religion**	700–799	**Arts and Recreation**
300–399	**Social Sciences**	800–899	**Literature**
400–499	**Languages**	900–999	**History and Geography**

RESEARCH

Using Call Numbers

A call number often has a decimal in it, followed by the first letters of an author's name. Note how the call numbers are arranged on the books below.

Understanding the Parts of a Book

The *title page* tells the title of the book, the author's name, and the publisher's name and city. It is usually the first page of a book. The *copyright page* comes next and includes the year the book was published. The *table of contents* lists the names and page numbers of sections and chapters in the book. Many books have at least one *appendix* near the back of the book, which holds extra information like maps, tables, and lists. The *index* is an alphabetical list of all topics and their page numbers in the book.

 Get a book from your library. Write down its title and call number, its publisher's name and city, the year it was published, and the page numbers for the section names of its table of contents.

Finding Books

To be sure students understand how call numbers are arranged, have them use the chart to answer these questions:

- What is the subject category of the books in the illustration? Explain how you know. (The category is history and geography. All the call numbers are between 900 and 999, which are the numbers for history and geography in the Dewey decimal system.)
- How are the call numbers arranged? (The call numbers are arranged sequentially by whole numbers. Between whole numbers, they are arranged sequentially by decimals.)
- How can you find a book if you know the call number and the author's last name? (Find the corresponding call number, and then look at the letter or letters after the call number. These letters are the initial letter or letters of the author's last name.)

Before students do the **Try It** activity with a library book, have them work in pairs to examine the parts of their *Write Source* book.

 Answers

Answers will vary.

Using Reference Materials

If possible, provide time for students to do the following:

- Create or print a list of encyclopedias, atlases, and dictionaries available in their school and public libraries.
- Find out what reference materials are available to them on their **library's Web site** *(see below)*.

Using Encyclopedias

Have on hand the index volume (hardbound) of an encyclopedia and several topic ideas.

- Suggest a topic.
- Invite a volunteer to find that topic in the encyclopedia's index and read aloud the entry.

Students can work independently on the **Try It** activity.

 Answers

1. volume H, page 222
2. volume M, page 864
3. volume M, page 228

Using Reference Materials

The reference section in a library contains materials such as encyclopedias, atlases, and dictionaries.

Using Encyclopedias

An **encyclopedia** is a set of books, a CD, or a Web site with articles on almost every topic you can imagine. The topics are arranged alphabetically. The tips below can guide your use of encyclopedias.

- If the article is long, skim any subheadings to find specific information.
- Encyclopedia articles are written with the most basic information first, followed by more detailed information.
- At the end of an article, you may find a list of related topics. Use them to learn more about your topic.
- The index lists all the places in the encyclopedia where you will find more information about your topic. (See the sample below.) The index is usually in the back of the last volume of a printed set.

Encyclopedia Index

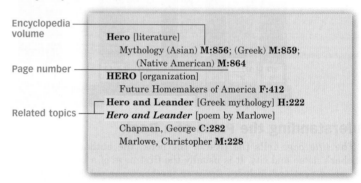

Using the index entries above, list the volume and page or pages where you might find the following information.

1. A description of Leander in Greek mythology
2. Native American mythic heroes
3. A biography of the English playwright Christopher Marlowe

English Language Learners

In the school library, guide students in examining and comparing reference materials. For example, point out that although all general encyclopedias contain the same basic type of information, some encyclopedias are harder to use and read than others.

Teaching Tip: Library Web Sites

Many libraries subscribe to online encyclopedias that are available through the library's Web site.

- Online encyclopedias are updated regularly, so the information is current.
- These and other reference materials can be easily accessed from any one of the library's computers.

Many libraries also offer at-home access to reference materials and databases for library cardholders.

- Usually, cardholders must go to the library's Web site and log in by typing in a library card number or a password.
- Explain that at-home access allows them to do research even when the library is closed.

371

Building Skills

Finding Magazine Articles

Periodical guides are found in the reference section of the library and list magazine articles about many different topics.

- **Locate the right edition** of the *Readers' Guide to Periodical Literature* (or a similar guide). The latest edition will have the newest information, but you may need information from an older edition.

- **Look up your subject**. Subjects are listed alphabetically. If your subject is not listed, try another word related to it.

- **Write down the information** about the article. Include the name of the magazine, the issue date, the name of the article, and its page numbers.

- **Find the magazine**. Ask the librarian for help if necessary.

Readers' Guide Format

RESEARCH

DINNER
Actually, America's still cooking, *USA Today* p6 Jn 21 2008.

DINOSAURS
Evidence of impact. J. Amadio. *Natural History* v113 no4 p15 M 2008
What wiped out the dinosaurs? E. Dobb. *Discover* v23 no6 p36–44 Jn 2006.
See also
Asteroid collisions

DIODES
Diodes and transistors demystified. Travis, Bill. *EDN* v45 no14 p28 Jl 2006.

DI SILVESTER, ROGER
Warmer climate threatens seas. Di Silvester, Roger. *National Wildlife* v42 no4 p10 Jl 2008.

Subject Entry
Title of Article
Page Number/Date
Name of Author
Cross-Reference
Name, Volume, and Number of Magazine
Author Entry

Internet-based databases are online subscription services that allow you to search for and read periodicals on the Internet.

 Using the sample entries above, write answers to these questions.

1. Under what additional heading can you find more articles about dinosaurs?
2. Who wrote the article "Evidence of Impact"?
3. Which periodicals contain articles about dinosaurs?

Finding Magazine Articles

As you review the information about periodicals and the *Readers' Guide* sample, point out the following:

- The most current information on periodicals probably will not be in a hardbound book. More likely, the latest editions of *Readers' Guide* will be available in a soft-covered booklet or in online form.

- Most libraries keep only the most recent editions of magazines and periodicals in the reference section. Older editions are usually archived, and each library has its own policy for requesting these materials. Students should find out how to request archived materials at their library.

Have students complete the **Try It** activity on their own.

Try It Answers

1. Asteroid collisions
2. J. Amadio
3. *Natural History, Discover*

For additional practice, have partners make up three questions based on the sample *Readers' Guide* entries. Then have partners exchange questions to answer.

Checking a Dictionary

Have volunteers take turns reading aloud each of the bulleted items.

- After each item is read, have students refer to the corresponding item on the sample dictionary page on PE page 373.
- For additional reinforcement, have students find and list other examples of each item from classroom or personal dictionaries.
- If there are not enough dictionaries to go around, have students work in pairs or small groups.

 Answers

Answers will vary.

372

Checking a Dictionary

A dictionary is the most reliable source for learning the meanings of words. It offers the following aids and information.

- **Guide words** are located at the top of every page. They show the first and last entry words on a page, so you can tell whether the word you're looking up is listed on that page.
- **Entry words** are the words that are defined on the dictionary page. They are listed in alphabetical order for easy searching.
- **Parts of speech** labels tell you the different ways a word can be used. For example, the word *Carboniferous* can be used as a noun or as an adjective.
- **Syllable divisions** show where you can divide a word into syllables.
- **Spelling and capitalization** (if appropriate) are given for every entry word. If an entry is capitalized, capitalize it in your writing, too.
- **Spelling of verb** forms is shown. Watch for irregular forms of verbs because the spelling can be a whole new word.
- **Illustrations** are often provided to make a definition clearer.
- **Accent marks** show which syllable or syllables should be stressed when you say a word.
- **Pronunciations** are special spellings of a word to help you say the word correctly.
- **Pronunciation keys** give symbols to help you pronounce the entry word correctly.
- **Etymology** gives the history of a word [in brackets]. Knowing a little about a word's history can make the definition easier to remember.

 Open a dictionary to any page and follow the directions below.

1. Write down the guide words on that page.
2. Find a verb and write down the verb forms listed.
3. Find an entry that gives the history of the word. Write out the etymology (history).

Dictionary Page

Guide words —

Entry word —

Part of speech —

Syllable division —

Spelling and capitalization —

Spelling of verb forms —

Illustration —

Accent marks —

Pronunciation —

Pronunciation key —

Etymology —

RESEARCH

carbon dioxide | carburetor 150

carbon dioxide *n.* A colorless or odorless gas that does not burn, composed of carbon and oxygen in the pro-portion CO_2 and present in the atmosphere or formed when any fuel containing carbon is burned. It is ex- haled from an animal's lungs during respiration and is used by plants in photosynthesis. Carbon dioxide is used in refrigeration, in fire extinguishers, and in carbonated drinks.

carbonic acid *n.* A weak acid having the formula H_2CO_3. It exists only in solution and decomposes readily into carbon dioxide and water.

car·bon·if·er·ous (kär′bə-nĭf′ər-əs) *adj.* Producing or containing carbon or coal.

Carboniferous *n.* The geologic time comprising the Mississippian (or Lower Carboniferous) and Pennsylvanian (or Upper Carboniferous) Periods of the Paleozoic Era, from about 360 to 286 million years ago. During the Carboniferous, widespread swamps formed in which plant remains accumulated and later hardened into coal. See table at **geologic time.—Carboniferous** *adj.*

car·bon·ize (kär′bə-nīz′) *tr. v.* **car·bon·ized, car·bon·iz·ing, car·bon·iz·es 1.** To change an organic compound into carbon by heating. **2.** To treat, coat, or combine with carbon.—**car′bon·i·za′tion** (kär′be-nī-zā′shən) *n.*

carbon monoxide *n.* A colorless odorless gas that is extremely poisonous and has the formula CO. Carbon monoxide is formed when carbon or a compound that contains carbon burns incompletely. It is present in the exhaust gases of automobile engines.

carbon paper *n.* A paper coated on one side with a dark coloring matter, placed between two sheets of blank paper so that the bottom sheet will receive a copy of what is typed or written on the top sheet.

carbon tet·ra·chlor·ide (tĕt′rə-klôr′īd′) *n.* A colorless poisonous liquid that is composed of carbon and chlorine, has the formula CCl_4, and does not burn although it vaporizes easily. It is used in fire extin-guishers and as a dry-cleaning fluid.

Car·bo·run·dum (kär′bə-rŭn′dəm) A trademark for an abrasive made of silicon carbide, used to cut, grind, and polish.

car·bun·cle (kär′bŭng′kəl) *n.* **1.** A painful inflammation in the tissue under the skin that is somewhat like a boil but releases pus from several openings. **2.** A deep-red garnet.

car·bu·re·tor (kär′bə-rā′tər *or* kär′byə-rā′tər) *n.* A device in a gasoline engine that vaporizes the gasoline with air to form an explosive mixture. [First written down in 1866 in English, from *carburet,* carbide, from Latin *carbō,* carbon.]

Illustration labels:
air — air filter
choke valve
gas
gas and air mixture
venturi
float
throttle valve
float chamber

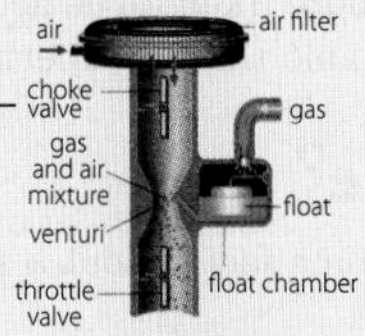

carburetor
cross section of a carburetor

Pronunciation key:

ă	pat	ôr	core
ā	pay	oi	boy
âr	care	ou	out
ä	father	ŏŏ	took
ĕ	pet	ōōr	lure
ē	be	ōō	boot
ĭ	pit	ŭ	cut
ī	bite	ûr	urge
îr	pier	th	thin
ŏ	pot	*th*	this
ō	toe	zh	vision
ô	paw	ə	about

If students have not yet read the entries on the dictionary page, have them do so now. You can also use this dictionary page to review

- parts of speech and their abbreviations,
- multiple-meaning words (*carbonize, carbuncle*),
- capitalization of geologic periods (*Carboniferous*) and trademarks (*Carborundum*), and
- adding suffixes to nouns (*carbon*) to create a different part of speech (*carbonize*).

Struggling Learners

Use this opportunity to review pronunciation strategies with students.

- Invite them to look through a dictionary to find words with challenging pronunciations.

- Copy each word on the board, including the syllable division and the respellings for pronunciation (with the stress marks).
- Together, work out the proper way to pronounce each word.

374

Evaluating Sources

Take time to discuss each of the questions and explanations for evaluating sources with students.

- Most students will have written research reports for other classes and previous grades. Ask them to describe what they have done in the past to evaluate a source.
- Be sure to emphasize how important this step is whenever students write a fact-based article or a research report.
- Point out that it takes only one incorrect or unreliable fact to discredit an otherwise well-researched and well-written report.

Evaluating Sources

Before you use any information in your writing, you must decide if it is trustworthy. Ask yourself the following questions to help judge the value of your sources.

Is the source a primary or a secondary source?

Firsthand facts are often more trustworthy than secondhand facts. However, many secondary sources are also trustworthy. (See page **364**.)

Is the source an expert?

An expert is an authority on a certain subject. You may need to ask a teacher, parent, or librarian for help when deciding how experienced a particular expert is.

Is the information accurate?

Sources that are well respected are more likely to be accurate. For example, a large city newspaper is much more reliable than a supermarket tabloid.

Is the information complete?

If a source of information provides some facts about a subject, but you still have questions, find an additional source.

Is the information current?

Be sure you have the most up-to-date information on a subject. Check for copyright dates of books and articles and for posting dates of online information.

Is the source biased?

A source is biased when it presents information that is one-sided. Some organizations, for example, have something to gain by using only some of the facts. Avoid such one-sided sources.

English Language Learners

Provide practice in evaluating sources. Present a collection of paired materials to students. Include sources such as

- a popular magazine and a scholarly journal,
- a story based on an event in nature and a science textbook, and

- a commercial Web site and a government Web site.

Engage students in discussing each pair of sources. Guide them in identifying the source that is more reliable, and encourage them to explain why.

Research Writing
Summary Paragraph

Have you ever noticed that when you explain an idea to someone else, you actually gain a better understanding of it yourself? That is why summary writing is such a valuable skill, both for writing reports and for learning new material.

When you write a summary paragraph about an article, you identify the main idea and important supporting details so that your reader gets a clear idea of what was in the original. In this chapter, you'll read an article about salt mines in Poland, as well as a student summary of the article. Then you'll find your own article and write a clear, concise summary paragraph about it.

Writing Guidelines

Subject: **A research article**
Form: **Summary paragraph**
Purpose: **To express the main idea**
Audience: **Classmates**

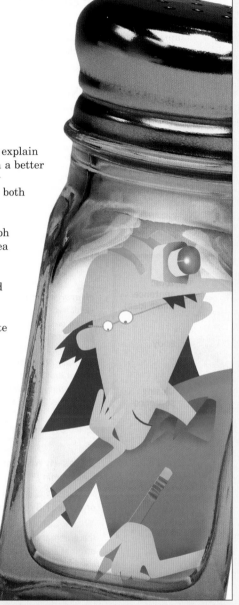

Summary Paragraph

Objectives
- understand the content, structure, and purpose of a summary paragraph
- choose an article to summarize
- plan, draft, revise, and edit a summary paragraph

A **summary paragraph** presents only the most important ideas from a longer piece of writing. Paragraphs have a topic sentence, the body, and a closing sentence.

Use the following questions to help students realize that they are summarizing whenever they tell someone about a book they read or a movie they saw.

- When you tell someone about a book or movie, do you tell every single thing that happened in the story? Why not? (It would take too long.)
- What parts do you usually tell? (The most important or exciting parts.)

English Language Learners

To help students understand what to include in a summary, use the overhead transparency for the T-chart (TR 10).

Ask students to tell about the highlights of a recent class or school event in a few sentences. Record their responses on the left side of the T-chart. For example:

- We went to an assembly yesterday afternoon.
- A guest speaker from a science center came to talk to us.
- She told us things that students can do to keep the environment clean.

Then ask students what they *didn't* tell about the event. Record

their responses on the right side of the chart. For example:

- We walked to the auditorium.
- It was hot in the auditorium.
- The speaker wore brown pants and a white blouse.

Point out that the details they left out were not important to a summary of the event.

Summary Paragraph

After students read the introduction, the article, and the summary of the article, have them find the main idea and the details in the original article that the summary writer used to write the topic sentence, body, and closing sentence.

Remind students that a summary
- retells only the most important ideas,
- is written in the writer's own words, and
- is presented in a much shorter form than the original article.

 Respond to the reading.

Answers

Ideas 1. Possible responses: details about specific ages of the mines and their specific distance and direction from Krakow, former uses of the salt and how the salt was mined, the statuary and chandeliers, underground lakes and sports facilities, cafeterias

Organization 2. by time

Word Choice 3. The first two sentences of the summary are simpler and much shorter.

376

Summary Paragraph

The following article, "Krakow's Salt Cellars," gives the history of two famous salt mines near Krakow, Poland. The paragraph "Polish Salt Mines" summarizes that article.

Krakow's Salt Cellars

Krakow, Poland, has two historic salt mines nearby, both of them dating back to the Middle Ages. Most famous is the 700-year-old Wieliczka mine about 20 km (12 miles) southeast of Krakow. The lesser-known Bochnia mine is 750 years old and lies about 30 km (18 miles) due east of the city.

Both mines tap into salt deposits that geologists say are left over from an inland sea that dried out 20 million years ago. Ever since the Stone Age, people have used salt from this region. At first, they boiled the brine from salt springs to get salt. In the 13th century, local farmers dug a few small shafts into the underground salt to keep themselves employed during the winter. Later, local rulers expanded the operations, using horse-powered winches to haul blocks of salt out of the mines. In the 20th century, electric power replaced the horses until the mines were finally emptied and closed in the 1990s.

Nowadays, the two mines are used mainly for guided tours. Visitors can see beautiful old chapels carved out of salt, decorated with salt statuary and chandeliers. They can view underground lakes and sports facilities where lords and ladies were once entertained. Underground museums document the history of salt mining, and cafeterias cater to the tourists. The Bochnia mine also has a sanitorium for people with respiratory ailments. The Wieliczka mine is on the United Nations' World Cultural Heritage list.

Topic sentence (main idea)

Body

Closing sentence

Polish Salt Mines
Less than 20 miles from Krakow, Poland, are two historic salt mines. The more famous is the Wieliczka mine, which dates back to the Middle Ages. The Bochnia mine is even older. Both mines were started in the 13th century and tap into deposits from a sea that dried up in prehistoric times. In the 1990s, both mines ran out of salt, but they remain open for tourists. Visitors can see chapels carved from salt, tour mining museums, and get treatment for breathing problems. The Wieliczka mine is on the United Nations' list of World Cultural Heritage sites.

 Respond to the reading. Answer the following questions.

☐ **Ideas** (1) What details from the original are not included in the summary?

☐ **Organization** (2) How is the summary paragraph organized? By importance? By location? By time?

☐ **Word Choice** (3) Compare the first two sentences of the summary with the wording of the first paragraph of the original article. Which is simpler?

English Language Learners

Because the original article may be challenging, first read and discuss the summary with students. Then put the original article on an overhead transparency.

- Read aloud the article to students.
- Engage them in locating facts that were included in the summary.

- As students locate each fact, use a transparency pen to highlight it in the article.

Have students look at the highlighted article and note which facts were included in the summary and which were left out.

Prewriting Selecting an Article

For this assignment, you must find an article to summarize. Choose an article that . . .

- relates to a subject you are studying,
- covers an interesting topic, and
- is fairly short (three to six paragraphs).

 Choose an article. Look through magazines and newspapers for an article to summarize. Choose one that has the three features listed above. Ask your teacher if the article will work for your summary paragraph.

Reading the Article

If possible, make a photocopy of your article so that you can underline important facts as you read. Otherwise, take brief notes on the article. The writer of the sample summary on page 376 underlined the key facts.

> Nowadays, the two mines are used mainly for guided tours. Visitors can see beautiful old chapels carved out of salt, decorated with salt statuary and chandeliers. They can view underground lakes and sports facilities where lords and ladies were once entertained. Underground museums document the history of salt mining, and cafeterias cater to the tourists. The Bochnia mine also has a sanitorium for people with respiratory ailments. The Wieliczka mine is on the United Nations' World Cultural Heritage list.

 Read your article. First read through the article. Then reread it and take notes or underline the important facts.

Finding the Main Idea

A summary focuses on the main idea of an article. Look over the material you underlined. What main idea do those facts and key details present? The writer of the sample summary wrote this main idea: "Less than 20 miles from Krakow, Poland, are two historic salt mines."

 Write the main idea. Review the facts you identified in your article. What main idea do they suggest? Write the main idea as a single sentence. This sentence (or a version of it) will be the topic sentence for your paragraph.

RESEARCH

Prewriting Selecting an Article

Have on hand a variety of current magazines (for both adults and children) and newspapers. Ask teachers from other curriculum areas to suggest or provide articles related to topics students are studying. Then have each student skim the materials and select an article on a topic of interest.

Prewriting Reading the Article

Direct students to read the article and find the most important facts.

- Tell students that as they read, they should list or underline at least three important facts.
- Point out that they are looking for related facts that will help them determine the main idea.

Prewriting
Finding the Main Idea

Remind students that the **main idea** *(see below)* of an article is the central thought the author develops; it is what the article is mostly about. The topic sentence of their summary should state this main idea as clearly and as concisely as possible.

✱ For more detailed instruction in writing a topic sentence, see PE page 525.

Teaching Tip: Recognizing the Main Idea

Students may need additional practice in identifying the main idea of an article.

Have students identify the main idea in an article that you provide. Tell them to follow these steps:

- Look at the title.
- Read the first paragraph. Find the sentence that all the other

sentences (and all the other paragraphs) support. Usually this sentence is the first or last sentence of the first paragraph.
- Look at the closing paragraph. Is an idea from the first paragraph restated there?
- Complete this sentence: *This article is mostly about . . .*

Offer guidance as needed.

Writing
Developing the First Draft

To help students get started, encourage them to use the topic sentence they wrote during prewriting.

- They can also refer to any notes they wrote and to ideas they underlined in the article.
- They will have a chance to revise and edit their drafts later.

Revising
Reviewing Your Writing

Have students review their summary paragraph with a partner before they revise it.

- Tell them to make sure that the topic sentence clearly states the article's main idea and that all the other sentences support the main idea of their summary.
- This will ensure that all their ideas go together and that the paragraph has unity.

✱ See PE page 538 for more information about creating unity in writing.

Editing
Checking for Conventions

As students edit, remind them to check the spelling and capitalization of names and places in the original article.

378

Writing Developing the First Draft

A summary paragraph includes a topic sentence, a body, and a closing sentence. As you write each part, follow these tips.

- **Topic sentence:** Introduce the main idea of the article.
- **Body:** Include just enough important facts to support or explain the main idea. As much as possible, use your own words and phrases to share these facts.
- **Closing sentence:** Restate the main idea of the summary in a different way.

 Write the first draft of your summary paragraph. Develop your topic sentence based on the main idea of the article. Add important facts that support the main idea. Then end your paragraph with a closing sentence.

Revising Reviewing Your Writing

As you revise, check your first draft for the following traits.

- ☐ **Ideas** Does my topic sentence correctly identify the main idea? Do I include only the most important facts to support it?
- ☐ **Organization** Is all of the information in a logical order?
- ☐ **Voice** Does my voice sound confident and informative?
- ☐ **Word Choice** Do I use my own words? Do I define any difficult terms?
- ☐ **Sentence Fluency** Do I use a variety of sentence types and lengths?

 Revise your paragraph. First reread the article and your summary. Then use the questions above as a guide for your revising.

Editing Checking for Conventions

Focus on conventions as you edit your summary.

- ☐ **Conventions** Have I checked the facts against the article? Have I checked for errors in punctuation, spelling, and grammar?

 Edit your work. Use the questions above as your editing guide. Make your corrections, write a neat final copy, and proofread it for errors.

Struggling Learners

Make an overhead transparency of a summary of an article. (Use a summary you have written or that was written by someone in another class.) As a class, highlight key parts of the summary and suggest ways to improve it (defining terms, replacing vague words, etc.).

Grammar Connection

Appositives
- **Proofreader's Guide** pages 586 (+), 587 (appositives)
- *Write Source* pages 472 (appositives), 513 (+)
- *SkillsBook* page 17
- **CD** Commas to Set Off Appositives

Semicolons
- **Proofreader's Guide** pages 594–595
- *SkillsBook* pages 19–20

Using the Right Word
- **Proofreader's Guide** pages 652–686 (+)
- *SkillsBook* pages 59–60

Research Writing
Research Report

There are some amazing places in this world—many of them closer to home than you might think. For example, how many people in Detroit know that a salt mine sprawls under a quarter of their city? And how many Nevada citizens know that some trees in the White Mountains are 5,000 years old? Every region of the country has its own natural wonders and historic sites.

In this chapter, you will write a report about an important place that interests you—a building, a historic site, a monument, or a natural feature. You will explain why the place you have chosen is important, tell its history, describe its condition today, and predict something about its future. In the process, you may become something of an expert about your chosen place.

Writing Guidelines

Subject:	An important place
Form:	Research report
Purpose:	To research and present information about an important place
Audience:	Classmates

Copy Masters/ Transparencies

5 W's chart (TE p. 383)

Research Report

Objectives
- understand what a research report is
- understand the purpose of a research report
- plan, draft, revise, edit, and publish a research report

A **research report** is a piece of writing that
- shares information on a topic that has been researched carefully, and
- presents the research results in a clear, well-organized way.

Have students brainstorm a list of interesting and important places they have visited, read about, heard about, or seen documentary films about.
- Keep the list on display in the classroom writing center, along with travel brochures, tour guides, posters, photographs, and Web-site addresses of interesting destinations.
- Students can refer to these materials when it's time to select a topic for their report.

Research Report

As you review this sample research report with the class, point out the elements that make it an interesting, well-organized, and unified report.

The three traits that are discussed on the next few pages relate to the development of the content and the form of the report. They provide a focus during prewriting, drafting, and revising.

- **Ideas**
- **Organization**
- **Voice**

Later, during the revising and editing stages, students will address the other three traits, which relate more to form.

- **Word Choice**
- **Sentence Fluency**
- **Conventions**

380

Research Report

Even though student writer Damek Soleny has lived in Detroit all of his life, he was surprised when he discovered that there is an enormous salt mine under the city. So Damek chose to write about that mine in his research report.

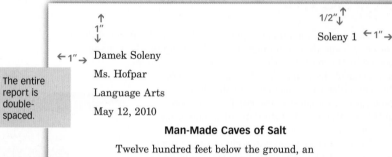

↑1"↓   1/2"↑↓   Soleny 1   ←1"→

←1"→   Damek Soleny

Ms. Hofpar

Language Arts

May 12, 2010

The entire report is double-spaced.

Man-Made Caves of Salt

Twelve hundred feet below the ground, an enormous mine has been operating almost nonstop for more than a century. A hundred miles of tunnels connect its huge chambers. It has underground roads for cars, trucks, and mining machines. This mine produces hundreds of tons of "rock" every day. However, the rock from this mine is not gold, or iron ore, or even coal; it is salt. This enormous, hundred-year-old salt mine lies beneath the city of Detroit, Michigan.

Beginning

The opening grabs the reader's attention.

The thesis (focus) statement identifies the topic (underlined).

Salt is much more important than most people realize. Wars have been fought over it. In some places, people have traded salt for gold in equal measures. In ancient China, salt coins were used for money, and Roman soldiers were often paid in salt, which is where the word "salary" comes from. In the human body, salt carries electrical signals that keep a person alive. To

 ↑1"↓

NOTE RESEARCH
organize summarize *cite*   **381**
Research Report

Soleny 2

Middle
The first middle paragraph explains why the topic is important.

stay healthy, a person needs to eat about three pounds of salt a year (Modern). Salt is also used to preserve meat and fish, to tan leather, to soften water, and to make many different chemicals. However, most of the salt from the Detroit mine is now used to melt ice and snow on streets and highways (Zacharias).

Headings help the reader to understand the paper's organization.

The Salt Mine's History

Scientists say that the Detroit mine digs into a bed of salt that is several hundred million years old. From 600 million to 230

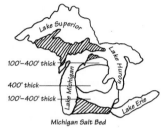

100'–400' thick
400' thick
100'–400' thick
Michigan Salt Bed

A map helps the reader understand the size and location of the mine.

million years ago, seawater flooded the middle of North America many times. As sun and wind evaporated the water, sea salt was deposited on the submerged land. Trillions of tons of salt, collected in a layer 400 to 1,600 feet thick, reached from western Michigan all the way to New York. Eventually, it was covered by silt that became rock more than 1,000 feet thick. When people later came to the area, they found springs of salty water bubbling from the ground. Early settlers would collect that liquid and boil away the water to get the salt ("Dry").

The history of the place is explained.

In 1896, the Detroit salt mine was started in order to dig the salt out of the ground. It began as a shaft

RESEARCH

Ideas
- The thesis statement identifies the main idea.
- Interesting details support the topic sentence of each middle paragraph.

English Language Learners

Provide students with a basic gathering chart to help them follow the research paper as you slowly read it aloud to them. Label the chart with the following headings: thesis statement, the salt mine's history, the salt mine today, and the salt mine's future. Help students fill in the chart with important details as you go along.

Struggling Learners

To help students recognize the organization of Damek's writing, tell them to look at the headings in his report. Then refer them to the requirements of the research assignment, which are outlined in the second paragraph on PE page 379. Ask students these questions:

- Did Damek follow the guidelines for organization?
- How can you tell? (time order)

Organization
- The beginning paragraph grabs the reader's attention.
- The middle paragraphs explain why the place is important, tell about the history of the place, and describe it as it exists today.
- The ending paragraph provides information about the place's future and makes a final observation for the reader.
- Headings help the writer create unity within the paper and identify for the reader what a section is mainly about.

382

Soleny 3

1,200 feet deep and about 6 feet wide. At first, the salt was used mainly for storing meat and fish and for making ice cream (Detroit 167). In 1940, though, Detroit became the first city to use rock salt on icy roads. Other cities soon followed Detroit's example, and the mine began selling most of its salt to road crews ("Dry"). In 1983, however, low sales and competition from Canadian mines caused the Detroit mine to close. Crystal Mines bought the mine, hoping to store hazardous wastes there. In 1985, while waiting for a permit, they ran public tours of the mine. In 1997, after the permit was denied, Crystal Mines sold the mine to the Detroit Salt Company, according to Kim Roberts, manager of the mine. The mine was reopened, and it again became one of the main sources of road salt in the United States.

A source and page number are identified in parentheses.

The Salt Mine Today

Some people call the Detroit salt mine a city beneath a city. It covers 1,400 acres under Detroit and its suburbs. That's equal to 1,300 football fields. Also, it has more than 50 miles of roads where construction equipment, trucks, and cars drive. All these vehicles had to be taken apart, carried down the shaft in pieces, and reassembled in underground workshops. The seven-foot-tall tires for the dump trucks had to be compressed and bound with straps to fit down the shaft (Zacharias).

The place is described as it exists today.

RESEARCH

Soleny 4

The writer's last name and page number appear on every page.

The mining equipment includes many different types of big electric trucks. One type has a giant chain saw on the front, which cuts a deep groove into a salt wall at floor level. Then a drilling-machine truck bores a pattern of holes 20 feet deep into the wall to hold dynamite or other explosives. The blast from these explosives breaks hundreds of tons of rock from the wall in huge chunks. Trucks with giant shovels then scoop up tons at a time and drop them into dump trucks. The dump trucks carry the chunks back to the shaft, where a crusher breaks them into smaller pieces and sorting machines separate the pieces by size. Finally, buckets that can hold nine tons of salt run up a conveyor to the surface. There the salt is packaged and shipped ("Dry").

Each paragraph begins with a topic sentence, followed by supporting details.

The Salt Institute explains that the mine is carved out in a "room-and-pillar" method. Each room is as big and high as a school gymnasium. Between rooms, the miners leave pillars of salt about 60 feet wide to hold up the ceiling. This type of mining gets about 70 percent of the salt from the ground, leaving the other 30 percent as support pillars. Because the salt bed has never had an earthquake or other shock, it lies very flat, so the pattern of rooms and pillars stretches level from one end of the mine to the other. According to the Salt Institute, this mine "has never experienced a collapse or mine fatality" ("Dry").

A quotation is used for emphasis.

Voice

- Specific, interesting facts throughout the report and the use of a quotation create a knowledgeable voice.
- Anecdotes about the importance of salt, wars, trading salt for gold, the word *salary,* and vital electric signals in the body show the writer's interest in the topic.

Advanced Learners

In his report, Damek explains the value of salt in earlier civilizations (PE page 380).

- Invite students to research the use of salt as money and then prepare a brief report for the class.

- Remind students to use the 5 W and H questions to gather their information and to note their sources.
- Provide photocopies of the reproducible 5 W's chart (TE page 792), and have students write *How* in the right-hand margin.

If there is time, have students reread the report, paying particular attention to the parts of the report that illustrate the notes in the margins of the report.

To reinforce the idea that every supporting paragraph in a research report should have its own unity while reinforcing the unity of the entire report, ask students to

- identify the topic sentence in each middle paragraph,
- identify the details that support that topic sentence,
- tell how that paragraph supports the main idea of the section (importance, history, present day, future), and
- tell how each section supports the idea stated in the thesis (focus) statement of the report.

Soleny 5

Miners say that the mine is a very clean and healthy place to work. The temperature stays a cool 58 degrees year-round, and the salt keeps the humidity at an even 55 percent. There are no bugs, rats, or other animals living in the mine, because there is nothing for them to eat (Zacharias). The air itself is very clean in a salt mine, with no mold or other allergens like on the surface (Modern).

The Salt Mine's Future

The Detroit salt mine could have a very interesting future. According to geologists, there is enough salt underneath Michigan to last for 70 million years ("Dry"). Many people worry, though, that the runoff from road salt is having a negative effect on our rivers and lakes. If people stop using salt on icy streets and highways, there may not be enough business to keep the Detroit mine open. In that case, the mine could be used to store important documents, films, and artwork, as some other salt mines do (Tanner). If nothing else, the Detroit salt mine could be turned into a public museum because it is an important part of the city's history.

Ending
The final paragraph states something about the place's future and leaves the reader with something to think about.

Struggling Learners

Point out that Damek provides a detailed description of the mines.

- Have students share examples with the class.
- Tell students to close their eyes and imagine what it's like to be there. Then have volunteers describe the salt mines, using their senses.
- Discuss the value of description in a research report.

Advanced Learners

Remind students that the value of salt has changed over time.

- Refer them to Damek's final paragraph, where he questions the future of the salt mine because of the harmful effects of road salt on the environment.
- Invite students to brainstorm other products that were once considered to contribute to "progress" but later turned out to be harmful to the environment.
- Consider having students role-play debates between advocates for a product and experts from the Environmental Protection Agency.

Soleny 6

Works Cited

A separate page alphabetically lists sources cited in the paper.

Detroit Almanac. Detroit: Detroit Free Press, 2004.

"Dry (Rock Salt) Mining." Salt Institute. Salt Institute.
10 May 2008 <http://www.saltinstitute.org/
mich-1.html>.

Modern Marvels: Salt Mines. Videocassette. A&E
Television Networks, 2004.

Roberts, Kim. E-mail to the author. 4 May 2008.

Tanner, Beccy. "Salt Mine Museum Could Spark Tourist
Trade." Wichita Eagle 8 May 2004: A9.

Zacharias, Patricia. "The Ghostly Salt City Beneath
Detroit." Detnews.com. The Detroit News. 11 May
2008 <http://info.detnews.com/history/story/
index.cfm?id=17&category=business>.

RESEARCH

Respond to the reading. After you have finished reading the sample research report, answer the following questions about the traits of writing.

☐ **Ideas** (1) What is the main idea of the report? (2) List at least four details that emphasize the age and size of the mine.

☐ **Organization** (3) How do the headings help organize the paper?

☐ **Voice** (4) What words does the writer use to show his interest in this topic? Give at least two examples.

Respond to the reading.

Answers

Ideas **1.** An enormous, hundred-year-old salt mine lies beneath the city of Detroit, Michigan.
2. Possible choices:

■ **size:** hundred miles of tunnels connect huge chambers, hundreds of tons of "rock" every day, trillions of tons of salt, a layer 400 to 1,600 feet thick, shaft 1,200 feet deep and 6 feet wide, covers 1,400 acres, has 50 miles of roads

■ **age:** bed of salt several hundred million years old, early settlers found springs, 1896 Detroit salt mine started

Organization **3.** The headings

■ help the writer organize and present related historical facts in chronological (time) order,

■ break the text into manageable sections for the reader, and

■ help ideas flow smoothly.

Voice **4.** Possible choices:

■ more important than most people realize

■ wars have been fought

■ traded salt for gold

■ word *salary* comes from

■ carries electrical signals

■ could have very interesting future

Struggling Learners

When considering voice, explain that not only does a writer need to show strong interest in the subject, she or he also needs to engage the curiosity of the audience.

Discuss with students whether Damek was successful in engaging their curiosity. Ask the following questions:

● When you read the title, did you expect the report to be interesting?

● Did Damek manage to engage your curiosity and interest? How?

● How did your expectations about the topic compare to what you actually learned?

Prewriting

Keys to Effective Prewriting

Remind students of the purpose of the prewriting stage in the writing process. (It's when the writer gets ready to write.)

Keys to Effective Prewriting explains the process students will be guided through on PE pages 387–394.

- Direct students' attention to item 3. Emphasize that they should choose a topic (place) that has a good balance of details about its past, present, and future.
- If, as they take notes (item 4), they notice that they have a predominance of details in one area but a lack of details in another, they should do more research or consider changing their topic.
- Students may be concerned about citing sources correctly (mentioned in items 5 and 6). Assure them that they will receive specific guidelines for citing sources later in this section.

386

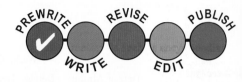

Prewriting

"Well begun is half done," Aristotle once said. When it comes to writing a research paper, a good beginning means choosing a good topic, taking careful notes during your research, writing a solid thesis statement, and preparing a good plan. Use these keys as a guide to your prewriting.

Keys to Effective Prewriting

1. For your topic, choose an important place that interests you.

2. Make a list of questions you want to have answered about that place.

3. Make sure that there are enough details about its past, present, and future.

4. Use a gathering grid and note cards to organize your research questions and the answers you find.

5. Be careful to list your sources when paraphrasing or quoting exact words.

6. Write down the publication details of all your sources for making a works-cited page.

Selecting a Topic

To find a topic for your research paper, make a list of important places that interest you. Answer the following questions to help generate ideas. (See Damek's list below as an example.)

● What interesting places have I visited?

● What interesting places have I seen on TV, in magazines, or on the Web?

● What interesting places does my social studies text mention?

TOPICS LIST

I have visited these interesting places:
- *The current Michigan State Capitol*
- *The Graystone International Jazz Museum in Detroit*
- *Yerkes Observatory in Williams Bay, Wisconsin*
- *The U.S.S. Constitution in Boston*

I have seen these places on TV, on the Web, or in a magazine:
- *The cliff dwellings at Mesa Verde, Colorado*
✱ - *The salt mine under Detroit*
- *The "Avenue of Giants," sequoia trees in California*
- *Fort Knox's gold vault in Kentucky*

My textbook mentions these interesting places:
- *Monticello, Thomas Jefferson's home*
- *The Alamo, a famous battle site in Texas*
- *Ellis Island, where many immigrants landed*
- *The International Space Station*

Make your list. Try to list at least three possible topics under each heading. Then choose the one that interests you the most.

RESEARCH

Prewriting Selecting a Topic

As you read the instruction and Damek's topics list with students, keep in mind that some students may not have had many travel opportunities beyond school (or community) field trips.

■ As part of a brainstorming session on topics, encourage students to recall the different field trips they have taken over the years, with school or other community groups.

■ If students still have trouble coming up with ideas for their topics list, suggest that they refer to the list of ideas they generated and the travel materials that you placed in the writing center (TE page 379).

English Language Learners

Some students may have lived in one or more other countries. Encourage them to consider writing about an interesting place in their homeland or another country they traveled through in making their way from their homeland to the United States.

Advanced Learners

Provide students with the option of participating in a group project based on their social studies curriculum.

● Have them limit their research choices to places that have significant historical value in the United States.

● Encourage each student to choose a different place that reflects a different time period. Have students work independently to research and complete their report.

● When the reports are completed, have students work together to create a time line and/or a map of the places in their reports to present a journey through America's past.

Prewriting Sizing Up Your Topic

Tell students to use Damek's notes as a model as they begin their research.

- Point out that if they look back at Damek's report (PE pages 380–385), they will see that this page of notes serves as a rough outline for the organization of ideas in his report.
- Students may want to follow a similar pattern of organization when they write their report.
- Make sure students understand how long they have to spend on each part of the report. If you want them to submit topic ideas, notes, outlines, first drafts, and final drafts in stages, prepare a schedule ahead of time and distribute it to students.
- To help students stay on schedule, write reminders on the board at least one week before, as well as the day before, something is due.

388

Prewriting Sizing Up Your Topic

A good research report about a place should say something about the place's importance, its past, its present, and its future. Damek decided to write about the salt mine under Detroit. He searched the Internet and learned the following major facts about that mine. With this information to start with, Damek was sure he could write a good research report about the mine.

Details List

> Notes About the Detroit Salt Mine
>
> Its importance
> - The salt has been used for making chemicals, softening water, preserving food, and making ice cream.
> - Today, it is used mainly for melting road ice.
>
> Its past
> - The salt bed is left from an ancient sea.
> - The first mine shaft was dug in 1896.
> - During the '80s its owners gave public tours.
>
> Its present
> - It has 100 miles of tunnels and 50 miles of roads.
> - The rooms are each as big as a school gymnasium.
> - Huge electric trucks do the digging and hauling.
>
> Its future
> - There's enough salt for 70 million years of mining.
> - If demand for salt goes down, the mine might close.
> - It could be used as a storage place or as a museum.

Size up your topic. Look up your chosen topic in an encyclopedia or on the Internet. List the key details you find. Are there enough details to support a research report? If not, think of another topic.

Struggling Learners

Before the due date for each stage of the project, schedule conference times so students can share their progress with you. Instruct students to discuss what they've accomplished. Ask questions if anything is unclear and offer suggestions for improvements.

RESEARCH

Using a Gathering Grid

A gathering grid can help you organize the information from your research. Damek made a grid during his research about the Detroit salt mine. Down the left-hand side, he listed questions about his topic. Across the top, he listed sources he found to answer those questions. For answers too long to fit in the grid, Damek used note cards. (See pages **390–391**.)

Gathering Grid

Detroit's Salt Mine	Detroit Almanac	Salt Institute	Detroit News Web site	Wichita Eagle
Importance: What is its purpose?			Rock salt for icy roads and making chemicals	
History: What is its past?	People dug a 1,200-foot shaft in 1896	See note card #1.		
Present: What does it look like?		Rooms the size of gymnasiums, pillars 60 feet wide	100 miles of tunnels, 50 miles of roads	
Future: How might it be used in the future?			It can't be use for toxic storage.	Some salt mines are used as museums.

Create a gathering grid. Make a list of questions in the left-hand column of your grid. Across the top, list the sources that you use. Fill in the squares with answers you find. Use note cards for longer, more detailed answers.

Prewrite

Prewriting

Using a Gathering Grid

It will be helpful for students to refer back to Damek's report to see how he used the details from the grid on this page and the note cards on PE page 390.

Point out the features of the grid, and instruct students to follow a similar pattern as they create their own grid.

Teaching Tip: Punctuation for Titles of Sources

Review the conventions for titles in a handwritten text and in a printed document.

Remind students to follow the conventions for titles in their grids, on note cards, and wherever they cite a source. Provide these guidelines:

- Italicize (or underline) the titles of books, newspapers, magazines, CD-ROMs, videos, films, television shows, and Web sites.

- Put quotation marks around titles of short stories, poems, magazine or newspaper articles, book chapters, songs, specific television episodes, lectures, and speeches.

✻ For more about how to treat titles, see PE pages 403–404.

Prewriting Creating Note Cards

Chances are, students are going to have more than one note card for each question.

- Have students color-code the note cards for each question. Then, when it's time to write their report, they can quickly find the details they gathered for that question by looking for all the cards with that color.
- Provide (or ask students to use) different colored index cards for each question. If students use white index cards instead, have them use different colored markers to highlight the question.
- Students can use the sample note cards as models, but suggest that they leave a space between the number and question. This will allow them to add a letter after the number to show the order of the cards (for example, 1. a, 1. b, 1. c, and so on) if they run out of space on a card. This will help them keep their notes in order.

Prewriting Creating Note Cards

While a gathering grid is a great way to see all your research at one glance, sometimes an answer needs more space. You can use note cards to keep track of details from your research.

Number each new card and write a question at the top. Then answer the question with a paraphrase, a list, or a quotation. At the bottom, identify the source of the information (including a page number if appropriate). Here are three sample cards Damek made for his report on the Detroit salt mine.

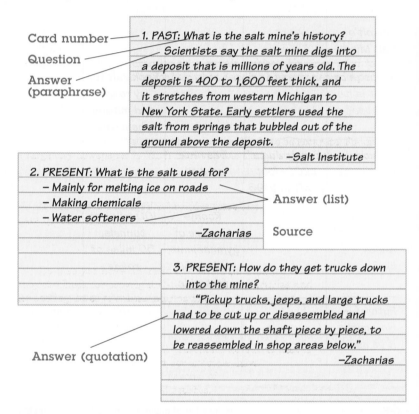

 Create note cards. Make note cards like the examples above whenever your answers are too long to fit on your gathering grid.

NOTE *RESEARCH* summarize *cite* *organize* 391

Research Report

Avoiding Plagiarism

Your research will lead you to many interesting facts and ideas to include in your paper. However, you must give credit for facts and ideas that are not common knowledge. Using other people's words and ideas without giving them credit is called plagiarism, and it is a form of stealing. Here are two good ways to avoid plagiarism.

■ **Paraphrase:** Usually it's best to put the ideas from a source into your own words so that your paper sounds like you. This is called *paraphrasing*. Remember, though, to give credit to the source of the ideas. (See page **396**.)

■ **Quote exact words:** When a source states something so perfectly that it makes sense to use those words exactly, you may include them in quotation marks and give credit to the source. (See page **396**.)

RESEARCH

Paraphrasing

4. PRESENT: How safe is the salt mine?
The Detroit salt mine has never had a
cave-in, and no one has ever died in a mining
accident there.
Salt Institute Web site

Quoting Exact Words

4. PRESENT: How safe is the salt mine?
"The mine, which consists of 100 miles
of tunnels, has never experienced a collapse
or mine fatality."
Salt Institute Web site

  Read the following excerpt from "Salt in the Michigan Basin." Then label two note cards with the question "What is salt used for?" On one card, *quote* a sentence from the excerpt. On the other, *paraphrase* the selection.

Chemically, there are several different types of salt, and they are used for many different purposes. When most people say "salt," they're talking about sodium chloride. In its purest form, sodium chloride is used for table salt. Mined rock salt usually has some impurities in it and is used for other purposes. Road crews use rock salt to melt ice and snow. Chemical companies use it to make rayon, soap, and bleach. It is also used in water softeners and as salt licks.

Prewriting Avoiding Plagiarism

Point out to students that
■ they should select quotations that develop the main ideas in their reports, and
■ quotations should be added logically and selectively, to support the writer's own ideas.

Before assigning the **Try It** activity, make sure students understand **how to paraphrase** *(see below)*.

Try It Answers

Answers and wording will vary. Possible responses are given.
1. What is salt used for? (quotation)
   "In its purest form, sodium chloride is used for table salt." "Salt in the Michigan Basin"
1. What is salt used for? (paraphrase)
   The most familiar form of sodium chloride is the salt we sprinkle on our food. "Salt in the Michigan Basin"

Teaching Tip: How to Paraphrase

Help students understand that a paraphrase

● expresses ideas from another source in your own words, and
● may be the same length or longer than the original work.

Show how the sample paraphrase says the same thing as the quotation, but in the writer's own words. Ask these questions:

● What is the main idea of the quotation? (The mine has never experienced a collapse or a fatality.)
● How did the writer put this idea into his or her own words? (The mine has never had a cave-in, and no one has ever died.)
● What information is left out of the paraphrase? (consists of 100 miles of tunnels)

Have students work in groups to paraphrase a newspaper article. Assign each group one paragraph of the article. Tell students to work together to rewrite each sentence in their paragraph in their own words, using the sample as a model. Have each group read aloud the original paragraph (in the order in which it appears in the article) and their paraphrase of it.

Prewriting
Keeping Track of Your Sources

Review the different kinds of sources students may encounter as they do their research, along with the sample source notes.

- Remind students to list all their sources as they do research and gather information, so they will have all the information they need at their fingertips when it's time to check a fact or create their works-cited page.

- Invite volunteers to create a poster showing a variety of examples of sources, and display it in your writing center or in the reference section of the school library.

- Students can also tag this page with a sticky note or flag for a quick reference when writing their works-cited page (PE pages 403–404).

392

Prewriting Keeping Track of Your Sources

Write down the following information about the sources you find.

Encyclopedia entry: Author's name (if listed). Entry title. Encyclopedia title. Edition (if given). Publication date.

Book: Author's name. Title. Publisher and city. Copyright date.

Magazine: Author's name. Article title. Magazine title. Date published. Page numbers.

Newspaper: Author's name. Article title. Newspaper title. City (for a local paper, if it isn't in the title). Date published. Section. Page numbers.

Internet: Author's name (if listed). Page title. Site title. Date posted or copyright date (if listed). Site sponsor. Date found. Electronic address.

Videocassette: Title. Distributor. Release date.

My Source Notes

Book
Mark Kurlansky. *Salt: A World History.* Penguin USA. East Rutherford, NJ. 2007.

Magazine
Don Hallett. "The Wieliczka Salt Mine." *Geology Today.* September/October 2006. Pages 182-185.

Newspaper
Beccy Tanner. "Salt Mine Museum Could Spark Tourist Trade." *Wichita Eagle.* May 8, 2004. Section A. Page 9.

Internet
No author. "Dry (Rock Salt) Mining." *Salt Institute.* The Salt Institute. No date posted. Visited May 10, 2008. www.saltinstitute.org/mich-1.html.

Video
Modern Marvels: Salt Mines. Videocassette. A&E Television Networks. 2004.

Interview
Kim Roberts. E-mail. May 4, 2008.

List sources. Keep a list of each of your sources with the information shown above. Whenever you find a new source, add it to the list.

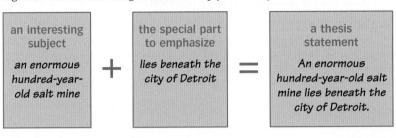

NOTE *RESEARCH* *organize* summarize *cite*   **393**
Research Report

Writing Your Thesis Statement

After your research is completed, you will need to write a thesis statement to guide your writing. The thesis is the main idea you want to emphasize in your report. It serves as a focus for your report to make sure all the parts work together. Use the following formula to help you write your thesis statement.

an interesting subject		the special part to emphasize		a thesis statement
an enormous hundred-year-old salt mine	**+**	lies beneath the city of Detroit	**=**	An enormous hundred-year-old salt mine lies beneath the city of Detroit.

RESEARCH

Sample Thesis Statements

> The 100-year-old Yerkes Observatory in Williams Bay, Wisconsin,
> (an interesting subject)
> has the largest refracting telescope in the world.
> (the part to emphasize)

> The "Avenue of the Giants" in northern California
> (an interesting subject)
> includes some giant sequoia trees that are 2,000 years old.
> (the part to emphasize)

> The International Space Station
> (an interesting subject)
> is the combined project of 16 different countries.
> (the part to emphasize)

Prewrite

Form your thesis statement. Review your research notes and choose a special part to emphasize about your topic. Using the formula above, write a thesis statement for your report.

Prewriting

Writing Your Thesis Statement

Discuss the sample thesis statements. Make sure students understand the purpose of the two parts before moving on.

Practice creating two-part thesis statements together as a class.

- Draw a graphic on the board like the one shown and use the same headings (an interesting subject, the special part to emphasize, a thesis statement).
- Invite students to suggest ideas for thesis statements, based on their report topics.
- Students who are willing to share their ideas can benefit from having their thesis statement written by the group during the practice.

Struggling Learners

To help students understand what to emphasize in a thesis statement, ask them the following questions:

- What is the most interesting thing you learned about the topic?
- Why does it interest you?
- What really surprised or impressed you?
- What do you think everyone should know about it?

Modeling the process may also help students recognize what to emphasize in a thesis statement.

Prewriting Outlining Your Ideas

Specify whether students will be required to write a topic outline or a sentence outline, or allow them to choose the type they prefer.

Before students make their own outlines, give them time to review the elements of the sample outline and to compare it to the finished report.

- For additional practice, have students work together to fill in the remainder of the outline for the report on PE pages 380–385.
- Completing that outline will help them to see that an outline is actually the framework of a report.

After you have practiced creating an outline together, have students work independently to create their own outlines.

- Circulate among students to offer guidance as needed.
- Caution them to avoid beginning their topic sentences with *It, This,* or *There.*

✽ For more about outlines, see PE page 550. For strategies for writing topic sentences, see PE pages 552–553.

394

Prewriting Outlining Your Ideas

Making an outline is one way to organize your details and plan your report. You can use either a topic outline or a sentence outline to list the main ideas of your report. A topic outline lists ideas as words or phrases. A sentence outline puts ideas into full sentences. (Also see page **550**.)

Sentence Outline

Below is the first part of a sentence outline for the report on pages 380–385. Notice that the outline begins with the thesis statement for the report. Then it lists a topic sentence for each middle paragraph, followed by details to support that topic sentence. Compare this partial outline to the finished report.

Thesis Statement	**THESIS STATEMENT:** This enormous, hundred-year-old salt mine lies beneath the city of Detroit, Michigan.
I. Topic Sentence (for first middle paragraph)	I. Salt is much more important than most people realize.
A. B. C. D. Supporting Ideas	A. Wars have been fought over salt, and it has been used for money.
	B. It helps keep the body alive and healthy.
	C. It is used to preserve food, to soften water, and to make chemicals.
	D. It is used to melt the ice on roads.
II. Topic Sentence (for second middle paragraph)	II. Scientists say that the Detroit mine digs into a bed of salt that is several hundred million years old.
	A. . . .
	B. . . .

Remember: In an outline, if you have a I, you must also have a II. If you have an A, you must also have a B.

Create your outline. Write a sentence outline for your report. Be sure that each topic sentence (I, II, III, . . .) supports the thesis statement and that each detail (A, B, C, . . .) supports its topic sentence. Use your outline as a guide when you write the first draft of your report.

Struggling Learners

✽ Have students examine different options for their report. Then discuss why it might be easier for them to start an organized list (PE page 550) or a topic outline instead of a sentence outline. Explain that listing details as phrases helps writers jot down key information and gives them ideas to write about.

Writing

With your research finished and a plan prepared, you're ready to begin writing the first draft of your paper. You don't have to get everything perfect in this draft. Just get your ideas down on paper in a way that makes sense to you. Use the following keys to guide your writing.

Keys to Effective Writing

1. Use your first paragraph to introduce your topic, get your reader's attention, and present your thesis statement.

2. In the second paragraph, explain why the place you have chosen is important.

3. In the next few paragraphs, tell about the history of the place.

4. Next, describe the place as it exists today.

5. End your paper with a few comments about the place's future.

6. Remember to cite your sources in your paper and list those sources alphabetically on a works-cited page.

RESEARCH

Writing Keys to Effective Writing

Remind students that the writing stage is when they get to write, or draft, their ideas on paper.

Keys to Effective Writing explains the process students will be guided through on PE pages 396–404.

Emphasize the idea that students do not have to get everything exactly right at this stage in the process. Instead, their goal should be to get down all the ideas they researched and developed during prewriting. Tell them to be sure to refer to their
- gathering grid,
- note cards,
- list of sources,
- thesis statement, and
- outline.

As you review Keys to Effective Writing, direct students' attention to item 2. Students should have developed interesting topic sentences for each main idea in their outline.

Challenge students to show why a place is important without saying, "This place is important because . . ."

Struggling Learners

Some students may need help in explaining why a place is important.
- Refer students back to the second paragraph on PE pages 380–381. Ask them to notice how Damek succeeded by using interesting examples.
- Guide a discussion that leads to options for explaining why a place is important.
- Record the options on a chart for classroom reference.

English Language Learners

Rather than asking students to compose a few paragraphs about the history of the place (item 3), have them write just one paragraph about its past. Explain that one paragraph for each main idea (items 1–5) can be sufficient.

Writing
Citing Sources in Your Report

Before assigning the **Try It** activity, have students explain in their own words

- when to include the author's last name (or first and last name, if authors share the same surname),
- when to omit the author's name,
- when and how to shorten a title, and
- how to cite sources without authors, page numbers, or both.

 Answers

Wording may vary. Possible answers:

For centuries, people have believed that bathing in saltwater springs restores and encourages good health. (Kemper, 78)

Steve Kemper explains that throughout history, people have believed that bathing in salt springs would make them healthier. (78)

For additional practice, have students try different ways of citing sources for their reports, based on the ideas shown.

396

Citing Sources in Your Report

Remember: It's very important that you give credit for each of the sources you use in your report.

When You Have All the Information

- The most common type of credit (citation) lists the author's last name and the page number in parentheses.
  "Marco Polo discovered that Tibetans used salt cakes stamped with the imperial seal of the great Kublai Khan as money" (Kemper 70).

- If you already name the author in your report, just include the page number in parentheses.
  Steve Kemper explains that during the Civil War, the North sent troops to attack the South's salt producers in order to make the South weaker (71).

When Some Information Is Missing

- Some sources do not list an author. In those cases, use the title and page number. (If the title is long, use only the first word or two.)
  At first, the salt was used mainly for storing meat and fish and for making ice cream (Detroit 167).

- Some sources (especially Internet sites) do not use page numbers. In those cases, list just the author.
  The seven-foot-tall tires for the dump trucks had to be compressed and bound with straps to fit down the shaft (Zacharias).

- If a source does not list the author or page number, use the title.
  Early settlers would collect that liquid and boil away the water to get the salt ("Dry").

 Rewrite the following sentence, citing Steve Kemper's article, "Salt of the Earth," from the *Smithsonian*, page 78.

Throughout history, people have soaked themselves in salt springs, believing that the salty water makes them healthier.

NOTE *organize* **RESEARCH** **summarize** *cite*   **397**
Research Report

Writing Starting Your Research Report

The opening paragraph of your report should grab the reader's attention, introduce your topic, and present your thesis statement. To start your opening paragraph, try one of these three approaches.

> Beginning
>
> Middle
>
> Ending

- **Start with an interesting fact.**
   Twelve hundred feet below the ground, an enormous mine has been operating almost nonstop for more than a century.

- **Ask an interesting question.**
   How many people know that there are cars and trucks driving on roads more than 1,200 feet below the city of Detroit?

- **Start with a quotation.**
   "The only dirty part of this job is getting to work," says salt miner Joel Payton.

Beginning Paragraph

> The beginning paragraph starts with an interesting detail and ends with the thesis (focus) statement (underlined).

> *Twelve hundred feet below the ground, an enormous mine has been operating almost nonstop for more than a century. A hundred miles of tunnels connect its huge chambers. It has underground roads for cars, trucks, and mining machines. This mine produces hundreds of tons of "rock" every day. However, the rock from this mine is not gold, or iron ore, or even coal; it is salt. <u>This enormous, hundred-year-old salt mine lies beneath the city of Detroit, Michigan.</u>*

Write your opening paragraph. Start with something to grab the reader's attention; then introduce your topic and end with a clear thesis statement.

RESEARCH

Writing
Starting Your Research Report

Encourage students to experiment with the three different approaches for grabbing the reader's attention (an interesting fact, an interesting question, or a quotation). Students can share their ideas in small groups for immediate feedback. Tell students to

- fold a piece of paper horizontally into thirds to create three rows,
- write a different opening sentence at the top of each row, and
- pass their paper around the group to get reactions.

Each group member can put a check mark next to the beginning he or she likes best.

- Students should not spend a long time deciding on their favorite beginning.
- The goal here is to see which beginning grabs their interest right away and makes them want to know more.

Remind students to use the thesis statement they created during prewriting in their opening paragraph (PE page 393).

Writing
Developing the Middle Part

Provide time for students to read and discuss the sample middle paragraphs, along with the notes in the margins of the report.

Point out to students that if they have written a complete sentence outline, they should be well prepared to write their middle paragraphs. In fact, depending on the amount of detail they included in their outline, they probably have at least the basic framework for each middle paragraph already in place. All they have to do is to

- use transitions to link sentences and paragraphs to create a smooth flow of ideas,
- refer to their gathering grid and note cards to flesh out details and check for accuracy, and
- integrate some quotations, along with citations.

✳ For specific guidelines for creating a first draft and writing effective paragraphs, see PE page 530.

398

Writing Developing the Middle Part

The middle part of your report should begin by explaining why the place you have chosen is important. Next tell about its history, and then describe the place as it exists today.

Each middle paragraph should start with a topic sentence covering one main idea. Additional sentences in each paragraph should support that one idea. Refer to your sentence outline to guide your writing. (See page 394.)

Beginning
Middle
Ending

Middle Paragraphs

All the details support the topic sentence (underlined).

The first middle paragraph explains why the place is important.

Salt is much more important than most people realize. Wars have been fought over it. In some places, people have traded salt for gold in equal measures. In ancient China, salt coins were used for money, and Roman soldiers were often paid in salt, which is where the word "salary" comes from. In the human body, salt carries electrical signals that keep a person alive. To stay healthy, a person needs to eat about three pounds of salt a year (Modern). Salt is also used to preserve meat and fish, to tan leather, to soften water, and to make many different chemicals. However, most of the salt from the Detroit mine is now used to melt ice and snow on streets and highways (Zacharias).

The Salt Mine's History

The author tells about the history of the place.

Scientists say that the Detroit mine digs into a bed of salt that is several hundred million years old. From 600 million to 230 million years ago, seawater flooded the middle of North America many times. As sun and wind evaporated the water, sea salt was

---

English Language Learners

If students have created a topic outline, model how they can turn their notes into sentences.

- Ask a volunteer to put one of her or his notes onto an overhead transparency.
- Engage students in collaborating to compose a sentence that conveys the idea in the note.

- After students are satisfied with the sentence, have them identify the subject and verb to double-check that the thought is actually a sentence.

Tell students to use this method for turning their own notes into sentences.

Struggling Learners

✳ Have students turn to PE pages 572–573.

- Ask how the transitions are organized (by usage). Then ask how their reports are organized.
- Help students make the connection between the grouping of the transitions and the order of ideas in their reports.
- Encourage volunteers to identify places where they can use specific transitions.

RESEARCH

deposited on the submerged land. Trillions of tons of salt, collected in a layer 400 to 1,600 feet thick, reached from western Michigan all the way to New York. Eventually, it was covered by silt that became rock more than 1,000 feet thick. When people later came to the area, they found springs of salty water bubbling from the ground. Early settlers would collect that liquid and boil away the water to get the salt ("Dry").

In 1896, the Detroit salt mine was started in order to dig the salt out of the ground. It began as a shaft 1,200 feet deep and about 6 feet wide. At first, the salt was used mainly for storing meat and fish and for making ice cream (<u>Detroit</u> 167). In 1940, though, Detroit became the first city to use rock salt on icy roads. Other cities soon followed Detroit's example, and the mine began selling most of its salt to road crews ("Dry"). In 1983, however, low sales and competition from Canadian mines caused the Detroit mine to close. Crystal Mines bought the mine, hoping to store hazardous wastes there. In 1985, while waiting for a permit, they ran public tours of the mine. In 1997, after the permit was denied, Crystal Mines sold the mine to the Detroit Salt Company, according to Kim Roberts, manager of the mine. The mine was reopened, and it again became one of the main sources of road salt in the United States.

Sentences are arranged so that the reader can easily follow the ideas.

Sources are included in parentheses.

Each paragraph has a topic sentence and supporting details.

Many students will write at least part of their research report outside of the classroom. Remind them to keep all their prewriting materials and their drafts together.

English Language Learners

In order to support students in the writing they will need to do outside of class, try to make available some time for extra assistance.

- For instance, you might offer students the option of using your classroom as a writing workshop before and after school and at lunchtime.

- In this setting, they will have available the resources and models they need, and they will be able to ask questions of you as they encounter any problems.

Advanced Learners

Encourage students to question some information in Damek's research report. Make it a scientific challenge. Have students scan the paragraph and ask questions about any uses of salt that are new or puzzling to them. For example, why is salt used on icy roads? Invite students to research the information and report their brief scientific explanations to the class.

Students who are working on a computer should be reminded to save their work periodically and to make backup copies of their drafts after each writing session.

The author describes the place as it is today.

The author shares interesting details with the reader.

The Salt Mine Today

Some people call the Detroit salt mine a city beneath a city. It covers 1,400 acres under Detroit and its suburbs. That's equal to 1,300 football fields. Also, it has more than 50 miles of roads where construction equipment, trucks, and cars drive. To get these vehicles down the shaft, they had to be taken apart, carried down in pieces, and reassembled in underground workshops. The seven-foot-tall tires for the dump trucks had to be compressed and bound with straps to fit down the shaft (Zacharias).

The mining equipment includes many different types of big electric trucks. One type has a giant chain saw on the front, which cuts a deep groove into a salt wall at floor level. Then a drilling-machine truck bores a pattern of holes 20 feet deep into the wall to hold dynamite or other explosives. The blast from these explosives breaks hundreds of tons of rock from the wall in huge chunks. Trucks with giant shovels then scoop up tons at a time and drop them into dump trucks. The dump trucks carry the chunks back to the shaft, where a crusher breaks them into smaller pieces and sorting machines separate the pieces by size. Finally, buckets that can hold nine tons of salt run up a conveyor to the surface. There the salt is packaged and shipped ("Dry").

Advanced Learners

The salt-mine tunnels Damek described could become a wonderful setting for a mystery.

- Engage students in a discussion of how Damek's details could be used to create an atmosphere of suspense.
- Encourage students to incorporate some of Damek's descriptions into a short story.

RESEARCH

A comparison of size helps the reader understand a complex idea.

The Salt Institute explains that the mine is carved out in a "room-and-pillar" method. Each room is as big and high as a school gymnasium. Between rooms, the miners leave pillars of salt about 60 feet wide to hold up the ceiling. This type of mining gets about 70 percent of the salt from the ground, leaving the other 30 percent as support pillars. Because the salt bed has never had an earthquake or other shock, it lies very flat, so the pattern of rooms and pillars stretches level from one end of the mine to the other. According to the Salt Institute, this mine "has never experienced a collapse or mine fatality" ("Dry").

Miners say that the mine is a very clean and healthy place to work. The temperature stays a cool 58 degrees year-round, and the salt keeps the humidity at an even 55 percent. There are no bugs, rats, or other animals living in the mine, because there is nothing for them to eat (Zacharias). The air itself is very clean in a salt mine, with no mold or other allergens like on the surface (Modern).

Write your middle paragraphs. Keep these tips in mind as you write.
1. Support the topic sentence for each paragraph with details.
2. Refer to your outline for help with your organization. (See page 394.)
3. Give credit to your sources in your paper. (See page 396.)

Some students may need additional guidance as they attempt to turn the sections of their outline into paragraphs of a report. If students are not sure how to proceed, they can schedule a **writing conference** *(see below)* with you for additional guidance.

After students have written their middle paragraphs, encourage them to exchange papers with a partner. Tell the partner to check each paragraph for
- a clearly stated topic sentence,
- relevant details that support the topic sentence, and
- accurate quotations and citations, correctly punctuated.

The partner should also politely point out any details that are unnecessary or that do not support the main idea of the paragraph.

Teaching Tip: Writing Conferences

In individual conferences with students, model how to structure middle paragraphs from their outlines.

- Point to the first main idea (I.) in the student's outline. Explain that this idea becomes the topic sentence for the first middle paragraph of the report. Show the student how to begin.
- Ask the student to point to the supporting details (A, B, C, D) for I. Explain that these become the main supporting sentences for the rest of the paragraph (although more details will probably be needed).
- Read the paragraph together. Point out where ideas could be combined, where more details are needed, and where transitions would make ideas flow more smoothly.

Writing
Ending Your Research Report

Have students analyze how the writer used all three strategies in the sample ending.

- First strategy: Remind the reader of the thesis (focus) of the report. (There is enough salt underneath Michigan to last 70 million years.)
- Second: Provide information about the place's future. (If people stop using salt on roads, there may not be enough business to keep the mine open. Perhaps the mine could be used for storage or as a museum.)
- Third: Make a final observation for the reader. (The mine is an important part of the city's history.)

Encourage students to use one or more of these strategies to write their own ending paragraphs.

✱ For other strategies for ending paragraphs (including models), refer students to the Index (PE page 800).

Suggest that as they look over the first draft of their report, students check each paragraph to be sure it has a topic sentence, supporting details, and a closing sentence.

Writing Ending Your Research Report

Your ending paragraph should sum up your report and bring it to a thoughtful close. To do that, you might . . .

- **Remind the reader of the thesis of the report.**
- **Provide information about the place's future.**
- **Make a final observation for the reader.**

Ending Paragraph

The writer includes an interesting fact.

Some final possibilities leave the reader with something to think about.

The Salt Mine's Future

The Detroit salt mine could have a very interesting future. According to geologists, there is enough salt underneath Michigan to last for 70 million years ("Dry"). Many people worry, though, that the runoff from road salt is having a negative effect on our rivers and lakes. If people stop using salt on icy streets and highways, there may not be enough business to keep the Detroit mine open. In that case, the mine could be used to store important documents, films, and artwork, as some other salt mines do (Tanner). If nothing else, the Detroit salt mine could be turned into a public museum because it is an important part of the city's history.

Write your final paragraph. Draft your final paragraph using one or more of the three strategies listed above.

Look over your report. Read your report, checking your notes and outline to make sure you haven't forgotten anything. In the margins and between the lines, make notes about anything you should change.

Struggling Learners

Point out that Damek never used the words *I* and *you* in his report.

Ask students why. (Those pronouns are too personal for a research report.)

- Encourage students to check their own writing to see if they've used those pronouns.
- Discuss alternative ways to write their ideas.

NOTE RESEARCH
organize summarize *cite* **403**
Research Report

Creating Your Works-Cited Page

To create your works-cited page, first format each of your sources; then list them in alphabetical order. The purpose of a works-cited page is to help other people find the sources you used. Not every source will match these formats exactly, but if you give as much detail as possible, your works-cited page will do its job.

Encyclopedias

Author (if available). Article title (in quotation marks). Title of the encyclopedia (underlined). Edition (if available). Date published.

> "Sodium Chloride." Columbia Encyclopedia.
> 2000.

Books

Author or editor (last name first). Title (underlined). City where the book was published: Publisher, copyright date.

> Kurlansky, Mark. Salt: A World History.
> East Rutherford, NJ: Penguin USA,
> 2007.

Magazines

Author (last name first). Article title (in quotation marks). Title of the magazine (underlined) Date (day/month/year): Page numbers of the article.

> Hallett, Don. "The Wieliczka Salt Mine."
> Geology Today Sept./Oct. 2006:
> 182-185.

Newspapers

Author (if available, last name first). Article title (in quotation marks). Title of the newspaper (underlined) Date (day/month/year), edition (if listed): Section letter and page numbers of the article.

> Tanner, Beccy. "Salt Mine Museum Could
> Spark Tourist Trade." Wichita Eagle
> 8 May 2004: A9.

RESEARCH

Writing

Creating Your Works-Cited Page

Review the formatting for each of the different types of sources here and on PE page 404.

Students may wonder how to alphabetize the sources when they don't know the author.

- Explain that sources are alphabetized according to the first word in the work cited, whether that is an author's name or the title of an article, a book, or other source (see PE page 385). Point out that the words *A*, *An*, and *The* are not used as the first word when alphabetizing titles.
- Explain that when students are citing more than one work by the same author, they should list the articles chronologically.

Tell students to follow the directions at the bottom of the page to format their sources. Make sure students follow the guidelines for treating titles as shown in the sample citations.

✱ See PE pages 598, 600, and 602 for specific instruction on using quotation marks, italics, and underlining to punctuate titles.

Technology Connections

At www.thewritesource.com, students can also find more help with documenting sources according to MLA style.

404

Internet

Author (if available). Page title (if available, in quotation marks). Site title (underlined). Date posted (day/month/year, if available). Name of sponsor (if available). Date found <electronic address>.

> "Dry (Rock Salt) Mining." Salt Institute.
> Salt Institute. 10 May 2008
> <http://www.saltinstitute.org/
> mich-1.html>.

Film, Video, and So On

Title (underlined). Type of medium (filmstrip, slide program, and so on). Distributor, date released.

> Modern Marvels: Salt Mines. Videocassette.
> A&E Television Networks, 2004.

Letter or E-Mail to the Author (Yourself)

Writer (last name first). Subject line title (if any) in quotation marks. Type of message ("Letter to the author" or "E-mail to the author"). Date addressed (day, month, year).

> Roberts, Kim. E-mail to the author. 4 May
> 2008.

Format your sources. Check your report and your list of sources (page 392) to see which sources you actually used. Then follow these directions.

1 Write your sources using the guidelines above and on the previous page. You can write them on a sheet of paper or on note cards.

2 Alphabetize your sources.

3 Create your works-cited page. (See the example on page 385.)

Struggling Learners

Review the samples of how to cite sources on PE pages 403–404.

- Before students try to format their own sources, help them recognize how and when to use quotation marks, italics, and underlining.
- Remind them especially that titles that are underlined by hand are italicized on the computer.
- Also review when periods and commas are used.

Together, make a chart of guidelines, and post it in the classroom for students to use as a reference as they write.

Revising

A good research report needs more than one draft. The first time through, you work mainly with organization and ideas. In the second draft, you fill in missing information, rearrange ideas for clarity, and polish your word choice. Take the time to make your report as good as it can be.

Keys to Effective Revising

1. Read your entire draft to get an overall sense of your report.

2. Review your thesis statement to be sure that it clearly states your main point about the topic.

3. Make sure your beginning draws the reader in. Then check that your ending leaves the reader with something to think about.

4. Make sure you sound knowledgeable and interested in the topic.

5. Check for correct, specific words and complete sentences.

6. Use the editing and proofreading marks inside the back cover of this book.

RESEARCH

Revising
Keys to Effective Revising

Remind students that revising is the stage in the writing process during which they examine their writing to make sure that their ideas and details are interesting, well organized, and clearly stated.

Suggest that students refer back to the Keys to Effective Revising throughout the revising process.

- Because of the length and complexity of a research report, students may experience a bit of a "burnout" once they finish their first draft. In this case, they may not be able or willing to see places in their draft that need improvement.

- If possible, suggest that students set aside their report for at least a day or two. When they return to it with a new perspective, hopefully, they will be eager to create a second and improved draft.

Grammar Connection

Active and Passive Verbs
- **Proofreader's Guide** page 726 (+)

Sentence Variety and Ellipses
- **Proofreader's Guide** pages 614–615
- **SkillsBook** pages 127–128, 129–130

Sentence Expanding
- **Write Source** pages 511, 521–522
- **SkillsBook** pages 121–122

Dashes and Parentheses
- **Write Source** pages 612–613
- **SkillsBook** pages 36, 37–38

Struggling Learners

In a one-on-one writing conference, slowly read the student's report aloud. Put a check next to sentences or parts that may need work. Discuss these parts with the student.

Revising
Improving Your Writing

If students need a refresher, review the use of proofreading marks as shown here and on the inside back cover of the pupil edition.

- To illustrate how revising can improve the sound of a piece of writing, have a volunteer read aloud the sample paragraphs without the revisions.
- Then have a second volunteer read aloud the revised sample paragraphs.
- Discuss how the revisions improve the sound of the whole piece.

Consider using **peer response groups** (*see below*) and response sheets for feedback during revisions.

406

Revising Improving Your Writing

A first draft is never a finished paper. There is always room for improvement. In the following sample paragraphs, Damek makes several important revisions. Each change improves the *ideas, organization, voice, word choice,* or *sentence fluency* in the writing.

Two sentences are combined for smoother reading.

An "It has" beginning is changed to improve sentence style.

Twelve hundred feet below the ground, lies an enormous mine. It has been operating almost nonstop for more than a century. It has a hundred miles of tunnels connecting its huge chambers. It has underground roads for cars, trucks, and mining machines. This mine produces hundreds of tons of "rock" every day. However, the rock from this mine is not gold, or iron ore, or even coal; it is salt. This enormous, hundred-year-old salt mine lies beneath the city of Detroit, Michigan.

A sentence is moved for better organization.

Salt is much more important than most people realize. In some places, people have traded salt for gold in equal measures. In ancient China, salt coins were used for money, and Roman soldiers were often paid in salt, which is where the word "salary" comes from. Wars have been fought over it. In the human body, salt carries electrical signals that keep a person

A detail is added for clarity.

alive. Salt is also used to preserve meat and fish . . .
To stay healthy, a person needs to eat about three pounds of salt a year (*Modern*).

Teaching Tip: Peer Responding

Peer response groups provide students with an opportunity to share their work and get immediate and honest feedback from their classmates.

Divide students into groups of five. Assign each group member a different trait (ideas, organization, voice, word choice, or sentence fluency). Tell him or her to listen for that trait as writers read aloud their reports.

(Responders should also have a written copy of the paper to refer to.)

As they listen to and/or read the paper, responders can provide feedback about each trait on a peer response sheet. Students can then use the peer-response sheets to revise their reports.

✳ For more about peer responding, see PE pages 29–32.

English Language Learners

To help these students with fluency, review the use of transitions, such as *however* and *in the past*. Help students add transitions to improve sentence fluency and combine sentences if necessary.

✳ For more about sentence fluency, see PE pages 122–123.

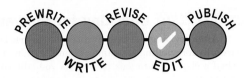

PREWRITE · REVISE · PUBLISH · WRITE · EDIT ✓

Editing

Once you have finished revising your report, edit your work for *conventions:* spelling, punctuation, capitalization, and grammar.

RESEARCH

Keys to Effective Editing

1. Use a dictionary, a thesaurus, your computer's spell-checker, and the "Proofreader's Guide" in the back of this book.

2. Read your essay out loud and listen for words or phrases that may be incorrect.

3. Look for errors in punctuation, capitalization, spelling, and grammar.

4. Check your report for proper formatting. (See pages 380–385 and 409.)

5. If you use a computer, edit on a printed computer copy. Then enter your changes on the computer.

6. Use the editing and proofreading marks inside the back cover of this book.

Editing Keys to Effective Editing

Remind students that during the editing stage, they have a chance to find and correct errors in

- punctuation,
- capitalization,
- spelling, and
- grammar.

Encourage students to refer to the Keys to Effective Editing as they check their reports for punctuation, capitalization, spelling, and grammar errors.

Struggling Learners

✴ Review the list of *Commonly Misspelled Words* on PE pages 645–651.

- Have students review the list to recognize words she or he has often misspelled in the past.
- Help students scan their reports for misspelled words and make the appropriate corrections.

Grammar Connection

Comma Rules Review

- **Proofreader's Guide** pages 582–591 (+)
- *SkillsBook* pages 15–16

Sentence Problems Review

- *Write Source* pages 506 (+), 507 (+), 508 (+), 509 (+), 510 (+)
- *SkillsBook* pages 93–94

Using the Right Word

- **Proofreader's Guide** pages 652–686 (+)
- *SkillsBook* pages 61–62

Editing
Checking for Conventions

Point out to students that writers often overlook their own mistakes because they know what they *meant* to say. Also, the more times someone reads his or her own work, the more common it is for minor errors to become invisible. For these reasons, it is almost impossible to proofread one's own writing perfectly. That is why it is so important that students have help with their editing. Here is one possible peer editing group activity.

- Have students work in groups of four.
- Members pass their reports around the group.
- Each member of the group edits reports for one type of error—punctuation, capitalization, spelling, or grammar—using a different colored pencil. (Students can choose which type of error to correct based on their own strengths, or you can assign responsibilities.)
- After each report has been edited, the writer can use the Proofreader's Guide (PE pages 579–749) to make final corrections.

408

Editing Checking for Conventions

After revising the first draft of his report, Damek checked the new version carefully for spelling, grammar, capitalization, and punctuation errors. He also asked a classmate to look it over. As you edit your own report, use the editing and proofreading marks inside the back cover of this book.

An error in subject-verb agreement is fixed.	Scientists says that the Detroit mine digs into a bed of salt that is several hundred million years old. From 600 million to 230 million years ago, seawater flooded the middle of North America many times.
A spelling error is corrected.	*evaporated* As sun and wind evaperated the water, sea salt was deposited on the submerged land. Trillions of tons of salt, collected in a layer 400 to 1,600 feet thick, reached from western Michigan all the way to New York. Eventually, it was covered by silt that became rock more than 1,000 feet thick. When people later
A missing comma is added.	came to the area, they found springs of salty water bubbling from the ground. Early settlers would collect that liquid and boil away the water to get the
A period is moved to its proper place.	salt. ("Dry")

In 1896, the Detroit salt mine was started in order to dig the salt out of the ground. It began . . .

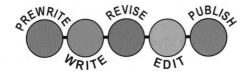

Research Report
409

Publishing
Sharing Your Report

After you have written and improved your report, you'll want to make a neat-looking final copy to share. You may also decide to prepare your report as an electronic presentation, an online essay, or an illustrated report.

Make a final copy. Use the following guidelines to format your report. (If you are using a computer, see page 60.) Create a clean final copy and carefully proofread it.

Focus on *Presentation*

- Use blue or black ink and double-space the entire paper.
- Write your name, your teacher's name, the class, and the date in the upper left corner of page 1.
- Skip a line and center your title; skip another line and start your writing.
- Indent every paragraph and leave a one-inch margin on all four sides.
- For a research paper, you should write your last name and the page number in the upper right corner of every page of your report.

Creating a Title Page

If your teacher requires a title page, follow his or her requirements. Usually you center the title one-third of the way down from the top of the page. Then go two-thirds of the way down and center your name, your teacher's name, the name of the class, and the date. Put each piece of information on a separate line.

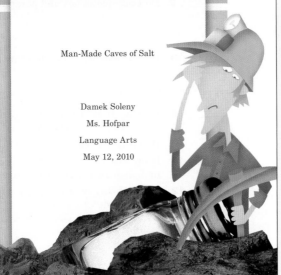

Man-Made Caves of Salt

Damek Soleny
Ms. Hofpar
Language Arts
May 12, 2010

RESEARCH

Publishing **Sharing Your Report**

Have students read the instruction and the guidelines for presentation before they make their final, clean copy.

- Remind students that visuals (for example, labeled diagrams, illustrations, charts, and graphs) can add impact and interest to their reports.

✳ See PE page 574 for more on adding graphics to writing.

- Suggest that students follow the sample formatting shown here for creating a title page, or provide students with the specific directions to meet your requirements for a title page and presentation.
- Allow time for students to share their reports with the class, or arrange for them to present their reports to students in other classes.

Research Paper Checklist

In their eagerness to be finished with the report, students may answer "yes" to all the questions in the checklist without really thinking about them.

- Be sure students have reviewed their reports several times for all the traits and conventions covered in the checklist before they actually use the checklist.
- For a more objective evaluation of their report, have students exchange papers with a partner who can use the checklist to decide if the report is ready to be handed in.
- Partners should give specific, constructive feedback for making final revisions or corrections.

410

Research Paper Checklist

Use the following checklist for your research paper. When you can answer all of the questions with a "yes," your paper is ready to hand in.

Ideas

_____ **1.** Is my research paper interesting and informative?

_____ **2.** Are my sources current and trustworthy?

Organization

_____ **3.** Does my paper have a thesis statement in the opening paragraph and a topic sentence in all other paragraphs?

_____ **4.** Does my ending paragraph cover the future of this place?

Voice

_____ **5.** Do I sound knowledgeable and interested in my topic?

Word Choice

_____ **6.** Have I explained any technical terms or unfamiliar words?

_____ **7.** Do I use quotations and paraphrasing effectively?

Sentence Fluency

_____ **8.** Do my sentences flow smoothly from one to another?

Conventions

_____ **9.** Does my first page include my name, my teacher's name, the name of the class, the date, and a title? (See page 380.)

_____ **10.** Do I correctly cite my sources? (See pages 381–384 and 396.)

_____ **11.** Is my works-cited page set up correctly? Are the sources listed in alphabetical order? (See pages 385 and 403–404.)

_____ **12.** If my teacher requires a title page, is mine done correctly? (See page 409.)

Research Writing
Multimedia Presentations

Anyone who uses a computer has seen multimedia in action on encyclopedia CD's, on Internet sites, and even in word-processing software. A multimedia presentation is a powerful means of expression that can be presented to a large group. When you can add pictures, sounds, animation, and video to a report, you bring your writing to life and keep the audience interested.

There are several kinds of software that you can use to produce multimedia presentations. With assistance from some of this software, and a little imagination, you'll be able to connect with your audience in a new, dynamic way.

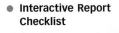

What's Ahead

- **Creating Interactive Reports**
- **Interactive Report Checklist**

Multimedia Presentations

Objectives

- select a topic and details for an interactive report
- plan, write, revise, and edit an interactive report

If possible, provide one or more examples of interactive reports for your students to watch and analyze. You can use examples from the following sources:

- reports by former students,
- student reports that other content-area teachers have on file,
- teacher-created reports,
- appropriate and suitable presentations that are available online.

If possible, ask the school's technology expert to assist students as they work through the process.

Advanced Learners

Invite students who are experienced in creating multimedia presentations to share their knowledge with the class. Discuss possible topics with them, such as the following:

- basic "how-to" information
- common pitfalls
- common misconceptions
- exciting features and options

Encourage students to create a "help manual" and print it for classmates to refer to as they work on their presentations.

Creating Interactive Reports

Prewriting
Selecting a Topic and Details

Suggest that students consider using the research report they wrote for this unit for their interactive report. If they have recently finished the report (or if they are still working on it), the ideas will be fresh in their minds.

- Make sure students understand that they will be creating a series of slides that show the main ideas of the report, using a condensed version of the text as their copy.
- Encourage them to include graphics and sound to add interest and drama to the story that the slides tell.

Review the sample media grid before asking students to do the **Try It** activity on their own. If students are using their research report for their interactive report, they can quickly identify main ideas by looking at the following:

- their gathering grid
- their note cards
- their outline

 **Answers**

Answers will vary but should contain a variety of ideas for sounds and graphics.

Creating Interactive Reports

With the help of a computer, you can design a report that other people can interact with. Your computer-generated slides, graphics, and sound effects will make the important parts of your report clearer and more interesting.

Prewriting Selecting a Topic and Details

For your interactive report, you will want to use something you've already written, something that interests both you and your audience. After you've chosen your piece of writing, make a list of its main ideas. Then find or create one or more of the following graphics or sound effects:

- **Pictures** such as photos or clip art
- **Animations** that show a process or tell a story
- **Videos** of something you've filmed yourself
- **Sounds and music** to use as background or to make a point

 Make a plan and organize your ideas by creating a list or media grid like the one below.

Media Grid

Main Ideas	Pictures or Videos	Animations or Music	Sounds
1. A hundred-year-old salt mine lies under Detroit.	photo of Detroit skyline	background music	
2. Early settlers found saltwater spring; mine opened in 1896.	picture of 1896 mine operation		mining sounds

 Gather details. Select ideas from your list or from your media grid for graphics and sounds to include with each slide. Create the graphics or sounds yourself or find them on the Internet. Save the images (credit any sources) and sounds on your computer in a special folder created for this report.

Advanced Learners

Students with advanced computer skills can be of great assistance to those who are less savvy in those areas. For example, the "experts" could help others

- find and download sounds,
- capture images,
- design their storyboards, and
- create their interactive reports.

RESEARCH

Writing **Preparing the Report**

Before you prepare your report, you need to make a *storyboard*. A storyboard is a "map" of the slides you plan to use in your report. (See the sample storyboard on the next page.) Using your list or media grid as a guide, include each main idea in one box in the storyboard. Then add links from these boxes to additional information.

Use your computer software to design the slides. Choose a typestyle that is easy to read. Use the graphics and sounds you found earlier, and consider using bulleted lists and graphs to organize your information. Show the user how to get around in the report using easy-to-follow navigation buttons, such as arrows or the words "Next" and "Back."

 Create a storyboard. Refer to your list or media grid to help you map out your report on a storyboard. Include details of what your audience will see and hear. This kind of preparation will give you an idea of how the slides should look before you actually make them on the computer.

Revising **Improving Your Report**

Since your audience is on their own with this type of report, it's important to double-check to make sure that it works as it should. Have several friends or family members test it for you. Ask them to tell you if it is clear, interesting, and easy to get around.

 Get feedback. If your "testers" have good suggestions, revise the text and design of your report where necessary.

Editing **Checking for Conventions**

Check the text on each slide for spelling, punctuation, grammar, and capitalization errors. Consider asking an adult or a classmate to check your slides, too.

 Make corrections. After you've made corrections, go through the report once more to make sure it works well.

Grammar Connection

Spelling Review

- **Proofreader's Guide** page 642 (+)
- **CD** Spelling Review—1 (+)

Writing **Preparing the Report**

Have students turn to the storyboard on PE page 414 before they try to create their own storyboards. Help students navigate through the sample.

- Explain that the gold boxes, which are connected to slides by dotted lines, appear only when the user clicks on the slide. Point out that clicking on a slide is the same as clicking on a link on a Web site.
- Before students create their own storyboards, review the suggestion on TE page 414 for a method you can use to make the process easier.

Revising **Improving Your Report**

Some students who do not have a computer at home won't be able to test their own reports there. If possible, allocate time for these students to use a classroom computer before or after school or at lunchtime.

- Invite students with good computer skills to help.
- Not only can these "testers" check to see if a report is easy to navigate, but they can also help the writer fix anything that doesn't work.

Editing

Checking for Conventions

Have partners edit each other's slides for conventions.

Interactive Report Storyboard

The following method will allow students to practice arranging their ideas easily as they create a storyboard manually before using the computer.

- Give each student some large and small note cards and a large piece of construction paper.
- Tell students to use a separate large note card to write their notes for each slide and a separate small note card for each piece of linked information. Remind them to include details to show where they want sound and graphics to appear in the presentation. (Many software programs have a text-to-speech function that allows students to record their voices. Encourage students to use this function.)
- Have students arrange the note cards on the construction paper. When they are satisfied with the arrangement, they can tape or glue the note cards to the paper. Then they can use arrows and dotted lines, as in the sample, to show the flow of the slides (arrows) and the placement of linked information (dotted lines).

414

Interactive Report Storyboard

Here is the map, or storyboard, for an interactive report based on the research report "Man-Made Caves of Salt." (See pages 380–385.) Since each user goes through the report on his or her own, it needs to share the essay's information as completely and clearly as possible. (The gold boxes contain additional information available by clicking a link on the original slide.)

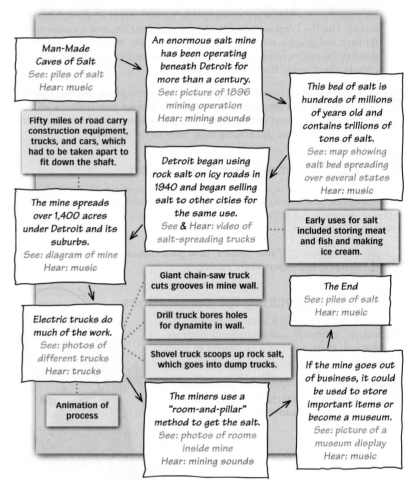

Advanced Learners

Once students have demonstrated competency using a particular type of software, encourage them to write a student-friendly guide for the process.

- Since this guide is for the beginner, remind the writers to include basic information, helpful hints, and a step-by-step outline for the procedure.

- Suggest that they include a troubleshooting section for the kinds of difficulties that are often encountered.
- Encourage writers to print out and bind the guide into a booklet for classmates to use.

RESEARCH

Interactive Report Checklist

Use the following checklist to make sure your report is the best it can be. When you can answer all of the questions with a "yes," it's ready!

Ideas

____ 1. Have I chosen a strong essay or report for my interactive report?

____ 2. Do my graphics help communicate my ideas clearly?

____ 3. Does each slide fit the audience and the purpose of the report?

Organization

____ 4. Do I introduce my topic clearly in the beginning?

____ 5. Do I include the important main points in the middle part?

____ 6. Do I end with a summary or wrap-up thought?

Voice

____ 7. Do I use an interested, somewhat formal voice?

____ 8. Does my voice fit my audience and topic?

Word and Multimedia Choices

____ 9. Are the words on my slides easy to read?

____ 10. Have I chosen the best pictures and sounds for my ideas?

Presentation Fluency

____ 11. Does my report flow smoothly from slide to slide?

Conventions

____ 12. Is my report free of grammar, spelling, capitalization, and punctuation errors?

Interactive Report Checklist

Have each student use the checklist to review his or her interactive report and make sure it is ready for presentation. When all the reports are on the computer, allocate time for students to take turns viewing their classmates' reports.

After students have completed this assignment, ask them to reflect on the process. Use these questions:

- What part of creating an interactive report did you enjoy most?
- What part did you find most difficult?
- Were you able to communicate your ideas better in writing or in the multimedia presentation? Explain.
- What do you think is more interesting to read, a traditional written report or an interactive report? Explain.

The Tools of Learning Overview

Unit Objectives

The writing standards listed below are based on a blending of state and NCTE standards.

- Use graphic organizers and clustering, listing, and freewriting to organize ideas.
- Take notes to remember information and organize a persuasive speech.
- Develop listening skills for classroom lectures and group work.
- Construct new concepts by keeping journals and learning logs, by summarizing and paraphrasing information, and by hypothesizing about and synthesizing new information.
- Demonstrate strong oral presentation skills.

Skills

- listening in class
- participating in a group
- speaking in class
- preparing and delivering a persuasive speech

Tools and Techniques

- journals
- learning logs
- writing-to-learn activities

Test Taking

- test preparation
- four basic types of objective tests (true/false, matching, multiple-choice, and fill-in-the-blanks)
- essay tests

The chapters in "The Tools of Learning" section provide students with strategies to improve their study and learning skills. Many of the "Tools" chapters are incorporated into the yearlong timetable (see TE pages 46–49). For example, the note-taking chapter is incorporated into the research-writing unit. You should determine when to implement the other chapters depending on the needs and nature of your students and the standards of instruction mandated in your district or state. Of course, students may refer to some of the chapters in this section again and again throughout the school year. For example, they may review the test-taking chapter before they take exams or the speech-making chapter during the planning of any oral presentations. In this way, you should think of "Tools of Learning" as a reference section, ready to aid students when they need help with their learning.

Special Note: Remind teachers across the curriculum that the *Write Source* contains chapters that will help students with their note taking, test taking, and other learning skills.

Teacher's Notes for The Tools of Learning

This overview for the tools of learning includes some specific teaching suggestions for the unit.

Listening and Speaking (pages 417–422)

This chapter focuses on improving listening and speaking skills. Listening in class, participating in a group, and speaking in class are featured.

Making an Oral Presentation (pages 423–430)

Speaking to classes and other groups is something students will be called on to do throughout their school years and adult lives. The ability to speak clearly, confidently, and persuasively is a skill that will serve students well. This chapter is a step-by-step guide to preparing and giving a speech, from knowing the purpose of the speech to delivering it well.

Keeping Journals and Learning Logs (pages 431–440)

Logs and journals help students learn as well as keep important information close at hand. Examples of different kinds of journals and learning logs are presented, including logs kept for classes across the curriculum.

Taking Notes (pages 441–448)

Students don't always understand how important notes can be. In addition, students need guidance for taking good notes. Guidelines (and examples) for classroom notes and reading notes are included here.

Completing Writing Assignments (pages 449–458)

As students' assignments—and their lives—become more complex, they need to know how to set goals, plan their time well, and manage stress. This chapter offers strategies and guidelines that will help them complete their assignments. A sample assignment schedule ends the chapter.

Taking Classroom Tests (pages 459–467)

As every teacher knows, doing well on a test is partly a matter of knowing the material and partly a matter of knowing how to take a test. This chapter helps students with both. It begins with a few tips for learning and remembering material and then focuses on test-taking skills, from how to handle objective tests to the best approach for essay tests.

Minilessons

Stage Fright
Listening and Speaking

- **LIST** the things you find difficult about speaking in class. **SHARE** the list with a classmate and **DISCUSS** ways you each can improve, using pages 419 and 422 in your textbook as a guide.

Practice, Practice
Making an Oral Presentation

- **FIND** a selection in one of your textbooks on a topic that interests you. **READ** that selection in a small group as though you were giving a speech. **ASK** for suggestions about your volume, tone, and speed. Also, **ASK** for comments on your eye contact and posture. **REVIEW** your classmates' suggestions, and then **READ** the paragraph again using their helpful ideas. **TAKE** turns until each group member has had a turn.

Journaling Pros & Cons
Keeping Journals and Learning Logs

- **READ** page 432 in your textbook. **FREEWRITE** for several minutes reflecting on why keeping a journal would be fun and beneficial. Then **WRITE** about the opposite side of the issue: why you would not want to keep a journal. **DISCUSS** your thoughts with a partner.

Vocabulary Log
Keeping Journals and Learning Logs

- **READ** "Writing in a Learning Log" on page 435. **CHOOSE** a word that's new to you from your class notes for one of your subjects. **USE** the model on page 435 as a guide and **WRITE** a similar entry in your learning log for the new word. Your learning log can be another section in your class notes, or it can be a completely separate notebook.

How to Take Notes
Taking Notes

- **READ** pages 442–444. **STUDY** the sample class notes on page 443. **NOTICE** that the student does not record everything the teacher says during a lecture. **TAKE** notes while watching a television program (perhaps a documentary). Check with your teacher to see if your notes include key material.

Time Line
Completing Writing Assignments

- **GET** a calendar for the year (banks often provide calendars for no charge). In the spaces for the days, **LIST** important test dates, due dates for long-range assignments, mid-semester report dates, and end-of-the semester dates. **INCLUDE** extra-curricular activities such as play practices, sporting events or practices, campouts, and so on. **USE** this to guide your plans for completing assignments. **NOTE** the amount of

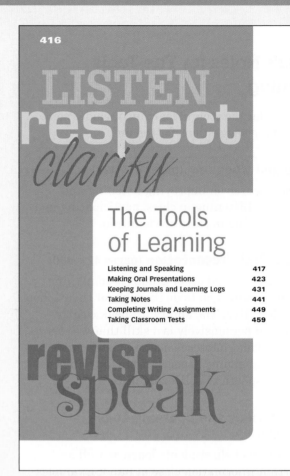

LISTEN
respect
clarify

The Tools of Learning

revise
speak

time available and how much time is needed for each assignment. If assignments and outside activities occur on the same days, plan accordingly so that you can complete your assignments on time.

Test Making
Taking Classroom Tests

- **WRITE** questions for a topic you will be tested on in class. **GENERATE** at least three of the four types of questions featured on pages 462–463. **EXCHANGE** "test" papers with a partner. **TAKE** one another's exams. **DISCUSS** the results.

Listening and Speaking

Is being a good listener the same thing as having good hearing? Not really. If your ears are doing one thing and your mind is doing something else, you aren't really listening. Listening, like other skills, takes practice and concentration.

Similarly, there is a big difference between speaking and merely talking. Speaking takes effort. Learning to speak effectively and listen closely will make you more successful in school and in life.

"Be a good listener. Your ears will never get you in trouble."
—Frank Tyger

What's Ahead

- **Listening in Class**
- **Participating in a Group**
- **Speaking in Class**

Copy Masters/ Transparencies

5 W's chart (TE p. 418)

Listening and Speaking

Objectives
- understand how to listen and speak effectively
- use tips for skillful listening in class
- understand and use guidelines for participating successfully in group discussions

Emphasize that **listening** involves hearing but requires a focused effort. Similarly, **speaking** involves talking but requires preparation and thought.

Listening in Class

Before reading the text, discuss how people listen differently in different circumstances. Here are two examples:

- During a conversation, people can get distracted and listen intermittently. They may think about other things or formulate responses to what is being said.

- In a group discussion, people need to listen to multiple speakers and focus on the ideas conveyed by each speaker.

Then discuss how students need to listen in the classroom, where they must focus on important facts and information.

Review the four tips for listening in class. Direct students to choose a set of notes they took for a previous class. Then have them identify which tip or listening strategy they used.

418

Listening in Class

When you really listen, you're doing more than simply hearing what is being said. Listening involves effort. The following tips will help you become a better listener.

1 **Know why you're listening.** What is the speaker trying to tell you? Is there going to be a test? Are you being given an assignment?

2 **Listen for the facts.** Listen for *who, what, when, where, why,* and *how.* The 5 W's and H will help you identify the most important information.

3 **Take notes.** When you hear important information, write it down in your notebook. Also write down questions you have and ask them later so that you can complete your notes.

4 **Put the lecture into your own words.** Paraphrase the speaker's statements as you take notes. Add your own comments and draw conclusions about the main points.

 Take notes in your own words. The next time you take notes in class, practice putting the ideas in your own words. Also add your own comments as you think about the main points.

> Westward Expansion
> 1800 to mid-1800s
>
> Pioneer women—status different in West than in East
> - Laura Ingalls Wilder—wrote stories of westward movement (stories still popular)
> - Annie Bidwell—social activist, Chico, CA
> - Slave women—gained freedom in West
> - Wyoming—gave women right to vote in 1869 (Was it the first state to do that?)

English Language Learners

Students may need help processing and recording spoken information. Here are two suggestions:

- Before students take notes, provide them with a photocopy of the reproducible 5 W's chart on TE page 792 and have them add a column for *H* in the right margin. Then have them fill in the chart as they listen.

- If filling in the chart while they listen is too difficult, have students take running notes during the lecture. Then, after class, they can transpose those notes onto the 5 W's and H chart.

Struggling Learners

To give students practice paraphrasing, ask them to

- select short paragraphs from chapters they are studying in their social studies and science textbooks,
- read them aloud, and
- work with classmates to restate the information in their own words.

LISTEN speak clarify observe respect   **419**
Listening and Speaking

A Closer Look at Listening and Speaking

Improving your listening and speaking skills will help you increase your confidence and effectiveness in school. Follow these basic guidelines to become a better listener and a better speaker.

Good Listeners . . .
- think about what the speaker is saying.
- pay attention to the speaker's tone of voice, gestures, and facial expressions.
- interrupt only when necessary to ask questions.

Good Speakers . . .
- speak loudly and clearly.
- maintain eye contact with their listeners.
- emphasize their main ideas by changing the tone and volume of their voice.

LEARNING

 Focus on speaking and listening skills by doing the activity below.

1. Gather two classmates and number yourselves 1, 2, and 3.
2. Person 1 will take person 2 aside and read the paragraph below.
3. Person 2 will then take person 3 aside and repeat the paragraph from memory.
4. Person 3 will repeat the paragraph from memory to the other two classmates.
5. Compare the original paragraph to what person 3 reports.

   Lieutenant Colonel Arthur Whitson was a United States Air Force pilot for 21 years. He spent some of his time flying weather planes into typhoons in the South Pacific. His crew also tracked radioactive winds, which were clues to when and where the Soviets were testing nuclear bombs. Once Whitson's plane was shot at over Vietnam. He had to dump his cargo of jet fuel, but he and his crew survived.

A Closer Look at Listening and Speaking

Point out the importance of voice and body language in communication. Albert Mehrabian's classic study reveals the following insights:

- Most of what people communicate (55 percent) comes from body language.
- Tone is almost as important: 38 percent of the message is perceived from the *way* the words are spoken.
- Only 7 percent of meaning comes from the actual words.

Try It Answers

Answers will vary, but much of the information in the original paragraph may be lost by the time the third person reports.

Struggling Learners

To show students how changing the tone and volume of different words in a sentence can completely change the meaning, read aloud the following sentence, stressing the words in boldface:

- I **wish** I'd taken the gift to Pete's house. *(I forgot it.)*
- I wish **I'd** taken the gift to Pete's house. *(Someone else took it.)*

- I wish I'd **taken** the gift to Pete's house. *(I mailed it instead.)*
- I wish I'd taken the **gift** to Pete's house. *(I took something else.)*
- I wish I'd taken the gift to **Pete's** house. *(I took it to someone else's house.)*

- I wish I'd taken the gift to Pete's **house**. *(I took it to school.)*

Invite students to repeat the exercise, using variations of their own sentences to show how meanings can change as different words are emphasized.

Participating in a Group

After reading the guidelines for group discussion, explain that other jobs can be assigned, depending on the task at hand. Some other possibilities include the following:

- timekeeper
- researcher
- mediator
- reporter

Have students practice group discussion.

- After each group chooses a topic, have them label a card *Speaker* and pass it around, so that each member has a turn to speak.
- Remind group members to speak only when they are holding the card. This makes everyone aware of how often and how long each person speaks.

* Refer students to PE pages 546–547 for topic ideas.

 Answers

Situation 1 Select a record keeper. (guideline)

Situation 2 Before you speak, think about what others have said. (tip)

Situation 3 Choose a chairperson. (guideline)

420

Participating in a Group

Working with others requires planning. Even if everyone listens politely and speaks clearly, the group needs leadership and a common goal. The guidelines below will help you organize a group discussion.

Guidelines for Group Discussion

- **Choose a chairperson.** This leader should keep the group focused and make sure everyone gets a chance to participate. Rather than choosing the same chairperson for each meeting, let each group member have a turn.
- **Select a record keeper.** The group needs someone to take notes and write down important decisions.
- **Define the topic or focus.** Be sure everyone participates when deciding on the group's goals.

Group Discussion Tips

- **Before you speak,** think about what others have said.
- **Share your thoughts** in a positive and constructive way.
- **Always be respectful,** especially when you disagree with someone.
- **Stick to the topic** or focus.

 Imagine yourself in the situations below. Which of the group guidelines or discussion tips above might have prevented each situation from happening?

Situation 1	There is a disagreement about what the group decided last week.
Situation 2	You realize that you are repeating something that has already been said.
Situation 3	One group member speaks twice as often as anyone else, and another member doesn't speak at all.

Struggling Learners

If some groups are having difficulty taking turns, try the following approach:

- Give each group member three counters (such as game chips, dry beans, or small erasers).
- Have students put one counter in a container on the table each time they speak.
- When a speaker's counters are gone, he or she must remain silent, but the discussion should continue until everyone has used up his or her counters.
- If all group members wish to continue the discussion, counters may be redistributed so that everyone can participate again.

LISTEN speak clarify observe respect **421**
Listening and Speaking

Group Skills

It's fun to belong to a group that gets something done. When each member listens closely and responds clearly, the whole group can succeed. Listening and speaking in a group is actually a step-by-step process, and when everyone practices these "steps," meetings will go smoothly.

Begin by **listening.**

1
- Think about what the speaker is saying.
- Make eye contact with the speaker.
- Take notes on the speaker's main ideas.

Follow up by **clarifying.**

2
- Ask questions about things that confuse you.
- Repeat what you've heard in your own words to see if your understanding is correct.

Continue by **responding.**

3
- Think before you speak.
- Comment on the issue, not on the person.
- Be honest and respectful.

 Read the sentences and questions below and discuss your answers with two or three of your classmates. Remember to listen, clarify, and respond.

1. Jasmine thinks that it would be rude to criticize another person in her group.
   Is Jasmine correct?
2. Raul already has his mind made up about what Steve is talking about.
   Should he sit quietly, looking out the window, until Steve finishes speaking?

LEARNING

Group Skills

For additional practice with this meeting technique, allow students to become familiar with the three steps (listening, clarifying, and responding) while working in small groups. Provide some new topics for discussion, if necessary. Circulate among the groups to monitor their progress.

Try IT Answers

Answers will vary, but discussion may focus on keeping comments polite and constructive—focusing on ideas, not individual people. In addition, they may discuss the importance of body language (see TE page 419).

Struggling Learners

To help students participate in a group discussion, try the following suggestions for each of the steps shown above:

- Step 1: Remind students that they can use the 5 W's chart (TE page 792) to record the speaker's main ideas or they can use a cluster or an outline to take notes.

- Step 2: Students may need additional time to process information. Suggest pauses between speakers so students can review their notes and formulate any questions or comments.
- Step 3: Encourage students to check their notes before responding so they can ask more specific questions.

Speaking in Class

In a typical group of students, some will dominate discussions, while others hesitate to contribute anything at all.

- To achieve more balanced participation, the class may need practice. Be sure to provide many opportunities for every student to speak in class, and keep a class-discussions log.

- After class discussions, take time to jot down notes about who participated and who did not. Keep track of the kinds of topics that get students talking, and continue to initiate discussions that lead to widespread **student involvement** (see below).

422

Speaking in Class

Speaking in class is a skill everyone needs to master. A good classroom discussion depends on cooperation. These basic strategies will help you and your classmates become better speakers.

Before You Speak . . .

- Listen carefully and take notes.
- Think about what others are saying.
- Wait until it's your turn to speak.
- Plan how you can add something positive to the discussion.

When You Speak . . .

- Use a loud, clear tone.
- Stick to the topic.
- Avoid repeating what's already been said.
- Support your ideas with examples.
- Maintain eye contact with others in the group or class.

 Play "Who Am I and Where Am I?" Warm up your speaking skills by playing the following game.

1 Form groups of five students. Have each group choose a speaker.

2 The speaker looks at the lists below and chooses one person and one place. Then the speaker begins to speak like that person in that place.

3 The first person to correctly guess the person and place becomes the next speaker.

People	Places
teacher	at the beach
athlete	in school
doctor	on a bus
police officer	in the dentist's chair
rock star	on a cattle ranch
carpenter	standing in line

Teaching Tip: Student Involvement

To help students become more comfortable with speaking and to give yourself more time to monitor their participation, institute a weekly discussion group that will be led by student volunteers.

- Invite students to list on chart paper topics they enjoy discussing. Keep the list on display.
- Each week, ask a volunteer to choose a topic and lead a short discussion so that you can monitor behaviors (participation, attention, interrupting, side conversations, and so on) and provide feedback.

Struggling Learners

If students need ideas for discussion topics, suggest a modified form of show-and-tell:

- a favorite item from childhood
- an interesting word in the dictionary
- an unusual item from a "junk drawer" at home
- an intriguing newspaper article
- an advertisement for something the student would never buy

practice EXPRESS demonstrate
speak show   423

Making Oral Presentations

You may not realize it, but you've been making oral presentations ever since you started school. In the early grades, your teachers coaxed you to say your name or to tell about your favorite toy. Later, you probably told your class about a book you had read or about a family vacation. Perhaps you even gave a demonstration speech or presented a report. Each year, your oral presentations become more complex, so your skill at making them should also improve.

In this chapter, you will learn how to make a persuasive speech based on an essay you have already written. You will find helpful tips for every step of the process, from planning your speech to making the presentation.

What's Ahead

- **Preparing Your Presentation**
- **Organizing a Persuasive Speech**
- **Delivering Your Speech**

Making Oral Presentations

Objectives

- understand how to make an effective oral presentation
- choose an essay on which to base a persuasive speech
- prepare a presentation by adapting an essay: write a strong beginning and ending, use visual aids, organize notes on cards, and practice delivering the speech

A **persuasive speech** attempts to convince the audience to agree with the speaker.

- The opening grabs the listener's attention.
- Visual aids help reinforce the speaker's points.
- The organization is clear and logical.
- The ending restates the main point.
- The delivery enhances the message.

Preparing Your Presentation

Ideally, students will already have written at least one persuasive essay that can be adapted into a speech.

❋ If students need to review how to write a persuasive essay, postpone this section and begin with PE pages 218–281.

Rewriting in Action

Give students a specific time limit for the speech (3–5 minutes should be sufficient). Have students practice presenting the speech while using a timer or a clock to make sure they adhere to the time frame. If the speech runs too long, help them focus on highlighting their main points.

424

Preparing Your Presentation

Adapting an essay into a persuasive speech is a different process than writing a speech from scratch. For one thing, you already have a topic and information, and you know what type of speech you will make. The following tips will help you transform your persuasive essay into a good speech.

Get Noticed	Plan Visuals	State Your Case	Cut, Cut, Cut
Use a question, fact, or anecdote to get listeners' attention. (See below.)	Note when you should use visual aids or gestures. (See page 425.)	Focus on the main persuasive points of your presentation.	Include only details that strongly support your main point.

Rewriting in Action

Below is the opening of the persuasive essay on pages 235–238. Notice that the new beginning (on gold paper) has been revised so it grabs the listeners' attention and makes an appropriate opening for an oral presentation.

Students at Belmer Junior High are used to looking out the windows of the school and seeing Belmer Woods. Now when they look out, they see a sign: "For Sale, 20 acres, Zoned Residential/Commercial." Belmer Woods is about to change, and there are many different ideas about how it should change. The best way to develop Belmer Woods would be to make it a park.

When you look out the windows of Belmer Junior High, would you rather see the back of a strip mall or a beautiful green space? As it is now, a huge "For Sale" sign blocks the view, but the sign could be replaced by something even worse. Students should speak up now before it's too late. The best way to develop Belmer Woods is to make it a park.

Adapt your persuasive essay. Choose a persuasive essay you've written that would make a good oral presentation. Rewrite the opening so that it gets the audience's attention. Then think of the main persuasive points that you will use in your speech.

Teaching Tip

As students prepare their speeches, remind them to review their word choice and their writing voice. Encourage them to include sensory details, action verbs, and active voice in their oral presentations.

English Language Learners

Schedule a teacher's conference with any student who needs extra support in adapting a persuasive essay to speech format. Encourage students who are nervous about speaking in front of the entire class to practice with a tape recorder or with a small, friendly audience first.

Advanced Learners

Have students write three different types of openings:

● a question,
● a fact, and
● an anecdote.

Then have them use peer feedback to select the one that most effectively grabs the listener's attention.

practice *speak* show EXPRESS demonstrate **425**
Making Oral Presentations

Using Visual Aids

Once you have written the opening of your speech and chosen your most persuasive points, you should decide where to use visual aids. Visual aids like the ones below can help you make your presentation clear and convincing.

Posters	show words, pictures, or both.
Photographs	help your audience "see" who or what you are talking about.
Charts	compare ideas or explain main points.
Transparencies	highlight key words, ideas, or graphics.
Maps	show specific places being discussed.
Objects	allow your audience to see the real thing.

Here are some tips for preparing your visual aids.

1 **Make them big.** Everyone in the room should be able to see your visual aids.

2 **Keep them simple.** Don't use sentences and paragraphs. Labels and short phrases are more effective.

3 **Design them to catch the eye.** Use color, bold lines, and basic shapes to attract attention.

 List visual aids. Think about the visual aids you could use in your presentation. Then select two that would help make your points clear. Write down how you will use them.

Poster	list reasons to create park in Belmer Woods
Map	show layout of possible park in Belmer Woods

LEARNING

Using Visual Aids

Encourage students to provide or create effective visual aids for their presentations. Emphasize that these graphics should be more than decorative; they should create an impact by clarifying and highlighting important points.

Help students understand what type of visual aid might enhance their presentations. Provide a set of guidelines or a list of visual aids they could include, such as

- posters,
- charts,
- graphs,
- dioramas, or
- maps.

Remind students to choose visual aids that clarify and are relevant to their topics.

English Language Learners

If students have difficulty deciding which kind of visual aid to use, suggest that they try out a few of the ideas in the chart on this page. Encourage them to make a rough sketch or mock-up of the visual aid and confer with you about it before they begin to make a detailed version. This will allow you to monitor whether they are choosing effective topics for visuals.

Organizing a Persuasive Speech

Review the relationship between the opening and closing of the speech. Discuss different patterns that could be used to **organize the details in a presentation** (see below).

Using Note Cards

Remind students to number their cards in order of discussion as they write their notes. Point out that the sample note cards on PE page 427 are numbered in the order in which the speaker will refer to them. As you review the Note-Card Guidelines, ask students to explain how the sample note cards follow each guideline.

- Card #1, the introduction, is written out word for word.
- Cards #2, 3, and 4 are written as notes. Each card has a main idea at the top, with supporting details below.
- Card #5, the ending, is also written out word for word. It includes a note about a visual aid.

426

Organizing a Persuasive Speech

Now that you've written an opening and planned visual aids, you are ready to organize your speech. The purpose of a persuasive speech is to convince your audience to agree with you, so your organization should be clear and logical. Use the following tips.

Beginning	Middle	Ending
Get your listeners' attention and focus on the main persuasive point.	Put your persuasive details in the best order possible.	Close by restating your main point in a memorable way.

Using Note Cards

Writing out note cards is a simpler and more efficient way to organize your speech than writing on notepaper. Each card contains a main point that will guide you as you deliver the speech. Using cards also helps you make eye contact with your audience.

The student who adapted the essay on pages 235–238 into a speech used note cards. He included the opening, the closing, and the main ideas on cards that he used during the speech.

Note-Card Guidelines

- Write your introduction word for word on the first note card.
- Place each main idea on a separate card.
- Number each card.
- Note the main idea at the top of each card.
- Write the supporting details on the lines below the main idea.
- Mark cards that call for visual aids.
- Write your ending word for word on the last note card.

 Create your note cards. Look over the note cards on the next page. Then create a note card for each important part of your persuasive speech—introduction, main points, and ending. Note where you will use visual aids.

Teaching Tip: Organize the Details in a Presentation

Students may need to review different ways to arrange details for maximum impact. Choose a topic (for example, why it is important to keep art in the school curriculum), and use a list or an outline to demonstrate how to put supporting details into the best order to make a point. Discuss the following ways to organize the details:

- chronological order
- order of importance
- comparison-contrast
- logical order

✻ For more information about organizing details, see PE pages 550–551.

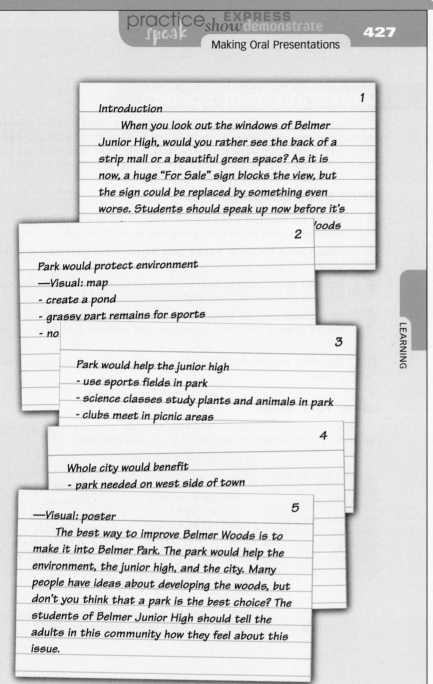

Introduction
When you look out the windows of Belmer Junior High, would you rather see the back of a strip mall or a beautiful green space? As it is now, a huge "For Sale" sign blocks the view, but the sign could be replaced by something even worse. Students should speak up now before it's

Woods

Park would protect environment
—Visual: map
- create a pond
- grassy part remains for sports
- no

Park would help the junior high
- use sports fields in park
- science classes study plants and animals in park
- clubs meet in picnic areas

Whole city would benefit
- park needed on west side of town

—Visual: poster
The best way to improve Belmer Woods is to make it into Belmer Park. The park would help the environment, the junior high, and the city. Many people have ideas about developing the woods, but don't you think that a park is the best choice? The students of Belmer Junior High should tell the adults in this community how they feel about this issue.

LEARNING

Emphasize that students should not write out their entire presentation word for word on their cards. Reexamine the sample note cards.

- Compare the two cards for the beginning and ending (#1 and #5) with the cards for the body of the speech (#2, 3, and 4).
- Point out that only the cards for the sample introduction and ending are written in complete sentences. The others are written in phrases.
- Explain that it is important to make eye contact with the audience (see PE page 428) even when reading parts of the speech.
- Explain that referring to a set of notes instead of reading complete sentences will allow them to look up and speak naturally.

Delivering Your Speech

Assure students that the more they practice their speeches, the easier it will be to look at the audience and use good body language.

Using Body Language

- Remind students to refer to the checklist on PE page 429 for help in focusing on specifics that will improve the presentation.
- Suggest that students try to make eye contact with members of the audience during their presentation, but point out that they should not do so in a methodical way (moving from one student to the next in each row).

Using Your Voice

Have students form groups so they can rehearse their speeches. Review the **qualities of good speakers** (*see below*) and listeners on PE page 419. Have group members give constructive feedback to each speaker, using the checklist on the bottom of PE page 429 as a guide.

428

Delivering Your Speech

The words are just the beginning of your speech. Your posture, gestures, and facial expressions communicate meaning as strongly as what you say. In order to persuade your audience, you should make sure your voice and body send the same message as your words. The following suggestions can help.

Using Body Language

1. **Stand up straight but stay relaxed.** If you look confident, your audience is more likely to be persuaded by what you say.
2. **Pause for a moment before you begin.** Take a breath and think about what you're going to say.
3. **Look at your audience.** If maintaining direct eye contact with your listeners distracts you, look slightly above their heads.
4. **Be natural and let your facial expressions reflect what you're saying.** Artificial expressions and gestures can distract your audience.
5. **Use your hands.** In a relaxed way, point to a visual aid or emphasize a point.

Using Your Voice

Your voice is the instrument that adds meaning to what you say. The three expressive characteristics of voice are *volume, tone,* and *speed.*

Volume	Tone	Speed
Speak loudly enough so that everyone can hear you.	Change your tone to show how you feel (upset, excited) about an idea or to emphasize a point.	Slow down. The most common vocal fault of oral presenters is speaking too fast.

 Practice and present. Using the tips above, practice with a friend or in front of family members so that they can give you suggestions.

Advanced Learners

If you do not have time to prepare for the **Teaching Tip** activity or do it with the entire class, have student volunteers

- research famous speakers and speeches,
- share a great speech with the class, and
- lead a discussion about the effectiveness of both the delivery and the content of the speech.

Teaching Tip: Qualities of Good Speakers

Discuss situations in which people speak to an audience (political speeches, a class lesson, a lecture, a press conference, and so on).

- Ask students to brainstorm a list of people who are effective public speakers.
- Ask your librarian to help you find DVDs, videotapes, or audio recordings of famous speakers and speeches, such

as the "I have a dream" speech of Martin Luther King, Jr., various presidents' inaugural speeches, and so on.

- Listen to the speeches as a class, and discuss what the speakers do to make their speeches effective.
- If time permits, allow volunteers to give their speeches more than once, after additional practice.

Overcoming Stage Fright

Most people feel nervous about speaking in front of a group. It's normal to have stage fright sometimes, but there are things that you can do to help yourself relax.

1 Be prepared.

Practice makes a big difference. Rehearse your speech often, especially in front of friends or family. Get used to having an audience.

2 Pause before you start.

When you get in front of the audience, pause to lay out your notes, think about what you're going to say, and take a deep breath.

3 Focus.

Concentrate on giving your speech. Visualize what comes next. Avoid distractions.

Using a Checklist

Practice your presentation using the checklist below. Videotape yourself or have someone evaluate your performance. That way you can identify areas that you need to improve.

_____ **1.** I stand up straight, and I look relaxed.

_____ **2.** I keep my head up and maintain eye contact with my audience.

_____ **3.** My voice is loud and clear.

_____ **4.** My voice and appearance both send the same message.

_____ **5.** I speak at a natural pace (not too fast or too slow).

_____ **6.** I avoid "stalling" words like _um, er,_ and _like._

_____ **7.** My visual aids are large and easy to understand.

_____ **8.** I use my hands for emphasis and to point out my visual aids.

LEARNING

Overcoming Stage Fright

To reduce potential nervousness when students are first presenting their speeches, dim the room lights in the "audience" section of the room. Remind the class to listen quietly and respectfully, so that each speaker will be able to focus on her or his speech.

Advanced Learners

Invite volunteers who are skilled at making audio or videotapes to help other students practice their speeches without an audience before they give their presentations to the entire class. Allocate time for this activity before or after class or at lunchtime, and monitor the activity and the results.

Presentation Tips

Prior to the presentation day, make sure students understand precisely where and how they will deliver their speeches. This will eliminate confusion and will help put students' minds at ease.

Consider having each student present his or her speech to a partner as a final dress rehearsal.

- Speakers should use their visual aids and have the listener time the speech.
- Remind students to be aware of their speaking pace. If they rush when they are nervous, their presentations will be too short and listeners will not fully appreciate the speech.
- Discuss ways to be a polite and encouraging listener. Also discuss what a speaker should do in awkward situations, such as when she loses her place.

430

Presentation Tips

Before your presentation . . .

- **Get organized.**
  Use note cards to put your information in order. Also make visual aids.
- **Time your speech.**
  If you are under or over a time limit, adjust your speech by adding or removing note cards.
- **Prepare.**
  The more you remember without looking at your notes, the easier it will be to give your presentation.

During your presentation . . .

- **Speak loudly, slowly, and clearly.**
  Be sure that everyone can hear you. Don't rush through your speech.
- **Connect with your audience.**
  Make eye contact.
- **Use body language.**
  Stand straight and tall with your arms relaxed. Face your audience and use appropriate gestures and facial expressions.
- **Hold visual aids so that everyone can see them.**
  Make the most out of your visuals. Use them to make your point.

After your presentation . . .

- **Answer questions.**
  Clarify any information that your listeners ask about.
- **Make closing comments.**
  Summarize the listeners' questions and concerns.

 Practice and present. Deliver your speech one final time before a friend or someone at home. Then present your speech to the class. Afterward, listen for suggestions from your teacher and classmates.

CLUSTER draw learn record freewrite **431**

Keeping Journals and Learning Logs

Your brain is a cornucopia overflowing with thoughts. One fruitful way to sort out all these thoughts is to write in a journal or a learning log.

A journal provides a space to reflect on your experiences. As you write, you come to understand what's important to you. Journal writing also helps you keep track of events in your daily life so you can reflect on them later.

A learning log focuses on classroom experiences. Writing in a learning log allows you to organize information and more fully understand your schoolwork.

The following chapter will teach you more about journals, learning logs, and other writing-to-learn activities.

What's Ahead

- Writing in a Specialized Journal
- Writing in Other Journals
- Writing in a Learning Log
- Writing-to-Learn Activities

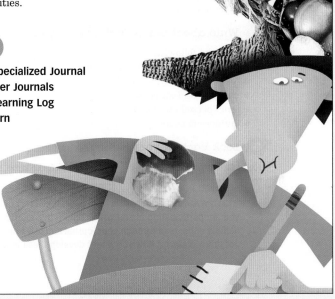

Keeping Journals and Learning Logs

Objectives
- understand how to keep journals and learning logs
- learn strategies for writing in journals and learning logs

A **journal** records reflections on experiences in daily life. A **learning log** focuses on classroom lessons.

Encourage students to keep a journal of their summer and vacation activities. Such entries will provide them with ideas for writing during the school year.

Writing in a Specialized Journal

Encourage students to use a composition notebook (with bound pages) for their journals. The bound pages will discourage students from tearing out entries and starting again. Explain that every thought recorded in the journal, complete or not, is important.

Consider having students begin keeping a Readers' Notebook where they make regular journal entries about the reading they do for class or on their own. Have the class brainstorm a list of sentence starters for these entries, and post them on a chart in the classroom. Suggestions for entries could include the following:

- The author did a really good job of . . .
- One thing that really confused me was . . .
- The character I most identified with was . . .
- I would/would not recommend this book to a friend because . . .

Refer to PE page 434 for additional ideas about reading journals.

Writing in a Specialized Journal

A specialized journal focuses on an ongoing event or experience. You could use this kind of journal to explore your thoughts while practicing for a school play, making a sculpture, or playing a sport. You don't have to write an essay—just record your thoughts and impressions.

Getting Started

To get started on your specialized journal, follow these steps:

1 Collect your supplies.

Paper and a pen (or pencil) are all you really need. If you wish, you can buy a blank book or a special notebook for your journal. You can also use a portable computer if one is available.

2 Decide on a time to write.

Set aside a time every day to write in your journal. Maybe early in the morning will be best for your schedule, or later at night, just before you go to bed. Also choose a comfortable place where you won't be disturbed.

3 Write freely for at least 10 minutes.

Writing freely for this long may seem difficult at first, but soon you'll get into a comfortable pattern and write for even longer periods of time.

4 Write about things that interest you.

Consider the following:
- things that catch your attention,
- personal thoughts and feelings,
- failures and successes,
- unexpected challenges, and
- humorous events.

5 Look back at your writing.

Read through your journal entries from time to time. Mark ideas you might like to develop into stories or poems.

 Start your specialized writing. Choose an ongoing event or activity that you are participating in and write about it in a journal. A week or two after the activity ends, read through your journal and mark the most interesting entries. Jot down ideas on how you might develop these entries into longer pieces.

Struggling Learners

Students who have never kept a journal or a diary may have difficulty writing a journal entry. Share with them published journal or diary entries (real or fictional) to help them get a sense of how journal entries can be written. Distribute photocopies of a bibliography of published journals compiled by classmates (see **Advanced Learners** box).

Advanced Learners

Ask students to compile a bibliography for classmates who would like to read examples of published journals or diaries (see **Struggling Learners** box). Some titles that might be listed include:

- *Anne Frank: The Diary of a Young Girl* by Anne Frank
- *I, Columbus: My Journal 1492–1493* by Peter Roop
- *Catherine, Called Birdy* by Karen Cushman
- *This Vast Land: A Young Man's Journal of the Lewis and Clark Expedition* by Stephen E. Ambrose

Specialized Journal Entry

In the journal entry below, a student writes about his experiences in his school's production of *You're a Good Man, Charlie Brown*. He tried out for a part in the play and wrote this journal entry after the first cast meeting.

Oct. 1

When Mrs. Walsh told us that the school play would be <u>You're a Good Man, Charlie Brown</u>, I started thinking about how much fun it would be to play Snoopy. I didn't audition for the play last year because it was a musical, and I'm afraid to sing on stage. <u>You're a Good Man</u> is a musical, too, but Snoopy doesn't talk in the cartoons, so I figured he wouldn't sing, either. After English class, I signed up to try out for the part.

We had the auditions yesterday after school, and all that the director, Mr. Goodwin, had us do was stand on the stage and say one sentence. When I looked at the cast list on the bulletin board this morning, there was my name next to Snoopy!

At the first cast meeting after school today, Mr. Goodwin congratulated us and handed out scripts. He also assigned practice times for the singers. "Linus and Schroeder practice on Mondays, Lucy and Charlie Brown on Tuesdays," and then he grinned at me, "and Snoopy on Wednesdays, Thursdays, and Fridays because he has the most songs."

What key does a beagle sing in?

LEARNING

To help you get started on a specialized journal entry, focus on an important personal experience. These two questions will help you.

What surprised or impressed me about this experience?
How did I react to what happened?

Specialized Journal Entry

Explain that the key difference between taking notes and writing a journal entry is the reflective nature of the journal entries.

Review the sample journal entry. Ask students to point out the personal reflections that the writer includes (fun to play Snoopy, afraid to sing on stage).

Writing in Other Journals

If your school has a specific policy on sharing entries from diaries or journals, review it with the class.

Ask students to brainstorm a list of situations in which keeping a journal might provide useful insights. Encourage them to think of hobbies or occupations that might lend themselves to keeping a journal. For example,

- professionals (doctors, lawyers, explorers, soldiers, meteorologists, naturalists, teachers, or social workers) might record their observations and reflections;
- students who study karate, perform in music recitals, or babysit might write about their experiences.

Engage the class in a discussion of the potential benefits (to writers and readers) of keeping a journal. If the journal is to be shared or published, ask the class what kinds of information (such as names of patients, clients, or students) should be kept private.

434

Writing in Other Journals

Specialized journals help you think about ongoing experiences. Here are some other types of journals you can try.

Personal Journal and Diary

Journals and diaries are very similar. Journals contain reflections and observations about your life and your experiences. Writers often develop longer pieces from their journal entries. Diaries, on the other hand, focus more on daily events. The entries are often shorter than those in journals, and together they form a history of your day-to-day life.

Dialogue Journal

A dialogue journal records a conversation between you and a teacher, family member, or friend. You and your partner take turns writing entries in a dialogue journal.

Travel Journal

In a travel journal, you write your impressions of a trip you are taking. Many people write in their journals while they are on the way from one place to another.

Reader-Response Journal

Writing journal entries about a book or an article that you're reading will increase your understanding and enjoyment of the material. Here are some questions that will help you write about what you read.

1 How did I feel after key points in the book, such as the opening, the ending, or a crisis?

2 What did I learn? Do I understand something now that I didn't before?

3 Is there a personal connection between the reading and my life?

4 What's really important about the reading? A character? An event? An idea?

5 Would I recommend this book or article to someone else? Why?

 Start a dialogue journal. Choose a friend or family member who would be a good partner for a dialogue journal. Make your first entry in a notebook and then give it to your partner to write a response. Continue your dialogue.

Struggling Learners

Remind students that e-mail messages might contain ideas for journal entries.

- Encourage them to mine their "sent mail" folder for topics that could be addressed in a journal.
- Suggest that they consider printing out an e-mail message that could be used as a starting point for an entry.

Advanced Learners

Students might enjoy keeping a specialized reader-response journal called "Thought for the Day," in which they reflect on quotations.

- Discuss places to find quotations, including novels, poems, biographies, newspapers, magazines, and Web sites (screen these for suitability).

- Ask students to choose a different quotation each day.
- On the top of the page, they should copy the quotation and record the author and source.
- On the rest of the page, they should write about the quotation and their reactions to it.

CLUSTER record freewrite
draw learn
435
Keeping Journals and Learning Logs

Writing in a Learning Log

Learning logs can be very helpful in school, and they can be adapted to any subject. Writing in a log is an especially good way to make sense of unfamiliar or difficult material. The following tips will give you some ideas.

1 **Start a learning log for any subject.**
Your most difficult subject might be the best choice.

2 **Organize your learning log.**
Keep a separate notebook or section of a notebook for each subject. Date each entry and leave margins for adding information later.

3 **Use charts and drawings.**
Illustrations can help you remember difficult or key ideas.

4 **Write freely about any of the following:**
- key ideas from assignments, lectures, or class discussions;
- questions you have; or
- how new material relates to things that you've already learned.

LEARNING

English Class   Jan. 12

Parallelism = Repeating the same grammatical structure to . . .
    —show equality among items or ideas, or
    —emphasize contrast between items or ideas.

Examples:
    Sally likes talking on the phone, hanging out with friends, and shopping at the mall. (equality)
    Harper went to his room every night after supper, took out his math book, opened it to that day's assignment, and watched TV until he fell asleep. (contrast)

    When I think of parallels, I usually think of geometry. Parallel lines run side by side. They are sort of the same. I guess it works in English, too. For instance, two "ing" words are parallel (running, swimming) and so are two prepositional phrases (on the land, in the water). So, I could talk about

---

Writing in a Learning Log

Most students will need specific guidance to begin a learning log. Help familiarize them with the concept by doing the following:

- Point out that a learning log should show the name of the class and the date at the top of each page. Discuss the kind of information the student recorded in the sample log on this page. Ask students to think of some examples of charts or drawings that they might include in their own learning logs.

- Have the class do a quick freewrite about how a learning log may prove helpful. Provide this sentence starter for the freewrite: "A learning log will help me understand . . ."

- Ask students to write a learning-log entry for two other classes they have during the day. On the next day, circulate among the class and review these entries with individual students.

This practice should help prepare students to write regularly on their own. In addition, ask other teachers to encourage students to keep learning logs for their classes as well.

Struggling Learners

Provide additional support for students who need help starting or keeping a learning log. Remind them that the log can include diagrams as well as written notes. Encourage students to jot down questions about any ideas or concepts that may be unclear.

Advanced Learners

Invite volunteers to take turns keeping a daily learning log for the entire class.

- Have different students record what the class covered in each subject.
- Students who have been absent can refer to the notes in the class log to catch up on the work they missed.

Science Log

A science log could also include
- lab procedures,
- hypotheses for experiments, and
- reflections on lab exercises.

Explain the difference between a science log entry, which may contain personal reactions and reflections, and an observation report that discusses a scientific experiment, as detailed on PE pages 210–211.

436

Science Log

Science logs are most effective if you put difficult ideas in your own words. Also include drawings and examples from your own experience. The learning log below was written after a science class lesson on momentum.

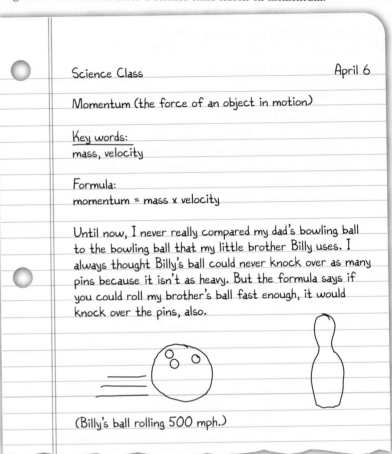

Science Class   April 6

Momentum (the force of an object in motion)

Key words:
mass, velocity

Formula:
momentum = mass x velocity

Until now, I never really compared my dad's bowling ball to the bowling ball that my little brother Billy uses. I always thought Billy's ball could never knock over as many pins because it isn't as heavy. But the formula says if you could roll my brother's ball fast enough, it would knock over the pins, also.

(Billy's ball rolling 500 mph.)

Log on in science. On your own paper, name the science subject you are currently studying. Then write a learning-log entry about the subject. Focus on something interesting, surprising, or confusing about it.

Math Log

A math log can help you think about concepts taught in your math class. One way to set up a math log is to ask a question related to a lesson and then answer it in your own words. Providing your own examples and thoughts will help you understand the concept. Examples are shown below.

> Math Class   Oct. 19
> Question: What is theoretical probability?
> Answer: Theoretical probability is a way to predict what will happen by doing math. You count the number of possibilities and then figure out the percentage chance of each one happening.
> Example: A coin has two sides, heads and tails. When you toss the coin, the probability of it landing heads is 50% and the probability of it landing tails is 50%.
>   Oct. 20
>
> Question: What is experimental probability?
> Answer: Experimental probability is based on the results of an experiment, or actually counting what happens.
> Example: You flip a coin a certain number of times and record how many times it lands heads and how many times it lands tails. You divide each number of heads and each number of tails by the total number of tosses, and you get the experimental results.
>   In 100 tosses, the coin lands heads 37 times and tails 63 times. The experimental results are 37% heads and 63% tails.
>   I think people should be more careful with statistics on probability. There can be big differences between theoretical statistics and what really happens.

 Log on in math. On your own paper, write a learning-log entry for math. First write down a question about a math concept you are studying. Then answer it and provide examples in your own words.

LEARNING

Math Log

Encourage students to use a math log to explain their thought processes as they worked on word problems and complex mathematical equations.

English Language Learners

Before students write their entries, have them do a warm-up exercise:

- Ask them to think of a math procedure they know well, such as multiplication.
- Have them write a math-log entry that they might give to a younger sibling to help her or him understand and remember the concept.

- Encourage them to use pictures as well as words in their examples, to make their explanations clear.
- Once students have successfully completed this practice log entry, encourage them to use the same skills to explain, review, and summarize a math concept from a current unit of study.

Social Studies Log

Suggest that students use social studies logs to explore their thoughts concerning events in history. They can also provide commentary on current political events. Remind students that they should focus on their feelings and thoughts about what happened.

Social Studies Log

A social studies log focuses on what a student learns in social studies class. In the entry below, a student briefly summarizes something that interests her, adding her own feelings and thoughts.

Social Studies   Sept. 14

Deborah Samson

Mr. Kronus told us an amazing story in class today. He was talking about how Americans think women weren't soldiers until just recently. But before the army was as organized as it is now, women sometimes dressed like men, sneaked onto battlefields, and fought. A number of women did this in the Revolutionary War, including Deborah Samson.

Deborah called herself Robert Shirtliffe and got away with this for three years. She performed many military duties and was wounded twice. The first time, she got a sword cut on the side of the head. Then, a few months later, she was shot through the shoulder. Even though she was wounded, no one figured that she was a woman until she caught a serious fever and had to go to a doctor.

Mr. Kronus said that after the war, Deborah got married. She was called to Washington and rewarded for her bravery. Paul Revere played a part in honoring her and recognizing her as a soldier.

I think it's interesting to find out about the people in history who aren't so famous. "Robert," with all that she had to do to fight for her country, seems more real to me than "taxation without representation" or "the shot heard round the world."

Log on in social studies. In your learning log, write the name of the topic you are now studying in social studies. Write an entry about something that interests you about that topic. Include your own thoughts and feelings.

English Language Learners

To help students connect with a topic, allow them to include comparisons to events or reactions in their homeland. For example:

- If they are studying a particular war, they may want to add comments about how their country of origin was affected by the conflict, if at all.

- Or if they are studying a particular culture, they can compare that culture to their homeland as well as to the United States.

CLUSTER record freewrite
draw learn
439
Keeping Journals and Learning Logs

Writing-to-Learn Activities

There are many strategies for writing in learning logs. This page describes three basic strategies, and five more ideas appear on the next page.

The Basic Three

1 **Clustering** Clustering helps you see how ideas fit together. Write the subject you are studying in the center of a page and circle it. Then write words and phrases about the subject around it. Circle each one and draw a line connecting it to the most closely related words. (See page 95.)

2 **Listing** Listing is another way to find ideas that relate to each other. Think about a subject and write a list of feelings, questions, and ideas that come to mind.

3 **Freewriting** When you write quickly and openly about a subject, you are freewriting. Write down everything that comes to mind, thinking about as many aspects of the subject as you can. Don't worry about sentence structure, spelling, or any of the other rules—just write continuously until you run out of ideas.

> In PE today, the teacher asked us to think about which of our favorite sports keeps you the most physically fit and would be a good activity to continue through life. Baseball is really my favorite sport, but I don't think I really get a lot of exercise playing it, although I'm pretty tired after I pitch 4 or 5 innings. Swimming is my second favorite, and I think that's really good exercise. I like soccer too, and you run constantly in that game. Baseball's out. It's between swimming and soccer. I guess swimming would be best, because you don't have to get a bunch of other people together to do it. My grandpa and grandma both swim in the pool at their condo, and they're in great shape!

LEARNING

 Freewrite on a topic you are studying in one of your classes. Write continuously until you run out of ideas. Create a focus statement that summarizes the most important idea in your freewriting.

Writing-to-Learn Activities

Students need to practice each of the three strategies presented here in order to use them effectively.

The Basic Three

Students will find clustering and listing to be fairly straightforward, but they may not realize that freewriting is another strategy they can use to gather ideas. Because most students have been taught to think about ideas before they write them down, some students may find it difficult to write down their thoughts, nonstop, for a given period of time. Spend some time practicing **freewriting** *(see below)* with students.

 **Answers**

Answers will vary.

Teaching Tip: Freewriting

Provide several freewriting practice sessions so that students can become comfortable with writing freely.

- Remind students to keep their pens moving. Encourage them to write whatever comes into their mind about the topic.

- Begin with a small amount of time, perhaps 2 minutes, and gradually build up to a 10-minute freewrite.
- Freewrite with your students the first few times, and read back what you have written or display it as a model on an overhead transparency.

Struggling Learners

Provide extra practice with the Basic Three strategies.

- Invite students to suggest topics from science, math, and social studies.
- Have them complete sample clusters, lists, and brief freewrites.
- Discuss which strategy worked best for them and why.

Special Writing Activities

Review the different **special writing activities** (*see below*) that can be used in learning logs.

- Brainstorm a list of situations when each kind of activity on PE page 440 might be useful.
- Using the sample reporter's "broadcast" report as a model, point out how students can combine creativity and information when giving a personal perspective on an event or a person in history.
- Display the different approaches on a bulletin board or in a booklet.

The more often students write in these forms, the more skilled and inventive their writing will become.

 **Answers**

Answers will vary.

440

Special Writing Activities

The learning-log activities on this page can be used for a wide variety of purposes. As you read them, try to think of a class in which each one would be helpful.

First Thoughts When you begin a new unit in a class, write down the first things that come to mind. Is the new material totally unfamiliar, or can you connect it to something you've learned before?

Stop 'n' Write This is similar to "first thoughts," but wait until you get into the middle of the new material before you stop and assess it. Make note of what you understand and write questions about things that you find difficult.

Unsent Letters Unsent letters are a more personal way for you to reflect on what you're learning. Write a letter to a historical figure about something that the person is famous for, or imagine that you have a friend to write to in a place that you are studying.

Personal Summary Summarize a lecture or a reading assignment in your own words. Putting your own slant on the material will help you understand and remember it.

Role-Playing Imagine that you are an eyewitness to some important event. Write an account of what happened as though you were a reporter or a bystander.

> Gettysburg, Pennsylvania
> November 19, 1863
> This is Chad Thackery reporting for CNN from a hilltop near Gettysburg. Today President Lincoln dedicated this battlefield as a memorial to the soldiers who died here during the current rebellion. His speech was amazingly short and took only a few minutes to deliver. He did not seem to have much confidence in the quality of his speech, saying at one point, "The world will little note, nor long remember, what we say here." The president concluded by vowing to carry on, in his words, "the unfinished work."
> Only time will tell whether this little speech will be remembered, but the men who fell here will be remembered in this cemetery. Back to you, Wolf.

 Write an account of an event you have studied. Imagine that you are an eyewitness to the event.

Advanced Learners

Extend the **Try It** activity. In addition to writing a first-person account as an imaginary eyewitness, encourage students to write a second account of the event from the point of view of the main character (for example, as President Lincoln instead of as a reporter).

Teaching Tip: Special Writing Activities

Students will benefit from additional practice in different kinds of learning-log activities.

Invite students to choose one of these three activities:

- Unsent letter: Suggest that students write an imaginary letter to an author, a current celebrity, or a historical figure.
- Personal summary: Students can write a summary of a lesson in this class or of an assignment or a lesson in another class.
- Role-playing: Students can write their own eyewitness accounts of an important historical or current event.

Have students share their work in small groups or as a class.

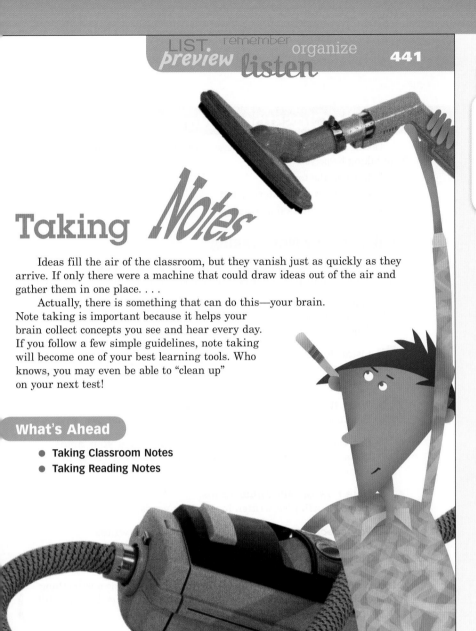

LIST. remember organize
preview listen
441

Taking *Notes*

Ideas fill the air of the classroom, but they vanish just as quickly as they arrive. If only there were a machine that could draw ideas out of the air and gather them in one place. . . .

Actually, there is something that can do this—your brain. Note taking is important because it helps your brain collect concepts you see and hear every day. If you follow a few simple guidelines, note taking will become one of your best learning tools. Who knows, you may even be able to "clean up" on your next test!

What's Ahead

- Taking Classroom Notes
- Taking Reading Notes

Taking Notes

Objectives

- learn and apply guidelines for taking notes in the classroom and while reading
- use graphic organizers to arrange reading notes

When taking notes, students should try to capture only the main points of information. They should *not* write in complete sentences or try to list every detail.

Note taking is often a difficult skill for students. Because they don't understand how to **listen for key points** *(see below),* they attempt to write down every word they hear. They soon fall behind and miss whole sections of a lesson. Students need to see how to take good notes and practice doing it themselves.

Teaching Tip: Listening for Key Points

Help students learn how to listen for the main points in a lesson by doing this activity:

- Read aloud a paragraph from a social studies or science textbook. Have students take notes on it as you read.
- Have students compare their notes as a class. List some examples on the board. Then discuss which ideas are key points and which ones are less

important details that could be left out.
- Read aloud another paragraph. Have each student compare his or her notes with a partner and come up with a final list of key points.
- Have partners share their final lists with the class. Help students reach a consensus on the key points.

Copy Masters/ Transparencies

T-chart (TE pp. 445, 446)

Time line (TE pp. 445, 448)

Taking Classroom Notes

Initially, keep daily note-taking sessions short, and allow time for students to review their classroom notes each day. They should rewrite them as needed, organizing the information according to the guidelines provided here or your own guidelines.

Have students share their revised notes in the next class, as a review of both the lesson and note taking. As students become more familiar with the skill, they will take more organized notes and will not have to rewrite them each day.

Guidelines for Note Taking

Review the guidelines with the class. Then have students work in pairs to review their notes and combine their information. If one partner has written down a point that the other has missed, the second student should add that fact or idea.

 Answers

Answers will vary, but students should select at least one guideline to implement in their own notes.

442

Taking Classroom Notes

Taking notes can help you understand new material and prepare for tests. Note taking helps you . . .

- focus on the topic,
- understand new material, and
- remember what's important.

Guidelines for Note Taking

1 **Write the topic and date at the top of each page.**
Number your pages so that you can sort them out if they get mixed up.

2 **Listen for main ideas.**
If your teacher tells you that there were three main causes of the American Revolution, get ready to list them in your notes.

3 **Listen for key words.**
Key words like *first, most importantly,* and *finally* tell you how ideas relate to each other.

4 **Write the main ideas in your own words.**
You understand things better if you say them in your own way.

5 **Use numbers, words, or symbols to organize your notes.**
Use an asterisk (✱) to mark a main idea. Number the steps in a process.

6 **Note new or unfamiliar terms.**
Include a definition written in your own words.

7 **Pay special attention to what the teacher writes on the board.**
This information is often on the test at the end of the unit.

Listen carefully for the main points. Don't try to write down everything the teacher says. If you miss something, you can always go back and fill in your notes later.

Try IT Review the guidelines above. What areas of your own note taking could you improve?

English Language Learners

If possible, allow students to record lectures so that they can replay the information and supplement their notes when needed. Also, assign note-taking partners. Allow class time for pairs of students to share their notes, discuss the lectures, and revise or add to what they wrote for a more complete record.

LIST. remember
preview listen organize
Taking Notes
443

Setting Up Your Notes

Keep separate notes for each subject. You might use a different notebook for each class or a three-ring binder with dividers. Binders allow you to remove and replace pages, which is especially helpful if you write on only one side of each sheet. The side notes below give additional tips.

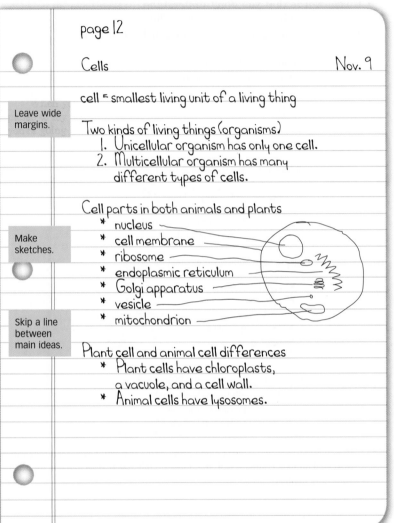

Leave wide margins.

Make sketches.

Skip a line between main ideas.

> page 12
>
> Cells   Nov. 9
>
> cell = smallest living unit of a living thing
>
> Two kinds of living things (organisms)
>   1. Unicellular organism has only one cell.
>   2. Multicellular organism has many
>   different types of cells.
>
> Cell parts in both animals and plants
>   * nucleus
>   * cell membrane
>   * ribosome
>   * endoplasmic reticulum
>   * Golgi apparatus
>   * vesicle
>   * mitochondrion
>
> Plant cell and animal cell differences
>   * Plant cells have chloroplasts,
>   a vacuole, and a cell wall.
>   * Animal cells have lysosomes.

LEARNING

Setting Up Your Notes

Provide students with a strategic format for their notes. Recommend that they use the layout as presented on this page. Or provide them with specific layout guidelines that you or your school may have previously established.

English Language Learners

Discuss each portion of the sample notes. Point out and discuss the following features:

- Most of the notes are written as short phrases, not complete sentences.
- The student used an equals sign to note a definition.
- The student used numbers and asterisks to list points of equal importance.

- The student made a drawing and labeled it by extending lines from the list to show where each cell feature appears.

Stress that the form of the notes can vary: For example, in the final section of the sample notes, the student could have used a Venn diagram to show how plant and animal cells differ.

Struggling Learners

Encourage students to incorporate diagrams in their notes, but remind them that the main function of a chart or sketch is to help a person remember ideas clearly—not to be artistic or creative.

Reviewing Your Notes

Emphasize that notes are a work in progress, not a clean, final copy. When students review their notes, suggest that they make any further notations in the margins with a different colored pen or pencil. These notations can include questions, revelations, references to other ideas, or anything else that students might want to record.

444

Reviewing Your Notes

Take time every day to review your notes.

- **If you have any questions, write them in the margins.**
  Follow up by checking with your teacher or a classmate and add explanations to clarify your notes.
- **Circle words that you don't understand.**
  Look up the definitions and correct spellings.
- **Rewrite anything that is confusing or hard to read.**
  Keep your notes organized and easy to read.
- **Review your notes before the next class.**
  Be ready for class discussions and quizzes.

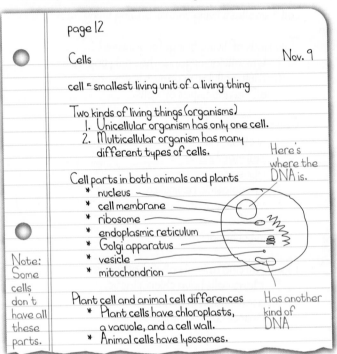

 Review your work. Check some class notes that you have taken recently. How well do they compare with the notes on this page? How can you improve your note taking?

Taking Reading Notes

Taking notes as you read will help you understand and remember the information. Pause during your reading to write down important ideas and questions. Here are some tips for taking reading notes.

1 Quickly skim the assignment.

Read the title, introduction, headings, and chapter summaries. Look at the charts, pictures, and illustrations. Your preview will help you when you start reading for details.

2 Read carefully and take notes.

Write down the main ideas and important details.

- **Write down each heading or subtopic.** Then write the most important information.
- **Use your own words.** You'll remember more than if you copy directly from the reading.
- **Pay attention to pictures, maps, and other graphics.** Make notes or drawings about the information.
- **Read difficult material out loud.** Hearing the information often helps you better understand and remember it.
- **Make a list of new words.** Look up the definitions in a dictionary or the glossary so that you fully understand the reading.
- **Review your notes.** After you finish reading, look over your notes and write down any questions you have.

3 Add graphic organizers whenever possible.

Graphic organizers can help you arrange your notes in a clear, logical order. You can use any of the helpful organizers on the next three pages for taking notes.

 Review the tips above. Which ones do you think will be the most valuable for you the next time that you have a reading assignment?

LEARNING

Taking Reading Notes

Students can take notes on their reading in much the same way that they record classroom notes, using the strategic note-taking format shown on TE page 443.

✳ Refer students to PE pages 548–549 for examples of graphic organizers to use. Also, provide photocopies of the reproducible charts on TE pages 789–793.

Review the tips for taking reading notes. Point out that one advantage of taking good notes is that it is easy to return to the original material to check for any important information students might have missed.

 **Answers**

Answers will vary.

Using a Before-After Organizer

This strategy is especially useful in social studies or science, where students can either explore the cause-and-effect relationships among historical events or analyze the results of an experiment.

Students can also use this type of organizer to analyze plots and character development in novels.

Some students may prefer to use a T-chart to create their own before-after organizer for the **Try It** activity. Provide photocopies of the reproducible T-chart on TE page 789.

 Answers

Event: When a piece of white paper burns, the chemical reaction causes a drastic increase in temperature and a dramatic change in color.

Before

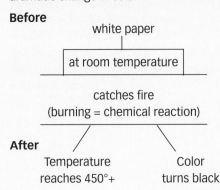

white paper

at room temperature

catches fire
(burning = chemical reaction)

After

Temperature reaches 450°+

Color turns black

446

Using a Before-After Organizer

Important events sometimes result in big changes. A **before-after organizer** can help you identify these changes by listing the way that things were before and after the event. This type of organizer can be used to help you understand what you read, especially in social studies and science.

Read the following paragraph and then note how the graphic organizer shows the main ideas.

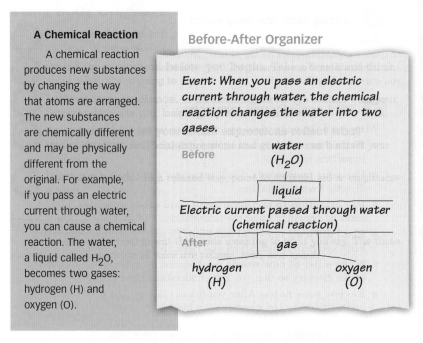

A Chemical Reaction

A chemical reaction produces new substances by changing the way that atoms are arranged. The new substances are chemically different and may be physically different from the original. For example, if you pass an electric current through water, you can cause a chemical reaction. The water, a liquid called H_2O, becomes two gases: hydrogen (H) and oxygen (O).

Before-After Organizer

Event: When you pass an electric current through water, the chemical reaction changes the water into two gases.

Before

water (H_2O)

liquid

Electric current passed through water (chemical reaction)

After   gas

hydrogen (H)   oxygen (O)

Read the following paragraph about chemical reactions. Then create a before-after organizer to diagram the information.

1   Chemical reactions often cause changes in temperature
2   and appearance. For example, burning is a chemical reaction.
3   When a piece of room-temperature white paper catches fire, its
4   temperature jumps to over 450° F, and its color changes from
5   white to black.

Struggling Learners

If students have trouble using the before-after organizer, they may find it easier to use a cause-effect diagram:

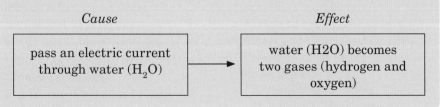

Cause

pass an electric current through water (H_2O)

Effect

water (H2O) becomes two gases (hydrogen and oxygen)

LIST. remember organize
preview listen

447

Taking Notes

Using a Comparison-Contrast Chart

You can graph, or record, two topics' similarities and differences in a comparison-contrast chart. In this type of organizer, list the characteristics for each of the topics. After the lists are finished, underline the differences. Read the paragraphs and the corresponding comparison-contrast chart below.

Free Verse and Blank Verse

Free verse is poetry that has no regular pattern of rhyme or rhythm. Much modern poetry is free verse.

Blank verse is poetry that has a regular pattern of rhythm but does not rhyme. Blank verse became very popular during Shakespeare's time.

Comparison-Contrast Chart

Free Verse	Blank Verse
- poetry	- poetry
- no regular rhythm	- regular rhythm
- unrhymed	- unrhymed
- modern	- Shakespeare's time

LEARNING

 Read the following paragraph comparing folktales and fables. Then create a comparison-contrast chart listing the characteristics of the two forms of writing. Underline the characteristics that are different.

1   People often confuse fables and folktales. A fable is a brief
2   story that teaches a lesson. Fables sometimes feature animals.
3   A folktale is a brief story that is passed from generation to
4   generation. Folktales sometimes contain animals but are usually
5   told to entertain rather than teach.

Using a Comparison-Contrast Chart

Model this note-taking strategy by teaching a topic that lends itself to this type of analysis (a ballad and a tall tale, haiku and cinquain, etc.). Ask student volunteers to identify features of each topic. List their suggestions on a comparison-contrast chart that you display on the board or on the overhead. Underline those features that differ.

 Answers

Fable: brief story, <u>teaches lesson</u>, sometimes features animals

Folktale: brief story, <u>passed from generation to generation</u>, sometimes features animals, <u>told to entertain</u>

Using a Time Line

Students generally think of time lines in terms of a series of events that span years, such as battles in a war, or expeditions of explorers.

Explain that they can also **use a time line to plan a story** (see below). Point out that a time line can help a writer plot what occurs in a scene or a series of scenes that take place over a period of hours or days.

Provide photocopies of the reproducible time line on TE page 790 for students to use for the **Try It** activity and the **Teaching Tip** activity.

 Answers

Gwendolyn Brooks

```
1917 ┼─ Born

1950 ┼─ First African American author
     │   to receive a Pulitzer Prize

1968 ┼─ Named poet laureate of
     │   Illinois
2000 ┼─ Died
     │
```

448

Using a Time Line

Some types of writing are organized chronologically, or according to when things happen. In histories, biographies, and narratives, for example, the order of the events is very important. When you want to take notes on this kind of writing, a time line can help you keep the flow of events organized.

Read the following short biography. Then look at the time line to see how the details are arranged.

Louisa May Alcott

By the time Louisa May Alcott died in 1888, she was famous for writing a very successful book, *Little Women*.

Louisa was born in 1832 and was raised in Massachusetts. Her first poem was published in 1851, and by 1854, she had published a book of stories and poems. *Little Women* was published in 1869. From then until her death, she wrote several other books, including several sequels to *Little Women*.

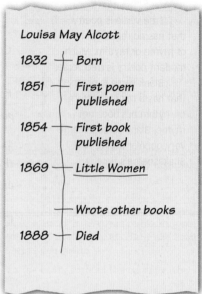

Time Line

Louisa May Alcott

```
1832 ┼─ Born

1851 ┼─ First poem
     │   published

1854 ┼─ First book
     │   published

1869 ┼─ Little Women

     ┼─ Wrote other books

1888 ┼─ Died
```

 Read the following brief biography. Then create a time line that lists the important events.

1 In 1950, Gwendolyn Brooks became the first African
2 American author to receive a Pulitzer Prize. She was recognized
3 for her collection of poetry titled *Annie Allen*. Born in 1917,
4 Gwendolyn grew up in Chicago, where her parents encouraged
5 her to write. She was widely admired for her writing, being
6 named poet laureate of Illinois in 1968. She died in 2000.

Struggling Learners

Students may be confused by the time jumps that occur in both the sample and the **Try It** passage. Explain that, for greater impact, a biography may begin by focusing on a person's most important achievement.

Teaching Tip: Use a Time Line to Plan a Story

Show students how they can use a time line to analyze or develop a story plot:

- Choose a short story students have recently read, or a well-known fable or fairy tale.
- On a copy of the time line (TE page 790), have students list the key events in the order in which they occur.

- Using a transparency (TR 11), compile a time line for the story, using ideas from the entire class.
- Next, ask students to create a time line for an important time in their own lives.
- Then have them use this time line to write a simple personal story.
- Display the time lines and the stories.

recall *apply* UNDERSTAND
analyze   evaluate   **449**
synthesize

Completing Writing Assignments

Completing writing assignments is more than simply finishing your work before the bell goes off. Teachers give you writing assignments to make you think and "use your brains."

Did you know that your brain is more powerful than the biggest supercomputer on the planet? Computers can do certain tasks very well—recalling information, analyzing it according to a program, and applying it in a specific way. However, computers don't really understand the information, nor can they really evaluate its worth. Your brain, on the other hand, can do these things.

Next time you get a writing assignment, remember not only that you can beat the clock, but also that you can beat the computer.

What's Ahead

- **Understanding the Assignment**
- **Thinking Through Each Assignment**
- **Setting Up an Assignment Schedule**

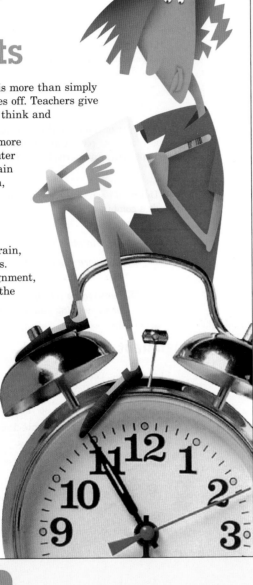

Copy Masters/ Transparencies

T-chart (TE p. 452)

Completing Writing Assignments

Objectives

- learn how to interpret what a writing assignment requires
- use recalling, understanding, applying, analyzing, synthesizing, or evaluating to complete a writing assignment
- set up a schedule for completing the steps of the writing process

A **writing assignment** can be
- specific (the topic is provided),
- open-ended (you select a topic),
- or a combination (part is chosen for you, but you choose the rest).

Discuss the connection between writing and different subject areas. Students often don't realize that they can use the writing skills and strategies they learn in this class to complete their assignments in other subject areas.

Have students brainstorm to fill in a chart showing the kinds of writing assignments they have in each subject area. Include class work and homework, such as
- research reports,
- essays,
- tests,
- lab reports, and
- short stories.

Understanding the Assignment

Help students develop a system for responding to "short term" writing assignments. Encourage them to use the checklist on this page as a starting point.

If students must complete a piece of writing in a single class period (45 minutes), they should try to set aside 5 to 10 minutes for prewriting and planning, 25 to 30 minutes for drafting, and about 10 minutes at the end to make any necessary changes.

On PE page 458 students will learn about setting up a schedule for writing assignments that have a longer time frame.

 Answers

1. specific
2. combination
3. open-ended

450

Understanding the Assignment

Writing assignments can take many forms, including these three basic types.

Specific
If the topic is chosen for you, the assignment is specific. (Explain what causes earthquakes.)

Open-Ended
If you are allowed to select your own topic, the assignment is open-ended. (Describe a historical period in which you would like to live.)

Combination
If part of the topic is chosen for you but you are allowed to choose another part, the assignment is a combination of open-ended and specific. (Compare chimpanzees to another type of great ape.)

 Decide if each of the assignments listed below is open-ended, specific, or a combination.

1. *Explain what makes planets revolve around the sun.*
2. *Compare the effects of smoking cigarettes with the effects of some other unhealthful activity.*
3. *Persuade a parent to agree with you about a family rule or something you want to do.*

Assignment Checklist

Be sure that you completely understand a writing assignment before you begin. Use the following checklist as a guide.

_____ 1. **Plan your time** so that you aren't rushed at the last minute.
_____ 2. **Ask what is expected** on the assignment.
_____ 3. **Read the directions** carefully and ask questions if necessary.
_____ 4. **Focus on key words**—*explain, contrast, describe*—so you know exactly what your writing should do.
_____ 5. **Review and revise** your writing.

Thinking Through Each Assignment

Different writing assignments ask you to use different levels of thinking. These levels can range from simply recalling information to understanding, applying, analyzing, synthesizing, or evaluating it. The chart below briefly describes these thinking tasks, and the next six pages give you a closer look at each one.

Recalling means remembering information. Use this basic level of thinking when you are asked to . . .

- fill in the blanks
- define terms
- list facts or words
- label parts of something

Understanding means knowing what information means. Use understanding when you are asked to . . .

- explain something
- choose the best answer
- tell if something is true or false
- summarize something

Applying means using information. Use applying when you are asked to . . .

- follow directions
- solve a problem

Analyzing means breaking information down into different parts. Use analyzing when you are asked to . . .

- compare things
- divide things into groups
- give reasons for something
- tell why something is the way it is

Synthesizing means using information to create something new. Use synthesizing when you are asked to . . .

- create something
- add new ideas
- combine things
- predict something

Evaluating means using information to tell the value of something. Use this advanced level of thinking when you are asked to . . .

- assess something
- give your opinion of something

LEARNING

Thinking Through Each Assignment

Review with students the chart describing the six levels of thinking. Explain that recalling is the most basic level; after that, the levels become increasingly complex.

- Point out that different types of thinking are useful for different purposes; many assignments require a combination of skills.
- Explain that the more advanced levels require some mastery of the basic levels. For example, in order to apply, analyze, synthesize, or evaluate, one must first be able to recall and understand information.

Reassure students that they do not have to remember all the details about the levels of thinking at this point, but encourage them to refer back to this page as a reference.

Struggling Learners

Choose a short nonfiction reading selection, and make sure each student has a copy. Read it aloud as students follow along. Together, write at least one question about the article or suggest an activity that would involve each level of thinking, using the information on this page.

Recalling

Point out that there are specific correct answers for these sample test questions. Students either know the required information or they do not. Stress that the more students put into taking accurate notes and reviewing them, the more they will likely be able to recall.

 Answers

Answers will vary.

452

Recalling

When you remember information, you are *recalling* it. You can strengthen this type of thinking by listening and reading carefully, taking notes, and then reviewing the information so that you don't forget it.

You recall when you . . .

- give details.
- identify or define key terms.
- remember main points.

The following test questions ask the student to recall.

DIRECTIONS: Fill in the blanks below with the correct answers.

1. The American Civil War lasted _____ (number) years.

2. The United States rapidly expanded toward the _____ (direction) after the Civil War.

DIRECTIONS: Circle the correct answer in each set of parentheses.

1. The expansion into new territories was known as (Manifest Destiny, Emancipation Proclamation).

2. The "Cowboy Era" lasted from about (1865–1885, 1910–1930).

DIRECTIONS: Define each term by completing the sentence.

1. Suffragettes were _____ .

2. The Underground Railroad was organized to help _____ .

recall

 Review your notes from a recent reading assignment. Set the notes aside and see how many key ideas you can recall. The next time you review your notes, underline the key ideas to help you remember them.

Advanced Learners

Have students lead a class discussion of the benefits and drawbacks of requiring students to memorize information. Ideas generated by the discussion can be recorded as *Pros* and *Cons* on a T-chart (TE page 789). For example:

- *Pro:* Knowing number facts makes solving math problems simpler; knowing dates helps keep history in perspective.
- *Con:* With calculators and computers, information can be retrieved with the push of a button; the less time students spend on memory drills, the more time they can spend on understanding the concepts and on creative pursuits.

recall *apply* UNDERSTAND synthesize evaluate **453**
analyze
Completing Writing Assignments

Understanding

When you *understand* something, you can explain what you have learned. If you can rewrite information in your own words, you are showing that you understand it.

You understand when you . . .

- **explain how something works.**
- **provide examples.**
- **summarize information in your own words.**

The following test question asks the student to show understanding, and the answer does that.

DIRECTIONS: Explain how Amendment XV to the Constitution affected voting rights in the United States.

Amendment XV of the Constitution was written to give African Americans the right to vote. It says that this right cannot be held back or changed in any way just because of a person's outer appearance. The amendment gave voting rights to people of any race or color and also applied to former slaves.

understand

 Write a paragraph explaining your understanding of something you've recently learned in social studies class.

LEARNING

Understanding

Ask students to find the key words in the directions for the sample assignment (*explain, affected*).

- Point out that students should find it easier to meet the requirements of the assignment if they have taken good class and reading notes in their own words.
- Studying with a partner or a small group is also helpful. If you can explain something to a classmate, you demonstrate that you **understand the information** (see below).

 Answers

Paragraphs will vary.

Teaching Tip: Understand the Information

Provide opportunities for students to study together. This will allow them to reinforce their own understanding by explaining concepts and information to each other. Have them quiz each other by posing questions that they think may appear on a test.

Applying

In order to apply information, students need to recall and understand the facts and make connections to a new situation.

- Ask students to find the key words in the sample assignment (*change, relate*).
- Point out that for this assignment, students need to have a number of facts at their command, and they need to organize their writing clearly in a way that leads the reader to see a relationship between the historical data and the present.

 **Answers**

Paragraphs will vary.

Applying

Applying information means using it. You need to understand something very well in order to apply it to a new situation or specific need.

You apply when you . . .

- **think about how you can use information.**
- **organize the information so that it meets your specific needs.**

In this assignment, the writer reviews information and chooses the most important details.

> **ASSIGNMENT:** How did the Fair Labor Standards Act change the use of child labor in the United States? Relate these changes to the present.
>
> Before the Fair Labor Standards Act, the United States had not put many limits on child labor. The act set minimum wages and limited the number of hours children could work. What these requirements really did was make it illegal to employ children under 16 in factories and mines. Eventually more adults realized that young people should remain in school, not get jobs. Today, most people agree that it's better to get a high school diploma than to work full-time. Some states require students to attend school until they are 18.

 Write a paragraph about how a law passed a long time ago still has an impact on the present day.

analyze apply UNDERSTAND synthesize evaluate **455**
Completing Writing Assignments

Analyzing

In order to *analyze* information, you need to break it down into parts so that you can see how it works.

You analyze when you . . .

- show how things are similar or different.
- identify which things are most important.
- arrange things in groups.
- give reasons.

In this assignment, the writer analyzes why some children are working more than the child-labor laws permit.

ASSIGNMENT: There are still children who work more than the labor laws allow. Give some reasons for this situation.

> Children of immigrants might work rather than go to school. In farming areas, young migrant laborers move from place to place, so schools and others can't keep track of them. In big cities, young illegal immigrants often become victims of child-labor abuse because they are hidden in their neighborhoods. These children must work to help the family make enough money to support the family.

analyze

 Think of something that you are good at. Write a paragraph that tells the most important skills involved in this activity.

LEARNING

Analyzing

To analyze information, students may need to compare and contrast, find causes and effects, figure out relative importance, or group related facts.

Have students find the key words in this sample assignment (*give some reasons*).

 Answers

Paragraphs will vary.

Synthesizing

Emphasize that **synthesizing** (*see below*) requires that students add original thoughts to information they have learned. This sometimes-creative response must be based on accurate factual information.

■ Have students point out the key words in this assignment (*imagine, diary entries*).

■ Then ask students to identify those parts of the sample entries that seem to be factual and those parts that seem to be fiction.

 **Answers**

Answers will vary.

456

Synthesizing

When you use information you have already learned to create something new, you are *synthesizing*.

You synthesize when you . . .

● add new ideas to existing information.
● use information to create a story or other creative writing.
● predict what will happen based on information that you already know.

In this assignment, the writer uses information to write an imaginary diary about being part of the Underground Railroad.

> **ASSIGNMENT:** Imagine that you are living during the period of the Underground Railroad. Write several diary entries about your experiences.
>
> February 8, 1864—I arrived at the Milton House Inn, where Mr. Goodrich has employed me as a maid.
> February 22, 1864—Today, Mr. Goodrich spoke to me about the troubles of the runaway slaves. I told him that I support their cause. Then he told me that Milton House Inn is a station on the Underground Railroad. I said I would like to help slaves escape to freedom.
> March 19, 1864—I was serving the evening meal when Mr. Goodrich suddenly said, "Mary, attend to the cabin." Going to the cellar of the inn, I crawled into the secret tunnel and up the ladder through the trapdoor into the cabin. There I met a surprised slave named Andrew Hamilton. I hid him in the basement of the inn.
>
> synthesize

 Imagine living during an important time in history. Write several diary entries about your experiences.

Teaching Tip: Synthesizing

Students will benefit from practice in using factual information to write creative applications such as diary entries.

● Consult with the social studies teacher to find out the period of history that students are studying.

● Ask students to brainstorm a list of several major events they have learned about.

● Students should write at least three diary entries about one event, from the perspective of someone who was affected by the event. For example, if they have been studying the Civil War, they might write about an event from the perspective of a Northern soldier, a Southern plantation owner, or a slave.

English Language Learners

As a warm-up activity, have students imagine that they are a character in a favorite story, movie, or television program, or a member of a favorite sports team. Have them write diary entries based on their interactions with the other characters, players, or fans.

recall *apply* UNDERSTAND synthesize evaluate **457**
analyze
Completing Writing Assignments

Evaluating

When you assess the value of something, you *evaluate* it. Before you can evaluate something, you must fully understand it.

You evaluate when you . . .

- tell your opinion.
- identify the good points and bad points about something.

In this assignment, the writer evaluates a historical event.

> **ASSIGNMENT: What is your opinion about the westward expansion of the United States after the Civil War?**
>
> Westward expansion after the Civil War was both good and bad. On one hand, the United States is a stronger and richer nation because of the land that was settled at that time. What would this country be like without the lands west of the Mississippi? On the other hand, people should not be proud of the things that were done to Native Americans and others living in the West. It's hard to judge something that happened more than 100 years ago. To settlers, the westward expansion probably seemed like a great victory, but to Native Americans and Mexicans, it was a time of real tragedy.

 Think of something that you understand very well, like a favorite sport or type of music. Write a paragraph telling both the good and bad points of the subject you have chosen.

LEARNING

Evaluating

Ask students to find the key phrase in this assignment (*your opinion*). Explain that when you evaluate something, you

- form an opinion about a topic,
- decide on its pros and cons, and
- generally assess its value, based on information you recall and thoroughly understand.

Emphasize that to be valid, an opinion (evaluation) should be supported with accurate data.

Try IT Answers

Paragraphs will vary.

Setting Up an Assignment Schedule

Students are accustomed to following a schedule supplied by a teacher. It is also important that they learn how to set up a schedule on their own, so they can work independently and take responsibility for meeting deadlines for "long term" assignments.

- Provide students with a detailed calendar or day-planner pages, and mark the overall schedule together for a real or imagined long-term assignment.
- Using the sample schedule as a guide, set the final deadline for the assignment, and then work through each step in the writing process.
- Talk about obstacles and opportunities as a group. Discuss upcoming vacations, exams, and major projects that are due in other subject areas.
- Suggest that students make scheduling modifications as necessary to accommodate their individual commitments.
- Circulate around the classroom and initial each student's schedule.
- Create a schedule of interim and final deadlines on a big calendar, and post it for the class.

458

Setting Up an Assignment Schedule

Your teacher may give you a schedule to follow for completing a writing assignment. If not, you can set up your own. Let's say that you have been asked to write a persuasive essay, and it is due in two weeks. Here's a suggested schedule.

Day	Week One	Day	Week Two
1	Prewriting: • Review the assignment and the assessment rubric. • Begin a topic search.	1	Revising: • Revise the completed draft for ideas and organization.
2	Prewriting: • Choose a writing topic. • Start gathering details.	2	Revising: • Revise the draft for voice. • Ask a peer to review it.
3	Prewriting: • Gather and organize details. • Find a focus for the writing.	3	Revising: • Check for word choice and sentence fluency.
4	Writing: • Begin the first draft.	4	Editing: • Check the writing for convention errors. • Proofread the final copy.
5	Writing: • Complete the first draft.	5	Publishing: • Share the final copy.

 Change this schedule to fit your assignment. For example, if you have a week to do your work, you could focus on one step in the writing process per day.

Scheduling a Timed Writing

If you must complete a piece of writing in a single class period (for example, 45 minutes), it is very important to plan your work. Try to set aside 5 to 10 minutes at the beginning of the period to plan your writing, 25 to 30 minutes for drafting, and about 10 minutes at the end to make any necessary changes.

review prepare
study plan check 459

Taking Classroom Tests

In archery, hitting a bull's-eye doesn't just happen. It starts with the proper stance, a correctly nocked arrow, a steady draw, an eagle eye, and that all-important smooth release. In other words, a bull's-eye begins long before the arrow actually touches the target.

In the same way, an A on a test begins long before you answer the questions. By paying attention in class, taking notes, keeping up with assignments, and studying before the test, you are more likely to hit the bull's-eye. This chapter will help you learn the best way to prepare for classroom tests.

What's Ahead

- Preparing for a Test
- Taking Objective Tests
- Taking Essay Tests

Taking Classroom Tests

Objectives

- learn to prepare for a test by listening and asking questions in class, taking notes, doing assignments, and studying the information
- understand test-taking tips and strategies
- study how to approach objective and essay-test questions

Preparation for **taking classroom tests** can be simplified if students meet specific goals for studying each day. Clarify what you expect from students on tests. Emphasize that if they keep up with their work each day, test preparation should not be overwhelming.

Struggling Learners

Together, brainstorm examples of successes that don't "just happen." Have students discuss the preparation involved in the following:

- shooting a free throw
- performing in a piano recital
- babysitting
- painting a portrait
- building a bookshelf

Preparing for a Test

Ask students to duplicate this pyramid in their writing journals. Then have them label each of the ten boxes with one of the following designations, depending on how often they follow that step:

- *A* = always use
- *S* = sometimes use
- *N* = never use

Most students will be able to place an *A* only in the very top box, since they cannot avoid taking a test. Some may be able to place an *A* on some of the blocks in the bottom row. Point out that as they begin to follow the daily steps in the pyramid, students should find that they are better prepared when they begin to study for a test.

Ask students to brainstorm alternative studying strategies that have helped them. For example, they might find it useful to

- share notes with a partner,
- study with a friend, or
- have a family member quiz them.

 Answers

Answers will vary, but many students will find that they did not follow all the steps.

Preparing for a Test

Preparing for a test is like building a pyramid. You begin by creating a solid foundation. You pay attention in class, take good notes, and keep up with assignments. On top of that foundation, you can build toward success. Read the chart below from the bottom up.

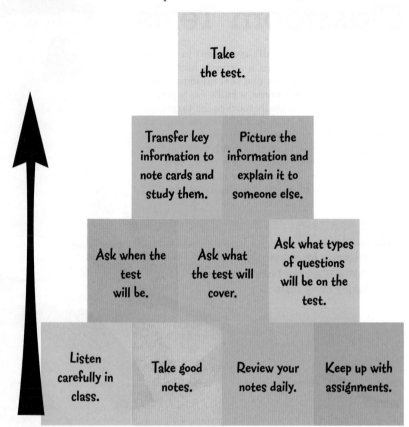

 Think about a test that you took recently. Then check the illustration above. Starting from the bottom and moving up, did you follow all of the steps before taking your test?

Struggling Learners

Create a reproducible Test-Prep Checklist that includes the following items:

- each step on the pyramid
- a place for students to check off each item
- space to fill in any details (such as when the test will be, what it will cover, and what types of questions it will include)

Hand out copies to students, so they will remember to prepare effectively for tests.

Test-Taking Tips

Before you begin . . .

- **Listen** carefully to the instructions.
- **Ask** questions about any instructions that you don't understand.
- **Check the clock** to see how much time you have.

During the test . . .

- **Skim the whole test** so that you can plan your time.
- **Read and answer** each question carefully.
- **Skip difficult questions** and come back to them later.
- **Watch the time** so that you can answer all of the questions.

After you've finished the test . . .

- **Go back** and check your answers, if you have time.
- **Be sure** that your name is on the test.
- **Remember** the questions that were the hardest for you, in case they appear on another test.

One of the most important ways to prepare for a test is to get a good night's sleep beforehand. Also make sure to eat a good breakfast. If your body is rested and fed, your mind is free to work.

Test-Taking Tips

Add your own test-taking tips here, along with any pointers that might apply specifically to testing in your state.

Tell students that these tips will help them on both classroom tests and standardized tests.

Be sure that students understand how to skim to **preview a test** *(see below)*. Remind them that although they do not want to use up too much of their test time on this step, they do need to look over the test in order to plan how long to spend on each section and item.

Teaching Tip: Preview a Test

Students may not have had much experience with skimming to preview a test.

- Explain that the purpose is not to read for content details. Instead, if the testing situation allows them to do so, they should look through each section of the test, noting the number of objective and essay questions it contains.
- They should look at the directions to determine what they must do within the total time allowed. For example, the directions may tell them to choose only *three* of five essay questions to answer.
- Once they have reached the end, students will have a sense of the length and demands of the test and will be able to allocate their time appropriately.

Advanced Learners

To expand on the tip to eat a good breakfast, assign this activity:

- Research what nutritionists consider "brain foods."
- Generate breakfast menu ideas for the class.
- Compare the cafeteria's menus with the "brain foods."
- If the cafeteria doesn't serve "brain foods," write polite letters to request a change.

Taking Objective Tests

Discuss these additional hints.

- True/False: Don't ever leave one blank. With a 50–50 chance of getting the correct answer, it's best to make an educated guess.
- Matching: Pay attention to **parts of speech** *(see below)*. Sometimes the type of word (noun, verb, adjective, adverb) that is needed to satisfy a definition provides a clue to the correct answer.

 Answers

Answers will vary.

462

Taking Objective Tests

An objective test can contain four different types of questions: true/false, matching, multiple-choice, and fill-in-the-blanks.

True/False

On this type of question, you decide whether a statement is true or false.

- Read carefully. If *any* part of the statement is false, the answer is "false."

  False **Light-years are used to measure time.**
  (Light-years measure distance, not time.)

- Words like *always, all, every, never, none,* or *no* can be misleading. Few things are always or never true.

  False **Every solution is either acidic or basic.**
  (The word "every" makes this statement false. Some solutions are neutral.)

- Pay special attention to words meaning "not": *doesn't, don't, isn't, wasn't.* Be sure that you understand what the statement means.

  True **The different kinds of molecules in a living organism aren't all the same size.**

Matching

Matching is connecting the items from one list to the items in another.

- Read both lists and then match the items you are sure of. Next, match the more difficult items using the process of elimination. Cross out each answer after you've used it.

  B 1. Mass per unit volume   A. velocity
  C 2. Upward force on an object in fluid   B. density
  A 3. Direction and speed of an object   C. buoyancy

- The items in a list that seem to have the closest meaning can be the hardest to match. Think about them carefully before you choose your answers.

  On your own paper, answer the following questions:
  Which questions are harder for you, true/false or matching? Why?

Teaching Tip: Parts of Speech

Some students may need to review the basic parts of speech. Help them to identify and define:

- noun—a word that names a person, a place, a thing, or an idea
- pronoun—a word used in place of a noun
- verb—a word that either shows action or links the subject to another word in the sentence

- adjective—a word that describes or modifies a noun or pronoun
- adverb—a word that describes or modifies a verb, an adjective, or another adverb

✱ For more information on using these parts of speech, direct students to PE pages 469–498.

463
Taking Classroom Tests

Multiple-Choice

A multiple-choice question gives you several possible answers to choose from. Follow these tips:

- Be sure to follow the directions carefully. On most tests you are asked to choose the best answer, but sometimes you can choose more than one.

    1. Two of the authors of the Federalist Papers were
    A. James Madison   **C.** Alexander Hamilton
    B. Franklin Roosevelt   **D.** Ronald Reagan

- Pay special attention to words like *always, all, none,* and *never.*

    2. All of the following influenced the writing of the U.S. Constitution except the
    A. Magna Carta   **C.** English Bill of Rights
    B. Mayflower Compact   **D.** Emancipation Proclamation

- Some questions have answers like "both A and B" or "all of the above." Consider those options carefully.

    3. The women's suffrage movement was advanced by women like
    A. Elizabeth Cady Stanton **D.** both A and B
    B. Susan B. Anthony   **E.** all of the above
    C. Hillary Rodham Clinton

First eliminate answers that you know are incorrect and then focus on the remaining answers.

Fill-in-the-Blanks

On a fill-in-the-blanks test, you fill in what's missing.

- Each blank usually stands for one missing answer, so three blanks mean that you should fill in three answers.

    1. The three states of matter are _____solid_____ , _____liquid_____ , and _____gas_____ .

- The questions sometimes give you clues about the answers. For example, if the word before the blank is *a*, the answer you fill in should start with a consonant sound.

    2. A _____comet_____ is a small, icy object in space with a cloudy "tail."

LEARNING

Point out these additional tips.

- Multiple-Choice: If you aren't sure of the answer at first, use the facts that you know to rule out any choices that cannot be right. For example, in question 3, if you know when the suffrage movement took place, then you know that Hillary Rodham Clinton is an incorrect answer because she wasn't alive then.

- Fill-in-the-Blanks: Look for patterns in questioning. Are the blanks key vocabulary words, details, or characters? Does the number of blanks reflect related patterns in vocabulary or terms?

Taking Essay Tests

Remind students to keep an eye on the amount of time they have to complete essay questions. They may need time to go back to other test questions as well.

❶ Understand and Restate the Question

Encourage students to first look for the key word(s) in a writing prompt. Read through the list here, and discuss what they must do for each term.

Tell students that as a regular part of essay assignments and taking tests, they should circle or underline the key word in each question that explains the expectation for the response.

 **Answers**

Answers will vary, but each response should restate the question as a focus statement for an essay.

464

Taking Essay Tests

When you answer an essay-test question, you write an essay. First, you must make sure you understand the question fully. Then you need to organize your thoughts, write your essay, and check your work, all in a limited amount of time. The information on this page and on pages 465–467 will help you write effective essay-test answers.

❶ Understand and Restate the Question

- Read the question very carefully.
- Identify the key word that explains what you have to do. Here are some key words and an explanation of what each asks you to do.

Compare	. . . tell how things are alike.
Contrast	. . . tell how things are different.
Define	. . . give a clear, specific meaning of a word or an idea.
Describe	. . . tell how something looks, sounds, and feels.
Diagram	. . . explain using lines, a web, or other graphic organizer.
Evaluate	. . . give your opinion about the value of something.
Explain	. . . tell what something means or how something works.
Identify	. . . answer the 5 W's about a topic.
Illustrate	. . . show how something works by using examples.
Prove	. . . present facts that show something is true.
Review	. . . give an overall picture of a topic.
Summarize	. . . tell just the key information about a topic.

- Turn the question into a statement. This often makes a good focus statement for your essay.

 For each of the following essay-test questions, restate the question as a focus statement for an essay answer.

1. Identify three causes of the Civil War.
2. Describe what happens when water boils.
3. Evaluate the importance of voting in the United States.
4. How would you define the concept of democracy?

English Language Learners

Before tackling the activities on PE pages 464–467, gradually build students' confidence in their ability to answer timed essay questions.

- First, discuss examples of prompts using each key word on the page.
- Then assign a simple one-paragraph essay as homework. During the next day, go over their completed assignments, giving positive feedback whenever possible.
- Next, have them do a similar assignment in class, with a limited time limit.

Maintain a consistent practice schedule of a homework assignment, a review discussion, and an in-class assignment, gradually increasing the difficulty.

❷ Plan a One-Paragraph Answer

The following guidelines will help you plan and write a one-paragraph answer for an essay-test question. Jot your planning notes on a piece of scrap paper.

● Study the essay-test question and write a focus statement.

● Use a list, an outline, or a graphic organizer to arrange the details.

Review = give an overall picture

Focus: Ireland's poor economic conditions in the 1840s forced 1.5 million of its people to come to the United States.

List
1. Economy declined for generations.
2. Government policies left farmers with little land.
3. Potato blight wiped out almost entire crop in one year.
4. Irish government encouraged people to leave country.

Social Studies Test

Review why one particular national, racial, or ethnic group immigrated to the United States during the 1800s.

Economic conditions in Ireland became so bad that 1.5 million of its people came to the United States beginning in the 1840s. For generations, the Irish people had been steadily getting poorer. Most of them were farmers, and government policies had made their farms smaller until they had only enough land to grow potatoes for their own food. Finally, the potato blight wiped out almost the entire crop in one year. The only choice the government gave the Irish was to leave Ireland or starve.

❷ Plan a One-Paragraph Answer

Point out the key word *(review)* and its explanation on the sample notes (Reviews give an overall picture).

■ Emphasize the importance of writing the focus statement and organizing the details before writing the response.

■ Explain that doing this preparation will make the essay more effective.

3 Plan an Essay Answer

Review the Assignment Checklist on PE page 450 and the teacher's edition suggestions that accompany it, and the suggestions at the bottom of PE page 458 for planning how to complete a timed writing assignment.

Emphasize the importance of prewriting in a timed test situation, even though the pressure of the time limit will make students feel that they need to skip this step. Explain that by making a quick list of ideas before they write, they will be able to write an organized essay that needs little revision.

 **Answers**

Lists will vary.

466

3 Plan an Essay Answer

An essay-test prompt may require you to write an answer longer than one paragraph. For example, the response to the question below should be longer than one paragraph.

- Study the essay-test question and write a focus statement.
- Quickly list the main points of your essay, leaving room under each point for details.
- Add your specific details under each main point. (See below.)

Social Studies Test Question:

Compare and contrast the reasons that two different racial, ethnic, or national groups immigrated to the United States.

Quick List

Focus Statement: Two of the largest groups to immigrate to the U.S. in the mid-1800s were the Germans and the Irish.

1. Opportunities in U.S. in 1840s
   - plenty of land   – mfg. jobs
   - land easy to get   – gold in CA

2. Other reasons Germans came
   - Ger. gov. not democratic
   - reformers came for freedom
   - brought $ to invest

3. Contrasting reasons Irish came
   - gov. reduced farm sizes
   - had only potatoes for food
   - blight wiped out crop in 1847
   - gov. told Irish to emigrate
   - Irish came to make $

Think of two historical events that you could compare and contrast. Make a quick list of main points and details for your essay.

Essay Answer

The essay below uses the main points and details from the quick list on page 466.

a new constitution were ended by force. Some
reformers were put in prison, and others began
ates.
ll, but
aved

erately
ey

Social Studies Test: Immigration

Compare and contrast the reasons that two
different racial, ethnic, or national groups
immigrated to the United States.

and
naller,
toes
wiped
nly
leave

Two of the largest groups to immigrate to
the United States in the middle 1800s were the
Germans and the Irish. Both groups came for
some of the same basic reasons that have drawn
others, but there were also big differences between
them. Those differences had a great deal to do
with the conditions in their native countries.

People who came to the United States at that
time were attracted by the opportunities that
were available. There was a huge amount of land in
America, and it was easy to get. Manufacturing
jobs were increasing rapidly, and these jobs were a
big attraction to those who wanted to live in the
cities. Finally, there was the discovery of gold in
California that lured those who wanted to get rich.

The Germans had some additional reasons
to leave their native country. They had been trying
to change their country's government to make it
more democratic. In 1849 their efforts to write

LEARNING

Essay Answer

Examine the essay-test prompt to find the key words (*compare and contrast the reasons*).

- Ask students to explain differences between the Quick List on PE page 466 and the essay on this page. Be sure to note that although the focus statement is exactly the same in both places, the list itself consists of phrases rather than sentences.
- Have students study how the list notes are transformed into complete sentences in the essay.
- Have students practice how to transform the notes in a list into complete sentences, using the quick list they made for the **Try It** activity on PE page 466.

Writing Paragraphs Level 8 *Write Source* (One Week)

Day	Writing and Skills Units	In the *Write Source* book			On the CD-ROM	*SkillsBook*
		Pages	Proofreader's Guide—basic grammar rules	Basic Grammar practice	Interactive Grammar Exercises	grammar practice pages
1	**Writing Paragraphs:** (Model)	523–524				
	(Topic Sentences)	525				
2	(Guidelines and Details)	530–533				
	(Models and Order)	534–537				
3–4	(Unity)	538–539				
	Revising Skills Activities: Kinds of Sentences			518 (+)		
	Editing Skills Activities: Capitalization and Abbreviations		620–621, 622–623, 634–635, 636–637, 638 (+), 640 (+)		Abbreviations	49–50
	Plurals		630 (+), 632 (+)		Plurals (+)	52
	Numbers		638–639, 640–641		Numbers	47–48
5 *opt.*	**Paragraph to Essay**	540				

Note: For specifics about reading the chart above, see page TE 33.

Constructing Strong Paragraphs (pages 523–541)

A paragraph is a group of sentences focusing on one specific topic or idea. Students can develop paragraphs as stories, descriptions, explanations, or opinions. The type of paragraph depends upon the topic, the kinds of details the writer is able to gather, and the audience. A paragraph must contain enough details to give the reader a complete picture of the topic. Paragraphs have three basic parts: the topic sentence, the body, and the closing sentence.

Paragraphs are building blocks of stories, essays, and articles. Sentences within paragraphs, and paragraphs within longer texts, require linking words and transitions. Paragraphs help readers make sense of longer pieces of writing, so learning to write and identify paragraphs is important.

468

agree vary

Basic Grammar and Writing

CONNECT organize model

Working with Words

According to the *Oxford English Dictionary,* our language contains over a quarter of a million words—more than most other languages. No wonder a dictionary is so heavy! Lifting a dictionary can strengthen your arm, but opening one will strengthen your mind.

A sentence won't work as well without some words—*adjectives, adverbs,* and *conjunctions,* for instance. It won't work at all without certain other words—*nouns* or *pronouns,* and *verbs.* So, as you continue to read, write, and speak the English language, it will be helpful to know how, when, and where to use its parts . . . to keep it running smoothly.

What's Ahead

- Using Nouns
- Using Pronouns
- Choosing Verbs
- Describing with Adjectives
- Describing with Adverbs
- Connecting with Prepositions
- Connecting with Conjunctions

Using Nouns

A noun is a word that names a person, a place, a thing, or an idea in your writing. (See page 702.)

Person	meteorologist, Jacob Kern, students, Mayor Blain
Place	city, Chicago, sky, Tampa, middle school
Thing	Manx cat, clouds, stopwatches, thunder
Idea	day, Sunday, strength, truth, Veterans Day

 Number from 1 to 8 on a piece of paper. For each of the eight underlined nouns in the paragraph below, write whether it is a person, a place, a thing, or an idea.

1 Weather has a very big **(1)** effect on all of the world's
2 **(2)** citizens. In the **(3)** United States, the National Weather Service
3 (NWS) keeps track of the **(4)** weather. Specialized **(5)** equipment
4 at **(6)** offices across the country helps the NWS collect weather
5 data. Its **(7)** scientists prepare forecasts and issue severe weather
6 **(8)** warnings when necessary.

Proper and Common Nouns

Proper nouns name specific people, places, things, or ideas. Proper nouns are always capitalized. A **common noun** is any noun that is not a proper noun.

	Person	Place	Thing	Idea
Common	meteorologist	school	hurricane	event
Proper	Hank Rhodes	University of Oklahoma	Irma	El Niño

Common nouns A weather event warms the surface water of the ocean and affects weather on a faraway continent.

Proper nouns El Niño warms the surface water of the Pacific Ocean and affects weather as faraway as Africa.

 Make a chart like the one above. Add four of your own common nouns and four of your own proper nouns. Be sure to capitalize the proper nouns.

Concrete, Abstract, and Collective Nouns

Concrete nouns name things that can be seen, heard, or touched.
Abstract nouns name something that you can think about but cannot see or touch.

Concrete	water	mountain	street	tree
Abstract	joy	August	dread	kindness

 Identify each underlined noun in the following sentences as concrete or abstract.

Example: The fury of a tornado is hard to imagine.
abstract, concrete

1. Often a twister is preceded by a series of thunderstorms.
2. An eerie calm might settle over the area when the wind stops.
3. You won't hear a sound—no thunder, no flocks of birds, no rustling leaves.
4. Suddenly, another wave of powerful winds begins, bending the trees horizontally.
5. Tornadoes inspire fear and awe, even for a team of storm chasers.

Collective nouns name a collection of persons, animals, or things.

Persons	group	clan	tribe	squad	family
Animals	herd	flock	litter	pod	pride

 In the six sentences above, identify the three collective nouns. (They are not underlined in the activity.)

General and Specific Nouns

When you use **specific nouns** in your writing, you give the reader a clear picture of people, places, things, and ideas. The following chart shows the difference between **general nouns** and specific nouns.

General	weatherperson	the Midwest	tool	thought
Specific	Robert Fitzroy	central Missouri	rain gauge	belief

 Write specific nouns for these general nouns: *newscaster, county, storm, emotion, housing, road, animal.* Then write a brief paragraph, using as many of your specific nouns as possible.

Try It Answers

1. idea
2. person
3. place
4. idea
5. thing
6. place
7. person
8. idea

Try It Answers

1. concrete, concrete
2. abstract
3. concrete, concrete
4. abstract, concrete
5. abstract, abstract, concrete

Try It Answers

1. series
2. flocks
3. team

Try It Answers

Answers will vary.

What can I do with nouns in my writing?

Show Possession

You can make your writing more specific by naming who (or what) possesses something. See the guidelines below. (Also see 604.4 and 606.1.)

Forming the Singular Possessive

- Add an apostrophe and an *s* to a singular noun: Emiko's **raincoat**.
- For multisyllable nouns ending in an *s* or *z* sound, the possessive may be formed in two ways: Carlos' **umbrella** or Carlos's **umbrella**.

Forming the Plural Possessive

- Add an apostrophe for most plural nouns ending in *s*: the boys' **galoshes**.
- Add an apostrophe and an *s* for plural nouns not ending in *s*: the women's **boots**.

 On a piece of paper list five singular nouns and five plural nouns. (Include at least one or two singular nouns that end in an *s* or a *z* sound.) Skip one or two lines after each noun. Then write one sentence for each noun, using the possessive form of the word.

Rename the Subject

An **appositive** renames the noun that comes before it. An appositive phrase, which is set off with commas, contains a noun.

Meteorologists predict weather changes using a barometer, a device that measures air pressure.

Cari Casey, a National Weather Service employee, **gave us a tour.**

 List the appositive phrase in each of the following sentences.

1. Dust whirls, rotating dust clouds, surround the base of tornadoes.
2. If you live near a large lake, you may have seen a waterspout, a tornado occurring over water.
3. During the summer months, downpours, heavy and intense rains, will occur.
4. In science class we talked about humidity, the amount of moisture in the air.
5. A cap, the layer of warm air near the ground, may delay the development of a thunderstorm.

Make the Meaning of the Verb Complete

Some sentences are not complete with just a subject and a verb.

Gray clouds release. (*What* do the clouds release?)

A radio report alerted. (*Whom* did the report alert?)

When you use a transitive verb like *release* or *alerted* in a sentence, you need to include a **direct object** to make the meaning of the verb complete. The direct object is a noun (or pronoun) that answers the question "what" or "whom."

Gray clouds release a downpour.   **A radio report alerted** the family.

To add further information, you might include a noun (or pronoun) that answers the question "to whom" or "for whom." This type of noun is called an **indirect object**. In order for a sentence to have an indirect object, it must also have a direct object. (For more about direct and indirect objects see 692.4–692.5.)

The storm gave Iesha **a scare.** (The storm gave a scare *to Iesha*.)

Dad built his parents **a storm shelter behind their house.** (Dad built a shelter *for his parents*.)

 Write the direct object in each of the following sentences. If there is an indirect object as well, write it and underline it.

Example: Each year, Texas gets many tornadoes.
          tornadoes

1. A recent tornado damaged many garage roofs.
2. Most thunderstorms, fortunately, do not trigger tornadoes.
3. The incredible winds show people the power of nature.
4. The twisting winds rip trees from the ground by their roots.

Add Specific Information

Another kind of object noun is the **object of a preposition**. A prepositional phrase (see 704.7) begins with a preposition and ends with an object (a noun or a pronoun). Prepositional phrases can add specific information to sentences. The object noun(s) in each prepositional phrase (underlined) below is highlighted in blue.

Tornadoes often appear at the end of a storm.

They begin high off the ground **with a specific** combination of wind, temperature, and moisture.

 Write a brief weather-related paragraph that includes at least five prepositional phrases. Underline the object of each prepositional phrase. (For a list of prepositions, see page 742.)

 Answers

Answers will vary.

 Answers

1. rotating dust clouds
2. a tornado occurring over water
3. heavy and intense rains
4. the amount of moisture in the air
5. the layer of warm air near the ground

Try It Answers

1. roofs
2. tornadoes
3. power, people
4. trees

 Answers

Answers will vary.

Using Pronouns

A pronoun is a word used in place of a noun. The noun replaced, or referred to, by the pronoun is called the pronoun's **antecedent**. The arrows below point to each pronoun's antecedent. (Also see **706.1**.)

The day's temperature was so high that it broke a record.

Ms. Johnson said that she never saw people sweat so much.

The personal pronouns listed below are the most common pronouns used by writers. (For a complete list of personal pronouns, see page **710**.)

Personal Pronouns						
I	you	he	she	it	we	they
me		him	her		us	them

Person and Number of a Pronoun

Pronouns show "person" and "number" in writing. The following chart shows which nominative, or subject, pronouns are used for the three different persons (*first, second, third*) and the two different numbers (*singular* or *plural*).

		Singular	Plural
First Person	(The person speaking)	I **talk.**	We **talk.**
Second Person	(The person spoken to)	You **talk.**	You **talk.**
Third Person	(The person spoken about)	He **talks.** She **talks.**	They **talk.**

 Number your paper from 1 to 4. Write original sentences that use the pronouns described below as subjects.

Example: first-person singular pronoun
(I) I don't like windy days.

1. third-person singular pronoun
2. third-person plural pronoun
3. second-person singular pronoun
4. first-person plural pronoun

Indefinite Pronouns

An indefinite pronoun refers to people or things that are not specifically named. Some indefinite pronouns are singular, while some are plural, and some can be either.

Indefinite Pronouns					
Singular				**Plural**	**Singular or Plural**
another	each	more	one	both	all
anybody	everybody	nobody	some	few	any
anyone	everyone	no one	somebody	many	most
anything	everything	nothing	someone	several	none

When you use a singular indefinite pronoun as a subject, the verbs (in red below) and other pronouns that refer to the subject must also be singular. If the indefinite pronoun is plural, the verbs and other pronouns must be plural.

Singular Everybody checks his or her **rain gauge in the morning.**

Plural Many **of the gauges** have **more than an inch of water in** them.

To tell if the pronouns *all, any, most,* and *none* are singular or plural, you must check the noun in the prepositional phrase following the pronoun.

Singular All of the rain **is over for today, but** it **will return tomorrow.**

or Plural (The subject *all* is singular because the noun in the prepositional phrase, *rain,* is singular.)

All **of the** gauges **are checked daily, and then** they **are emptied.** (The subject *all* is plural because the noun in the prepositional phrase, *gauges,* is plural.)

 Number your paper from 1 to 5. Choose the correct pronoun to complete each of the following sentences. (See page **714** for more help.)

1. One of the boys left *(their, his)* umbrella at school.
2. I guess nobody thought *(they, he or she)* would need it.
3. Few of the students even wore *(their, his or her)* raincoats.
4. Most of the trail is muddy, and *(their, its)* bridges are slippery.
5. If anyone gets wet, that's *(their, his or her)* own fault.

> If using *his or her* is clumsy, try changing the singular pronoun to a plural pronoun. For example, the first sample sentence above could be rewritten like this: **All** *of the students* check **their** *rain gauges in the morning.*

BASIC GRAMMAR

How can I use pronouns correctly?
Avoid Agreement Problems

You can make your writing clear by using pronouns properly. Remember that you must use pronouns that agree with their antecedents. (An antecedent is the noun or pronoun that a pronoun replaces or refers to.) Pronouns must agree with their antecedents in number, person, and gender. (See 712.1–712.4.)

A cloud's electrical charges create lightning when they become separated.

Warm winds blow the positive charges high into the cloud, so its underside is full of negative charges, or electrons.

Agreement in Number

The **number** of a pronoun is either singular or plural. The pronoun must match the antecedent in number.

- A singular pronoun refers to a singular antecedent.

  Since the ground does not have a lot of negative charges, it attracts the cloud's electrons.

- A plural pronoun refers to a plural antecedent.

  The electrons are pulled to the ground, crashing into air molecules on their way down.

 Select the correct pronouns from the following list to complete the paragraphs below. (You will use one pronoun twice.)

its	them	they	it

(1) The molecules create more charged ions as _____ are pulled down to the ground, too. **(2)** The stream of electrons moves at 240 miles per second as _____ races toward the ground.

(3) The air molecules become extremely hot when the electrons collide with _____. **(4)** As hot air expands, _____ produces the sudden earsplitting noise we know as thunder. **(5)** The lightning has completed _____ electrical connection in less than a second.

Agreement in Person

You must choose either first, second, or third person pronouns, depending on the situation. If you start a sentence in one "person," don't shift to another "person" later in the sentence.

Pronoun shift: I have learned a lot about lightning, and with all that knowledge you can stay safe in a storm.

Correct: I have learned a lot about lightning, and with all that knowledge I can stay safe in a storm.

 For each sentence below, change the underlined pronoun so it doesn't cause a shift in person.

1. We are learning about weather in their science class.
2. If people knew some of the facts we're learning, you would be amazed.
3. Weather fascinates us, and they want to study it in college.
4. Once you learn about a particular kind of weather, I wish to see it up close.

Agreement in Gender

The **gender** of a pronoun (*her, his, its*) must be the same as the gender of its antecedent. Pronouns can be feminine (female), masculine (male), or neuter (neither male nor female).

Roy Sullivan, a park ranger, was struck by lightning seven times, but his injuries were never life threatening.

Grandma likes to watch lightning from her front porch.

 For each of the following sentences, write the correct pronoun. Make sure it is the same gender as its antecedent.

1. The first time lightning struck Roy, _____ big toenail was knocked off.
2. One of the strikes Roy endured caused _____ to lose consciousness.
3. Roy learned that the saying "Lightning never strikes the same place twice" isn't true; _____ can, in fact, do just that.
4. Aunt Jia insists that _____ is not frightened by lightning but asks me to stay with _____ during storms anyway.

Try IT Answers

1. they
2. it
3. them
4. it
5. its

Try IT Answers

1. our
2. they
3. we
4. you

Try IT Answers

1. his
2. him
3. it
4. she, her

Working with Words **478-479**

478

479

vary modify *compare* CONNECT
choose
Working with Words

What else should I know about pronouns?

Check for Agreement with Compound Subjects and Objects

As you know, a pronoun must agree with its antecedent. When a compound subject or object is the antecedent, different rules apply depending on the conjunction that is used.

- If the compound subject or object is joined by the word *and,* use a **plural** pronoun to refer to the antecedent.
  Andre and **Jerry** got out their **snowboards.**
  (The compound subject joined by *and* requires the plural pronoun *their.*)

- If the compound subject or object is joined by the word *or* or *nor,* do one of these:
  - Use a **singular** pronoun when both subjects or objects or only the second one is singular.
    The attendant would allow neither Andre nor **Jerry to ride the lift without** his **ticket.** (The compound object joined by *nor* requires the singular pronoun *his* because *Andre* and *Jerry* are both singular.)
  - Use a **plural** pronoun when both subjects or objects or only the second one is plural.
    A blizzard or **snow squalls could hamper the fun if** they **occur.** (The compound subject joined by *or* requires the plural pronoun *they* because *squalls* is plural.)

 For each of the following sentences, write the correct choice of pronouns (and verbs, in some cases) from those in parentheses.

Example: The cold, snow, and ice can be dangerous when *(they arrive, it arrives).*
they arrive

1. The cold causes hypothermia and frostbite, and *(this, these)* can result in physical damage to fingers and toes.
2. A collapsed roof or downed power lines *(is, are)* not only inconvenient; *(it is, they are)* also unsafe to approach.
3. Ice is treacherous for either a motorist or a pedestrian when *(they, he or she)* must travel.
4. People should wear hats when it's cold, but neither Shelby nor Selena will wear *(theirs, hers).*
5. Skis or a sled can prove *(their, its)* worth when a car can't get through the snow.

Use Intensive and Reflexive Pronouns

A pronoun with *self* attached—*myself, yourself, herself,* and so on—is either an **intensive pronoun** or a **reflexive pronoun.** The following chart shows how they differ. (Also see 708.2 and 708.3.)

Reflexive Pronoun
- *Necessary* to complete the meaning of the sentence
  Nomi fanned *(what?)* **with some paper.**
- Used as an object in a sentence (direct or indirect object, object of a preposition)
  Nomi fanned herself **with some paper.**

Intensive Pronoun
- *Not necessary* to complete the meaning of the sentence
  The temperature was not so bad.
- Used to emphasize the noun before it
  The temperature itself **was not so bad.**

 In the sentences below, label each pronoun as either reflexive or intensive.

1. When my grandmother finds herself in the midst of a heat wave, she goes to the air-conditioned library.
2. The newspaper suggests that people wearing dark clothing while in the sun are making it very difficult for themselves.
3. Sometimes my dad pushes himself in hot weather, and that makes his body work to maintain its normal temperature.
4. I myself don't have to worry about that; I always push myself just enough.
5. Most doctors themselves know enough to avoid the extreme heat.
6. If you find yourself feeling sick because of the heat, seek shelter immediately.

 Write two sentences of your own. Use a reflexive pronoun in one of the sentences and an intensive pronoun in the other one. Exchange papers with a partner. Underline the reflexive pronoun and circle the intensive pronoun in each other's sentences.

Try It Answers

1. these
2. are, they are
3. he or she
4. hers
5. its

Try It Answers

1. reflexive
2. reflexive
3. reflexive
4. intensive; reflexive
5. intensive
6. reflexive

 **Answers**

Answers will vary.

Choosing Verbs

The main verb either shows action or links the subject to another word in the sentence. A helping verb "helps" to complete the main verb.

Action Verbs

An **action verb** tells what the subject is doing. Strong action verbs can bring your writing to life.

The hurricane slammed into the coast.

High winds hurl objects through the air.

Linking Verbs

A **linking verb** connects (links) a subject to a noun or an adjective in the predicate.

Common Linking Verbs	
Forms of "be"	be, is, are, was, were, am, been, being
Other linking verbs	appear, become, feel, grow, look, remain, seem, smell, sound, taste

A hurricane is a tropical cyclone.
(The linking verb *is* connects the subject *hurricane* to the noun *cyclone*. *Cyclone* is a **predicate noun**.)

The storm grows larger, often covering a circle 500 miles wide.
(The linking verb *grows* connects the subject *storm* to the adjective *larger*. *Larger* is a **predicate adjective**.)

 For each sentence in the paragraph below, write the linking verb and the predicate noun or predicate adjective that follows it. (The complex sentence has two linking verbs.)

(1) In the Pacific Ocean, the term for a "hurricane" is "typhoon." **(2)** Whatever these storms are called, they can remain a threat for up to 30 days. **(3)** They are dangerous because of their strong winds and floods. **(4)** Although some people seem fearless against the rage of such storms, many people feel powerless. **(5)** For most people it is best to evacuate the area.

Helping Verbs

The simple predicate may include a **helping verb** plus the main verb. A helping verb completes the main verb in many sentences.

A category 1 hurricane will result in minimal harm.
(The helping verb *will* helps express future tense.)

A category 3 hurricane has hit the town of Burnley.
(The helping verb *has* helps express the present perfect tense. See page **724.1**.)

A category 5 hurricane does cause unbelievable damage.
(The helping verb *does* helps express ongoing action.)

 Select a helping verb from the following list to complete each sentence in the paragraph below.

must	do	will	may	has	can

The United States **(1)** _____ endured two category 5 hurricanes, in 1935 and 1969. In any such storm, high winds **(2)** _____ cause the most loss of property and life. Flooding **(3)** _____ also result in losses. The government **(4)** _____ issue an order to evacuate when a hurricane strikes. Often, people **(5)** _____ leave their homes even if they **(6)** _____ not want to.

Irregular Verbs

Irregular verbs do not follow the *ed* rule. Instead of adding *ed* to show past tense, as you would with a regular verb, an irregular verb might change. (See the list of irregular verbs on page **722**.) The chart below gives the three main parts for *write* and *swim*.

Present	Past	Past participle
I write.	Yesterday I wrote.	I have written.
She swims.	Yesterday she swam.	She has swum.

 On your own paper, write six sentences using the given tense of the irregular verbs listed below.

1. tear *(past)*
2. sit *(past participle)*
3. choose *(past)*
4. give *(present)*
5. get *(past participle)*
6. know *(present)*

Answers

1. is, "typhoon"
2. remain, threat
3. are, dangerous
4. seem, fearless; feel, powerless
5. is, best

Answers

1. has
2. will or can
3. can or will
4. may
5. must
6. do

Possible Answers

1. I tore my new coat.
2. She has sat on that bench for hours every day.
3. We chose to go to the movies first.
4. They give me candy.
5. He has gotten a cold each year.
6. I know her phone number.

How can I use verbs effectively?

Show When Something Happens

You can use different verb tenses to "tell time" in sentences. The three simple tenses are "present," "past," and "future." (See page **720**.)

Weather controls **our actions.** *(present)*

We left **before the thunderstorms.** *(past)*

The teams will play **tomorrow.** *(future)*

Avoid Unnecessary Tense Shift

It may happen that you will shift from one verb tense to another in the same sentence.

Sean reported *(past)* **on hurricanes, which** are *(present)* **tropical storms that often** strike *(present)* **the Atlantic coast.**

However, in most sentences, you need to avoid a shift in verb tense because it will be confusing to the reader.

Unnecessary shift in tense:

People predicted *(past)* **the weather after they** study *(present)* **its patterns.** (The verb tense incorrectly shifts from past to present.)

Corrected sentence:

People predicted *(past)* **the weather after they** studied *(past)* **its patterns.** (Both the verbs are correctly in the past tense.)

 Rewrite the following sentences to eliminate the tense shift in each one.

1. In the past, people tried to predict the weather; they use methods such as studying animal behavior and observing the heavens.
2. In the early 1600s, people invented tools that allow their users to record weather data.
3. Scientists began to understand the atmosphere, so they start making predictions.
4. Of course, it was hundreds of years later when forecasts really will become accurate.
5. Today, weather forecasters told how storms threaten this area.

 Write a brief paragraph about a weather-related experience. Afterward, exchange papers with a classmate and check each other's sentences for any confusing shifts in verb tense.

Show Special Types of Action

You need perfect tense verbs to express certain types of times and actions. (See page **724** in the "Proofreader's Guide.") There are three perfect tenses.

	Singular	Plural
Present perfect tense states an action that *began in the past but continues or is completed in the present.*		
Present perfect (use *has* or *have* + past participle)	I have studied. You have studied. He or she has studied.	We have studied. You have studied. They have studied.
Past perfect tense states an action that *began in the past and was completed in the past.*		
Past perfect (use *had* + past participle)	I had studied. You had studied. He or she had studied.	We had studied. You had studied. They had studied.
Future perfect tense states an action that *will begin in the future and will be completed by a specific time in the future.*		
Future perfect (use *will have* + past participle)	I will have studied. You will have studied. He or she will have studied.	We will have studied. You will have studied. They will have studied.

 Write a sentence using the stated tense of each of the following verbs. (See the list of irregular verbs on page **722**.)

Example: try *(present perfect)*
　　　　Raekwon has tried to find each constellation.

1. rain *(past perfect)*
2. listen *(present perfect)*
3. grow *(future perfect)*
4. make *(past perfect)*
5. look *(present perfect)*
6. see *(future perfect)*
7. learn *(past perfect)*
8. talk *(present perfect)*
9. want *(past perfect)*
10. finish *(future perfect)*

BASIC GRAMMAR

Try IT Answers

1. In the past, people tried to predict the weather; they used methods such as studying animal behavior and observing the heavens.
2. In the early 1600s, people invented tools that allowed their users to record weather data.
3. Scientists began to understand the atmosphere, so they started making predictions.
4. Of course, it was hundreds of years later when forecasts really became accurate.
5. Today, weather forecasters tell how storms threaten this area.

Try IT Answers

Answers will vary.

Try IT Possible Answers

1. It had rained the entire day.
2. I have listened to that CD a thousand times.
3. By that time, he will have grown at least 4 inches!
4. He had made that meal many times before.
5. Who has looked for it?
6. Blake will have seen that play.
7. I thought you had learned chemistry already.
8. Annabelle has talked about her trip.
9. Originally, I had wanted that sweater.
10. They will have finished by dinnertime.

How else can I use verbs?

Transfer Action to an Object

You will use both transitive and intransitive verbs to express specific ideas in your writing.

Transitive verbs are always action verbs. A transitive verb needs a direct object to make its meaning complete. Remember that a direct object is a noun or a pronoun that answers the question "what" or "whom." (See page 473 and 692.4.)

> **Mountains, cold fronts, and the jet stream** cause **air to rise.**
> (The meaning of the transitive verb *cause* would not be complete without the direct object *air.*)
>
> **The cool, expanding air** holds **moisture.**
> (The direct object *moisture* completes the meaning of the transitive verb *holds.*)

An **intransitive verb's** meaning is complete without a direct object.

> **The moisture** condenses **into droplets.**
> (The meaning of the intransitive verb *condenses* is complete without a direct object. *Into droplets* is a prepositional phrase.)
>
> **Ice crystals** form **in high altitudes.**
> (The meaning of the intransitive verb *form* is complete without a direct object. *In high altitudes* is a prepositional phrase.)

Depending on how a verb is used in a sentence, it may be transitive or intransitive.

> **All rain actually** begins **its life as snow.**
> (*Begins* is followed by a direct object, *life. Begins* is a transitive verb.)
>
> **All rain actually** begins **as snow.**
> (*Begins* is intransitive because there is no direct object. *As snow* is a prepositional phrase.)

 Write whether the underlined verbs in the following paragraph are transitive or intransitive. For each transitive verb, write the direct object that follows it.

> Ice crystals in a cloud **(1)** grow in size and weight. After a while, their weight **(2)** prevents them from staying in the cloud. As ice crystals **(3)** fall toward the earth, the warmer air below the cloud **(4)** melts the ice. As long as the surface **(5)** produces warm air, rain is the result. Otherwise, the crystals **(6)** change into snow.

Form Verbals

Verbals are words that are made from verbs but are used as other parts of speech. Verbals are used as nouns, adjectives, or adverbs, and they are often used in phrases. (See 730.2–730.4.)

Gerunds

A **gerund** is a verb form that ends in *ing* and is used as a noun.

> **A** warning **alerted us that a storm was approaching.**
> (The gerund *warning* acts as a subject noun.)
>
> **I heard the** ringing of the wind chimes. (The gerund phrase *ringing of the wind chimes* acts as a direct object.)

Participles

A **participle** is a verb form that ends in *ing* or *ed* and is used as an adjective.

> **The** pounding **waves rocked the boats in the bay.**
> (The participle acts as an adjective describing *waves.*)
>
> **The wind** whipping through town **tore shingles loose.**
> (The participial phrase acts as an adjective describing *wind.*)

Infinitives

An **infinitive** is a verb with "to" before it. An infinitive can be used as a noun, an adjective, or an adverb.

> To protect ourselves **was our number one goal.**
> (The infinitive phrase *to protect ourselves* acts as a subject noun.)
>
> **Our plan** to shut the windows **was never carried out.**
> (*To shut the windows* acts as an adjective modifying the noun *plan.*)
>
> **We watched carefully** to evaluate the danger.
> (*To evaluate the danger* acts as an adverb modifying the verb *watched.*)

 Write a separate sentence for each of the verbals listed below. Refer to the model sentences above as a guide.

1. breaking down the trees *(gerund phrase)*
2. to find shelter *(infinitive phrase)*
3. blowing *(participle)*
4. frightened by the wind *(participial phrase)*

Try It Answers

1. intransitive
2. transitive (them)
3. intransitive
4. transitive (ice)
5. transitive (air)
6. intransitive

Try It Possible Answers

1. Breaking down the trees is not an easy job.
2. They knew they needed to find shelter before nightfall.
3. Blowing roofs off houses, the wind was the most powerful they had ever seen.
4. The dog, frightened by the wind, hid under the car.

Describing with Adjectives

Adjectives are words that describe or modify nouns or pronouns. Sensory adjectives help the reader see, hear, feel, smell, and taste what writers are describing. (Also see pages **732** and **734**.)

Without Adjectives

Today's weather allows us to be outside. Clouds dot the sky. We can soak up the sun as we eat lunch.

With Adjectives

Today's summer-like weather allows us to be outside. Fluffy clouds dot the blue sky. We can soak up the sun as we eat our picnic lunch.

Adjectives answer four questions: *what kind? how much? how many?* or *which one?* Remember that proper adjectives can be made from proper nouns (Africa, *African*; Japan, *Japanese*) and are capitalized.

What kind?	Spanish **moss**	tall **tree**	green **apple**
How many (Much)?	six **horses**	few **computers**	some **rain**
Which one?	that **desk**	those **papers**	last **test**

 For each blank in the sentences below, write an adjective of the type called for in parentheses.

1. Yesterday was a *(what kind?)* day.
2. *(What kind?)* rain fell off and on all day.
3. We had *(how many?)* separate storms go through overnight.
4. The *(which one?)* storm was the worst.
5. It left *(what kind?)* debris everywhere.
6. The window in the *(which one?)* wall was shattered.
7. Today the forecast is for a *(what kind?)* day.
8. Predictions show a *(what kind?)* chance for rain in the morning.
9. *(Which one?)* afternoon, I'll go biking.
10. A *(how much?)* exercise will energize me.

Comparative and Superlative Forms

You can use comparative adjectives to compare two things. For most one-syllable adjectives, add *er* to make the **comparative form**. To compare three or more things, add *est* to make the **superlative form**.

Positive	Comparative	Superlative
small	smaller	smallest

Comparative: Today's rainbow is smaller than the one we saw last week.
Superlative: It's probably the smallest one I've ever seen.

Add *er* and *est* to some two-syllable words and use *more* or *most* (or *less* or *least*) with others. Always use *more* or *most* with three-syllable adjectives.

Positive	Comparative	Superlative
tiny	tinier	tiniest
forceful	more forceful	most forceful

Comparative: The wind last night was more forceful than it is tonight.
Superlative: The wind is most forceful during a tornado.

NOTE Some adjectives use completely different words to express comparison. For example, *bad, worse, worst.* (See **734.6.**)

Write the positive, comparative, or superlative form of the underlined adjective to fill in the blanks in each of the following sentences.

1. There were some violent storms last summer, but this past week's storms have been _____ than those. I think the _____ storm occurred last night.
2. Fargo, North Dakota, is a snowy city, and Buffalo, New York, is a _____ city, but the _____ city in the United States is Blue Canyon, California.
3. It gets _____ in Chicago, but it's _____ in Dodge City, Kansas. Mt. Washington, New Hampshire, with gusts of more than 200 miles per hour, is the windiest place in the nation.
4. Yuma, Arizona, is not a very _____ place; however, Las Vegas is even less humid than Yuma. The _____ city in the United States is Milford, Utah.

Try IT Possible Answers

1. rainy
2. Heavy
3. three
4. last
5. huge
6. living room
7. cloudy
8. small
9. This
10. little

Try IT Answers

1. more violent, most violent
2. snowier, snowiest
3. windy, windier
4. humid, least humid

How can I strengthen my writing with adjectives?

Use Effective Adjectives

If you avoid overused adjectives (*nice, big, pretty, small, nice, good,* and so on) and use specific, colorful adjectives instead, your writing will be clear and powerful.

> **With Overused Adjectives**
>
> A bad **storm knocked down a** big **tree in our yard.**

> **With Stronger Adjectives**
>
> A fierce summer **storm knocked down a** century-old oak **tree in our yard.**

 List three adjectives in the following passage that seem especially strong and two adjectives that seem overused. Then write an effective adjective next to each overused one.

> I listened to the growling thunder in the distance while watching the blue-black clouds. I wondered if we would get a nice rain. The parched ground in the fields was criss-crossed with ugly cracks. The curled leaves were turned bottom side up, like hands begging for help. I hoped that the bad drought would be over.

Use Adjectives with the Right Feeling

Your choice of adjectives can really change the feeling of your writing. What an adjective suggests—its **connotation**—has a significant effect on your writing. Look at this example:

The blustery **wind blew Isaac's homework against the brick wall.**
What does the word *blustery* suggest to you? What if you changed it to *howling* wind or *brisk* wind? These adjectives are similar, yet each one gives the sentence a different feeling.

 If you need help, check a thesaurus. This reference book offers synonyms and antonyms for words. Pick words that best fit the meaning and feeling you want to express.

 Write a brief paragraph about a windy day. Concentrate on how the wind makes you feel and use adjectives with the right connotation.

Be Selective

While adjectives can make your writing engaging, don't overuse them. Compare these two sets of descriptive phrases:

Awkward, over-modified phrases	*Stronger phrases*
a sunny, inviting, warm, balmy day	a balmy, sunny day
the gray, threatening, windy, cloudy sky	the gray, threatening sky

Although the phrases in the first column have more words, they don't really say more than the second descriptions. In fact, they actually slow the reader down and disrupt the flow of ideas.

 Rewrite each of the following over-modified phrases by cutting back on the number of adjectives. Keep only those adjectives that make the phrase strong. Then use each of the new phrases in an effective sentence.

1. a frigid, dark, raw, dangerous winter night
2. the intense, bright, white, shocking lightning
3. a calm, peaceful, quiet, still evening
4. the fiery, colorful, vibrant, red maple leaves
5. a plodding, struggling, weary, demoralized hiker

Be General or Specific

You can use **indefinite adjectives**, such as *few, many, more,* and *some,* to give the reader approximate (rather than *specific*) information.

Some **thunderstorms produce funnel clouds.**
Most **storms don't cause** much **harm.**

A **demonstrative adjective** points to a specific noun. The demonstrative adjectives are *this, that, these,* and *those.*

Those **clouds over there look threatening.**
This **weather is not so bad.**

Note that both indefinite and demonstrative adjectives must come before the nouns they modify. If they appear alone, they are pronouns.

 Write about a rainy experience using two sentences with indefinite adjectives and two sentences with demonstrative adjectives. Exchange papers with a classmate and underline each other's indefinite adjectives and circle the demonstrative adjectives.

 **Possible Answers**

STRONG	OVERUSED
growling	nice (needed)
blue-black	bad (terrible)
parched	
criss crossed	
curled	

Answers

Answers will vary.

 **Answers**

Answers will vary.

Answers

Answers will vary.

Describing with Adverbs

Adverbs describe or modify verbs, adjectives, or other adverbs. Adverbs answer *how? when?* (or *how often?*) *where?* or *how much?* in a sentence. (See pages 736 and 738.)

How?	carefully	Dad drove carefully through the fog.
When?	later	We hope it clears up later.
Where?	everywhere	The fog seems to be everywhere.
How Much?	completely	It completely blocks my view of our yard.

 Team up with a partner, and list at least 10 adverbs from the following narrative. (There are more than 10, so keep listing if you want to.) Then write *how? when?* (or *how often?*) *where?* or *how much?* next to each adverb in your list, depending on the question it answers. If you're not sure, leave the space blank.

1 Grandma Abby was very disappointed when her flight was
2 cancelled due to fog, but she probably should have expected the
3 cancellation. Her home in the Appalachian Mountains has fog on
4 more than 100 days annually. On those foggy days, she will go out
5 if absolutely necessary. The morning of her flight, she optimistically
6 journeyed to the airport, hoping that the fog would go away soon.
7 When it didn't, she headed homeward with a heavy heart.
8   Obviously, Grandma could not have done anything to change
9 the situation. Fog happens often in the Appalachians, especially in
10 the valleys there. Nightly, the surface air cools rapidly. This colder
11 air, full of moisture, slowly sinks into low spots. This ground fog
12 can entirely block visibility and make driving dangerous. I'm glad
13 Grandma stays inside when fog blankets her valley.

Special Challenge: Answer the following questions about the narrative above and about your own writing.

1. Which adverbs seem necessary to understand the story?

2. Which adverbs seem not as important?

3. Do you use adverbs very often in your writing? Explain after reviewing one of your latest pieces of writing.

Comparative and Superlative Adverbs

You can use adverbs to compare two things. The **comparative form** of an adverb compares two people, places, things, or ideas. The **superlative form** of an adverb compares three or more people, places, things, or ideas.

 For most one-syllable adverbs, add *er* to make the comparative form and *est* to make the superlative form.

Positive	Comparative	Superlative
soon	sooner	soonest

While you add *er* and *est* to some two-syllable adverbs, you need to use *more* or *most* (or *less* or *least*) with others. Always use *more* or *most* with adverbs of three or more syllables.

Positive	Comparative	Superlative
early	earlier	earliest
quickly	more quickly	most quickly
importantly	more importantly	most importantly

Comparative: **It rained harder last night than it did on Sunday.**
It rains more frequently in Ohio than it does in Nevada.

Superlative: **During a storm last summer, it rained the hardest ever.**
Hawaii is the state where it rains most frequently.

 Make sure that you write a complete comparison: *It rained harder last night than it did on Sunday* rather than *It rained harder last night than Sunday.*

 Write two sentences for each adverb listed below. In the first sentence, use the comparative form of the adverb; in the second sentence, use the superlative form. Reword each sentence as needed.

Example: softly
        The snow falls more softly now that it did this morning.
        The snow falls most softly in the evenings.

1. early
2. loudly
3. late
4. effectively

Try It Answers

line 1.   very (how much?)
line 2.   probably (how?)
line 4.   annually (how often?)
          out (where?)
line 5.   absolutely (how much?)
          optimistically (how?)
line 6.   away (where?)
          soon (when?)
line 7.   homeward (where?)
line 8.   obviously (how)
          not (how?)
line 9.   often (how often?)
          especially (how much?)
line 10. there (where?)
          nightly (when?)
          rapidly (how?)
line 11. slowly (how?)
line 12. entirely (how much?)
line 13. inside (where?)

Try It Answers

1. earlier, earliest
2. more (less) loudly, most (least) loudly
3. later, latest
4. more (less) effectively, most (least) effectively

How can I use adverbs effectively?

Describe Actions

You can make your writing more descriptive by using adverbs. Since adverbs can often appear in more than one position in a sentence, always consider the best place to include them. Remember that each different position may slightly change the meaning of the adverb.

For many years, people have tried tirelessly to control the weather.
For many years, people have tirelessly tried to control the weather.
Tirelessly, people have tried to control the weather for many years.

 Rewrite the following sentences, placing the adverb (in parentheses) where you think it fits best.

1. It would be satisfying to control when and where it rains. *(certainly)*
2. Having the ability to stop severe storms would be awesome! *(absolutely)*
3. There is only one method in use that controls the weather. *(currently)*
4. "Seeding" a cloud with chemicals will produce rain. *(possibly)*
5. Whether they realize it or not, humans affect the weather. *(unfortunately)*
6. Man-made structures that trap heat and pollution can cause natural weather patterns to be unstable. *(actually)*

Special Challenge: Rewrite any four of the above sentences a second time. In each of these new sentences, place the adverb in a different position.

Add Emphasis

You can stress the importance of an idea with adverbs. Generally, use adverbs of degree—those that answer *how much?*—for this job. (See **736.4**.)

It was an unbelievably strong wind.
An extremely windy day can be scary.

 Write a short paragraph about this picture that shows a windy scene. Use a few adverbs to add emphasis.

Express Frequency

With adverbs, you can describe how often something happens or how often something is done. Adverbs that tell how often include words like *sometimes, often, usually, occasionally, always,* and so on.

Storms with high winds are often frightening.
They never fail to scare me.

 Write three sentences about fall weekends. Use one of the "how often" adverbs below per sentence.

| regularly | never | occasionally | always | seldom | frequently |

Be Precise

With adverbs, you can tell the readers exactly when or where something happens.

Adverbs answering *when?* first then yesterday now right away
Adverbs answering *where?* here there nearby inside outside

Shayla saw the lightning first.
Then we heard the thunder and ran inside.

 Write two sentences about winter mornings using one "when" adverb per sentence. Then write two sentences about the same subject using one "where" adverb per sentence.

Connect Ideas

A **conjunctive adverb** is a special word used as a connection between two independent clauses (or complete sentences). The two sentences below show how conjunctive adverbs are used.

We wore ponchos during the storm; however, we still were drenched.
(A semicolon comes before the conjunctive adverb, and a comma follows it.)
Within a few days, I came down with a cold. Nevertheless, I didn't miss a day of school. (The conjunctive adverb starts the second sentence, and a comma follows the word.)

Common conjunctive adverbs: *also, then, however, meanwhile, therefore, as a result, for example,* and *for instance.* (Also see **738.1**.)

Write sentences using three of the conjunctive adverbs listed above. Make sure that you punctuate each of your sentences correctly.

 **Answers**

Answers will vary.

 Answers

Answers will vary.

 **Answers**

Answers will vary.

 **Answers**

Answers will vary.

 **Answers**

Answers will vary.

Connecting with Prepositions

A preposition is a word or words that show how one word or idea is related to another. A preposition is the first word of a prepositional phrase, a phrase that acts as an adjective or an adverb in a sentence. (See page **742** for a complete list of prepositions.)

Weather events occur even in outer space.
(The preposition *in* shows the relationships between the verb *occur* and the object of the preposition *outer space*. The prepositional phrase acts as an adverb telling "where.")

These cosmic storms release jets of hot gas.
(The preposition *of* shows the relationship between the noun *jets* and the object of the preposition *gas*. The prepositional phrase acts as an adjective telling "what kind.")

■ **A word that is used as a preposition may also be used as an adverb.**
If a word that sometimes is used as a preposition appears alone in a sentence, that word is probably an adverb.

Ten million light-years away, space hurricanes whirl around the universe. (*Around the universe* is a prepositional phrase.)

In the eye of these hurricanes, winds of hot gas spin around.
(*Around* is an adverb that modifies the verb *spin*.)

■ **"To" is either a preposition or part of an infinitive phrase.**
If the words that follow "to" include the object of the preposition (a noun or pronoun), then "to" is a preposition. If "to" is followed by a verb or verb phrase, then "to" is part of an infinitive or infinitive phrase. (See page **485**.)

Although I might like traveling to space, **I would not like getting caught in a space hurricane's million-mile-per-hour winds.**
(*To space* is a prepositional phrase.)

Scientists use the Hubble Space Telescope to look deep into space.
(*To look deep into space* is an infinitive phrase used as an adverb.)

Try It Write four sentences about your favorite kind of weather. Use the word "around" as a preposition in one sentence and as an adverb in another sentence. Use the word "to" as a preposition in one sentence and as part of an infinitive in another.

How can I use prepositional phrases?
Add Information

You can use a prepositional phrase as an adjective to describe either a noun or a pronoun. Adjectives answer *what kind? how many? how much?* or *which one?*

        Which one?   What kind?

The weather report on channel 33 **predicts a cool night** with clear skies.

Try It Write each prepositional phrase that is used as an adjective in the following paragraph. (You should find seven.)

1   Yesterday's forecast for a warm, sunny day was absolutely
2 wrong. In Atlanta, we got the worst storm of the season instead.
3 The rumbling thunder along the storm front got closer, and the
4 lightning flashes got more intense. High winds throughout the area
5 brought hail, and many cars across the county were damaged by
6 it. One tree in front of our house lost a large branch. Heavy rain
7 clogged the storm sewers. Fortunately, we still have a roof over
8 our heads!

You can also use a prepositional phrase as an adverb to describe a verb, an adjective, or another adverb. Adverbs answer *how? when? where? how long? how often?* or *how much?*

        Where?   How long?

It hasn't rained in Middleville for three weeks.

Try It Write a prepositional phrase that could complete each sentence below. Tell what question each one answers.

Example: The storm was heading _____.
    toward Middleville (where)

1. Clouds were heavy _____.
2. The rain began to fall early _____.
3. The rain did not stop _____.
4. Some neighborhoods appeared vulnerable _____ forcing people to flee their homes.
5. The police department acted quickly _____ to help people find shelter.

Try It Answers

Answers will vary.

Try It Answers

line 1. for a warm, sunny day
line 2. of the season
line 3. along the storm front
line 4. throughout the area
line 5. across the county
line 6. in front of our house
line 7. over our heads

Try It Possible Answers

1. for miles (where)
2. at noon (when)
3. for hours (how long)
4. near the river (where)
5. in town (which one)

Connecting with Conjunctions

Conjunctions connect words, groups of words, and sentences. There are three kinds of conjunctions: *coordinating, subordinating,* and *correlative.* The following sentences show some of the ways to use conjunctions. (See page **744** for a list of common conjunctions.)

Coordinating Conjunctions
Connect Words and Phrases

Shawn wants to report the news and the weather on a radio station.

Does he need a science degree or a communications degree?

Connect Compound Subjects and Predicates

Hassan and Francisco want to become TV weathermen.

They continually study the weather or read about it.

Connect Sentences

Many weather reporters are meteorologists, but not all of them are.

Weather will always be a topic of interest, so reporters will never run out of work.

Subordinating Conjunctions
Connect Dependent Clauses to Independent Clauses

Jalisa hopes to work at a TV station while she attends college.

Although she is a good student, she wants job experience, too.

Correlative Conjunctions
Connect Phrases

Many weather forecasts today are based not only on scientific instruments and observations but also on satellite images.

People either believe the forecasts or ignore them.

Try It Choose three of the sentences above to use as models. Write three sentences of your own imitating the three you've chosen. (Make sure to write original sentences.) Underline the conjunctions you use.

How can I use conjunctions?

Connect Phrases

You can use **coordinating** and **correlative conjunctions** to connect different types of phrases: noun phrases, verb phrases, prepositional phrases, verbal phrases, and so on. Coordinating conjunctions include words like *and, but, or, yet,* and so on. Correlative conjunctions are used in pairs: *either/or, both/and, not only/but also,* and so on. Correlative conjunctions show a relationship between the phrases.

"Black blizzards" of the Dust Bowl (the severe drought during the 1930s) blew dry soil off the farm fields and into the air. (The coordinating conjunction *and* connects two prepositional phrases.)

A long period without rain either damages crops or prevents them from growing. (The correlative conjunctions *either* and *or* connect two verb phrases and show that they are alternatives.)

Try It Complete each sentence below using a coordinating conjunction or a set of correlative conjunctions to fill in the blanks. (See **744.2**.)

1. _____ natural elements _____ human actions were causes of the Dust Bowl.
2. Farmers learned that they must _____ change their farming practices _____ find another occupation.
3. As a result, farmers increased crop yields _____ reduced soil erosion.
4. The southern Great Plains experienced serious droughts _____ in the 1930s _____ in the 1950s.
5. High temperatures _____ low rainfall led to the five-year drought of the '50s.
6. The effects of a major drought are serious _____ for nature _____ for society.
7. Drought increases the risk of forest fires, _____ fires are necessary for certain trees to release their seeds.
8. A water shortage prevents activities as different as hog farming _____ river recreation.
9. _____ hydroelectric power _____ some manufacturing processes will work correctly during a drought.
10. To avoid the effects of drought, we can conserve water _____ find new water supplies.

Try It Possible Answers

1. Henry hopes to ride his bike <u>while</u> he is on vacation.
2. Vallery <u>and</u> Tannika want to become writers.
3. I will <u>either</u> play tennis <u>or</u> go swimming today.

Try It Answers

1. Not only, but also
2. either, or
3. and
4. both, and
5. and
6. not only, but also
7. but
8. and
9. Neither, nor
10. or

Expand Sentences (with Subordinating Conjunctions)

You can use a **subordinating conjunction** to connect a dependent clause to another sentence. A dependent clause (one that *cannot* stand alone as a sentence) must be connected to an independent clause (one that *can* stand alone as a sentence). In the expanded sentences below, the dependent clause is underlined, and the subordinating conjunction is in blue.

Before people used satellite images to explain and predict the weather, they used folklore. As early people observed changes in the weather, they noticed how it affected insects, animals, birds, and the skies. People believed much of the weather folklore until some of it was disproved by modern science.

■ When a dependent clause begins the sentence, follow it with a comma. The comma is usually not needed when the dependent clause follows the independent clause.

 Use the given subordinating conjunction (in parentheses) to combine each of the following pairs of statements into one complex sentence. Place some dependent clauses first.

Example: Some folklore turned out to be accurate. Scientists studied the weather. *(after)*
After scientists studied the weather, some folklore turned out to be accurate.

1. Other folklore was myth. It did not stop people from using the sayings anyway. *(although)*
2. Sea birds sit on the sand. There truly is a storm at hand. *(when)*
3. Wind and daylong rain is nigh. Yellow streaks the sunset sky. *(if)*
4. You see a rainbow at noon. There will be more rain soon. *(when)*
5. The dew is on the grass. Rain will never come to pass. *(as long as)*
6. We'll have a long winter over all the land. A wooly bear caterpillar has a wide brown band. *(since)*
7. A cow tries to scratch her ear. It means a shower is very near. *(whenever)*
8. I hear these different myths. I can only shake my head in wonder. *(as)*
9. I won't trust these sayings. They are proven true. *(unless)*
10. I go on a long hike. I will check the forecast for the day. *(before)*

Building Effective Sentences

Our world is a diverse place. Snow-capped mountains tower more than five miles high, and ocean trenches delve more than six miles deep. In one place, the sun pours its life-giving light on a dense tropical rain forest, while in another, it bakes sand dunes until nothing can survive. Golden fields of grain, rocky shorelines, flat-topped mesas, mazelike everglades—the beauty of the world is its diversity.

Diversity is also the beauty of writing. If every sentence is the same, a reader will soon get bored. Instead, if the sentences vary, containing pleasant surprises around some of the turns, the reader will want to keep reading. This chapter will help you create sentences that are clear, complete, and varied so that you can build beautiful landscapes of ideas.

What's Ahead

You will learn about . . .
● writing complete sentences.
● fixing sentence problems.
● improving your sentence style.
● combining sentences.
● using different types and kinds of sentences.
● expanding and modeling sentences.

TryIT Answers

1. Although other folklore was myth, it did not stop people from using the sayings anyway.
2. When sea birds sit on the sand, there truly is a storm at hand.
3. Wind and daylong rain is nigh if yellow streaks the sunset sky.
4. When you see a rainbow at noon, there will be more rain soon.
5. As long as the dew is on the grass, rain will never come to pass.
6. We'll have a long winter over all the land since a wooly bear caterpillar has a wide brown band.
7. Whenever a cow tries to scratch her ear, it means a shower is very near.
8. I can only shake my head in wonder as I hear these different myths.
9. I won't trust these sayings unless they are proven true.
10. Before I go on a long hike, I will check the forecast for the day.

agree model EXPAND combine
order

Building Effective Sentences

Writing Complete Sentences

Every sentence has two basic parts: a complete subject (which tells who or what is doing something) and a complete predicate (which tells what the subject is doing or tells something about the subject).

Complete Subject	Complete Predicate
Who or what does something?	*What does the subject do?*
The Amazon River	winds through the jungle.
The Nile River	empties into the sea.

 Divide a piece of paper into two columns. For each of the sentences below, write the complete subject in the left column and write the complete predicate in the right column.

> In the following sentences, the words that come before the verb are part of the *complete subject*. The verb and all the words that follow it are part of the *complete predicate*.

Example: Old Faithful, a geyser in Yellowstone National Park, erupts for about four minutes every hour.

| *Old Faithful, a geyser in* | *erupts for about four* |
| *Yellowstone National Park,* | *minutes every hour.* |

1. The Royal Gorge Bridge in Colorado ranks as the highest suspension bridge in the world.
2. Australia's Great Barrier Reef stretches for about 1,250 miles.
3. A moat surrounds the Imperial Palace in Tokyo, Japan.
4. Timbuktu served as the chief trading center in western Africa.
5. More than 250,000 workers built the Panama Canal for wages of about 10 cents an hour.
6. The only species of wild ape in Europe lives on Gibraltar Rock.
7. Residents of Venice, Italy, travel through canals by boat.
8. The volcano Mount Vesuvius made Pompeii, Italy, famous.
9. Antarctica is not owned by any country.
10. Jim White, a cowboy, discovered the Carlsbad Caverns in New Mexico.

Subjects and Predicates

Every sentence has a subject and a predicate. A simple subject consists of the subject without the words that modify it. A simple predicate is the verb without the words that modify it or complete the thought. In the sentences below, the simple subjects are orange, and the simple predicates are blue.

Simple Subject	Simple Predicate
Ancient Egyptians	worshiped the Nile River.
The distance from New York City to Los Angeles	matches the length of the Nile.

A simple subject may be compound, which means that it includes two or more subjects sharing the same predicate (or predicates). A simple predicate may also be compound, which means that it includes two or more verbs sharing the same subject (or subjects).

Compound Subject	Compound Predicate
Crocodiles and hippos	live and thrive in the Nile.

 Number a piece of paper from 1 to 5, skipping a line between numbers. For each sentence below, write the simple subject on one line and the simple predicate on the next line. (Remember to look for compound subjects and predicates.)

Example: Part of the Nile River, the Blue Nile, originates in Ethiopia.
part
originates

1. Sand accumulates in the Blue Nile and turns the water brownish blue.
2. The clear White Nile gathers no sand.
3. The Blue Nile and the White Nile combine at Khartoum, Sudan.
4. The Nile River becomes dark blue at Khartoum and continues to the Mediterranean Sea.
5. The word *Nile* means "dark blue."

 Write NOW Write one sentence with a single simple subject and a compound simple predicate. Then write another sentence with a compound simple subject and a compound simple predicate. Ask a classmate to underline the simple subjects once and the simple predicates twice in each sentence.

BASIC WRITING

Try It Answers

1. The Royal Gorge Bridge in Colorado | ranks as the highest suspension bridge in the world.
2. Australia's Great Barrier Reef | stretches for about 1,250 miles.
3. A moat | surrounds the Imperial Palace in Tokyo, Japan.
4. Timbuktu | served as the chief trading center in western Africa.
5. More than 250,000 workers | built the Panama Canal for wages of about 10 cents an hour.
6. The only species of wild ape in Europe | lives on Gibraltar Rock.
7. Residents of Venice, Italy, | travel through canals by boat.
8. The volcano Mount Vesuvius | made Pompeii, Italy, famous.
9. Antarctica | is not owned by any country.
10. Jim White, a cowboy, | discovered the Carlsbad Caverns in New Mexico.

Try It Answers

1. sand
   accumulates, turns
2. White Nile
   gathers
3. Blue Nile, White Nile
   combine
4. Nile River
   becomes, continues
5. word
   means

How can I make sure my sentences are complete?

Check Your Subjects and Predicates

Incomplete thoughts are called fragments. Fragments may be missing a subject, a predicate, or both. Study the fragments below. Then read the complete sentences made from them. Notice that a subject, a predicate, or both have been added to make the corrections.

Fragment	Sentence
Consists of four large islands and more than 3,000 small ones.	Japan consists of four large islands and more than 3,000 small ones. (A subject is added.)
In Japan.	Mount Fuji is the highest mountain in Japan. (A subject and predicate are added.)
Shinto pilgrims this sacred mountain.	Shinto pilgrims climb this sacred mountain. (A predicate is added.)

 Number your paper from 1 to 7. Read each group of words below. If the group of words is a complete sentence, write "C" next to the number. If it is a fragment, write "F" and tell if it needs a subject, a predicate, or both to become a complete sentence.

Example: Stands on Honshu, the largest island.
　　　　 F–subject

1. Mount Fuji is named for an ancient Japanese goddess of fire.
2. Lake Biwa, Japan's largest lake, near Mount Fuji.
3. Of Japan's more than 250 volcanoes, Mount Fuji the largest.
4. In the past few hundred years, has erupted almost 20 times.
5. To hike the trail up the slopes of Mount Fuji about nine hours.
6. Open to the public only during July and August.
7. Mount Fuji remains a top tourist attraction.

 Correct any fragments above by adding the missing parts to form complete sentences. Exchange papers with a classmate and check each other's work.

Check for Dependent Clauses

A dependent clause (also called a subordinate clause) contains a subject and a verb but does not express a complete thought. It cannot stand by itself as a sentence. A dependent clause needs to be connected to an independent clause to compete its meaning. A dependent clause plus an independent clause creates a complex sentence. (See 698.3.)

Dependent Clauses (They cannot stand alone.)	Combined with Independent Clauses (Complex sentences are created.)
Where the wilderness is mostly untouched	The Yukon Territory is located in a northerly region where the wilderness is mostly untouched.
Because the sun never sets during some of the summer season	Because the sun never sets during some of the summer season, people go to bed with the sun still shining.
That are extremely cold	Winters that are extremely cold can turn gasoline to slush.

 A comma is needed after a dependent clause that comes at the beginning of a sentence. A comma is usually not needed if the dependent clause comes at the end. A dependent clause in the middle of a sentence may or may not need to be set off by commas. (See 584.1 and 590.1.)

 Read the paragraph below. How many dependent clauses do you find? Now rewrite the paragraph, connecting each dependent clause to an independent clause that comes before or after it.

1　　　When the gold rush occurred in the 1800s. Thousands rushed to
2　the Klondike River in the Yukon. Though many had jobs. They left home
3　to seek their fortune. Because of the gold rush. The Royal Canadian
4　Mounted Police went north to police the miners. The Mounties stopped
5　travelers to be sure they had adequate supplies. Before the Mounties
6　let them go on. Once the gold rush began. Dawson City, Yukon, grew
7　from a tiny town to a city of 30,000. After the gold rush, only 700
8　residents remained in Dawson City. Suddenly the Yukon area was left
9　with many empty log cabins. That were built earlier by the miners.

 Write a brief paragraph explaining the history of a place in your city or hometown or a place you have visited or read about. Include at least two complex sentences.

Try It Answers

1. C
2. F–predicate
3. F–predicate
4. F–subject
5. F–predicate
6. F–both
7. C

Try It Answers

There are six dependent clauses.

Try It Possible Answers

　　When the gold rush occurred in the 1800s, thousands rushed to the Klondike River in the Yukon. Though many had jobs, they left home to seek their fortunes. Because of the gold rush, the Royal Canadian Mounted Police went north to police the miners. The Mounties stopped travelers to be sure they had adequate supplies before the Mounties let them go on. Once the gold rush began, Dawson City, Yukon, grew from a tiny town to a city of 30,000. After the gold rush, only 700 residents remained in Dawson City. Suddenly the Yukon area was left with many empty log cabins that were built earlier by the miners.

504–505   Basic Grammar and Writing

504

agree model EXPAND *combine*
order
Building Effective Sentences
505

Fixing Sentence Problems

Avoid Run-On Sentences

Sometimes you may accidentally write a run-on sentence by putting together two or more sentences. One type of run-on is called a *comma splice*, in which the sentences are connected with a comma only. Another type of run-on has no punctuation at all.

One way to fix run-on sentences is to add a coordinating conjunction (*and, so, or, for, but, yet,* or *nor*) and a comma (if not already present). Another way is to connect the two sentences with a semicolon.

Run-On Sentence	Corrected Sentences
The Rock of Gibraltar stands between Europe and Africa less than eight miles separate the continents.	The Rock of Gibraltar stands between Europe and Africa, and less than eight miles separate the continents.
	The Rock of Gibraltar stands between Europe and Africa; less than eight miles separate the continents.

 On your own paper, correct the run-on sentences below by adding a comma and a coordinating conjunction.

> **Example:** The Gibraltar peninsula is a thin, hilly strip of land it is connected to Spain.
> *The Gibraltar peninsula is a thin, hilly strip of land, and it is connected to Spain.*

1. Many cargo and passenger ships visit Gibraltar's harbor the safe harbor and mild climate make it a great place to stop for repairs.
2. Storks spend winters in Africa and summers in Europe they migrate over Gibraltar.
3. This limestone mountain was legendary to Ancient Greeks they called it one of the Pillars of Hercules.
4. In ancient times, the African Moors occupied Gibraltar it has also been controlled by Spain and England.
5. People use the Rock of Gibraltar as a symbol of strength they say something strong is "as solid as the Rock of Gibraltar."

 Select two of the run-on sentences above. Correct them by adding a semicolon.

Eliminate Rambling Sentences

A rambling sentence occurs when you connect too many ideas with the word *and.* Study the rambling sentence below and two ways it can be corrected.

Rambling Sentence	Corrected Sentences *(The* and*'s have been eliminated.)*
Loch Ness is a large lake in northern Scotland and it is famous for its legendary monster and many tourists visit the loch and hope they see the monster. 	Loch Ness, a large lake in northern Scotland, is famous for its legendary monster. Many tourists, hoping to see the monster, visit the loch. (An appositive phrase [see page 513] is used in the first sentence, and a participial phrase [see page 520] is used in the second sentence.)
	Loch Ness is a large lake in northern Scotland that is famous for its legendary monster. Many tourists, who hope to see the monster, visit the loch. (Two complex sentences have been created. The dependent clause in each sentence begins with a relative pronoun: *that* and *who.* See pages 515 and 517.)

 It is not necessary to eliminate all of the *and*'s in a rambling sentence. Some *and*'s may be needed to connect compound sentences, compound subjects and predicates, and so on.

 Rewrite the following rambling sentences so they contain fewer *and*'s. Whenever possible, make complex sentences. (See pages 515 and 517.)

1. The water in Loch Ness stays about 42 degrees Fahrenheit (6 degrees Celsius) and it is very deep and it never freezes.
2. Scientists searched the lake with sonar equipment in the 1960s and numerous sightings of a monster were reported and this made people even more curious about the Loch Ness monster.
3. In 1972 an underwater camera took pictures in Loch Ness and scientists studied the evidence of a monster and the scientists say the creature might be a sea cow.
4. The monster legend began around the year 565 C.E. and children were not allowed to play by the lake and people began fearing attacks by the monster.

Try IT Possible Answers

1. Many cargo and passenger ships visit Gibraltar's harbor, for the safe harbor and mild climate make it a great place to stop for repairs.
2. Storks spend winters in Africa and summers in Europe, so they migrate over Gibraltar.
3. This limestone mountain was legendary to ancient Greeks, and they called it one of the Pillars of Hercules.
4. In ancient times, the African Moors occupied Gibraltar, but it has also been controlled by Spain and England.
5. People use the Rock of Gibraltar as a symbol of strength, so they say something strong is "as solid as the Rock of Gibraltar."

Try IT Possible Answers

1. The water in Loch Ness is very deep. It stays about 42 degrees Fahrenheit (6 degrees Celsius), so it never freezes.
2. When numerous sightings of a monster were reported, scientists searched the lake with sonar equipment in the 1960s. This made people even more curious about the Loch Ness monster.
3. In 1972, when an underwater camera took pictures in Loch Ness, scientists studied the evidence of a monster and said the creature might be a sea cow.
4. After the monster legend began around the year 565 C.E., people began fearing attacks by the monster, and children were not allowed to play by the lake.

Check for Wordy Sentences

Unnecessary repetition creates wordy sentences. Removing unnecessary words improves the sentence. Study the wordy sentence below and the two ways in which it is corrected.

Wordy Sentence	Corrected Sentences *(Unnecessary words are eliminated.)*
Huge, giant stones stand on end upright in England.	Huge stones stand on end in England.
	Giant stones stand upright in England.

 Rewrite each of the sentences below so that the unnecessary words are eliminated.

1. Approximately 4,000 years ago, 2000 B.C.E., the stones were set in place.
2. Each year thousands of visitors annually go to Stonehenge as tourists.
3. Britain has approximately about 900 stone site locations.
4. In the evening at dusk, visitors especially like to see Stonehenge while the sun is setting.
5. The rocks that make Stonehenge come from great distances far away.
6. No one is certain exactly how these gigantic stones were transported and moved.
7. Because one stone in the middle aligns in a straight line with the sun, some scientists think that people used the stones as a calendar.
8. In Great Britain, Stonehenge sits by itself on the Salisbury Plain in the southern part of England.
9. Some people think that alien beings who came from outer space created Stonehenge.
10. Careful studies show that Stonehenge was built over a long period of time taking hundreds of years.

Move Misplaced Modifiers

Misplaced modifiers occur when a descriptive phrase is improperly located in a sentence and appears to describe the wrong word or idea. To correct this error, locate descriptive phrases as close as possible to the words they modify.

Misplaced Modifier	Corrected Sentences
The largest desert in the world, Africa contains the Sahara Desert. (This sentence incorrectly makes it sound as if Africa is the desert.)	Africa contains the Sahara Desert, the largest desert in the world.
	The Sahara Desert, the largest desert in the world, is contained in Africa. (In both sentences the descriptive phrase is moved closer to the word it modifies.)

 Rewrite each sentence below so that the descriptive modifier clearly describes the correct word or idea. (Change the sentences as needed.)

Example: Ninety percent gravel and boulders, sand actually covers a small portion of the Sahara Desert.
Sand actually covers a small portion of the Sahara Desert, which is 90 percent gravel and boulders.

1. Burrowing during the heat of the day, a visitor might see centipedes and scorpions.
2. Wearing long, protective robes and turbans, camels carry Bedouin nomads through the Sahara.
3. Supplying enough water to support a small city, people can live around a large desert oasis.
4. In sandstone shelters, the Sahara contains carvings and paintings drawn by ancient people.
5. Currently dried up, aerial photographs show that ancient rivers and lakes existed near the Sahara.

Write NOW **Write two sentences containing misplaced modifiers. Base your sentences on the facts below. Then exchange sentences with a classmate and correct each other's work.**

Animals in the Sahara

– survive a harsh environment
– squeeze into abandoned burrows
– seek shade during the day
– are active mostly at night
– live near an oasis

BASIC WRITING

Try IT Possible Answers

1. Approximately 4,000 years ago, the stones were set in place.
2. Each year thousands of visitors go to Stonehenge.
3. Britain has about 900 stone sites.
4. Visitors especially like to see Stonehenge while the sun is setting.
5. The rocks that make Stonehenge come from far away.
6. No one is certain exactly how these gigantic stones were transported.
7. Because one stone in the middle aligns with the sun, some scientists think that people used the stones as a calendar.
8. Stonehenge sits by itself on the Salisbury Plain in the southern part of England.
9. Some people think that aliens from outer space created Stonehenge.
10. Careful studies show that Stonehenge was built over hundreds of years.

Try IT Possible Answers

1. A visitor might see centipedes and scorpions burrowing during the heat of the day.
2. Bedouin nomads, wearing long, protective robes and turbans, ride camels through the Sahara.
3. People can live around a large desert oasis that supplies enough water to support a small city.
4. Ancient people drew carvings and paintings in sandstone shelters of the Sahara.
5. Aerial photographs show that ancient rivers and lakes, currently dried up, existed near the Sahara.

What can I do to write clear sentences?

Make Subjects and Verbs Agree

Subjects and verbs in each sentence you write must agree. That means a singular subject needs a singular verb, and a plural subject needs a plural verb. (Also see **728.1**.)

Single Subjects

A verb must agree with its subject in number.

■ If a subject is singular, the verb must be singular, too.
Brazil is the largest country in South America.

■ If a subject is plural, the verb must be plural.
Most beaches in Brazil have beautiful white sand.

(Don't forget that nouns ending in *s* or *es* are very often plural, and verbs ending in *s* are very often singular.)

■ If an indefinite pronoun is singular, its verb must be singular, too.
Almost everyone in Brazil lives near the Atlantic coast.

■ If an indefinite pronoun is plural, its verb must be plural also.
Many of Brazil's people speak Portuguese.

 Some indefinite pronouns are tricky because they can be singular or plural when used as a subject. (See the chart on page **475**.)

 Number your paper from 1 to 7. For each of the following sentences, correctly write the verb to agree with the subject. If the verb or verbs are correct, write a "C" on your paper.

Example: The Amazon River flow through Brazil.
flows

1. Only some of the plants in the Amazon rain forest has been classified.
2. Amazingly, rain forest spiders grows bigger than this book.
3. Now the rain forests are endangered by civilization.
4. Something are needed to protect animals from heavy river traffic.
5. Tourists doesn't see as many animals in the rain forest.
6. Plants is also disappearing.
7. Some agencies, however, are starting to counteract the damage.

Compound Subjects Connected by "And"

A compound subject connected by the word *and* usually needs a plural verb.
Ecuador and Chile are the only South American countries that don't touch Brazil's border.

Compound Subjects Connected by "Or"

A compound subject connected by the word *or* needs a verb that agrees in number with the subject nearest to the verb.
Either concerned citizens or the World Bank manages a new rain forest conservation program.
(*World Bank*, the subject nearer the verb, is singular, so the singular verb *manages* is used.)

Unusual Word Order

When the subject is separated from the verb by words or phrases, be sure that the verb agrees with the subject.
The Amazon River basin, which extends for more than 4,000 miles, is the largest river basin in the world.
(*Basin*, not *miles*, is the subject, so the singular verb *is* is used.)

When the subject comes after the verb in a sentence, be sure that the verb agrees with the "true subject."
There is more water carried by the Amazon than by the world's 10 next largest rivers combined.
(The subject *water* and the verb *is* are both singular.)
Feeding this great river are more than 1,000 tributaries.
(The subject *tributaries* and the verb *are* are both plural.)

 Number your paper from 1 to 5. Write the correct verb choice for each of these sentences.

1. The Nile and the Amazon (*is, are*) the world's longest rivers.
2. In a square mile of Amazon rain forest (*is, are*) many types of trees.
3. My aunt and uncle (*lives, live*) in Rio de Janeiro, Brazil.
4. Either Rio or the giant trees (*was, were*) highlights of my trip.
5. The screech of monkeys or the call of parrots still (*pierces, pierce*) my dreams.

 Write five sentences of your own: one with a compound subject connected by "and," one with a compound subject connected by "or," and three with unusual word order. Share your work with a classmate.

Answers

1. have
2. grow
3. C
4. is
5. don't
6. are
7. C

Answers

1. are
2. are
3. live
4. were
5. pierces

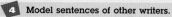
What should I do to avoid nonstandard sentences?

Avoid Double Negatives

Two negative words used together in the same sentence form a double negative (*not no, barely nothing, not never*). Double negatives also happen if you use contractions ending in *n't* with a negative word (*can't hardly, didn't never*). Your writing will not be accurate if you use double negatives.

Negative Words								
nothing	nowhere	neither	never	not	barely	hardly	nobody	none

Negative Contractions							
don't	can't	won't	shouldn't	wouldn't	couldn't	didn't	hadn't

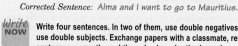 Number your paper from 1 to 5. List the double negatives you find in the sentences below and then correctly rewrite each sentence. *Hint:* There is usually more than one way to correct a double negative.

Example: My sister and I never have no fun on family vacations.
>   never no
>   My sister and I never have any fun on family vacations.

1. We can't go nowhere we want to.
2. I don't hardly want to hear what the plan is this year.
3. Nobody doesn't want to go to Aunt Jessica's house again.
4. We just go there because it doesn't cost nothing.
5. Why don't we never just go to a giant water park?

Avoid Double Subjects

Avoid sentences in which a personal pronoun is used immediately after the subject—the result is usually a double subject.

Double Subject: **Mauritius it** is an island in the Indian Ocean.
Corrected Sentence: Mauritius is an island in the Indian Ocean.

Double Subject: **Alma she** and I want to go to Mauritius.
Corrected Sentence: Alma and I want to go to Mauritius.

Write NOW Write four sentences. In two of them, use double negatives. In the other two, use double subjects. Exchange papers with a classmate, rewrite each other's sentences correctly, and then check each other's work.

Improving Your Sentence Style

There are a number of ways to add variety to your sentences and improve your writing style. Here are four of the most common ways.

1 Combine short sentences.

2 Use different types of sentences.

3 Expand sentences by adding words and phrases.

4 Model sentences of other writers.

When too many sentences in a paragraph are the same length or follow the same pattern, the paragraph sounds choppy. Read the following paragraph.

Little Variety

> Part of Turkey is in Europe. Part of Turkey is in Asia. Turkey is a very interesting country. Ankara is the capital. The largest city is Istanbul. It exists on two continents. No other major city does this. The Bosporus Strait splits the city in two. The European part is on the western side. The Asian part is on the eastern side.

Read the following version, which has a better variety of sentences. See how using different types of sentences helps this paragraph flow more smoothly.

Good Variety

> Turkey is an interesting country because part of it is in Europe and part is in Asia. Ankara is the capital city; however, the largest city is Istanbul. Istanbul is the only major city in the world that exists on two continents. The Bosporus Strait splits the city in two, with the European part on the western side and the Asian part on the eastern side.

 Read the paragraph below. Then, on your own paper, rewrite the paragraph to create more sentence variety.

1   Turkish food is partly Asian. Turkish food is partly European. There
2 are many kinds of dishes. Kebabs are from Turkey. Kebabs usually
3 have meat. Some kebabs are made just with vegetables. Puddings are
4 popular in Turkey. There are at least twelve kinds of milk pudding.
5 There are many delicious pastries. Turkish coffee is a common drink.
6 Turkish coffee is very strong. Tea is a common drink, too.

Possible Answers

1. can't nowhere
   We can't go anywhere we want to.
2. don't hardly
   I don't want to hear what the plan is this year.
3. Nobody doesn't
   Nobody wants to go to Aunt Jessica's house again.
4. doesn't nothing
   We just go there because it doesn't cost anything.
5. don't never
   Why don't we ever just go to a giant water park?

Possible Answers

Turkish food is partly Asian and partly European. There are many kinds of dishes, such as kebabs. Kebabs usually have meat, but some are made with just vegetables. At least 12 kinds of milk pudding are popular in Turkey. There are also many delicious pastries. Turkish coffee, which is very strong, and tea are common drinks.

512-513   Basic Grammar and Writing

512

agree model EXPAND
order combine
Building Effective Sentences
513

How can I make my sentences flow more smoothly?

Writers often combine sentences to help their writing flow more smoothly. Too many short sentences can make writing sound choppy. Combining some sentences will add variety to your writing and improve your overall writing style.

Combine with a Series

You can combine sentences using a series of words, phrases, or clauses.

Combine with a Series

Short Sentences	Combined Using a Series of Words
The Mississippi River was carved by melting glaciers. The Missouri and Ohio rivers were carved by melting glaciers.	The Mississippi, Missouri, and Ohio rivers were carved by melting glaciers.

Short Sentences	Combined Using a Series of Words
The Pacific Northwest has many ecosystems. It is home to over 15 million people. It is a world leader in technology industries.	The Pacific Northwest has many ecosystems, is home to over 15 million people, and is a world leader in technology industries.

The items in any series must be alike (or parallel). For example, if the first item is a phrase, all the items must be phrases worded in the same way. (See page 559.) Use commas to separate items in a series.

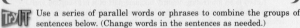 Use a series of parallel words or phrases to combine the groups of sentences below. (Change words in the sentences as needed.)

1. The Pacific Northwest was claimed by Russia and by Spain at different times in history. It was also claimed by Britain.
2. The Rocky Mountains are in the Pacific Northwest. The Cascade Range and the Coast Ranges are also there.
3. Visitors to Olympic National Park in Washington State can take pictures of snow-topped mountains. They can also relax on ocean beaches. They can hike in rain forests.
4. Tide pools at the park are a great place to view anemones. People can also see starfish in the tide pools. They can see sand dollars in the tide pools, too.

Combine with Phrases

You can combine sentences by using appositives (see 586.1) or prepositional phrases (see 742.1). An appositive is a word or phrase that comes after a noun or pronoun and renames it.

Combine Using an Appositive Phrase

Short Sentences	Combined Sentences
Sumo wrestling began as a religious ritual. It is Japan's national sport.	Sumo wrestling, Japan's national sport, began as a religious ritual.

Combine Using a Prepositional Phrase

Sumo wrestlers weigh as much as 265 kilograms. In pounds, that's about 580.	Sumo wrestlers weigh as much as 265 kilograms, or about 580 pounds.

 Combine each of the following sets of sentences by using the method given in parentheses.

Example: The wrestling ring is a circle. The ring has a diameter of about 15 feet. *(two prepositional phrases)*
The wrestling ring is a circle with a diameter of about 15 feet.

1. The wrestling ring is raised so spectators can better see. The wrestling ring is a clay platform. *(appositive phrase)*
2. The wrestlers wear silk robes. They wear the robes before their matches. *(prepositional phrase)*
3. One way to win is to pull or push an opponent. A wrestler tries to pull or push his opponent out of the ring. *(prepositional phrase)*
4. At any one time, there are from one to four yokozuna. *Yokozuna* is the Japanese word for grand champions. *(appositive phrase)*
5. A sumo tournament consists of either seven or fifteen bouts held over two weeks. A sumo tournament is properly called a "basho." *(appositive phrase)*

Write NOW **Write two sentences about a sport you enjoy. Use an appositive phrase in the first sentence. Use at least one prepositional phrase in the second sentence.**

Try It Answers

1. The Pacific Northwest was claimed by Russia, Spain, and Britain at different times in history.
2. The Rocky Mountains, the Cascade Range, and the Coast Range are in the Pacific Northwest.
3. Visitors to Olympic National Park in Washington State can take pictures of snow-topped mountains, relax on ocean beaches, or hike in rain forests.
4. Tide pools at the park are great places to view anemones, starfish, and sand dollars.

Try It Answers

1. The wrestling ring, a clay platform, is raised so spectators can better see.
2. The wrestlers wear silk robes before their matches.
3. One way to win is to pull or push an opponent out of the ring.
4. At any one time, there are from one to four *yokozuna*, the Japanese word for grand champions.
5. A sumo tournament, a "basho," consists of either seven or fifteen bouts held over two weeks.

Combine with Infinitive or Participial Phrases

You can combine short sentences by using infinitive phrases (see 730.4) or participial phrases (see 730.3).

Combine Using an Infinitive Phrase

Short Sentences	Combined Sentences
Gina interviewed her grandmother. She was interested in learning about her ancestors.	Gina interviewed her grandmother to learn about her ancestors.

Combine Using a Participial Phrase

Gina's ancestors hoped for a better future. They emigrated from Italy to New York State.	Hoping for a better future, Gina's ancestors emigrated from Italy to New York State.

 On your own paper, combine each of the following sets of short sentences using the method given in parentheses.

Example: Between 1884 and 1920, about 7 million Italians immigrated to the United States. They escaped poverty and malnutrition. *(infinitive phrase)*
Between 1884 and 1920, about 7 million Italians immigrated to the United States to escape poverty and malnutrition.

1. Gina's great-great-grandfather arrived in New York City in 1912. He was equipped with only a suitcase. *(participial phrase)*
2. Gina's great-great-grandfather settled in the Hudson Valley. He wanted a better life. *(participial phrase)*
3. Even today many immigrants come to the Hudson Valley. They can improve their lives. *(infinitive phrase)*
4. Jorge Garcia was urged to move by his uncle. Jorge Garcia came to the Hudson Valley from Mexico and now owns a restaurant. *(participial phrase)*
5. Gina is planning a trip to the Hudson Valley. She will see it for herself. *(infinitive phrase)*

Write NOW Write two sentences about your ancestors. Use an infinitive phrase in the first sentence. Use a participial phrase in the second sentence.

Combine with Relative Pronouns

You can also combine sentences by using a relative pronoun to connect a dependent clause to an independent clause. Relative pronouns include words such as *who, which, that, whose, whom,* and so on.

Combine with Relative Pronouns

Two Short Sentences	Combined Using a Relative Pronoun
George Washington has many places named after him. George Washington was our first president.	George Washington, who has many places named after him, was our first president.
	George Washington, who was our first president, has many places named after him.

 A dependent clause beginning with the relative pronoun *which* is always set off by commas. A dependent clause beginning with *who* or *whose* is also set off by commas if the dependent clause contains information that is not necessary to understand the independent clause.

 Combine each set of sentences below by using the relative pronoun in parentheses.

Example: In the United States, "Washington" is the name of seven counties. They range from New York to Oregon. *(which)*
In the United States, "Washington" is the name of seven counties, which range from New York to Oregon.

1. Amazingly, James Madison has twenty counties named for him. James Madison was our fourth president. *(who)*
2. John Adams was the second president. His home was in Braintree, Massachusetts. *(whose)*
3. Five of the first ten presidents were all from Virginia. They were born before the U.S. became a country. *(who)*
4. Schools help us honor them. These schools are named for presidents. *(that)*
5. I attend Jefferson Middle School. It holds the best science fair in our county. *(which)*

Write NOW Write freely about an adult you admire (a relative, a teacher, a coach). Explain places or organizations that could be named for this person. Afterward, underline any sentences containing relative pronouns. Also find two shorter sentences in your writing that you could combine using a relative pronoun.

Try It Answers

1. Equipped with only a suitcase, Gina's great-great-grandfather arrived in New York City in 1912.
2. Wanting a better life, Gina's great-great-grandfather settled in the Hudson Valley.
3. Even today many immigrants come to the Hudson Valley to improve their lives.
4. Urged to move by his uncle, Jorge Garcia came to the Hudson Valley from Mexico and now owns a restaurant.
5. Gina is planning a trip to the Hudson Valley to see it for herself.

Try It Possible Answers

1. Amazingly, James Madison, who was our fourth president, has twenty counties named for him.
2. John Adams, whose home was in Braintree, Massachusetts, was the second president.
3. Five of the first ten presidents, who were all from Virginia, were born before the U.S. became a country.
4. Schools that are named for presidents help us honor them.
5. I attend Jefferson Middle School, which holds the best science fair in our county.

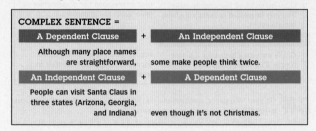
What can I do to add variety to my writing?

Varying sentence types can make your writing come alive. A good writer uses a variety of sentences to make writing clear and interesting.

Create Compound Sentences

A **compound sentence** is made up of two or more simple sentences (independent clauses) joined by a comma and a coordinating conjunction (*and, for, but, or, so, nor,* and *yet*) or by a semicolon. (See 590.2 and 594.1.)

> **Compound Sentence = Two Independent Clauses**
>
> **The Bay of Bengal has an area of 1,300,000 square miles,** and **it is the largest bay in the world.** (A comma and the conjunction *and* join the two independent clauses.)
>
> **Eight countries border the Bay of Bengal; its west coast is formed by India.** (A semicolon joins the two independent clauses.)

 On your own paper, join each of the following sets of sentences using either a comma and a coordinating conjunction or a semicolon.

Example: Ancient Greek and Roman traders sailed to the Bay of Bengal. "Modern" Europeans didn't discover the bay until the 1500s.
Ancient Greek and Roman traders sailed to the Bay of Bengal, but "modern" Europeans didn't discover the bay until the 1500s.

1. Approximately two million tons of fish are caught in the Bay of Bengal each year. The fishing industry is threatened by pollution.
2. One-fourth of the world's population lives in the countries bordering the bay. Seafood from the Bay of Bengal is very important.
3. Monsoons blow across the Bay of Bengal from the southwest in the summer. They blow from the northeast in the winter.
4. Monsoons are strong winds. They bring heavy rains.
5. Much of the country of Bangladesh is a fertile delta. Dangerous flooding there has killed many people.

 Write two compound sentences about a body of water that you know about. Make sure you punctuate your sentences correctly.

Develop Complex Sentences

When you join a dependent clause to an independent clause, you form a **complex sentence**. In complex sentences, relative pronouns and subordinating conjunctions are used to connect the dependent clause to the independent clause. Subordinating conjunctions include words such as *after, although, because, before, even though, until, when,* and *while.* (See page 744 for more subordinating conjunctions.)

> **COMPLEX SENTENCE =**
>
> | A Dependent Clause | + | An Independent Clause |
> |---|---|---|
> | Although many place names are straightforward, | | some make people think twice. |
>
> | An Independent Clause | + | A Dependent Clause |
> |---|---|---|
> | People can visit Santa Claus in three states (Arizona, Georgia, and Indiana) | | even though it's not Christmas. |

 Number your paper from 1 to 5. Then write the dependent clause in each of the following complex sentences. (Also see 698.2–698.3.)

Example: You'd better be careful of what you say if you visit Secret, Nevada.
if you visit Secret, Nevada

1. Until I traveled to Rhode Island, I didn't know there was a town named Common Fence Post.
2. After you visit the town of Brothers, Oregon, you should drive on to the town of Sisters, Oregon.
3. The Romans named the Canary Islands ("Island of the Dogs" in Latin) because they found wild dogs there.
4. Because its name is only one syllable long, Maine is unique among the states.
5. Enola, Oregon, might be a solitary place since its name comes from "alone" spelled backward.

 Write a short paragraph about your name. (How did you get it? How is it working for you? Or, what has happened to you because of that name?) When you finish, underline any complex sentences you use. Also try to find two shorter sentences that you could combine into a complex sentence.

Try It Possible Answers

1. Approximately two million tons of fish are caught in the Bay of Bengal each year, but the fishing industry is threatened by pollution.
2. One-fourth of the world's population lives in the countries bordering the bay, so seafood from the Bay of Bengal is very important.
3. Monsoons blow across the Bay of Bengal from the southwest in the summer; they blow from the northeast in the winter.
4. Monsoons are strong winds, and they bring heavy rains.
5. Much of the country of Bangladesh is a fertile delta, but dangerous flooding there has killed many people.

Try It Answers

1. Until I traveled to Rhode Island
2. After you visit the town of Brothers, Oregon
3. because they found wild dogs there
4. Because its name is only one syllable long
5. since its name comes from "alone" spelled backward

Use Questions and Commands

Writers add variety to their sentences by making statements, asking questions, giving commands, or showing strong emotion. See the chart below.

Kinds of Sentences			
Declarative .	Makes a statement about a person, a place, a thing, or an idea	The diameter of Mars is slightly more than half the diameter of Earth.	This is the most common kind of sentence.
Interrogative ?	Asks a question	Does Mars have any interesting physical features?	A question gets the reader's attention.
Imperative .	Gives a command or makes a strong request	Read about it and find out.	Commands or requests often appear in dialogue and directions.
Exclamatory !	Shows strong emotion or feeling	What an amazing place it is!	Use these sentences for occasional emphasis.

 On a piece of paper, write the numbers 1 to 9. Classify each of the sentences below by writing "D" for declarative, "INT" for interrogative, "IMP" for imperative, or "EX" for exclamatory. Then write the correct end punctuation.

1. Did you know that Mars has two main areas
2. They are the northern lowlands and the southern highlands
3. Study the information about lava flows in the northern lowlands
4. Wow, the southern highlands are almost four miles higher than the northern lowlands
5. In the south, the Hellas Basin is more than 5.5 miles deep
6. What a crater it must be
7. When can we visit
8. For now, just read about it
9. Instead, think of the Grand Canyon, which is "only" one mile deep

Write NOW Write four sentences—one of each kind—about an unusual place that you would like to visit. Be sure you punctuate your sentences correctly.

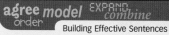
What can I do to add details to my sentences?
Expand with Prepositional Phrases

Writers add details to their sentences using prepositional phrases. These phrases function as adjectives or adverbs. *Remember:* A prepositional phrase begins with a preposition and ends with the object of a preposition. (See page **742** for a list of prepositions.)

- Prepositional phrases used as adjectives answer the questions *How many? Which one? What kind?*
- Prepositional phrases used as adverbs answer the questions *When? How? How often? How long? Where? How much?*

Prepositional Phrase	Function in Sentence
Centuries ago, settlers from Scotland and France settled Cape Breton Island.	The phrase *from Scotland and France* acts as an **adjective** to describe the noun *settlers*.
Cape Breton Island lies on Canada's eastern coast.	The phrase *on Canada's eastern coast* acts as an **adverb** to modify the verb *lies*.

 Write the 10 prepositional phrases that you find in sentences 1 to 6 below.

Example: The Cabot Trail winds along Cape Breton's mountainsides.
along Cape Breton's mountainsides

1. From the road, drivers can view the ocean.
2. People often see pods of whales along the coast.
3. Moose graze near lakes and streams.
4. Visitors take tours through a museum of French history.
5. Alexander Bell, the inventor of the telephone, settled in Cape Breton.
6. Though he traveled to many places, he said, "For simple beauty, Cape Breton outrivals them all."

Write NOW Use one or two prepositional phrases to add information to each of the sentences below.

1 I can imagine going through the mountains.
2 I'd see whales and eagles.
3 The sunset would be beautiful.

Answers

1. INT   ?
2. D   .
3. IMP   .
4. EX   !
5. D   .
6. EX   !
7. INT   ?
8. IMP   .
9. IMP   .

Answers

1. From the road
2. of whales, along the coast
3. near lakes and streams
4. through a museum, of French history
5. of the telephone, in Cape Breton
6. to many places, for simple beauty

Expand with Infinitive and Participial Phrases

Writers sometimes make their sentences more interesting by adding infinitive or participial phrases. (Also see 730.3 and 730.4.)

● An infinitive phrase consists of the word "to" plus the basic form of a verb plus any modifiers. An infinitive phrase can serve as a noun, an adjective, or an adverb.

● A participial phrase consists of a participle (a verb form usually ending in *ed* or *ing*) plus any modifiers. It serves as an adjective in a sentence.

Infinitive Phrases

To visit Death Valley **is a goal of mine.**
(The phrase serves as a noun—the subject of the sentence.)

Someday, I will have a chance to take this trip.
(The phrase serves as an adjective that modifies the noun *chance*.)

Many people travel to enjoy good weather.
(The phrase serves as an adverb that modifies the verb *travel*.)

Participial Phrases

Hearing about Death Valley, **I thought it would be an amazing place.**
(The *ing* phrase is an adjective that modifies the pronoun *I*.)

In Death Valley, recognized as one of earth's hottest places, **the temperature reaches 130 degrees Fahrenheit.**
(The *ed* phrase is an adjective that modifies the noun *Death Valley*.)

 There is one infinitive or participial phrase in each sentence below. Copy each phrase and label it "I" for infinitive or "P" for participial.

Example: To view all of Death Valley, you should climb Telescope Peak.
to view all of Death Valley, I

1. Earth scientists, having a deep understanding of geology, can "read" Death Valley's rocks.
2. Plants and animals living in the harsh conditions are amazing.
3. Somehow, prehistoric humans were able to survive there.
4. Borax, mined in Death Valley in the late 1800s, still exists there.
5. I can't wait to visit this amazing place in person.

How can I make my sentences more interesting?
Model Sentences

You can learn a great deal about writing by studying the sentences of other writers. When you come across sentences that you like, practice writing some of your own using the same pattern. This process is called *modeling*.

Professional Models

I walked along the Grand Canyon, gazing down into its rocky gorges and dizzyingly sheer cliffs.

Goats can go where wolves cannot, following routes that spiral down canyon walls.
—*National Geographic*

Student Models

I strolled down the beach, looking out across the crashing surf and foaming breakers.

My brothers slipped through the trapdoor of the fort, swinging down ladders that hung to the ground.

Guidelines for Modeling

● Find a sentence or a short passage that you like and write it down.
● Think of a topic for your practice writing.
● Follow the pattern of the sentence or passage as you write about your own subject. (You do not have to follow the model exactly.)
● Build each sentence one part at a time and check your work when you are finished. (Take your time.)
● Review your work and change any parts that seem confusing or unclear.
● Share your new sentences with your classmates.
● Find other sentences to model and keep practicing.

Write NOW On your own paper, model the following sentences. *Remember:* You do not have to follow a model sentence exactly.

1 I can tell you that when I spotted the slithery streak in the grass, my heart started to race, but my feet wouldn't move.

2 The children jumped up with surprise, broke into smiles, doubled over with laughter, and shouted for joy.

3 Although the heavy, wet snow soaked through their gloves, Tim and Matt continued building their fort.

 Answers

1. having a deep understanding of geology, P
2. living in the harsh conditions, P
3. to survive there, I
4. mined in Death Valley in the late 1800s, P
5. to visit this amazing place in person, I

Develop a Sentence Style

The following techniques and strategies will help you improve your writing style. (Also see page 42.)

Varying Sentence Beginnings

To add some variety to the common subject-verb pattern, try beginning a sentence with a phrase or a dependent clause.

One evening after sundown, **we drove in a buggy past old Dorset's house.**

—"The Ransom of Red Chief" by O. Henry

To judge by his face, **Dussel is dreaming of food.**

—*The Diary of a Young Girl* by Anne Frank

Moving Adjectives

Usually, you write adjectives before the nouns they modify. You can also emphasize adjectives by placing them after the nouns.

A long, low moan, indescribably sad**, swept over the moor.**

—*The Hound of the Baskervilles* by Sir Arthur Conan Doyle

Repeating a Word

You can repeat a word or phrase to emphasize a particular idea or feeling.

They could see **her cheeks going up and down,** they could see **the trickle of milk leaking out of one side of her mouth, but** they couldn't see **what she was thinking.**

—*The Fledgling* by Jane Langton

Creating a Balanced Sentence

You can write a sentence that uses parallel words, phrases, or clauses for emphasis.

Home! That was what they meant, those caressing appeals, those soft touches **wafted through the air,** those invisible little hands **pulling and tugging, all one way!**

—*The Wind in the Willows* by Kenneth Grahame

 Write NOW Study the sample sentences above. Then write your own sentences that follow each sample pattern. Share your sentences with your classmates.

Constructing Strong Paragraphs

What's the best way to build strong muscles? Most forms of exercise build muscle, but other factors are also important. Eating right, relaxing between workouts, and sleeping well help muscles develop.

What's the best way to build strong paragraphs? Starting with a well-written topic sentence is essential, but a paragraph doesn't stop there. The sentences in the body need to support the topic sentence and provide interesting and well-organized details. Last of all, the closing sentence should summarize or restate the topic. In the following chapter, you will exercise your brain by building strong paragraphs.

What's Ahead

You will learn about . . .

- the parts of a paragraph.
- types of paragraphs.
- writing effective paragraphs.
- adding details to paragraphs.
- gathering details.
- organizing your details.
- refining your details.
- turning paragraphs into essays.
- using a checklist.

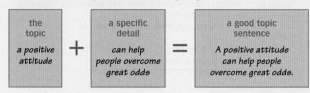

The Parts of a Paragraph

Most paragraphs have three main parts: a topic sentence, a body, and a closing sentence. Paragraphs usually begin with a **topic sentence** that tells what the paragraph is about. The sentences in the **body** share details about the topic, and the **closing sentence** brings the paragraph to a close.

Topic Sentence

Body

Closing Sentence

Attitude Is Everything

A positive attitude can help people overcome great odds. Walt Disney didn't let a learning disability stop him from creating the best-known amusement park in the world. Helen Keller's positive attitude helped her become the first person who was hearing-, sight-, and speech-impaired to earn a bachelor of arts degree. She went on to write many books and became one of America's greatest speakers. When the famous scientist Stephen Hawking was asked about having ALS, a serious muscular disease, he said, "I try to lead as normal a life as possible and not think about my condition or regret the things it prevents me from doing." That's a positive attitude in action! Whenever people face a difficult challenge, they should remember these individuals and the power of a positive attitude.

 Respond to the reading. How many examples of positive attitude are mentioned? What do they all have in common?

A Closer Look at the Parts
The Topic Sentence

The topic sentence tells the reader what a paragraph is going to be about. A good topic sentence (1) names the topic and (2) states a specific detail or a feeling about it. Here is a simple formula for writing a topic sentence.

the topic		a specific detail		a good topic sentence
a positive attitude	+	can help people overcome great odds	=	A positive attitude can help people overcome great odds.

The topic sentence is usually the first sentence in a paragraph, although sometimes it comes later. It guides the direction of the sentences in the rest of the paragraph.

A positive attitude can help people overcome great odds.

The Body

The sentences in the body of the paragraph include the details needed to understand the topic.

- **Use specific details to make your paragraph interesting.**
  The specific details below are shown in red.
  Walt Disney didn't let a learning disability stop him from creating the best-known amusement park in the world.
- **Organize your sentences in the best possible order.**
  Five common ways to organize sentences are chronological (time) order, order of location, order of importance, comparison-contrast order, and logical order. (See page 551.)

The Closing Sentence

The closing sentence comes after all the details in the body. It will often restate the topic or give the reader something to think about. In an essay, it can provide a transition into a following paragraph.

Whenever people face a difficult challenge, they should remember these individuals and the power of a positive attitude.

 Answers

Respond to the reading.

three
Each person had a positive attitude despite having a disability.

Types of Paragraphs

There are four basic types of paragraphs: *narrative, descriptive, expository,* and *persuasive*. Each type requires a different way of thinking and planning.

Write Narrative Paragraphs

In a **narrative paragraph**, you share a personal story or an important experience with the reader. The details in a narrative paragraph should answer the 5 W's *(who? what? when? where?* and *why?)*. A narrative is often organized according to time *(what happened first, next, then, finally)*.

Topic Sentence ·········

Body

Closing Sentence ·········

> ### Champions
>
> With only 15 seconds left on the clock, we needed a basket to win the Midwest Wheelchair Basketball Tournament. My teammates and I were racing toward our end of the court, and I had the ball. I scrambled between two guys and gave a strong push to the basket. Though my eyes were on all the players, my mind was on scoring. We'd worked too hard to get this far—we just had to win. When I was near the top of the key, I heard my coach yell, "Shoot it, Mo!" In one smooth motion, I squared up and let the ball fly. I remember thinking the shot was right on line, but the ball hit the back of the rim and went straight up into the air. Everyone tried to get in position under the basket. Then, just as the buzzer sounded, the ball slipped cleanly through the net. We had won the game 38-37, and the championship was ours.

 Respond to the reading. How does the closing sentence connect with the topic sentence? How is suspense built into the story?

 Write a narrative paragraph. Write a paragraph that tells about some memorable experience you've had. Make sure to answer the 5 W's.

Develop Descriptive Paragraphs

When you write a **descriptive paragraph**, you give a detailed picture of a person, a place, an object, or an event. Descriptive paragraphs include many sensory details (sight, sound, smell, taste, touch).

Topic Sentence ·········

Body

Closing Sentence ·········

> ### My Guide Dog
>
> I know my golden retriever Misha just about as well as I know myself. She has a firm, wide head with floppy ears that are covered with curly, silky fur. My hands slide down the top of her head and over her eyes, the eyes that see for me. Then I find her cold, damp nose and thick, smooth tongue. I can feel her warm breath on my hands. She wears a thick collar around her neck and a leather harness around her broad sides. Her silky fur ruffles in my fingers and smells like the outdoors. Her nails are stubby and hard, and her round toes are rough. Little tufts of fur, called feathers, stick out between her toes. When I hold Misha's paw, her tail thumps against the floor, almost like a greeting. Misha is an incredible dog, and I often wonder what my life would be like without her.

 Respond to the reading. How many of the five senses are covered in the paragraph? Which two or three details are especially descriptive?

 Write a descriptive paragraph. Write a paragraph that describes an animal. Use sensory details in your description.

BASIC ELEMENTS

 ## Answers

Respond to the reading.

Both the topic sentence and the closing sentence mention winning.

Suspense is built into the story by having the shot miss at first before going into the basket.

 ## Answers

Respond to the reading.

sound: tail thumps against floor
smell: fur smells like the outdoors
touch: curly, silky fur; cold, damp nose; smooth tongue; warm breath; fur ruffles in fingers; nails are stubby and hard

Answers will vary.

Construct Expository Paragraphs

In an **expository paragraph**, you share information. You can tell how to do something, give directions, or explain a subject. Transition words like *first, next, then,* and *finally* are often used in expository writing.

Topic Sentence · · · · · · · · ·

Body

Closing Sentence · · · · · · · · ·

> ### What Is a TDD?
>
> A telecommunications device for the deaf, or TDD, works like instant messaging on a computer. The TDD is made up of a keyboard, display screen, modem, and printer. First, the user types a message on the keyboard and then sends it to another TDD. When the message reaches its destination, it appears on the other user's display screen. The TDD does not ring like a regular telephone does. Instead, a flashing light tells the person at the other end that a message is waiting. Some TDD systems include a vibrating wristband to alert the person that a message has arrived. There are also message relay centers so that people using regular telephones can send messages to TDD's. Today, more than four million people in the United States have TDD's. This communication tool makes it easy for people with severe hearing disabilities to "reach out and touch somebody" with a message.

 Respond to the reading. What type of information about the topic is included in the paragraph? Think in terms of definitions, materials needed, and so on.

 Write an expository paragraph. Write a paragraph that explains a device, small appliance, or piece of equipment that you know well. Make sure to include different types of information.

Build Persuasive Paragraphs

In a **persuasive paragraph**, you share your opinion (or strong feeling) about a topic. To be persuasive, you must include plenty of reasons, facts, and details to support your opinion. Persuasive writing is usually organized by order of importance (as in the paragraph below) or by logical order.

Topic Sentence · · · · · · · · ·

Body

Closing Sentence · · · · · · · · ·

> ### Volunteer for Special Olympics
>
> Students at Parkwood Middle School should volunteer to help with the Special Olympics. First of all, volunteering for this worthy event will get students involved in the community. Over time, this involvement will help them become better citizens and neighbors. Secondly, working with these special athletes will allow students to put into practice what they have learned. Parkwood coaches have taught students a lot about sports and training, so it would be satisfying to share this knowledge with other athletes. Most importantly, volunteering will help students better understand and appreciate people with different abilities and gifts. As they work with these athletes, they will surely learn a lot from them, just as they will learn from the volunteers. There are plenty of things that students can do, from working with individual athletes to helping out at the local events. How they help out doesn't matter. What is important is that students volunteer their services and make the Special Olympics a rewarding experience for everyone involved.

 Respond to the reading. What is the writer's opinion in the paragraph? Name two or three reasons that support her opinion. When is the most important reason given?

 Write a persuasive paragraph. Write to promote a worthwhile cause. Include at least three strong reasons that support your opinion.

 ## Answers

Respond to the reading.

The paragraph presents information about what a TDD is and how it works. The paragraph also includes information about the equipment and about how many people use TDD's.

 ## Answers

Respond to the reading.

The writer's opinion is that students should volunteer to help with the Special Olympics. Her reasons include involvement in the community, the sharing of knowledge and skills, and a better understanding of and appreciation for people with different abilities. The most important reason is given last.

Writing Effective Paragraphs

Use the following general guidelines whenever you write paragraphs.

Prewriting Selecting a Topic and Details

■ Select a specific topic.
■ Collect facts, examples, and details about your topic.
■ Write a topic sentence that states what your paragraph
  is going to be about. (See page 525 for help.)
■ Decide on the best way to arrange your details.

Writing Creating the First Draft

■ Start your paragraph with the topic sentence.
■ Write sentences in the body that support your topic.
  Use the details you collected as a guide.
■ Connect your ideas and sentences with transitions.
■ End with a sentence that restates your topic, leaves the reader
  with a final thought, or (in an essay) leads into the next paragraph.

Revising Improving Your Writing

■ Add information if you need to say more about your topic.
■ Move sentences that aren't in the correct order.
■ Delete sentences that do not support the topic.
■ Rewrite any sentences that are not clear.

Editing Checking for Conventions

■ Check the revised version of your writing for capitalization,
  punctuation, grammar, and spelling errors.
■ Then write a neat final copy and proofread it.

When you write a paragraph, remember that readers want . . .
  ● original ideas. *(They want to learn something new and interesting.)*
  ● personality. *(They want to hear the writer's voice.)*

How can I find interesting details?

Every paragraph needs good supporting details. Some details will come from personal experience, especially when you are writing narrative and descriptive paragraphs. Other details will come from other sources of information, especially when you are writing expository and persuasive paragraphs.

Use Personal Details

Personal details are those that you gather by using your senses, your memory, or your imagination.

  ● **Sensory details** are things that you see, hear, smell, taste, and touch. (These details are important in descriptive paragraphs.)

      Then I find her cold, damp nose and thick, smooth tongue. I can feel her warm breath on my hands.

  ● **Memory details** are things you remember from experience. (These details are important in narrative paragraphs.)

      I remember thinking the shot was right on line, but the ball hit the back of the rim and went straight up into the air.

  ● **Reflective details** are things you wonder about, hope for, or imagine. (These details are often used in narrative and descriptive paragraphs.)

      Misha is an incredible dog, and I often wonder what my life would be like without her.

Use Other Sources of Details

To collect details from other sources, use the following tips.

1 **Talk with someone you know.** Parents, neighbors, friends, or teachers may know a lot about your topic.

2 **Write for information.** If you think a museum, a business, or a government office has information you need, send for it.

3 **Read about your topic.** Gather details from books, magazines, and newspapers.

4 **Use the Internet.** The quickest source of information is the Internet. Remember to check Internet sources carefully for reliability. (See page 374.)

BASIC ELEMENTS

532–533 Basic Grammar and Writing

532

organize *share* **explain** *tell*
describe

Constructing Strong Paragraphs

533

How do I know what kinds of details to gather?

The following tips will help you collect the right kinds of details for your paragraphs about people, places, objects, events, and definitions.

Writing About a Person

When writing about or describing a person, make sure you collect plenty of details that deal with his or her appearance and personality. The following guidelines will help.

Observe ■ If possible, carefully watch the person. Maybe the person laughs in a special way or wears a certain type of clothing.

Interview ■ Talk with your subject if you can. Write down words and phrases that the person uses.

Research ■ Use whatever sources are necessary—books, articles, the Internet—to find out more about this person.

Compare ■ Can your subject be compared to some other person?

Describe ■ List any physical characteristics and personality traits.

Writing About a Place

When describing or writing about a place, use details that help the reader understand why the place is important to you.

Observe ■ Study the place you plan to write about. Use photos, postcards, or videos if you can't observe the place in person.

Remember ■ Think of a story (or an anecdote) about this place.

Describe ■ Include the sights, sounds, and smells of the place.

Compare ■ Compare your place to other places.

Writing About an Object

When writing about an object, tell your reader what kind of object it is, what it looks like, how it is used, and why this object is important to you.

Observe ■ Think about these questions: How is it used? Who uses it? How does it work? What does the object look like?

Research ■ Learn about the object. Try to find out when it was first made and used. Ask other people about it.

Define ■ What class or category does this object fit into? (See "Writing a Definition" on the next page.)

Remember ■ Recall interesting stories about this object.

Writing About an Event

When writing about or describing an event, focus on the important actions or on one interesting part. Try to collect sensory details and details that answer the 5 W's. The following guidelines will help.

Observe ■ Study the event carefully. What sights, sounds, tastes, and smells come to mind? Listen to what people around you are saying.

Remember ■ When you write about something that has happened to you, recall as many details connected with the event as you can.

List ■ Answer the *who? what? when? where?* and *why?* questions for facts about the event.

Investigate ■ Read about the event and ask other people what they know about it.

Evaluate ■ Decide why the event is important to you.

Writing a Definition

When you write a definition, you need to think about three things.

● First put the **term** you are defining (*snowboard*) into a **class** or category of similar things (*ski-like board*).

● Then list special **characteristics** that make this object different from others in that class (*ridden downhill over snow*).

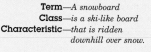

        Term—*A snowboard*
        Class—*is a ski-like board*
Characteristic—*that is ridden downhill over snow.*

BASIC ELEMENTS

What can I do to organize my details effectively?

After gathering your details, you need to organize them in the best possible way. You can organize a paragraph by *time, location, importance, comparison-contrast,* or *logical* order. Graphic organizers can help you keep your details in order.

Use Chronological Order

Chronological means "according to time." Transition words and phrases (*first, second, then,* and *finally*) are often used in narrative and expository paragraphs. A time line can help you organize details chronologically.

		Kwanzaa Time Line					
week before	Dec. 26	Dec. 27	Dec. 28	Dec. 29	Dec. 30	Dec. 31	Jan. 1
decorate house	each evening light a candle, discuss family unity and community theme, tell a story or sing, and exchange gifts					Karamu feast and dancing	faith in leaders

Topic Sentence

Body

Closing Sentence

Celebrating Kwanzaa

Kwanzaa is a seven-day festival that celebrates African American culture. The week before the celebration, family members decorate the home. A traditional symbol, a candleholder with seven candles, is placed on a straw mat. The candles symbolize the African Americans' struggles in the past and their hopes for the future. The celebration actually begins on the evening of December 26. Families gather, and a child lights a candle. Then the family members discuss unity of the family and the community. Next a story or song is used to illustrate the principle. Afterward, gifts may be exchanged. On each of the following four nights, this ceremony is repeated. Families discuss self-determination, community togetherness, economic cooperation, and purpose. On December 31, in addition to talking about creativity, a special feast called Karamu takes place. It features traditional food, music, and dancing. The last day of the celebration is spent discussing faith in other people, teachers, and leaders. After the seven days, the bonds of family, culture, and community have been reinforced.

 Respond to the reading. Is "Celebrating Kwanzaa" a narrative paragraph or an expository paragraph? How is time order used to organize this paragraph?

Use Order of Location

Often, you can organize descriptive details spatially, by order of location. For example, a description may move from left to right, from top to bottom, from one direction (north) to another (south), or from the whole to its parts. Words or phrases like *next to, before, above, below, east, west, north,* and *south* may be used to show location. A drawing or map can help you organize your details.

Topic Sentence

Body

Closing Sentence

Dancing Chinese Dragon

The grand finale of the San Francisco Chinese New Year's Parade is a giant dragon dancing down the street. As 600,000 firecrackers explode, a group of 100 people carries the 200-foot-long dragon. This special creation is made up of 29 sections of brightly colored silk and velvet. Underneath the layers of fabric, a bamboo frame supports the dragon. From head to tail, its skin is decorated with colored lights, white fur, and silver rivets. The dragon's enormous head is modeled after a camel's head. A set of curved deer horns rest on top. Between the head and the body is a serpent's slithery neck. The long, twisting body is covered in a rainbow of fish scales. The lower belly looks like the belly of a frog. A writhing, whiplike tail completes the dancing dragon. As the dragon passes, another new year begins.

 Respond to the reading. How are the details in this paragraph arranged—from left to right, from top to bottom, or in another order?

BASIC ELEMENTS

 ## Answers

Respond to the reading.

expository paragraph

The time order explains what occurs the week before the ceremony, on the first five days of the week-long festival, and on the two last days, in that order.

 ## Answers

Respond to the reading.

The sensory details in the paragraph are arranged from the dragon's head to its tail.

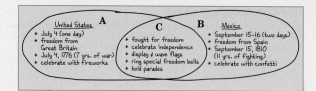

Use Order of Importance

Expository and persuasive paragraphs are often organized by order of importance—from *most* to *least* important, or from *least* to *most* important.

> Most important
> 1. _____
> 2. _____   or
> 3. _____
> Least important
>
> Least important
> 3. _____
> 2. _____
> 1. _____
> Most important

Topic Sentence

Ethnic Celebrations Connect People

Throughout the year, people in the United States honor and celebrate different ethnic groups. These celebrations, some lasting for an entire month, are important for many reasons. First of all, people have an opportunity to share their culture. Food is one way they can share. Pizza is Italian, egg rolls are Chinese, and so on. With these many celebrations, people have a chance to try more authentic ethnic foods such as beignets, fry bread, or pierogies.

Body

Helping ethnic groups gain a better understanding of each other is another reason for the celebrations. For example, during February, the country explores the contributions African Americans have made in science, politics, and entertainment. Most importantly, during these special times, young people get a chance to discover their own heritage. As members of different generations celebrate together, they share food, traditions, memories, and more. A bond is made that keeps each family's culture alive. As long as the celebrations continue, people will be able to appreciate the wonderful mix of cultures in this country.

Closing Sentence

 Respond to the reading. How are the details organized in this paragraph? On your own paper, list them in reverse order (most to least or least to most). Does one order seem to work better?

Use Comparison-Contrast Order

Expository paragraphs are often organized by comparison-contrast order, which shows how two subjects are both alike and different. A Venn diagram can be used to show differences (**A** and **B**) and similarities (**C**).

United States **A** — July 4 (one day) • freedom from Great Britain • July 4, 1776 (7 yrs. of war) • celebrate with fireworks

C — fought for freedom • celebrate independence • display & wave flags • ring special freedom bells • hold parades

B Mexico — September 15-16 (two days) • freedom from Spain • September 15, 1810 (11 yrs. of fighting) • celebrate with confetti

Topic Sentence

Two Independence Days

Both the United States and Mexico fought for their independence. July 4, 1776, marks the date when the United States declared its independence from Great Britain. It took seven years of fighting before freedom was won. Similarly, Mexico overcame Spain's control. On September 15, 1810, Father Hidalgo rang his church's bell as a signal for revolution. Mexico's battle for independence lasted 11 years. Although both countries honor freedom by celebrating their independence days, the celebrations vary slightly. Each July 4, people in the United States wave flags, hold parades, and watch fireworks. Many places have special events. For example, in Philadelphia, the Liberty Bell is rung. In Mexico, the fiesta begins on September 15, Independence Day Eve, when the Mexican president rings the same bell Father Hidalgo rang and shouts "viva Mexico, viva la independencia." Across Mexico, at the same time, people repeat the cry and throw confetti. The celebration continues through September 16 with flag-waving parades. No matter how the people celebrate, both countries enjoy the freedom that was won for them many years ago.

Body

Closing Sentence

 Respond to the reading. Find two body sentences that include similar details. What words show the comparison?

 Write a paragraph. Choose two festivals or holidays to compare. Use a Venn diagram to organize your details. Then write your paragraph.

 ## Answers

Respond to the reading.

The details in the paragraph are arranged from least to most important.

most to least important:
- Young people can discover their heritage.
- Ethnic groups can better understand each other.
- People can share their culture; one way is with food.

Answers

Respond to the reading.

Similarly, Mexico overcame Spain's control. (similarly)
Although both countries honor freedom by celebrating their independence days . . . (both)

How can I be sure all my details work well?
Create Unity in Your Writing

In a well-written paragraph, each detail tells something about the topic. If a detail does not tell something about the topic, it breaks the *unity* of the paragraph and should probably be cut.

The detail shown in blue in the following passage does not fit with the rest of the paragraph. It disrupts the unity and should be cut.

> **The Pittsburgh Pirates struggled during the 1960 World Series. During series play, the Pirates had only 27 runs compared to the New York Yankees' 55 runs. In addition, the Yankees hit the ball 91 times, while the Pirates could manage only 60 hits.** The Pirates were the first modern National League champions in 1901. **However, the Pirates were victorious in the seventh game and claimed the series title for 1960 because Bill Mazeroski hit a game-winning home run in the bottom of the ninth inning.**

 In the paragraph below, find three details (sentences) that *do not* support the topic sentence. Then read the paragraph aloud without those sentences. How does cutting those details affect the paragraph's unity?

1   Star baseball player Roberto Clemente was born in Puerto
2 Rico in 1934. Baseball is my favorite sport, too. At first, he played
3 amateur baseball in Puerto Rico. Then he signed on with the
4 Brooklyn Dodgers and played for their minor league team, the
5 Montreal Royals. I don't know much about how he did with that
6 team. However, he is most famous for the 18 years, 1955 through
7 1972, that he played with the Pittsburgh Pirates. By the way, the
8 Pirates are doing great this year. He played in two World Series,
9 won four batting titles and twelve Gold Glove awards, and was
10 once voted most valuable player. Roberto was also a humanitarian.
11 In 1972, he was on a plane carrying supplies to help people who
12 had been in an earthquake in Nicaragua. The plane crashed, and
13 Clemente died at the age of 38. Today he is remembered as a
14 great athlete and the first Latino to be inducted into the National
15 Baseball Hall of Fame.

 Look at your paragraph. Study the comparison-contrast paragraph you wrote (page 537). Do all your details support your topic? Would the unity of your paragraph be improved if you cut a detail or two?

Develop Coherence from Start to Finish

An effective paragraph reads smoothly and clearly. When all the details in a paragraph are tied together well, the paragraph has *coherence* and is easy for the reader to follow. Transitions help make your writing smooth and coherent.

 Number your paper from 1 to 6. Use the transitions from the following list to help tie the paragraph below together. (Use each transition only once.) Then reread the paragraph. Does it read smoothly? If not, switch some transitions.

between	after	when	until	before	finally

The Underground Railroad was made up of people who

helped slaves escape from the South to the North before the

Civil War. _____ escaping from a slaveholder, slaves often
      (1)

traveled by foot, usually at night, _____ they came to a
             (2)

"station." A station was a house or business owned by someone

willing to help the slaves escape. The slaves rested and hid

there _____ moving on. Then the next "stationmaster" was
    (3)

alerted that people were coming. Once they were safe, the

slaves were given food and clothing for their journey. _____
               (4)

it was safe, slaves moved from station to station with the help

of the stationmasters. _____ , they crossed the border to
        (5)

freedom in the North. _____ 1810 and 1850, approximately
       (6)

100,000 slaves escaped to start new lives as free persons. Many

of them used the Underground Railroad.

 Read your paragraph. Read your comparison-contrast paragraph from page 537. Underline any parts that don't flow smoothly. Then use transitions to make the writing smoother. (See pages 572–573.)

BASIC ELEMENTS

Baseball is my favorite sport, too.
I don't know much about how he did with that team.
By the way, the Pirates are doing great this year.

Cutting these sentences (details) improves the paragraph's unity.

1. After
2. until
3. before
4. When
5. Finally
6. Between

How can I write essays containing strong paragraphs?

Use an Essay Plan

Writing an essay is not simply a matter of putting together a group of paragraphs. To begin with, each paragraph needs to be well written and well organized. Then follow the guidelines listed below.

1 Plan the organization.

Organize your essay in a way that fits your topic—chronological order, order of importance, order of location, and so on.

2 State the topic and focus in the first paragraph.

Begin with an interesting fact or example to catch the reader's attention. Then tell what your essay is about in a focus or thesis statement. This statement should identify the topic and a main idea or feeling about it.

3 Develop your writing idea in the middle paragraphs.

Use each paragraph in the body of your essay to explain and support one part of your focus statement. Each paragraph must have a topic sentence followed with supporting details.

4 Finish with a strong ending.

The final paragraph is usually a review of the main points in the essay. Your ending may emphasize the importance of the topic or may leave the reader with something to think about.

5 Use transition words or phrases to connect paragraphs.

For a complete list of transitions, see pages 572–573.

A paragraph has . . .	An essay has . . .
a topic sentence.	a thesis or focus statement.
sentences that support the topic sentence.	middle paragraphs that support the focus.
a closing sentence.	an ending paragraph.

How do I know if I have a strong paragraph?

Use a Paragraph Checklist

You'll know that you have a strong paragraph if it gives the reader complete information on a specific topic. One sentence should identify the topic, and the other sentences should support it. Use the checklist below to help you plan and write effective paragraphs.

Ideas
_____ **1.** Do I focus on an interesting idea?
_____ **2.** Do I use enough specific details?

Organization
_____ **3.** Is my topic sentence clear?
_____ **4.** Have I organized the details in the best order?

Voice
_____ **5.** Do I show interest in—and knowledge of—my topic?
_____ **6.** Does my voice fit my audience? My purpose? My topic?

Word Choice
_____ **7.** Do I use specific nouns and active verbs?
_____ **8.** Do I use specific adjectives and adverbs?

Sentence Fluency
_____ **9.** Have I written clear and complete sentences?
_____ **10.** Do I use a variety of sentence beginnings and lengths?

Conventions
_____ **11.** Do I use correct punctuation and capitalization?
_____ **12.** Do I use correct spelling and grammar?

improve
support

A Writer's Resource

organize
REFERENCE
select

A Writer's Resource

Writing is a complex job. Sometimes even experienced authors have trouble knowing what to write about, where to start, or how to sound interesting. Although practice certainly helps a writer become more skillful and self-confident, everyone needs a little help once in a while.

"A Writer's Resource" contains information, tips, and guidelines to get you through your writing problems. You'll find strategies for selecting topics, ways to improve your style, and ideas on techniques to enrich your writing.

What's Ahead

You will learn how to . . .

- find topics and get started.
- collect and organize details.
- write terrific topic sentences.
- use new forms and techniques.
- improve your voice and writing style.
- increase your vocabulary.
- improve your sentences.
- improve your presentation.

How can I find the best topics to write about?

Try a Topic-Selecting Strategy

A distinguished writer once said, "There are few experiences quite so satisfactory as getting a good writing idea." This may be overstating it a little, but getting a good writing idea is certainly an important step in the writing process. Let's say, for example, you are asked to write an essay about a controversial issue in your school or community. Your first job would be to select a specific topic to write about.

> **General Subject Area:** school or community controversy
>
> **Specific Writing Topic:** new auditorium

The following strategies will help you select interesting topics that you can feel good about.

Clustering Begin a cluster (also called a web) by selecting a key word that is related to your writing assignment. Write the key word in the middle of your paper and cluster related words around it. (See page 264.)

Journal Writing Write on a regular basis in a personal journal, recording your thoughts and experiences. Review your entries from time to time and underline ideas that you would like to write more about later, as in the model below. (See also pages 431–434.)

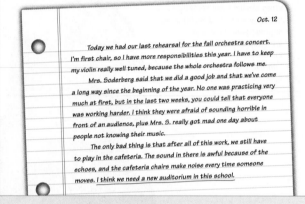

Oct. 12

Today we had our last rehearsal for the fall orchestra concert. I'm first chair, so I have more responsibilities this year. I have to keep my violin really well tuned, because the whole orchestra follows me.

Mrs. Soderberg said that we did a good job and that we've come a long way since the beginning of the year. No one was practicing very much at first, but in the last two weeks, you could tell that everyone was working harder. I think they were afraid of sounding horrible in front of an audience, plus Mrs. S. really got mad one day about people not knowing their music.

The only bad thing is that after all of this work, we still have to play in the cafeteria. The sound in there is awful because of the echoes, and the cafeteria chairs make noise every time someone moves. I think we need a new auditorium in this school.

Listing Write your general subject at the top of your paper and list related ideas as they come to mind. Keep your list going as long as you can. Then look for words in your list that you feel would make good writing topics.

Freewriting Write nonstop for 5 to 10 minutes to discover possible writing ideas. Begin writing with a particular subject or idea in mind (one related to the writing assignment). Underline the ideas that might work as topics for your assignment.

Sentence Starters Complete an open-ended sentence in as many ways as you can. Try to word your sentence so that it leads you to a topic you can use for your writing assignment.

People disagree about . . .	I learned a lesson when . . .
This community should . . .	My favorite experience was . . .
There are differences between . . .	It would be interesting to meet . . .

Review the "Basics of Life" List

The words listed below name many of the categories or groups of things that people need in order to live a full life. The list provides an endless variety of possibilities for topics. Consider the first category, food. You could write about . . .

- the most unusual meal you've ever eaten,
- what's good for you and what's not, or
- the first time you tried to cook something.

food	senses	rules/laws
work/occupation	machines	tools/utensils
clothing	intelligence	heat/fuel
faith/religion	history/records	natural resources
communication	agriculture	personality/identity
exercise	land/property	recreation/hobbies
education	community	trade/money
family	science	literature/books
friends	plants/vegetation	health/medicine
purpose/goals	freedom/rights	art/music
love	energy	

Selecting Ideas **546-547**

546

organize
select support improve

A Writer's Resource

547

What can I do to get started?

Use a List of Writing Topics

The writing prompts listed below and the sample topics listed on the next page provide plenty of starting points for writing assignments.

Writing Prompts

Every day is full of experiences that make you think. You do things that you feel good about. You hear things that make you angry. You wonder how different things work. You are reminded of a past experience. These common, everyday thoughts can make excellent prompts for writing.

Describe (Descriptive)
An influential person
Your favorite celebrity
A solar eclipse
Hermit crabs
Life before television

Tell Your Story (Narrative)
Learning something about life
Overcoming a challenge
Meeting an unusual person
Visiting a special place
A sudden revelation
The perfect day
Facing a disappointment
A surprise

Classify (Expository)
Clothing styles
Scooters
Extreme sports
Types of pets
Constellations
Kinds of diets
Birds of prey

Compare-Contrast (Expository)
Soccer and football
Living in a small town/large city
Two seasons
Heroes and celebrities
Fashions now and twenty years ago
Jobs and professions

Defend (Persuasive)
Starting school later in the morning
Eating wisely and exercising
Service learning
Individuality
Sports in school
A worthwhile cause

Respond to . . .
(Response to Literature)
A book that made you think
A poem that explained something
A character you identify with
The biography of someone
  you admire

Research (Report)
Aquifers, hot springs, glaciers
Oil wells, salt mines
Mud slides, forest fires

Sample Topics

You come across many people, places, experiences, and things every day that could be topics for writing. A number of possible topics are listed below for descriptive, narrative, expository, and persuasive writing.

Descriptive

People: best friend, favorite relative, personal idol, great leader, person you're comfortable with, someone who overcomes difficulty, teacher, coach, brother or sister

Places: hangout, garage, room, rooftop, historical place, zoo, park, hallway, barn, bayou, lake, cupboard, yard, empty lot, alley, valley, campsite, river, city street

Things: billboard, poster, video game, cell phone, bus, boat, gift, drawing, rainbow, doll, junk drawer, flood, mascot, movie

Animals: dolphin, elephant, snake, armadillo, eagle, deer, toad, spoonbill, squirrel, pigeon, pet, coyote, catfish, octopus, beaver, turtle

Narrative

moving to a new home, scoring a goal in a game, making a new friend, losing a pet, going to camp, learning a skill or sport, traveling to an interesting place

Expository

Classification: animal camouflage, natural disasters, kinds of music, types of government, religious beliefs, scientific principles, fads

Comparison-Contrast: friends, places, jobs, teachers, pets, transportation, a house cat and a lion, lakes and oceans

The causes of . . . sunburn, acne, hiccups, tornadoes, school dropouts, computer viruses, arguments

Kinds of . . . crowds, friends, commercials, dreams, neighbors, pain, clouds, joy, stereos, heroes, chores, homework, frustration

Persuasive

Community: building a skate park, beautifying the city, losing a local movie theater, opening a teen center, building sidewalks, building a superstore on the edge of town

School: assigning less homework, air-conditioning classrooms, providing more computers and printers, changing the school mascot, starting a school drama department

How can I collect details for my writing?

Try Graphic Organizers

Graphic organizers can help you gather and organize your details for writing. Clustering is one method. (See page 264.) These two pages list other useful organizers.

Cause-Effect Organizer

Use to collect and organize details for cause-effect essays.

Subject:

Causes	Effects
•	•
•	•
•	•
•	•
•	•

Problem-Solution Web

Use to map out problem-solution essays.

Time Line (Step-by-Step)

Use to collect details for personal narratives and how-to essays.

Subject:

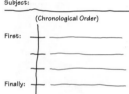

Before-After Chart

Use to collect details for narratives or expository essays.

Venn Diagram

Use to collect details to compare and contrast two subjects.

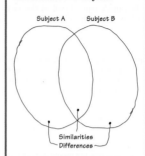

Process Chain (5-Step)

Use to collect details for science-related writing, such as how a process or cycle works.

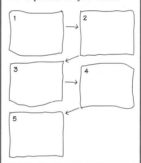

5 W's Chart

Use to collect the *Who? What? When? Where?* and *Why?* details for personal narratives and news stories.

Subject:

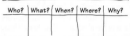

Who?	What?	When?	Where?	Why?

Line Diagram

Use to collect and organize details for classification or other expository essays.

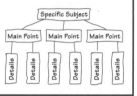

Sensory Chart

Use to collect details for descriptive essays and observation reports.

Subject:

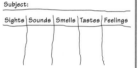

Sights	Sounds	Smells	Tastes	Feelings

RESOURCE

What can I do to organize my details better?

Make Lists and Outlines

List Your Details

You can use a variety of ways to organize details as you prepare to write an essay or a report. For most writing, you can make a simple list.

> The importance of salt
> – wars fought over it
> – used for money
> – helps keep us alive
> – preserves food
> – softens water
> – used to make chemicals
> – melts ice on roads
>
> How Detroit salt bed formed
> – seawater flooded the area
> – seawater evaporated, leaving salt
> – layer 400 to 1,600 feet thick
> – covered by layers of silt

Outline Your Information

After gathering facts and details, select two or three main points that best support your focus. Write an outline to organize your information.

> I. Salt is much more important than most people realize.
>   A. Wars have been fought over it.
>   B. In ancient China, salt coins were used for money.
>   C. In the human body, salt carries electrical signals that keep a person alive.
>   D. Salt is used to preserve meat and fish and to tan leather.
>   E. Salt is also used to make chemicals.
> II. Scientists say that the Detroit mine digs into a bed of salt that is several hundred million years old.
>   A. From 600 million to 230 million years ago, seawater flooded the middle of North America many times.
>   B. As the sun and wind evaporated the water . . .

Use Patterns of Organization

- **Chronological (Time) Order** or **Step-by-Step** You can arrange your details in the order in which they happen *(first, then, next)*. Use these patterns for narratives, history reports, and explaining a process. (See page 534.)

  > In 1896, the Detroit salt mine was started in order to dig the salt out of the ground. It began as a shaft 1,200 feet deep and about 6 feet wide. At first, the salt was used mainly for storing meat and fish and for making . . .

- **Order of Location** You can arrange details in the order in which they are located *(above, below, beside,* and so on). Use order of location for descriptions, explanations, and directions. (See page 535.)

  > Rosa and her once-white jumpsuit look like the paint-chip aisle at the hardware store—splattered with color from the top of her head to the toes of her now rainbow-colored canvas shoes.

- **Order of Importance** You can arrange details from the most important to the least—or from the least important to the most. Persuasive and expository essays are often organized this way. (See page 536.)

  > First of all, an open study hall would let hardworking students go where they need to go to get more work done. . . . Secondly, an open study hall would motivate students to take study hall more seriously. . . . Most importantly, open study hall would teach responsibility.

- **Comparison-Contrast** You can write about two or more subjects by showing how they are alike and how they are different. Compare each subject separately or compare both, point by point, as in the example below. (See page 537.)

  > The same juice comes in two different packages. Which is cheaper, a 12-pack of cans that costs $3.95 or a 6-pack of bottles that costs $2.50? The cans contain 12 ounces each, and the bottles are 16.9 ounces. Dividing the cost of each package by its total number of ounces indicates that the juice in the 12-pack is .027 cents per ounce, and the juice in the 6-pack is .025 cents per ounce. The 6-pack is a better deal.

- **Logical Order** You can organize information by beginning with a main idea followed by details, or by starting with details and leading up to the main point.

  > Studies show that by eating fewer calories people can lose weight. They can also lose weight by increasing how much they exercise. However, if people eat less and exercise more, they will lose more weight and keep it off longer. Combining these methods of losing weight makes sense.

How can I write terrific topic sentences?

Try Eight Special Strategies

Writing a good topic sentence is a key to writing a great paragraph. A good topic sentence names the topic and states a specific feeling about it. Use the following strategies the next time you need to write a terrific topic sentence. (Also see page 525.)

Use a Number

Topic sentences can use number words to tell what the paragraph will be about.

> Several **problems need to be looked at more carefully.**

> **I have** three **pet peeves that drive me crazy.**

Number Words		
two	a couple	a pair
few	three	a number
several	four	many
a variety	five	a list

Create a List

A topic sentence can list the things the paragraph will talk about.

> **Squeaky had to** take care of her brother **and** train for the race **at the same time.**

> Heat, light, **and** moisture **can affect a plant's growth.**

Start with "To" and a Verb

A topic sentence that starts with "to" and a verb helps the reader know why the information in the paragraph is important.

> To identify **the theme in a story, consider the thoughts and actions of the main character.**

> To persuade **others to change their minds, you have to make a convincing argument.**

Use Word Pairs

Word pairs or correlative conjunctions that come in pairs can help organize a topic sentence.

> Whether **you're the best player on the team** or **just average, you need to practice hard.**

> Both **fables** and **folktales are entertaining, but fables are more likely to teach a lesson.**

Word Pairs
if . . . then
either . . . or
not only . . . but also
both . . . and
whether . . . or
as . . . so

Join Two Ideas

A topic sentence can combine two equal ideas (in independent clauses) by using a comma and a coordinating conjunction: *and, but, or, for, so, nor, yet.*

> **Living in a small town sounds peaceful,** but **I think I would miss the excitement of the city.**

> **Some fashions seem to come around every 10 or 20 years,** so **you can't really say that clothing stores always have new clothes, can you?**

Use a "Why-What" Word

A "why-what" word is a subordinating conjunction that shows how ideas are connected.

> Before **you tell a story, think about the main point that you want to make.**

> Since **we're trying to beautify the city, could we do something about the weeds along the highways?**

"Why-What" Words	
So that	Once
Before	Since
Until	Whenever
Because	While
If	As long as
As	After
In order that	When

Use a "Yes, But" Word

A "yes, but" word is a subordinating conjunction that tells how two ideas are different.

> Instead of **discouraging strip malls, we should be sure that any new ones are well designed.**

> **Some people think that it's all right to lie** unless **the lie hurts someone.**

"Yes, But" Words
Although
Even though
Even if
Unless
Whether
Whereas

Quote an Expert

Sometimes the best way to start a paragraph is to quote someone who knows about your topic.

> **Even though I dislike football practice, I think Joe Paterno was right when he said,** "The will to win is important, but the will to prepare is vital."

> **Helen Keller's statement** "Keep your face to the sunshine and you cannot see the shadow" **is a good way to define optimism.**

What other forms can I use for my writing?

Try These Forms of Writing

Finding the right *form* for your writing is just as important as finding the right topic. When you are selecting a form, be sure to ask yourself who you're writing for (your audience) and why you're writing (your purpose).

Anecdote	A brief story that makes a point
Autobiography	A writer's story of his or her own life
Biography	A writer's story of some other person's life
Book review	A brief essay giving a response or an opinion about a book (See pages 287–322.)
Character sketch	Writing that describes a specific character in a story
Composition	A longer piece of writing, such as a story or an essay
Descriptive writing	Writing that uses details to help the reader clearly imagine a certain person, a place, a thing, or an idea (See pages 71–91.)
Editorial	Newspaper letter or article giving an opinion
Essay	A piece of writing in which ideas are presented, explained, argued, or described in an interesting way
Expository writing	Writing that explains by presenting the steps, the causes, or the kinds of something (See pages 157–217.)
Fable	A short story that often uses talking animals as the main characters and teaches a lesson or moral
Fantasy	A story set in an imaginary world in which the characters usually have supernatural powers or abilities
Freewriting	Writing whatever comes to mind about any topic
Historical fiction	A made-up story based on something real in history in which fact is mixed with fiction
Myth	A traditional story intended to explain a mystery of nature, religion, or culture
Narrative	Writing that relates an event, an experience, or a story (See pages 93–155.)

Novel	A book-length story with several characters and a well-developed plot
Personal narrative	Writing that shares an event or experience from the writer's personal life (See pages 93–142.)
Persuasive writing	Writing that is meant to persuade the reader to agree with the writer about someone or something (See pages 219–281.)
Play	A form that uses dialogue to tell a story and is meant to be performed in front of an audience
Poem	Writing that uses rhythm, rhyme, and imagery (See pages 353–361.)
Proposal	Writing that includes specific information about an idea or a project that is being considered for approval
Research report	An essay that shares information on a topic that has been researched well and organized carefully (See pages 379–410.)
Response to literature	Writing that is a summary or a reaction to something the writer has read (novel, short story, poem, article, and so on)
Science fiction	Writing based on real or imaginary science and often set in the future
Short story	A short piece of literature with only a few characters and one problem or conflict (See pages 343–349.)
Summary	Writing that presents only the most important ideas from a longer piece of writing (See pages 375–378.)
Tall tale	A humorous, exaggerated story (often based on the life of a real person) about a character or animal who does impossible things
Tragedy	Literature in which the hero is destroyed because of some serious flaw or defect in his or her character

How can I create a voice in my writing?

You can create a strong writing voice by using dialogue and by "showing instead of telling."

Use Dialogue

Each person you write about has a unique way of saying things, and well-written dialogue lets the reader *hear* the speaker's personality and thoughts. For example, notice how the message below can be spoken in several different ways.

Message: The family trip to the Grand Canyon was fun.

Speaker 1: **"The whole thing was boring until we got to ride the donkeys."**

Speaker 2: **"The view was certainly beautiful and peaceful, but those people were standing too close to the edge."**

Speaker 3: **"Wasn't the Grand Canyon great? Now, if we skip lunch, we can make it to Zion Canyon this afternoon."**

Each of the speakers above delivers the same message in a unique way. The dialogue tells as much about the speaker as it does about the topic.

One way to improve your dialogue is to think about the speaker and his or her personality. Look at the three personality webs below and try to decide which one is *Speaker 1, Speaker 2,* or *Speaker 3* from above. How does the dialogue show their personalities?

pleasant   worrying
Grace
old-fashioned

young
Jake
active   daring

impatient   in charge
Lucius
middle-aged

Tips for Punctuating Dialogue

- Indent every time a different person speaks.
- Put the exact words of a speaker in quotation marks.
- Set off the quoted words from the rest of the sentence by using a comma.
- At the end of quoted words, put a period or comma inside the quotation marks.

For more information and examples on how to punctuate dialogue, see 588.1, 598.1, and 600.1 in the "Proofreader's Guide."

Show, Don't Tell

When you tell someone that a movie is "good" or that the weather was "awful," what have you really told that person? Not much. If you really want to get your idea across, you have to *show* the details so that your reader experiences what you're describing. Notice the difference in the accounts below.

Telling: **It was really hot riding across the desert on the back of Dad's motorcycle, so we went to a movie in Phoenix.**

Showing: Before Dad and I started on our trip through the Southwest, I thought that riding on a motorcycle would cool us off. I was wrong. It was so hot and dry in the desert that we baked. The sun beat down from above, the heat radiated up from the pavement, and the engine temperature surrounded us like an oven on wheels. Our lips were burning, and our eyes got dry. One day we just stopped at a Phoenix movie theater and "chilled" all afternoon.

The sentence above *tells* the reader that the motorcycle ride was "really hot." The paragraph *shows* why the writer and his father needed to "chill."

Key Strategies for Showing

Next time you realize your writing is telling rather than showing, try one of these strategies.

- **Add sensory details.** Include sights, sounds, smells, tastes, and touch sensations. That way the reader can "experience" the event.

  Telling: **My little brother had trouble with his ice-cream cone.**

  Showing: The blast of hot air went to work on my little brother's chocolate-swirl ice-cream cone. Little streams began to drip off the rim. Jimmy licked at the sweet, sticky liquid, but he couldn't keep up, and the chocolate goo ran down his arm. As he tried to lick his arm, the ice cream tumbled out of the cone onto the sidewalk.

- **Explain body language.** Write about facial expressions and the way people stand, gesture, and move.

  Telling: **Aunt Elsa was glad to see me.**

  Showing: When I walked into the room, Aunt Elsa grinned, jumped out of her chair, and ran over to hug me.

- **Use dialogue.** Let the people in your writing speak for themselves.

  Telling: **Latrell was happy about his test.**

  Showing: Latrell gave me a high five, shouting, "Getting an A on my science test is the greatest thing I've done all year!"

Creating Voice **558-559**

558

organize
select support REFERENCE improve
A Writer's Resource

569

What can I do to improve my writing style?

Learn Some Writing Techniques

Writers put special effects into their stories and essays in different ways. Look over the following writing techniques and then experiment with some of them in your own writing.

Analogy
A comparison of similar objects to help clarify one of the objects
> Personal journals are like photograph albums. They both share personal details and tell a story.

Anecdote
A brief story used to illustrate or make a point
> Abe Lincoln walked two miles to return several pennies he had overcharged a customer. (This anecdote shows Lincoln's honesty.)

Exaggeration
An overstatement or a stretching of the truth used to make a point or paint a clearer picture (See *overstatement*.)
> After getting home from summer camp, I slept for a month.

Foreshadowing
Hints or clues that a writer uses to suggest what will happen next in a story
> Halfway home, Sarah wondered whether she had locked her locker.

Irony
A technique that uses a word or phrase to mean the opposite of its normal meaning
> Marshall just loves cleaning his room.

Local color
The use of details that are common in a certain place or local area (A story taking place on a seacoast would contain details about the water and the life and people near it.)
> Everybody wore flannel shirts to the Friday fish fry.

Metaphor
A figure of speech that compares two things without using the word *like* or *as* (See page 360.)
> In our community, high school football is king.

Overstatement
An exaggeration or a stretching of the truth (See *exaggeration*.)
> When he saw my grades, my dad hit the roof.

---

phobia *[fear]*
acrophobia (a fear of high places)
agoraphobia (a fear of public, open places)

phon *[sound]*
phonics (related to sounds)
symphony (sounds made together)

photo *[light]*
photo-essay (a story told mainly with photographs)
photograph (picture made using light rays)

pop *[people]*
population (number of people in an area)
populous (full of people)

port *[carry]*
export (to carry out)
portable (able to be carried)

psych *[mind, soul]*
psychiatry (the study of the mind)
psychology (science of mind and behavior)

sci *[know]*
conscious (being aware)
omniscient (knowing everything)

scope *[instrument for viewing]*
kaleidoscope (instrument for viewing patterns and shapes)
periscope (instrument used to see above the water)

scrib, script *[write]*
manuscript (something written by hand)
scribble (to write quickly)

spec *[look]*
inspect (to look at carefully)
specimen (an example to look at)

spir *[breath]*
expire (to breathe out; die)
inspire (to breathe into; give life to)

tele *[over a long distance; far]*
telephone (machine used to speak to people over a distance)
telescope (machine used to see things that are very faraway)

tempo *[time]*
contemporary (from the current time period)
temporary (lasting for a short time)

tend, tens *[stretch, strain]*
extend (to stretch and make longer)
tension (stretching something tight)

terra *[earth]*
terrain (the earth or ground)
terrestrial (relating to the earth)

therm *[heat]*
thermal (related to heat)
thermostat (a device for controlling heat)

tom *[cut]*
anatomy (the science of cutting apart plants and animals for study)
atom (a particle that cannot be cut or divided)

tract *[draw, pull]*
traction (the act of pulling)
tractor (a machine for pulling)

typ *[print]*
prototype (the first printing or model)
typo (a printing error)

vac *[empty]*
vacant (empty)
vacuum (an empty space)

vid, vis *[see]*
supervise (to oversee or watch over)
videotape (record on tape for viewing)

vor *[eat]*
carnivorous (flesh-eating)
herbivorous (plant-eating)

zoo *[animal or animals]*
zoo (a place where animals are kept)
zoology (the study of animal life)

How can I expand my writing vocabulary?

Study Writing Terms

This glossary includes terms used to describe the parts of the writing process. It also includes terms that explain special ways of stating an idea.

Antonym	A word that means the opposite of another word: *happy* and *sad; large* and *small* (See page 563.)
Audience	The people who read or hear what has been written
Body	The main or middle part in a piece of writing that comes between the *beginning* and the *ending* and includes the main points
Brainstorming	Collecting ideas by thinking freely about all the possibilities
Closing	The ending or final part in a piece of writing (In a paragraph, the closing is the last sentence. In an essay or a report, the closing is the final paragraph.)
Coherence	Tying ideas together in your writing (See page 539.)
Connotation	The "feeling" a word suggests (See page 106 and 488.)
Denotation	The dictionary meaning of a word
Dialogue	Written conversation between two or more people
Figurative language	Special comparisons, often called figures of speech, that make your writing more creative (See page 360.)
Focus statement	The statement that tells what specific part of a topic is written about in an essay (See *thesis statement* and page 393.)
Form	A type of writing or the way a piece of writing is put together (See pages 554–555.)
Grammar	The structure of language; the rules and guidelines that you follow in order to speak and write acceptably
Jargon	The special language of a certain group, occupation, or field **Computer jargon: byte digital upload**
Journal	A notebook for writing down thoughts, experiences, ideas, and information (See pages 431–434.)

Limiting the subject	Taking a general subject and narrowing it down to a specific topic General subject → sports → golf → golf skills → putting Specific topic
Modifiers	Words, phrases, or clauses that describe another word Our black **cat** slowly **stretched and** then **leaped** onto the wicker chair. (Without the blue modifiers, all we know is that a "cat stretched and leaped.")
Point of view	The angle from which a story is told (See page 352.)
Purpose	The specific reason that a person has for writing **to describe to narrate to persuade to explain**
Style	How an author writes (choice of words and sentences)
Supporting details	Facts or ideas used to tell a story, explain a topic, describe something, or prove a point
Synonym	A word that means the same thing as another word (*dog* and *canine*) (See page 563.)
Theme	The main point, message, or lesson in a piece of writing
Thesis statement	A statement that gives the main idea of an essay (See *focus statement.*)
Tone	A writer's attitude toward his or her subject **serious humorous sarcastic**
Topic	The specific subject of a piece of writing
Topic sentence	The sentence that contains the main idea of a paragraph (See page 525.) **Blue jeans are a popular piece of American clothing.**
Transition	A word or phrase that connects or ties two ideas together smoothly (See pages 572–573.) **also however lastly later next**
Usage	The way in which people use language (*Standard usage* generally follows the rules of good grammar. Most of the writing you do in school will require standard usage.)
Voice	A writer's unique, personal tone or feeling that comes across in a piece of writing (See pages 40 and 119.)

What can I do to increase my vocabulary skills?

Try Vocabulary-Building Techniques

Technique	Description	Why It Works
Learn common roots, prefixes, and suffixes.	If you know common word parts, you will be able to figure out many new words. (See pages 564–569.)	Tens of thousands of English words come from Greek and Latin word parts.
Use context.	Look at the passage surrounding a word you don't know. (See page 563.)	Words and ideas around a word often give hints as to what the word means.
Look up words in the dictionary.	Read the dictionary meaning. Also read the history of the word. (See pages 372–373.)	Sometimes the word history helps you connect the new word with one you already know.
Keep a vocabulary notebook.	Write down words you don't know. Find out their meaning and use each word in a sentence.	Writing reinforces your learning. The notebook is also a handy study guide.
Say your new words out loud.	Read your new words out loud and look for places in your writing where you can use them effectively.	Saying new words out loud means you hear them. Using that extra sense helps you remember.
Use your new words often.	Concentrate on using new words whenever possible in your writing.	Research shows that you need to use a new word to make it your own.

Use Context

When you come across a word you don't know, you can often figure out its meaning from the other words in the sentence. The other words form a familiar context, or setting, for the unfamiliar word. Looking closely at the surrounding words will give you clues to the meaning of the new word.

When you come to a word you don't know . . .

■ Look for a synonym—a word or words that have the same meaning as the unknown word.

> Sara had an ominous feeling when she woke up, but the feeling was less threatening when she saw she was in her own room.
> (An *ominous* feeling is a threatening one.)

■ Look for an antonym—a word that has the opposite meaning as the unknown word.

> Boniface had always been quite heavy, but he looked gaunt when he returned from the hospital.
> (*Gaunt* is the opposite of *heavy*.)

■ Look for a comparison or contrast.

> Riding a mountain bike in a remote area is my idea of a great day, but some people like to ride motorcycles on busy six-lane highways.
> (A *remote* area is out of the way, in contrast to a *busy* area. The word *but* also emphasizes a contrast.)

■ Look for a definition or description.

> Manatees, large aquatic mammals (sometimes called sea cows), can be found in the warm coastal waters of Florida.
> (An *aquatic* mammal is one that lives in the water.)

■ Look for words that appear in a series.

> The campers spotted blue jays, chickadees, and indigo buntings on Saturday morning.
> (An *indigo bunting*, like a *blue jay* or *chickadee*, is a bird.)

■ Look for a cause-and-effect relationship.

> The amount of traffic at 6th and Main doubled last year, so crossing lights were placed at that corner to avert an accident.
> (*Avert* means "to prevent.")

How can I build my vocabulary across the curriculum?

On the next several pages, you will find many of the most common prefixes, suffixes, and roots in the English language. Learning these word parts can help you increase your writing vocabulary.

Learn About Prefixes

A **prefix** is a word part that is added before a word to change the meaning of the word. For example, when the prefix *un* is added to the word *fair (unfair)*, it changes the word's meaning from "fair" to "not fair."

ambi *[both]*
ambidextrous (skilled with both hands)

anti *[against]*
antifreeze (a liquid that works against freezing)
antiwar (against wars and fighting)

astro *[star]*
astronaut (person who travels among the stars)
astronomy (study of the stars)

auto *[self]*
autobiography (writing that is about yourself)

bi *[two]*
bilingual (using or speaking two languages)
biped (having two feet)

circum *[in a circle, around]*
circumference (the line or distance around a circle)
circumnavigate (to sail around)

co *[together, with]*
cooperate (to work together)
coordinate (to put things together)

ex *[out]*
exhale (to breathe out)
exit (the act of going out)

fore *[before, in front of]*
foremost (in the first place, before everyone or everything else)
foretell (to tell or show beforehand)

hemi *[half]*
hemisphere (half of a sphere or globe)

hyper *[over]*
hyperactive (overactive)

im *[not, opposite of]*
impatient (not patient)
impossible (not possible)

in *[not, opposite of]*
inactive (not active)
incomplete (not complete)

inter *[between, among]*
international (between or among nations)
interplanetary (between the planets)

macro *[large]*
macrocosm (the entire universe)

mal *[bad, poor]*
malnutrition (poor nutrition)

micro *[small]*
microscope (an instrument used to see very small things)

mono *[one]*
monolingual (using or speaking only one language)

non *[not, opposite of]*
nonfat (without the normal fat content)
nonfiction (based on facts; not made-up)

over *[too much, extra]*
overeat (to eat too much)
overtime (extra time; time beyond regular hours)

poly *[many]*
polygon (a figure or shape with three or more sides)
polysyllable (a word with more than three syllables)

post *[after]*
postscript (a note added at the end of a letter, after the signature)
postwar (after a war)

pre *[before]*
pregame (activities that occur before a game)
preheat (to heat before using)

re *[again, back]*
repay (to pay back)
rewrite (to write again or revise)

semi *[half, partly]*
semicircle (half a circle)
semiconscious (half conscious; not fully conscious)

sub *[under, below]*
submarine (a boat that can operate underwater)
submerge (to put underwater)

trans *[across, over; change]*
transcontinental (across a continent)
transform (to change from one form to another)

tri *[three]*
triangle (a figure that has three sides and three angles)
tricycle (a three-wheeled vehicle)

un *[not]*
uncomfortable (not comfortable)
unhappy (not happy; sad)

under *[below, beneath]*
underage (below or less than the usual or required age)
undersea (beneath the surface of the sea)

uni *[one]*
unicycle (a one-wheeled vehicle)
unisex (a single style that is worn by both males and females)

Numerical Prefixes

deci *[tenth of a part]*
decimal system (a number system based on units of 10)

centi *[hundredth of a part]*
centimeter (a unit of length equal to 1/100 meter)

milli *[thousandth of a part]*
millimeter (a unit of length equal to 1/1,000 meter)

micro *[millionth of a part]*
micrometer (one-millionth of a meter)

deca, dec *[ten]*
decade (a period of 10 years)
decathlon (a contest with 10 events)

hecto, hect *[one hundred]*
hectare (a metric unit of land equal to 100 ares)

kilo *[one thousand]*
kilogram (a unit of mass equal to 1,000 grams)

mega *[one million]*
megabit (one million bits)

Building Word Choice   566-567

566

organize
select support improve

REFERENCE
A Writer's Resource

567

Study Suffixes

A **suffix** is a word part that is added after a word. Sometimes a suffix will tell you what part of speech a word is. For example, many adverbs end in the suffix *ly*.

able *[able, can do]*
 agreeable (able or willing to agree)
 doable (can be done)

al *[of, like]*
 magical (like magic)
 optical (of the eye)

ed *[past tense]*
 called (past tense of call)
 learned (past tense of learn)

ess *[female]*
 lioness (a female lion)

ful *[full of]*
 helpful (giving help; full of help)

ic *[like, having to do with]*
 symbolic (having to do with symbols)

ily *[in some manner]*
 happily (in a happy manner)

ish *[somewhat like or near]*
 childish (somewhat like a child)

ism *[characteristic of]*
 heroism (characteristic of a hero)

less *[without]*
 careless (without care)

ly *[in some manner]*
 calmly (in a calm manner)

ology *[study, science]*
 biology (the study of living things)

s *[more than one]*
 books (more than one book)

ward *[in the direction of]*
 westward (in the direction of west)

y *[containing, full of]*
 salty (containing salt)

Comparing Suffixes

er *[comparing two things]*
 faster, later, neater, stronger

est *[comparing more than two]*
 fastest, latest, neatest, strongest

Noun-Forming Suffixes

er *[one who]*
 painter (one who paints)

ing *[the result of]*
 painting (the result of a painter's work)

ion *[act of, state of]*
 perfection (the state of being perfect)

ist *[one who]*
 violinist (one who plays the violin)

ment *[act of, result of]*
 amendment (the result of amending, or changing)
 improvement (the result of improving)

ness *[state of]*
 goodness (the state of being good)

or *[one who]*
 actor (one who acts)

Understand Roots

A **root** is a word or word base from which other words are made by adding a prefix or a suffix. Knowing the common roots can help you figure out the meaning of difficult words.

aster *[star]*
 asteroid (resembling a star)
 asterisk (starlike symbol [*])

aud *[hear, listen]*
 audible (can be heard)
 auditorium (a place to listen to speeches and performances)

bibl *[book]*
 Bible (sacred book of Christianity)
 bibliography (list of books)

bio *[life]*
 biography (book about a person's life)
 biology (the study of life)

chrome *[color]*
 monochrome (having one color)
 polychrome (having many colors)

chron *[time]*
 chronological (in time order)
 synchronize (to make happen at the same time)

cide *[the killing of; killer]*
 homicide (the killing of one person by another person)
 pesticide (bug killer)

cise *[cut]*
 incision (a thin, clean cut)
 incisors (the teeth that cut or tear food)
 precise (cut exactly right)

cord, cor *[heart]*
 cordial (heartfelt)
 coronary (relating to the heart)

corp *[body]*
 corporation (a legal body; business)
 corpse (a dead human body)

cycl, cyclo *[wheel, circular]*
 bicycle (a vehicle with two wheels)
 cyclone (a very strong circular wind)

dem *[people]*
 democracy (ruled by the people)
 epidemic (affecting many people at the same time)

dent, dont *[tooth]*
 dentures (false teeth)
 orthodontist (dentist who straightens teeth)

derm *[skin]*
 dermatology (the study of skin)
 epidermis (outer layer of skin)

fac, fact *[do, make]*
 factory (a place where people make things)
 manufacture (to make by hand or machine)

fin *[end]*
 final (the last of something)
 infinite (having no end)

flex *[bend]*
 flexible (able to bend)
 reflex (bending or springing back)

flu *[flowing]*
 fluent (flowing smoothly or easily)
 fluid (waterlike, flowing substance)

forc, fort *[strong]*
 forceful (full of strength or power)
 fortify (to make strong)

fract, frag *[break]*
 fracture (to break)
 fragment (a piece broken from the whole)

RESOURCE

organize
select *support*
REFERENCE
improve
A Writer's Resource
569

Learn More Roots

gen *[birth, produce]*
congenital (existing at birth)
genetics (the study of inborn traits)

geo *[of the earth]*
geography (the study of places on the earth)
geology (the study of the earth's physical features)

graph *[write]*
autograph (writing one's name)
graphology (the study of handwriting)

homo *[same]*
homogeneous (of the same birth or kind)
homogenize (to blend into a uniform mixture)

hydr *[water]*
dehydrate (to take the water out of)
hydrophobia (the fear of water)

ject *[throw]*
eject (to throw out)
project (to throw forward)

log, logo *[word, thought, speech]*
dialogue (speech between two people)
logic (thinking or reasoning)

luc, lum *[light]*
illuminate (to light up)
translucent (letting light come through)

magn *[great]*
magnificent (great)
magnify (to make bigger or greater)

man *[hand]*
manicure (to fix the hands)
manual (done by hand)

mania *[insanity]*
kleptomania (abnormal desire to steal)
maniac (an insane person)

mar *[sea, pool]*
marine (of or found in the sea)
mariner (sailor)

mega *[large]*
megalith (large stone)
megaphone (large horn used to make voices louder)

meter *[measure]*
kilometer (a thousand meters)
voltmeter (device to measure volts)

mit, miss *[send]*
emit (to send out; give off)
transmission (sending over)

multi *[many, much]*
multicultural (of or including many cultures)
multiped (an animal with many feet)

numer *[number]*
innumerable (too many to count)
numerous (large in number)

omni *[all, completely]*
omnipresent (present everywhere at the same time)
omnivorous (eating all kinds of food)

onym *[name]*
anonymous (without a name)
pseudonym (false name)

ped *[foot]*
pedal (lever worked by the foot)
pedestrian (one who travels by foot)

phil *[love]*
Philadelphia (city of brotherly love)
philosophy (the love of wisdom)

phobia *[fear]*
acrophobia (a fear of high places)
agoraphobia (a fear of public, open places)

phon *[sound]*
phonics (related to sounds)
symphony (sounds made together)

photo *[light]*
photo-essay (a story told mainly with photographs)
photograph (picture made using light rays)

pop *[people]*
population (number of people in an area)
populous (full of people)

port *[carry]*
export (to carry out)
portable (able to be carried)

psych *[mind, soul]*
psychiatry (the study of the mind)
psychology (science of mind and behavior)

sci *[know]*
conscious (being aware)
omniscient (knowing everything)

scope *[instrument for viewing]*
kaleidoscope (instrument for viewing patterns and shapes)
periscope (instrument used to see above the water)

scrib, script *[write]*
manuscript (something written by hand)
scribble (to write quickly)

spec *[look]*
inspect (to look at carefully)
specimen (an example to look at)

spir *[breath]*
expire (to breathe out; die)
inspire (to breathe into; give life to)

tele *[over a long distance; far]*
telephone (machine used to speak to people over a distance)
telescope (machine used to see things that are very faraway)

tempo *[time]*
contemporary (from the current time period)
temporary (lasting for a short time)

tend, tens *[stretch, strain]*
extend (to stretch and make longer)
tension (stretching something tight)

terra *[earth]*
terrain (the earth or ground)
terrestrial (relating to the earth)

therm *[heat]*
thermal (related to heat)
thermostat (a device for controlling heat)

tom *[cut]*
anatomy (the science of cutting apart plants and animals for study)
atom (a particle that cannot be cut or divided)

tract *[draw, pull]*
traction (the act of pulling)
tractor (a machine for pulling)

typ *[print]*
prototype (the first printing or model)
typo (a printing error)

vac *[empty]*
vacant (empty)
vacuum (an empty space)

vid, vis *[see]*
supervise (to oversee or watch over)
videotape (record on tape for viewing)

vor *[eat]*
carnivorous (flesh-eating)
herbivorous (plant-eating)

zoo *[animal or animals]*
zoo (a place where animals are kept)
zoology (the study of animal life)

RESOURCE

What can I do to write more-effective sentences?

Study Sentence Patterns

Sentences in the English language follow the basic patterns below. Use a variety of patterns to add interest to your writing. (Also see page 571.)

1 Subject + Action Verb

      S   AV

The storm ended. (Some action verbs, like *ended,* are intransitive, which means that they *do not need* a direct object to express a complete thought. See 728.3.)

2 Subject + Action Verb + Direct Object

      S   AV   DO

One mistake cost the game. (Some action verbs, like *cost,* are transitive. This means that they *need* a direct object to express a complete thought. See 728.2.)

3 Subject + Action Verb + Indirect Object + Direct Object

      S   AV IO   DO

Jim's friends gave him a surprise party.

4 Subject + Action Verb + Direct Object + Object Complement

      S   AV   DO   OC

The director named Joyce the stage manager.

5 Subject + Linking Verb + Predicate Noun

      S LV   PN

Roger is an amateur ventriloquist.

6 Subject + Linking Verb + Predicate Adjective

      S LV   PA

Broccoli is very tasty.

In the patterns above, the subject comes before the verb. In the patterns below, the subject comes after the verb (called a *delayed subject*).

7
  LV   S   PA
Is anyone absent? (A question)

8
     LV   S
There were two storms last night.
(A sentence beginning with *there* or *here*)

Practice Sentence Diagramming

Diagramming sentences can help you understand how the different parts of a sentence fit together. Here are the most common diagrams.

1   S   AV   **The storm ended.**

Note: Modifiers (including *a, an,* and *the*) are placed under the word they modify.

2   S   AV   DO   **One mistake cost the game.**

3   S   AV   IO   DO   **Jim's friends gave him a surprise party.**

4   S   AV   DO   OC   **The director named Joyce the stage manager.**

5   S   LV   PN   **Roger is an amateur ventriloquist.**

6   S   LV   PA   **Broccoli is very tasty.**

RESOURCE

How can I connect my sentences and paragraphs?

Use Transitions

Transitions can be used to connect one sentence to another sentence or one paragraph to another within a longer essay or report. The lists below show a number of transitions and how they are used.

Note: Each colored list below is a group of transitions that could work well together in a piece of writing.

Words that can be used to show location

above	around	between	inside	outside
across	behind	by	into	over
against	below	down	near	throughout
along	beneath	in back of	next to	to the right
among	beside	in front of	on top of	under

Above	Beside	On top of	To the right
Below	In back of	Next to	
Beneath	In front of	To the left	

Words that can be used to show time

about	during	yesterday	until	finally
after	first	meanwhile	next	then
at	second	today	soon	as soon as
before	to begin	tomorrow	later	in the end

After	First	Now	Third
Before	In the end	Second	To begin
During	Later	Soon	To conclude
Finally	Next	Then	To continue

Words that can be used to compare two things

also	both	like	one way
as	in the same way	likewise	similarly

Also	In the same way
Another way	One way
Both	Similarly

Words that can be used to contrast things (show differences)

although	even though	on the other hand	still
but	however	otherwise	yet

Although	Nevertheless
Even though	Still
On the other hand	Yet

Words that can be used to emphasize a point

again	for this reason	to emphasize	truly
especially	in fact	to repeat	

Especially	In fact	To repeat
For this reason	To emphasize	Truly

Words that can be used to conclude or summarize

all in all	because	in conclusion	therefore
as a result	finally	lastly	to sum it up

All in all	Because	In conclusion	To sum it up
All in all	Finally	Therefore	

Words that can be used to add information

additionally	and	finally	moreover
again	another	for example	other
along with	as well	for instance	next
also	besides	in addition	

Additionally	Another	Finally	Moreover
Also	As well	For example	Next
Along with	Besides	For instance	

Words that can be used to clarify

for example	for instance	in other words	that is

Equally important	For instance
For example	In other words

Polishing Presentations **574-575**

574

575

organize
select support
REFERENCE
improve
A Writer's Resource

What can I do to make my final copy look better?

Add Graphics to Your Writing

You can add information and interest to essays and reports by using diagrams, tables, and graphs.

Diagrams are drawings that show the parts of something.

Picture diagrams show how something is put together. A diagram may leave out some parts to show only the parts you need to learn.

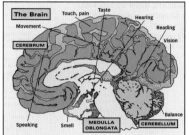

Line diagrams show something you can't really see. Instead of objects, line diagrams show ideas and relationships. The problem-solving diagram helps you understand how to solve a scientific problem.

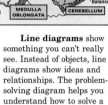

Tables are another form of diagram. Tables have two parts: rows and columns. Rows go across and show one kind of information or data. Columns go up and down and show a different kind of data.

To read a distance or mileage table, find the place you're starting from and the place you're going to. Then find the place where the row and the column meet—that will show the distance and the driving time from one place to the other.

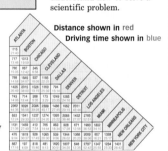

Distance shown in red
Driving time shown in blue

Graphs are pictures of information. **Bar graphs** show how things compare to one another. The bars on a bar graph may be vertical or horizontal. (*Vertical* means "up and down." *Horizontal* means "from side to side.") Sometimes the bars on graphs are called *columns*. The part that shows numbers is called the *scale*.

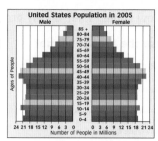

Pie graphs show how all the parts of something add up to make the whole. A pie graph often shows percentages. (A percentage is the part of a whole stated in hundredths: $35\% = 35/100$.) It's called a pie graph because it is usually in the shape of a pie or circle.

The pie graph to the left shows the sources of carbon monoxide emissions in 2007 and what percentage of total emissions each source produced.

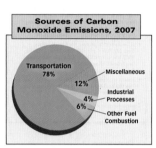

Line graphs show how something changes as time goes by. A line graph always begins with an L-shaped grid. One axis of the grid shows passing time; the other axis shows quantities.

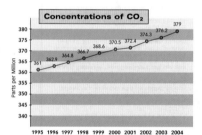

How should I set up my practical writing?

Use the Proper Format

Memos

A memo is a brief written message that you can share with a teacher, a coach, or a principal. Memos create a flow of information—asking and answering questions, giving instructions, describing work to be done, or reminding people about meetings.

Date: Friday, March 6, 2009

To: Mrs. Lee, Technical Director

From: Corrine Stier, Student Director

Subject: Progress on the *Brigadoon* Sets

Here is my first weekly update on the progress of the *Brigadoon* sets.

- Dave Dye has sketched a 15-foot-long set. One side will show the living room of the Campbell cottage, with a thatched roof on top and a window at the back. The other side will be cathedral ruins for the wedding scene. The whole piece will be on wheels, so we can spin it around for scene changes.

- Julie Reynolds primed the four old flats from *My Fair Lady* and drew trees on them. We'll use them on a dark stage along with two freestanding trees to make the forest for the chase scene.

- I want to repaint an old drop curtain to look like the backdrop in the movie. I've attached my drawings for your approval.

Thanks for your confidence in me, Mrs. Lee.

Date: January 12, 2009
To: Mrs. Munn, Room 210
From: The Titan Group: Todd Davis, LaToya Wilson, Jacque Trevino, Becky Jackson
Subject: Volunteer Tutoring

Project Description: An article in our school paper stated that Lincoln Elementary School needed eighth-grade students to tutor third graders in reading. We would like to volunteer our services starting February 3.

What We Need: We need written permission from you, our parents, and our principal. We also need written approval from the principal and the third-grade teachers of Lincoln Elementary School.

What We Will Do: On Tuesdays and Thursdays, during our fourth period study hall, we will walk across the playground to Lincoln School to our assigned classrooms. We will help third-grade students by listening to them read, helping them with their reading assignments, and reading to them.

Outcome: At the end of this project, we will report on the students' progress and show a videotape of our students reading during one of our last sessions. It will show how the tutoring helped.

We hope you will approve our proposal. If you have any suggestions or changes, please let us know.

Proposals

A proposal is a detailed plan for doing a project, solving a problem, or meeting a need.

Follow Guidelines

Letters

A letter is a written message sent through the mail. Letters follow a set format, including important contact information, a salutation (greeting), a body, and a closing signature. (See pages 274–277 for more information.)

1080 Burns Road
Orange Park, FL 32000
May 5, 2008

Principal Joseph Rodriguez
Greenberg Middle School
116 Shelton Street
Orange Park, FL 32000

Dear Mr. Rodriguez:

As a soccer team member at Greenberg Middle School, I have a suggestion. We need lights for nighttime games. When school starts in the fall, it gets darker earlier and earlier. It's hard for our teams to finish games safely.

I realize that lighting is expensive. However, a lighted field could be used by the whole community, so the community could help pay for it. The soccer team could even run a citywide fund-raiser.

Adding lights to our soccer field would make a huge difference for my teammates and me. Please make the request at the next school board meeting.

Sincerely,

Alex Hastings

Alex Hastings

Envelope Addresses

Place the return address in the upper left corner, the destination address in the center, and the correct postage in the upper right corner.

ALEX HASTINGS
1080 BURNS RD
ORANGE PARK FL 32000

PRINCIPAL JOSEPH RODRIGUEZ
GREENBERG MIDDLE SCHOOL
116 SHELTON ST
ORANGE PARK FL 32000

U.S. Postal Service Guidelines

1. Capitalize everything and leave out ALL punctuation.
2. Use the list of common address abbreviations at 634.1. Use numerals rather than words for numbered streets and avenues (9TH AVE NE, 3RD ST SW).
3. If you know the ZIP + 4 code, use it.

RESOURCE

578

Proofreader's Guide

579

Marking Punctuation

Periods

Use a **period** to end a sentence. Also use a period after initials, after abbreviations, and as a decimal point.

579.1
At the End of Sentences

Use a period to end a sentence that makes a statement or a request. Also use a period for a mild command, one that does not need an exclamation point. (See page 518.)

> The Southern Ocean surrounds Antarctica. (statement)
> Please point out the world's largest ocean on a map. (request)
> Do not use a laser pointer. (mild command)

NOTE It is not necessary to place a period after a statement that has parentheses around it if it is part of another sentence.

> The Southern Ocean is the fourth-largest ocean (it is larger than the Atlantic).

579.2
After Initials

Place a period after an initial.

> J. K. Rowling (author)
> Colin L. Powell (politician)

579.3
After Abbreviations

Place a period after each part of an abbreviation. Do not use periods with acronyms or initialisms. (See page 636.)

> Abbreviations: Mr. Mrs. Ms. Dr. B.C.E. C.E.
> Acronyms: AIDS NASA
> Initialisms: NBC FBI

NOTE When an abbreviation is the last word in a sentence, use only one period at the end of the sentence.

> My grandfather's full name is William Ryan James Koenig, Jr.

579.4
As Decimal Points

Use a period to separate dollars and cents and as a decimal point.

> The price of a loaf of bread was $1.54 in 1992.
> That price was only 35 cents, or 77.3 percent less, in 1972.

Related Skills Activities

■ **Basic Grammar and Writing**
Kinds of Sentences, p. 518

■ *SkillsBook*
End Punctuation, pp. 3–4

Question Marks

A **question mark** is used after an interrogative sentence and also to show doubt about the correctness of a fact or figure. (See page 518.)

580.1
At the End of Direct Questions

Use a question mark at the end of a direct question (an interrogative sentence).

Is a vegan a person who eats only vegetables?

580.2
At the End of Indirect Questions

No question mark is used after an indirect question. (An indirect question tells about a question you or someone else asked.)

Because I do not eat meat, I'm often asked if I am a vegetarian.
I asked the doctor if going meatless is harmful to my health.

580.3
To Show Doubt

Place a question mark within parentheses to show that you are unsure that a fact or figure is correct.

By the year 2020 (?) the number of vegetarians in the United States may approach 15 percent of the population.

Exclamation Points

An **exclamation point** may be placed after a word, a phrase, or a sentence to show emotion. (The exclamation point should not be overused.)

580.4
To Express Strong Feelings

Use an exclamation point to show excitement or strong feeling.

Yeah! Wow! Oh my!

Surprise! You've won the million-dollar sweepstakes!

Caution: Never use more than one exclamation point in writing assignments.

Incorrect: Don't ever do that to me again!!!

Correct: Don't ever do that to me again!

Grammar Practice

End Punctuation

 On your own paper, write whether each of the following sentences needs a period, a question mark, or an exclamation point at the end.

Example: I want to get a pet
period

1. Did you ever think about getting a ferret
2. They are from the same animal family that minks, skunks, and otters are from
3. Ferrets are active creatures and need a lot of exercise
4. The word *ferret* comes from a Latin word meaning *little thief,* so the animals also require patience
5. Oh no, a ferret might take your keys or your pens and hide them
6. Make sure you lock away anything valuable
7. A ferret's cage should be large enough to hold some toys, a water dish, and a food bowl
8. What should you feed a ferret if you can't find ferret food
9. Many ferret owners feed their animals cat food
10. Just like a cat, a ferret can be trained to use a litter box
11. Wow, a baby ferret is even called a kit
12. You might ask if ferrets need their own toys
13. They do, but they'll be happy as can be with an old sock
14. In general, ferrets will live 8 to 10 years
15. Enjoy your new pet

Next Step: Write three sentences about a pet or other animal. Use different end punctuation for each one.

Related Skills Activities

■ **Basic Grammar and Writing**
Kinds of Sentences, p. 518

■ *SkillsBook*
End Punctuation, pp. 3–4

 ## Answers

1. question mark
2. period
3. period
4. period
5. exclamation point
6. period OR exclamation point
7. period
8. question mark
9. period
10. period
11. exclamation point
12. period
13. period
14. period
15. period OR exclamation point

582

Commas

Use a **comma** to indicate a pause or a change in thought. This helps to keep words and ideas from running together so that the writing is easier to read. For a writer, no other form of punctuation is more important to understand than the comma.

582.1
Between Items in a Series

Use commas between words, phrases, or clauses in a series. (A series contains at least three items.) (See page 512.)

> **Chinese, English, and Hindi** are the three most widely used languages in the world. (words)

> **Being comfortable with technology, working well with others, and knowing another language** are important skills for today's workers. (phrases)

> **My dad works in a factory, my mom works in an office, and I work in school.** (clauses)

582.2
To Keep Numbers Clear

Use commas to separate the digits in a number in order to distinguish hundreds, thousands, millions, and so on.

> More than **104,000** people live in Kingston, the capital of Jamaica.

> The population of the entire country of Liechtenstein is only **29,000.**

NOTE Commas are not used in years.

> The world population was **6.1 billion by 2003.**

582.3
In Dates and Addresses

Use commas to distinguish items in an address and items in a date.

> On **August 28, 1963,** Martin Luther King, Jr., gave his famous "I Have a Dream" speech.

> The address of the King Center is 449 Auburn Avenue NE, Atlanta, Georgia 30312.

NOTE No comma is placed between the state and ZIP code. Also, when only the month and year are given, no comma is needed.

> In **January 2029** we will celebrate the 100th anniversary of Reverend King's birth.

583

Grammar Practice

Commas 1

■ Between Items in a Series
■ To Keep Numbers Clear
■ In Dates and Addresses

 For each sentence below, write the words or numbers that need commas. Then insert the commas correctly.

Example: I started first grade on September 2 1998.
September 2, 1998

1. There are more than 1200 students at my brother's high school.
2. He has been going there since August 18 2001.
3. The school's address is 1010 Water Street Arlo Texas 80989.
4. Nikki Rasheed and Collin are hall monitors.
5. They started their "jobs" in March 2000, which was more than 1000 days ago.
6. Javier woke up late missed the bus and forgot his homework.
7. He thought of about 50000 excuses he could give the teacher.
8. The teacher gave him until October 9 2003 to turn it in.
9. Javier walked to Frank's house at 2105 Juniper Road Catalpa Texas 80990.
10. Javier did his homework Frank read a magazine and Frank's little brother bothered them.

Next Step: Write full sentences that answer each of the following questions. Be sure to use commas correctly.
● When were you born?
● What is your home address?
● What are your three favorite foods?
● What is the sum of 500 + 525?

Related Skills Activities

■ **Basic Grammar and Writing**
Combine with a Series, p. 512

■ *SkillsBook*
Commas between Items in a Series, pp. 5–6

 ## Answers

1. 1,200
2. August 18, 2001
3. 1010 Water Street, Arlo, Texas
4. Nikki, Rasheed, and Collin
5. 1,000
6. late, missed the bus, and
7. 50,000
8. October 9, 2003,
9. 2105 Juniper Road, Catalpa, Texas
10. homework, Frank read a magazine, and

Commas . . .

584.1
To Set Off Nonrestrictive Phrases and Clauses

Use commas to set off nonrestrictive phrases and clauses—those not necessary to the basic meaning of the sentence.

> People get drinking water from surface water or groundwater, which makes up only 1 percent of the earth's water supply.

(The clause *which makes up only 1 percent of the earth's water supply* is additional information; it is nonrestrictive—not required. If the clause were left out, the meaning of the sentence would remain clear.)

Restrictive phrases or clauses—those that are needed in the sentence—restrict or limit the meaning of the sentence; they are not set off with commas.

> Groundwater that is free from harmful pollutants is rare.

(The clause *that is free from harmful pollutants* is restrictive; it is needed to complete the meaning of the basic sentence and is not set off with commas.)

584.2
To Set Off Titles or Initials

Use commas to set off a title, a name, or initials that follow a person's last name. (Use only one period if an initial comes at the end of a sentence.)

> Melanie Prokat, M.D., is our family's doctor. However, she is listed in the phone book only as Prokat, M.

NOTE Although commas are not necessary to set off "Jr." and "Sr." after a name, they may be used as long as a comma is used both before and after the abbreviation.

584.3
To Set Off Interruptions

Use commas to set off a word, phrase, or clause that interrupts the main thought of a sentence. These interruptions usually can be identified through the following tests:

1. You can leave them out of a sentence without changing its meaning.

2. You can place them other places in the sentence without changing its meaning.

> Our school, as we all know, is becoming overcrowded again. (clause)
> The gym, not the cafeteria, was expanded a while ago. (phrase)
> My history class, for example, has 42 students in it. (phrase)
> There are, indeed, about 1,000 people in my school. (word)
> The building, however, has room for only 850 students. (word)

Grammar Practice

Commas 2

- ■ To Set Off Nonrestrictive Phrases and Clauses
- ■ To Set Off Titles or Initials
- ■ To Set Off Interruptions

 For each sentence below, write the parts that should be set off with commas. If commas are not necessary, write "none."

Example: When was music which plays a big role in every culture invented?
which plays a big role in every culture

1. Some scientists think it was the sounds of nature that originally inspired people to create music.

2. The songs of birds for example probably inspired many composers.

3. People were in fact making music as long as 50,000 years ago.

4. Prehistoric bone flutes which were played by cave dwellers are evidence of music's long history.

5. Egyptian paintings that show people playing instruments are also evidence of music's ancient beginnings.

6. By the Middle Ages which covered the thousand-year period from 450 to 1450 many different musical instruments were being used.

7. During the Renaissance, the recorder and reed instruments in general were very popular.

8. The years from 1825 to 1900 known as the Romantic period introduced many talented composers to the world.

9. Johann Strauss Jr. was one of these famous musicians.

Next Step: What instrument do you play (or wish you could play)? Write one sentence about it. Include a nonrestrictive phrase or clause, setting it off with commas.

Related Skills Activities

■ **CD-ROM**
Commas with Non restrictive Clauses
584.1
Commas to Set Off Initials and
Interruptions   584.2, 584.3

■ *SkillsBook*
Commas to Set Off Nonrestrictive Phrases and
Clauses, pp. 7–8
Commas to Set Off Dialogue, Interruptions, and
Interjections, pp. 9–10

Answers

1. none
2. for example
3. in fact
4. which were played by cave dwellers
5. none
6. which covered the thousand-year period from 450 to 1450
7. in general
8. known as the Romantic period
9. none OR Jr.

586

Commas . . .

586.1
To Set Off Appositives

Commas set off an appositive from the rest of the sentence. An appositive is a word or phrase that identifies or renames a noun or pronoun. (See page 513.)

> **The capital of Cyprus, Nicosia, has a population of almost 643,000.** (*Nicosia* renames *capital of Cyprus,* so the word is set off with commas.)

> **Cyprus, an island in the Mediterranean Sea, is about half the size of Connecticut.** (*An island in the Mediterranean Sea* identifies *Cyprus,* so the phrase is set off with commas.)

Do not use commas with appositives that are necessary to the basic meaning of the sentence.

> **The Mediterranean island Cyprus is about half the size of Connecticut.** (*Cyprus* is not set off because it is needed to make the sentence clear.)

586.2
To Separate Equal Adjectives

Use commas to separate two or more adjectives that equally modify the same noun.

> **Comfortable, efficient cars are becoming more important to drivers.** (*Comfortable* and *efficient* are separated by a comma because they modify *cars* equally.)

> **Some automobiles run on clean, renewable sources of energy.** (*Clean* and *renewable* are separated by a comma because they modify *sources* equally.)

> **Conventional gasoline engines emit a lot of pollution.** (*Conventional* and *gasoline* do not modify *engines* equally; therefore, no comma separates the two.)

Use these tests to help you decide if adjectives modify equally:

1. Switch the order of the adjectives; if the sentence is clear, the adjectives modify equally.

   Yes: Efficient, comfortable cars are becoming more important to drivers.

   No: Gasoline conventional engines emit a lot of pollution.

2. Put the word *and* between the adjectives; if the sentence reads well, use a comma when *and* is taken out.

   Yes: Comfortable and efficient cars are becoming more important to drivers.

   No: Conventional and gasoline engines emit a lot of pollution.

Grammar Practice

Commas 3

■ To Set Off Appositives

 For each numbered sentence below, write the appositive phrase and the noun it renames. Set off the appositive with commas.

Example: Kit houses "build-it-yourself" homes were popular in the early 1900s.
Kit houses, "build-it-yourself" homes,

(1) Sears the nationwide department store chain sold kit houses between 1908 and 1940. **(2)** One of the most popular models was the Osborn a small bungalow. **(3)** All the materials 30,000 or more pieces were neatly packed into two boxcars for rail delivery. **(4)** The home designers architects hired by the store could make changes to the floor plan the buyers wanted. **(5)** In a few months, the owners of this new house once just a big pile of materials could move in.

■ To Separate Equal Adjectives

 For each numbered sentence below, write the adjectives that need commas between them. Add the commas.

Example: The catalog offered 90 fashionable unique home designs.
fashionable, unique

(1) It's amazing to think that these big roomy houses—many still standing today—came from a department store catalog! **(2)** A complete ready-to-assemble kit included everything that was needed. **(3)** When people ordered their houses from the catalog, they would also order attractive modern light fixtures and sturdy plumbing fixtures. **(4)** All the pieces were delivered by rail, along with a thick detailed instruction book. **(5)** Then the buyers, along with anyone who could be persuaded to help, began the long challenging construction process.

Related Skills Activities

■ Basic Grammar and Writing
Combine with Phrases, p. 513

■ CD-ROM
Commas to Set Off Appositives
  586.1
Initials, Interruptions, and Interjections
Commas to Set Off Equal Adjectives
  586.2

■ *SkillsBook*
Commas to Separate Equal
  Adjectives, p. 13
Commas with Appositives, p. 17

Answers

1. Sears, the nationwide department store chain,
2. the Osborn, a small bungalow
3. the materials, 30,000 or more pieces,
4. home designers, architects hired by the store,
5. this new house, once just a big pile of materials,

Answers

1. big, roomy
2. complete, ready-to-assemble
3. attractive, modern
4. thick, detailed
5. long, challenging

588

Commas . . .

588.1
To Set Off Dialogue

Use commas to set off the exact words of a speaker from the rest of the sentence. (Also see page 556.)

> The firefighter said, "When we cannot successfully put out a fire, we try to keep it from spreading."

> "When we cannot successfully put out a fire, we try to keep it from spreading," the firefighter said.

NOTE Do not use a comma or quotation marks for indirect quotations. The words *if* and *that* often signal dialogue that is being reported rather than quoted.

> The firefighter said that when they cannot successfully put out a fire, they try to keep it from spreading. (These are not the speaker's exact words.)

588.2
In Direct Address

Use commas to separate a noun of direct address from the rest of the sentence. (A noun of direct address is a noun that names a person spoken to in the sentence.)

> Hanae, did you know that an interior decorator can change wallpaper and fabrics on a computer screen?

> Sure, Jack, and an architect can use a computer to see how light will fall in different parts of a building.

588.3
To Set Off Interjections

Use commas to separate an interjection or a weak exclamation from the rest of the sentence.

> No kidding, you mean that one teacher has to manage a class of 42 pupils? (weak exclamation)

> Uh-huh, and that teacher has other classes that size. (interjection)

588.4
To Set Off Explanatory Phrases

Use commas to separate an explanatory phrase from the rest of the sentence.

> English, the language computers speak worldwide, is also the most widely used language in science and medicine.

> More than 750 million people, about an eighth of the world's population, speak English as a foreign language.

PUNCTUATION

Grammar Practice

Commas 4

- To Set Off Dialogue
- In Direct Address
- To Set Off Interjections

 For each numbered sentence below, write the word or words that should be followed by commas. Add the commas.

Example: "Class we'll discuss oceans today" said the teacher.
Class, today,

1. The teacher asked "Who can define *ocean*?"
2. "It's a sea covering a large expanse Ms. Jackson" said Ralph.
3. She said "Wow that's right Ralph. Who knows which ocean is the largest?"
4. Renatta asked "Is it the Pacific?"
5. "Yes Renatta" replied Ms. Jackson.

- To Set Off Explanatory Phrases

 For each numbered sentence below, write the explanatory phrase that should be set off with commas.

Example: The Pacific Ocean the world's largest ocean contains nearly 50 percent of earth's water.
the world's largest ocean

1. The majority of the world's water supply 98 percent of it comes from the oceans.
2. Oceans provide fish a major source of food for many people.
3. Many huge ships cruise liners and cargo freighters provide people with opportunities for both work and play.
4. Also, shells and coral commonly used in building materials come from the oceans.
5. Ocean water which contains a lot of salt is not safe to drink.

Related Skills Activities

- **Basic Grammar and Writing**
  Write Narrative Paragraphs, p. 526

- **CD-ROM**
  Commas to Set Off Interjections   588.3

- ***SkillsBook***
  Commas to Set Off Dialogue, Interruptions, and Interjections, pp. 9–10

 Answers

1. asked,
2. expanse, Jackson,
3. said, Wow, right,
4. asked,
5. Yes, Renatta,

 Answers

1. 98 percent of it
2. a major source of food for many people
3. cruise liners and cargo freighters
4. commonly used in building materials
5. which contains a lot of salt

590

Commas . . .

590.1
To Separate Introductory Clauses and Phrases

Use a comma to separate an adverb clause or a long phrase from the independent clause that follows it.

> If every automobile in the country were a light shade of red, we'd live in a pink-car nation. (adverb clause)

> According to some experts, solar-powered cars will soon be common. (long modifying phrase)

590.2
In Compound Sentences

Use a comma between two independent clauses that are joined by a coordinating conjunction (such as *and, but, or, nor, for, so,* and *yet*), forming a compound sentence. An independent clause expresses a complete thought and can stand alone as a sentence. (Also see page **516**.)

> Many students enjoy working on computers, so teachers are finding new ways to use them in the classroom.

> Computers can be valuable in education, but many schools cannot afford enough of them.

Avoid Comma Splices: A comma splice results when two independent clauses are "spliced" together with only a comma—and no conjunction. (See page **504**.)

SCHOOL DAZE

Ann, we've completed two-thirds of the quarter, and you haven't turned in one assignment. What do you have to say for yourself?

Ah . . . is there anything I can do for extra credit?

Grammar Practice

Commas 5

■ To Separate Introductory Clauses and Phrases
■ In Compound Sentences

 Number your paper from 1 to 13. For each line, write the words that should be followed by a comma, and put the commas after them. (Not every line needs a comma.) You should add nine commas.

Example: I didn't do my homework but I have an excuse.
homework,

1 This might come as a surprise to you but doing homework can
2 be very dangerous. As I began to work on a math worksheet last
3 night three dangerous felons grabbed me from behind and stuffed
4 me into the trunk of a rusty, old car. After driving for quite a while
5 the car came to a sudden stop and my kidnappers left the car. I
6 knew I had to do something quickly or it would be too late. I didn't
7 want to yell and alert the kidnappers so I wrote a note on the back
8 of my worksheet and stuck it through one of the rust holes in the
9 car. Fortunately, a passerby saw the note and notified the police.
10 Soon after the police came and captured the kidnappers. Since
11 the police kept my worksheet as evidence I couldn't complete my
12 homework. For some reason my math teacher didn't buy my excuse
13 for not having my homework done.

Next Step: Take a normal, everyday experience, such as doing homework, walking to school, taking a test, or playing a game, and turn it into a "tall tale" like the one above. Use commas with introductory word groups and in compound sentences.

Related Skills Activities

■ **Basic Grammar and Writing**
Avoid Run-on Sentences, p. 504
Create Compound Sentences, p. 516

■ *SkillsBook*
Commas to Separate Introductory Clauses and Phrases, pp. 11–12
Commas in Compound Sentences, p. 14

Answers

line 1.   you,
line 3.   night,
line 5.   while,
               stop,
line 6.   quickly,
line 7.   kidnappers,
line 10.   after,
line 11.   evidence,
line 12.   reason,

592-593   Proofreader's Guide

592

punctuate *edit* *capitalize*
improve SPELL
Marking Punctuation   593

PUNCTUATION

Test Prep!

For each underlined part of the paragraphs below, choose the letter (on the next page) of the best way to punctuate it.

The bumps on your tongue are not your taste <u>buds but</u> they do
                                                    (1)
contain taste buds. The bumps are called <u>papillae</u> An average person
                                              (2)
has about <u>10000</u> taste <u>buds and</u> each bud contains between 50 and 100
          (3)   **(4)**
taste cells. Taste buds are mostly located on your <u>tongue but</u> can also be
                                                        (5)
found on the roof of <u>your mouth your throat and part</u> of the esophagus.
                          (6)

What happens when you put food in your <u>mouth</u> It gets mixed with
                                            (7)
your saliva so that the taste buds can detect the flavor. At the same

time, the odor of the food in your mouth travels up into your <u>nose so</u>
                                                                  (8)
specialized cells in your <u>nose olfactory receptors</u> also play an important
                              (9)
role in tasting. Your taste buds and olfactory receptors work together to

sense true flavor.

Taste buds enable a person to experience tastes that are <u>sweet salty</u>

<u>sour bitter and umami.</u> <u>Umami a newly recognized taste</u> is experienced
      (10)   **(11)**
in protein-rich foods like aged cheese. Every taste cell can respond to all

five <u>sensations but</u> responds mostly to only one of them. Did you know
      (12)
that people are actually born liking sweet flavors and disliking <u>bitterness</u>
                                                                      (13)
These traits evolved to help people desire <u>sugars the chemicals we need</u>
                                              (14)
<u>for energy and growth</u> and reject bitter tastes as a protection against

eating poisons.

1
  Ⓐ buds, but
  Ⓑ buds. but
  Ⓒ buds; but
  Ⓓ correct as is

2
  Ⓐ papillae?
  Ⓑ papillae.
  Ⓒ papillae,
  Ⓓ correct as is

3
  Ⓐ 100,00
  Ⓑ 1,0000
  Ⓒ 10,000
  Ⓓ correct as is

4
  Ⓐ buds, and
  Ⓑ buds and,
  Ⓒ buds. and
  Ⓓ correct as is

5
  Ⓐ tongue, but
  Ⓑ tongue. but
  Ⓒ tongue but,
  Ⓓ correct as is

6
  Ⓐ your mouth, your throat and part
  Ⓑ your mouth, your throat, and part
  Ⓒ your mouth your throat, and part
  Ⓓ correct as is

7
  Ⓐ mouth?
  Ⓑ mouth.
  Ⓒ mouth,
  Ⓓ correct as is

8
  Ⓐ nose. so
  Ⓑ nose, so
  Ⓒ nose so,
  Ⓓ correct as is

9
  Ⓐ nose olfactory receptors,
  Ⓑ nose, olfactory receptors,
  Ⓒ nose, olfactory receptors
  Ⓓ correct as is

10
  Ⓐ sweet, salty, sour, bitter, and umami
  Ⓑ sweet, salty, sour, bitter and umami
  Ⓒ sweet salty, sour, bitter and umami
  Ⓓ correct as is

11
  Ⓐ Umami, a newly recognized taste
  Ⓑ Umami a newly, recognized taste
  Ⓒ Umami, a newly recognized taste,
  Ⓓ correct as is

12
  Ⓐ sensations, but
  Ⓑ sensations but,
  Ⓒ sensations. but
  Ⓓ correct as is

13
  Ⓐ bitterness.
  Ⓑ bitterness,
  Ⓒ bitterness?
  Ⓓ correct as is

14
  Ⓐ sugars, the chemicals we need for energy and growth,
  Ⓑ sugars, the chemicals, we need for energy and growth,
  Ⓒ sugars, the chemicals we need for energy and growth
  Ⓓ correct as is

Related Skills Activities

■ **SkillsBook**
Commas Rules, pp. 15–16
Comma Review, p. 18

Answers

1. A   9. B
2. B   10. A
3. C   11. C
4. A   12. D
5. D   13. C
6. B   14. A
7. A
8. B

Semicolons

Use a **semicolon** to suggest a stronger pause than a comma indicates.
A semicolon may also serve in place of a period.

594.1
To Join Two Independent Clauses

In a compound sentence, use a semicolon to join two independent clauses that are not connected with a coordinating conjunction. (See 744.1.)

> The United States has more computers than any other country; its residents own more than 164 million of them.

594.2
With Conjunctive Adverbs

A semicolon is also used to join two independent clauses when the clauses are connected by a conjunctive adverb (such as *as a result, for example, however, therefore,* and *instead*). (See 738.1.)

> Japan is next on that list; however, the Japanese have only 50 million computers.

> You might think that the billion people of China own a lot of computers; instead, the smaller country of Germany has twice as many computers as China.

594.3
To Separate Groups That Contain Commas

Use a semicolon between groups of words in a series when one or more of the groups already contain commas.

> Many of our community's residents separate their garbage into bins for newspapers, cardboard, and junk mail; glass, metal, and plastic; and nonrecyclable trash.

SCHOOL DAZE

It's true that I have only a few minutes to finish this; however, I am not worried.

Well, that makes one of us.

 Grammar Practice

Semicolons

 Write the numbers of the lines that need a semicolon in the following paragraphs. Then write the two words, separated by the semicolon.

Example: The Nintendo Playing Card Company was begun in 1889 in Japan today it's a familiar video game company.
Japan; today

1   In the 1960s, a Japanese company called Service Games started
2   up the company's name was later shortened to Sega. At first, Sega
3   created pinball games. Interactive video games were introduced
4   in 1968 however, the first *popular* interactive game, Pong, was
5   not developed until 1972. These early arcade video games were
6   big machines that included speakers, video screens, and coin slots
7   knobs, flippers, and joysticks and computer processors and software.
8   Things changed in 1976 when people could play video games at
9   home on their televisions. Less than 10 years later, home computers
10 were becoming more common as a result, Tetris became one of
11 the first popular computer games. The first handheld video game,
12 Nintendo's Game Boy, was introduced in 1989 it had a black-and-
13 white screen! By 2001, online games allowed thousands of gamers to
14 play at once.
15   What does the future hold for video games? One possibility is
16 games that can "think" for themselves another is games that are
17 controlled by eye movements. Whatever the case, these games are
18 almost guaranteed a big audience!

Next Step: Write a compound sentence about any kind of game you've played. Punctuate it with a semicolon. Then write another compound sentence using a conjunctive adverb; again, use a semicolon to join the independent clauses.

Related Skills Activities

■ **Basic Grammar and Writing**
Create Compound Sentences, p. 516

■ **SkillsBook**
Semicolons, pp. 19–20

Answers

line 2.	up; the
line 4.	1968; however,
line 6.	slots; knobs
line 7.	joysticks; and
line 10.	common; as
line 12.	1989; it
line 16.	themselves; another

Colons

A **colon** may be used to introduce a list or an important point. Colons are also used in business letters and between the numbers in time.

596.1
To Introduce Lists

Use a colon to introduce a list. The colon usually comes after words describing the subject of the list (as in the first example below) or after summary words, such as *the following* or *these things*. Do not use a colon after a verb or preposition.

Certain items are still difficult to recycle: foam cups, car tires, and toxic chemicals.

To conserve water, you should do the following three things: fix drippy faucets, install a low-flow showerhead, and turn the water off while brushing your teeth.

Incorrect: To conserve water, you should: install a low-flow showerhead, turn the water off while brushing your teeth, and fix drippy faucets.

596.2
To Introduce Sentences

A colon may be used to introduce a sentence, a question, or a quotation.

This is why air pollution is bad: We are sacrificing our health and the health of all other life on the planet.

Answer this question for me: Why aren't more people concerned about global warming?

Joaquin shared this with us: "Iceland is the world's leader in the use of renewable energy."

596.3
After Salutations

A colon may be used after the salutation of a business letter.

Dear Ms. Manners: Dear Dr. Warmle: Dear Professor Potter:

Dear Captain Elliot: Dear Senator:

596.4
For Emphasis

Use a colon to emphasize a word or phrase.

The newest alternative energy is also the most common element on earth: hydrogen.

Here's one thing that can help save energy: a programmable thermostat.

596.5
Between Numbers in Time

Use a colon between the parts of a number that indicates time.

My thermostat automatically sets my heat to 60 degrees between 11:00 p.m. and 6:00 a.m.

Grammar Practice

Colons

Which words or numbers in the letter below should be followed by or contain a colon? Write each one and place the colon correctly.

Example: Kangaroos are known for these features their pouches, their long legs, and their long tails.
features:

1 Dear Mr. Sei

2   Last night around 815 p.m., I saw one of the largest kangaroos

3 I have ever seen. It entered our camping area, seemingly unafraid,

4 and ate the plants near our tent. As I silently watched, I studied its

5 features the long claw, the big ears, the strong forelimbs, and the

6 soft muzzle. Although there was very little light, I could tell by the

7 size that it could only be the giant of kangaroos the red.

8   I remembered a friend asking me this How much ground can a

9 red cover in a single jump? I have seen these kangaroos easily cover

10 20 feet while they cruised along. I don't know if that is any kind of

11 record, but it sure is a long hop. A park ranger says that the female

12 red, which is gray blue in color, can hit 30 miles per hour.

13   After eating as much as it wanted, the big red finally

14 disappeared into the darkness about 945 p.m. Sadly, I've heard this

15 comment Kangaroos are giant jumping rats and cause nothing but

16 trouble. Some kangaroos may be pests, but the one I saw makes me

17 think only one thing They are a marvelous part of Australia.

18 With regards,

19 Franklin

Next Step: Write a brief reply to Franklin. Use colons as necessary.

Related Skills Activities

■ **SkillsBook**
Colons, pp. 21–22

Answers

line 1:   Sei:
line 2:   8:15
line 5:   features:
line 7:   kangaroos:
line 8:   this:
line 14:   9:45
line 15:   comment:
line 17:   thing:

598

Quotation Marks

Quotation marks are used in a number of ways:
- to set off the exact words of a speaker,
- to punctuate material quoted from another source,
- to punctuate words used in a special way, and
- to punctuate certain titles.

598.1
To Set Off a Speaker's Exact Words

Place quotation marks before and after a speaker's words in dialogue. Only the exact words of the speaker are placed within quotation marks.

Marla said, "I've decided to become a firefighter."

"A firefighter," said Juan, "can help people in many ways."

598.2
For Quotations Within Quotations

Use single quotation marks to punctuate a quotation within a quotation.

Sung Kim asked, "Did Marla just say, 'I've decided to become a firefighter'?"

When titles occur within a quotation, use single quotation marks to punctuate those that require quotation marks.

Juan said, "Springsteen's song 'The Rising' really inspired her."

598.3
To Set Off Quoted Material

When quoting material from another source, place quotation marks before and after the source's exact words.

In her book *Living the Life You Deserve*, Tess Spyeder explains, "Choose a job you'll enjoy doing day after day over one that will fatten your bank account."

598.4
To Set Off Long Quoted Material

If more than one paragraph is quoted from a single source, quotation marks are placed before each paragraph and at the end of the last paragraph.

"
————
"
———— .
"
————
"   "

Quotations that are more than four lines are usually set off from the rest of the paper by indenting each line 10 spaces from the left. Quotations that are set off in this way require no quotation marks either before or after the quoted material.

———— .
————
————
————
———— .

---

punctuate *edit* capitalize SPELL
improve
Marking Punctuation

599

Grammar Practice

Quotation Marks 1

- To Set Off a Speaker's Exact Words
- For Quotations Within Quotations
- To Set Off Quoted Material

For each paragraph below, write the quotation marks along with the words that come after and before them, or write "none needed."

Example: Principal Krenz announced, A hurricane is coming!
"A . . . coming!"

1. Jamilah shouted, Next week the Hurricane Sisters are coming to our school! They're going to sing their new song, Eye of the Storm.

2. David said, Did you just say, Next week the Hurricane Sisters are coming to our school? I can't believe it! They rock!

3. Did you know there's a new book about them, too? Jamilah asked. Here, check this out. It's called *Coast to Coast Hurricane.*

4. David read the following passage from the Hurricane Sisters' book:
   The Hurricane Sisters, Jill and Lily, were actually born during a hurricane. In August 1983, Hurricane Alicia hit Galveston, Texas, and the twins' mother was unable to leave the area before she went into labor. Luckily, the birth was an uncomplicated one, and mother and daughters rode out the hurricane together.

5. He flipped a few more pages and read, Jill and Lily began singing at church picnics and talent shows at age three. By the age of six, both girls were learning how to play the guitar.

6. David remarked, Wow! They've been performing together for years. Maybe that's why they've become so popular.

Related Skills Activities

- **Basic Grammar and Writing**
  Write Narrative Paragraphs, p. 526
  Parts of a Paragraph, p. 524

- **CD-ROM**
  Punctuating Dialogue   598.1, 598.2

- *SkillsBook*
  Punctuating Dialogue, pp. 23–24

Answers

1. "Next . . . Storm."
2. "Did . . . 'Next . . . school?' . . . rock!"
3. "Did . . . too?" "Here, . . . *Hurricane.*"
4. none needed
5. "Jill . . . guitar."
6. "Wow! . . . popular."

Quotation Marks . . .

600.1 Placement of Punctuation

Always place periods and commas inside quotation marks.

"I don't know," said Lac.

Lac said, "I don't know."

Place an exclamation point or a question mark inside the quotation marks when it punctuates the quotation.

Ms. Wiley asked, "Can you actually tour the Smithsonian on the Internet?"

Place it outside when it punctuates the main sentence.

Did I hear you say, "Now we can tour the Smithsonian on the Internet"?

Place semicolons or colons outside quotation marks.

First, I will read the article "Sonny's Blues"; then I will read "The Star Café" in my favorite music magazine.

600.2 For Special Words

Quotation marks also may be used (1) to set apart a word that is being discussed, (2) to indicate that a word is slang, or (3) to point out that a word or phrase is being used in a special way.

1. Renny uses the word "like" entirely too much.
2. Man, your car is really "phat."
3. Aunt Lulu, an editor at a weekly magazine, says she has "issues."

600.3 To Punctuate Titles

Use quotation marks to punctuate titles of songs, poems, short stories, lectures, episodes of radio or television programs, chapters of books, and articles found in magazines, newspapers, or encyclopedias. (Also see 602.3.)

"21 Questions" (song)
"The Reed Flute's Song" (poem)
"Old Man at the Bridge" (short story)
"Birthday Boys" (a television episode)
"The Foolish and the Weak" (a chapter in a book)
"Science Careers Today" (lecture)
"Teen Rescues Stranded Dolphin" (newspaper article)

NOTE When you punctuate a title, capitalize the first word, last word, and every word in between—except for articles (a, an, the), short prepositions (at, to, with, and so on), and coordinating conjunctions (and, but, or). (See 624.2.)

Grammar Practice

Quotation Marks 2

- Placement of Punctuation
- To Punctuate Titles

 Rewrite the following sentences, correctly placing quotation marks where they are needed.

Example: Have you read the poem Spring Dragon?
Have you read the poem "Spring Dragon"?

1. Caleb shouted, Hey, I saw your picture in the paper!
2. My picture appeared in the article McCabe Scores in Finals.
3. Duante couldn't get the song When Doves Cry out of his head.
4. I have one suggestion for your short story Mama's Reading Lamp: Change the title.
5. Today Dr. Nguyen is presenting his speech Get Fit! in the gym.
6. Guillermo asked, Did you see *The Smiths* on TV last night?
7. No, I didn't, Tom said.
8. Did you ever see the episode The Genius?
9. The funniest episode ever was Lisa on Ice!
10. This quarter we are reading *Fahrenheit 451*, the teacher said.
11. We must read the last chapter, Burning Bright, by the end of the month.

Next Step: Write two or three sentences about a song you like, a poem you're familiar with, and a newspaper article you have read.

Related Skills Activities

CD-ROM
Punctuating Dialogue   600.1
Punctuating Titles   600.3

SkillsBook
Quotation Marks and Italics, pp. 25–26

Answers

1. Caleb shouted, "Hey, I saw your picture in the paper!"
2. My picture appeared in the article "McCabe Scores in Finals."
3. Duante couldn't get the song "When Doves Cry" out of his head.
4. I have one suggestion for your short story "Mama's Reading Lamp": Change the title.
5. Today Dr. Nguyen is presenting his speech "Get Fit!" in the gym.
6. Guillermo asked, "Did you see *The Smiths* on TV last night?"
7. "No, I didn't," Tom said.
8. Did you ever see the episode "The Genius"?
9. The funniest episode ever was "Lisa on Ice"!
10. "This quarter we are reading *Fahrenheit 451*," the teacher said.
11. We must read the last chapter, "Burning Bright," by the end of the month.

602

Italics and Underlining

Italics is slightly slanted type. In this sentence, the word *happiness* is typed in italics. In handwritten material, each word or letter that should be in italics is **underlined**. (See an example on page 403.)

602.1
In Printed Material

Print words in italics when you are using a computer.

In *Tuck Everlasting*, the author explores what it would be like to live forever.

602.2
In Handwritten Material

Underline words that should be italicized when you are writing by hand.

In <u>Tuck Everlasting</u>, the author explores what it would be like to live forever.

602.3
In Titles

Italicize (or underline) the titles of books, plays, book-length poems, magazines, newspapers, radio and television programs, movies, videos, cassettes, CD's, and the names of aircraft and ships.

Walk Two Moons (book)	*Teen People* (magazine)
Fairies and Dragons (movie)	*Everwood* (TV program)
The Young and the Hopeless (CD)	*U.S.S. Arizona* (ship)
Columbia (space shuttle)	*Daily Herald* (newspaper)

Exception: Do not italicize or put quotation marks around your own title at the top of your written work.

A Day Without Water (personal writing: do not italicize)

602.4
For Scientific and Foreign Words

Italicize (or underline) scientific and foreign words that are not commonly used in everyday English.

Spinacia oleracea is the scientific term for spinach.

Many store owners who can help Spanish-speaking customers display an *Hablamos Español* sign in their windows.

602.5
For Special Uses

Italicize (or underline) a number, letter, or word that is being discussed or used in a special way. (Sometimes quotation marks are used for this same reason.)

Matt's hat has a bright red *A* on it.

Related Skills Activities

■ **CD-ROM**
Punctuating Titles   602.2, 602.3

■ *SkillsBook*
Quotation Marks and Italics, pp. 25–26

Grammar Practice

Italics and Underlining

 Write and underline the word or words that should be italicized in each sentence. If a word or words have been incorrectly italicized, write them down and circle them.

Example: Sylvia asked, "Did you read the book Undaunted Courage?"
<u>Undaunted Courage</u>

1. "No, but I saw the TV show The Lewis and Clark Expedition," replied Angela.

2. Sylvia wrote the article *Finding the Northwest Passage* for the student paper.

3. William Least Heat-Moon traveled that famous route in a boat he called Nikawa.

4. During their two-year journey, Lewis and Clark must have heard someone say tatonka, a Lakota word meaning "buffalo."

5. The scientific name for the American buffalo is Bison bison.

6. Buffalo are mentioned in the familiar song *Home on the Range.*

7. The book *Mystic Warriors of the Plains* talks about the *designs* hunters would paint on the bison skulls.

8. National Geographic magazine has released a large-format movie called *Lewis and Clark: The Journey West.*

9. The *Missouri Gazette* reported on many events that honored the 200th anniversary of the *Lewis and Clark expedition.*

Next Step: Write three sentences with movie, book, or CD titles, as well as poem and song titles. Exchange papers with a classmate and underline the titles that should be italicized.

Answers

1. The Lewis and Clark Expedition
2. (Finding the Northwest Passage)
3. Nikawa
4. tatonka
5. Bison bison
6. (Home on the Range)
7. (designs)
8. National Geographic
9. (Lewis and Clark expedition)

Apostrophes

Use **apostrophes** to form contractions, to form certain plurals, or to show possession.

604.1
In Contractions

Use an apostrophe to form a contraction, showing that one or more letters have been left out of a word.

Common Contractions

can't (cannot)	**couldn't** (could not)	**didn't** (did not)
doesn't (does not)	**don't** (do not)	**hasn't** (has not)
haven't (have not)	**isn't** (is not)	**I'll** (I will)
I'd (I would)	**I'm** (I am)	**I've** (I have)
they'll (they will)	**they'd** (they would)	**they've** (they have)
they're (they are)	**won't** (will not)	**wouldn't** (would not)
you'll (you will)	**you'd** (you would)	**you've** (you have)
you're (you are)		

604.2
In Place of Omitted Letters or Numbers

Use an apostrophe to show that one or more digits have been left out of a number, or that one or more letters have been left out of a word to show a special pronunciation.

> class of **'99** (*19* is left out)
>
> g'bye (the letters *ood* are left out of *good-bye*)

NOTE Letters and numbers should not be omitted in most writing assignments; however, they may be omitted in dialogue to make it sound like real people are talking.

604.3
To Form Some Plurals

Use an apostrophe and *s* to form the plural of a letter, a sign, a number, or a word being discussed as a word.

> A's   8's   +'s   to's
>
> Don't use too many *and*'s in your writing.

604.4
To Form Singular Possessives

To form the possessive of a singular noun, add an apostrophe and *s*.

> the game's directions   Dr. Mill's theory
> Ross's bike   Roz's hair

NOTE When a singular noun with more than one syllable ends with an *s* or *z* sound, the possessive may be formed by adding just an apostrophe.

> Texas' oil (or) Texas's oil   Carlos' mother (or) Carlos's mother

---

Grammar Practice

Apostrophes 1

■ In Contractions

For the sentences below, write the word pairs and the contractions they can be combined to form.

Example: Mom says it is time for me to do my own laundry.
it is—it's

1. She said she would teach me.
2. "Doing laundry is not hard," she said. "It just takes time."
3. "First separate your clothes. Do not wash the light-colored clothes with the dark ones."
4. She added, "It would not hurt to look at the washing instructions on the clothes tag."
5. "Next you are going to put detergent in the washing machine and select the water temperature."
6. After she explained that I would use hot water for whites and warm water for the rest, I put my clothes in.
7. "It will take about half an hour for the washer to finish."
8. Then she said, "You will want to clean the lint trap in the dryer before putting your clothes in," and she showed me how.
9. "When they are dry, fold them and put them away."

■ To Form Some Plurals

For the sentences below, correctly write the plurals of letters, numbers, symbols, and words being discussed.

Example: Marisa typed a line made of ~s on her computer.
~'s

1. Our last name is Patel, so Mom has Ps all over the house.
2. Tom's phone number has four 2s in it.
3. I took out all the &s in my paper and replaced them with *and*s.

Related Skills Activities

■ **Basic Grammar and Writing**
Avoid Double Negatives, p. 510
Show Possession, p. 472

■ **CD-ROM**
Apostrophes to Form Possessives
604.4

■ *SkillsBook*
Apostrophes 1, pp. 27–28
Apostrophes 2, pp. 29–30

Answers

1. she would—she'd
2. is not—isn't
3. do not—don't
4. would not—wouldn't
5. you are—you're
6. I would—I'd
7. it will—it'll
8. you will—you'll
9. they are—they're

Answers

1. P's
2. 2's
3. &'s, *and*'s

606

Apostrophes . . .

606.1
To Form Plural Possessives

The possessive form of plural nouns ending in *s* is usually made by adding just an apostrophe.

    students' homework   teachers' lounge

For plural nouns not ending in *s*, an apostrophe and *s* must be added.

    children's book   people's opinions

Remember: The word immediately before the apostrophe is the owner.

    student's project (*student* is the owner)
    students' project (*students* are the owners)

606.2
To Show Shared Possession

When possession is shared by more than one noun, add an apostrophe and *s* to the last noun in the series.

    Uncle Reggie, Aunt Rosie, and my mom's garden
    (All three own the garden.)

    Uncle Reggie's, Aunt Rosie's, and my mom's gardens
    (Each person owns a garden.)

606.3
To Form Possessives with Compound Nouns

The possessive of a compound noun is formed by placing the possessive ending after the last word.

    her sister-in-law's hip-hop music (singular)
    her sisters-in-law's tastes in music (plural)
    the secretary of state's husband (singular)
    the secretaries of state's husbands (plural)

606.4
To Form Possessives with Indefinite Pronouns

The possessive of an indefinite pronoun is formed by adding an apostrophe and *s*.

    no one's   anyone's   somebody's

NOTE In pronouns that use *else*, add an apostrophe and *s* to the second word.

    somebody else's   anyone else's

606.5
To Express Time or Amount

Use an apostrophe with an adjective that is part of an expression indicating time (month, day, hour) or amount.

    In today's Spanish class, we talked about going to Spain.
    My father lost more than an hour's work when that thunderstorm knocked out our power.
    I bought a couple dollars' worth of grapes at the roadside stand.

---

punctuate *edit* capitalize SPELL
improve
Marking Punctuation   **607**

PUNCTUATION

Grammar Practice

Apostrophes 2

■ To Form Possessives

 For each sentence below, write the word or words that need an apostrophe with the apostrophe placed correctly.

    Example: David G. Wilsons 1970 invention, the modern recumbent bicycle, is a "reclining" bicycle.
    Wilson's

1. Many engineers designs for these bicycles have been around since the late 1800s, but the bikes are just now gaining in popularity.
2. This bicycles seat enables riders to sit and lean back in it.
3. While the feet are on the pedals out front, the pedals power drives the back wheel, just as with a traditional bicycle.
4. The handlebar grips are at or below the riders shoulder level.
5. The recumbent design allows peoples bike riding to be free from neck strain, wrist pain, and sore seats.

■ To Show Shared Possession
■ To Form Possessives with Compound Nouns and Indefinite Pronouns

 Write the underlined word or words in the correct possessive form.

    Example: <u>Tyronica and Lanelle</u> bikes were falling apart.
    Tyronica's and Lanelle's

1. It was their <u>mom and dad</u> decision to get them new bikes.
2. They had seen <u>Deion and Terry</u> recumbent bikes.
3. The girls practiced riding the strange bikes around their <u>cul-de-sac</u> central garden.
4. They ignored <u>everyone</u> stares because they didn't care about <u>anyone else</u> opinion.
5. They just loved to see their <u>great-grandmother</u> smile!

Related Skills Activities

■ **Basic Grammar and Writing**
Show Possession, p. 472

■ **CD-ROM**
Apostrophes to Form Possessives
606.1, 606.2, 606.3, 606.4

■ *SkillsBook*
Apostrophe 1, pp. 27–28
Apostrophes 2, pp. 29–30
Apostrophes 3, pp. 31–32

 Answers

1. engineers'
2. bicycle's
3. pedals'
4. rider's
5. people's

 Answers

1. mom and dad's
2. Deion's and Terry's
3. cul-de-sac's
4. everyone's, anyone else's
5. great-grandmother's

Hyphens

Use a **hyphen** to divide words at the end of a line and to form compound words. Also use a hyphen between the numbers in a fraction and to join numbers that indicate the life span of an individual, the scores of a game, and so on.

608.1
To Divide Words

Use a hyphen to divide a word when you run out of room at the end of a line. A word may be divided only between syllables. Here are some additional guidelines:

- Never divide a one-syllable word: *raised, through.*
- Avoid dividing a word of five letters or fewer: *paper, study.*
- Never divide a one-letter syllable from the rest of the word: *omit-ted,* **not** *o-mitted.*
- Never divide abbreviations or contractions: *NASA, wouldn't.*
- Never divide the last word in more than two lines in a row or the last word in a paragraph.
- When a vowel is a syllable by itself, divide the word after the vowel: *epi-sode,* **not** *ep-isode.*

NOTE Refer to a dictionary if you're not sure how to divide a word.

608.2
In Compound Words

A hyphen is used in some compound words, including numbers from twenty-one to ninety-nine.

about-face	warm-up	time-out
down-to-earth	ice-skating	high-rise
thirty-three	seventy-five	

608.3
To Create New Words

A hyphen is often used to form new words beginning with the prefixes *self, ex, all,* and *great.* A hyphen is also used with suffixes such as *elect* and *free.*

self-cleaning	ex-friend	all-natural	mayor-elect
self-esteem	ex-president	great-aunt	germ-free

608.4
Between Numbers in a Fraction

Use a hyphen between the numbers in a fraction. Do not, however, use a hyphen between the numerator and denominator when one or both are already hyphenated.

four-tenths	five-sixteenths	seven thirty-seconds (7/32)

Grammar Practice

Hyphens 1

- To Divide Words
- To Create New Words
- Between Numbers in a Fraction

 For each of the following sentences, correctly write the words that need hyphens. If a word is hyphenated incorrectly, write it with the hyphen properly placed (or without the hyphen).

Example: Most people who fish are not self taught.
self-taught

1. They learn to fish from a parent or grandparent who probably also learned to fish from a relative.
2. When I was learning how to hook a worm, I did it over and over again until I got it right.
3. It takes about two thirds of an hour for me to find enough worms.
4. Some believe the best way to fish is to use a barbfree hook.
5. The fish that these anglers release back into the water aren't badly injured by the hooks.
6. In addition, this type of hook is easier to remove from yourself if it "catches" you!
7. Fishing is nine tenths patience.
8. My greatgrandparents like to fish, and I have to say that they're some of the most patient people I know.
9. Yesterday, they gave us one fourth of all the fish they caught.
10. They also gave their neighbor, an exmarine, some of their fish.
11. After Dad gutted and cleaned the fish, we cooked them for dinner that night.

Next Step: Write the following words as they could be hyphenated at the end of a line: *candle, maximum, protein,* and *tomorrow.*

Related Skills Activities

■ **CD-ROM**
Hyphens 608.1, 608.3

■ *SkillsBook*
Hyphens 1, pp. 33–34
Hyphens 2, p. 35

 Answers

1. also
2. over
3. two-thirds
4. barb-free
5. aren't
6. your-self
7. nine-tenths
8. great-grandparents, they're
9. one-fourth
10. ex-marine
11. din-ner

Next Step: **Answers**

can-dle, maxi-mum, pro-tein, to-morrow or tomor-row

Hyphens . . .

610.1
To Form Adjectives

Use a hyphen to join two or more words that work together to form a single-thought adjective before a noun. Generally, hyphenate any compound adjective that might be misread if it is not hyphenated—use common sense. (See page 488.)

smiley-face sticker   dress-up clothes   fresh-breeze scent

Use the tests below to determine if a hyphen is needed.

1. When a compound adjective is made of a noun plus an adjective, it should be hyphenated.

   microwave-safe cookware   book-smart student

2. When the compound adjective is made of a noun plus a participle (*ing* or *ed* form of a verb), it should be hyphenated.

   bone-chilling story   vitamin-enriched cereal

3. Hyphenate a compound adjective that is a phrase (includes conjunctions or prepositions).

   heat-and-serve meals   refrigerator-to-oven dishes

Do *not* hyphenate compound adjectives in these instances:

1. When words forming the adjective come after the noun, do not hyphenate.

   This cookware is microwave safe.
   The cereal was vitamin enriched.

2. If the first of the two words ends in *ly*, do not hyphenate.

   newly designed computer   rarely seen species

3. Do not use a hyphen when a number or letter is the final part of a one-thought adjective.

   grade A milk   level 6 textbook

610.2
To Join Letters to Words

Use a hyphen to join a capital letter to a noun or participle.

U-turn   Y-axis
PG-rated movie

610.3
To Avoid Confusion

Use a hyphen with prefixes or suffixes to avoid confusion or awkward spelling.

Re-collect (not recollect) **the reports we handed back last week.**
It has a shell-like (not shelllike) **texture.**

Grammar Practice

Hyphens 2

■ To Form Adjectives
■ To Join Letters to Words

For each of the following sentences, correctly write the words that need a hyphen. If no words need a hyphen, write "OK."

Example: A paper thin membrane called the *pleura* covers the lungs.
paper-thin

1. The diaphragm and the chest muscles are responsible for the up and down motion of the rib cage during breathing.

2. The trachea, the tube that carries air to and from the lungs, has 16 to 20 U shaped rings of hard cartilage in front.

3. The heart is a four chambered organ divided in two by the septum.

4. The right side of the heart pumps oxygen poor blood into the lungs.

5. The left side pumps oxygen enriched blood from the lungs all over the body.

6. Arteries carry the blood to barely visible capillaries in the body tissues.

7. Their single cell walls allow oxygen to pass into the tissues and carbon dioxide to be absorbed from them.

8. High blood pressure can result from slowly formed blockages in the blood vessels.

9. A once in a lifetime event might cause a brief spike in one's blood pressure.

10. Long term effects of high blood pressure can be serious.

11. A doctor will often X ray the chest of a person with high blood pressure to see if the condition is affecting the heart.

Next Step: Write sentences that include two words (*not* those on this page or the facing one) with letters joined to them.

Related Skills Activities

■ **CD-ROM**
Hyphens   610.2, 610.2

■ *SkillsBook*
Hyphens 1, pp. 33–34

Answers

1. up-and-down
2. U-shaped
3. four-chambered
4. oxygen-poor
5. oxygen-enriched
6. OK
7. single-cell
8. OK
9. once-in-a-lifetime
10. Long-term
11. X-ray

Dashes

The **dash** can be used to show a sudden break in a sentence, to emphasize a word or clause, and to show that someone's speech is being interrupted.

612.1
To Indicate a Sudden Break

A dash can be used to show a sudden break in a sentence.

The three of us came down with colds, lost our voices, and missed the football game—all because we had practiced in the rain.

612.2
For Emphasis

A dash may be used to emphasize or explain a word, a series of words, a phrase, or a clause.

Vitamins and minerals—important dietary supplements—can improve your diet.

The benefits of vitamin A—better vision and a stronger immune system—are well known.

612.3
To Indicate Interrupted Speech

Use a dash to show that someone's speech is being interrupted by another person.

Well—yes, I understand—no, I remember—oh—okay, thank you.

NOTE A dash is indicated by two hyphens--without spacing before or after the hyphens--in all typed material.

Parentheses

Parentheses are used around words that are included in a sentence to add information or to help make an idea clearer.

612.4
To Add Information

Use parentheses when adding information or clarifying an idea.

Cures for diseases (from arthritis to AIDS) may be found in plants in the rain forest.

Only about 10 percent (27,000) of the plant species in the world have been studied.

Grammar Practice

Dashes

 Rewrite the sentences below, adding dashes where appropriate.

Example: We'll be outside all afternoon don't forget the sunscreen.
We'll be outside all afternoon—don't forget the sunscreen.

1. Han said, "They were going I mean they *are* going to the mall."
2. *Taraxacum officinale* that is, the common dandelion is the curse of many lawns.
3. I don't let's just wait calm down.
4. "Good morning! Here are your oops eggs," Mom said as she dropped my scrambled eggs on my lap.
5. This is Reggie's bike the bike that was stolen!

Parentheses

 Write the parts of the sentences below that should be enclosed in parentheses. Add the parentheses.

Example: Simone's sisters Rachel, Gabby, and Naomi joined us.
(Rachel, Gabby, and Naomi)

1. Peter asked the clerk the one wearing glasses for some change.
2. Of the flower bulbs I planted, most of them 80 percent bloomed.
3. Fumiki looking quite pale excused herself from the table.
4. Vinnie my friend's first cousin has a job at the amusement park this summer.
5. Kat always peppers her e-mails with emoticons smiley faces.

Related Skills Activities

■ *SkillsBook*
Dashes, p. 36

 Answers

1. Han said, "They were going—I mean they are going—to the mall."
2. *Tarasacum officinale*—that is, the common dandelion—is the curse of many lawns.
3. I don't—let's just—wait—calm down.
4. "Good morning! Here are your—oops—eggs," Mom said as she dropped my scrambled eggs on my lap.
5. This is Reggie's bike—the bike that was stolen!

 Answers

1. (the one wearing glasses)
2. (80 percent)
3. (looking quite pale)
4. (my friend's first cousin)
5. (smiley faces)

614

Ellipses

Use an **ellipsis** (three periods) to show a pause in dialogue or to show that words or sentences have been left out. Leave one space before, after, and between each period.

614.1
To Show Pauses

Use an ellipsis to show a pause in dialogue.

"My report," said Reggie, "is on . . . ah . . . cars of the future. One place that I . . . uh . . . checked on the Internet said that cars would someday run on sunshine."

614.2
To Show Omitted Words

Use an ellipsis to show that one or more words have been left out of a quotation. Read this statement about hibernation.

Some animals, such as the chipmunk and the woodchuck, hibernate in winter. During this time, the animal's heart beats very slowly—only a few times per minute. Its body cools down so much that it nearly freezes, and this is called going into torpor.

Here's how you would type part of the above quotation, leaving some of the words out. If the words left out are at the end of a sentence, use a period followed by three dots.

Some animals . . . hibernate in winter. During this time, the animal's heart beats very slowly . . . and this is called going into torpor.

SCHOOL DAZE

615

Grammar Practice

Ellipses

 ■ **To Show Pauses**

Rewrite the following sentences, adding ellipses where they are needed.

Example: Oh no I forgot the tickets.

Oh no . . . I forgot the tickets.

1. Did you see the disgusting uh I mean the special food we are having for lunch?

2. It's well how can I describe it?

3. Hmm does it have something healthful in it?

4. Ah you hit the nail on the head.

5. We're having let's see "Martina's Tofu Surprise."

 ■ **To Show Omitted Words**

Rewrite the following paragraph as a quotation for a research paper. Insert ellipses where you decide to leave out less-important information.

Sandstone is a very simple kind of sedimentary rock. It is not much more than sand pressed tightly together and mixed with clay, which acts as a kind of cement. Sandstone is porous, which means that water can pass through it; each year's freeze and thaw breaks down the rock a little more. It erodes rapidly, so wind and water can carve sandstone into unusual shapes.

 ### Answers

1. Did you see the disgusting . . . uh . . . I mean . . . the special food we are having for lunch?

2. It's . . . well . . . how can I describe it?

3. Hmm . . . does it have something healthful in it?

4. Ah . . . you hit the nail on the head.

5. We're having . . . let's see . . . "Martina's Tofu Surprise."

 ### Possible Answers

Sandstone is . . . sedimentary rock. It is . . . sand pressed tightly together and mixed with clay, which acts as . . . cement. Sandstone is porous . . . each year's freeze and thaw breaks down the rock a little more . . . wind and water can carve sandstone into unusual shapes.

Test Prep!

Number your paper from 1 to 12. For each underlined part of the paragraphs below, write the letter (from the next page) of the best way to punctuate it.

Soon you'll be thinking about an upcoming <u>event: your</u> move from
    (1)
middle school to high school. <u>Its likely that you'll</u> be going to a bigger
    (2)
school with many more students than attend your current school. Don't

worry about getting <u>lost; Go</u> to the freshman orientation to get valuable
    (3)
information—including a map—that will make your move to ninth

grade easier.

You might be concerned about harder work in high <u>school: however,</u>
    (4)
most students find they can keep up with it. On the other hand, you can

look forward to having more choices in these <u>areas; courses,</u> friends, and
    (5)
cafeteria food.

In <u>Norton Wright</u> book <u>Eighth to Ninth,</u> Wright suggests, <u>'It's</u> a good
    (6)   (7)   (8)
idea to visit the high school in the spring before you attend." He goes

on to say, "If you can <u>'shadow'</u> another student, that's even <u>better</u>"! An
    (9)   (10)
article titled <u>"Casting Long Shadows"</u> in the newspaper <u>"High School</u>
    (11)   (12)
<u>Happenings"</u> agreed with his advice.

<table>
<tr><td>

1   (A) event: Your
    (B) event; your
    (C) event your
    (D) correct as is

2   (A) It's likely that you'll
    (B) Its' likely that you'll
    (C) It's likely that you'l
    (D) correct as is

3   (A) lost Go
    (B) lost; go
    (C) lost go
    (D) correct as is

4   (A) school, however;
    (B) school: However,
    (C) school; however,
    (D) correct as is

5   (A) areas: courses,
    (B) areas courses
    (C) areas: Courses
    (D) correct as is

6   (A) Norton Wrights
    (B) Norton Wright's
    (C) Norton Wrights'
    (D) correct as is

</td><td>

7   (A) "Eighth to Ninth"
    (B) *"Eighth to Ninth"*
    (C) Eighth to Ninth
    (D) correct as is

8   (A) 'Its
    (B) "Its
    (C) "It's
    (D) correct as is

9   (A) "shadow"
    (B) 'shadow'
    (C) "shadow'
    (D) correct as is

10   (A) better!
    (B) better!"
    (C) better"
    (D) correct as is

11   (A) Casting Long Shadows
    (B) *Casting Long Shadows*
    (C) "Casting Long Shadows"
    (D) correct as is

12   (A) "High School Happenings"
    (B) *High School Happenings*
    (C) High School Happenings
    (D) correct as is

</td></tr>
</table>

Related Skills Activities

■ ***SkillsBook***
Other Forms of Punctuation, pp. 37–38
Punctuation Review, pp. 39–40

Answers

1.	D	**7.**	D
2.	A	**8.**	C
3.	B	**9.**	D
4.	C	**10.**	B
5.	A	**11.**	D
6.	B	**12.**	B

618

Editing for Mechanics
Capitalization

618.1
Proper Nouns and Adjectives

Capitalize all proper nouns and all proper adjectives. A proper noun is the name of a particular person, place, thing, or idea. A proper adjective is an adjective formed from a proper noun.

> Common Noun: country, president, continent
>
> Proper Noun: **Canada, Andrew Jackson, Asia**
>
> Proper Adjective: **Canadian, Jacksonian, Asian**

618.2
Names of People

Capitalize the names of people and also the initials or abbreviations that stand for those names.

> **Samuel L. Jackson   Aung San Suu Kyi**
>
> **Mary Sanchez-Gomez**

618.3
Titles Used with Names

Capitalize titles used with names of persons; also capitalize abbreviations standing for those titles.

> **President Mohammed Hosni Mubarak   Dr. Linda Trout**
>
> **Governor Michael Easley   Rev. Jim Zavaski**
>
> **Senator John McCain**

618.4
Words Used as Names

Capitalize words such as *mother, father, aunt,* and *uncle* when these words are used as names.

> Uncle Marius **started to sit on the couch.** (*Uncle* is a name; the speaker calls this person "Uncle Marius.")
>
> **Then** Uncle **stopped in midair.** (*Uncle* is used as a name.)
>
> **"So,** Mom, **what are you doing here?" I asked.** (*Mom* is used as a name.)

Words such as *aunt, uncle, mom, dad, grandma,* and *grandpa* are usually not capitalized if they come after a possessive pronoun (*my, his, our*).

> My aunt **had just called him.** (The word *aunt* describes this person but is not used as a name.)
>
> **Then** my dad **and** mom **walked into the room.** (The words *dad* and *mom* are not used as names in this sentence.)

Grammar Practice

Capitalization 1

- Names of People
- Titles Used with Names
- Words Used as Names

 Some words in the following sentences are capitalized and should not be; others need to be capitalized. Write each of the words correctly.

Example: Before he was a Governor and a President, mr. Ronald Reagan was an actor.
governor, president, Mr.

1. The first African American Congresswoman was representative Shirley Chisholm.

2. A Famous Poet, dr. Maya Angelou, read a poem at president Clinton's inauguration.

3. Abigail Adams was the Mother of President John quincy Adams.

4. Mr. Adams called his mom's brother simply "uncle."

5. President john f. Kennedy's Brother is senator Ted Kennedy.

6. The first woman appointed to the United States Supreme Court was justice Sandra day O'Connor.

7. President George w. Bush's Father is a former president: george h. w. Bush.

8. In 1997, secretary of state madeleine K. Albright became the highest-ranking woman in the history of the U.S. government.

9. Greenville, South Carolina, is the birthplace of rev. jessie Jackson, who ran for President at one time.

Next Step: Write a sentence about a famous person you are studying in school. Use a title (Dr., Ms., Senator) for this person in your sentence. Check your capitalization.

Related Skills Activities

- **CD-ROM**
  Capitalization 1   618.3
  Capitalization 2   618.1

- *SkillsBook*
  Capitalization 1, pp. 41–42
  Capitalization 2, pp. 43–44

Answers

1. congresswoman, Representative
2. famous, poet, Dr., President
3. mother, Quincy
4. Uncle
5. John, F., brother, Senator
6. Justice, Day
7. W., father, George H.W.
8. Secretary, State, Madeleine
9. Rev., Jessie, president

Capitalization . . .

620.1
School Subjects

Capitalize the name of a specific educational course, but not the name of a general subject. (Exception—the names of all languages are proper nouns and are always capitalized: *French, English, Hindi, German, Latin.*)

> Roberto is studying accounting at the technical college. (Because *accounting* is a general subject, it is not capitalized.)

> He likes the professor who teaches Accounting Principles. (The specific course name is capitalized.)

620.2
Official Names

Capitalize the names of businesses and the official names of their products. (These are called trade names.) Do not, however, capitalize a general word like "toothpaste" when it follows the trade name.

Old Navy	Best Buy	Microsoft	Kodak
Sony Playstation	Tombstone pizza	Mudd jeans	

620.3
Races, Languages, Nationalities, Religions

Capitalize the names of languages, races, nationalities, and religions, as well as the proper adjectives formed from them.

Arab	Spanish	Judaism	Catholicism
African art	Irish linen	Swedish meatballs	

620.4
Days, Months, Holidays

Capitalize the names of days of the week, months of the year, and special holidays.

Thursday	Friday	Saturday
July	August	September
Arbor Day	Independence Day	

Do not capitalize the names of seasons.

> winter, spring, summer, fall (autumn)

620.5
Historical Events

Capitalize the names of historical events, documents, and periods of time.

World War II	the Bill of Rights	the Magna Carta
the Middle Ages	the Paleozoic Era	

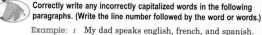
Grammar Practice

Capitalization 2

- School Subjects
- Races, Languages, Nationalities, Religions
- Historical Events

Correctly write any incorrectly capitalized words in the following paragraphs. (Write the line number followed by the word or words.)

Example: 1 My dad speaks english, french, and spanish.
1 *English, French, Spanish*

1   Last year I took a french language class. The class was
2 actually called french language and history, so we learned some
3 of that country's history, too. For instance, the french wars of
4 religion were fought by people of different christian faiths. While
5 France was ruled by catholic kings, an army attacked a protestant
6 church service. After many years of fighting between catholics and
7 protestants, the french people were allowed to choose their own
8 faith. Today, people of all faiths—christianity, judaism, hinduism,
9 islam, and others—have freedom to worship in France.
10   We also talked about Bastille Day, the french holiday that's
11 like Independence Day in the United States. In France, it celebrates
12 the beginning of the french revolution. The Bastille was the name
13 of a french prison for people who did not agree with the king and
14 queen's decisions. On July 14, 1789, a crowd of frenchmen stormed
15 the Bastille and released the prisoners. That revolution brought
16 great changes and new freedoms to France, just as the revolutionary
17 war gained freedom for early american colonists.

Next Step: Write two or three sentences about an American historical event you have recently studied or know something about.

Related Skills Activities

- **CD-ROM**
  Capitalization 1   620.2, 620.3
  Capitalization 2   620.5

- *SkillsBook*
  Capitalization 2, pp. 43–44

Answers

line 1:   French
line 2:   French, Language, History
line 3:   French
line 4:   Christian
line 5:   Catholic, Protestant
line 6:   Catholics
line 7:   Protestants, French
line 8:   Christianity, Judaism, Hinduism
line 9:   Islam
line 10: French
line 12: French Revolution
line 13: French
line 14: Frenchmen
line 16: Revolutionary
line 17: War, American

622

Capitalization . . .

622.1
Geographic Names

Capitalize the following geographic names.

Planets and heavenly bodies . . . . **Venus, Jupiter, Milky Way**

Lowercase the word "earth" except when used as the proper name of our planet, especially when mentioned with other planet names.

What on earth are you doing here?

Sam has traveled across the face of the earth several times.

Jupiter's diameter is 11 times larger than Earth's.

The four inner planets are Mercury, Venus, Earth, and Mars.

Continents	**Europe, Asia, South America, Australia, Africa**
Countries . . .	**Morocco, Haiti, Greece, Chile, United Arab Emirates**
States	**New Mexico, Alabama, West Virginia, Delaware, Iowa**
Provinces	**Alberta, British Columbia, Quebec, Ontario**
Counties	**Sioux County, Kandiyohi County, Wade County**
Cities	**Montreal, Baton Rouge, Albuquerque, Portland**
Bodies of water	**Delaware Bay, Chickamunga Lake, Indian Ocean, Gulf of Mexico, Skunk Creek**
Landforms	**Appalachian Mountains, Bitterroot Range**
Public areas	**Tiananmen Square, Sequoia National Forest, Mount Rushmore, Open Space Park, Vietnam Memorial**
Roads and highways	**New Jersey Turnpike, Interstate 80, Central Avenue, Chisholm Trail, Mutt's Road**
Buildings . . .	**Pentagon, Paske High School, Empire State Building**
Monuments	**Eiffel Tower, Statue of Liberty**

622.2
Particular Sections of the Country

Capitalize words that indicate particular sections of the country. Also capitalize proper adjectives formed from names of specific sections of a country.

Having grown up on the hectic East Coast, I find life in the South to be refreshing.

Here in Georgia, Southern hospitality is a way of life.

Words that simply indicate a direction are not capitalized; nor are adjectives that are formed from words that simply indicate direction.

The town where I live, located east of Memphis, is typical of others found in western Tennessee.

Grammar Practice

Capitalization 3

■ Geographic Names
■ Particular Sections of the Country

For each sentence below, write the word or words that should be capitalized but aren't. If a sentence has correct capitalization, write "correct."

Example: Kennebunk, ocean city, and St. Augustine are cities on the east coast.
Ocean City, East Coast

1. You can see giant pandas in china at the beijing zoological gardens.
2. Honolulu, Hawaii, is on the southeast coast of the island of Oahu.
3. The San Andreas Fault runs northwest to southeast along california's coastline.
4. The queen lives in buckingham palace in london, england.
5. Mt. rushmore and the crazy horse monument are in the black hills of south dakota.
6. The mississippi river runs from minnesota to the gulf of mexico.
7. Mount kilimanjaro, near the border of kenya, is the highest point in africa.
8. There are many historic trails and landmarks in the western united states.
9. The will rogers highway is one of the names for route 66, which runs from chicago to los angeles.
10. Indiana, wisconsin, iowa, and ohio are states in the midwest.

Next Step: Write complete sentences to answer the following questions. Be sure to use correct capitalization.
● What large body of water is closest to your home?
● What city in the state of New York has the greatest population?

Related Skills Activities

■ **CD-ROM**
Capitalization 1   622.1
Capitalization 2   622.1, 622.2

■ *SkillsBook*
Capitalization 1, pp. 41–42
Capitalization 2, pp. 43–44

Answers

1. China, Beijing Zoological Gardens
2. correct
3. California's
4. Buckingham Palace, London, England
5. Rushmore, Crazy Horse Monument, Black Hills, South Dakota
6. Mississippi River, Minnesota, Gulf, Mexico
7. Kilimanjaro, Kenya, Africa
8. United States
9. Will Rogers Highway, Route, Chicago, Los Angeles
10. Wisconsin, Iowa, Ohio, Midwest

624

Capitalization . . .

624.1
First Words

Capitalize the first word of every sentence and the first word in a direct quotation.

> In many families, pets are treated like people, according to an article in the *Kansas City Star.* (sentence)

> Marty Becker, coauthor of *Chicken Soup for the Pet Lover's Soul,* reports, "Seven out of ten people let their pets sleep on the bed." (direct quotation)

> "I get my 15 minutes of fame," he says, "every time I come home." (Notice that *every* is not capitalized because it does not begin a new sentence.)

> "It's like being treated like a rock star," says Becker. "Now I have to tell you that feels pretty good."

Do not capitalize the first word in an indirect quotation.

> Becker says that in the last 10 years, pets have moved out of kennels and basements and into living rooms and bedrooms. (indirect quotation)

624.2
Titles

Capitalize the first word of a title, the last word, and every word in between except articles *(a, an, the)*, short prepositions, and coordinating conjunctions. Follow this rule for titles of books, newspapers, magazines, poems, plays, songs, articles, movies, works of art, pictures, stories, and essays.

> *Locked in Time* (book)
> *Boston Globe* (newspaper)
> *Dog Fancy* (magazine)
> "Roses Are Red" (poem)
> *The Phantom of the Opera* (play)
> *Daddy Day Care* (movie)
> "Intuition" (song)
> *Mona Lisa* (work of art)

Grammar Practice

Capitalization 4

■ First Words
■ Titles

 For each of the following sentences, correctly write any word that is incorrectly capitalized.

Example: Laura Ingalls Wilder once said that She had no idea she was writing history.
she

1. A collection of her letters can be found in the book *West From Home.*

2. Laura's book *Little house in The Big Woods* is about her life in Wisconsin.

3. Pa played and sang songs like "My old kentucky home."

4. the television series *Little House On the Prairie* was based on Laura's books.

5. Laura wrote articles for the *Missouri ruralist* and other magazines.

6. Laura's sister Carrie worked for a while at the *De Smet news.*

7. "I love the *Little House* books," said Heather, "Because of their descriptions about life during the 1800s."

8. Heather told us That she has all of Laura Ingalls Wilder's books.

9. "My favorite is *Little Town on the prairie*," she said. "It's the one where Laura meets Almanzo Wilder."

Next Step: Write a short paragraph about a favorite author and include the titles of some of his or her works. Exchange papers with a classmate. Are first words and titles capitalized correctly?

Related Skills Activities

■ **SkillsBook**
Capitalization 1, pp. 41–42

 Answers

1. *from*
2. *House, the*
3. Old Kentucky Home
4. The, *on*
5. *Ruralist*
6. *News*
7. because
8. that
9. *Prairie*

626

Capitalization . . .

626.1
Abbreviations

Capitalize abbreviations of titles and organizations.

Dr. (Doctor)	**M.D.** (Doctor of Medicine)
Mr. (Mister)	**UPS** (United Parcel Service)
SADD (Students Against Destructive Decisions)	

626.2
Organizations

Capitalize the name of an organization, an association, or a team.

New York State Historical Society	**the Red Cross**
General Motors Corporation	**the Miami Dolphins**
Republicans	**the Democratic Party**

626.3
Letters

Capitalize the letters used to indicate form or shape.

T-shirt   U-turn   A-frame   T-ball

Capitalize	**Do Not Capitalize**
American	un-American
January, February	winter, spring
Missouri and Ohio rivers	the rivers Missouri and Ohio
The South is humid in summer.	Turn south at the stop sign.
Duluth Middle School	a Duluth middle school
Governor Bob Taft	Bob Taft, our governor
President Luiz Lula Da Silva	Luiz Lula Da Silva, Brazil's president
Nissan Altima	a Nissan automobile
The planet Earth is egg shaped.	The earth on Grandpa's farm is rich.
I'm taking World Cultures.	I'm taking social studies.

Related Skills Activities

- **CD-ROM**
  Capitalization 2   626.2

- *SkillsBook*
  Capitalization 1, pp. 41–42
  Capitalization 2, pp. 43–44
  Capitalization and Abbreviations, pp. 45–46

Grammar Practice

Capitalization 5

- Abbreviations
- Organizations

 Capitalize the words in the following paragraphs that need to be capitalized. (Write the line number followed by the word or words.)

Example: 1 The ad council donates services to organizations
          2 like the girl scouts of America.

          1 *Ad Council*
          2 *Girl Scouts*

1   The ad council is a group of volunteers in the advertising
2 industry. They make and promote public service announcements
3 (psa's) for many organizations. For instance, they created McGruff
4 the Crime Dog for the National crime prevention Council. They also
5 created Smokey Bear for the usfs (United States forest service) and
6 Vince and Larry, the Crash Test Dummies, for the government's dot
7 (department of transportation).
8   When members of the ad council see a problem that concerns
9 people, they try to draw attention to it. Some of their recent
10 campaigns include increasing environmental awareness (sponsored
11 by earth share) and getting parents involved in school (sponsored
12 by the National pta). The ad council's programs encourage people to
13 give these subjects the notice they deserve. The hope is that positive
14 social change will result as people take action.

Next Step: Write a brief paragraph about an issue that concerns you. Include the name of an organization that you would create to deal with the problem.

Answers

line 1.	Ad Council
line 3.	PSA's
line 4.	Crime Prevention
line 5.	USFS, Forest Service
line 6.	DOT
line 7.	Department, Transportation
line 8.	Ad Council
line 11.	Earth Share
line 12.	PTA, Ad Council's

MECHANICS

Test Prep!

For each sentence below, write the letter of the line that contains a mistake. If there is no mistake, choose "D."

1
(A) "Do you want to go
(B) with me and my Dad?"
(C) Ryan asked.
(D) correct as is

2
(A) S. e. hinton
(B) is the author of a book
(C) called *Rumble Fish*.
(D) correct as is

3
(A) Tony Blair, former prime
(B) Minister of Great Britain,
(C) was born in Scotland.
(D) correct as is

4
(A) my best friend, Cory,
(B) likes the new teacher
(C) who teaches biology.
(D) correct as is

5
(A) Our english teacher
(B) speaks Spanish,
(C) French, and German.
(D) correct as is

6
(A) The Fourth of July
(B) is a nickname
(C) for independence day.
(D) correct as is

7
(A) Canada, the United
(B) States, and Mexico are
(C) countries in north America.
(D) correct as is

8
(A) At Wilson's Observatory,
(B) we saw Mars, Jupiter,
(C) and the Milky Way.
(D) correct as is

9
(A) The east coast runs along
(B) the Atlantic Ocean and has
(C) many interesting beaches.
(D) correct as is

10
(A) The story was printed
(B) in the *Seattle times*
(C) last winter.
(D) correct as is

11
(A) "When you're a singer,"
(B) she told the reporter,
(C) "Every song is an adventure."
(D) correct as is

12
(A) Maria says that
(B) there are only seven
(C) questions on the test.
(D) correct as is

13
(A) Franky plans to
(B) build a large
(C) a-frame storage shed.
(D) correct as is

14
(A) Kayle's family wants
(B) to drive North to Canada
(C) later this summer.
(D) correct as is

For each underlined part of the following paragraph, choose the letter (below) that shows the correct capitalization. If the underlined part is correct, choose "D."

Our <u>Social Studies class</u> is learning about the <u>cdc (Centers for</u>
                    (15)   (16)
<u>disease control</u>). The CDC is located in <u>atlanta, Georgia</u>, and its director
                                                        (17)
is <u>dr. Julie L. Gerberding</u>. This agency works to improve the health of
      (18)
<u>the people of the United States</u>. The CDC is a part of the <u>Department of</u>
                (19)   (20)
<u>Health and human services</u>.

15
(A) Social studies class
(B) social Studies Class
(C) social studies class
(D) correct as is

16
(A) CDC (Centers for Disease Control)
(B) CDC (centers for disease control)
(C) cdc (Centers for Disease Control)
(D) correct as is

17
(A) Atlanta, georgia
(B) Atlanta, Georgia
(C) atlanta, georgia
(D) correct as is

18
(A) dr. julie l. Gerberding
(B) Dr. Julie L. gerberding
(C) Dr. Julie L. Gerberding
(D) correct as is

19
(A) The people of the United States
(B) the People of the United States
(C) the people of the united states
(D) correct as is

20
(A) Department of Health and Human Services
(B) department of Health and Human Services
(C) Department of health and human services
(D) correct as is

MECHANICS

Answers

1. B	8. D
2. A	9. A
3. B	10. B
4. A	11. C
5. A	12. D
6. C	13. C
7. C	14. B

Answers

15. D	18. C
16. A	19. D
17. B	20. A

Related Skills Activities

■ *SkillsBook*
Mechanics Review, pp. 49–50

630

Plurals

630.1
Most Nouns

The **plurals** of most nouns are formed by adding *s* to the singular.

cheerleader — **cheerleaders**   wheel — **wheels**
bubble — **bubbles**

630.2
Nouns Ending in *ch, sh, s, x,* and *z*

The plural form of nouns ending in *ch, sh, s, x,* and *z* is made by adding *es* to the singular.

lunch — **lunches**   dish — **dishes**   mess — **messes**
buzz — **buzzes**   fox — **foxes**

630.3
Nouns Ending in *o*

The plurals of nouns ending in *o* with a vowel just before the *o* are formed by adding *s*.

radio — **radios**   studio — **studios**   rodeo — **rodeos**

The plurals of most nouns ending in *o* with a consonant just before the *o* are formed by adding *es*.

echo — **echoes**   hero — **heroes**   tomato — **tomatoes**

Exceptions: Musical terms and words of Spanish origin always form plurals by adding *s*.

alto — **altos**   banjo — **banjos**   taco — **tacos**
solo — **solos**   piano — **pianos**   burro — **burros**

630.4
Nouns Ending in *ful*

The plurals of nouns that end with *ful* are formed by adding an *s* at the end of the word.

three platefuls   six tankfuls   four cupfuls   five pailfuls

630.5
Nouns Ending in *f* or *fe*

The plurals of nouns that end in *f* or *fe* are formed in one of two ways: If the final *f* sound is still heard in the plural form of the word, simply add *s;* if the final sound is a *v* sound, change the *f* to *ve* and add *s.*

roof — **roofs**   chief — **chiefs**   belief — **beliefs**
(plural ends with *f* sound)

wife — **wives**   loaf — **loaves**   leaf — **leaves**
(plural ends with *v* sound)

Grammar Practice

Plurals 1

- Nouns Ending in *ch, sh, s, x,* and *z*
- Nouns Ending in *o*
- Nouns Ending in *ful*
- Nouns Ending in *f* or *fe*

 For each sentence below, write the correct plural for the underlined word. If the plural is correct, write "C."

Example: Today's four o'clock meeting is for <u>coachs</u> only.
          coaches

1. The cooks used a whole bag of <u>potatoes</u> to make this soup.
2. During the night, <u>thiefs</u> took three signs from the parking lot.
3. Randy ate three <u>bowlsful</u> of his favorite cereal.
4. Sometimes countries use special <u>taxs</u> to control the number of imported goods.
5. These extra charges are called <u>tariffes</u>.
6. The winning lumberjack used six different <u>axs</u> during the competition.
7. The eighth-grade choir wants five more girls to be <u>sopranoes</u>.
8. Some people say that cats have nine <u>lifes</u>.
9. Allan figured he needed four <u>bucketfuls</u> of red paint to complete the job.
10. Angelica likes to eat <u>mangos</u>.
11. The newspaper reported that there were more than 50 <u>canoes</u> in the race.
12. In the movie *Aladdin*, does the genie grant three or four <u>wishs</u>?

Next Step: Write three sentences that include the plurals of these words: *studio, spoonful,* and *wax.*

Related Skills Activities

- **CD-ROM**
  Plurals   630.1, 630.2, 630.3, 630.4, 630.5

- ***SkillsBook***
  Plurals and Spelling 1 and 2, pp. 51–52

 ## Answers

1. C
2. thieves
3. bowlfuls
4. taxes
5. tariffs
6. axes
7. sopranos
8. lives
9. C
10. mangoes
11. C
12. wishes

Next Step: **Answers**

studios, spoonfuls, waxes

632

Plurals . . .

632.1
Nouns Ending in *y*

The plurals of common nouns that end in *y* with a consonant letter just before the *y* are formed by changing the *y* to *i* and adding *es*.

    fly — flies   baby — babies   cavity — cavities

The plurals of common nouns that end in *y* with a vowel before the *y* are formed by adding only *s*.

    key — keys   holiday — holidays   attorney — attorneys

The plurals of proper nouns ending in *y* are formed by adding *s*.

    There are three Circuit Citys in our metro area.

632.2
Compound Nouns

The plurals of some compound nouns are formed by adding *s* or *es* to the main word in the compound.

    brothers-in-law   maids of honor   secretaries of state

632.3
Plurals That Do Not Change

The plurals of some words are the same in singular and plural form.

    deer   sheep   trout   aircraft

632.4
Irregular Spelling

Some words (including many foreign words) form a plural by taking on an irregular spelling; others are now acceptable with the commonly used *s* or *es* ending.

    child — children   woman — women   man — men
    goose — geese   mouse — mice   ox — oxen
    tooth — teeth   octopus — octopi or octopuses
    index — indices or indexes

632.5
Adding an 's

The plurals of letters, figures, symbols, and words discussed as words are formed by adding an apostrophe and an *s*.

    Dr. Walters has two Ph.D.'s.
    My dad's license plate has three 2's between two B's.
    You've got too many but's and so's in that sentence.

For information on forming plural possessives, see 606.1.

 Grammar Practice

Plurals 2

- Nouns Ending in *y*
- Compound Nouns
- Plurals That Do Not Change
- Irregular Spelling

For each of the following sentences, write the plural form of the word or words in parentheses.

Example: My favorite author writes (story) about (child) in other (country).
stories, children, countries

1. The (boy) rode (donkey) into the Valley of the Kings.
2. There are (county) in Nebraska named after (antelope) and (buffalo).
3. There were six (Bobby) at the Malloy family reunion.
4. (Passer-by) saw the injured animal and called the Humane Society.
5. We saw at least two dozen (species) of birds on our nature walk.
6. (Mushroom) are edible, fleshy (fungus).
7. Marcus and Tyisha packed the old (textbook) into (box).
8. The zoo bought two ring-tailed lemurs and three howler (monkey).
9. Medical school is where (man) and (woman) study to become (doctor).
10. There were three (runner-up) in the Battle of the Bands.
11. Many Asian American (family) live in my neighborhood.

Next Step: Write sentences using plurals of the following words: *cavity, goose, octopus,* and *holiday.*

Related Skills Activities

- **CD-ROM**
  Plurals   632.1, 632.3, 632.4

- ***SkillsBook***
  Plurals and Spelling 1 and 2, pp. 51–52

 Answers

1. boys, donkeys
2. counties, antelope, buffalo
3. Bobbys
4. Passers-by
5. species
6. Mushrooms, fungi
7. textbooks, boxes
8. monkeys
9. men, women, doctors
10. runners-up
11. families

Next Step: **Answers**

cavities, geese, octopuses or octopi, holidays

Abbreviations

An **abbreviation** is the shortened form of a word or phrase. The following abbreviations are always acceptable in any kind of writing:

Mr.   Mrs.   Ms.   Dr.   a.m., p.m. (A.M., P.M.)

B.C.E. (before the Common Era)   **C.E.** (Common Era)

B.A.   M.A.   Ph.D.   M.D.   Sr.   Jr.

Caution: Do not abbreviate the names of states, countries, months, days, or units of measure in formal writing. Also, do not use signs or symbols (%, &) in place of words.

Common Abbreviations

AC alternating current	**kg** kilogram	**pd.** paid
a.m. ante meridiem	**km** kilometer	**pg.** (or p.) page
ASAP as soon as possible	**kw** kilowatt	**p.m.** post meridiem
COD cash on delivery	**l** liter	**ppd.** postpaid, prepaid
DA district attorney	**lb.** pound	**qt.** quart
DC direct current	**m** meter	**R.S.V.P.** please reply
etc. and so forth	**M.D.** doctor of medicine	**tbs., tbsp.** tablespoon
F Fahrenheit	**mfg.** manufacturing	**tsp.** teaspoon
FM frequency modulation	**mpg** miles per gallon	**vol.** volume
GNP gross national product	**mph** miles per hour	**vs.** versus
i.e. that is (Latin *id est*)	**oz.** ounce	**yd.** yard

Address Abbreviations

	Standard	Postal		Standard	Postal		Standard	Postal
Avenue	Ave.	AVE	Lake	L.	LK	Route	Rt.	RTE
Boulevard	Blvd.	BLVD	Lane	Ln.	LN	South	S.	S
Court	Ct.	CT	North	N.	N	Square	Sq.	SQ
Drive	Dr.	DR	Park	Pk.	PK	Station	Sta.	STA
East	E.	E	Parkway	Pky.	PKY	Street	St.	ST
Expressway	Expy.	EXPY	Place	Pl.	PL	Terrace	Ter.	TER
Heights	Hts.	HTS	Plaza	Plaza	PLZ	Turnpike	Tpke.	TPKE
Highway	Hwy.	HWY	Road	Rd.	RD	West	W.	W

Grammar Practice

Abbreviations 1

For each of the following sentences, write the correct abbreviation for the underlined word or words.

Example: Coach Chen told us to get off the field <u>as soon as possible</u>.
ASAP

1. On my cousin's wedding invitation, it said "<u>please reply</u> by May 10."
2. The <u>district attorney</u> for our county is <u>Mister</u> John B. Stepanek, <u>Senior</u>.
3. I wonder how long I could play my stereo on one <u>kilowatt</u> of electricity.
4. Grandpa always says that an <u>ounce</u> of prevention is worth a <u>pound</u> of cure.
5. At 238 <u>miles per hour</u>, an "Indy" car covers 350 feet of track per second.
6. Most banana plants stop growing when the temperature drops below 53 degrees <u>Fahrenheit</u>.
7. Noah Blain, <u>doctor of medicine</u>, operated on my sister's shoulder.
8. The television set we take camping uses <u>direct current</u>.
9. I listen mostly to <u>frequency modulation</u> radio stations.
10. Mom's new car averages 36 <u>miles per gallon</u>.
11. The cake recipe calls for one <u>teaspoon</u> of vanilla.
12. I was named after my uncle, Juan L. Martinez, <u>Junior</u>.
13. The Greek philosopher Aristotle was born in 384 <u>before the Common Era</u>.

Next Step: Rewrite these addresses using standard abbreviations.

123 Greenwillow Parkway   13 South Linden Station
10 North Lincoln Boulevard   258 Willmore Terrace
1659 Standish Court

Related Skills Activities

- **CD-ROM**
  Abbreviations   634.1

- ***SkillsBook***
  Abbreviations and Numbers, pp. 47–48

Answers

1. R.S.V.P.
2. DA, Mr., Sr.
3. kw
4. oz., lb.
5. mph
6. F
7. M.D.
8. DC
9. FM
10. mpg
11. tsp.
12. Jr.
13. B.C.E.

Next Step: ## Answers

123 Greenwillow Pky.
10 N. Lincoln Blvd.
1659 Standish Ct.
13 S. Linden Sta.
258 Willmore Ter.

636

Abbreviations . . .

636.1
Acronyms

An **acronym** is an abbreviation that can be pronounced as a word. It does not require periods.

WHO — World Health Organization   **ROM** — read-only memory

FAQ — frequently asked question

636.2
Initialisms

An **initialism** is similar to an acronym except that it cannot be pronounced as a word; the initials are pronounced individually.

PBS — Public Broadcasting System

BLM — Bureau of Land Management

WNBA — Women's National Basketball Association

Common Acronyms and Initialisms

AIDS	acquired immunodeficiency syndrome	ORV	off-road vehicle
CETA	Comprehensive Employment and Training Act	OSHA	Occupational Safety and Health Administration
CIA	Central Intelligence Agency	PAC	political action committee
FAA	Federal Aviation Administration	PIN	personal identification number
FBI	Federal Bureau of Investigation	PSA	public service announcement
FCC	Federal Communications Commission	ROTC	Reserve Officers' Training Corps
FDA	Food and Drug Administration	SADD	Students Against Destructive Decisions
FDIC	Federal Deposit Insurance Corporation	SSA	Social Security Administration
FHA	Federal Housing Administration	SUV	sport utility vehicle
FmHA	Farmers Home Authority	SWAT	special weapons and tactics
FTC	Federal Trade Commission	TDD	telecommunications device for the deaf
IRS	Internal Revenue Service	TMJ	temporomandibular joint
MADD	Mothers Against Drunk Driving	TVA	Tennessee Valley Authority
NAFTA	North American Free Trade Agreement	VA	Veterans Affairs
NASA	National Aeronautics and Space Administration	VISTA	Volunteers in Service to America
		WAC	Women's Army Corps
NATO	North Atlantic Treaty Organization	WAVES	Women Accepted for Volunteer Emergency Service
OEO	Office of Economic Opportunity		
OEP	Office of Emergency Preparedness		

Grammar Practice

Abbreviations 2

■ Acronyms
■ Initialisms

 Write the correct abbreviation for each phrase below. Tell whether it is an acronym or an initialism.

Example: Federal Emergency Management Agency
FEMA—acronym

1. American Kennel Club
2. telecommunications device for the deaf
3. National Basketball Association
4. personal identification number
5. Federal Bureau of Investigation
6. National Aeronautics and Space Administration
7. attention deficit disorder
8. North Atlantic Treaty Organization
9. special weapons and tactics
10. Internal Revenue Service
11. Federal Aviation Administration
12. Food and Drug Administration
13. parental guidance
14. also known as

Next Step: Make up a slogan for your school that can be abbreviated as an acronym.

Related Skills Activities

■ **CD-ROM**
Abbreviations   636.1, 636.2

■ *SkillsBook*
Abbreviations and Numbers, pp. 47–48

 ## Answers

1. AKC (initialism)
2. TDD (initialism)
3. NBA (initialism)
4. PIN (acronym)
5. FBI (initialism)
6. NASA (acronym)
7. ADD (initialism)
8. NATO (acronym)
9. SWAT (acronym)
10. IRS (initialism)
11. FAA (initialism)
12. FDA (initialism)
13. PG (initialism)
14. AKA (initialism)

Numbers

638.1
Numbers Under 10

Numbers from one to nine are usually written as words; all numbers 10 and over are usually written as numerals.

    two   seven   nine   10   25   106

638.2
Numerals Only

Use numerals to express any of the following forms:

money **$2.39**
decimals **26.2**
percentages . . . . **8 percent**
chapters . . . . **chapter 7**
pages . . . . **pages 287–289**
time (with "a.m." or "p.m.") . . . . **4:30 p.m.**
telephone numbers **1-800-555-1212**
dates . . . . **44 B.C.E.; July 6, 1942**
identification numbers . . . . **Highway 36**
addresses . . . . **2125 Cairn Road**
ZIP codes **60004**
statistics . . . . **a vote of 23 to 4**

When abbreviations and symbols are used (for instance, in science or math), always use numerals with them.

    12° C   **7%**   **33 kg**   **9 cm**   **55 mph**

638.3
Very Large Numbers

You may use a combination of numerals and words for very large numbers.

Of the 17 million **residents of the three Midwestern states, only** 1.3 million **are blonds.**

You may spell out a large number that can be written as two words. If more than two words are needed, use the numeral.

More than nine thousand **people attended the concert.**

About 3,011 **people missed the opening act.**

Grammar Practice

Numbers 1

- Numbers Under 10
- Numerals Only
- Very Large Numbers

 For each of the following sentences, write the underlined number the correct way. If it is already in the correct form, write "correct."

    Example: In the <u>nineteen sixties</u>, Americans drove large, heavy cars.
        1960s

1. Many cars of that decade got only <u>nine</u> miles per gallon.
2. A car built in <u>two thousand four</u> is quite a bit more efficient than those built <u>40</u> years ago.
3. It is safest to drive under <u>fifty-five</u> miles per hour.
4. In 1965, there were more than <u>90,300,000</u> cars registered in the United States.
5. Today, there are about <u>240 million</u> cars in use on our nation's roads.
6. In 2006, there were about <u>201,000,000</u> drivers in the United States, each averaging <u>14,000</u> miles per year.
7. Many roads in major cities get traffic jams between <u>seven</u> a.m. and <u>nine</u> a.m.
8. People would save fuel and face less traffic if more cars carried at least <u>2</u> people.
9. The business located at <u>two forty-nine</u> South Cheps Road requires all its employees to carpool or use public transportation.

Next Step: Complete the following sentence with your own numbers:
Today, _____(date)_____, at _____(time)_____ it was _____(temperature)_____ degrees.

Related Skills Activities

■ **CD-ROM**
  Numbers 638.1, 638.2, 638.3

■ ***SkillsBook***
  Abbreviations and Numbers, pp. 47–48

 ### Answers

1. correct
2. 2004, correct
3. 55
4. 90.3 million
5. correct
6. 201 million
7. 7:00, 9:00
8. two
9. 249

Numbers . . .

640.1
Comparing Numbers

If you are comparing two or more numbers in a sentence, write all of them the same way: as numerals or as words.

Students from 9 to 14 years old are invited.

Students from nine to fourteen years old are invited.

640.2
Numbers in Compound Modifiers

A compound modifier may include a numeral.

The floorboards come in 10-foot lengths.

When a number comes before a compound modifier that includes a numeral, use words instead of numerals.

We need eleven 10-foot lengths to finish the floor.

Ms. Brown must grade twenty 12-page reports.

640.3
Sentence Beginnings

Use words, not numerals, to begin a sentence.

Nine students had turned in their homework. Fourteen students said they were unable to finish the assignment.

640.4
Time and Money

When time or money is expressed with an abbreviation, use numerals. When either is expressed with words, spell out the number.

6:00 a.m. or six o'clock

$25 or twenty-five dollars

SCHOOL DAZE

Jerry, haven't you finished your paper yet?

No, it's not due until three o'clock, and Mrs. Wright told me to add a few new twists and wrinkles.

Grammar Practice

Numbers 2

■ Sentence Beginnings
■ Time and Money

 If a number in the following sentences is not in the right form, write it correctly.

Example: 14 teams compete in the girls' softball league.
Fourteen

1. The softball games at Carrey Middle School start at four p.m.
2. 40 girls from my school signed up to play softball this season.
3. It costs the school about $5 hundred a month to support all of its teams.
4. The teams practice after school on Tuesdays and Thursdays until five-thirty p.m.
5. Each player must pay 25 dollars for equipment and supplies.

■ Comparing Numbers
■ Numbers in Compound Modifiers

 Rewrite the underlined parts of the following sentences so that they are correct.

Example: Girls from nine to 14 years old compete in the league.
9 to 14 years old (or) nine to fourteen years old

1. Players may participate in ten to 16 games each month.
2. We have seven home games and 10 away games this season.
3. Carlos Moy is an umpire for 3 90-minute games each week.
4. Each team has at least 3 twelve-inch softballs.
5. Our school has 4 nine-player teams.

Related Skills Activities

■ **CD-ROM**
Numbers 640.1, 640.2, 60.3, 640.4

 ## Answers

1. 4:00
2. Forty
3. $500
4. 5:30
5. $25

 ## Answers

1. 10 to 16 or ten to sixteen
2. 7 home games and 10 away games or seven home games and ten away games
3. three 90-minute games
4. three 12-inch softballs
5. four 9-player teams

Improving Spelling

642

642.1
i before e

Write *i* before *e* except after *c*, or when sounded like *a* as in *neighbor* and *weigh*.

Some Exceptions to the Rule: *counterfeit, either, financier, foreign, height, heir, leisure, neither, science, seize, sheik, species, their, weird*

642.2
Silent e

If a word ends with a silent *e*, drop the *e* before adding a suffix that begins with a vowel. There are exceptions, for example, *knowledgeable* and *changeable*.

state — stating — statement		use — using — useful
like — liking — likeness		nine — ninety — nineteen

NOTE You do not drop the *e* when the suffix begins with a consonant. Exceptions include *truly, argument,* and *ninth*.

642.3
Words Ending in y

When *y* is the last letter in a word and the *y* comes just after a consonant, change the *y* to *i* before adding any suffix except those beginning with *i*.

fry — fries — frying	happy — happiness
hurry — hurried — hurrying	beauty — beautiful
lady — ladies	

When forming the plural of a word that ends with a *y* that comes just after a vowel, add *s*.

toy — toys	play — plays	monkey — monkeys

642.4
Consonant Endings

When a one-syllable word ends in a consonant *(bat)* preceded by one vowel *(bat)*, double the final consonant before adding a suffix that begins with a vowel *(batting)*.

sum — summary	god — goddess

When a multisyllable word ends in a consonant preceded by one vowel *(contról)*, the accent is on the last syllable *(contról)*, and the suffix begins with a vowel *(ing)*—the same rule holds true: double the final consonant *(controlling)*.

prefer — preferred	begin — beginning

Grammar Practice

Spelling 1

■ *i before e*
■ Silent *e*
■ Words Ending in *y*
■ Consonant Endings

 For each sentence below, write the correct spelling of any misspelled word. If no word is misspelled, write "correct."

Example: Dragon boat races are an interesting and exciteing part of Chinese history.
exciting

1. The colorful boats look like feirce dragons with scary heads, scaly bodyes, and long tails.

2. Actually, they're quite beautiful.

3. Centurys ago, some Chinese people believed that dragon boat racing would bring them bountyful crops.

4. They rowed on the river in thier boats, beatting drums to scare fish and water dragons away.

5. They also wraped rice in leaves and threw them into the river.

6. Today, people race the dragon boats cheifly for amusement during Chinese festivals.

7. The festivals and races are enjoied by people in cities around the world.

8. Observers can expereince the thrill of all the druming and yelling.

9. Identifiing which boat will win isn't easy.

10. I am beting that the rowers are no longer nerveous about water dragons comeing to get them.

Next Step: Review the list of spelling words on pages 645–651. Choose three words that give you trouble. Write a sentence for each that will help you remember its correct spelling.

Related Skills Activities

■ **CD-ROM**
Spelling 1—*i before e* 642.1
Spelling 2—silent *e* 642.2
Spelling 3—words ending in *y* 642.3
Spelling 4—Consonant endings 642.4

■ *SkillsBook*
Plurals and Spelling 1 and 2, pp. 51–52

 ## Answers

1. fierce, bodies
2. correct
3. Centuries, racing, bountiful
4. their, beating
5. wrapped
6. chiefly, amusement
7. enjoyed
8. experience, drumming
9. Identifying
10. betting, nervous, coming

Grammar Practice

Spelling 2
- *i* before *e*
- Silent *e*
- Words Ending in *y*
- Consonant Endings

For each sentence below, write the correct spelling of any word that is misspelled. If no word is misspelled, write "correct."

Example: Angelica spent time at the art museum admireing the Renaissance paintings.
admiring

1. Ryan prefered to read about the anceint kingdoms of Egypt.
2. Borna thought that the science assignment was sensless.
3. Viu likes decorating her room with fresh flowers.
4. Our science teacher's cheif complaint is the condition of the school's microscopes.
5. He has identifyd the brand he would like to purchase.
6. Five students measured the boundarys of the school property.
7. On a hot day, Hamal faned himself with a peice of paper.
8. Everyone is talking about the wierd weather we're haveing.
9. Every morning, Principal Phipps reads the day's announcments.
10. The aviation industry plans to improve the guidance systems for its aircraft.
11. Although Shania likes shoping, she knows she is not very good at bargainning.
12. Sam twisted his right ankle, so he was hoping around on his left foot.
13. Rozene could not beleive how much snow was falling.
14. For your own safty, do not eat any food that appears to be roting.

Yellow Pages Guide to Improved Spelling

Be patient. Becoming a good speller takes time.

Check your spelling by using a dictionary or list of commonly misspelled words (like the list that follows). And, remember, don't rely too much on computer spell-checkers.

Learn the correct pronunciation of each word you are trying to spell. Knowing the correct pronunciation of a word will help you remember how it's spelled.

Look up the meaning of each word as you are checking the dictionary for pronunciation. (Knowing how to spell a word is of little use if you don't know what it means.)

Practice spelling the word before you close the dictionary. Look away from the page and try to see the word in your mind's eye. Write the word on a piece of paper. Check the spelling in the dictionary and repeat the process until you are able to spell the word correctly.

Keep a list of the words that you misspell.

Write often. As noted educator Frank Smith said, "There is little point in learning to spell if you have little intention of writing."

A

abbreviate	account	after	almost
aboard	accurate	afternoon	already
about	accustom (ed)	afterward	although
above	ache	again	altogether
absence	achieve (ment)	against	aluminum
absent	acre	agreeable	always
absolute (ly)	across	agree (ment)	amateur
abundance	actual	ah	ambulance
accelerate	adapt	aid	amendment
accident	addition (al)	airy	among
accidental (ly)	address	aisle	amount
accompany	adequate	alarm	analyze
accomplice	adjust (ment)	alcohol	ancient
accomplish	admire	alike	angel
according	adventure	alive	anger
	advertise (ment)	alley	angle
	advertising	allowance	angry
	afraid	all right	animal

Answers

1. preferred, ancient
2. senseless
3. correct
4. chief
5. identified
6. correct
7. fanned, piece
8. weird, having
9. announcements
10. correct
11. shopping, bargaining
12. hopping
13. believe
14. safety, rotting

Related Skills Activities

- **CD-ROM**
  Spelling 1, 2 and 3
    642.1, 642.2, 642.3, 642.4
  Spelling Review 1
    642.1, 642.2, 642.3, 642.4

- ***SkillsBook***
  Plurals and Spelling 1 and 2, pp. 51–52

anniversary	asleep	basement	brother
announce	assassin	basis	brought
annoyance	assign (ment)	basket	bruise
annual	assistance	battery	bubble
anonymous	associate	beautiful	bucket
another	association	beauty	buckle
answer	assume	because	budget
Antarctic	athlete	become	building
anticipate	athletic	becoming	bulletin
anxiety	attach	before	buoyant
anxious	attack (ed)	began	bureau
anybody	attempt	beggar	burglar
anyhow	attendance	beginning	bury
anyone	attention	behave	business
anything	attitude	behavior	busy
anyway	attorney	being	button
anywhere	attractive	belief	
apartment	audience	believe	
apiece	August	belong	**C**
apologize	author	beneath	
apparent (ly)	authority	benefit (ed)	cabbage
appeal	automobile	between	cafeteria
appearance	autumn	bicycle	calendar
appetite	available	biscuit	campaign
appliance	avenue	blackboard	canal
application	average	blanket	cancel (ed)
appointment	awful (ly)	blizzard	candidate
appreciate	awkward	bother	candle
approach		bottle	canister
appropriate		bottom	cannon
approval	**B**	bough	cannot
approximate		bought	canoe
architect	baggage	bounce	can't
Arctic	baking	boundary	canyon
aren't	balance	breakfast	capacity
argument	balloon	breast	captain
arithmetic	ballot	breath (n.)	carburetor
around	banana	breathe (v.)	cardboard
arouse	bandage	breeze	career
arrange (ment)	bankrupt	bridge	careful
arrival	barber	brief	careless
article	bargain	bright	carpenter
artificial	barrel	brilliant	carriage

carrot	colossal	cooperate	deceive
cashier	column	corporation	decided
casserole	comedy	correspond	decision
casualty	coming	cough	declaration
catalog	commercial	couldn't	decorate
catastrophe	commission	counter	defense
catcher	commit	counterfeit	definite (ly)
caterpillar	commitment	country	definition
catsup	committed	county	delicious
ceiling	committee	courage	dependent
celebration	communicate	courageous	depot
cemetery	community	court	describe
census	company	courteous	description
century	comparison	courtesy	desert
certain (ly)	competition	cousin	deserve
certificate	competitive (ly)	coverage	design
challenge	complain	cozy	desirable
champion	complete (ly)	cracker	despair
changeable	complexion	cranky	dessert
character (istic)	compromise	crawl	deteriorate
chief	conceive	creditor	determine
children	concerning	cried	develop (ment)
chimney	concert	criticize	device (n.)
chocolate	concession	cruel	devise (v.)
choice	concrete	crumb	diamond
chorus	condemn	crumble	diaphragm
circumstance	condition	cupboard	diary
citizen	conductor	curiosity	dictionary
civilization	conference	curious	difference
classmates	confidence	current	different
classroom	congratulate	custom	difficulty
climate	connect	customer	dining
climb	conscience	cylinder	diploma
closet	conscious		director
clothing	conservative		disagreeable
coach	constitution	**D**	disappear
cocoa	continue		disappoint
cocoon	continuous	daily	disapprove
coffee	control	dairy	disastrous
collar	controversy	damage	discipline
college	convenience	danger (ous)	discover
colonel	convince	daughter	discuss
color	coolly	dealt	discussion

disease
dissatisfied
distinguish
distribute
divide
divine
divisible
division
doctor
doesn't
dollar
dormitory
doubt
dough
dual
duplicate

eager (ly)
economy
edge
edition
efficiency
eight
eighth
either
elaborate
electricity
elephant
eligible
ellipse
embarrass
emergency
emphasize
employee
employment
enclose
encourage
engineer
enormous
enough

entertain
enthusiastic
entirely
entrance
envelop (v.)
envelope (n.)
environment
equipment
equipped
equivalent
escape
especially
essential
establish
every
evidence
exaggerate
exceed
excellent
except
exceptional (ly)
excite
exercise
exhaust (ed)
exhibition
existence
expect
expensive
experience
explain
explanation
expression
extension
extinct
extraordinary
extreme (ly)

F

facilities
familiar
family

famous
fascinate
fashion
fatigue (d)
faucet
favorite
feature
February
federal
fertile
field
fierce
fiery
fifty
finally
financial (ly)
foliage
forcible
foreign
forfeit
formal (ly)
former (ly)
forth
fortunate
forty
forward
fountain
fourth
fragile
freight
friend (ly)
frighten
fulfill
fundamental
further
furthermore

G

gadget
gauge
generally

generous
genius
gentle
genuine
geography
ghetto
ghost
gnaw
government
governor
graduation
grammar
grateful
grease
grief
grocery
grudge
gruesome
guarantee
guard
guardian
guess
guidance
guide
guilty
gymnasium

H

hammer
handkerchief
handle (d)
handsome
haphazard
happen
happiness
harass
hastily
having
hazardous
headache
height

hemorrhage
hesitate
history
hoarse
holiday
honor
hoping
hopping
horrible
hospital
humorous
hurriedly
hydraulic
hygiene
hymn

I

icicle
identical
illegible
illiterate
illustrate
imaginary
imaginative
imagine
imitation
immediate (ly)
immense
immigrant
immortal
impatient
importance
impossible
improvement
inconvenience
incredible
indefinitely
independence
independent
individual
industrial

inferior
infinite
inflammable
influential
initial
initiation
innocence
innocent
installation
instance
instead
insurance
intelligence
intention
interested
interesting
interfere
interpret
interrupt
interview
investigate
invitation
irrigate
island
issue

J

jealous (y)
jewelry
journal
journey
judgment
juicy

K

kitchen
knew
knife
knives

knock
knowledge
knuckles

L

label
laboratory
ladies
language
laugh
laundry
lawyer
league
lecture
legal
legible
legislature
leisure
length
liable
library
license
lieutenant
lightning
likable
likely
liquid
listen
literature
living
loaves
loneliness
loose
lose
loser
losing
lovable
lovely

M

machinery
magazine
magnificent
maintain
majority
making
manual
manufacture
marriage
material
mathematics
maximum
mayor
meant
measure
medicine
medium
message
mileage
miniature
minimum
minute
mirror
miscellaneous
mischievous
miserable
missile
misspell
moisture
molecule
monotonous
monument
mortgage
mountain
muscle
musician
mysterious

SPELLING

N

naive
natural (ly)
necessary
negotiate
neighbor (hood)
neither
nickel
niece
nineteen
nineteenth
ninety
ninth
noisy
noticeable
nuclear
nuisance

O

obedience
obey
obstacle
occasion
occasional (ly)
occur
occurred
offense
official
often
omission
omitted
operate
opinion
opponent
opportunity
opposite
ordinarily
original
outrageous

P

package
paid
pamphlet
paradise
paragraph
parallel
paralyze
parentheses
partial
participant
participate
particular (ly)
pasture
patience
peculiar
people
perhaps
permanent
perpendicular
persistent
personal (ly)
personnel
perspiration
persuade
phase
physician
piece
pitcher
planned
plateau
playwright
pleasant
pleasure
pneumonia
politician
possess
possible
practical (ly)
prairie
precede
precious

precise (ly)
precision
preferable
preferred
prejudice
preparation
presence
previous
primitive
principal
principle
prisoner
privilege
probably
procedure
proceed
professor
prominent
pronounce
pronunciation
protein
psychology
pumpkin
pure

Q

quarter
questionnaire
quiet
quite
quotient

R

raise
realize
really
receipt
receive
received

recipe
recognize
recommend
reign
relieve
religious
remember
repetition
representative
reservoir
resistance
respectfully
responsibility
restaurant
review
rhyme
rhythm
ridiculous
route

S

safety
salad
salary
sandwich
satisfactory
Saturday
scene
scenery
schedule
science
scissors
scream
screen
season
secretary
seize
sensible
sentence
separate
several

sheriff
shining
similar
since
sincere (ly)
skiing
sleigh
soldier
souvenir
spaghetti
specific
sphere
sprinkle
squeeze
squirrel
statue
stature
statute
stomach
stopped
straight
strength
stretched
studying
subtle
succeed
success
sufficient
summarize
supplement
suppose
surely
surprise
syllable
sympathy
symptom

T

tariff
technique
temperature
temporary
terrible
territory
thankful
theater
their
there
therefore
thief
thorough (ly)
though
throughout
tired
tobacco
together
tomorrow
tongue
touch
tournament
toward
tragedy
treasurer
tried
tries
trouble
truly
Tuesday
typical

U

unconscious
unfortunate (ly)
unique
university
unnecessary
until
usable
useful
using
usual (ly)
utensil

V

vacation
vacuum
valuable
variety
various
vegetable
vehicle
very
vicinity
view
villain
violence
visible
visitor
voice
volume
voluntary
volunteer

W

wander
wasn't
weather
Wednesday
weigh
weird
welcome
welfare
whale
where
whether
which
whole
wholly
whose
width
women
worthwhile
wouldn't
wreckage
writing
written

Y

yellow
yesterday
yield

SPELLING

652

Using the Right Word

652.1
a, an

A is used before words that begin with a consonant sound; *an* is used before words that begin with any vowel sound except long "u."

a **heap**, a **cat**, an **idol**, an **elephant**, an **honor**, a **historian**, an **umbrella**, a **unicorn**

652.2
accept, except

The verb *accept* means "to receive"; the preposition *except* means "other than."

Melissa graciously accepted defeat. (verb)

All the boys except Zach were here. (preposition)

652.3
affect, effect

Affect is almost always a verb; it means "to influence." *Effect* can be a verb, but it is most often used as a noun that means "the result."

How does population growth affect us?

What are the effects of population growth?

652.4
allowed, aloud

The verb *allowed* means "permitted" or "let happen"; *aloud* is an adverb that means "in a normal voice."

We aren't allowed to read aloud in the library.

652.5
allusion, illusion

An *allusion* is a brief reference to or mention of a famous person, place, thing, or idea. An *illusion* is a false impression or idea.

The Great Dontini, a magician, made an allusion to Houdini as he created the illusion of sawing his assistant in half.

652.6
a lot

A lot is not one word, but two; it is a general descriptive phrase meaning "plenty." (It should be avoided in formal writing.)

652.7
all right

All right is not one word, but two; it is a phrase meaning "satisfactory" or "okay." (Please note, the following *are* spelled correctly: *always, altogether, already, almost.*)

Related Skills Activities

- **CD-ROM**
  Using the Right Word 1
  652.2, 652.3, 652.5, 652.7

Grammar Practice

Using the Right Word 1

■ accept, except; affect, effect; allusion, illusion; all right

For each of the following sentences, write the correct choice from each set of words in parentheses.

Example: Dennis thought he saw pools of water in the parking lot on that hot, hot day, but it was just an *(allusion, illusion)*.
illusion

1. I guess the sun can *(affect, effect)* us in many ways!

2. We will give away all the kittens *(accept, except)* the two that we're keeping.

3. Will it be *(all right, alright)* with your mom if you take one of the kittens?

4. Ms. Whitsom thinks constant cloudy weather has a bad *(affect, effect)* on a person's outlook.

5. In order for a magician to be successful, the audience must believe in the *(allusions, illusions)* he or she creates.

6. Your outfit looks *(all right, alright)* to me.

7. All the mail was addressed to Dad *(accept, except)* for one handwritten letter, which was addressed to me.

8. "Please *(accept, except)* my apology," the letter began.

9. Some students did not understand Roy's *(allusion, illusion)* to *Star Trek* in his speech during science class.

Next Step: Write three sentences that show you know the meaning of these words: *allusion, effect,* and *except.*

Answers

1. affect
2. except
3. all right
4. effect
5. illusions
6. all right
7. except
8. accept
9. allusion

654

654.1 already, all ready	*Already* is an adverb that tells when. *All ready* is a phrase meaning "completely ready." **We have** already **eaten breakfast; now we are** all ready **for school.**
654.2 altogether, all together	*Altogether* is always an adverb meaning "completely." *All together* is used to describe people or things that are gathered in one place at one time. **Ms. Monces held her baton in the air and said, "Okay, class,** all together **now: sing!"** **Unfortunately, there was** altogether **too much street noise for us to hear her.**
654.3 among, between	*Among* is used when speaking of more than two persons or things. *Between* is used when speaking of only two. **The three friends talked** among **themselves as they tried to choose** between **trumpet or trombone lessons.**
654.4 amount, number	*Amount* is used to describe things that you cannot count. *Number* is used when you can actually count the persons or things. **The** amount **of interest in playing the tuba is shown by the** number **of kids learning to play the instrument.**
654.5 annual, biannual, semiannual, biennial, perennial	An *annual* event happens once every year. A *biannual* (or *semiannual*) event happens twice a year. A *biennial* event happens once every two years. A *perennial* event happens year after year. **The** annual **PTA rummage sale is so successful that it will now be a** semiannual **event.** **The neighbor has some wonderful** perennial **flowers.**
654.6 ant, aunt	An *ant* is an insect. An *aunt* is a female relative (the sister of a person's mother or father). **My** aunt **is an entomologist, a scientist who studies** ants **and other insects.**
654.7 ascent, assent	*Ascent* is the act of rising or climbing; *assent* is agreement. **After the group's** ascent **of five flights of stairs to the meeting room, plans for elevator repairs met with quick** assent.

Grammar Practice

Using the Right Word 2

■ altogether, all together; among, between; amount, number; annual, biannual, semiannual, biennial, perennial; ascent, assent

For each of the following sentences, write the correct choice from each set of words in parentheses.

Example: The *(ascent, assent)* of Mount Everest is hard and dangerous.
ascent

1. The *(amount, number)* of climbers who successfully climb Mount Everest varies from year to year.

2. For the people of Tibet and Nepal, the arrival of climbing teams every May has become *(an annual, a biennial, a perennial)* event.

3. Some climbing routes on the mountain are more dangerous than others because of the *(amount, number)* of snow on the ridges.

4. The *(amount, number)* of days with good weather is very low.

5. Some critics believe that there are *(altogether, all together)* too many inexperienced climbers on Mount Everest.

6. Mountaineers must scramble *(among, between)* numerous ice-covered rocks.

7. Prior to a climb, each hiker must *(ascent, assent)* to doing his or her part for the team.

8. *(Altogether, All together)*, team members decide on tasks for the day.

9. As two climbers make their way up the mountain, the distance *(among, between)* them is usually not very great.

10. One man who climbs once in May and once in October says his *(biannual, biennial)* climbs keep him in shape.

11. After reaching the top of Mount Everest each year during a five-year period, a seasoned mountaineer said that these *(annual, semiannual)* climbs had worn him out.

Related Skills Activities

■ *SkillsBook*
Using the Right Word 1, pp. 53–54

Answers

1. number
2. an annual or a perennial
3. amount
4. number
5. altogether
6. among
7. assent
8. All together
9. between
10. biannual
11. annual

656

656.1 **bare, bear**	The adjective *bare* means "naked." A *bear* is a large, heavy animal with shaggy hair. Despite his bare feet, the man chased the polar bear across the snow. The verb *bear* means "to put up with" or "to carry." Shondra could not bear another of her older sister's lectures.
656.2 **base, bass**	*Base* is the foundation or the lower part of something. *Bass* (pronounced like "base") is a deep sound or tone. The stereo speakers are on a base so solid that even the loudest bass tones don't rattle it. *Bass* (rhymes with "mass") is a fish. Jim hooked a record-setting bass, but it got away . . . so he says.
656.3 **beat, beet**	The verb *beat* means "to strike, to defeat," and the noun *beat* is a musical term for rhythm or tempo. A *beet* is a carrot-like vegetable (often red). The beat of the drum in the marching band encouraged the fans to cheer on the team. After they beat West High's team four games to one, many team members were as red as a beet.
656.4 **berth, birth**	*Berth* is a space or compartment. *Birth* is the process of being born. We pulled aside the curtain in our train berth to view the birth of a new day outside our window.
656.5 **beside, besides**	*Beside* means "by the side of." *Besides* means "in addition to." Besides a flashlight, Kedar likes to keep his pet boa beside his bed at night.
656.6 **billed, build**	*Billed* means either "to be given a bill" or "to have a beak." The verb *build* means "to construct." We asked the carpenter to build us a birdhouse. She billed us for time and materials.
656.7 **blew, blue**	*Blew* is the past tense of "blow." *Blue* is a color and is also used to mean "feeling low in spirits." As the wind blew out the candles in the dark blue room, I felt more blue than ever.

Grammar Practice

Using the Right Word 3

- bare, bear; base, bass; berth, birth; beside, besides

 For each of the following sentences, write a word from the list above to fill in the blank.

Example: At the _____ of the Statue of Liberty is a plaque that says her lamp is a sign of welcome to those seeking freedom.
base

1. _____ the European countries, immigrants to the United States come from Africa, Asia, and South America.

2. Pictures of immigrants in the early 1900s show children with _____ hands in cold weather.

3. The desire for freedom and opportunity was at the _____ of many immigrants' decisions to endure the journey.

4. They brought with them only the _____ minimum of belongings.

5. Many immigrants would spend most of the long voyage in a crowded _____ below the waterline of the ship.

6. From there, the passengers could hear and sometimes feel the deep _____ sound of the ship's engines.

7. The ship's crew members were occasionally called on to assist in the _____ of a baby.

8. After a two-week voyage, many passengers couldn't _____ another day at sea.

9. Tugboats _____ the ocean liners guided them into the harbor as the weary travelers celebrated.

Next Step: Find the other definitions for *bear* and *bass* explained on the facing page. Write two sentences that show your understanding of those definitions.

Related Skills Activities

- ***SkillsBook***
  Using the Right Word 1, pp. 53–54

 Answers

1. Besides
2. bare
3. base
4. bare
5. berth
6. bass
7. birth
8. bear
9. beside

658

658.1
board, bored

A *board* is a piece of wood. *Board* also means "a group or council that helps run an organization."

The school board approved the purchase of 50 pine boards for the woodworking classes.

Bored means "to become weary or tired of something." It can also mean "made a hole by drilling."

Dulé bored a hole in the ice and dropped in a fishing line. Waiting and waiting for a bite bored him.

658.2
borrow, lend

Borrow means "to *receive* for temporary use." *Lend* means "to *give* for temporary use."

I asked Mom, "May I borrow $15 for a CD?"

She said, "I can lend you $15 until next Friday."

658.3
brake, break

A *brake* is a device used to stop a vehicle. The verb *break* means "to split, crack, or destroy"; as a noun, *break* means "gap or interruption."

After the brake on my bike failed, I took a break to fix it so I wouldn't break a bone.

658.4
bring, take

Use *bring* when the action is moving toward the speaker; use *take* when the action is moving away from the speaker.

Grandpa asked me to take the garbage out and bring him today's paper.

658.5
by, buy, bye

By is a preposition meaning "near" or "not later than." *Buy* is a verb meaning "to purchase."

By tomorrow I hope to buy tickets for the final match of the tournament.

Bye is the position of being automatically advanced to the next tournament round without playing.

Our soccer team received a bye because of our winning record.

658.6
can, may

Can means "able to," while *may* means "permitted to."

"Can I go to the library?"

(This actually means "Are my mind and body strong enough to get me there?")

"May I go?"

(This means "Do I have your permission to go?")

Grammar Practice

Using the Right Word 4

■ borrow, lend; brake, break; bring, take; by, buy, bye; can, may

 For each of the following sentences, write the correct choice from each set of words in parentheses.

Example: When I was sick at home, I asked Salvatore to *(bring, take)* me my homework.
bring

1. Suddenly the car's *(brake, break)* pedal wasn't working.

2. By pulling up on the parking *(brake, break)* lever, Sanji was able to make the car stop.

3. Our team will sit out the first round if we are given a *(by, buy, bye)* in the tournament schedule.

4. Vanessa has some black pants that she'll *(borrow, lend)* me for the choir concert.

5. I still need to *(by, buy, bye)* a white shirt, though.

6. We need to ask if we *(can, may)* hold a party for Alex.

7. We don't mind if we have to *(bring, take)* our own food.

8. I can't find the pen that is usually kept right here *(by, buy, bye)* the phone.

9. All you need is a library card to *(borrow, lend)* books, CD's, or magazines from any library in the system.

10. You never have to *(by, buy, bye)* any of that again!

11. A city's crime record is one record that its citizens really don't want to *(brake, break)*.

12. "Here, let me *(bring, take)* that for you," Maura offered as I carried my heavy suitcase.

13. "No, thanks. I *(can, may)* carry it," I said.

Next Step: Write two sentences that show your understanding of the words *borrow* and *lend*.

Answers

1. brake
2. brake
3. bye
4. lend
5. buy
6. may
7. bring
8. by
9. borrow
10. buy
11. break
12. take
13. can

660

660.1 canvas, canvass	*Canvas* is a heavy cloth; *canvass* means "ask people for votes or opinions." **Our old canvas tent leaks.** **Someone with a clipboard is canvassing the neighborhood.**
660.2 capital, capitol	*Capital* can be either a noun, referring to a city or to money, or an adjective, meaning "major or important." *Capitol* is used only when talking about a building. **The capitol building is in the capital city for a capital (major) reason: The city government contributed the capital (money) for the building project.**
660.3 cell, sell	*Cell* means "a small room" or "a small unit of life basic to all plants and animals." *Sell* is a verb meaning "to give up for a price." **Today we looked at a human skin cell under a microscope.** **Let's sell those old bicycles at the rummage sale.**
660.4 cent, sent, scent	*Cent* (1/100 of a dollar) is a coin; *sent* is the past tense of the verb "send"; *scent* is an odor or a smell. **After our car hit a skunk, we sent our friends a postcard that said, "One cent doesn't go far, but skunk scent seems to last forever."**
660.5 chord, cord	*Chord* may mean "an emotion or a feeling," but it is more often used to mean "the sound of three or more musical tones played at the same time." A *cord* is a string or rope. **The band struck a chord at the exact moment the mayor pulled the cord on the drape covering the new statue.**
660.6 chose, choose	*Chose* (chōz) is the past tense of the verb *choose* (chōōz). **This afternoon Mom chose tacos and hot sauce; this evening she will choose an antacid.**
660.7 coarse, course	*Coarse* means "rough or crude." *Course* means "a path" or "a class or series of studies." **In our cooking course, we learned to use coarse salt and freshly ground pepper in salads.**

---

punctuate *edit* capitalize
improve   SPELL   **661**
Using the Right Word

Grammar Practice

Using the Right Word 5

■ canvas, canvass; capital, capitol; chord, cord; coarse, course

 Write a word from the above list to properly complete each of the following sentences.

Example: Phil used _____ sandpaper to remove the paint from the old dresser.
coarse

1. When Tasha was learning how to play the guitar, she played the same _____ over and over again.

2. The class trip included a tour of the _____ building in Washington, D.C.

3. Elaine's family fits into one huge _____ tent when they go camping.

4. They tie the bulky, heavy tent to the car roof with lots of nylon _____.

5. Last year the high school offered its first _____ in German.

6. Jackson is the state _____ of Mississippi.

7. Whenever our dog would get lost, we would _____ the neighborhood looking for him.

8. On my way to school yesterday, I took a _____ through the woods that I hadn't taken before.

Next Step: Write two sentences that show your understanding of *capital* and *capitol*.

Related Skills Activities

■ **CD-ROM**
Using the Right Word 4
660.1, 660.2, 660.5, 660.7

■ *SkillsBook*
Using the Right Word 1, pp. 53–54

 ## Answers

1. chord
2. capitol
3. canvas
4. cord
5. course
6. capital
7. canvass
8. course

662

662.1 complement, compliment	*Complement* means "to complete or go with." *Compliment* is an expression of admiration or praise. **Aunt Athena said, "Your cheese sauce really complements this cauliflower!"** **"Thank you for the compliment," I replied.**
662.2 continual, continuous	*Continual* refers to something that happens again and again; *continuous* refers to something that doesn't stop happening. **Sunlight hits Peoria, Iowa, on a continual basis; but sunlight hits the earth continuously.**
662.3 counsel, council	When used as a noun, *counsel* means "advice"; when used as a verb, *counsel* means "to advise." *Council* refers to a group that advises. **The student council asked for counsel from its trusted adviser.**
662.4 creak, creek	A *creak* is a squeaking sound; a *creek* is a stream. **I heard a creak from the old dock under my feet as I fished in the creek.**
662.5 cymbal, symbol	A *cymbal* is a metal instrument shaped like a plate. A *symbol* is something (usually visible) that stands for or represents another thing or idea (usually invisible). **The damaged cymbal lying on the stage was a symbol of the band's final concert.**
662.6 dear, deer	*Dear* means "loved or valued"; *deer* are animals. **My dear, old great-grandmother leaves corn and salt licks in her yard to attract deer.**
662.7 desert, dessert	A *desert* is a barren wilderness. *Dessert* is a food served at the end of a meal. **In the desert, cold water is more inviting than even the richest dessert.** The verb *desert* means "to abandon"; the noun *desert* (pronounced like the verb) means "deserving reward or punishment." **A spy who deserts his country will receive his just deserts if he is caught.**

Grammar Practice

Using the Right Word 6

- complement, compliment; continual, continuous; counsel, council; dear, deer; desert, dessert

For each numbered sentence below, write the correct choice from the set of words in parentheses.

Example: Some *(dear, deer)* appeared on the edge of the field.
deer

(1) After a light dinner, Kiana brought some *(desert, dessert)* to the table. **(2)** She said, "I also have the perfect *(complement, compliment)* for these brownies—hazelnut ice cream."

As she and Juwan ate, he kept making "mmm" sounds. **(3)** "I'll take that as a *(complement, compliment)*," Kiana said.

(4) Then she said, "Juwan, I've noticed there's a *(continual, continuous)* buzz coming from the refrigerator recently. It just won't stop. Do you think I should have it checked?"

(5) Juwan said, "Do you want my *(counsel, council)*, or do you want me to actually check it?"

(6) "Well, yes, please see if you can fix it yourself, *(dear, deer)*. And while you're at it, take a look at the humidifier, too. **(7)** It feels like a *(desert, dessert)* in here," Kiana said.

(8) "Kiana," Juwan said, "your *(continual, continuous)* requests for me to check things are a signal. Your apartment is falling apart!"

"I know. **(9)** I'm going to bring it up at the next renters' *(counsel, council)* meeting," she said. "In the meantime, thanks for being so handy!"

Next Step: Write a few lines of dialogue between two friends. Include at least two of the words from the list at the top of the page.

Related Skills Activities

- ***SkillsBook***
  Using the Right Word 2, p. 55

Answers

1. dessert
2. complement
3. compliment
4. continuous
5. counsel
6. dear
7. desert
8. continual
9. council

664.1 **die, dye**	*Die* (dying) means "to stop living." *Dye* (dyeing) is used to change the color of something. **The young girl hoped that her sick goldfish wouldn't** die. **My sister** dyes **her hair with coloring that washes out.**
664.2 **faint, feign, feint**	*Faint* means "feeble, without strength" or "to fall unconscious." *Feign* is a verb that means "to pretend or make up." *Feint* is a noun that means "a move or an activity that is pretended in order to divert attention." **The actors** feigned **a sword duel. One man staggered and fell in a** feint. **The audience gave** faint **applause.**
664.3 **farther, further**	*Farther* is used when you are writing about a physical distance. *Further* means "additional." **Alaska reaches** farther **north than Iceland. For** further **information, check your local library.**
664.4 **fewer, less**	*Fewer* refers to the number of separate units; *less* refers to bulk quantity. **I may have** less **money than you have, but I have** fewer **worries.**
664.5 **fir, fur**	*Fir* refers to a type of evergreen tree; *fur* is animal hair. **The Douglas** fir **tree is named after a Scottish botanist.** **An arctic fox has white** fur **in the winter.**
664.6 **flair, flare**	*Flair* means "a natural talent" or "style"; *flare* means "to light up quickly" or "burst out" (or an object that does so). **Jenrette has a** flair **for remaining calm when other people's tempers** flare.
664.7 **for, four**	The preposition *for* means "because of" or "directed to"; *four* is the number 4. **Mary had grilled steaks and chicken** for **the party, but the dog had stolen one of the** four **steaks.**

Grammar Practice

Using the Right Word 7

■ faint, feign, feint; farther, further; fewer, less; flair, flare; for, four

For each sentence below, write the word "correct" if the underlined word is used correctly. If it is incorrect, write the right word.

Example: During a marathon, which is just over 26 miles long, some runners <u>feint</u> along the way.
faint

1. Some of the runners have <u>less</u> stamina than others.
2. Those who can endure run <u>further</u> than many who begin the race.
3. <u>Less</u> runners finish the race than start it.
4. Near the end, a few minutes may feel like <u>fore</u> hours.
5. Only a surge of energy that <u>flares</u> up at this point will get the runner to the finish line.
6. Occasionally, a competitor will <u>feign</u> a move to one side before giving a burst of speed.
7. Most marathoners practice <u>four</u> at least a year prior to the race.
8. A few people run a marathon every year, but many are not interested in <u>farther</u> marathons once they've run one.
9. One runner, who has a definite <u>flare</u> for humor, wears a funny hat as he runs.
10. He also seems to stumble a lot, perhaps as some sort of <u>faint</u>.

Next Step: Write two sentences about some kind of race to show your understanding of the words *farther* and *further*.

Answers

1. correct
2. farther
3. Fewer
4. four
5. correct
6. correct
7. for
8. further
9. flair
10. feint

666.1 good, well	*Good* is an adjective; *well* is nearly always an adverb. **The strange flying machines flew** well. (The adverb *well* modifies *flew*.) **They looked** good **as they flew overhead.** (The adjective *good* modifies *they*.) When used in writing about health, *well* is an adjective. **The pilots did not feel** well, **however, after the long, hard race.**
666.2 hare, hair	A *hare* is an animal similar to a rabbit; *hair* refers to the growth covering the head and body of mammals and human beings. **When a** hare **darted out in front of our car, the** hair **on my head stood up.**
666.3 heal, heel	*Heal* means "to mend or restore to health." *Heel* is the back part of a human foot. **I got a blister on my** heel **from wearing my new shoes. It won't** heal **unless I wear my old ones.**
666.4 hear, here	You *hear* sounds with your ears. *Here* is the opposite of *there* and means "nearby."
666.5 heard, herd	*Heard* is the past tense of the verb "to hear"; *herd* is a group of animals. **The** herd **of grazing sheep raised their heads when they** heard **the collie barking in the distance.**
666.6 heir, air	An *heir* is a person who inherits something; *air* is what we breathe. **Will the next generation be** heir **to terminally polluted** air?
666.7 hole, whole	A *hole* is a cavity or hollow place. *Whole* means "entire or complete." **The** hole **in the ozone layer is a serious problem requiring the attention of the** whole **world.**
666.8 immigrate, emigrate	*Immigrate* means "to come into a new country or area." *Emigrate* means "to go out of one country to live in another." **Martin Ulferts** immigrated **to this country in 1882. He was only three years old when he** emigrated **from Germany.**

Grammar Practice

Using the Right Word 8

■ good, well; heal, heel; hear, here; hole, whole; immigrate, emigrate

Each sentence below has a choice of words in parentheses. Write the word that makes the sentence correct.

Example: Did you *(hear, here)* the latest news?
    hear

1. After her heart surgery, Granny Kasten is feeling surprisingly *(good, well)*.
2. The doctor said it may take a few months for her to *(heal, heel)* completely.
3. When she *(immigrated, emigrated)* to this country, she was only 12 years old.
4. My sister Alison spends her *(hole, whole)* morning fixing her hair.
5. When Sybil broke her *(heal, heel)*, she had to stay off her foot for two months.
6. My dad's parents *(immigrated, emigrated)* from Laos.
7. We often *(hear, here)* them talk about their lives there.
8. My grandparents adjusted *(good, well)* to living in this country.
9. I can't play in this weekend's concert because there is a *(hole, whole)* in my drum.
10. Deshawn is *(good, well)* at coming up with creative ideas for art projects.
11. Will this school still be *(hear, here)* in 50 years?

Next Step: Write three sentences that show you know the meaning of these words: *good, well,* and *heal.*

Answers

1. well
2. heal
3. immigrated
4. whole
5. heel
6. emigrated
7. hear
8. well
9. hole
10. good
11. here

668

668.1 imply, infer	*Imply* means "to suggest indirectly"; *infer* means "to draw a conclusion from facts." "Since you have to work, may I infer that you won't come to my party?" Guy asked. "No, I only meant to imply that I would be late," Rochelle responded.
668.2 it's, its	*It's* is the contraction of "it is." *Its* is the possessive form of "it." It's a fact that a minnow's teeth are in its throat.
668.3 knew, new	*Knew* is the past tense of the verb "know." *New* means "recent or modern." If I knew how to fix it, I would not need a new one!
668.4 know, no	*Know* means "to recognize or understand." *No* means "the opposite of yes." Phil, do you know Cheri? No, I've never met her.
668.5 later, latter	*Later* means "after a period of time." *Latter* refers to the second of two things mentioned. The band arrived later and set up the speakers and the lights. The latter made the stage look like a carnival ride.
668.6 lay, lie	*Lay* means "to place." (*Lay* is a transitive verb; that means it needs a word to complete the meaning.) *Lie* means "to recline." (*Lie* is an intransitive verb.) Lay your sleeping bag on the floor before you lie down on it. (*Lay* needs the word *bag* to complete its meaning.)
668.7 lead, led	*Lead* (lēd) is a present tense verb meaning "to guide." The past tense of the verb is *led* (lĕd). The noun *lead* (lĕd) is the metal. Guides planned to lead the settlers to safe quarters. Instead, they led them into a winter storm. Peeling paint in old houses may contain lead.
668.8 learn, teach	*Learn* means "to get information"; *teach* means "to give information." I want to learn how to sew. Will you teach me?

 Grammar Practice

Using the Right Word 9

■ imply, infer; later, latter; lay, lie; learn, teach

For each numbered word below, write the word "correct" if it is used correctly. If it is incorrect, write the right word.

Example: Are you <u>inferring</u> that I'm not smart enough?
implying

Mr. Levine was attempting to **(1)** <u>learn</u> us a difficult scientific concept. After answering some questions, he said, "From the looks on some of your faces, I **(2)** <u>imply</u> that you still don't get it."

"Mr. Levine," Davion said, "isn't there another way that we can **(3)** <u>learn</u> this?"

Albert added, "Why do we need to know this, anyway?"

Without being too obvious, Mr. Levine **(4)** <u>implied</u> that we would all fail the exam if we didn't understand it. "Furthermore," he said, "if you don't have some basic curiosity, you might as well just **(5)** <u>lay</u> down and sleep away your life."

(6) <u>Latter</u> in the week, Mr. Levine came up with a different way to **(7)** <u>teach</u> us about the characteristics of atoms. He asked Chaya to **(8)** <u>lie</u> her fleece jacket on some carpet. (He had brought a piece of the **(9)** <u>later</u> from home.) Then he shut off the light and told Chaya to drag her jacket back and forth on the carpet. There were sparks! Mr. Levine explained to us that static forms when one material pulls electrons away from the other. And, just like that, we had **(10)** <u>learned</u> something!

Next Step: Here is an easy way to remember the difference between *imply* and *infer:* "When **you** (with a *y*) imply, **I** infer." Try to think of something that will help you remember the difference between *lay* and *lie*.

Related Skills Activities

■ **SkillsBook**
Using the Right Word 2, p. 55

 Answers

1. teach
2. infer
3. correct
4. correct
5. lie
6. Later
7. correct
8. lay
9. latter
10. correct

670

670.1 leave, let	*Leave* means "fail to take along." *Let* means "allow." Rozi wanted to leave her boots at home, but Jorge wouldn't let her.
670.2 like, as	*Like* is a preposition meaning "similar to"; *as* is a conjunction meaning "to the same degree" or "while." *Like* usually introduces a phrase; *as* usually introduces a clause. The glider floated like a bird. The glider floated as the pilot had hoped it would. As we circled the airfield, we saw maintenance carts moving like ants below us.
670.3 loose, lose, loss	*Loose* (lüs) means "free or untied"; *lose* (lo͞oz) means "to misplace or fail to win"; *loss* (lôs) means "something lost." These jeans are too loose in the waist since my recent weight loss. I still want to lose a few more pounds.
670.4 made, maid	*Made* is the past tense of "make," which means to "create," "prepare," or "put in order." A *maid* is a female servant; *maid* is also used to describe an unmarried girl or young woman. The hotel maid asked if our beds needed to be made. Grandma made a chocolate cake for dessert. A maid strolled in the garden before the concert.
670.5 mail, male	*Mail* refers to letters or packages handled by the postal service. *Male* refers to the masculine sex. My little brother likes getting junk mail. The male sea horse, not the female, takes care of the fertilized eggs.
670.6 main, mane	*Main* refers to the most important part. *Mane* is the long hair growing from the top or sides of the neck of certain animals, such as the horse, lion, and so on. The main thing we noticed about the magician's tamed lion was its luxurious mane.
670.7 meat, meet	*Meat* is food or flesh; *meet* means "to come upon or encounter." I'd like you to meet the butcher who sells the leanest meat in town.

Grammar Practice

Using the Right Word 10

■ like, as; loose, lose, loss; mail, male; main, mane

For each of the following sentences, write the correct choice from the set of words in parentheses.

Example: The road crew set up detour signs and began repairing the village's *(main, mane)* street.
main

1. Bianca wears her hair in *(loose, lose, loss)* curls around her face.

2. For thousands of years, people have dreamed of flying *(like, as)* a bird.

3. In the 1980s, rock stars sported big, wild *(mains, manes)* of hair.

4. Most people know to avoid a bull moose, which is a *(mail, male)* moose, but a mother moose with a calf is equally dangerous.

5. Is California or Florida the *(main, mane)* producer of oranges in the United States?

6. The basketball players from Orson Middle School celebrated their victory *(like, as)* their fans screamed with joy.

7. The opposing team took their *(loose, lose, loss)* well, even though it was their last game.

8. Worrying causes many people to *(loose, lose, loss)* sleep.

9. In the hottest parts of Africa, some lions have almost no *(main, mane)*.

10. More and more people around the world now send and receive *(mail, male)* electronically.

11. I wish I had a friend *(like, as)* you.

Next Step: Write three sentences that show your understanding of the words *loss, loose,* and *lose*.

Related Skills Activities

■ **CD-ROM**
Using the Right Word 3
670.2, 670.3, 670.5, 670.6

■ *SkillsBook*
Using the Right Word 3, p. 56

Answers

1. loose
2. like
3. manes
4. male
5. main
6. as
7. loss
8. lose
9. mane
10. mail
11. like

672

672.1
medal, metal, meddle, mettle

A *medal* is an award. *Metal* is an element like iron or gold. *Meddle* means "to interfere." *Mettle*, a noun, refers to quality of character.

> Grandpa's friend received a medal for showing his mettle in battle. Grandma, who loves to meddle in others' business, asked if the award was a precious metal.

672.2
miner, minor

A *miner* digs in the ground for valuable ore. A *minor* is a person who is not legally an adult. *Minor* means "of no great importance" when used as an adjective.

> The use of minors as miners is no minor problem.

672.3
moral, morale

Moral relates to what is right or wrong or to the lesson to be drawn from a story. *Morale* refers to a person's attitude or mental condition.

> The moral of this story is "Everybody loves a winner."
> After the unexpected win at football, morale was high throughout the town.

672.4
morning, mourning

Morning refers to the first part of the day (before noon); *mourning* means "showing sorrow."

> Abby was mourning her test grades all morning.

672.5
oar, or, ore

An *oar* is a paddle used in rowing or steering a boat. *Or* is a conjunction indicating choice. *Ore* refers to a mineral made up of several different kinds of material, as in iron ore.

> Either use one oar to push us away from the dock, or start the boat's motor.
> Silver-copper ore is smelted and refined to extract each metal.

672.6
pain, pane

Pain is the feeling of being hurt. A *pane* is a section or part of something.

> Dad looked like he was in pain when he found out we broke a pane of glass in the neighbor's front door.

672.7
pair, pare, pear

A *pair* is a couple (two); *pare* is a verb meaning "to peel"; *pear* is the fruit.

> A pair of doves nested in the pear tree.
> Please pare the apples for the pie.

 Grammar Practice

Using the Right Word 11

■ meddle, mettle; moral, morale; morning, mourning; pain, pane

 For each of the following sentences, write a word from the list above to fill in the blank.

> Example: People's _____ often sags when winter drags on.
> *morale*

1. Some people, _____ the long, warm summer days that have passed, can't see the beauty of autumn.

2. When Kaleb picked up the pile of heavy, wet clothes, he felt a sharp _____ in his back.

3. Once last winter, the extreme cold formed delicate frost flowers on the window _____.

4. Grandma thinks that the _____ values of young people have sunk to a new low.

5. "I appreciate your interest," said Alejandra, "but I really don't need you to _____ in this situation."

6. Thad is _____ the loss of his beloved dog.

7. Sometimes only time will ease the _____ of such a loss.

8. A firefighter's _____ is tested every time an emergency requires swift action.

9. I find that _____ is the best time for me to work out.

10. Is it a person's _____ obligation to help someone in need?

11. The team's high _____, despite a string of defeats, was inspiring.

Next Step: Write some sentences using one word from each of the four word groups at the top of the page.

Related Skills Activities

■ *SkillsBook*
Using the Right Word 3, p. 56

 Answers

1. mourning
2. pain
3. pane
4. moral
5. meddle
6. mourning
7. pain
8. mettle
9. morning
10. moral
11. morale

674

674.1 past, passed	*Passed* is always a verb; it is the past tense of *pass*. *Past* can be used as a noun, as an adjective, or as a preposition. A motorcycle passed my dad's 'Vette. (verb) The old man won't forget the past. (noun) I'm sorry, but I'd rather not talk about my past life. (adjective) Old Blue walked right past the cat and never saw it. (preposition)
674.2 peace, piece	*Peace* means "harmony, or freedom from war." A *piece* is a part or fragment of something. In order to keep peace among the triplets, each one had to have an identical piece of cake.
674.3 peak, peek, pique	A *peak* is a "high point" or a "pointed end." *Peek* means "brief look." *Pique*, as a verb, means "to excite by challenging"; as a noun, it means "a feeling of resentment." Just a peek at Pike's Peak in the Rocky Mountains can pique a mountain climber's curiosity. In a pique, she marched away from her giggling sisters.
674.4 personal, personnel	*Personal* means "private." *Personnel* are people working at a job. Some thoughts are too personal to share. The personnel manager will be hiring more workers.
674.5 plain, plane	A *plain* is an area of land that is flat or level; it also means "clearly seen or clearly understood" and "ordinary." It's plain to see why the early settlers had trouble crossing the Great Plains. *Plane* means "a flat, level surface" (as in geometry); it is also a tool used to smooth the surface of wood. When I saw that the door wasn't a perfect plane, I used a plane to make it smooth.
674.6 pore, pour, poor	A *pore* is an opening in the skin. *Pour* means "to cause a flow or stream." *Poor* means "needy." People perspire through the pores in their skin. Pour yourself a glass of water. Your poor body needs it!

Grammar Practice

Using the Right Word 12

■ past, passed; peace, piece; peak, peek, pique; pore, pour, poor

 For each sentence below, write the word "correct" if the underlined word is used correctly. If it is incorrect, write the right word.

Example: I looked up from my book and realized that my bus was now more than a mile <u>past</u> my stop.
correct

1. I <u>peaked</u> at my watch and wondered if I could possibly get to my dentist appointment in time.

2. I took out what I thought was my bus schedule and discovered that it was only a small <u>peace</u> of blank paper.

3. I got off the bus and saw just the <u>pique</u> of the building where I needed to be in 15 minutes.

4. I walked as fast as I could, and soon I was sweating from every <u>pour</u> on my body.

5. That would <u>pique</u> anyone's thirst, so I got a bottle of water from my backpack.

6. When I'd had enough, I decided to <u>poor</u> the rest of it on a small tree before throwing the empty bottle in a city waste can.

7. I was so focused on satisfying my thirst that I almost <u>past</u> the dentist's office.

8. I gratefully sat at <u>piece</u> in the waiting room.

9. My <u>pore</u> feet needed the rest.

10. I was glad that this experience was now in my <u>passed</u>.

Next Step: Write a paragraph about a time when you were late. Use as many of the words in the list at the top of the page as you can.

Related Skills Activities

■ **SkillsBook**
Using the Right Word 3, p. 56

 ## Answers

1. peeked
2. piece
3. peak
4. pore
5. correct
6. pour
7. passed
8. peace
9. poor
10. past

676

676.1
principal,
principle

As an adjective, *principal* means "primary." As a noun, it can mean "a school administrator" or "a sum of money." *Principle* means "idea or doctrine."

> My mom's principal goal is to save money so she can pay off the principal balance on her loan from the bank.
>
> Hey, Charlie, I hear the principal gave you a detention.
>
> The principle of freedom is based on the principle of self-discipline.

676.2
quiet, quit, quite

Quiet is the opposite of "noisy." *Quit* means "to stop." *Quite* means "completely or entirely."

> I quit mowing even though I wasn't quite finished.
>
> The neighborhood was quiet again.

676.3
raise, rays, raze

Raise is a verb meaning "to lift or elevate." *Rays* are thin lines or beams. *Raze* is a verb that means "to tear down completely."

> When I raise this shade, bright rays of sunlight stream into the room.
>
> Construction workers will raze the old theater to make room for a parking lot.

676.4
real, very, really

Do not use the adjective *real* in place of the adverbs *very* or *really*.

> The plants scattered throughout the restaurant are not real.
>
> Pimples are very embarrassing.
>
> Her nose is really small.

676.5
red, read

Red is a color; *read*, pronounced the same way, is the past tense of the verb meaning "to understand the meaning of written words and symbols."

> "I've read five books in two days," said the little boy.
>
> The librarian gave him a red ribbon.

Grammar Practice

Using the Right Word 13

■ principal, principle; quiet, quit, quite; raise, rays, raze; real, very, really

For each sentence below, write the word "correct" if the underlined word is used correctly. If it is incorrect, write the right word.

Example: The National Aeronautics and Space Administration (NASA) plans to <u>raise</u> some buildings to make way for new construction.
raze

1. A <u>principle</u> concern of NASA is the amount of debris left in space from previous space flights.

2. Although scientists keep track of the space debris, they are not <u>quit</u> sure they know where it all is.

3. Sound waves cannot travel in airless space, so space is a <u>quite</u> place.

4. At times, the <u>raze</u> of the sun are reflected by the shiny orbiting objects.

5. NASA worries about space debris, which is <u>real</u> small.

6. Even a tiny fleck of paint in space can be a <u>real</u> threat because it could be speeding along at almost 18,000 miles per hour.

7. Unfortunately, these <u>very</u> small objects cannot be tracked.

8. They <u>rays</u> the danger for flight crews.

9. In spite of the danger, the <u>principle</u> of exploration drives astronauts to travel into space again and again.

10. For a variety of reasons, some people think that the United States should <u>quit</u> sending rockets into space.

Next Step: Write two sentences on your thoughts about the space program. Use the words *real* and *really* correctly.

Related Skills Activities

■ **CD-ROM**
Using the Right Word 2
676.1, 676.2, 676.3, 676.4

Answers

1. principal
2. quite
3. quiet
4. rays
5. really or very
6. correct
7. correct
8. raise
9. correct
10. correct

678

678.1
right, write, rite

Right means "correct or proper"; *right* is the opposite of "left"; it also refers to anything that a person has a legal claim to, as in "copyright." *Write* means "to record in print." *Rite* is a ritual or ceremonial act.

We have to write an essay about how our rights are protected by the Constitution.

Turn right at the next corner.

A rite of passage is a ceremony that celebrates becoming an adult.

678.2
scene, seen

Scene refers to the setting or location where something happens; it also means "sight or spectacle." *Seen* is a form of the verb "see."

The scene of the crime was roped off. We hadn't seen anyone go in or out of the building.

678.3
seam, seem

A *seam* is a line formed by connecting two pieces of material. *Seem* means "appear to exist."

Every Thanksgiving, it seems, I stuff myself so much that my shirt seams threaten to burst.

678.4
sew, so, sow

Sew is a verb meaning "to stitch"; *so* is a conjunction meaning "in order that." The verb *sow* means "to plant."

In Colonial times, the wife would sew the family clothes, and the husband would sow the family garden so the children could eat.

678.5
sight, cite, site

Sight means "the act of seeing" or "something that is seen." *Cite* means "to quote or refer to." A *site* is a location or position (including a Web site on the Internet).

The Alamo at night was a sight worth the trip. I was also able to cite my visit to this historical site in my history paper.

678.6
sit, set

Sit means "to put the body in a seated position." *Set* means "to place." (*Set* is a transitive verb; that means it needs a direct object to complete its meaning.)

How can you just sit there and watch as I set up all these chairs?

Grammar Practice

Using the Right Word 14

■ scene, seen; seam, seem; sew, so, sow; sit, set

For each of the following sentences, write a word from the list above to fill in the blank.

Example: Because even a little moisture can damage wood, please do not _____ that wet towel on the table.
set

1. "Did you notice that the _____ of this jacket is coming apart?" Mia asked.

2. "Yes," I replied, "I'm going to try to _____ it up myself."

3. Theo finally had to _____ down after standing for three hours during the football game.

4. When he _____ his soda on the bench, someone knocked it over.

5. Janelle and Rhonda stopped Craig to ask him if he had _____ their lost dog.

6. Landon wants to design his diorama to look like a _____ from the Battle of New Orleans.

7. Looking around, Jay said, "I _____ to have lost my hat."

8. Sharon promised to help her mother _____ some flower seeds in their little garden.

9. I'm trying to get extra pet-sitting jobs _____ that I will have enough money to get two kittens.

10. We _____ in assigned seats in this class.

11. My aunt does not like to be _____ without her makeup.

12. Although lemmings might _____ to jump off a ledge into the sea, they actually are looking for food and accidentally fall.

13. Khadijah is tired of her long hair, _____ she's going to get it cut short this weekend.

 Answers

1. seam
2. sew
3. sit
4. set
5. seen
6. scene
7. seem
8. sow
9. so
10. sit
11. seen
12. seem
13. so

680.1 sole, soul	*Sole* means "single, only one"; *sole* also refers to the bottom surface of a foot or shoe. *Soul* refers to the spiritual part of a person. **Maggie got a job for the** sole **purpose of saving for a car.** **The** soles **of these shoes are very thick.** **"Who told you dogs don't have** souls?" **asked the kind veterinarian.**
680.2 some, sum	*Some* means "an unknown number or part." *Sum* means "the whole amount." **The** sum **in the cash register was stolen by** some **thieves.**
680.3 sore, soar	*Sore* means "painful"; to *soar* means "to rise or fly high into the air." **Craning to watch the eagle** soar **overhead, we soon had** sore **necks.**
680.4 stationary, stationery	*Stationary* means "not movable"; *stationery* is the paper and envelopes used to write letters. **Grandpa designed and printed his own** stationery. **All of the built-in furniture is** stationary, **of course.**
680.5 steal, steel	*Steal* means "to take something without permission"; *steel* is a metal. **Early iron makers had to** steal **recipes for producing** steel.
680.6 than, then	*Than* is used in a comparison; *then* tells when. **Since tomorrow's weather is supposed to be nicer** than **today's, we'll go to the zoo** then.
680.7 their, there, they're	*Their* is a possessive pronoun, one that shows ownership. *There* is an adverb that tells where. *They're* is the contraction for "they are." **They're upset because** their **dog got into the garbage over** there.
680.8 threw, through	*Threw* is the past tense of "throw." *Through* means "passing from one side to the other" or "by means of." **Through sheer talent and long practice, Nolan Ryan** threw **baseballs** through **the strike zone at more than 100 miles per hour.**

Grammar Practice

Using the Right Word 15

■ sole, soul; sore, soar; stationary, stationery; than, then; threw, through

 If a word from the list above is used incorrectly in one of the following numbered sentences, write the correct word; otherwise, write "OK."

Example: When I finished reading Vilma's letter, I through it away.
threw

(1) I had noticed that Vilma's stationary had drawings of kites along the side of the page. That got me wondering: Why do people fly kites? (2) I guess the sole motive for most people is to have fun. (3) They would rather embrace the wind then try to fight it.

(4) Often I fly a kite, standing stationary against the raging gusts. (5) I watch my flying piece of art struggle in the wind, and then I gradually let out more string. (6) For me, the sole of kite flying is imagining myself as the kite. (7) Attached to the ground by only a thin string, I sore on the breeze. (8) I dart in and out through the clouds before diving toward earth again. (9) Eventually, my soar fingers mean the kite flying must end for the day. (10) It is time to slowly reel in the string than and put the kite away . . . until the next time a dream and the wind call me once again.

Next Step: Write two sentences about an activity you enjoy. Use the words *than* and *then* correctly.

Related Skills Activities

■ **SkillsBook**
Using the Right Word 4, pp. 57–58t

 Answers

1. stationery
2. OK
3. than
4. OK
5. OK
6. soul
7. soar
8. OK
9. sore
10. then

682

682.1
to, too, two

To is the preposition that can mean "in the direction of." (*To* also is used to form an infinitive. See **730.4**.) *Too* is an adverb meaning "very or excessive." *Too* is often used to mean "also." *Two* is the number 2.

> Only two of Columbus's first three ships returned to Spain from the New World.

> Columbus was too restless to stay in Spain for long.

682.2
vain, vane, vein

Vain means "worthless." It may also mean "thinking too highly of one's self; stuck-up." *Vane* is a flat piece of material set up to show which way the wind blows. *Vein* refers to a blood vessel or a mineral deposit.

> The weather vane indicates the direction of wind.

> A blood vein determines the direction of flowing blood.

> The vain mind moves in no particular direction and thinks only about itself.

682.3
vary, very

Vary is a verb that means "to change." *Very* can be an adjective meaning "in the fullest sense" or "complete"; it can also be an adverb meaning "extremely."

> Garon's version of the event would vary from day to day. His very interesting story was the very opposite of the truth.

682.4
waist, waste

Waist is the part of the body just above the hips. The verb *waste* means "to wear away" or "to use carelessly"; the noun *waste* refers to material that is unused or useless.

> Don't waste your money on fast-food meals. What a waste to throw away all this food because you're concerned about the size of your waist!

682.5
wait, weight

Wait means "to stay somewhere expecting something." *Weight* is the measure of heaviness.

> When I have to wait for the bus, the weight of my backpack seems to keep increasing.

682.6
ware, wear, where

Ware means "a product to be sold"; *wear* means "to have on or to carry on one's body"; *where* asks the question "in what place or in what situation?"

> Where can you buy the best cookware to take on a campout—and the best rain gear to wear if it rains?

Grammar Practice

Using the Right Word 16

■ to, too, two; vain, vane, vein; vary, very; ware, wear, where

For each of the following sentences, write the correct choice from the set of words in parentheses.

Example: Angelica braids her hair *(to, too, two)* keep it out of her face.
to

1. The school's weather *(vain, vane, vein)* shows that the wind is from the north today.

2. A cold breeze makes me want to *(ware, wear, where)* a sweater.

3. Although the school ordered a reference guide for every class, only *(to, too, two)* arrived.

4. After searching for 15 minutes, Tony finally asked the librarian *(ware, wear, where)* the biographies were located.

5. As long as he had to talk to her, he asked her to point out the bathrooms, *(to, too, two)*.

6. In a *(vain, vane, vein)* attempt to open the window, Ms. Jenkins discovered that it had been painted shut.

7. When Char glanced at the clock and realized only 20 minutes had gone by, she knew it was going to be a *(vary, very)* long day.

8. Grandpa says that sometimes a nurse cannot find a good *(vain, vane, vein)* from which to draw his blood.

9. Darren and I went *(to, too, two)* the mall yesterday.

10. Fatima is an artist who works with metal; she sells her *(wares, wears, wheres)* at festivals and county fairs.

11. Although we were told that the lunch menu would *(vary, very)* from week to week, it always seems the same to me.

12. Many fast foods have *(to, too, two)* much salt.

Next Step: Write one sentence that uses *to, too,* and *two.* For an extra challenge, write one with *vary* and *very.*

Related Skills Activities

■ **SkillsBook**
Using the Right Word 4, pp. 57–58

Answers

1. vane
2. wear
3. two
4. where
5. too
6. vain
7. very
8. vein
9. to
10. wares
11. vary
12. too

684

684.1 way, weigh	*Way* means "path or route" or "a series of actions." *Weigh* means "to measure weight." What is the correct way to weigh liquid medicines?
684.2 weather, whether	*Weather* refers to the condition of the atmosphere. *Whether* refers to a possibility. The weather will determine whether I go fishing.
684.3 week, weak	A *week* is a period of seven days; *weak* means "not strong." Last week when I had the flu, I felt light-headed and weak.
684.4 wet, whet	*Wet* means "soaked with liquid." *Whet* is a verb that means "to sharpen." Of course, going swimming means I'll get wet, but all that exercise really whets my appetite.
684.5 which, witch	*Which* is a pronoun used to ask "what one or ones?" out of a group. A *witch* is a woman believed to have supernatural powers. Which of the women in Salem in the 1600s were accused of being witches?
684.6 who, which, that	When introducing a clause, *who* is used to refer to people; *which* refers to animals and nonliving beings but never to people (it introduces a nonrestrictive, or unnecessary, clause); *that* usually refers to animals or things but can refer to people (it introduces a restrictive, or necessary, clause). The idea that pizza is junk food is crazy. Pizza, which is quite nutritious, can be included in a healthful diet. My mom, who is a dietician, said so.
684.7 who, whom	*Who* is used as the subject in a sentence; *whom* is used as the object of a preposition or as a direct object. Who asked you to play tennis? You beat whom at tennis? You played tennis with whom? **NOTE** To test for *who/whom*, arrange the parts of the clause in a subject–verb–direct-object order. *Who* works as the subject, *whom* as the object. (See page **570**.)

Grammar Practice

Using the Right Word 17

■ way, weigh; wet, whet; which, witch; who, which, that; who, whom

If a word from the list above is used incorrectly in one of the following sentences, write the correct word; otherwise, write "OK."

Example: Ms. Fridley, whom is our homeroom teacher, is helping us plan our year-end picnic.
who

1. The planning has really wet our desire for the end of the school year to come quickly!

2. The picnic which we planned for last year was rained out.

3. Most of us know the way to the park.

4. Lauren, that is new to the area, might not know how to get there.

5. We will use a picnic shelter that offers electricity and water.

6. Arlan suggested bringing ice for the soda, but it may way too much.

7. If Luis brings a wagon, which he did last year, we could use that for the ice.

8. Ms. Fridley still needs to decide who she will ask to organize the games.

9. I hope we play the game with water balloons that gets everyone wet!

10. A which wouldn't play that game because, according to legend, she will melt if water touches her.

11. The girl whom wore her swimsuit last year was the smart one.

Next Step: Read 584.1 and 706.3 to learn more about using *which* and *that* correctly. Then write two sentences that show your understanding of the words.

Related Skills Activities

■ *SkillsBook*
Using the Right Word 4, pp. 57–58

Answers

1. whet
2. that
3. OK
4. who
5. OK
6. weigh
7. OK
8. whom
9. OK
10. witch
11. who

686

686.1
who's, whose

Who's is the contraction for "who is." *Whose* is a possessive pronoun, one that shows ownership.

Who's **the most popular writer today?**

Whose **bike is this?**

686.2
wood, would

Wood is the material that comes from trees; *would* is a form of the verb "will."

Sequoia trees live practically forever, but would **you believe that the** wood **from these giants is practically useless?**

686.3
your, you're

Your is a possessive pronoun, one that shows ownership. *You're* is the contraction for "you are."

You're **the most important person in** your **parents' lives.**

SCHOOL DAZE

David, you know **you're** supposed to be doing **your** homework.

I am, Mom. I'm doing firsthand research on energy conservation.

Grammar Practice

Using the Right Word 18

■ who's, whose; wood, would; your, you're

 For each of the following sentences, write a word from the list above to fill in the blank.

Example: Please bring _____ journals to class tomorrow.
your

1. Five students said that they _____ be willing to help serve at the Wing Road Soup Kitchen.
2. Can anyone tell me _____ watch this is?
3. _____ planning to go on the Washington, D.C., trip?
4. The manager said, "After you put away the weights and sweep the workout room, _____ free to go."
5. This old desk is made completely of _____.
6. Make sure you have _____ lunch, and then get on the bus.

Using the Right Word Review

 For each of the following sentences, write the correct choice from each set of words in parentheses.

1. My uncle living in Cuba wants to *(immigrate, emigrate)* to the United States.
2. The *(stationary, stationery)* bike is *(to, too, two)* heavy for you to move by yourself.
3. Have you *(scene, seen)* the city bus that's painted to look *(as, like)* a shark?
4. Scuba divers need a *(continual, continuous)* supply of air.
5. The magician asked Frank to *(borrow, lend)* her a coin for an *(allusion, illusion)* she would perform.
6. Larry wasn't *(quiet, quit, quite)* ready to leave the lake and the *(base, bass)* *(who, which, that)* got away.

Related Skills Activities

■ *SkillsBook*
Using the Right Word 4, pp. 57–58

 Answers

1. would
2. whose
3. Who's
4. you're
5. wood
6. your

Answers

1. emigrate
2. stationary, too
3. seen, like
4. continuous
5. lend, illusion
6. quite, bass, that

Test Prep!

For each underlined part of the paragraphs below, choose the letter (on the next page) that shows the correct usage.

Last year, the company <u>which</u> put together the Fourth of July
        (1)
fireworks display was Fire in the Sky. <u>Its owned bye</u> Carlos's Uncle
                                              (2)
Diaz, <u>whom</u> enjoys creating the <u>biannual July 4 scene</u> in the sky. During
      (3)   (4)
several visits to the factory, Carlos <u>piqued at four</u> new projects on the
                                       (5)
tables. He was <u>as a</u> reporter, constantly asking questions. His uncle
               (6)
would laugh and say, "Your questions are <u>like a</u> string of firecrackers."
                                          (7)

On Independence Day, Uncle Diaz let Carlos walk <u>through the mane</u>
                                                  (8)
area of the display setup. Uncle Diaz pointed out an extra-special
rocket, <u>that</u> was much louder and had greater special <u>affects then</u> any
        (9)   (10)
of the other fireworks. The big rocket's slow <u>assent would sit</u> the stage
                                               (11)
for a dramatic explosion at the end of the show. A bit later, Uncle Diaz
surprised Carlos with the news that he <u>would learn</u> him how to fire the
                                        (12)
last rocket—the big rocket. Wow! What <u>a moral</u> booster. When it was
                                        (13)
launched, the great rocket exploded with a tremendous boom, filling the
sky with <u>really long flairs</u> of light. It <u>seemed like the birth</u> of a star. The
          (14)   (15)
crowd loved it! Carlos felt <u>good about the complement</u> his uncle had given
                            (16)
him. He wants to help his uncle again this summer.

1 Ⓐ who
Ⓑ whom
Ⓒ that
Ⓓ correct as is

2 Ⓐ Its' owned by
Ⓑ It's owned by
Ⓒ It's owned bye
Ⓓ correct as is

3 Ⓐ who
Ⓑ which
Ⓒ that
Ⓓ correct as is

4 Ⓐ biannual July 4 seen
Ⓑ annual July 4 scene
Ⓒ annual July 4 seen
Ⓓ correct as is

5 Ⓐ peaked at for
Ⓑ peeked at four
Ⓒ peaked at four
Ⓓ correct as is

6 Ⓐ as an
Ⓑ like a
Ⓒ like an
Ⓓ correct as is

7 Ⓐ as an
Ⓑ as a
Ⓒ like an
Ⓓ correct as is

8 Ⓐ through the main
Ⓑ threw the main
Ⓒ threw the mane
Ⓓ correct as is

9 Ⓐ who
Ⓑ whom
Ⓒ which
Ⓓ correct as is

10 Ⓐ affects than
Ⓑ effects then
Ⓒ effects than
Ⓓ correct as is

11 Ⓐ assent would set
Ⓑ ascent would sit
Ⓒ ascent would set
Ⓓ correct as is

12 Ⓐ wood learn
Ⓑ would teach
Ⓒ wood teach
Ⓓ correct as is

13 Ⓐ a morale
Ⓑ an moral
Ⓒ an morale
Ⓓ correct as is

14 Ⓐ real long flares
Ⓑ real long flairs
Ⓒ really long flares
Ⓓ correct as is

15 Ⓐ seamed like the birth
Ⓑ seamed like the berth
Ⓒ seemed like the berth
Ⓓ correct as is

16 Ⓐ good about the compliment
Ⓑ well about the compliment
Ⓒ well about the complement
Ⓓ correct as is

RIGHT WORD

Related Skills Activities

■ *SkillsBook*
Using the Right Word 1and 2, pp. 59–62

Answers

1. C
2. B
3. A
4. B
5. B
6. B
7. D
8. A

9. C
10. C
11. C
12. B
13. A
14. C
15. D
16. A

690

Understanding Sentences

Sentences

A **sentence** is a group of words that expresses a complete thought. A sentence must have both a subject and a predicate. A sentence begins with a capital letter; it ends with a period, a question mark, or an exclamation point.

> I like my teacher this year.
> Will we go on a field trip?
> We get to go to the water park!

Parts of a Sentence

690.1 **Subjects**	A subject is the part of a sentence that does something or is talked about. The kids on my block play basketball at the local park. We meet after school almost every day.
690.2 **Simple Subjects**	The simple subject is the subject without the words that describe or modify it. (Also see page **501**.) My friend Chester plays basketball on the school team.
690.3 **Complete Subjects**	The complete subject is the simple subject and all the words that modify it. (Also see page **500**.) My friend Chester plays basketball on the school team.
690.4 **Compound Subjects**	A compound subject has two or more simple subjects. (See page **501**.) Chester, Malik, and Meshelle play on our pickup team. Lou and I are the best shooters.

Grammar Practice

Parts of a Sentence 1
■ Simple, Complete, and Compound Subjects

For each of the numbered sentences that follow, write the complete subject. Underline the simple subject. (Watch for compound subjects.)

Example: Cesar Chavez was a Spanish-speaking migrant worker.
Cesar Chavez

(1) Cesar Chavez was born in Arizona in 1927. **(2)** He became an activist for farmworkers. **(3)** Many of these workers were Spanish-speaking migrants. **(4)** Chavez earned respect for using nonviolent ways to improve the working conditions on farms.

(5) In the early 1960s, Chavez organized grape pickers in California. **(6)** The workers held marches and strikes. **(7)** They picketed unfair employers. **(8)** As a result, many major growers offered farmworkers better wages, health insurance, and safer working conditions.

(9) Later in the '60s, Chavez continued his effort, and he drew attention to the situation. **(10)** People who shopped at grocery stores were asked to avoid buying grapes. **(11)** More Americans became aware of the troubles of the farmworkers. **(12)** The United Farm Workers Union gained the respect of farm employers.

(13) Chavez died in 1993. **(14)** Since then, seven states and several Southwestern cities have declared a holiday in honor of the labor leader. **(15)** Phoenix, Tempe, Los Angeles, Denver, and Santa Fe celebrate Chavez's accomplishments on his birthday, March 31. **(16)** He is remembered for making a peaceful stand for farmworkers.

Next Step: Did you remember that a compound sentence has two subjects? Review the sentences above for any of these you may have missed.

SENTENCES

Related Skills Activities

■ **Basic Grammar and Writing**
Writing Complete Sentences, pp. 500–501

■ *SkillsBook*
Subjects and Predicates, pp. 65–66
Compound Subjects and Predicates, pp. 67–68

Answers

1. Cesar <u>Chavez</u>
2. <u>He</u>
3. Many of these <u>workers</u>
4. <u>Chavez</u>
5. <u>Chavez</u>
6. The <u>workers</u>
7. <u>They</u>
8. many major <u>growers</u>
9. <u>Chavez</u>, <u>he</u>
10. <u>People</u> who shopped at grocery stores
11. More <u>Americans</u>
12. The United Farm Workers <u>Union</u>
13. <u>Chavez</u>
14. seven <u>states</u> and several Southwestern <u>cities</u>
15. <u>Phoenix</u>, Tempe, Los Angeles, <u>Denver</u>, and <u>Santa Fe</u>
16. <u>He</u>

692

Parts of a Sentence . . .

692.1 Predicates

The predicate, which contains the verb, is the part of the sentence that shows action or says something about the subject.

Hunting has reduced the tiger population in India.

692.2 Simple Predicates

The simple predicate is the predicate (verb) without the words that describe or modify it. (See page 501.)

In the past, poachers killed too many African elephants. Poaching is illegal.

692.3 Complete Predicates

The complete predicate is the simple predicate with all the words that modify or describe it. (See page 500.)

In the past, **poachers** killed too many African elephants. **Poaching** is illegal.

692.4 Direct Objects

The complete predicate often includes a direct object. The direct object is the noun or pronoun that receives the action of the simple predicate—directly. The direct object answers the question *what* or *whom*. (See page 570.)

Many smaller animals need friends who will speak up for them.

The direct object may be compound.

We all need animals, plants, wetlands, deserts, and forests.

692.5 Indirect Objects

If a sentence has a direct object, it may also have an indirect object. An indirect object is the noun or pronoun that receives the action of the simple predicate—indirectly. An indirect object names the person *to whom* or *for whom* something is done. (See page 570.)

I showed the class my multimedia report on endangered species. (*Class* is the indirect object because it says *to whom* the report was shown.)

Remember, in order for a sentence to have an indirect object, it must first have a direct object.

692.6 Compound Predicates

A compound predicate is composed of two or more simple predicates. (See page 501.)

In 1990 the countries of the world met and banned the sale of ivory.

Grammar Practice

Parts of a Sentence 2

■ Simple, Complete, and Compound Predicates

 For each sentence below, write the complete predicate (or predicates for a compound sentence). Circle the simple or compound predicate.

Example: Ancient people were the first to work with copper.
(were) the first to work with copper

1. It was easy to find, and it was a fairly simple process to melt the copper.

2. Bronze is probably the first invented metal.

3. Metal workers, or smelters, melted copper and threw tin into it.

4. Smelters gradually added other substances to copper and created even stronger metals.

■ Direct and Indirect Objects

 Write the direct object or objects that are part of the predicate in each sentence below. If the sentence has an indirect object, write it after the direct object and underline it.

Example: Metal workers produced bronze pins, jewelry, and oil lamps.
pins, jewelry, lamps

1. Sculptors could cast lifelike statues in bronze.

2. Kings sometimes gave great warriors bronze swords.

3. Wealthy people bought their families bronze trinkets.

4. Archaeologists have found many bronze artifacts.

5. Museum displays show visitors bronze objects that are thousands of years old.

6. Even today, one can see the fine designs carved into them.

7. Artists still like bronze and work with it often.

Related Skills Activities

■ **Basic Grammar and Writing**
Make the Meaning of the Verb Complete, p. 473
Transfer Action to an Object, p. 484
Writing Complete Sentences, pp. 500–501

■ **CD-ROM**
Direct and Indirect Objects 692.4, 692.5

■ *SkillsBook*
Subjects and Predicates, pp. 65–66
Compound Subjects and Predicates, pp. 67–68

 ## Answers

1. (was) easy to find, and . . . (was) a fairly simple process to melt the copper
2. (is) probably the first invented metal
3. (melted) copper and (threw) tin into it
4. gradually (added) other substances to copper and (created) even stronger metals

 ## Answers

1. statues
2. swords, <u>warriors</u>
3. trinkets, <u>families</u>
4. artifacts
5. objects, <u>visitors</u>
6. designs
7. bronze

694

Parts of a Sentence . . .

694.1
Understood Subjects and Predicates

Either the subject or the predicate (or both) may not be stated in a sentence, but both must be clearly understood.

[You] **Get involved!** (*You* is the understood subject.)

Who needs your help? Animals [do]. (*Do* is the understood predicate.)

What do many animals face? [They face] **Extinction.** (*They* is the understood subject, and *face* is the understood predicate.)

694.2
Delayed Subjects

In sentences that begin with *there* followed by a form of the "be" verb, the subject usually follows the verb. (See page **570**.)

There are laws that protect endangered species. (The subject is *laws; are* is the verb.)

The subject is also delayed in questions.

How can we preserve the natural habitat? (*We* is the subject.)

SCHOOL DAZE

John, I've got all the projects. Now which one is yours?

I'm not sure. See if there's one with a missing piece.

694.3
Modifiers

A modifier is a word (adjective, adverb) or a group of words (phrase, clause) that changes or adds to the meaning of another word. (See pages **486–493**.)

Many North American **zoos and aquariums** voluntarily **participate** in breeding programs that help prevent extinction.

The modifiers in this sentence include the following: *many, North American* (adjectives), *voluntarily* (adverb), *in breeding programs* (phrase), *that help prevent extinction* (clause).

 Grammar Practice

Parts of a Sentence 3

- Understood Subjects and Predicates
- Delayed Subjects

 Write the simple subject in the numbered sentences below. If the simple subject is understood, write "you."

Example: There are ticks that carry disease.
ticks

(1) Imagine a tick embedded in your arm. **(2)** How do you remove it? **(3)** First of all, do not try to pull it off by force. **(4)** A portion of its head could break off and remain inside the flesh. **(5)** There is a better way to remove it. **(6)** To begin, cover the tick with rubbing alcohol, heavy salad oil, or petroleum jelly, and wait for it to relax its grip. **(7)** Then carefully remove the tick with tweezers. **(8)** What is the final step? To wash the affected area thoroughly with soap and water.

Next Step: In the last sentence above, neither the subject nor the predicate is stated, but they are understood. Rewrite the sentence, stating both the subject and the predicate.

- Modifiers

 List the adjectives and adverbs in each of the sentences below.

Example: Fortunately, fleas are usually not dangerous.
fortunately, usually, not, dangerous

1. An intense itch is often the only result of a flea bite.
2. Fleas really like to hide in pet fur.
3. All fleas are wingless.
4. They do not fly, but they can jump incredibly far!

Related Skills Activities

- **Basic Grammar and Writing**
Describing with Adjectives, pp. 486–489
Describing with Adverbs, pp. 490–493

- *SkillsBook*
Adjectives, pp. 165–166
Adverbs 1 and 2, pp. 171–172

 Answers

1. you
2. you
3. you
4. portion
5. way
6. you
7. you
8. step

Next Step: **Answers**

It (or the final step) is to wash the affected area thoroughly with soap and water.

Answers

1. intense, often, only, flea
2. really, pet
3. all, wingless
4. not, incredibly, far

Test Prep!

For each underlined part in the sentences below, choose the letter or letters from the following list that best describes it.

Ⓐ simple subject   Ⓓ simple predicate
Ⓑ complete subject   Ⓔ complete predicate
Ⓒ compound subject   Ⓕ compound predicate

1 <u>Many diseased birds</u> have been tagged with identification bands.

2 We <u>decorated the gym for the dance and set the refreshment tables.</u>

3 After school, Owen <u>registered</u> for the Tuesday softball league.

4 <u>Lists and charts</u> are two helpful brainstorming tools.

5 In the late 1800s, many <u>pioneers</u> traveled on the Oregon Trail.

6 Ralph Waldo Emerson <u>was a famous American writer.</u>

7 <u>My oldest brother, Michael,</u> likes to rebuild old cars.

8 <u>One</u> of the kittens has a kink in her tail.

9 Rachelle noisily <u>sips and slurps</u> her soup.

10 We <u>are reading</u> a pretty good book in English class.

11 Wild <u>animals and birds</u> in my neighborhood stay away from my dog.

12 I <u>saw</u> Maria talking to Jennifer after algebra class.

13 <u>Benjamin Franklin and Alexander Hamilton</u> are two of America's founding fathers.

14 I <u>visited</u> the Smithsonian <u>and saw</u> the White House in Washington, D.C.

Select the letter that best indicates what the direct and indirect objects are in each sentence below.

15 In the future, people will invent methods of transportation that are faster and more economical.
  Ⓐ *direct object:* methods
  Ⓑ *direct object:* transportation; *indirect object:* methods
  Ⓒ *direct object:* transportation
  Ⓓ *direct object:* faster

16 Derrick aimed his arrow at the bull's-eye on the target.
  Ⓐ *direct object:* bull's-eye
  Ⓑ *direct object:* arrow; *indirect object:* bull's-eye
  Ⓒ *direct object:* arrow
  Ⓓ *direct object:* target

17 I showed my sister the essay that I wrote for social studies class.
  Ⓐ *direct object:* sister
  Ⓑ *direct object:* essay; *indirect object:* sister
  Ⓒ *direct object:* sister; *indirect object:* essay
  Ⓓ *direct object:* class

18 Jacob gave Indira his telephone number last week.
  Ⓐ *direct object:* Indira
  Ⓑ *direct object:* Indira; *indirect object:* number
  Ⓒ *direct object:* number; *indirect object:* Indira
  Ⓓ *direct object:* week

19 Mr. Juarez coaches the girls' volleyball team.
  Ⓐ *direct object:* girls'
  Ⓑ *direct object:* volleyball; *indirect object:* team
  Ⓒ *direct object:* volleyball
  Ⓓ *direct object:* team

20 With this equation, you can calculate the percentage of a number.
  Ⓐ *direct object:* percentage
  Ⓑ *direct object:* percentage; *indirect object:* number
  Ⓒ *direct object:* number
  Ⓓ *direct object:* equation

SENTENCES

Answers

1. B
2. E, F
3. D
4. B, C
5. A
6. E
7. B
8. A
9. F
10. D
11. C
12. D
13. B, C
14. F

Answers

15. A
16. C
17. B
18. C
19. D
20. A

Parts of a Sentence . . .

698.1
Clauses

A clause is a group of related words that has both a subject and a verb. (Also see pages 515–517.)

> **a whole chain of plants and animals is affected**
> (*Chain* is the subject, and *is affected* is the verb.)

> **when one species dies out completely**
> (*Species* is the subject; *dies out* is the verb.)

698.2
Independent Clauses

An independent clause presents a complete thought and can stand alone as a sentence.

> **This ancient oak tree may be cut down.**

> **This act could affect more than 200 different species of animals!**

> **Why would anyone want that to happen?**

698.3
Dependent Clauses

A dependent clause does not present a complete thought and cannot stand alone as a sentence. A dependent clause *depends* on being connected to an independent clause to make sense. Dependent clauses begin with either a subordinating conjunction (*after, although, because, before, if*) or a relative pronoun (*who, whose, which, that*). (See pages **710** and **744** for complete lists.)

> **If this ancient oak tree is cut down, it could affect more than 200 different species of animals!**

> **The tree, which experts think could be 400 years old, provides a home to many different kinds of birds and insects.**

SCHOOL DAZE

Boy, are you in for a real blockbuster next hour!

Yeah . . . Mr. Runge is showing a movie called *A Day in the Life of a Dependent Clause.*

 Grammar Practice

Parts of a Sentence 4

■ Clauses

 For the even-numbered sentences, write the dependent clause. (If there is no dependent clause, write "none.") Write the independent clause for the odd-numbered sentences.

Odd-numbered
example: Although digital cameras take excellent pictures, they still do not see as well as the human eye.
although digital cameras take excellent pictures

1. The eye sends nerve signals through the optic nerve to the brain, which interprets the signals as sight.

2. The cornea, pupil, lens, and retina are the key parts of the eye.

3. The cornea is a clear membrane that covers the front of the eye.

4. The retina, which focuses light, is located in the back of the eye and is filled with rods and cones.

5. Cones, which are not functional in every person, make it possible to see in color.

6. Because rods sense light in black, white, and gray, they allow people to see in low light.

7. A person can also see in low light because the pupil enlarges.

8. When the light is bright, the pupil contracts.

9. Muscles stretch or compress the lens in each eye so that a person can see near or far.

10. The lenses of a person who has cataracts are not clear.

11. If someone's eye shape isn't quite right, he or she will have trouble seeing clearly.

12. Although surgery can solve many vision problems, glasses or contact lenses are still the simplest remedy.

Next Step: Write two complex sentences about your eyes. Remember that a complex sentence has both an independent and a dependent clause.

Related Skills Activities

■ **Basic Grammar and Writing**
Combine with Relative Pronouns, p. 515
Create Compound Sentences, p. 516
Develop Complex Sentences, 517

■ **CD-ROM**
Sentence Combining   698.2, 698.3

■ *SkillsBook*
Phrases and Clauses 1 and 2, pp. 69–72

Answers

1. The eye sends nerve signals through the optic nerve to the brain

2. none

3. The cornea is a clear membrane

4. which focuses light

5. Cones . . . make it possible to see in color.

6. Because rods sense light in black, white, and gray,

7. A person can also see in low light

8. When the light is bright,

9. Muscles stretch or compress the lens in each eye

10. who has cataracts

11. he or she will have trouble seeing clearly

12. Although surgery can solve many vision problems,

700

Parts of a Sentence . . .

700.1
Phrases

A phrase is a group of related words that lacks either a subject or a predicate (or both). (See pages **519–520**.)

guards the house (The predicate lacks a subject.)

the ancient oak tree (The subject lacks a predicate.)

with crooked old limbs (The phrase lacks both a subject and a predicate.)

The ancient oak tree with crooked old limbs guards the house. (Together, the three phrases form a complete thought.)

700.2
Types of Phrases

Phrases usually take their names from the main words that introduce them (prepositional phrase, verb phrase, and so on). They are also named for the function they serve in a sentence (adverb phrase, adjective phrase).

The ancient oak tree (noun phrase)

with crooked old limbs (prepositional phrase)

has stood its guard, (verb phrase)

very stubbornly, (adverb phrase)

protecting the little house. (verbal phrase)

For more information on verbal phrases, see page **730**.

SCHOOL DAZE

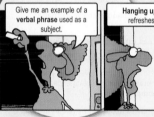

Give me an example of a **verbal phrase** used as a subject.

Hanging upside down refreshes my brain.

Grammar Practice

Parts of a Sentence 5

■ Types of Phrases

Make three columns labeled "noun phrases," "verb phrases," and "prepositional phrases." Write each of the following phrases in the correct column.

Example:

Noun Phrases	Verb Phrases	Prepositional Phrases
a big drooling dog	quickly turned its head	toward the front door

1. my best friend's bike
2. in Washington, D.C.
3. the brown gym bag
4. ate a big dinner
5. was the captain
6. many weary people
7. at the graduation dance
8. could not swim
9. his dog's sharp teeth
10. on the piano
11. over the fence
12. traveled a long way
13. dropped a contact lens
14. an aquarium shark
15. took a walk
16. under a grocery cart
17. the modern telephone
18. through some mulberry bushes

Next Step: Choose two of the phrases above and write a sentence for each.

Related Skills Activities

■ **Basic Grammar and Writing**
Combine with Phrases,
   pp. 513–514
What Can I Do to Add Details
   to My Sentences?, pp. 519–520

■ *SkillsBook*
Phrases and Clauses 1 and 2,
   pp. 69–72

Answers

Noun Phrase	Verb Phrase	Prepositional Phrase
my best friend's bike	ate a big dinner	in Washington, D.C.
the brown gym bag	was the captain	at the graduation dance
many weary people	could not swim	on the piano
his dog's sharp teeth	traveled a long way	over the fence
an aquarium shark	dropped a contact lens	under a grocery cart
the modern telephone	took a walk	through some mulberry bushes

Using the Parts of Speech

Nouns

A **noun** is a word that names a person, a place, a thing, or an idea.

Person: **John Ulferts** (uncle)	Thing: **"Yankee Doodle"** (song)
Place: **Mississippi** (state)	Idea: **Labor Day** (holiday)

Kinds of Nouns

702.1
Common Nouns

A common noun is any noun that does not name a specific person, place, thing, or idea. These nouns are not capitalized.

woman   museum   book   weekend

702.2
Proper Nouns

A proper noun is the name of a specific person, place, thing, or idea. Proper nouns are capitalized.

Hillary Clinton   Central Park   *Maniac McGee*   Sunday

702.3
Concrete Nouns

A concrete noun names a thing that is physical (can be touched or seen). Concrete nouns can be either proper or common.

space station   pencil   Statue of Liberty

702.4
Abstract Nouns

An abstract noun names something you can think about but cannot see or touch. Abstract nouns can be either common or proper.

Judaism   poverty   satisfaction   illness

702.5
Collective Nouns

A collective noun names a group or collection of persons, animals, places, or things.

Persons: **tribe, congregation, family, class, team**
Animals: **flock, herd, gaggle, clutch, litter**
Things: **batch, cluster, bunch**

702.6
Compound Nouns

A compound noun is made up of two or more words.

football (written as one word)
high school (written as two words)
brother-in-law (written as a hyphenated word)

Related Skills Activities

■ **Basic Grammar and Writing**
Using Nouns, pp. 470–471

■ ***SkillsBook***
Concrete, Abstract, and Collective Nouns, pp. 133–134

---

punctuate *edit* capitalize **SPELL**
improve
Using the Parts of Speech   **703**

Grammar Practice

Nouns 1

■ **Concrete and Abstract Nouns**

 For each of the following sentences, write whether the underlined noun is "concrete" or "abstract."

Example: Pilots enjoy the <u>challenge</u> of flying a sailplane.
abstract

1. It's as close to soaring like a <u>bird</u> as a person is likely to get.
2. Fliers talk about the sense of <u>peace</u> they have when gliding.
3. To keep the <u>flight</u> going, a pilot might have to put the sailplane into a dive.
4. The dive gives the craft <u>speed</u>, which means more air time.
5. After the flight, the <u>pilot</u> returns the glider to its storage trailer so that it is ready for another day.

■ **Compound and Collective Nouns**

 For each sentence below, write any compound or collective nouns you find. Circle the collective nouns.

Example: West of the Great Plains, groups of glider pilots take advantage of winds blowing against or over mountains.
Great Plains,(groups)

1. A glider's light weight and long wings, along with a small cluster of instruments, allow a pilot to take advantage of updrafts in the air.
2. With the right conditions, gliders (or sailplanes) can travel over great distances by moving along a mountain range.
3. A pilot will travel southeast along with a flock of geese over several miles.
4. Pilots can join gliding clubs that support this unique sport.
5. I think this "unique sport" would give me a stomachache.

 Answers

1. concrete
2. abstract
3. abstract
4. abstract
5. concrete

 Answers

1. (cluster,) updrafts
2. sailplanes, (range)
3. southeast, (flock)
4. (clubs)
5. stomachache

Nouns . . .

Number of Nouns

The number of a noun is either singular or plural.

704.1
Singular Nouns

A singular noun names one person, place, thing, or idea.

boy   group   audience   stage   concert   hope

704.2
Plural Nouns

A plural noun names more than one person, place, thing, or idea.

boys   groups   audiences   stages   concerts   hopes

Gender of Nouns

704.3
Noun Gender

Nouns are grouped according to gender: *feminine, masculine, neuter,* and *indefinite.*

Feminine (female): **mother, sister, women, cow, hen**

Masculine (male): **father, brother, men, bull, rooster**

Neuter (neither male nor female): **tree, cobweb, closet**

Indefinite (male or female): **president, duckling, doctor**

Uses of Nouns

704.4
Subject Nouns

A noun that is the subject of a sentence does something or is talked about in the sentence.

The roots of rap can be traced back to West Africa and Jamaica.

704.5
Predicate Nouns

A predicate noun follows a form of the *be* verb (*am, is, are, was, were, being, been*) and renames the subject.

In the 1970s, rap was a street art.

704.6
Possessive Nouns

A possessive noun shows possession or ownership.

Early rap had a drummer's beat but no music.

The rapper's words are set to music.

704.7
Object Nouns

A noun is an object noun when it is used as the direct object, the indirect object, or the object of the preposition.

Some rappers tell people their story about life in the city.
(indirect object: *people;* direct object: *story*)

Rap is now a common music choice in this country. (object of the preposition: *country*)

---

punctuate edit capitalize
improve SPELL **705**
Using the Parts of Speech

Grammar Practice

Nouns 2

■ Uses of Nouns

Write whether the underlined noun in each of the following sentences is a "subject," "predicate," "possessive," or "object" noun.

Example: Last year, <u>Danika's</u> dad found a good used all-terrain wheelchair for her.
possessive

1. It's a big <u>improvement</u> over her old one.

2. This <u>wheelchair's</u> frame and tires are very sturdy.

3. Danika recently competed in a wheelchair <u>race</u>.

4. A local business <u>owner</u> arranged the loan of a racing wheelchair for Danika.

5. The business owner is also a wheelchair <u>user</u>.

6. Racing <u>wheelchairs</u> are not the same as ordinary wheelchairs.

7. Regular wheelchairs have two large and two small <u>wheels</u>.

8. The made-for-racing chair features two large angled wheels but only one small wheel in the <u>front</u>.

9. The large side wheels tilt so the <u>rider</u> can more easily push the wheels.

10. The <u>city's</u> parks department has approved plans to make all the parks accessible to wheelchairs.

11. The parks' redesign is a definite <u>move</u> in the right direction.

Next Step: Write two sentences about someone in a wheelchair. Use a predicate noun and an object noun somewhere in your sentences. Underline and label each one appropriately.

Related Skills Activities

■ **Basic Grammar and Writing**
Show Possession, p. 472
Make the Meaning of the Verb Complete, p. 473

■ **CD-ROM**
Nouns 1—Uses   704.4, 704.5, 704.6, 704.7

■ *SkillsBook*
Uses of Nouns, pp. 135–136

Answers

1. predicate
2. possessive
3. object
4. subject
5. predicate
6. subject
7. object
8. object
9. subject
10. possessive
11. predicate

706

Pronouns

A **pronoun** is a word used in place of a noun. Some examples are *I, you, he, she, it, we, they, his, hers, her, its, me, myself, us, yours,* and so on.

Without pronouns:	Kevin said Kevin would be going to Kevin's grandmother's house this weekend.
With pronouns:	Kevin said he would be going to his grandmother's house this weekend.

706.1
Antecedents

An antecedent is the noun that the pronoun refers to or replaces. All pronouns (except interrogative and indefinite pronouns) have antecedents. (See page **474**.)

Jamal and Rick tried out for the team, and they both made it. (*They* refers to *Jamal* and *Rick; it* refers to *team.*)

NOTE Pronouns must agree with their antecedents in number, person, and gender.

Types of Pronouns

There are several types of pronouns. The most common type is the personal pronoun. (See the chart on page **710**.)

706.2
Personal Pronouns

A personal pronoun takes the place of a specific person (or thing) in a sentence. Some common personal pronouns are *I, you, he, she, it, we,* and *they.*

Suriana would not like to live in Buffalo, New York, because she does not like snow.

706.3
Relative Pronouns

A relative pronoun is both a pronoun and a connecting word. It connects a dependent clause to an independent clause in a complex sentence. Relative pronouns include *who, whose, which,* and *that.* (See **684.6**.)

Buffalo, which often gets more than eight feet of snow in a year, is on the northeast shore of Lake Erie.

The United States city that gets the most snow is Valdez, Alaska.

706.4
Interrogative Pronouns

An interrogative pronoun helps ask a question.

Who wants to go to Alaska?

Which of the cities would you visit?

Whom would you like to travel with?

What did you say?

Grammar Practice

Pronouns 1

■ Antecedents
■ Personal Pronouns
■ Relative Pronouns

 For each blank in the sentences below, write the missing pronoun. (The type of pronoun is in parentheses.) Also write its antecedent.

Example: Field trips are enjoyable because ___(personal)___ allow students to learn outside of the classroom.
they (trips)

1. The student ___(relative)___ suggests the best field trip may propose ___(personal)___ to the principal.
2. The Adler Planetarium, ___(relative)___ is in Chicago, is a favorite field trip destination.
3. Mrs. Bogart said ___(personal)___ would like to go to a film festival in Boston.
4. Ben said that ___(personal)___ thought the class should visit a veterinary hospital.
5. Mr. Andrews suggested, " ___(personal)___ would like to take the class to Washington, D.C., for several days."
6. The state capitol, ___(relative)___ is a popular place to visit, is where we plan to go next Tuesday.
7. The students ___(relative)___ names are on Mr. Daly's list should attend the field trip meeting.
8. The field trip ___(relative)___ Susan liked best was sailing on a tall ship.
9. Mrs. Bogart and Mr. Andrews announced, " ___(personal)___ will discuss all your suggestions."

Next Step: Write two sentences about a field trip you have taken. Use pronouns in each sentence and underline them. Exchange papers with a classmate and circle the antecedents in each other's sentences.

Related Skills Activities

■ **Basic Grammar and Writing**
Using Pronouns, p.474
How Can I Use Pronouns?, pp. 476–478
Combine with Relative Pronouns, p. 515

■ **CD-ROM**
Pronouns 1—Types   706.2, 706.3, 706.4

■ *SkillsBook*
Pronouns, pp. 139–140
Pronouns and Antecedents 1and 2,
   pp. 141–144

 ## Answers

1. who (student), it (trip)
2. which (Adler Planetarium)
3. she (Mrs. Bogart)
4. he (Ben)
5. I (Mr. Andrews)
6. which (capital)
7. whose (students)
8. that (trip)
9. We (Mrs. Bogart and Mr. Andrews)

Pronouns . . .
Types of Pronouns

708.1
Demonstrative Pronouns

A demonstrative pronoun points out or identifies a noun without naming the noun. When used together in a sentence, *this* and *that* distinguish one item from another, and *these* and *those* distinguish one group from another. (See page **710**.)

> This **is a great idea;** that **was a nightmare.**

> These **are my favorite foods, and** those **are definitely not.**

NOTE When these words are used before a noun, they are *not* pronouns; rather, they are demonstrative adjectives.

> **Coming to** this **picnic was fun—and** those **ants think so, too.**

708.2
Intensive Pronouns

An intensive pronoun emphasizes, or *intensifies,* the noun or pronoun it refers to. Common intensive pronouns include *itself, myself, himself, herself,* and *yourself.*

> **Though the chameleon's quick-change act protects it from predators, the lizard** itself **can catch insects 10 inches away with its long, sticky tongue.**

> **When a chameleon changes its skin color—seemingly matching the background—the background colors** themselves **do not affect the chameleon's color changes.**

NOTE These sentences would be complete without the intensive pronoun. The pronoun simply emphasizes a particular noun.

708.3
Reflexive Pronouns

A reflexive pronoun refers back to the subject of a sentence, and it is always an object (never a subject) in a sentence. Reflexive pronouns are the same as the intensive pronouns—*itself, myself, himself, herself, yourself,* and so on.

> **A chameleon protects** itself **from danger by changing colors.** (direct object)

> **A chameleon can give** itself **tasty meals of unsuspecting insects.** (indirect object)

> **I wish I could claim some of its amazing powers for** myself. (object of the preposition)

NOTE Unlike sentences with intensive pronouns, these sentences would *not* be complete without the reflexive pronouns.

Grammar Practice

Pronouns 2
■ **Demonstrative Pronouns**

For the sentences below that have a demonstrative pronoun, write "DP." Rewrite the other sentences so that they also have demonstrative pronouns.

Example: This CD is awesome.
This is an awesome CD.

1. That was the best concert I've been to.
2. Those tickets were very expensive.
3. That drummer is the one you told me about!
4. These are my favorite cuts from the album.
5. Do you know anything about this?

■ **Intensive Pronouns**
■ **Reflexive Pronouns**

Write whether the pronouns that end in "self" or "selves" in the following sentences are intensive or reflexive.

Example: On July 4, 1845, Henry David Thoreau went by himself to live in the woods and write.
reflexive

1. Thoreau became an admired author, but he himself earned little from his writing.
2. When he went to Walden Pond, he hoped to better himself by living off the earth with just the bare essentials.
3. He himself planned and built a small cottage where he wrote in his journal and drafted his first book.
4. The cottage itself is no longer there, but the area is now a public park.
5. Someday, you may want to go somewhere by yourself to experience living quietly with just the bare essentials.

Related Skills Activities

■ **Basic Grammar and Writing**
Use Intensive and Reflexive Pronouns, p. 479

■ **CD-ROM**
Pronouns 1—Types   708.1, 708.2, 708.3

■ *SkillsBook*
Intensive and Reflexive Pronouns, pp. 145–146

Answers

1. DP
2. Those were very expensive tickets.
3. That is the drummer you told me about!
4. DP
5. DP

Answers

1. intensive
2. reflexive
3. intensive
4. intensive
5. reflexive

710

Pronouns . . .
Types of Pronouns

710.1
Indefinite
Pronouns

An indefinite pronoun is a pronoun that does not have a specific antecedent (the noun or pronoun it replaces). (See page **475**.)

Everything about the chameleon is fascinating.

Someone donated a chameleon to our class.

Anyone who brings in a live insect can feed our chameleon.

Types of Pronouns

Personal Pronouns

I, me, mine, my, we, us, our, ours, you, your, yours, they, them, their, theirs, he, him, his, she, her, hers, it, its

Relative Pronouns

who, whose, whom, which, what, that, whoever, whomever, whichever, whatever

Interrogative Pronouns

who, whose, whom, which, what

Demonstrative Pronouns

this, that, these, those

Intensive and Reflexive Pronouns

myself, himself, herself, itself, yourself, yourselves, themselves, ourselves

Indefinite Pronouns

all	both	everything	nobody	several
another	each	few	none	some
any	each one	many	no one	somebody
anybody	either	most	nothing	someone
anyone	everybody	much	one	something
anything	everyone	neither	other	such

---

punctuate edit capitalize
improve **SPELL**
Using the Parts of Speech **711**

Grammar Practice

Pronouns 3

■ Indefinite Pronouns

Write the indefinite pronoun in each of the following sentences.

Example: Many recognize Sondre Norheim as the father of modern skiing.
Many

1. Norheim created a new kind of ski for himself and others.
2. Each had a heel binding and curved sides.
3. Sondre had a remarkable style of skiing that everyone admired.
4. No one can deny that he promoted the joy of skiing.
5. Most credit Norheim with making skiing a popular sport.

Pronoun Review

Identify the underlined pronouns in the sentences below as "personal," "relative," or "indefinite."

1. Ralph Samuelson, <u>who</u> was from Minnesota, invented water-skiing in 1922.
2. <u>Most</u> didn't believe the eighteen-year-old when he talked about skiing on water.
3. Ralph and his brother Ben set out to prove that <u>they</u> could do it.
4. They tried skis made from pieces of a barrel, <u>which</u> did not work well.
5. <u>Neither</u> thought twice about using a window-sash cord as a ski rope.
6. Ralph made <u>his</u> own skis from leather strips and lumber that he purchased.
7. <u>Everything</u> worked fine!
8. In 1925, during an exhibition <u>that</u> was held on Lake Pepin, Ralph made his first successful water-ski jump.

Related Skills Activities

■ **Basic Grammar and Writing**
Indefinite Pronouns, p. 475

■ ***SkillsBook***
Indefinite Pronouns, pp. 147–148

 ## Answers

1. others
2. Each
3. everyone
4. No one
5. Most

Answers

1. relative
2. indefinite
3. personal
4. relative
5. indefinite
6. personal
7. indefinite
8. relative

Pronouns . . .

Number of a Pronoun

712.1
Singular and Plural Pronouns

Pronouns can be either singular or plural in number.

Singular: I, you, he, she, it   Plural: we, you, they

NOTE The pronouns *you*, *your*, and *yours* may be singular or plural.

Person of a Pronoun

The person of a pronoun tells whether the pronoun is speaking, being spoken to, or being spoken about. (See page **474**.)

712.2
First Person Pronouns

A first-person pronoun is used in place of the name of the speaker or speakers.

I am speaking.   We are speaking.

712.3
Second Person Pronouns

A second-person pronoun is used to name the person or thing spoken to.

Eliza, will you please take out the garbage?

You better stop grumbling!

712.4
Third Person Pronouns

A third-person pronoun is used to name the person or thing spoken about.

Bill should listen if he wants to learn the words to this song.

Charisse said that she already knows them.

They will perform the song in the talent show.

Uses of Pronouns

A pronoun can be used as a subject, as an object, or to show possession. (See the chart on page **714**.)

712.5
Subject Pronouns

A subject pronoun is used as the subject of a sentence (*I, you, he, she, it, we, they*).

I like to surf the Net.

A subject pronoun is also used after a form of the *be* verb (*am, is, are, was, were, being, been*) if it repeats the subject. (See "Predicate Nouns," **704.5**.)

"This is she," Mom replied into the telephone.

"Yes, it was I," admitted the child who had eaten the cookies.

---

punctuate *edit* capitalize
SPELL
improve   **713**
Using the Parts of Speech

Grammar Practice

Pronouns 4

- Number of a Pronoun
- Person of a Pronoun

 Write the personal pronouns in each of the following sentences and identify each as "singular" or "plural." Also tell whether it is "first," "second," or "third" person.

Example: We studied the Industrial Revolution in our history class.

We—plural, first person   our—plural, first person

1. My history teacher asked me, "Would you do a report on the Industrial Revolution and child-labor issues?

2. It was a time when machines replaced skilled labor.

3. Many people lost their jobs during that period in history.

4. Samuel Slater and his textile mill began the Industrial Revolution.

5. Inventors Watt, Kay, and Hargreaves are known for their contributions to the textile industry.

6. My American ancestors were probably affected by the Industrial Revolution.

7. In 1886, workers formed a labor union that they called the American Federation of Labor.

8. Samuel Gompers was its first president.

9. Early unions protected workers' rights and made sure that they were paid a fair wage.

10. Of course, the teacher gave us a test on this era.

11. My friend Chris said, "I know I passed!"

Next Step: Write a short paragraph about a subject you're studying in school. Make sure your pronouns agree with their antecedents in person and number.

Related Skills Activities

■ **Basic Grammar and Writing**
How Can I Use Pronouns Correctly?, pp. 476–477

■ **CD-ROM**
Pronouns 2—Number and Person
712.1, 712.2, 712.3, 712.4
Pronouns 3—Uses
712.5

■ **SkillsBook**
Number and Person of Pronouns, pp. 149–150
Uses of Pronouns, pp. 151–152

 Answers

1. My—singular, first person
   me—singular, first person
   you—singular, second person
2. It—singular, third person
3. their—plural, third person
4. his—singular, third person
5. their—plural, third person
6. My—singular, first person
7. they—plural, third person
8. its—singular, third person
9. they—plural, third person
10. us—plural, first person
11. My—singular, first person
    I—singular, first person

Pronouns . . .
Uses of Pronouns

714.1
Object Pronouns

An object pronoun (*me, you, him, her, it, us, them*) can be used as the object of a verb or preposition. (See **692.4, 692.5,** and **742.1.**)

> I'll call her as soon as I can. (direct object)
>
> Hand me the phone book, please. (indirect object)
>
> She thinks these flowers are from you. (object of the preposition)

714.2
Possessive Pronouns

A possessive pronoun shows possession or ownership. These possessive pronouns function as adjectives before nouns: *my, our, his, her, their, its,* and *your.*

> School workers are painting our classroom this summer. Its walls will look much better.

These possessive pronouns can be used after verbs: *mine, ours, hers, his, theirs,* and *yours.*

> I'm pretty sure this backpack is mine and that one is his.

NOTE An apostrophe is not needed with a possessive pronoun to show possession.

Uses of Personal Pronouns

	Singular Pronouns			Plural Pronouns		
	Subject Pronouns	Possessive Pronouns	Object Pronouns	Subject Pronouns	Possessive Pronouns	Object Pronouns
First Person	I	my, mine	me	we	our, ours	us
Second Person	you	your, yours	you	you	your, yours	you
Third Person	he	his	him	they	their, theirs	them
	she	her, hers	her			
	it	its	it			

Grammar Practice

Pronouns 5

■ Uses of Pronouns

For each sentence below, identify each personal pronoun as a "subject pronoun" (712.5), an "object pronoun," or a "possessive pronoun."

Example: She thinks that the invitation to the dance is from you.
She—subject pronoun, you—object pronoun

1. They asked me not to bring my brother to basketball practice.
2. When we think of our fourth-grade teacher, Mr. Wong, we remember his funny skits in the variety show.
3. Angela admits that algebra is not easy for her; it is difficult for me, too.
4. Before the game, she was afraid that her team might lose.
5. Max said, "Sunan and Elena went to the band concert without us, even after we asked them to wait."
6. The dirt bike hit some debris that caused it to crash.
7. It suffered quite a bit of damage.
8. Her sister sings in a band that plays at their school's dances.
9. Hank was late for practice today; he has been late for everything lately.
10. The coach is going to have a talk with him.
11. I thought the ball was mine, but then Jack jumped up and caught it.
12. You should check with the teacher before posting your ad on the bulletin board.

Next Step: Write a sentence with a subject pronoun and an object or a possessive pronoun. Trade sentences with a classmate. Underline the subject pronoun and circle the object or possessive pronoun.

Related Skills Activities

■ **CD-ROM**
Pronouns 2—Number and Person   714.1, 714.2
Pronouns 3—Uses   714.1, 714.2

■ *SkillsBook*
Uses of Pronouns, pp. 151–152

Answers

1. They—subject pronoun, me—object pronoun, my—possessive pronoun
2. we—subject pronoun, our—possessive pronoun, we—subject pronoun, his—possessive pronoun
3. her—object pronoun, it—subject pronoun, me—object pronoun
4. she—subject pronoun, her—possessive pronoun
5. us—object pronoun, we—subject pronoun, them—object pronoun
6. it—object pronoun
7. It—subject pronoun
8. Her—possessive pronoun, their—possessive pronoun
9. he—subject pronoun
10. him—object pronoun
11. I—subject pronoun, mine—possessive pronoun, it—object pronoun
12. You—subject pronoun, your—possessive pronoun

Test Prep!

For each underlined word in the sentences below, write the letter from the following list that best describes it.

- Ⓐ subject noun
- Ⓑ predicate noun
- Ⓒ object noun
- Ⓓ subject pronoun
- Ⓔ object pronoun
- Ⓕ possessive noun/pronoun

Early in the twentieth century, <u>Lloyd Loar</u> invented an electric
<u>(1)</u>
<u>guitar</u>. The new invention, however, was not very popular in <u>its</u>
<u>(2)</u>   <u>(3)</u>
early years. Many musicians didn't like the distorted <u>sound</u> that the
<u>(4)</u>
guitars made.

In the 1940s, Les Paul was a well-known <u>musician</u> and guitarist.
<u>(5)</u>
<u>He</u> made some changes to the <u>instrument's</u> design. Paul created an
<u>(6)</u>   <u>(7)</u>
electric guitar with a solid body rather than a hollow <u>one</u>. The new
<u>(8)</u>
<u>design</u> helped reduce feedback and made a better <u>sound</u>. About the
<u>(9)</u>   <u>(10)</u>
same <u>time</u>, Leo Fender was developing electric guitars as a hobby. <u>His</u>
<u>(11)</u>   <u>(12)</u>
legendary Stratocaster was introduced in 1954. Together, these men are

the "<u>fathers</u>" of the electric guitar.
<u>(13)</u>

Jazz and country music increased the electric <u>guitar's</u> popularity
<u>(14)</u>
in the 1950s. By the 1960s, rock musicians had discovered <u>it</u>, and the
<u>(15)</u>
instrument had gone mainstream. Despite an uncertain start, <u>it</u> now
<u>(16)</u>
has many <u>fans</u>. In fact, <u>retailers</u> in the United States now sell more
<u>(17)</u>   <u>(18)</u>
electric guitars than acoustic ones.

---

punctuate *edit* *capitalize*
improve **SPELL** **717**
Using the Parts of Speech

For each underlined pronoun in the sentences below, write the letter that best describes its type.

19 Darius wanted Nita and Tyree to go to the game with <u>him</u>.
Ⓐ personal   Ⓑ reflexive   Ⓒ indefinite   Ⓓ relative

20 It is the first game of the season and the only <u>one</u> at North Park.
Ⓐ reflexive   Ⓑ personal   Ⓒ indefinite   Ⓓ relative

21 <u>That</u> is my seat there in the third row.
Ⓐ relative   Ⓑ demonstrative   Ⓒ personal   Ⓓ indefinite

22 <u>Who</u> left this sandwich in the refrigerator?
Ⓐ personal   Ⓑ interrogative   Ⓒ relative   Ⓓ intensive

23 Clay said that he already gave the concert tickets to <u>you</u>.
Ⓐ interrogative   Ⓑ personal   Ⓒ indefinite   Ⓓ relative

24 Fortunately, the man <u>whose</u> sleeve caught fire didn't get burned.
Ⓐ relative   Ⓑ demonstrative   Ⓒ personal   Ⓓ reflexive

25 Does <u>anyone</u> know how this happened?
Ⓐ demonstrative   Ⓑ indefinite   Ⓒ intensive   Ⓓ personal

26 Jenica <u>herself</u> doesn't understand what happened.
Ⓐ demonstrative   Ⓑ reflexive   Ⓒ intensive   Ⓓ personal

27 They asked <u>me</u> to volunteer at my little brother's day-care center.
Ⓐ relative   Ⓑ demonstrative   Ⓒ personal   Ⓓ interrogative

28 "Make sure you share <u>those</u> with your friends," Dad said.
Ⓐ demonstrative   Ⓑ reflexive   Ⓒ intensive   Ⓓ personal

29 Graciela began drinking the milk <u>that</u> had turned sour.
Ⓐ personal   Ⓑ interrogative   Ⓒ relative   Ⓓ demonstrative

30 I think I'll get <u>myself</u> a new pair of jeans.
Ⓐ personal   Ⓑ reflexive   Ⓒ intensive   Ⓓ relative

Answers

1. A
2. C
3. F
4. C
5. B
6. D
7. F
8. E
9. A
10. C
11. C
12. F
13. B
14. F
15. E
16. D
17. C
18. A

Answers

19. A
20. C
21. B
22. B
23. B
24. A
25. B
26. C
27. C
28. A
29. C
30. B

Related Skills Activities

■ *SkillsBook*
Nouns Review, pp. 17–138

718

Verbs

A **verb** is a word that shows action or links a subject to another word in a sentence.

Tornadoes cause tremendous damage. (action verb)

The weather is often calm before a storm. (linking verb)

Types of Verbs

718.1
Action Verbs

An action verb tells what the subject is doing. (See page **480**.)

Natural disasters hit the globe nearly every day.

718.2
Linking Verbs

A linking verb connects—or links—a subject to a noun or an adjective in the predicate. The most common linking verbs are forms of the verb *be (is, are, was, were, being, been, am).* Verbs such as *smell, look, taste, feel, remain, turn, appear, become, sound, seem, grow,* and *stay* can also be linking verbs. (See page **480**.)

The San Andreas Fault is an earthquake zone in California. (The linking verb *is* connects the subject to the predicate noun *zone*.)

Earthquakes there are fairly common. (The linking verb *are* connects the subject to the predicate adjective *common*.)

718.3
Helping Verbs

A helping verb (also called an auxiliary verb) helps the main verb express tense and voice. The most common helping verbs are *shall, will, should, would, could, must, might, can, may, have, had, has, do, did,* and the forms of the verb *be— is, are, was, were, am, being, been.* (See page **481**.)

It has been estimated that 500,000 earthquakes occur around the world every year. (These helping verbs indicate that the tense is present perfect and the voice is passive.)

Fortunately, only about 100 of those will cause damage. (*Will* helps express the future tense of the verb.)

---

punctuate *edit* capitalize SPELL
improve
Using the Parts of Speech **719**

Grammar Practice

Verbs 1

■ Action, Linking, and Helping Verbs

For each numbered sentence in the following paragraphs, write the verb or verbs. (Remember that clauses also have verbs.) Identify each as an "action verb," a "linking verb," or a "helping verb."

Example: Pizza, which is one of the most popular foods in the world today, was also eaten by ancient people.
is–linking verb, was–helping verb, eaten–action verb

(1) Pizza is one type of food with a long history. **(2)** Its origins reach back to ancient Middle Eastern times. **(3)** People of that era ate flat bread that had been cooked in mud ovens. **(4)** Soon the Mediterraneans were eating the same flat bread with olive oil and native spices on it.

(5) Much later, in 1889, Queen Margherita was touring her Italian kingdom. **(6)** She noticed peasants who were enjoying the flat bread with spices on top. **(7)** An Italian baker, Raffaele Esposito, created a special pizza for the queen. **(8)** He topped it with tomatoes, mozzarella cheese, and fresh basil. **(9)** The pizza became the queen's favorite treat. **(10)** Today, it is known as pizza Margherita.

(11) Pizza was not a standard American food until after World War II. **(12)** American soldiers tried it for the first time while they were staying in areas of Italy. **(13)** It tasted wonderful! **(14)** When the soldiers returned home, they were hungry for this Italian treat. **(15)** Before long, everyone in America knew about pizza.

Next Step: Write a paragraph about one of your favorite foods. Use action, linking, and helping verbs. Exchange papers with a classmate. List and identify all of the verbs.

Related Skills Activities

■ **Basic Grammar and Writing**
Choosing Verbs, pp. 480–481

 ## Answers

1. is—linking verb
2. reach—action verb
3. ate—action verb, had—helping verb, been—helping verb, cooked—action verb
4. were—helping verb, eating—action verb
5. was—helping verb, touring—action verb
6. noticed—action verb, were—helping verb, enjoying—action verb
7. created—action verb
8. topped—action verb
9. became—linking verb
10. is—helping verb, known—action verb
11. was—linking verb
12. tried—action verb, were—helping verb, staying—action verb
13. tasted—linking verb
14. returned—action verb, were—linking verb
15. knew—action verb

punctuate *edit* capitalize
improve   SPELL   **721**
Using the Parts of Speech

Verbs . . .

Tenses of Verbs

A verb has three principal parts: *present, past,* and *past participle.* (The part used with the helping verbs *has, have,* or *had* is called the past participle.)

All six of the tenses are formed from these principal parts. The past and past participle of regular verbs are formed by adding *ed* to the present tense. The past and past participle of irregular verbs are formed with different spellings. (See the chart on page **722**.)

720.1
Present Tense Verbs

The present tense of a verb expresses action (or a state of being) that is happening now or that happens continually or regularly. (See page **482**.)

The universe **is** gigantic. It **takes** my breath away.

720.2
Past Tense Verbs

The past tense of a verb expresses action (or a state of being) that was completed in the past. (See page **482**.)

To most people many years ago, the universe **was** the earth, the sun, and some stars. The universe **reached** only as far as the eye could see.

720.3
Future Tense Verbs

The future tense of a verb expresses action that *will* take place. (See page **482**.)

Maybe I **will visit** another galaxy in my lifetime.

Somebody **will find** a way to do it.

SCHOOL DAZE

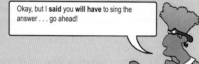

I **know** the answer!

Okay, but I **said** you **will have** to sing the answer . . . go ahead!

Grammar Practice

Verbs 2

■ Present Tense, Past Tense, and Future Tense Verbs

For each of the sentences below, identify the underlined verbs as "present tense," "past tense," or "future tense."

Example: The United States Naval Academy <u>founded</u> its drum and bugle corps in 1914.
past tense

1. Today it <u>boasts</u> being the oldest drum and bugle corps in America.

2. The corps, consisting of 16 men, first <u>performed</u> at a baseball game.

3. It <u>was</u> active for eight years until it <u>disbanded</u> in 1922.

4. The academy's superintendent, Henry B. Wilson, <u>said</u>, "It <u>is</u> a luxury, not a necessity."

5. Some of the students <u>thought</u>, "The corps <u>will return</u> someday."

6. In 1926, the corps <u>came</u> back bigger and better.

7. Seeing them take the field again in full dress uniforms <u>was</u> an awesome sight.

8. Today the U.S. Naval Academy Drum and Bugle Corps <u>has</u> about 100 members.

9. The corps still <u>plays</u> "Anchors Away," just as it <u>did</u> almost a century ago.

10. You <u>will hear</u> its members shout, "Go, Navy!"

11. The corps <u>provides</u> enjoyable entertainment for people of all ages.

Next Step: Write a sentence in the present tense about some music you enjoy. Exchange papers with a classmate and write each other's sentence in the past and future tenses.

Related Skills Activities

■ **Basic Grammar and Writing**
How Can I Use Verbs Effectively?, p. 482

■ *SkillsBook*
Simple Verb Tenses, pp. 153–154

Answers

1. present tense
2. past tense
3. past tense, past tense
4. past tense, present tense
5. past tense, future tense
6. past tense
7. past tense
8. present tense
9. present tense, past tense
10. future tense
11. present tense

722

Common Irregular Verbs and Their Principal Parts

The principal parts of the common irregular verbs are listed below. The part used with the helping verbs *has, have,* or *had* is called the **past participle**. (Also see page 481.)

Present Tense:	I write.	She hides.
Past Tense:	Earlier I wrote.	Earlier she hid.
Past Participle:	I have written.	She has hidden.

Present Tense	Past Tense	Past Participle	Present Tense	Past Tense	Past Participle
am, is, are	was, were	been	lead	led	led
begin	began	begun	lie (recline)	lay	lain
bid (offer)	bid	bid	lie (deceive)	lied	lied
bid (order)	bade	bidden	make	made	made
bite	bit	bitten	ride	rode	ridden
blow	blew	blown	ring	rang	rung
break	broke	broken	rise	rose	risen
bring	brought	brought	run	ran	run
burst	burst	burst	see	saw	seen
buy	bought	bought	set	set	set
catch	caught	caught	shake	shook	shaken
come	came	come	shine (polish)	shined	shined
dive	dived, dove	dived	shine (light)	shone	shone
do	did	done	shrink	shrank	shrunk
draw	drew	drawn	sing	sang, sung	sung
drink	drank	drunk	sink	sank, sunk	sunk
drive	drove	driven	sit	sat	sat
eat	ate	eaten	sleep	slept	slept
fall	fell	fallen	speak	spoke	spoken
fight	fought	fought	spring	sprang, sprung	sprung
flee	fled	fled	steal	stole	stolen
fly	flew	flown	strive	strove	striven
forsake	forsook	forsaken	swear	swore	sworn
freeze	froze	frozen	swim	swam	swum
get	got	gotten, got	swing	swung	swung
give	gave	given	take	took	taken
go	went	gone	tear	tore	torn
grow	grew	grown	throw	threw	thrown
hang (execute)	hanged	hanged	wake	woke, waked	woken, waked
hang (dangle)	hung	hung	wear	wore	worn
hide	hid	hidden, hid	weave	wove	woven
know	knew	known	wring	wrung	wrung
lay (place)	laid	laid	write	wrote	written

---

punctuate *edit* *capitalize*
improve SPELL
Using the Parts of Speech **723**

 Grammar Practice

Verbs 3

■ Irregular Verbs

 For the sentences below, fill in each blank with the correct past tense or past participle form of the verb or verbs in parentheses.

Example: Mr. Malone had _____ me permission to leave early.
(give)
given

1. Ron _____ at the ball and hit it. *(swing)*

2. It _____ in the air for a few seconds before a fielder _____ it. *(hang, catch)*

3. The alarm _____ me, but I _____ back down and _____ for another hour. *(wake, lie, sleep)*

4. When the tornado _____ through town and _____ out windows, we _____ for cover. *(tear, blow, run)*

5. I have never _____ as many e-mails as I _____ last weekend. *(write, do)*

6. My hands had almost _____ after I had _____ out in the cold temperatures for so long. *(freeze, am)*

7. Although I had _____ to the principal, we _____ detentions anyway. *(speak, get)*

8. If we had _____ that Vandana was in the track meet, we would have _____ to watch her race. *(know, come)*

9. The marching band _____ a huge crowd. *(draw)*

10. I just _____ that new action-adventure film at the cinema. *(see)*

11. I have _____ all of the movies in that series. *(see)*

12. At last night's party, I had _____ so much that the snap on my jeans _____. *(eat, break)*

13. My sister has _____ my sweater more often than I have! *(wear)*

Next Step: Write three sentences using the present tense, past tense, and past participle of the word *fly*.

Related Skills Activities

■ **CD-ROM**
Verbs 1—Irregular
722

■ *SkillsBook*
Irregular Verbs, pp. 157–158

Answers

1. swung
2. hung, caught
3. woke, lay, slept
4. tore, blew, ran
5. written, did
6. frozen, been
7. spoken, got
8. known, come
9. drew
10. saw
11. seen
12. eaten, broke
13. worn

724

Verbs . . .
Tenses of Verbs

724.1
Present Perfect Tense Verbs

The present perfect tense verb expresses action that began in the past but continues or is completed in the present. The present perfect tense is formed by adding *has* or *have* to the past participle. (Also see page **483**.)

I have wondered for some time how the stars got their names.

A visible star has emitted light for thousands of years.

724.2
Past Perfect Tense Verbs

The past perfect tense verb expresses action that began in the past and was completed in the past. This tense is formed by adding *had* to the past participle. (Also see page **483**.)

I had hoped to see a shooting star on our camping trip.

724.3
Future Perfect Tense Verbs

A future perfect tense verb expresses action that will begin in the future and will be completed by a specific time in the future. The future perfect tense is formed by adding *will have* to the past participle. (Also see page **483**.)

By the middle of this century, we probably will have discovered many more stars, planets, and galaxies.

724.4
Present Continuous Tense Verbs

A present continuous tense verb expresses action that is not completed at the time of stating it. The present continuous tense is formed by adding *am, is,* or *are* to the *ing* form of the main verb.

Scientists are learning a great deal from their study of the sky.

724.5
Past Continuous Tense Verbs

A past continuous tense verb expresses action that was happening at a certain time in the past. This tense is formed by adding *was* or *were* to the *ing* form of the main verb.

Astronomers were beginning their quest for knowledge hundreds of years ago.

724.6
Future Continuous Tense Verbs

A future continuous tense verb expresses action that will take place at a certain time in the future. This tense is formed by adding *will be* to the *ing* form of the main verb.

Someday astronauts will be going to Mars.

This tense can also be formed by adding a phrase noting the future (*are going to*) plus *be* to the *ing* form of the main verb.

They are going to be performing many experiments.

punctuate *edit* *capitalize*
improve   **SPELL**   **725**
Using the Parts of Speech

Grammar Practice

Verbs 4

■ Perfect Tense Verbs
■ Continuous Tense Verbs

 For each of the sentences below, write the correct form of the verb given in parentheses.

Example: Geologists _____ some strange rocks.
(discover, present perfect)
have discovered

1. During years of careful study, scientists _____ some of the ordinary-looking rocks to ultraviolet light.
(expose, past continuous)

2. The rocks _____ with brilliant colors! *(glow, past continuous)*

3. Oddly, the rocks _____ to glow, even without the light on them. *(continue, past perfect)*

4. Now researchers _____ different levels of ultraviolet light on the rocks. *(test, present continuous)*

5. Scientists _____ these minerals unusual names, such as willemite, selenite, fluorite, aragonite, and Texas calcite. *(give, present perfect)*

6. As interest in these glow-in-the-dark minerals grows, more people _____ for them. *(look, future continuous)*

7. Geologists hope that rock hunters _____ more of these interesting objects by 2025. *(find, future perfect)*

8. In the meantime, people _____ museum displays of the minerals. *(visit, present continuous)*

9. The displays _____ museum visitors for years to come. *(amaze, future continuous)*

Next Step: Write two sentences about an interesting mineral or metal. Use continuous tense verbs.

PARTS OF SPEECH

Related Skills Activities

■ **Basic Grammar and Writing**
Show Special Types of Action, p. 483

■ *SkillsBook*
Perfect Verb Tenses, pp. 155–156

 ## Answers

1. were exposing
2. were glowing
3. had continued
4. are testing
5. have given
6. will be looking or are going to be looking
7. will have found
8. are visiting
9. will be amazing or are going to be amazing

726

Verbs . . .
Forms of Verbs

726.1
Active or Passive Voice

The voice of a verb tells you whether the subject is doing the action or is receiving the action. A verb is in the active voice (in any tense) if the subject is doing the action in a sentence. (See page 118.)

I dream of going to galaxies light-years from Earth.

I will travel in an ultrafast spaceship.

A verb is in the passive voice if the subject is not doing the action. The action is done *by* someone or something else. The passive voice is always indicated with a helping verb plus a past participle or a past tense verb.

My daydreams often are shattered **by reality.** (The subject *daydreams* is not doing the action.)

Of course, reality can be seen **differently by different people.** (The subject *reality* is not doing the action.)

Tense	Active Voice		Passive Voice	
	Singular	**Plural**	**Singular**	**Plural**
Present Tense	I find	we find	I am found	we are found
	you find	you find	you are found	you are found
	he/she/it finds	they find	he/she/it is found	they are found
Past Tense	I found	we found	I was found	we were found
	you found	you found	you were found	you were found
	he found	they found	he/she/it was found	they were found
Future Tense	I will find	we will find	I will be found	we will be found
	you will find	you will find	you will be found	you will be found
	he will find	they will find	he/she/it will be found	they will be found
Present Perfect	I have found	we have found	I have been found	we have been found
	you have found	you have found	you have been found	you have been found
	he has found	they have found	he/she/it has been found	they have been found
Past Perfect	I had found	we had found	I had been found	we had been found
	you had found	you had found	you had been found	you had been found
	he had found	they had found	he/she/it had been found	they had been found
Future Perfect	I will have found	we will have found	I will have been found	we will have been found
	you will have found	you will have found	you will have been found	you will have been found
	he will have found	they will have found	he/she/it will have been found	they will have been found

---

punctuate *edit* capitalize **SPELL**
improve
Using the Parts of Speech   727

Grammar Practice

Verbs 5

■ Active or Passive Voice

 For each sentence below, write the verb and tell whether it is in the active or passive voice.

Example: Elvis Presley has been called the King of Rock and Roll.
has been called (passive)

1. He is recognized by many people as an American music legend.

2. He soared to popularity with teenagers in the late 1950s.

3. By the end of his career, Elvis had recorded 81 albums and 51 singles.

4. In addition to his recording career, Elvis starred in movies.

5. Most of his best-known songs can be heard in his movies.

6. Elvis Presley died in 1977 at the age of 42.

7. His talent will be remembered for a very long time.

 Rewrite each of the following sentences in the active voice. Add or delete words as necessary.

Example: Elvis Presley's movies have been enjoyed by several generations.
Several generations have enjoyed Elvis Presley's movies.

1. His films have been seen by millions of people.

2. In *Jailhouse Rock,* the part of Vince Everett was played by Elvis.

3. Elvis's films have been appreciated by audiences around the world.

4. Elvis was made famous by his singing and acting talents.

Next Step: Write a sentence in the passive voice about a famous performer. Exchange papers with a classmate and rewrite each other's sentence in the active voice.

PARTS OF SPEECH

 ## Answers

1. is recognized (passive)
2. soared (active)
3. had recorded (active)
4. starred (active)
5. can be heard (passive)
6. died (active)
7. will be remembered (passive)

Answers

1. Millions of people have seen his films.
2. In *Jailhouse Rock,* Elvis played the part of Vince Everett.
3. Audiences around the world have appreciated Elvis's films.
4. Elvis's singing and acting talents made him famous.

Verbs . . .
Forms of Verbs

728.1 Singular and Plural Verbs

A singular subject needs a singular verb. A plural subject needs a plural verb. For action verbs, only the third-person singular verb form is different: *I wonder, we wonder, you wonder, she wonders, they wonder.* Some linking verbs, however, have several different forms.

First Person **Singular:** I am (or was) a good student.
Plural: We are (or were) good students.

Second Person **Singular:** You are (or were) a cheerleader.
Plural: You are (or were) cheerleaders.

Third Person **Singular:** He is (or was) on the wrestling team.
Plural: They are (or were) also on the team.

728.2 Transitive Verbs

A transitive verb is a verb that transfers its action to a direct object. The object makes the meaning of the verb complete. A transitive verb is always an action verb (never a linking verb). (See pages **484** and **570**.)

An earthquake shook **San Francisco in 1906.** (*Shook* transfers its action to the direct object *San Francisco*. Without *San Francisco* the meaning of the verb *shook* is incomplete.)

The city's people spent **many years rebuilding.** (Without the direct object *years*, the verb's meaning is incomplete.)

A transitive verb transfers the action directly to a direct object and indirectly to an indirect object.

Fires destroyed **the city.** (direct object: *city*)

Our teacher gave **us the details.** (indirect object: *us*; direct object: *details*)

See **692.4** and **692.5** for more on direct and indirect objects.

728.3 Intransitive Verbs

An intransitive verb does not need an object to complete its meaning. (See pages **484** and **570**.)

Abigail was shopping. (The verb's meaning is complete.)

Her stomach felt **queasy.** (*Queasy* is a predicate adjective describing *stomach*; there is no direct object.)

She lay **down on the bench.** (Again, there is no direct object. *Down* is an adverb modifying *lay*.)

Grammar Practice

Verbs 6
■ Transitive and Intransitive Verbs

For each sentence below, write whether the underlined verb is "transitive" or "intransitive."

Example: My best friend's mother <u>writes</u> poetry and short stories.
transitive

1. The wolf <u>snarled</u> fearsomely.
2. The coach <u>gave</u> the player a penalty for poor sportsmanship.
3. The leaves on this bush <u>are</u> purple.
4. Near the end of the race, Taylor <u>ran</u> faster than ever before.
5. Jorge <u>has been transferred</u> to Jackson Park Middle School.
6. Casey <u>told</u> the truth when he said that he didn't do it.
7. I <u>read</u> a letter to the editor about rising energy costs.
8. Ted <u>worked</u> quietly.
9. The sound of the fire alarm <u>blasted</u> through the halls.
10. Eva <u>plays</u> the drums in a band that she and her friends put together.
11. Before eating his breakfast, Najee <u>took</u> a vitamin.
12. <u>Have</u> you ever <u>seen</u> a telephone with a dial?
13. The sky <u>seems</u> a little green this afternoon.
14. The maintenance staff <u>cleans</u> the pool once a week.
15. The housekeeping staff <u>cleans</u> regularly.

Next Step: Write two sentences with transitive verbs and two with intransitive verbs. Exchange papers with a classmate and identify each other's verbs correctly.

Related Skills Activities

■ **Basic Grammar and Writing**
Transfer Action to an Object, p. 484
Make Subjects and Verbs Agree, pp. 508–509

■ **CD-ROM**
Verbs 2—Transitive and Intransitive
Verbs 728.2, 728.3

■ *SkillsBook*
Transitive and Intransitive Verbs, pp. 159–160

Answers

1. intransitive
2. transitive
3. intransitive
4. intransitive
5. intransitive
6. transitive
7. transitive
8. intransitive
9. intransitive
10. transitive
11. transitive
12. transitive
13. intransitive
14. transitive
15. intransitive

Verbs . . .
Forms of Verbs

730.1
Transitive or Intransitive Verbs

Some verbs can be either transitive or intransitive.

Transitive: She reads my note.   Albert ate an apple.

Intransitive: She reads aloud.   Albert ate already.

Verbals

A **verbal** is a word that is made from a verb but acts as another part of speech. Gerunds, participles, and infinitives are verbals.

730.2
Gerunds

A gerund is a verb form that ends in *ing* and is used as a *noun*. A gerund often begins a gerund phrase.

Worrying is useless. (The gerund is the subject noun.)

You should stop worrying about so many things. (The gerund phrase is the direct object.)

730.3
Participles

A participle is a verb form ending in *ing* or *ed*. A participle is used as an *adjective* and often begins a participial phrase.

The idea of the earth shaking **and** splitting **both fascinates and frightens me.** (The participles modify *earth*.)

Rattling in the cabinets, **the dishes were about to crash to the floor.** (The participial phrase modifies *dishes*.)

Why doesn't this tired **earth just stand still?** (The participle modifies *earth*.)

730.4
Infinitives

An infinitive is a verb form introduced by *to*. It may be used as a *noun*, an *adjective*, or an *adverb*. It often begins an infinitive phrase.

My need to whisper **is due to this secret.** (The infinitive is an adjective modifying *need*.)

I am afraid to swim. (The infinitive is an adverb modifying the predicate adjective *afraid*.)

To overcome this fear is my goal. (The infinitive phrase is used as a noun and is the subject of this sentence.)

Grammar Practice

Verbs 7

■ Verbals

 For each sentence below, identify the underlined verb form as a "gerund," a "participle," or an "infinitive."

Example: In the late 1800s, Ohio artist Richard Felton Outcault began to create comics for newspapers.
infinitive

(1) Richard Outcault's comic strips became popular in America when the New York Journal decided to print his comic strip, the "Yellow Kid." **(2)** The "Yellow Kid" got his name because his distinguishing nightshirt was always printed in the color yellow. **(3)** Printing in color was new to newspapers in those days. **(4)** Soon there were more of Outcault's cartoons appearing in newspapers. **(5)** Comic strips read by people of all ages became an important part of the Sunday paper. **(6)** Reading them was fun! **(7)** Outcault went on to create several more popular strips, including one called "Buster Brown." **(8)** Then, after a while, he grew weary of creating comics, and the tired artist moved on to other things. **(9)** Advertising became his new profession. **(10)** Richard Outcault's ability to develop characters for the Sunday funnies earned him the title the Father of the Comic Strip.

 For each sentence below, write the infinitive phrase and label how it is used—as a "noun," an "adjective," or an "adverb."

Example: To enjoy the funnies is a Sunday ritual.
To enjoy the funnies (noun)

1. It's a good way to begin a Sunday morning!
2. I want to read the comics before anything else.
3. I'm happy to read them to my little sister.

Related Skills Activities

■ **Basic Grammar and Writing**
Transfer Action to an Object, p. 484
Form Verbals, p. 485
Connect with Infinitives and Participial Phrases, p. 514

■ **CD-ROM**
Verbs 3—Verbals   730.2, 730.3, 730.4

■ *SkillsBook*
Transitive and Intransitive Verbs, pp. 159–160
Identifying Verbals, pp. 161–162

 ## Answers

1. infinitive
2. participle
3. gerund
4. participle
5. participle
6. gerund
7. infinitive
8. participle
9. gerund
10. infinitive

 ## Answers

1. to begin a Sunday morning (adjective)
2. to read the comics (noun)
3. to read them (adverb)

Adjectives

An **adjective** is a word used to describe a noun or a pronoun. Adjectives tell *what kind, how many,* or *which one.* They usually come before the word they describe. (See pages 486–489.)

ancient **dinosaurs**   800 **species**   that **triceratops**

Adjectives are the same whether the word they describe is singular or plural.

small **brain**—or—small **brains**   large **tooth**—or—large **teeth**

732.1
Articles

The articles *a, an,* and *the* are adjectives.

A brontosaurus was an animal about 70 feet long.

The huge dinosaur lived on land and ate plants.

732.2
Proper Adjectives

A proper adjective is formed from a proper noun, and it is always capitalized. (See 618.1.)

A Chicago museum is home to the skeleton of one of these beasts. (*Chicago* functions as a proper adjective describing the noun *museum.*)

732.3
Common Adjectives

A common adjective is any adjective that is not proper. It is not capitalized (unless it is the first word in a sentence).

Ancient mammoths were huge, woolly creatures.

They lived in the ice fields of Siberia.

Special Kinds of Adjectives

732.4
Demonstrative Adjectives

A demonstrative adjective points out a particular noun. *This* and *these* point out something nearby; *that* and *those* point out something at a distance.

This mammoth is huge, but that mammoth is even bigger.

NOTE When a noun does not follow *this, these, that,* or *those,* these words are pronouns, not adjectives. (See 708.1.)

732.5
Compound Adjectives

A compound adjective is made up of two or more words. (Sometimes it is hyphenated.)

Dinosaurs were egg-laying animals.

The North American Allosaurus had sharp teeth and powerful jaws.

---

punctuate *edit* *capitalize*
improve   SPELL   733
Using the Parts of Speech

Grammar Practice

Adjectives 1

- ■ Demonstrative Adjectives
- ■ Compound Adjectives
- ■ Indefinite and Predicate Adjectives (See page **734.**)

 For each numbered sentence in the paragraphs below, identify the underlined word or words as one of the kinds of adjectives listed above.

Example: <u>Most</u> people know about the Great Chicago Fire.
indefinite

(1) On the night of October 8, 1871, an eerie, <u>reddish orange</u> glow filled the Chicago sky. **(2)** <u>Some</u> people believe that the Great Chicago Fire began in the O'Learys' barn when a cow kicked over a lantern. **(3)** (<u>That</u> theory was never proven, however, and the exact cause of the fire is still unknown.) **(4)** <u>Many</u> residents panicked and tried to flee the burning city. **(5)** <u>Kind-hearted</u> people did whatever they could to help, but most of Chicago was destroyed, and 300 people died.

(6) As bad as it was, <u>another</u> fire on the same day caused even more damage. **(7)** The Great Peshtigo Fire was <u>huge</u>; it covered more than a million acres in northeast Wisconsin and Michigan's upper peninsula. **(8)** Hundreds of miles of forest, dry from drought, were tinder for <u>this</u> firestorm. **(9)** <u>Hurricane-force</u> winds created by the fire pushed the blaze from town to town, and 1,500 people lost their lives. **(10)** To <u>this</u> day, the Great Peshtigo Fire ranks as the worst natural disaster to ever hit the United States.

Next Step: Write two or three sentences about fire safety. Use a predicate adjective, an indefinite adjective, and a demonstrative adjective in your sentences.

Related Skills Activities

- ■ **Basic Grammar and Writing**
  Describing with Adjectives, p. 486

- ■ **CD-ROM**
  Adjectives and Adverbs   732.2, 732.4

- ■ *SkillsBook*
  Adjectives, pp. 165–166

Answers

1. compound
2. indefinite
3. demonstrative
4. indefinite
5. compound
6. indefinite
7. predicate
8. demonstrative
9. compound
10. demonstrative

734

Adjectives . . .
Special Kinds of Adjectives

734.1
Indefinite Adjectives

An indefinite adjective gives approximate or indefinite information (*any, few, many, most,* and so on). It does not tell exactly how many or how much.

> Some **mammoths** were heavier than today's elephants.

734.2
Predicate Adjectives

A predicate adjective follows a linking verb and describes the subject.

> **Mammoths** were once abundant, but now they are extinct.

Forms of Adjectives

734.3
Positive Adjectives

The positive form describes a noun or pronoun without comparing it to anyone or anything else.

> The **Eurostar** is a fast **train** that runs between London, Paris, and Brussels.
> It is an impressive **train**.

734.4
Comparative Adjectives

The comparative form of an adjective (*er*) compares two persons, places, things, or ideas. (See page 487.)

> The **Eurostar** is faster than the Orient Express.

Some adjectives that have more than one syllable show comparisons by their *er* suffix, but many of them use the modifiers *more* or *less*.

> It is a speedier commuter **train** than the Tobu Railway trains in Japan.
> This **train** is more impressive than my commuter train.

734.5
Superlative Adjectives

The superlative form (*est* or *most* or *least*) compares three or more persons, places, things, or ideas. (See page 487.)

> In fact, the **Eurostar** is the fastest **train** in Europe.
> It is the most impressive commuter **train** in the world.

734.6
Irregular Forms

Some adjectives use completely different words to express comparison.

good, better, best	bad, worse, worst
many, more, most	little, less, least

---

punctuate *edit* capitalize
SPELL
improve   **735**
Using the Parts of Speech

Grammar Practice

Adjectives 2

■ Forms of Adjectives

Based on the clues in each sentence below, write the correct form (positive, comparative, or superlative) of the adjective shown in parentheses to complete each sentence.

Example: Giraffes are _____ than any other animal. *(tall)*
    taller

1. The _____ snake in the world is the reticulated python. *(long)*
2. A rabbit has _____ ears than a hare does. *(short)*
3. A cheetah is a _____ runner. *(fast)*
4. Even though the whale shark feeds mostly on plankton and small fish, it is the _____ fish in the sea. *(big)*
5. The common snail is probably the _____ animal on earth. *(slow)*
6. Is the warthog really the _____ animal? *(attractive)*
7. Many people believe the polar bear is _____ than the grizzly bear. *(powerful)*
8. The Indian elephant has a _____ forehead. *(square)*
9. Even the _____ human sprinter can't outrun an elephant. *(good)*
10. Some zebras have _____ stripes than other zebras. *(many)*
11. Compared to other animals in the United States, the wolverine seems to be the one with the _____ temper. *(bad)*
12. An arctic fox in the snow is _____ than a red fox in the forest. *(visible)*
13. Long ago, the Pacific salmon was the _____ source of food in the diet of the Yakima tribe. *(important)*

Next Step: Write three sentences about different animals. Use adjectives that are positive, comparative, and superlative in your sentences.

Related Skills Activities

■ **Basic Grammar and Writing**
Comparative and Superlative Forms, p. 487

■ **CD-ROM**
Adjectives and Adverbs   734.2

■ *SkillsBook*
Using Adjectives to Compare, pp. 169–170

Answers

1. longest
2. shorter
3. fast
4. biggest
5. slowest
6. least attractive
7. more powerful
8. square
9. best
10. more
11. worst
12. less visible
13. most important

736

punctuate *edit* capitalize
improve SPELL **737**
Using the Parts of Speech

Adverbs

An **adverb** is a word used to modify a verb, an adjective, or another adverb. It tells *how, when, where, how often,* or *how much.* Adverbs can come before or after the words they modify. (See pages **490–493.**)

Dad snores loudly. (*Loudly* modifies the verb *snores.*)

His snores are really **explosive.** (*Really* modifies the adjective *explosive.*)

Dad snores very **loudly.** (*Very* modifies the adverb *loudly.*)

Types of Adverbs

There are four basic types of adverbs: *time, place, manner,* and *degree.*

736.1
Adverbs of Time

Adverbs of time tell *when, how often,* and *how long.*

tomorrow   often   never   always

Jen rarely has time to go swimming.

736.2
Adverbs of Place

Adverbs of place tell *where, to where,* or *from where.*

there   backward   outside

We'll set up our tent here.

736.3
Adverbs of Manner

Adverbs of manner often end in *ly* and tell *how* something is done.

unkindly   gently   well

Ahmed boldly entered the dark cave.

Some words used as adverbs can be written with or without the *ly* ending. When in doubt, use the *ly* form.

slow, slowly   deep, deeply

NOTE Not all words ending in *ly* are adverbs. *Lovely,* for example, is an adjective.

736.4
Adverbs of Degree

Adverbs of degree tell *how much* or *how little.*

scarcely   entirely   generally   very   really

Jess is usually the leader in these situations.

Grammar Practice

Adverbs 1

■ Types of Adverbs

Write the adverb or adverbs that modify the underlined words in the sentences below. The number of adverbs is in parentheses. Label each as one of "time," "place," "manner," or "degree."

Example: America's national parks <u>are</u> always a great place to camp. *(1)*

always—time

1. Some parks, like Yosemite and Yellowstone, <u>are</u> often very <u>busy.</u> *(2)*

2. You might have to <u>wait</u> patiently to get a campsite. *(1)*

3. People must enjoy <u>sleeping</u> outside! *(1)*

4. Campers in national parks regularly <u>go</u> bicycling, canoeing, and hiking. *(1)*

5. Younger kids really <u>enjoy</u> meeting the park rangers. *(1)*

6. Frequently, national park campgrounds <u>offer</u> evening campfire activities. *(1)*

7. If someone <u>brings</u> a guitar there, people might start <u>dancing</u> around. *(2)*

8. Sometimes, national parks <u>have</u> programs to teach campers about nature and wildlife. *(1)*

9. Campers need to <u>react</u> quietly and cautiously when wild animals <u>are</u> nearby. *(3)*

10. Wherever you camp, it is important to <u>do</u> it safely. *(1)*

11. You should <u>follow</u> the park's camping rules exactly and faithfully. *(2)*

12. Never <u>hike</u> by yourself. *(1)*

13. Be extremely <u>careful</u> that your campfire <u>does</u> not accidentally <u>start</u> a forest fire. *(3)*

14. Always <u>remember</u> to carefully <u>inspect</u> your campsite before you leave. *(2)*

Related Skills Activities

■ **Basic Grammar and Writing**
Describing with Adverbs, p. 490
How Can I Use Adverbs Effectively?,
    pp. 492–493

■ **CD-ROM**
Adjectives and Adverbs
    536.1, 536.2, 536.3, 536.4

■ *SkillsBook*
Adverbs 1 and 2, pp. 169–172

Answers

1. often—time, very—degree
2. patiently—manner
3. outside—place
4. regularly—time
5. really—degree
6. frequently—time
7. there—place, around—place
8. sometimes—time
9. quietly—manner, cautiously—manner, nearby—place
10. safely—manner
11. exactly—manner, faithfully—manner
12. never—time
13. extremely—degree, not—time, accidentally—manner
14. always—time, carefully—manner

738

Adverbs . . .

Special Kinds of Adverbs

738.1
Conjunctive Adverbs

A conjunctive adverb can be used as a conjunction and shows a connection or a transition between two independent clauses. Most often, a conjunctive adverb follows a semicolon in a compound sentence; however, it can also appear at the beginning or end of a sentence. (Note that the previous sentence has an example of a conjunctive adverb.)

also	besides	however	instead
meanwhile	nevertheless	therefore	

Forms of Adverbs

Many adverbs—especially adverbs of manner—have three forms: *positive*, *comparative*, and *superlative*.

738.2
Positive Adverbs

The positive form describes but does not make a comparison.

Juan woke up late.

He quickly ate some breakfast.

738.3
Comparative Adverbs

The comparative form of an adverb (*er*) compares two things.

Juan woke up later than he usually did. (See page **491**.)

Some adverbs that have more than one syllable show comparisons by their *er* suffix, but many of them use the modifiers *more* or *less*.

He ate his breakfast more quickly than usual.

738.4
Superlative Adverbs

The superlative form (*est* or *most* or *least*) compares three or more things. (See page **491**.)

Of the past three days, Juan woke up latest on Saturday.

Of the past three days, he ate his breakfast least quickly on Saturday.

738.5
Irregular Forms

Some adverbs use completely different words to express comparison.

Positive	Comparative	Superlative
well	better	best
badly	worse	worst

---

punctuate *edit* capitalize SPELL
improve
Using the Parts of Speech
739

Grammar Practice

Adverbs 2

■ Comparative Forms

 For each of the sentences below, write the adverb and identify it as "positive," "comparative," or "superlative."

Example: This year, the school bus arrives earlier than it did last year.
earlier (comparative)

1. Makenna carelessly dripped paint on the floor.
2. Paul bakes walnut brownies better than I do.
3. Of everyone in our school's chorus, Marissa sings the best.
4. The play's director said, "For this role, Carmen, you have to act more mysteriously than that."
5. My old computer runs more slowly than this new one.
6. Ms. Green, who was formerly a marine, is a new teacher at our school.
7. Of any of the recent storms in the area, the wind blew the most forcefully during last night's storm.
8. My brother rides his dirt bike faster than I do.
9. Julian divided the popcorn equally among the four of us.
10. Of the Rosses' three regular babysitters, Bianca seems to be the least readily available.
11. Instant messaging was largely unknown until a few years after its introduction.
12. Shanice dresses the most plainly of anyone in her family.
13. Dimitri treats his dog roughly.
14. Paola gives classroom presentations more confidently than the other students give them.

Next Step: Write one sentence with a comparative adverb and one with a superlative adverb.

PARTS OF SPEECH

Related Skills Activities

■ **Basic Grammar and Writing**
Comparative and Superlative Adverbs, p. 491
Connect Ideas, p. 493

■ ***SkillsBook***
Types of Adverbs, p. 173

 ## Answers

1. carelessly (positive)
2. better (comparative)
3. best (superlative)
4. more mysteriously (comparative)
5. more slowly (comparative)
6. formerly (positive)
7. most forcefully (superlative)
8. faster (comparative)
9. equally (positive)
10. least readily (superlative)
11. largely (positive)
12. most plainly (superlative)
13. roughly (positive)
14. more confidently (comparative)

punctuate *edit* capitalize
improve **SPELL** **741**
Using the Parts of Speech

Test Prep!

For each of the following sentences, write the letter that shows the correct form of the verb in parentheses.

1 I *(see)* William when he left with his mom just before class.
  Ⓐ seed   Ⓑ saw   Ⓒ seen   Ⓓ see

2 Latisha has *(run)* in the Labor Day marathon before.
  Ⓐ runnen Ⓑ ran   Ⓒ run   Ⓓ runned

3 Last summer we *(freeze)* a lot of the beans from our garden.
  Ⓐ freezed Ⓑ froze   Ⓒ freezen Ⓓ frozen

4 The jockey *(lead)* the horse to the winner's circle.
  Ⓐ lead   Ⓑ leaded   Ⓒ led   Ⓓ leaden

5 I had *(buy)* this DVD for Cruz's birthday.
  Ⓐ bought Ⓑ boughten Ⓒ buy   Ⓓ buyed

6 These plants *(grow)* better inside than they did outside.
  Ⓐ growed Ⓑ grown   Ⓒ grew   Ⓓ grows

7 My aunt and uncle have *(drive)* their motorcycles across the country.
  Ⓐ driven Ⓑ drive   Ⓒ drove   Ⓓ drived

8 Since I use e-mail now, I haven't *(write)* a letter on paper in a while.
  Ⓐ wrote   Ⓑ writed   Ⓒ writ   Ⓓ written

Label the verb in each of the following sentences. Write "I" for intransitive or "T" for transitive.

9 The students named the new mascot.

10 Syed slipped on the ice in the parking lot.

11 The class laughed at Mr. Jenkin's dumb joke.

12 Thad broke the record for the 50-yard dash.

13 Olivia read my essay.

14 Isamar read aloud.

For each of the following sentences, write the letter that best describes the underlined word.
  Ⓐ comparative adverb   Ⓒ superlative adverb
  Ⓑ comparative adjective   Ⓓ superlative adjective

15 Could you talk <u>more quietly</u>, please?

16 Rocco's has the <u>least expensive</u> pizza in town.

17 You will have to wake up <u>earlier</u> when school starts in the fall.

18 This algebra test is the <u>hardest</u> one we've had all semester.

19 Kirstin sang <u>better</u> than she did yesterday.

20 This week is <u>warmer</u> than last week was.

21 Of everyone on the team, Claire played <u>most energetically</u>.

22 The classroom is <u>more comfortable</u> when the air conditioning is on.

23 Kevin is <u>funnier</u> than most of the other kids.

24 Everyone in the club worked hard, but Luis worked <u>hardest</u> of all.

25 Lisa's purse is the <u>heaviest</u> one here.

Answers

  1. B
  2. C
  3. B
  4. C
  5. A
  6. C
  7. A
  8. D

Answers

  9. T
  10. I
  11. I
  12. T
  13. T
  14. I

Answers

  15. A
  16. D
  17. A
  18. D
  19. A
  20. B
  21. C
  22. B
  23. B
  24. C
  25. D

742

Prepositions

Prepositions are words that show position, direction, or how two words or ideas are related to each other. Specifically, a preposition shows the relationship between its object and some other word in the sentence.

> **Raul hid under the stairs.** (*Under* shows the relationship between *hid* and *stairs*.)

742.1
Prepositional Phrases

A preposition never appears alone; it is always part of a prepositional phrase. A prepositional phrase includes the preposition, the object of the preposition, and the modifiers of the object. (See pages **494–495**.)

> **Raul's friends looked in the clothes hamper.** (preposition: *in;* object: *hamper;* modifiers: *the, clothes*)

A prepositional phrase functions as an adjective or as an adverb.

> **They checked the closet with all the winter coats.** (*With all the winter coats* functions as an adjective modifying *closet*.)

> **They wandered around the house looking for him.** (*Around the house* functions as an adverb modifying *wandered*.)

NOTE If a word found in the list of prepositions has no object, it is not a preposition. It is probably an adverb.

> **Raul had never won at hide 'n' seek before.** (*Before* is an adverb that modifies *had won*.)

Prepositions

aboard	apart from	beyond	from among	near	over	toward
about	around	but	from between	near to	over to	under
above	aside from	by	from under	of	owing to	underneath
according to	at	by means of	in	off	past	until
across	away from	concerning	in addition to	on	prior to	unto
across from	back of	considering	in front of	on account of	regarding	up
after	because of	despite	in place of	on behalf of	round	up to
against	before	down	in regard to	on top of	save	upon
along	behind	down from	in spite of	onto	since	with
along with	below	during	inside	opposite	through	within
alongside	beneath	except	inside of	out	throughout	without
alongside of	beside	except for	instead of	out of	till	
amid	besides	excepting	into	outside	to	
among	between	for	like	outside of	together with	

---

punctuate edit capitalize **SPELL**
improve
Using the Parts of Speech **743**

Grammar Practice

Prepositions

 Write the prepositional phrases you find in each numbered sentence below. Underline the prepositions and circle the objects of the prepositions.

Example: The Plains Indians were once the finest horse riders in the world.
in the (world)

(1) Plains Indians learned horse-riding skills at a very early age. **(2)** Tribesmen on horses could follow the buffalo herds, so mastering those skills meant food for the tribe. **(3)** Riding among the buffalo and using a bow involved great skill and daring. **(4)** Some of the Indian braves would ride with one foot on the top of the horse's hips while shooting arrows underneath the horse's neck at an enemy. **(5)** In the 1800s, nations like the Crow and the Lakota enjoyed a golden age because of their superb riding abilities.

 Write a prepositional phrase to complete each of the following sentences.

Example: I like tropical fish . . . *(what kind?)*
from the Caribbean Sea.

1. I was born . . . *(when?)*
2. The CD . . . *(which one?)* . . . is my favorite one right now.
3. My uncle grew up . . . *(where?)*
4. My notebook is the one . . . *(which one?)*
5. I keep my pens and pencils . . . *(where?)*
6. Please get me some candy . . . *(what kind?)*

Related Skills Activities

■ **Basic Grammar and Writing**
Connecting with Prepositions, pp. 494–495
Combine with Phrases, p. 513

■ **CD-ROM**
Prepositions   742.1

■ **SkillsBook**
Prepositions, p. 174

 ### Answers

1. at a very early (age)
2. on (horses,) for the (tribe)
3. among the (buffalo)
4. of the Indian (braves,) with one (foot,) on the (top,) of the horse's (hip,) underneath the horse's (neck,) at an (enemy)
5. In the (1800s,) like the (Crow) and the (Lakota,) because of their superb riding (abilities)

 ### Possible Answers

1. on the first day of the month
2. in the player
3. near Miami
4. with the red stripe
5. in a pencil box
6. with chocolate on it

744

Conjunctions

A **conjunction** connects individual words or groups of words. There are three kinds of conjunctions: *coordinating, correlative,* and *subordinating.* (See pages 496–498.)

744.1 **Coordinating Conjunctions**	A coordinating conjunction connects a word to a word, a phrase to a phrase, or a clause to a clause. The words, phrases, or clauses joined by a coordinating conjunction must be equal, or of the same type. Polluted rivers and streams can be cleaned up. (Two nouns are connected by *and*.) Ride a bike or plant a tree to reduce pollution. (Two verb phrases are connected by *or*.) Maybe you can't invent a pollution-free engine, but you can cut down on the amount of energy you use. (Two equal independent clauses are connected by *but*.) **NOTE** When a coordinating conjunction is used to make a compound sentence, a comma always comes before it.
744.2 **Correlative Conjunctions**	Correlative conjunctions are conjunctions used in pairs. We must reduce not only pollution but also excess energy use. Either you're part of the problem, or you're part of the solution.

Conjunctions

Coordinating Conjunctions
and, but, or, nor, for, so, yet

Correlative Conjunctions
either, or   neither, nor   not only, but also   both, and   whether, or   as, so

Subordinating Conjunctions
after, although, as, as if, as long as, as though, because, before, if, in order that, provided that, since, so, so that, that, though, till, unless, until, when, where, whereas, while

---

Related Skills Activities

■ **Basic Grammar and Writing**
Connecting with Conjunctions, pp. 496–497
Create Compound Sentences, p. 516

■ **CD-ROM**
Conjunctions 744.1, 744.2

■ *SkillsBook*
Coordinating Conjunctions, pp. 175–176
Correlative Conjunctions, pp. 177–178

---

punctuate *edit* *capitalize*
improve SPELL **745**
Using the Parts of Speech

Grammar Practice

Conjunctions 1

 ■ Coordinating Conjunctions

Use a coordinating conjunction to combine each pair of sentences below.

Example: Anyone may join the Polar Bear Club. He or she must be willing to swim in freezing water.
Anyone may join the Polar Bear Club, but he or she must be willing to swim in freezing water.

1. The members braved the subzero temperatures. They plunged into the icy water.
2. Club members could go into the water wearing swimsuits. They could go into the water wearing warmer clothing.
3. Participants get very cold. It is important to have a place to warm up when they get out of the water.
4. Polar Bear Club members like to have fun. They also like to help raise money for special causes.

 ■ Correlative Conjunctions

Use a different set of correlative conjunctions to combine each sentence pair below. Underline the conjunctions.

Example: Josh must decide if he wants to go to the game. Josh must decide if he wants to go to the movies.
Josh must decide whether he wants to go to the game or the movies.

1. Rain will not stop the football game. Snow will not stop the football game.
2. Volleyball is a team sport. Soccer is a team sport.
3. Sally has twin sisters. Sally also has twin cousins.
4. Maybe Ron's mom will pick us up after school. Maybe Ron's dad will pick us up after school.

 Possible Answers

1. The members braved the subzero temperatures and plunged into the icy water.
2. Club members could go into the water wearing swimsuits or warmer clothing.
3. Participants get very cold, so it is important to have a place to warm up when they get out of the water.
4. Polar Bear Club members like to have fun, but they also like to help raise money for special causes.

 Possible Answers

1. Neither rain nor snow will stop the football game.
2. Both volleyball and soccer are team sports.
3. Sally has not only twin sisters but also twin cousins.
4. Either Ron's mom or his dad will pick us up after school.

Conjunctions . . .

746.1
Subordinating Conjunctions

A subordinating conjunction is a word or group of words that connects two clauses that are not equally important. A subordinating conjunction begins a dependent clause and connects it to an independent clause to make a complex sentence. (See page 517 and the chart on page 744.)

> Fuel-cell engines are unusual because they don't have moving parts.

> Since fuel-cell cars run on hydrogen, the only waste products are water and heat.

As you can see in the sentences above, a comma sets off the dependent clause only when it begins the sentence. A comma is usually not used when the dependent clause follows the independent clause.

NOTE Relative pronouns and conjunctive adverbs can also connect clauses. (See 706.3 and 738.1.)

Interjections

An **interjection** is a word or phrase used to express strong emotion or surprise. Punctuation (a comma or an exclamation point) is used to separate an interjection from the rest of the sentence.

> Wow, would you look at that!   Oh no! He's falling!

SCHOOL DAZE

Forget it! We aren't using activity money for that.

Yikes, I've told everyone that we could buy a plasma-screen TV for our classroom!

---

punctuate edit capitalize
improve SPELL
Using the Parts of Speech **747**

Grammar Practice

Conjunctions 2

■ Subordinating Conjunctions

 Choose a subordinating conjunction (from the chart on page 744) to connect each pair of clauses below, forming complex sentences. Place the conjunction first in some of the sentences.

Example: Cicadas are easy to recognize. They make unique sounds.

Cicadas are easy to recognize because they make unique sounds.

1. It's not uncommon to hear dozens of them ticking, buzzing, and whining. It's hot outside.
2. They are capable of producing sounds in excess of 120 decibels. The noise might hurt your ears.
3. The king hornet preys on cicadas. Birds are even worse.
4. Unsuspecting cicadas are sitting high in the treetops. Hungry birds are watching.
5. It sounds disgusting. Some people eat cicadas.
6. You might hear the 17-year cicadas. You are in the United States east of the Great Plains.
7. These cicadas are called 17-year cicadas. They emerge in great numbers once every 17 years.
8. You know what a cicada looks like. You might mistake it for a locust or a giant fly.
9. A cicada's body temperature drops below 72 degrees Fahrenheit. It won't fly.
10. You might not like the racket that cicadas make. You have to admit that they are interesting insects.

Next Step: Would an interjection be appropriate in any of the sentences you just wrote? Add an interjection to at least four of them. Separate it from the rest of the sentence with either a comma or an exclamation point.

PARTS OF SPEECH

Related Skills Activities

■ **Basic Grammar and Writing**
Connecting with Conjunctions, p. 496
Develop Complex Sentences,
    p. 517

■ **CD-ROM**
Conjunctions   746.1

■ *SkillsBook*
Subordinating Conjunctions,
    pp. 179–180
Interjections, pp. 181–182

Possible Answers

1. It's not uncommon to hear dozens of them ticking, buzzing, and whining when it's hot outside.
2. Since they are capable of producing sounds in excess of 120 decibels, the noise might hurt your ears.
3. While the king hornet preys on cicadas, birds are even worse.
4. Unsuspecting cicadas are sitting high in the treetops as hungry birds are watching.
5. Although it sounds disgusting, some people eat cicadas.
6. You might hear the 17-year cicadas if you are in the United States east of the Great Plains.
7. These cicadas are called 17-year cicadas because they emerge in great numbers once every 17 years.
8. Unless you know what a cicada looks like, you might mistake it for a locust or a giant fly.
9. If a cicada's body temperature drops below 72 degrees Fahrenheit, it won't fly.
10. Though you might not like the racket that cicadas make, you have to admit that they are interesting insects.

Quick Guide: Parts of Speech

In the English language, there are eight parts of speech. Understanding them will help you improve your writing skills. Every word you write is a part of speech—a noun, a verb, an adjective, and so on. The chart below lists the eight parts of speech.

Noun	A word that names a person, a place, a thing, or an idea
	Alex Moya Belize ladder courage
Pronoun	A word used in place of a noun
	I he it they you anybody some
Verb	A word that shows action or links a subject to another word in the sentence
	sing shake catch is are
Adjective	A word that describes a noun or a pronoun
	stormy red rough seven grand
Adverb	A word that describes a verb, an adjective, or another adverb
	quickly today now bravely softer
Preposition	A word that shows position or direction and introduces a prepositional phrase
	around up under over between to
Conjunction	A word that connects other words or groups of words
	and but or so because when
Interjection	A word (set off by commas or an exclamation point) that shows strong emotion
	Stop! Hey, how are you?

punctuate *edit* *capitalize*
improve SPELL **749**
Using the Parts of Speech

Grammar Practice

Parts of Speech Review

 For each underlined word in the following paragraphs, write whether it is a "noun," a "pronoun," a "verb," an "adjective," an "adverb," a "preposition," a "conjunction," or an "interjection."

(1) There's a big change taking place in the Black Hills of South Dakota. (2) Not far from Mount Rushmore, a huge likeness of the Native American leader Crazy Horse is being carved into the side of a mountain. (3) Crazy Horse was a famous warrior of the Lakota tribe. (4) He was a committed leader who fought to preserve the traditions and values of his people. (5) Now, people are creating this memorial to his life. (6) Anyone who's in the area can see it in person.

(7) The sculptor Korczak Ziolkowski began work on the memorial in 1948. (8) In the beginning, he worked alone. (9) He worked diligently, and soon the image of Crazy Horse began taking shape.

(10) Surprisingly, he then decided to carve the entire 600-foot mountain instead of following his original plan to carve only the top 100 feet.

(11) Wow, Korczak worked on his amazing sculpture for 32 years!

(12) When he died unexpectedly in 1982 at the age of 74, he was buried in a tomb about 500 yards from the base of the mountain.

(13) Ziolkowski's project continues under the supervision of his wife. (14) The face portion of this gigantic sculpture was dedicated in 1998. (15) The crew will work faithfully until the project is finished.

(16) Oh, it will be years before the memorial is finished, but it will be well worth the wait.

Next Step: Write one word for each of the eight parts of speech and exchange lists with a partner. Write a sentence or two using all of each other's words.

Related Skills Activities

■ *SkillsBook*
Parts of Speech Review 1, pp. 183–184
Parts of Speech Review 2, pp. 185–185

Answers

1. noun
2. preposition
3. adjective
4. pronoun
5. verb
6. pronoun
7. noun
8. verb
9. conjunction
10. adverb
11. interjection
12. adverb
13. preposition
14. adjective
15. conjunction
16. interjection

RUBRICS

6-Point

Rubric for Narrative Writing

Ideas

6 The narrative captures an unforgettable time. The details make the story come alive.

5 The writer shares an interesting experience. Details help create the interest.

4 The writer tells about an interesting experience. More details are needed.

3 The writer tells about an experience or time. Many more details are needed.

2 The writer needs to focus more specifically on one experience or time.

1 The writer needs to select a topic suitable for a narrative.

Organization

6 The way the narrative is put together makes it enjoyable to read.

5 The narrative is well organized, with a clear beginning, middle, and ending. Transitions are used well.

4 The narrative is well organized. Most of the transitions are helpful.

3 The order of events needs to be corrected. More transitions need to be used.

2 The beginning, middle, and ending all run together. The order is unclear.

1 The narrative needs to be organized.

Voice

6 The voice in the narrative perfectly captures the special time or experience.

5 The writer's voice creates interest in the story.

4 The writer's voice could be stronger.

3 A voice can sometimes be heard. The writer needs to show more feelings.

2 The voice cannot be heard.

1 The writer has not gotten involved in the story.

Word Choice

6 The writer's exceptional word choice captures the experience.

5 Specific nouns, verbs, and modifiers create clear pictures.

4 Some of the words need to be more specific to create clear pictures.

3 Many more specific words need to be used.

2 The writer has given little consideration to word choice.

1 The writer has not yet considered word choice.

Sentence Fluency

6 The style of the sentences captures this time or experience.

5 The sentences are skillfully written and original.

4 The sentences show variety, but some should read more smoothly.

3 A better variety of sentences is needed. Sentences do not read smoothly.

2 Many short or incomplete sentences make the writing choppy.

1 Few sentences are written well. Help is needed.

Conventions

6 The narrative is error free.

5 The narrative has a few minor errors in punctuation, spelling, or grammar.

4 The narrative has some errors that may distract the reader.

3 Several errors confuse the reader.

2 Many errors make the narrative truly confusing and hard to read.

1 Help is needed to make corrections.

© Great Source. Permission is granted to copy this page.

6-Point

Rubric for Expository Writing

Ideas

6 The topic, focus, and details make the essay truly memorable.
5 The essay is informative with a clear focus and specific details.
4 The essay is informative with a clear focus. More specific details are needed.
3 The focus of the essay needs to be clearer, and more specific details are needed.
2 The topic needs to be narrowed or expanded. Many more specific details are needed.
1 A new topic needs to be selected.

Organization

6 The organization and transitions make the essay clear and easy to read.
5 The beginning interests the reader. The middle supports the focus. The ending works well. Transitions are used.
4 The essay is divided into a beginning, a middle, and an ending. Some transitions are used.
3 The beginning or ending is weak. The middle needs a paragraph for each main point. More transitions are needed.
2 The beginning, middle, and ending all run together. Paragraphs and transitions are needed.
1 The essay should be reorganized.

Voice

6 The writer's voice sounds confident, knowledgeable, and enthusiastic.
5 The writer's voice sounds knowledgeable and confident. It fits the audience.
4 The writer's voice sounds knowledgeable most of the time and fits the audience.
3 The writer sometimes sounds unsure, and the voice needs to fit the audience better.
2 The writer sounds unsure. The voice needs to fit the audience.
1 The writer needs to learn about voice.

Word Choice

6 The word choice makes the essay very clear, informative, and enjoyable to read.
5 Specific nouns and action verbs make the essay clear and informative.
4 Some nouns and verbs could be more specific.
3 Too many general words are used. Specific nouns and verbs are needed.
2 General or missing words make this essay difficult to understand.
1 The writer needs help finding specific words.

Sentence Fluency

6 The sentences are skillfully written, and readers will enjoy them.
5 The sentences read smoothly.
4 Most of the sentences read smoothly, but some are short and choppy.
3 Many short, choppy sentences need to be rewritten to make the essay read smoothly.
2 Many sentences are choppy or incomplete and need to be rewritten.
1 Most sentences need to be rewritten.

Conventions

6 The essay is error free.
5 The essay has a few minor errors in punctuation, spelling, or grammar.
4 The essay has some errors in punctuation, spelling, or grammar.
3 Several errors confuse the reader.
2 Many errors make the essay difficult to read.
1 Help is needed to make corrections.

6-Point

Rubric for Persuasive Writing

Ideas

6 My position is very well defended and compels the reader to act.

5 The essay has a clear position or opinion statement. Persuasive reasons support the writer's position.

4 The position statement is clear, and most reasons support the writer's position.

3 The position statement may be clear. More persuasive reasons are needed.

2 The position statement is unclear. Persuasive reasons are needed.

1 A new position statement and reasons are needed.

Organization

6 All the parts of the essay work together to build a thoughtful, convincing position.

5 The opening contains the position statement. The middle provides clear support. The ending reinforces the position.

4 The opening contains the position statement. The middle provides support. The ending needs work.

3 The beginning has an opinion statement. The middle and ending need more work.

2 The beginning, middle, and ending run together.

1 The organization is unclear and incomplete.

Voice

6 The writer's voice is confident, positive, and convincing.

5 The writer's voice is confident and persuasive.

4 The writer's voice is confident, but it may not be persuasive enough.

3 The writer's voice needs to be more confident and persuasive.

2 The writer's voice rambles on without any confidence.

1 The writer has not considered voice.

Word Choice

6 The writer's choice of words makes a powerful case.

5 The writer's word choice helps persuade the reader.

4 Some changes would make the word choice more persuasive.

3 Many more precise and persuasive words are needed.

2 The words do not create a clear message. Some unfair words are used.

1 Word choice has not been considered.

Sentence Fluency

6 The sentences spark the reader's interest in the essay.

5 Variety is seen in both the types of sentences and their beginnings.

4 Varied sentence beginnings are used. Sentence variety would make the essay more interesting to read.

3 Varied sentence beginnings are needed. Sentence variety would make the essay more interesting.

2 Most sentences begin the same way. Most of the sentences are simple. Compound and complex sentences are needed.

1 Sentence fluency has not been established. Ideas do not flow smoothly.

Conventions

6 The writing is error free.

5 Grammar and punctuation errors are few. The reader is not distracted by the errors.

4 Grammar and punctuation errors are seen in a few sentences. They distract the reader in those areas.

3 There are a number of errors that may confuse the reader.

2 Frequent errors make the essay difficult to read.

1 Nearly every sentence contains errors.

6-Point

Rubric for Response to Literature

Ideas

6 The ideas show a complete understanding of the reading.
5 The essay has a clear focus statement and all the necessary details.
4 The essay has a clear focus statement. Unnecessary details need to be cut.
3 The focus statement is too broad. Unnecessary details need to be cut.
2 The focus statement is unclear. More details are needed.
1 The essay needs a focus statement and details.

Organization

6 All the parts work together to create an insightful essay.
5 The organization pattern fits the topic and purpose. All parts of the essay are well developed.
4 The organization pattern fits the topic and purpose. A part of the essay needs better development.
3 The organization fits the essay's purpose. Some parts need more development.
2 The organization doesn't fit the purpose.
1 A plan needs to be followed.

Voice

6 The voice expresses interest and complete understanding. It engages the reader.
5 The voice expresses interest in and understanding of the topic.
4 The voice expresses interest but needs to show more understanding.
3 The voice needs to be more interesting and express more understanding.
2 The voice does not show interest in or an understanding of the topic.
1 The writer needs to understand how to create voice.

Word Choice

6 The word choice reflects careful thinking about the reading.
5 The word choice, including the use of literary terms, creates a clear message.
4 The word choice is clear, but more literary terms would improve the essay.
3 The word choice is too general and more literary terms are needed.
2 Little, if any, attention was given to word choice.
1 The writer needs help with word choice.

Sentence Fluency

6 The sentences in the essay make the ideas really stand out.
5 The sentences are skillfully written and keep the reader's interest.
4 No sentence problems exist. More sentence variety is needed.
3 A few sentence problems need to be corrected.
2 The essay has many sentence problems.
1 The writer needs to learn how to construct sentences.

Conventions

6 Grammar and punctuation are correct, and the copy is free of all errors.
5 The essay has one or two errors that do not interfere with the reader's understanding.
4 The essay has a few careless errors in punctuation and grammar.
3 The errors in the essay confuse the reader.
2 The number of errors make the essay hard to read.
1 Help is needed to make corrections.

5-Point

Rubric for Narrative Writing

Ideas

5 The narrative captures an unforgettable time. The details make the story come alive.
4 The writer shares an interesting experience. Details help create the interest.
3 The writer tells about an interesting experience. More details are needed.
2 The writer tells about an experience or time. Many more details are needed.
1 The writer needs to focus more specifically on one experience or time.

Organization

5 The way the narrative is put together makes it enjoyable to read.
4 The narrative is well organized, with a clear beginning, middle, and ending. Transitions are used well.
3 The narrative is well organized. Most of the transitions are helpful.
2 The order of events needs to be corrected. More transitions need to be used.
1 The beginning, middle, and ending all run together. The order is unclear.

Voice

5 The voice in the narrative perfectly captures the special time or experience.
4 The writer's voice creates interest in the story.
3 The writer's voice could be stronger.
2 A voice can sometimes be heard. The writer needs to show more feelings.
1 The voice cannot be heard.

Word Choice

5 The writer's exceptional word choice captures the experience.
4 Specific nouns, verbs, and modifiers create clear pictures.
3 Some of the words need to be more specific to create clear pictures.
2 Many more specific words need to be used.
1 The writer has given little consideration to word choice.

Sentence Fluency

5 The style of the sentences captures this time or experience.
4 The sentences are skillfully written and original.
3 The sentences show variety, but some should read more smoothly.
2 A better variety of sentences is needed. Sentences do not read smoothly.
1 Many short or incomplete sentences make the writing choppy.

Conventions

5 The narrative is error free.
4 The narrative has a few minor errors in punctuation, spelling, or grammar.
3 The narrative has some errors that may distract the reader.
2 Several errors confuse the reader.
1 Many errors make the narrative truly confusing and hard to read.

5-Point
Rubric for Expository Writing

Ideas
5 The topic, focus, and details make the essay truly memorable.
4 The essay is informative with a clear focus and specific details.
3 The essay is informative with a clear focus. More specific details are needed.
2 The focus of the essay needs to be clearer, and more specific details are needed.
1 The topic needs to be narrowed or expanded. Many more specific details are needed.

Organization
5 The organization and transitions make the essay clear and easy to read.
4 The beginning interests the reader. The middle supports the focus. The ending works well. Transitions are used.
3 The essay is divided into a beginning, a middle, and an ending. Some transitions are used.
2 The beginning or ending is weak. The middle needs a paragraph for each main point. More transitions are needed.
1 The beginning, middle, and ending all run together. Paragraphs and transitions are needed.

Voice
5 The writer's voice sounds confident, knowledgeable, and enthusiastic.
4 The writer's voice sounds knowledgeable and confident. It fits the audience.
3 The writer's voice sounds knowledgeable most of the time and fits the audience.
2 The writer sometimes sounds unsure, and the voice needs to fit the audience better.
1 The writer sounds unsure. The voice needs to fit the audience.

Word Choice
5 The word choice makes the essay very clear, informative, and enjoyable to read.
4 Specific nouns and action verbs make the essay clear and informative.
3 Some nouns and verbs could be more specific.
2 Too many general words are used. Specific nouns and verbs are needed.
1 General or missing words make this essay difficult to understand.

Sentence Fluency
5 The sentences are skillfully written, and readers will enjoy them.
4 The sentences read smoothly.
3 Most of the sentences read smoothly, but some are short and choppy.
2 Many short, choppy sentences need to be rewritten to make the essay read smoothly.
1 Many sentences are choppy or incomplete and need to be rewritten.

Conventions
5 The essay is error free.
4 The essay has a few minor errors in punctuation, spelling, or grammar.
3 The essay has some errors in punctuation, spelling, or grammar.
2 Several errors confuse the reader.
1 Many errors make the essay difficult to read.

5-Point

Rubric for Persuasive Writing

Ideas

5 My position is very well defended and compels the reader to act.

4 The essay has a clear position or opinion statement. Persuasive reasons support the writer's position.

3 The position statement is clear, and most reasons support the writer's position.

2 The position statement may be clear. More persuasive reasons are needed.

1 The position statement is unclear. Persuasive reasons are needed.

Organization

5 All the parts of the essay work together to build a thoughtful, convincing position.

4 The opening contains the position statement. The middle provides clear support. The ending reinforces the position.

3 The opening contains the position statement. The middle provides support. The ending needs work.

2 The beginning has an opinion statement. The middle and ending need more work.

1 The beginning, middle, and ending run together.

Voice

5 The writer's voice is confident, positive, and convincing.

4 The writer's voice is confident and persuasive.

3 The writer's voice is confident, but it may not be persuasive enough.

2 The writer's voice needs to be more confident and persuasive.

1 The writer's voice rambles on without any confidence.

Word Choice

5 The writer's choice of words makes a powerful case.

4 The writer's word choice helps persuade the reader.

3 Some changes would make the word choice more persuasive.

2 Many more precise and persuasive words are needed.

1 The words do not create a clear message. Some unfair words are used.

Sentence Fluency

5 The sentences spark the reader's interest in the essay.

4 Variety is seen in both the types of sentences and their beginnings.

3 Varied sentence beginnings are used. Sentence variety would make the essay more interesting to read.

2 Varied sentence beginnings are needed. Sentence variety would make the essay more interesting.

1 Most sentences begin the same way. Most of the sentences are simple. Compound and complex sentences are needed.

Conventions

5 The writing is error free.

4 Grammar and punctuation errors are few. The reader is not distracted by the errors.

3 Grammar and punctuation errors are seen in a few sentences. They distract the reader in those areas.

2 There are a number of errors that may confuse the reader.

1 Frequent errors make the essay difficult to read.

5-Point
Rubric for Response to Literature

Ideas
5 The ideas show a complete understanding of the reading.
4 The essay has a clear focus statement and all the necessary details.
3 The essay has a clear focus statement. Unnecessary details need to be cut.
2 The focus statement is too broad. Unnecessary details need to be cut.
1 The focus statement is unclear. More details are needed.

Organization
5 All the parts work together to create an insightful essay.
4 The organization pattern fits the topic and purpose. All parts of the essay are well developed.
3 The organization pattern fits the topic and purpose. A part of the essay needs better development.
2 The organization fits the essay's purpose. Some parts need more development.
1 The organization doesn't fit the purpose.

Voice
5 The voice expresses interest and complete understanding. It engages the reader.
4 The voice expresses interest in and understanding of the topic.
3 The voice expresses interest but needs to show more understanding.
2 The voice needs to be more interesting and express more understanding.
1 The voice does not show interest in or an understanding of the topic.

Word Choice
5 The word choice reflects careful thinking about the reading.
4 The word choice, including the use of literary terms, creates a clear message.
3 The word choice is clear, but more literary terms would improve the essay.
2 The word choice is too general and more literary terms are needed.
1 Little, if any, attention was given to word choice.

Sentence Fluency
5 The sentences in the essay make the ideas really stand out.
4 The sentences are skillfully written and keep the reader's interest.
3 No sentence problems exist. More sentence variety is needed.
2 A few sentence problems need to be corrected.
1 The essay has many sentence problems.

Conventions
5 Grammar and punctuation are correct, and the copy is free of all errors.
4 The essay has one or two errors that do not interfere with the reader's understanding.
3 The essay has a few careless errors in punctuation and grammar.
2 The errors in the essay confuse the reader.
1 The number of errors make the essay hard to read.

© Great Source. Permission is granted to copy this page.

4-Point

Rubric for Narrative Writing

Ideas

4 The narrative captures an unforgettable time. The details make the story come alive.

3 The writer shares an interesting experience. Details help create the interest.

2 The writer tells about an interesting experience. More details are needed.

1 The writer tells about an experience or time. Many more details are needed.

Organization

4 The way the narrative is put together makes it enjoyable to read.

3 The narrative is well organized, with a clear beginning, middle, and ending. Transitions are used well.

2 The narrative is well organized. Most of the transitions are helpful.

1 The order of events needs to be corrected. More transitions need to be used.

Voice

4 The voice in the narrative perfectly captures the special time or experience.

3 The writer's voice creates interest in the story.

2 The writer's voice could be stronger.

1 A voice can sometimes be heard. The writer needs to show more feelings.

Word Choice

4 The writer's exceptional word choice captures the experience.

3 Specific nouns, verbs, and modifiers create clear pictures.

2 Some of the words need to be more specific to create clear pictures.

1 Many more specific words need to be used.

Sentence Fluency

4 The style of the sentences captures this time or experience.

3 The sentences are skillfully written and original.

2 The sentences show variety, but some should read more smoothly.

1 A better variety of sentences is needed. Sentences do not read smoothly.

Conventions

4 The narrative is error free.

3 The narrative has a few minor errors in punctuation, spelling, or grammar.

2 The narrative has some errors that may distract the reader.

1 Several errors confuse the reader.

4-Point
Rubric for Expository Writing

Ideas
4 The topic, focus, and details make the essay truly memorable.
3 The essay is informative with a clear focus and specific details.
2 The essay is informative with a clear focus. More specific details are needed.
1 The focus of the essay needs to be clearer, and more specific details are needed.

Organization
4 The organization and transitions make the essay clear and easy to read.
3 The beginning interests the reader. The middle supports the focus. The ending works well. Transitions are used.
2 The essay is divided into a beginning, a middle, and an ending. Some transitions are used.
1 The beginning or ending is weak. The middle needs a paragraph for each main point. More transitions are needed.

Voice
4 The writer's voice sounds confident, knowledgeable, and enthusiastic.
3 The writer's voice sounds knowledgeable and confident. It fits the audience.
2 The writer's voice sounds knowledgeable most of the time and fits the audience.
1 The writer sometimes sounds unsure, and the voice needs to fit the audience better.

Word Choice
4 The word choice makes the essay very clear, informative, and enjoyable to read.
3 Specific nouns and action verbs make the essay clear and informative.
2 Some nouns and verbs could be more specific.
1 Too many general words are used. Specific nouns and verbs are needed.

Sentence Fluency
4 The sentences are skillfully written, and readers will enjoy them.
3 The sentences read smoothly.
2 Most of the sentences read smoothly, but some are short and choppy.
1 Many short, choppy sentences need to be rewritten to make the essay read smoothly.

Conventions
4 The essay is error free.
3 The essay has a few minor errors in punctuation, spelling, or grammar.
2 The essay has some errors in punctuation, spelling, or grammar.
1 Several errors confuse the reader.

© Great Source. Permission is granted to copy this page.

4-Point

Rubric for Persuasive Writing

Ideas

4 My position is very well defended and compels the reader to act.

3 The essay has a clear position or opinion statement. Persuasive reasons support the writer's position.

2 The position statement is clear, and most reasons support the writer's position.

1 The position statement may be clear. More persuasive reasons are needed.

Organization

4 All the parts of the essay work together to build a thoughtful, convincing position.

3 The opening contains the position statement. The middle provides clear support. The ending reinforces the position.

2 The opening contains the position statement. The middle provides support. The ending needs work.

1 The beginning has an opinion statement. The middle and ending need more work.

Voice

4 The writer's voice is confident, positive, and convincing.

3 The writer's voice is confident and persuasive.

2 The writer's voice is confident, but it may not be persuasive enough.

1 The writer's voice needs to be more confident and persuasive.

Word Choice

4 The writer's choice of words makes a powerful case.

3 The writer's word choice helps persuade the reader.

2 Some changes would make the word choice more persuasive.

1 Many more precise and persuasive words are needed.

Sentence Fluency

4 The sentences spark the reader's interest in the essay.

3 Variety is seen in both the types of sentences and their beginnings.

2 Varied sentence beginnings are used. Sentence variety would make the essay more interesting to read.

1 Varied sentence beginnings are needed. Sentence variety would make the essay more interesting.

Conventions

4 The writing is error free.

3 Grammar and punctuation errors are few. The reader is not distracted by the errors.

2 Grammar and punctuation errors are seen in a few sentences. They distract the reader in those areas.

1 There are a number of errors that may confuse the reader.

4-Point

Rubric for Response to Literature

Ideas

4 The ideas show a complete understanding of the reading.

3 The essay has a clear focus statement and all the necessary details.

2 The essay has a clear focus statement. Unnecessary details need to be cut.

1 The focus statement is too broad. Unnecessary details need to be cut.

Organization

4 All the parts work together to create an insightful essay.

3 The organization pattern fits the topic and purpose. All parts of the essay are well developed.

2 The organization pattern fits the topic and purpose. A part of the essay needs better development.

1 The organization fits the essay's purpose. Some parts need more development.

Voice

4 The voice expresses interest and complete understanding. It engages the reader.

3 The voice expresses interest in and understanding of the topic.

2 The voice expresses interest but needs to show more understanding.

1 The voice needs to be more interesting and express more understanding.

Word Choice

4 The word choice reflects careful thinking about the reading.

3 The word choice, including the use of literary terms, creates a clear message.

2 The word choice is clear, but more literary terms would improve the essay.

1 The word choice is too general and more literary terms are needed.

Sentence Fluency

4 The sentences in the essay make the ideas really stand out.

3 The sentences are skillfully written and keep the reader's interest.

2 No sentence problems exist. More sentence variety is needed.

1 A few sentence problems need to be corrected.

Conventions

4 Grammar and punctuation are correct, and the copy is free of all errors.

3 The essay has one or two errors that do not interfere with the reader's understanding.

2 The essay has a few careless errors in punctuation and grammar.

1 The errors in the essay confuse the reader.

Six-Trait Checklist

Ideas

☐ focuses on a specific topic
☐ has a clear focus statement
☐ contains specific details

Organization

☐ has a beginning, a middle, and an ending
☐ has a topic sentence for each paragraph
☐ has enough details to develop each topic sentence
☐ uses transitions to connect paragraphs

Voice

☐ speaks in an engaging way that keeps readers wanting to hear more
☐ shows that the writer really cares about the subject

Word Choice

☐ contains specific nouns and action verbs
☐ presents an appropriate level of language (not too formal or too informal)

Sentence Fluency

☐ flows smoothly from sentence to sentence
☐ shows variety in sentence beginnings and lengths
☐ uses transitions to connect sentences

Conventions

☐ follows the basic rules of grammar, spelling, capitalization, and punctuation

Narrative Writing

Puppy

1 I used to have these dreams. I used to dream that Beluga

2 was alive, and he ran to me, so happy to see me, wagging his tail,

3 tongue lolling out. Then my puppy Sophie came out from behind a

4 wall. Beluga would look at me, his dark, almost-human eyes filling

5 with sadness and confusion, asking me without words, "Who is this

6 stranger who has taken my place in your heart?"

7 And then I'd cry out, "No! No! Don't leave me!" But he would turn

8 around, tail between his legs, and walk away. Then I would wake up.

9 Beluga, my beautiful black Lab mix, was diagnosed with cancer

10 when he was only nine years old. They told us there was still hope.

11 They did an operation on his leg. In a later operation, no cancer cells

12 were found. There was a chance! Then one morning, my mom came

13 home from the vet with a gray, ashen face and red eyes.

14 "The cancer spread," she said. "They can't stop it. He won't live

15 out the year."

16 I remember the day we put him to sleep—a memory locked in my

17 brain like a bad dream. I hugged Beluga one last time, trying not to

18 look at his swollen, cancer-filled leg, not believing it would be the last

19 time I ever saw him.

20 After Beluga was put to sleep, we didn't even consider getting

21 another dog for a long time. We noticed his absence in every corner,

22 underneath every table. After a while, though, we started yearning,

23 not for a replacement, but for a new, quirky, individual dog that we

24 could love just as much.

25   My mom, my friend, and I started going to different shelters

26 looking at dogs, but nothing measured up. This dog was too old, this

27 one might not get along with our cat, this one had too much energy.

28   I voted strongly for getting a puppy, but my dad just wanted a

29 calm, loyal dog, and my brother insisted that a puppy would chew up

30 his shoes. My mom started calling breeders, just in case. Finally, she

31 found a breeder we liked. Unfortunately, they wouldn't have another

32 litter for months, so all we could do was wait.

33   Then one day, a couple of weeks later, we got a phone call. I was

34 at a friend's house playing with her guinea pig when my parents

35 called, excited. "I think this is the one," was all they would tell me. I

36 heard that line too many times, though.

37   "Dad, I'm busy. Call me if you come home with a dog," I snapped.

38   About two hours later, my dad called again. "Nope, no luck.

39 Someone got there before us, but you'd better come home. It's late."

40   On the way home my dad started talking about how disappointed

41 my mother was, and how I should be sensitive. I was almost to the

42 point of believing him when we pulled up in front of our house. I got

43 out and waved at my mom, ready to be sympathetic. Then I looked

44 down. Following behind her was an adorable, glossy, splay-footed,

45 rambunctious, little PUPPY! I absolutely screamed with delight.

46 Breathless, my mom explained, "Well, you see we got a call from

47 that really good breeder and he had this puppy that was so sweet-

48 tempered he saved her for a friend but they just found out the friend

49 is ill and can't raise a dog so he's giving her to US!"

50   I was thrilled. I reached down and pickup up this wonderful

51 bundle of energy. Wriggling in my arms, she immediately began

52 licking my face, my neck, my ears, my hands. I put her down and

53 smiled. I knew we were going to be best friends.

54   That's when I started having those horrible nightmares. Every

55 time I ran my hands over my new puppy's soft, velvety ears, every

56 time I scooped her small black body into my arms, every time I

57 laughed at her odd, lopsided walk, I felt a pang of guilt. I simply

58 couldn't love Sophie without feeling as though I was betraying Beluga.

59   Then one day I couldn't stand it any longer. I went up to my

60 room and pulled out a blank journal. Slowly at first, then faster and

61 faster still, I started writing page after page about Beluga. Everything

62 about him went into that book. Then, ever so slowly, I closed the book,

63 and right there and right then I knew that I'd never forget Beluga.

64 I carefully placed the book high in the corner of my bookshelf and

65 walked down the stairs, leaving Beluga behind, but a part of me now. I

66 bent down to greet my puppy, and for once nothing held me back.

Assessment Sheet

Title _Puppy_

_6_ Ideas

- You carry the dream idea through nicely.
- It would help to know how long Beluga had been gone before you got the puppy.

_6_ Organization

- You chose a difficult style of organization, beginning with the dream. Very well-done, with a nice use of transition into the story itself.
- You might try going back to the dream at the end to bring the main idea full circle.

_6_ Voice

- Your emotion is presented in a very natural way. The matter-of-fact way you present it makes it all the more effective.
- Excellent mix of dialogue and narrative in the section with your father.

_6_ Word Choice

- Your language is appropriate, with good word choice.
- Excellent descriptive words, such as "quirky" and "lopsided." I loved "splay-footed."

_5_ Sentence Fluency

- Your writing has an excellent rhythm, with a good variety of sentences, but watch out for rambling sentences, as in your mother's explanation of how you got the dog. There's also a run-on sentence where you pick up the puppy. Also, some of your shorter sentences could be combined.

Narrative Writing

A Message for Myself

1   I walked, slowly, rhythmically, as if in a half trance, the sand

2   creeping in between my bare toes. My reddish brown hung down my

3   back, occasionally lifted by a small breeze that cut through the humid

4   summer evening air like a piercing dagger. Even though the sun was

5   slowly losing it's light over the land as it fell into the cliffs; bordering

6   the open sea that lay open like a frame to a mural, the evening was

7   still warm and dry. The salty air seemed to be able to just sit on the

8   humid twilight atmosphere as if it was a solid block.

9   I continued down the outstretched beach along the waters edge

10 careful not to let even the slightest bit of water touch my toes. It was

11 a game the sea and I liked to play. Sometimes I let the ocean win,

12 treating myself to its cool waters. Sometimes I would even indulge

13 myself and walk out slowly, farther then just the rising wave's edge.

14 Each step caused tiny ripples in the water, as if I was plucking it's

15 placidness. The ripples, dozens of them, would then flee frantically

16 away from me as if I had a contagious disease. I looked out across the

17 open water, at the skywhich is slowly dimming from lack of the golden

18 light that illuminated the earth. The sky and the water met each other

19 at their illusion of an end, as if they were two long lost friends that

20 never wanted to release, ever so thoughtlessly referred to as a horizon.

21   This was what I did the summer my best friend moved to Arizona.

22   I walked the beaches alone. Everything I saw changed every day, and

23   I hated change. However, I found the water, the sand, the sea shells,

24   the wind, and the sky seemed not to mind changing. It was a mystery

25   to me because I hated change. I hated my mother for humming. I

26   hated my father for going to his job in the city. I hated the tuna fish

27   sandwiches for lunch. I hated my hair and my faded, pink swimsuit.

28   Then one day as I strode down the beach, I saw a lump of

29   something lying up ahead. As I approached it began to beat a wing

30   and flop around, scared to death. It was a young seagull with only

31   one wing and a terrible wound. I backed off until it stopped flopping

32   about. I sat down. I thought it might want some company. After awhile

33   I began to talk to it. I told it about Jessica leaving, about how I hated

34   everything, about how lonely I was. It seemed to be listening. I began

35   inching a bit closer. I told it about school and my birthday and dying

36   Easter eggs. Finally, I was close enough to touch it, but I didn't. I had

37   nothing else to say, so I hummed. Slowly, I started to move a hand

38   closer. The gull stayed still. I thought maybe it had died. After a long

39   time, I touched it. I could feel its heart beating. It wasn't dead. It

40   was dirty and it's feathers were full of dried blood. I let my hand rest

41   lightly on its back.

42   I knew I should be starting home. It was growing cooler. Instead, I

43   snuggled into the warm sand beside the gull. That's how Mom found us.

44   "Do you think you can pick it up?" Mom asked. The gull was

45 looking at me. Slowly I sat up. I began to talk to it . . .quietly and

46 calmly. It didn't flop around. I started to move my other hand nearer,

47 then under it. It didn't move. I held my breath. The next thing I knew

48 I was holding the gull. The three of us walked home.

49   Mom called Mrs. Crutcher who came over. She had been helping

50 hurt animals and birds all her life. Now everyday I go to Mrs.

51 Crutcher's to help her. My one-winged gull, Amelia, has filled out. She

52 follows me around as I clean cages, feed and hug animals. Sometimes

53 I carry her down to the beach. Now I don't hate anything anymore.

Assessment Sheet

Title *A Message for Myself*

_4_ Ideas

- *The delicacy of the hurt seagull is vividly presented.*
- *Your use of sensory details and personification is excellent, but try to limit your opening description to one paragraph.*
- *A clearer change is needed to show why the feelings of anger go away.*
- *The title should reflect the meaning of the story. What is the main idea?*

_3_ Organization

- *The main idea should come in sooner.*
- *The section with the gull is the clearest with the most logical transitions.*
- *The ending does not reflect the title or main idea. Tie it to the opening.*

_4_ Voice

- *Your emotion comes through most clearly in the paragraph about the seagull.*
- *Try for a more natural sound. The forced description makes your voice uneven.*

_3_ Word Choice

- *Flowery phrases and unusual words sound awkward. For example, "plucking its placidness" is unclear.*
- *Try for a more appropriate level of language. While I like that you experiment with different words, be sure the ones you choose sound like you.*

_3_ Sentence Fluency

- *Long, rambling sentences are hard to read (see your third sentence).*
- *I'm excited by your desire to write more complicated sentences, but be careful not to sacrifice clarity.*
- *Read your sentences out loud. If you run out of breath during a sentence, it's too long.*

_3_ Conventions

- *Go over the rules regarding "its" and "it's."*
- *When you proofread, watch out for missing words. Read it out loud.*
- *Be sure all your verbs agree with their subjects.*

Expository Writing

911!

1 When you hear a siren, what do you imagine is happening? Most

2 people picture someone who needs help in a hurry. Vehicles with

3 sirens carry emergency personnel—police, firefighters, and EMT's—

4 who serve the public during difficult times. These specialists are

5 trained to manage serious situations while risking their own lives and

6 health.

7 In an emergency, it is not unusual to see police, firefighters, and

8 EMT's (emergency medical technicians) on the scene at the same

9 time. Police sometimes arrive first, assessing the situation, controlling

10 traffic, and making sure that the area is clear for firefighters and

11 EMT's. When firefighters arrive, they often work to control whatever

12 is causing the problem. In fact, most calls to which firefighters

13 respond are for medical emergencies, not fires. EMT's are trained to

14 handle the most serious medical problems, and many of them are

15 qualified to take extreme measures to save a life.

16 All three types of emergency personnel are specially trained

17 for their jobs. Many police departments prefer hiring college

18 graduates, who are then given further instruction at a police academy.

19 Firefighters must pass written and physical requirements, go through

20 training at a local facility, and serve a period of apprenticeship. EMT's

21 progress through several levels of certification to gain more complex

22 medical skills. The first level of EMT training, known as First

23 Responder, is often taken by police and firefighters, as well.

24   The work of emergency personnel is dangerous, no matter how

25 well they are trained. Police often find themselves in life-threatening

26 situation, as do firefighters and EMT's. Criminals, accidents, and

27 hazardous materials are common problems for all three groups.

28 What is sometimes not recognized, though, is the almost constant

29 pressure of the jobs. Seeing people suffer and die can be very, very

30 upsetting, even for the most experienced personnel. Irregular working

31 hours and unpredictable conditions are difficult to del with year

32 after year. Stress is a very big problem in emergency work, and

33 probably accounts for more damage to individuals than the dangerous

34 situations that they face.

35   When you look at the duties, training, and risks connected with

36 emergency occupations, you realize that there are more similarities

37 than differences among the three groups of personnel. The jobs are

38 closely related and the hazards are similar. The next time you hear a

39 siren, you'll know that, no matter what type of vehicle is making the

40 noise, highly-qualified, dedicated help is on the way.

Assessment Sheet

Title _911!_ _____

_5_ Ideas
- You should place the explanation for a word such as EMT after it is first used.
- Your second paragraph topic sentence needs to be more specific to the paragraph content about duties.

_5_ Organization
- Excellent transitions. I like the way you mention the previous paragraph's idea in your body topic sentences.
- Make your introduction more specific, clearly naming your three main points.
- Don't introduce new ideas in your closing. You mention similarities of the jobs in your closing statement, but have not mentioned it before.

_5_ Voice
- Your voice is appropriately serious for the topic.
- You show obvious respect but could use a little more enthusiasm. Your best paragraph is your third point, where you mention the difficulties. You sound really concerned there.

_5_ Word Choice
- Nice use of specific words.
- Clear, informative language makes this essay easy to read and understand.
- There are an awful lot of "be" verbs. Could you use more action verbs?

_6_ Sentence Fluency
- Excellent variety in sentence length and complexity.
- Sentences flow smoothly from one to the next.

_5_ Conventions
- Try proofreading more carefully to avoid simple spelling errors. Even an electronic spell-checker can miss words like "del."

Expository Writing

Storm Cells

1 Single cell storms, also called "air mass" storms, the weakest type

2 of storm. Some hail and heavy rainfall, they are usually not very

3 dangerous. The single cell storm occurs beneath a high, mounded

4 cloud as it passes overhead. This type of storm has just one updraft/

5 downdraft sequence, which is unusual. It is more common for a storm

6 to have several cells. The storm is short, lasting around 20 to 30

7 minutes. It comes together quickly. Is of short duration. The single cell

8 storm is difficult to predict.

9 They are often large hail, flash floods, dangerous downbursts, and

10 even violent tornadoes. Even so, because of their continuous, rotating

11 updraft, they are the most predictable of storms. The winds rotate,

12 turn in circles. Which can build to a cyclone.

13 The clouds of the supercell storm have the appearance of different

14 types of clouds mixed together. Some are towering mounds.

15 Supercells, the strongest type of thunderstorms, are the rarest, most

16 dangerous storms. The storm's rotating winds feed it, so it continues

17 to build as it moves over a wide area.

Assessment Sheet

Title *Storm Cells*

_3_ Ideas
- *You have a lot of details, but they don't connect.*
- *Selecting a central focus for the essay will help you decide on details.*
- *You need to use a main point as the focus of each paragraph.*

_2_ Organization
- *You need to develop a separate beginning, middle, and ending.*
- *Use an organized list to help you group your ideas together and build your paragraphs from that.*
- *Use transitions to move from one paragraphs to the next and occasionally from one sentence to another.*

_4_ Voice
- *You have good facts and sound knowledgeable.*
- *You show interest, but your feelings about the power of storms could come out more.*

_3_ Word Choice
- *You include some nice descriptive words, such as "towering mounds."*
- *Let your words reflect your interest and the power of storms.*

_1_ Sentence Fluency
- *Combine some of your short, choppy sentences.*
- *It would help you to review the section on fragments.*
- *Read your sentences out loud to see if they connect with each other.*

_4_ Conventions
- *Review the use of conjunctions and articles.*
- *Excellent use of punctuation in phrases and clauses.*
- *Remember to indent your paragraphs.*

Persuasive Writing

Yes, Skateboarding

1   New signs have sprung up along the sidewalks and parking lots

2 of Bloomington. Do these signs protest war? Do they tell kids to stay

3 off drugs? No, they tell kids to stay off skateboards. The city council

4 wants to "take back" the downtown, so they have created laws and

5 fines to end skateboarding. However, skateboarding is not the cause

6 of the problems downtown, and outlawing it may do more harm than

7 good.

8   First of all, skateboarding has many benefits. It provides

9 exercise for kids who might otherwise sit around all day watching TV.

10 Skateboarding also helps kids be social. Too many teenagers spend

11 hours alone surfing the Internet, but skateboarding gets them out of

12 their homes and into groups of friends. Take away skateboards, and

13 more kids will be out of shape, lonely, and bored. That's a recipe for

14 real trouble.

15   The ban on skateboarding also tells teenagers that the city

16 disrespects them. Some adults think any group of teenagers is a gang.

17 The truth is that if kids are together on skateboards, they're almost

18 certainly not a gang. By outlawing skateboards, the city pushes

19 teenagers toward more destructive activities.

20   The most important reason to end the ban, though, is that

21   skateboarding isn't the cause of the big problems downtown.

22   Abandoned buildings, graffiti, crime, and substance abuse aren't

23   caused by kids on skateboards. Malls kill city centers, not kids doing

24   grinds on bridges. Instead of policing skateboarders, the city should

25   crack down on gangs and slum lords.

26   Of course, the city council argues that skateboarders cause

27   damage to handrails and benches downtown. However, most

28   skateboarders don't damage public property, and those who do won't

29   be stopped by the new ban. Outlawing skateboarding just takes the

30   activity away from law-abiding kids.

31   Instead of making skateboarders outlaws, the city should make

32   them "in-laws" by creating a skateboard park. When the MacNamara

33   Building burned last year, the city had to tear it down. The property is

34   still for sale, right there in the middle of the decaying downtown. Why

35   not turn it into a skateboard park so riders have a home in our city?

36   When the city council put up "No Skateboarding" signs

37   everywhere, they wanted to "turn the city around." The best way

38   to turn the city around, though, is to put up "Yes, Skateboarding"

39   signs. A skateboard park downtown would give skateboarders a safe

40   place to practice this healthy group sport, and would give downtown

41   Bloomington a park to be proud of.

Assessment Sheet

Title _Yes, Skateboarding_

_5_ Ideas

- It would help to explain why outlawing skateboards pushes kids toward destructive activities (see lines 15–19).
- Paragraph #3 is also a little short and could be expanded.
- Logic in paragraph #4 is a little fuzzy. The connection between the mall and skateboarders is unclear.
- Your strong opinion statement is very effective, but it doesn't match the ending. The idea of a skate park at the end seems a separate main idea.

_6_ Organization

- You list your arguments by order of importance, with clear transitions.
- Nice connection of introduction and closing through idea of signs.
- Excellent use of opposing argument and solution.

_5_ Voice

- Mainly well-balanced facts, although the comments on the mall don't quite fit.
- Strong, confident voice makes argument compelling and convincing.

_5_ Word Choice

- Good use of qualifiers such as "more," "most," and "almost certainly."
- You might want to soften the idea of the city "disrespecting" teenagers. It's a strong accusation.
- Although it's a good try for a cute twist, the word "in-laws" has a specific meaning that doesn't fit here.

_6_ Sentence Fluency

- Excellent use of sentence variety.
- Good variety in openings.

_6_ Conventions

- No errors in spelling, punctuation, or grammar.
- Excellent use of commas after opening words, phrases, and clauses

Persuasive Writing

Help the School Band

1 The school band is planning its annual trip to band camp during
2 summer break. And we need money to go. It would really help the
3 band if everybody would support it.

4 The camp was out of state last year. We have to rent a bus, and
5 stay over night in a motel on the way to camp. We had fun. There
6 is a competition on the last day of camp. We want to do good in the
7 competition this year.

8 Two years ago the band needed money to buy new uniforms. But
9 the uniforms still look good, so we don't have to replace them right
10 now.

11 Everybody is really excited about camp. The band members
12 practice really hard. They deserve to go on this trip.

13 So help the band. Buy treats at the bake sale buy buttons and
14 banners in the basketball games.

Assessment Sheet

Title _Help the School Band_

2 Ideas

- A stronger focus is needed. Eliminate unnecessary ideas (see lines 8–10).
- More facts and details are needed to persuade the reader.
- You need to present an objection and argue against it.

2 Organization

- You do have a beginning, a middle, and an ending, but they are not developed.
- Try listing and sorting your ideas so you can identify and expand your main points.
- You need to use transitions to move from one idea to the next.

3 Voice

- I like your enthusiasm in spots (see lines 6–7 and 11–12).
- Use your enthusiasm to build arguments.

3 Word Choice

- Use more precise words and action verbs to build a stronger argument.
- More persuasive words are needed. You want to make people feel the need.
- Watch out for weak modifiers like "really."
- Review the use of the words "good" and "well."

2 Sentence Fluency

- Don't start sentences with coordinating conjunctions like "and" or "but" very often.
- Combine short sentences wherever possible to avoid a choppy feel.

4 Conventions

- Be sure your tenses are consistent.
- Watch your spelling of compound words such as "overnight."
- Avoid run-on sentences (see lines 13–14).

Response to Literature

Number the Stars

1 The book *Number the Stars* by Lois Lowry is a story of the

2 Holocaust and its effects not only on Jews, but also on the many brave

3 people who tried to save them. In it, a young girl learns a lesson about

4 the strength of human decency and the importance of standing up for

5 something you believe in.

6 The setting of the story is Denmark during World War II. The

7 Nazis have taken over the country, but the people refuse to be beaten

8 down. The main character, Annemarie Johansen, lives there with her

9 mother, father, and little sister, Kirsti. An older sister, Lisle, has died

10 earlier, supposedly in an automobile accident.

11 The plot centers on Annemarie and her best friend Ellen Rosen,

12 a Jewish girl whose family is very close with the Johansens. Word

13 spreads that the Nazis are planning to "relocate" the Danish Jews.

14 The two families are horrified at the news, and Ellen's parents plan to

15 escape to freedom. They disappear one night, leaving Ellen with the

16 Johansens, where she pretends to be Annemarie's sister. The suspense

17 is heightened when the Nazis visit the house looking for the Rosens

18 and Annemarie must break off Ellen's Star of David necklace so she

19 won't get caught.

20 Then Annemarie, Kirsti, Ellen, and Mrs. Johansen make a trip to

21 the country, where Mrs. Johansen's brother, a fisherman, still lives on

22 the family farm. There the girls enjoy a taste of the freedom Denmark

23 once knew, even as a plot is swirling around them concerning the

24 death of "Great-Aunt Birte," a relative who never existed. The funeral

25 is visited by the Nazis, who leave the grieving family alone. We then

26 learn that the coffin is filled not with a person, but with supplies to

27 help Jews, including the Rosens, to escape to Sweden.

28   It turns out that Annemarie's uncle is one of the Danish

29 resistance fighters, smuggling Jews below his ship's decks to freedom.

30 After the Jews leave the house, Annemarie's mother finds a package

31 that is vital and must be delivered before they set sail. But when her

32 mother sprains her ankle, Annemarie must deliver the package, going

33 through Nazi patrols on her way. Despite the danger of the Nazi guard

34 dogs, Annemarie gets through, the package is delivered, and the Jews

35 are all safely smuggled away to Sweden.

36   Afterwards, Annemarie is amazed to learn that her sister Lisle

37 had died because of her participation in the Danish Resistance.

38 Annemarie is proud of Denmark's compassion and of her family's

39 bravery in helping others. She still has Ellen's Star of David, which

40 has become a symbol of human dignity and goodness, and vows to

41 return it to Ellen after the war. Annemarie understands now that the

42 strength of human decency was what her sister died for, and knows

43 that she would do the same.

Assessment Sheet

Title _Number the Stars_

_6_ Ideas

- _Your introduction, while brief, offers an excellent background of the story._
- _Your focus statement is powerful and makes the reader want to go on._

_6_ Organization

- _I like the way you tie in the ending with the focus statement in the opening._
- _Excellent job presenting the story line in a clear, concise manner._
- _Your beginning, middle, and ending flow smoothly and tie together well._

_6_ Voice

- _Your voice is compelling and engaging._
- _You sound interested—I can tell you really liked the book._

_6_ Word Choice

- _Excellent use of specific literary terms, including "plot," "character," "symbol," and "suspense."_
- _I love your use of descriptive phrases such s "a plot is swirling around them."_

_5_ Sentence Fluency

- _Although you use a great variety of sentence patterns, in some spots you rely too heavily on the subject-verb pattern. "Annemarie is proud," "Annemarie understands," "Annemarie must," and so on. Watch for this and try to reword some sentences to follow different patterns._

_6_ Conventions

- _Excellent job of proofreading. The paper is error-free._

Response to Literature

Across Five Aprils

1   *Across Five Aprils* by Irene Hunt tells the story of Jethro

2   Creighton. He is eight years old when the story begins. The story

3   takes place in southern Illinois. The Civil War is happening. Jethro

4   learns about hate. Jethro is the youngest Creighton. He worries most

5   about his brothers and his cousin. They have volunteered with the

6   Union army.

7   Jethro is planting potatoes with his mother when the story

8   starts. Jethro is especially sad when his school master, Shadrach Yale,

9   says he also is joining the Union Army. Jethro feels worse when his

10 brother, Bill, tells him that he is going to fight with the Confederate

11 army. Bill doesn't agree with the ways of the North. The Creighton

12 family respects Bill's decision. Jethro tries to understand the family

13 members' decisions.

14   With all of his brothers away at the war, Jethro is given new

15 responsibilities. On his first trip into town, some older men question

16 him about Bill's decision. Certain people feel Bill is being disloyal.

17 They want to punish the Creighton family. On Jethro's next trip to

18 town, troublemakers ambush him. They scare the horses. A man

19 named, Dave Burdow, controls the team of horses and protects Jethro.

20 Other strange things happen at the Creighton farm.

21   The situation gets worse when Jethro's dad has a heart attack.

22 Jethro becomes the "man" of the family. He now makes major

23 decisions about the farm. He also makes a decision that may endanger

24 his family. Soldiers desert. Jethro's cousin, Eb, deserts his troop. He

25 comes back home. Asks Jethro for help. Jethro writes to President

26 Lincoln about Eb's problem. He receives a reply.

27   Five years pass with the war beginning and ending in the

28 month of April. Jethro sees the effects of war. He hopes the treaty

29 will guarantee peace. Then Jethro learns about President Lincoln's

30 assassination. Jethro feels that peace won't last long.

Assessment Sheet

Title _Across Five Aprils_

_2_ Ideas

- _You need a focus statement to tell the reader the theme. What is the purpose of the story? What is the author trying to teach us?_
- _Try to select some quotations that will help the reader get a feel for the story._
- _Be sure to give important background information, such as that the family is on the side of the North when Bill decides to fight for the South._
- _Explain specific statements. What is President Lincoln's reply? What treaty? What is the decision that endangers his family? These might be important to the reader's understanding._

_2_ Organization

- _Without a theme, your essay is simply a synopsis of the book._
- _Chronological order is fine for a book report, but it doesn't present a theme or support the theme._

_2_ Voice

- _You need to establish a theme and show interest in it._

_3_ Word Choice

- _Having a specific theme would allow you to use literary terms._
- _Your word choice is general and needs to be more active and exciting._

_3_ Sentence Fluency

- _You need to work on combining your short, choppy sentences into longer, smoother ones. Review combining sentences._
- _Try to vary your sentences. Almost all of them follow the same pattern._

_4_ Conventions

- _Your punctuation and spelling are generally quite good, but you need to proofread more carefully for errors._

Assessment Sheet

 **Directions** Use one of the rubrics listed below to rate a piece of writing. Circle the rubric your teacher tells you to use. If you need information about assessing with a rubric, see pages 52 and 55 in your *Write Source* book.

Narrative Rubric (pages 130–131)   Expository Rubric (pages 194–195)
Persuasive Rubric (pages 256–257)   Response to Literature (pages 318–319)

Title _____

____ **Ideas**

____ **Organization**

____ **Voice**

____ **Word Choice**

____ **Sentence Fluency**

____ **Conventions**

Evaluator _____

Editing and Proofreading Marks

Use the symbols and letters below to show where and how your writing needs to be changed.
Your teachers may also use these symbols to point out errors in your writing.

Symbols	Meaning	Example	Corrected Example
=	Capitalize a letter.	Lorraine Hansberry wrote *A Raisin in the sun*.	Lorraine Hansberry wrote *A Raisin in the Sun*.
/	Make a capital letter lowercase.	Her play tells the story of the Younger Family.	Her play tells the story of the Younger family.
⊙	Insert (add) a period.	This play focuses on racial attitudes It also . . .	This play focuses on racial attitudes. It also . . .
◯ or *sp.*	Correct spelling.	Lena Younger, the family leader, is very (religous.)	Lena Younger, the family leader, is very religious.
⌒	Delete (take out) or replace.	Lena she makes a down payment on a nice house.	Lena makes a down payment on a nice house.
∧	Insert here.	The family wants to escape *ghetto* ∧ life.	The family wants to escape ghetto life.
∧ ∧ ∧	Insert a comma, a colon, or a semicolon.	Her son, Walter Lee, Jr. wants to buy a business.	Her son, Walter Lee, Jr., wants to buy a business.
∨ ∨∨ ∨∨	Insert an apostrophe or quotation marks.	Walter Lees wife hopes for a larger apartment.	Walter Lee's wife hopes for a larger apartment.
? ! ∧ ∧	Insert a question mark or an exclamation point.	What would Beneatha do with the money	What would Beneatha do with the money?
¶	Start a new paragraph.	¶The direction of the play clearly changes when . . .	The direction of the play clearly changes when . . .
∼	Switch words or letters.	Walter gets the possible worst news.	Walter gets the worst possible news.

T-Chart

Subject:

Time Line

Subject:

(Chronological Order)

1

2

3

4

5

6

7

8

Venn Diagram

Subject A

Differences

Subject B

Similarities

5 W's Chart

Subject: _____

Who?	What?	When?	Where?	Why?

Sensory Chart

Subject:

Sights	Sounds	Smells	Tastes	Feelings

Scavenger Hunt 1: Find the Fives

Directions Find the following "fives" in your book by turning to the pages listed in parentheses.

1. **Five** steps in the writing process (page 7)

   _____

   _____

2. **Five** transitions that show time in a narrative (page 38)

   _____

   _____

3. **Five** on a rubric means _____ . (page 46)

   _____

4. **Five** parts of a portfolio (page 67)

   _____

   _____

5. **Five** traits to look at while revising (page 204)

   _____

   _____

6. **Five** basic parts of a friendly letter (page 327)

   _____

   _____

7. **Five** story patterns (page 350)

   _____

   _____

8. **Five** types of primary sources (page 364)

   _____

   _____

9. **Five** points to remember when using the Internet (page 365)

   _____

   _____

10. **Five** ways to get started when writing a specialized journal (page 432)

   _____

   _____

Scavenger Hunt 2: What Is It?

 **Directions** Find the answers to the following questions using the index in the back of the book. The underlined words below tell you where to look in the index.

1. What is the correct <u>spelling</u> for the following misspelled words: *neice, hynm,* and *calender*?

_____

2. Which word—*lay* or *lie*—is correct in the following sentence? _____ the book on the table.

_____

3. What are three different <u>sentence beginnings</u> that you can use?

_____

_____

4. What is *paraphrasing*?

_____

5. What four thinking tasks might you do when *<u>recalling</u>*?

_____

6. What is a <u>compound noun</u>?

_____

7. What details could you include about a place in a piece of <u>descriptive writing</u>?

_____

_____

8. What are the three principal parts of the <u>irregular verb</u> *bite*?

_____

9. What <u>graphic organizer</u> can you use to compare and contrast two things?

_____

10. What information is often needed on a <u>title page</u> that you create?

_____

_____

Getting to Know *Write Source*

© Great Source. Permission is granted to copy this page.

Directions Locate the pages in *Write Source* where answers to the following learning tasks can be found. Both the index and the table of contents can help you.

_____ 1. You want to create a new club at your school. To do so you need to submit a proposal to your principal. You need to know how to write a proposal.

_____ 2. You ask your mother "Can I go to the movies?" Your mother says you may go as soon as you speak English properly. You need to know the different between *can* and *may*.

_____ 3. You have been asked to speak to fourth graders about research skills that they might use. You need to review research skills.

_____ 4. You want to enter the short story contest that a local author is sponsoring. The story must be science fiction. You need to check your understanding of science fiction.

_____ 5. Tomorrow your school's media center will start using a computer catalog. You want to know what a computer catalog is.

_____ 6. Your social studies teacher has asked you to review the keys to effective prewriting before starting your research paper. You need to find the keys to effective prewriting for research.

_____ 7. You want to get started writing a narrative, but you cannot think of a topic. You need a list of possible writing prompts for narratives.

_____ 8. Your essay about forest fires is excellent, but your teacher wants you to correct the subject-verb agreement problems. You need help making the subjects agree with their verbs.

_____ 9. Your math teacher thinks it will be okay if you go with your parents for a short vacation. She asks you to keep a math log. You need to discover what a math log is.

_____ 10. One of your classmates suggests that you experiment with word repetition in your poem. You need to know what word repetition is.

Getting Started Activity Answers

Scavenger Hunt 1: Find the Fives

1. The five steps are prewriting, writing, revising, editing, and publishing.

2. Some transitions that show time are *after, before, during, first, second, today, next,* and *then.*

3. A *5* means that the writing is very strong and clearly meets the main requirements for a trait.

4. The parts of a portfolio are a table of contents; a brief introductory letter; a collection of writing samples; a cover sheet for each sample; and evaluations, reflections, or checklists.

5. Review your work for ideas, organization, voice, word choice, and sentence fluency.

6. The parts of a letter are the heading, salutation, body, closing, and signature.

7. Five story patterns are the Rescue, the Union, the Underdog, the Decision, and Rivalry.

8. Some primary sources are diaries, journals, and letters; presentations; interviews; surveys and questionnaires; and observation and participation.

9. Remember to use the Web carefully, use a search site, look for links, be patient, and know your school's Internet policy.

10. To get started, collect your supplies, decide on a time to write, write freely for at least 10 minutes, write about things that interest you, and look back at your writing.

Scavenger Hunt 2: What Is It?

1. The correct spellings are *niece* (p. 650), *hymn* (p. 649), and *calendar* (p. 646).

2. The correct word is *lay.* (p. 668.6)

3. You can start with a single-word modifier, a participial phrase, or an infinitive phrase. (p. 43)

4. Paraphrasing is putting ideas from a source into your own words. (p. 391)

5. You might label parts of something, list facts or words, define terms, or fill in the blanks. (p. 451)

6. A compound noun is made up of two or more words. (p. 702.6)

7. You could include details that you observe or remember; you could also describe and compare the place to other places. (p. 532)

8. The parts are *bite* (present tense), *bit* (past tense), and *bitten* (past participle). (p. 722)

9. You could use a Venn diagram (p. 203 or 537) or a comparison-contrast chart. (p. 447)

10. A title page should include the title, your name, your teacher's name, the name of the class, and the date. (p. 409)

Getting to Know *Write Source*

1. 90–91 or 576
2. 658.6
3. 363–374
4. 555
5. 367
6. 386
7. 546 or 152–154
8. 508–509, 126–127, or 728.1
9. 437
10. 361

Unit Planning

Writing Form

PARAGRAPH

___ days

- FOCUS

- SKILLS

ESSAY 1

___ days

Prewriting

- FOCUS

- SKILLS

Writing

___ days

- FOCUS

- SKILLS

Revising

___ days

- IDEAS

- ORGANIZATION

- VOICE

- WORD CHOICE

- SENTENCE FLUENCY

See the yearlong timetable on pages TE 46–49.

Unit Planning (continued)

Editing ___ days

- PUNCTUATION

- CAPITALIZATION

- SPELLING

- GRAMMAR

Publishing ___ days

- OPTIONS

Evaluating ___ days

- SELF-ASSESSMENT

- BENCHMARK PAPERS

ESSAY 2 ___ days

- FOCUS

- SKILLS

ACROSS THE CURRICULUM ___ days

- SOCIAL STUDIES

- SCIENCE

- MATH

- PRACTICAL

Index

A

A/an, 652.1
A lot, 652.6
Abbreviations, 634, 636
    Acronyms, 636.1
    Address, 634
    Capitalization of, 626.1
    Common, 634
    Initialisms, 636.2
    Punctuation of, 579.3
Abstract noun, 471, 702.4
Accent marks, 372, 373
Accept/except, 652.2
Acronyms, 579.3, 636.1

Across-the-curriculum writing,
    Math, 86–87, 146–147, 208–
      209, 270–271, 437
    Practical writing, 90–91,
      150–151, 212–213, 274–277,
      334–335, 576–577
    Science, 88–89, 148–149,
      210–211, 272–273, 332–333,
      436
    Social studies, 84–85,
      144–145, 206–207, 268–269,
      330–331, 438

Action, in a story, 351
Action verbs, 480, 570, 571,
    718.1
Active voice, 41, 118, 726.1
Address,
    Abbreviations, 634
    Envelope, 577
    Punctuation of, 582.3
Address, direct, 588.2
Adjectives,
    79, 486–489, 732, 734
    Articles, 732.1
    Common, 732.3
    Comparative, 487, 734.4
    Compound, 610.1, 732.5
    Demonstrative, 489, 732.4
    Equal, 586.2

Forms, 487, 734.3–734.6
    Indefinite, 489, 734.1
    Irregular, 734.6
    Kinds of, 732.4, 732.5, 734.1,
      734.2
    Moving, 522
    Positive, 487, 734.3
    Predicate, 480, 570, 734.2
    Prepositional phrases as, 494,
      495, 519, 742.1
    Proper, 486, 618.1, 732.2
    Punctuation of, 586.2, 610.1
    Specific, 120
    Superlative, 487, 734.5
    Unnecessary, 185
Advanced learners, 3, 9, 15, 16,
    22, 26, 40, 41, 58, 60, 69, 73,
    84, 85, 89, 90, 100, 109, 129,
    139, 142, 144, 145, 151, 170,
    184, 189, 193, 197, 207, 220,
    223, 235, 240, 241, 254, 258,
    264, 267, 269, 270, 273, 291,
    299, 300, 307, 314, 316, 317,
    321, 331, 333, 346, 354, 355,
    356, 357, 358, 360, 361, 364,
    367, 371, 383, 384, 387, 399,
    400, 411, 412, 414, 424, 428,
    429, 432, 433, 434, 435, 440,
    452, 461
Adverbs, 490–493, 736, 738
    Comparative, 491, 738.3
    Conjunctive, 594.2, 738.1
    Forms, 491, 738
    Irregular, 738.5
    Positive, 491, 738.2
    Prepositional phrase as, 494,
      495, 519, 742.1
    Superlative, 491, 738.4
    Types of, 736
Affect/effect, 652.3
Agreement,
    Antecedent-pronoun, 252,
      476–479, 706.1
    Indefinite pronouns, 475, 508,
      710.1
    Subject-verb, 126, 127, 508–
      509, 728.1

Unusual word order, 509,
    694.2
Air/heir, 666.6
All-or-nothing statement, 240
All right, 652.7
Alliteration, 360
Allowed/aloud, 652.4
Allusion/illusion, 652.5
Already/all ready, 654.1
Altogether/all together, 654.2
Among/between, 654.3
Amount/number, 654.4
Analogy, 558
Analyzing,
    Information, 451, 455
    Themes, 287–322
Anecdote, 37, 554, 558
*Annual/biannual/
    semiannual/biennial/
    perennial*, 654.5
Answer, essay test, 464–467
Answering an objection, 230,
    241
Ant/aunt, 654.6
Antagonist, 351
Antecedent, 252, 474, 706.1
Antonym, 560, 563
Apostrophes, 190, 604, 606
Appendix, 369
Applying, information, 451, 454
Appositives,
    Phrase, 122, 472, 513
    Punctuating, 586.1
Argument, developing a
    statistical, 270–271
Arrangement,
    Of details, 534–537
    Of paragraphs, 243, 540
Article, summarizing, 375–378
Articles, 732.1
    Magazine, finding, 371
As/like, 670.2
Ascent/assent, 654.7
Assessing,
    Final copy, 27
    With a rubric, 45–53,
      130–131, 194–195,
      256–257, 318–319

Credits

Pupil Edition

Photos:

comstock.com: pages 1, 27, 33, 39, 43, 101, 107, 113, 125, 165, 171, 177, 189, 198, 199, 205, 223, 227, 233, 239, 251, 267, 283, 291, 295, 301, 313, 353, 375, 379, 386, 395, 405, 407, 409, 411, 413, 417, 421, 423, 429, 431, 441, 445, 449, 461, 521, 531, 547

Getty Images: pages xvi, 9, 27, 45, 60, 323, 363, 367, 374, 411, 413, 485, 533, 547, 555

Hemera: pages iii, v, x, xviii, 3, 5, 10, 11, 16, 57, 63, 65, 68, 71, 75, 83, 93, 97, 129, 135, 143, 157, 161, 193, 205, 219, 228, 238, 255, 261, 265, 267, 269, 287, 299, 317, 343, 347, 353, 360, 372, 431, 459, 469, 483, 499, 505, 523

Ulead Systems: pages 238, 379, 409

www.jupiterimages.com: pages 354, 355, 356, 358, 359, 360, 361, 492, 535

Text Credits:

Page 373: Copyright © 2007 by Houghton Mifflin Company. Adapted by permission from *The American Heritage Student Dictionary*.

Teacher's Edition

Photos:

comstock.com: pages TE 53, 819

Getty Images: page iii

Hemera: pages TE 51, v, ix, x, xii, xvi, 70A

Acknowledgements

We're grateful to many people who helped bring *Write Source* to life. First we must thank all the teachers and students from across the country who contributed writing models and ideas.

In addition, we want to thank our Write Source/Great Source team for all their help:

Steven J. Augustyn, Laura Bachman, Ron Bachman, April Barrons, William Baughn, Heather Bazata, Colleen Belmont, Lisa Bingen, Evelyn Curley, Sandra Easton, Chris Erickson, Mark Fairweather, Jean Fischer, Sherry Gordon, Mariellen Hanrahan, Kathy Henning, Tammy Hintz, Hillary Gammons, Mary Anne Hoff, Rob King, Lois Krenzke, Mark Lalumondier, Joyce Becker Lee, Ellen Leitheusser, Kevin Nelson, Sue Paro, Pat Reigel, Jason C. Reynolds, Susan Rogalski, Chip Rosenthal, Janae Sebranek, Lester Smith, Richard Spencer, Julie Spicuzza, Thomas Spicuzza, Jean Varley, Sandy Wagner, and Claire Ziffer.